The Church of Our Lady of Mount Carmel
and some conventual buildings at the
Whitefriars, Coventry

Charmian Woodfield

with contributions by

Chris Caple, John Cattell, Geof Egan, Helen Howard, Philip Kiberd, Helen List, Graham Morgan, James Rackham, Stephanie Ratkai, Charles Tracy, Hugh Willmott, Paul Woodfield

BAR British Series 389
2005

This title published by

Archaeopress
Publishers of British Archaeological Reports
Gordon House
276 Banbury Road
Oxford OX2 7ED
England
bar@archaeopress.com
www.archaeopress.com

BAR 389

The Church of Our Lady of Mount Carmel and some conventual buildings at the Whitefriars, Coventry

ISBN 1 84171 834 3

Printed in England by The Basingstoke Press

All BAR titles are available from:

Hadrian Books Ltd
122 Banbury Road
Oxford
OX2 7BP
England
bar@hadrianbooks.co.uk

The current BAR catalogue with details of all titles in print, prices and means of payment is available free from Hadrian Books or may be downloaded from www.archaeopress.com

Looking N across the masonry of the E bay of the nave, with piers and buttresses, and two Chapels of Our Lady and the Holy Rood (marked by ranging poles). To the right of the SW tower Pier lies the W crossing and transepts with diagonal buttresses.
The masonry extends for a width of 31m (102ft) from S to N.

CONTENTS

LIST OF ILLUSTRATIONS

LIST OF TABLES

ACKNOWLEDGEMENTS AND LIST OF CONTRIBUTORS

Charmian Woodfield gratefully acknowledges the help given by so many people during the course of the excavations and subsequently, during the preparation of this report. Without their generosity this work could never have been brought to fruition. The passage of several decades since the excavations will regrettably mean omissions in the Acknowledgement list of some of those worthy to have been mentioned, but I would particularly like to thank:

Lady Ann Aberconway, Nat Alcock, David Barker, Johan Bergstrom Allen, Julian Barnard, John Bateman, Martin Biddle, Claude Blair, Terry Blincham, Peter Brears, Jimmy Brown, Alison Cameron, Marion Campbell, Ray Cartwright, John Cattell, Lyndon Cave-Brown-Cave, Robert Charleston, Philip Chatwin, John Cherry, John Clark, Judith Clayton, Nick Cooper, Glyn Coppack, Fr. Richard Copsey, O. Carm, Coventry Record Office, Ian Davis, G. Demidowicz, J. Edward Dickinson, Murray Dixon, Gerald Dunning, Elizabeth Eames, Geoff Egan, Keith Egan, Anne Endean, John English, Janet Escritt (Supervisor), Myk Flitcroft, David Gaimster, Roberta Gilchrist, R. Gilyard Beer, John Goodall, Dr Arthur Gooder, Eileen Gooder, Pamela Graves, Murielle de Grey, Nick Griffiths, Ann Hamlin (Supervisor), Barbara Harbottle, Avril Hart, Martin Henig, R. J. Hilyard, John Hunt, Kate Hunter, Barbara Hurman, Gillian Hurst, John Hurst, John Inglis, Richard Ivens, Casper Johnson, Gill Johnson, Martyn Jope, Laurence Keen, George Lambrick, Philip Lindley, W. J. Lindsay, Malcolm Marjoram, Richard Marks, Maureen Mellor, Linda Monckton, David T. Moore, Graham Morgan, Ron Morgan, Richard Morris, Beverley Nenk, Philip Newton, Charles Oman, Tim Padley, Tony Page, David Park, Tim Pestell, Nicholas Phillips, Colin Platt, Public Record Office, Mark Redknap, Philip Rahtz, Stuart Rigold, Peter Salway, Cyril Scott, Linda Shaw, F. W. Shotton, Edna Simpson, Iain Soden, Brian Spencer, Kate Stanisland, Judith Stones, Fiona Sturdy, Gabriele Stutz, Bob Thompson, Paul Thompson, Roger Vaughan, Ray Wallwork, Graham Webster, Lady Wedgwood (Pamela Tudor Craig), Canon David Weston, Robert White, George Wigley and Linda Woolley.

The excavation would not have been possible without Mrs Woodfield's invaluable team – George Fowles, with Bill and Harry, from the City Engineers Department, and a later team from Winson Green Prison, Birmingham, particularly Mick and Jock.

Contributors

J. Ables, Father Jerome Bertram, Chris Caple, John Cattell, Mark Curteis, Geoff Egan, Ian Goodall, Edwin Holmes, Helen Howard, Philip Kibberd, Helen List, Richard Marks, David Moore, Graham Morgan, M. O'Hara, James Rackham, Stephanie Ratkai, Charles Tracy, Hugh Willmott and Paul Woodfield.

Illustrators

June Burbidge, Anne Endean, Nick Griffiths, Arthur Hillyer, Erica Jane Waters, David Watts and Paul Woodfield.

Charmian Woodfield gratefully acknowledges a financial contribution by the Carmelite Friars to the heavy cost of producing this report.

SUMMARY

Excavations carried out in the 1960s on the site of the Carmelite Friary at Coventry, England, revealed the lost church, of unexpected size and splendour, adjoining the standing cloister E range. It was founded in 1342 by Sir John Poulteney, a pre-eminent merchant and Draper, and Lord Mayor of London. The church had a six-bay choir and a central lantern tower. After structural failure, this was replaced by a square tower and spire, and transepts with a chapel; the nave with its slender piers was of nine bays, and this had eastern chapels, and elaborate tombs. Copious stonework was recovered giving some impression of its architectural character, mostly limewashed, but with some indications of wall paintings and a coloured and gilded tower tierceron vault and bosses. The tracery of the Great East Window was recovered and much other detail, including the remains of fine tombs, one with Renaissance dolphins. Large quantities (21,000 pieces) of painted window glass in the International Gothic style were recovered, perhaps the work of a London glazier, with a Tree of Jesse in the E window. Some interesting sculptural pieces were also recovered, including a Samson and the Lion and a costumed wildman probably relating to the Draper's Guild's Mystery Play. Encaustic tiles of over 200 types, of local origin, many hitherto unknown, came from the lavishly patterned floors, including mosaic tiles.

The report includes the first detailed examination of the standing E claustral range by the Royal Commission on Historic Monuments, probably the finest medieval friary claustral range to survive in N Europe. This is augmented by historical illustrations, many here published for the first time. There is also a study of the exceptionally fine surviving choir stalls, with the arms of several later London mayors, which originally seated up to 90 friars. These were set above acoustic chambers in the choir to amplify their singing. Only three other sets of friary choir stalls are known to exist in Britain.

Small finds include a rare oyster shell palette, uniquely with gold and red lake, also azurite; a unique enamelled roundel with twisted silver wire cloisons from a 15th-century Hungarian chalice, early 16th-century Venetian coloured millifiori glass, rare imported pottery from Spain and the Low Countries, and, surprisingly, among some dozen well-dated local wares, a bird whistle and a cucurbit. Pilgrim badges and a Valenciennes cloth seal, together with rare coins from Ireland and Scotland cast light on the internationalism of the Coventry friars. Other finds include a pair of spectacles, Nuremberg thimbles and sewing rings, and amber, jet and quartz rosary beads.

An attempt is made to reconstruct the appearance of the friary in its 10 acre (*c.*4ha) precinct in the 15th century, including the highly unusual architectural expression of the chapter house and the reredorter and the gate houses. Comparative plans of other Carmelite houses in Britain and Europe are illustrated for comparison, some for the first time.

The Coventry Whitefriars had early associations with the London Carmelites, and provided education in Theology as a counterpart to the Oxford Whitefriars' School of Philosophy. The friars were confessors to kings and the nobility, much respected for their works of mercy, and sought after for their singing. Reference is made to the visits of scholars, poets and philosophers and of Priors General of the European Order, Lawrence Burelli and Peter Terrasse, in 1494 and 1504.

After a short period as a palace for the renegade Carmelite John Bird as Bishop of Penrith, and a use of the reredorter, the eastern choir and the N transept as workshops, the friary was dissolved in 1538. It was purchased by John Hales in 1544 who set up a grammar and music school in the choir, and converted the E cloister range into a fine Elizabethan mansion, fit to accommodate the Queen. The church was finally destroyed by the City Corporation in 1573-4.

RÉSUMÉ

Les fouilles exécutées dans les années 1960 sur le site du monastêre de Carmes de Coventry, en Angleterre, ont mis au jour l'église disparue adjacente au cloître subsistant, qui s'est révélée de dimensions et d'une splendeur inattendues. Fondée en 1342 par Sir John Pulteney, un marchand drapier eminent, lord-maire de Londres, elle possédait un chœur à six travées et une tour lanterne centrale. S'étant effondrée, elle fut remplacée par une tour carrée a flêche, des transepts dotés d'une chapelle et une nef à neuf travées ; celle-ci possédait des chapelles à l'est, ainsi que des tombes ouvragées. On a retrouvé d'abondants fragments de maçonnerie qui donnent une idée du caractêre de son architecture. L'ensemble était enduit de chaux, mais on a découvert des traces de peintures murales, et la tour possédait une voûte à tiercerons ainsi que des bossages colorés. On a également dégagé le remplage du grand vitrail est et de nombreux autres détails, y compris de belles tombes, dont l'une ornée de dauphins Renaissance. On a mis au jour de grandes quantités (21 000 fragments) de verre de vitrail peint dans le style du gothique international, y compris un arbre de Jesse provenant du vitrail est, dont l'auteur était peut-être un verrier londonien. Des sculptures intéressantes ont été exhumées, entre autres un Samson au lion et un sauvage costumé ayant probablement un rapport avec le mystère de la Guilde des drapiers. Des carreaux émaillés de fabrication locale de plus de 200 types, dont un grand nombre jusqu'à présent inconnus, composaient les sols à la décoration luxueuse, y compris des carreaux de mosaïque.

L'exposé contient le premier examen de détaillé, par La Royal Commission on Historic Monuments, des bâtiments claustraux est qui sont encore debout et forment sans doute le plus bel ensemble claustral survivant en Europe. Il est accompagné d'illustrations historiques, dont de nombreuses sont publiées ici pour la première fois. Il comporte également une étude des stalles du chœur subsistantes qui, d'une beauté exceptionnelle, sont ornées des armes de plusieurs autres maires de Londres et pouvaient accueillir jusqu'à 90 moines. Elles avaient été installées au-dessus de chambres acoustiques creusées sous le chœur pour amplifier leurs chants.

Les petits objets découverts comprennent une rare palette en coquille d'huître, ornée d'or et de laque rouge ainsi que d'azurite ; un rondeau émaillé exceptionnel, à cloisons en argent torsadé provenant d'un calice hongrois du XVe siècle, du verre *millefiori* coloré de Venise datant du XVe siècle, des poteries importées rares venant d'Espagne et des Pays-Bas ainsi que, chose surprenante, un sifflet en forme d'oiseau et une cucurbite. Des insignes de pèlerins et un sceau de tissus de Valenciennes ainsi que des pièces rares d'Irlande et d'Écosse témoignent des liens qu'entretenaient les frères de Coventry avec l'étranger. On a également trouvé une paire de lunettes, des dés de Nuremberg et des anneaux de couture, ainsi que des perles de rosaire en ambre, en jais et en quartz.

Une tentative est faite pour reconstituer l'apparence du monastère dans son enceinte de quatre hectares au XVe siècle, ainsi que l'expression architecturale d'une grande originalité du chapitre et des latrines. Les plans d'autres monastères de Carmes d'Europe et de Grande-Bretagne sont illustrés à titre de comparaison, dont certains pour la première fois.

Les Carmes de Coventry entretenaient des le début des liens avec ceux de Londres et dispensaient un enseignement en théologie complémentaire de celui de l'école de philosophie des Carmes d'Oxford. Les frères étaient les confesseurs des rois et de la noblesse ; leurs œuvres de charité éveillaient unn grand respect et ils étaient très demandés pour leur chant. Les visites des Prieurs Généraux de l'ordre européen, Lawrence Burelli et Peter Terrasse sont mentionnées en 1494 et 1504.

Après une brève période durant laquelle il servit de palais au Carme renégat, John Bird, évêque de Penrith, puis d'ateliers, le monastère fut dissout en 1538. Il fut acheté par John Hales en 1544, qui fonda, dans le chœur, une école où l'on enseignait entre autres la musique et transforma les bâtiments du cloître est en tin beau manoir élisabéthain digne d'accueillir la reine. Le bâtiment fut enfin détruit par la City Corporation en 1573-1574.

ZUSAMMENFASSUNG

Am Standort des Karmeliterklosters in Coventry, England, wurde bei Ausgrabungen in den sechziger Jahren neben dem noch stehenden Kreuzgang die verlorene Kirche gefunden, die sich als unerwartet groß und prächtig herausstellte. Sie wurde im Jahr 1342 von Sir John Poulteney gegründet, prominenter Kaufmann, Tuchhändler und Oberbürgermeister von London. Die Kirche wies einen sechsgliedrigen Chor und einen zentralen Lichtturm auf. Wegen Baufälligkeit wurde dies später durch eine quadratische Turmspitze, Querschiffe mit Kapelle und einem neungliedrigen Schiff ersetzt. An der Ostseite wies dieses Gebäude Kapellen und kunstvolle Grabmale auf. Bausteine wurden in großer Zahl gefunden und vermittelten einen Eindruck ihrer architektonischen Gestaltung. Größtenteils waren sie weiß gekalkt, es gab aber auch Spuren von Wandgemälden sowie farbigen Rippen und Schlußsteinen im Turmgewölbe. Das Maßwerk des großen Ostfensters wurde wiederhergestellt sowie viele andere Einzelheiten, zum Beispiel feine Grabstätten, eine davon mit Delphinen der Renaissance. Große Mengen an farbigem Glas (21000 Stück) im internationalen gothischen Stil, mit einem Baum Isais im Ostfenster, wurden ebenfalls gefunden, womöglich die Arbeit eines Londoner Glasers. Einige interessante Skulpturen kamen ans Tageslicht, wie z.B. einem Samson mit Löwen und einem wilden Mann, die wahrscheinlich aus dem Mysterienspiel der Tuchhändlerzunft stammen. Von dem reichhaltig gemusterten Fußboden sind über 200 verschiedene Arten enkaustische Kacheln regionalen Ursprungs erhalten, viele davon vorher noch unbekannt, einschließlich Mosaikfliesen.

Der Artikel beinhaltet die erste Detailuntersuchung des noch bestehenden östlichen Klosterkomplexes durch die Royal Commission on Historic Monuments [Königliche Kommission für Historische Gebäude]. Dies ist wohl der bedeutendste noch erhaltene Klosterkomplex in Europa. Zusätzlich sind historische Illustrationen beigefügt, viele davon hier zum ersten Mal veröffentlicht. Außerdem finden sich eine Studie des außerordentlichen noch erhaltenen Chorgestühls, das ursprünglich 90 Mönchen Platz bot, mit den Wappen mehrerer späterer Oberbürgermeister von London. Zur Klangverstärkung befand es sich über akustischen Kammern.

Unter den kleineren Funden gab es zum Beispiel eine seltene Palette aus Austernschalen, einzigartig mit goldenem und rotem Lackpigment und Azurit sowie einem einzigartigen emaillierten Tablett mit gewundener Silberdekorarbeit, das zu einem ungarischen Kelch aus dem 15. Jahrhundert gehört. Außerdem fanden sich venezianisches millifiori Glas aus dem frühen 15. Jahrhundert, seltene Töpferarbeiten spanischer und niederländischer Herkunft, überraschenderweise eine Vogelpfeife und ein Destillierkolben. Pilgrimabzeichen und ein Tuchsiegel aus Valenciennes, wie auch seltene Münzen aus Irland und Schottland weisen auf den internationalen Bezugsbereich der Mönche hin. Weitere Funde sind zum Beispiel eine Brille, Nürnberger Fingerhüte und Nähringe sowie Rosenkranzperlen aus Bernstein, Jett und Quarz.

Der Artikel beinhaltet Rekonstruktionsvorschläge der 10 Morgen großen Klosteranlage im 15. Jahrhundert, sowie der sehr ungewöhnlichen architektonischen Erscheinung des Kapitelhauses und des Necessariums. Zum Vergleich finden sich Illustrationen von Plänen ähnlicher Karmeliterhäuser in Großbritannien und Europa; einige davon erscheinen hier zum ersten Mal.

Die Karmeliter von Coventry wiesen bereits früh Verbindungen zu den Karmelitern in London auf; ihre Theologieausbildung bot eine Alternative zur Philosophie der Karmeliterschule in Oxford. Beichtväter von Königen und Adligen, waren die Karmeliter respektiert für ihre Barmherzigkeit, und ihr Gesang war hoch angesehen. Ein Vermerk bezeugt den Besuch von Gelehrten, Poeten, Philosphen und Äbten des europäischen Ordens, Lawrence Burelli und Peter Terrasse, in den Jahren 1494 und 1504.

Das Kloster wurde für kurze Zeit als Palast des abtrünnigen Karmeliter John Bird, Bischof von Penrith, und später als Werkstatt benutzt, bevor es im Jahr 1538 aufgelöst wurde. 1544 wurde das Gebäude von John Hales aufgekauft, der dort ein Gymnasium und eine Musikschule errichtete; den östlichen Klosterkomplex verwandelte er in ein elisabethanisches Herrenhaus, das die Königin als Gast empfangen konnte.

Das Gebäude wurde schließlich in den Jahren 1573-74 von der Gemeinde zerstört.

SECTION A
THE RÉSUMÉ

C. Woodfield

Because of the length of this publication it has been thought realistic to preface it with a résumé of the main history and discoveries. The reader can then follow up those points of main interest to him or her. References are normally not given here, but in the full text.

SECTION B: HISTORICAL BACKGROUND

C. Woodfield.

The Order of Our Lady of Mount Carmel, the Carmelites, or Whitefriars, originated as a group of hermits on Mount Carmel in Israel, owing allegiance to the prophet Elijah (Elias), in the 9th century BC, but a formalised hermitic Order was not established until 1226 AD. The Crusaders' wars caused the Earl of Cornwall, brother to Henry III, to bring members of this Order over to England in 1240, when they became transformed from hermits into an active mendicant Order, embracing poverty, evangelising, preaching, teaching, and receiving confessions, from kings and paupers alike. They obtained patronage from royalty, nobility, Fig. 54, and the affluent laity, and at Coventry formed links with the City Guilds, who held their feasts at the Whitefriars. The friars were also scholars, philosophers, poets, historians, scientists and explorers (Hakluyt records a friar, Nicholas of Lynn, possibly a Carmelite (or a Franciscan), visiting in 1360 the circumpolar islands with his astrolabe, and recording a magnetic rock 13 miles in circumference under the North Pole); they were originators of the universities; and their cult of Mary resulted in a supportive attitude towards women, and meant they were known as 'women's brothers'. It is known that they played a courageous part in times of plague holding services for, and burying, those infected.

There were, however, disputes about precedence with other Orders of Friars, e.g. with the Dominican friars at Cambridge in 1369, who held it 'more honour to be named after a man than a mountain'! There was also an objection to the Whitefriars calling themselves 'the brothers of the blessed Virgin' and then 'by consequence, we all know whose uncles they pretend to be'.

The distribution of Carmelite houses in the British Isles is given on Fig. 3 and comparative plans of the houses on Figs 4-7.

The Coventry Whitefriars Establishment

Figures 12, 15, 20-21, 23, 25, 27, 32, 39, 44-46 and 56 (antiquarian drawings and paintings);
Figures 2, 4, 6, 30, 37-38, 40-43 and 47-52b (maps, plans and sections);
Figures 9-11 and 33 (recording of standing buildings);
Figures 31, 34-36 (reconstructions of friary buildings);
Figures 13-14, 16-19, 22, 24, 26, 28-29, 57, 59a-65b (photographs).

'As confessors particularly, and as buriers of the dead, the friars popularity amongst townspeople had brought them the wealth that had set up for example, an establishment as magnificent as the Carmelite house at Coventry' (Platt 1978, 212), Fig. 31.

The founder of this relatively late Coventry house was Sir John Poulteney, one of the wealthiest citizens of London in medieval times, a Draper and four times Lord Mayor of London. It was a House of Studies, in this case Theology, from the beginning, with close links with the Oxford House, with its School of Philosophy, and with Winchester. The choir stalls, Figs 82-93, suggest seating for some 90 persons, which would include visiting students, novices and the local clergy. Little information survives of the life of the Friary, but the presence of carrels in the cloister must relate to study and the preparation of manuscripts. The only document known to survive from the monastic period is Sir Henry Willoughby's (printed) Letter of Confraternity of 1512 (he owned coal mines at Wyken outside the City), Fig. 55.

The friary was dissolved in 1538, by which time the friars numbers had sunk to 14, but in 1536, to possibly 1544, there appears to have been an unusual period of use; this was the leasing of part of the Whitefriars by the Crown as an apparent 'Bishop's Palace' to John Bird, the Coventry-born renegade last Provincial of the English

Carmelite Order, for some eight years, Fig. 53. Bird was Suffragan Bishop of Penrith by 1536/7 and the Whitefriars would have provided lodging, stabling (a King's stable is known) and accommodation useful when making the long journey from almost the Scottish borders to London. As the lease was for life it may have continued through his subsequent holding of the Bishoprics of Bangor and Chester to 1544.

The Whitefriars was not spared at the Dissolution despite pleas of the City which surprisingly had only two parish churches (Norwich has 30). The Letters Patent granting the request of Sir Ralph Sadleir (a famous man of the day, who had just held the office of Principal Secretary of State) to purchase the property in 1544, list structures of which we are otherwise unaware, viz. a dovecote, fishponds, barns and a granary, and also gardens, ornamental ponds and orchards. A mill is also known to have existed, Fig. 37. Later in 1544 the property was bought by John Hales, a man with great interest in education and connections with important men of the day, not only Sir Ralph Sadleir but also with the Lord Protector of the realm, the Duke of Somerset. As an MP he made efforts to assist the poor by introducing parliamentary Bills such as that for the rebuilding of decayed dwelling houses. In 1545 Hales founded the Free Grammar School in the western choir of the church, still the only 16th-century Grammar School to have been excavated in this country. It unusually included a Music School, and an interesting range of small finds from there was published in a well-known report by this author (1981). The hostility of the City authorities caused the Grammar School to be moved to St John's Hospital in 1557-8, taking with them choir stalls which still largely survive, Figs 82-93. The City's aim was to retain the Carmelite church as a parish church, but this project was doomed to sink in a sea of squabbles. In 1573 the now ruinous and roofless church was partly demolished by the Corporation and in 1574 the tower and spire fell. The great bell was sold and moved to Holy Trinity, Coventry. Recast it now hangs in the cathedral of Christchurch, New Zealand (Pickford 1987, 465 and 468).

For his great Elizabethan mansion John Hales retained the E range of the cloister, Figs 9-30, 39, 44-46 and 56, with parts of its N and S ranges, together it seems (there are virtually no records) with part of the medieval courtyard S of the cloister, Fig. 15, and the adjoining Prior's House/Bishop's Palace, Figs 38 and 49. Unfortunately the nature and importance of this last building was not understood, and evidence for it was destroyed without record in the early 1980s. Two Elizabethan walled gardens are known W of the E cloister range, Figs 30 and 38, the northern one terminating against the standing S wall of the nave, apparently an early example of the use of a Gothick ruin as a garden feature; part of the vaulting of the W cloister range was likewise retained. The main entrance was through a fine reset doorway on the truncated S range, Figs 9 and 56. Two of the E cloister range garth windows were widened, Fig. 56; in summer these gave easy access to the gardens; in winter a covered and glazed walk was provided with a view of those gardens. The dorter was provided with a plaster ceiling and became perhaps an early long gallery with fireplace and oriel window, Figs 23 and 27-28.

To the S of the cloister lay what seemed basically to be an Inner (service) Court, Figs 15, 23, 29-30 and 38, although ranges of rooms of some quality are probable, most likely in the W and S areas of that Court. About these almost nothing is known except that some appear to have been three-storeyed, and to have involved the re-use of friary buildings, with some total rebuilding, (probably the western range at least). The E range was expanded to the E and connected at the S with a large building that related in some manner to the Prior's House, Fig. 25; both seem to have been three-storeyed. About these two E and S buildings almost nothing is known, particularly the S building, except for the *c.*1800 outline plans, Fig. 30.

The house was fit, and indeed used, to entertain monarchs, Elizabeth I, Mary Queen of Scots and later James I, it being presumably the largest and finest house in Coventry at that time.

SECTION C: THE STANDING BUILDING - THE EAST CLOISTER RANGE

J. Cattell and P. Woodfield

Figures 9-11, 13-30 and 37-39

The Coventry Whitefriars included, as well as an exceptionally large and important friary church, Figs 4-7, not only in British but in European terms (about which nothing had been known before the 1960s excavations), but also the important still standing E claustral range, probably the finest surviving friary cloister building in North Europe; its present neglected condition should be regarded as unacceptable, particularly as E cloister ranges rarely survive the Dissolution. It appears to have been constructed by royal master masons William Ramsay III and John Box. Ramsay is known to have connections with the founder Sir John Poulteney and Poulteney's great house at Penshurst, Kent, and the two doorways at the S of the standing Cloister with their male and female heads are thought likely to relate to Ramsay, Figs 14 and 66a-b.

The style of the cloister is that of the change from late Decorated to Perpendicular, and it is of elaborate design and high quality. Unusual features include the cut-water buttresses, Fig. 9, and the eleven bays of the cloister walks' elaborate tierceron, star and quatrefoil cusping vault; on the E side the simpler vaults are carried on corbels carved as cowled heads, Figs 16 and 66c, probably representing important Carmelites or benefactors; the use of stone vaults over cloister walks in friaries is rare. There is evidence (carrels) for *studia* and libraries, and for a unique quality night stair with extraordinary large torii mouldings, possibly by the master mason Robert Skyllington, Figs 21, 25 and 44-46.

The first floor tie beam, collars and queen struts roof, with purlins and windbraces, Fig. 22, is now dendrochronologically dated to the later last quarter of the 15th century. Might this work, which relates in time with the finishing of the nave, the rebuilding of the sacristy, and probably the tower and spire, (and also to the 60 year run for repairs mentioned in the Vatican document of 1423), relate to the visits of Lawrence Burelli the Prior General in 1494, Peter Terrasse the Prior General of the order in 1504, and in 1505 the election of the Provincial? The overall dimensions of the cloister garth are some 43m N to S, and some 46m E to W. The sculpture of a friar in the cloister walk is noteworthy, though pollution damaged, Fig. 66b.

The use of the two chambers at the E of the cloister are uncertain. Day room, inner parlour, common room, school room for novices or novices lodgings, early frater, misericord (dining room for the sick and elderly) and warming house, have all been suggested.

The chapter house of which only one bay is standing, was rebuilt in the later 14th century with an elaborate entrance arch leading into it from the cloister, the vault having parallels with Tewkesbury and Wells Cathedral, Fig. 18. At each side of the entry arch are curious opposed passages entered through plain ogee-arched openings, connecting the unusual chambers to the N and S of the chapter house. These passages are thought to be unique to Coventry Whitefriars, Fig. 19. The triangular buttresses of the chapter house, Figs 34 and 38, which differ from the cloister's cut water buttresses, are nearly identical with those of the Great Hall and flanking towers at Kenilworth Castle, built for John of Gaunt, son of Edward III, by the mason Robert Skyllington at the same period. Gaunt had strong Carmelite connections and confessors, and founded the Carmelite house at Doncaster. William Lubbenham, an important Carmelite, who was Provincial of the Order, was buried in 1361 'at the front of the entrance to the chapter house'.

SECTION D: RECONSTRUCTIONS AND RECORDING OF OUTLYING STANDING BUILDINGS

P. Woodfield

The *Chapter House*

Figures 34 and 38

This is a putative reconstruction, but the surviving remains indicate that this early rebuild of *c.* 1375-80 would have been a building of consequence, the vault having resemblances to Tewkesbury and Wells Cathedral. The surviving section of the internal vault of the chapter house determines the size of the bays; it is inconceivable that such a building would end in a half bay, and it is reconstructed as three bays. The weight is carried almost entirely on the triangular buttresses, presumably to allow for the intervening space to be fully glazed, as indicated. Triangular buttresses are paralleled at John of Gaunt's Kenilworth Castle a decade or so earlier, and Gaunt is a known patron of the Carmelites, so a connection is likely. Surviving evidence in the cloister suggests two storeys for this structure.

Inner Cloister Gate

Figures 12, 35 and 37

This gate had a fine lierne vault, the most spectacular of the surviving vaults, and three niches for statues on the outer face, with the Poulteney arms carried above the central niche. It was finally demolished in 1956.

The Reredorter

Figures 31, 36, 38 and 49

The reconstruction is of the unusual earlier 16th-century shortened reredorter, connected to the dorter by a two storey passage, all partly exposed during landscape clearance, and consisting of six substantial pier bases forming two E-W arcades with a secondary blocking wall at the E, with a narrowed opening leading to the eastern drain. Unfortunately no further clearance was done to the E, for a length of at least some five bays of the original building might be expected. The floor of heavy inward-sloping green sandstone flags continued outwards for one metre N and S of the arcade, presumably to bring in rainwater from overhanging water spouts to aid flushing, a system attested at Raglan Castle, Wales. The arcade would have supported the lavatories at first floor level. The nearest parallel to this form is the Benedictine Muchelney reredorter in Somerset. Jugs, of late medieval local wares, with hot-water lime deposits were found here, indicating that hot water was available to the friars for washing. Just before the Reformation the reredorter was replaced by a workshop.

The surviving Much Park Street outer Gate

Figures 33 and 37

The original stone fronted gateway (red sandstone, with decorative green sandstone banding on the front elevation only) was altered in the second half of the 14th century, but the present building dates largely from the 15th century. Few friary gateways survive in these urban settings. The reconstruction depicts its assumed original form with a statue niche, for which there is slight evidence, over the archway and with crenellations. The end walls are partly timber-framed and it may well be part of a larger *hospitium* range.

SECTION E: THE EXCAVATIONS

C. Woodfield

Figures 38, 40-43, 47-52 and 57-65

The site came under threat in the 1950s when a new ring road was planned, Fig. 57. The excavations in the 1960s (by Charmian Woodfield, at Dr. Graham Webster's suggestion, for the Ministry of Public Buildings and Works and Coventry Museum) revealed a church of unexpected size, and unexpected siting, for the standing cloister lay opposite the second and third W bays of the choir, not the expected E bay of the nave, Fig. 38. The 1960 trenches revealed not only the walls of a 10.5m wide choir, (the lack of aisles to the choir is common in friary churches) but resonance (acoustic) passages, and transepts, both these being rare in friary churches, Figs 42-43. The resonance passages were just over a metre square in section, and rock-cut as acoustic chambers, Fig. 51; they were supposed to resonate the singing coming through from those standing on the wooden boards of the choir stalls, Figs 82-4. A nave extending at least 55m to the W of the 1960 trenches was also attested, somewhat to the alarm of the tiny excavation team, Figs 41-2.

Further work in the 1960s revealed an aisled nave of nine bays, 48m. long, the W door, and the nature of the nave piers (they are identical in form even though the nave is of three phases). The pier bases reduce to very slender picrs to provide visibility for preacher and congregation, Fig. 76, No 1246. The lane, Fig. 38, - the space between the nave S aisle and cloister - is a feature of some friary churches including the London Whitefriars; it here carries an added buttress, because of the usual site problem of filled in quarry pits. Also recorded were two chapels, of the Holy Rood and Our Lady in the E nave transepts, and evidence for an early lantern tower and a 7 x 11m 'walking place', separating the choir from the preaching nave. It appears that the tower fell (or was replaced) and heavy buttressing added in the 15th to early 16th century, there being a constant battle to prevent falls of the tower. The later tower(s) are square-based, with a spire; a two-bay chapel at the NE of the N transept, later destroyed by the fall of the tower was also recorded. The area to the N of this chapel became a workshop at the end of the monastic period.

The choir was established as having six bays, and the multi-period plan of the sacristy and the passage from there to the presbytery were recorded. The sacristy had been much damaged *c.*1967 without record (the writer being then working in Sarawak), making interpretation from the Woodfield 1969 rescue excavation difficult. Examination of the NW corner of the cloister revealed the abandonment of an attempt to add a W range there in the early 16th century. The remains of elaborate painting was noted on walls and tombs, and clearances in 1977 produced painted roof bosses and other features, Figs 69, 71 and 73-8. Eight dated phases were established. It should be noted that the church is equivalent in length to Ripon or Hereford cathedrals.

The visits to England by the Prior General of the Order, Lawrence Burelli in 1494, and Peter Terrasse, also a Prior General in December, 1504, would have been occasions for a great international multitude to assemble here. Another important occasion is known in 1505, when friar Robert Lowe was elected Provincial at the Coventry house. This was probably the buildings' most spectacular period.

The City Wall enclosed the large ten-acre Whitefriars precinct on its S and E sides, Figs 2 and 37, and the friars are recorded as contributing to the cost of its construction; the waiving of the right to freedom from making contributions to the expense of the walling as religious men by the Carmelites is very unusual. The Salutation tower on that wall may have incorporated an earlier chapel of the Virgin Mary; it was on the London Road and housed a painted image of Our Lady, saluted by travellers. Orchards, gardens, a dovecote, the Kings Stable, St John's Hall and fishponds, are known to have existed, but they are now largely destroyed, as are the cemeteries. Fishponds are not normally attested in friaries but do occur at the Carmelite House at Appleby, Cumbria. The friars also had a water mill on the River Sherborne.

SECTION F: THE ARCHITECTURAL STONEWORK

P. Woodfield.

Figures 60a, 63a and 66-79

A total of 2,346 pieces of worked and shaped stone survived the post-excavation dispersal. Important groups come from the Great East Window (cusped tracery and oculi), and from the choir came fragments from wall tombs, shrines and canopies using colours including yellow and red ochre, a warm sienna ochre, blue and black, and gilding; there was also a crocketed and gilded ogee arch. A carved and painted boss came from the crossing, bearing the arms of Ferrers (vair, or and gules), possibly Ferrers de Groby? From the E end of the nave came again painted canopies from tombs, piscina and sedilia.

Most of the surviving masonry comes from the collapse of the tower, and comprises much blind lime-washed tracery in a bold and plain Perpendicular style of *c.*1450, but also includes painted floral bosses enlivened with vermilion, azurite, and gold leaf, probably from the tower complex cusped vault. The tracery would have formed a tierceron vault with a central star. and a smaller version formed the vault of the N transept chapel. Here there was also an arch with evidence of gilding, and a seven-lobed terminal enriched with leaves and pieces of a tomb or shrine with red white and blue stripes.

From the crossing, parts of the main chancel and transept arches survive.

From the southern nave chapel came fragments with a red ground and gilding and a piece in an early Renaissance style showing confronting dolphins, Fig. 75 No 1099.

Arch soffit mouldings probably from the nave arcades suggest the mouldings of the slender piers rose without interruption into the arches, with small capitals limited to the slender framing shafts. The indications are that a hall church may have been intended. This may be seen in large double-naved mendicant churches in France, such as Bordeaux and the Dominican church of Toulouse.

A high degree of masons' competence is present, though masons' marks (11) are surprisingly few, Fig. 79. The marks are not paralleled by any of those noted at St Michael's Coventry or St Mary's Guildhall.

SECTION G: ARCHITECTURAL SCULPTURE

H. List and P. Woodfield

Figures 80-81

Two figures are of more than local importance. Firstly, the gargoyle of Samson struggling with the Lion, unusual at this date, Fig. 80 No 1073. This is presumably from the tower, and was found in 1969 by one of Woodfields' workmen, 9m. NE of the N wall of the N chapel/porch. Note the hunting horn and detailed harness; a mid 14th- and a later 15th-century date are both suggested.

Secondly, the later 15th-century. figure of an apparent wild man or wodewose, Fig. 80 Nos 1076-77 and 1079, normally represents 'untamed humanity', but this figure in fact must relate to a dramatic performance or pageant, for his fur ends in cuffs at the wrist and below the knee; he is also provided with a codpiece, and the conclusion must be that he relates to Guild plays and pageants. His damaged bearded head, and a damaged hand, with fur and indications of a cuff, holding a torch, come from the same archaeological deposit and it is known that torches were carried in the Drapers play 'The Doom'. All the parts of this figure need to be considered together if we are not to seriously miss its significance. There is also a gargoyle spout in the form of a dog's head; unusually this appears to be a spaniel, Fig. 80 No 1072.

SECTION H: THE CHOIR STALLS

C. Tracy

Figures 82-93c

The Coventry stalls are one of only three sets of probable friary choir stalls to survive, and are of the very finest quality workmanship. This report identifies the workshop as probably that of the Lincoln Cathedral stalls, though there are parallels with those from London at St Katherine's-by-the-Tower. They were saved from destruction by John Hales who moved them from the church with his new-founded Grammar School to its new location in the medieval hall of St John's hospital, where they now languish neglected. There is a record of 32 of the original estimated 52 stalls. Most misericords represent foliage and secular subjects, but include an image of a wodewose with a chained lion, a green man, and three heads, one a fashionable lady in a crimpled veil. Ten of them are heraldic, particularly the lions, perhaps a reference to Sir John Poulteney's heraldic lion badges. Arms of mayors of London include Sir Nicholas Brembre, grocer, mayor in 1385; Sir William Walworth, fishmonger, mayor in 1381, and Sir John Philipot, grocer, mayor in 1378. Three earlier mayors are also represented: John Stodye, mayor in 1357, Adam Francis, mayor in 1352, and John Lovekin, fishmonger, mayor in 1348. Lovekin was also patron of the building of the W end of the London Whitefriars in 1348-50, and there is clear evidence for a close association between London mercantile interests and the Coventry house. The seating which is dated by Dr Tracy to the mid 1380s, had front benching for seating for novices, choir boys and visiting friars, Fig. 84a. The total seating would therefore have been 90 seats. A late 14th-century door head appears to be related, Fig. 93c.

SECTION I: THE MARBLES GAMING BOARD, CARVED ON THE CHOIR STALL DESKS

G. Egan with C. Woodfield

Figure 94

The marbles found in the Grammar School 1545-1558 deposits are the earliest found in England. It is not possible to date, with certainty, the gaming channels and scoring holes surviving on this desk, possibly multi-period in any case, but they are most likely to be of a similar date. Certainly an illustration of the Grammar School at St John's Hospital in 1801 shows the desks in place, but the boys are by then playing marbles on the floor, Fig. 84a.

SECTION J: THE PAINTED WINDOW GLASS

C. Woodfield

Figures 95-134

A total of some 21,000 pieces of painted medieval window glass was recovered, largely from the choir area. 900 of the 1640 drawings in the report are from the Tree (or rather vine) of Jesse in the Great East Window showing the descent of Christ from the royal house of David' Figs 95-114, and other Trees of Jesse are discussed. This assemblage records, unusually, a fossilised point of time in the 1540s for the precise destruction of images that then took place. The choir contained figures, the painting of costume being particularly fine, within pinnacled margins in the International Gothic style, the glass from the choir dating from *c.*1400. This earlier glass is of very high quality but cannot be tied to John Thornton or to other glaziers of the Coventry School, and it is possible that London glaziers were involved. Later glass of the third quarter of the 15th century from the crossing and the eastern nave shows a decline in quality. A comparison is made with other known Carmelite and friary glass.

SECTION K: SCIENTIFIC EXAMINATION OF AN OYSTER SHELL PALATE

H. Howard

Figures 135a-e and 135f-g

A later 15th-century oyster shell palette with gold leaf, azurite, red lake, lead white and carbon black, and a range of pinks and blues was recovered, similar to one from Clarendon Palace. This was the first case where red lake and gold leaf have been identified in a shell palette.

SECTION L: LATE FOURTEENTH AND FIFTEENTH-CENTURY STAMPED FLOOR TILE

C. Woodfield

Figures 136-147

Some 200 different tile patterns, are illustrated (this being more than the number known for, e.g. the county of Leicestershire). All are apparently products of the tile kiln at Stoke, Coventry, and it is estimated that tiling of the known floors alone would have required some 150,000 tiles. The larger tiles are here of earlier date than the smaller. All tiles are stamped and not inlaid. Sixteen-, nine-, and four-tile patterns are present, as well as 'endless repeating' patterns; heraldic, lettered, mosaic, border and cut plain tiles. A specialist report on the heraldry is presented. The significance of the different tile sizes and the manner and methods of laying are discussed and the importance of the complete pattern, which was what the tile maker intended and the client purchased, is emphasised. Full parallels are given with other sites. Analysis of the tile fabric and the manufacturing processes are given.

SECTION M: THE ROOF TILE

S. Ratkai and C. Woodfield

Figures 148-149

This report has established a chronology for the roof tile fabrics present, notably extending the date range of Chilvers Coton A tiles to the end of the 14th century. It has established the presence and the form of roof tiles made at the Stoke kilns; it has confirmed the chronology for crested ridge tiles, and suggested a new louvre type and other tile types; it draws attention to the presence of 'tiles and a half', their use being a sign of expensive roofing; it has also further indicated the decline of the use of glaze on roof tile in the later Middle Ages, and has established the use of women and children in the Stoke manufacturing process. The use of roof tile (and roof slate), for levelling courses in masonry walls has also been discussed. What buildings were roofed with tile has been established, together with the appearance of the perforated cloister sky line, with its brilliant green glaze colours.

SECTION N: TUDOR BRICK

P. Woodfield

Some 20 Tudor bricks are recorded, one at least being blue. Construction in brickwork including the last years of the friary (probably with diapered brickwork) can be anticipated, though perhaps only as chimney stacks. Certainly brick was used in grave 19, the chantry tomb in the SE nave.

SECTION O: SLATE

P. and C. Woodfield

Figure 150

The geology and occurrence of Stockingford Shale is described. This green laminating shale is generally used as roofing slate, but offcuts and laminates are used extensively for packing/levelling in masonry walls. It has been noted in the excavations at Much Park Street, Coventry, the Woodfield excavations on the Coventry City Wall, and at nearby Combe Abbey and Kenilworth Castle. All this seems to represent a substantial, but unlocated and undocumented, medieval industry, based probably in the Nuneaton area, perhaps at Griff.

SECTION P: PLASTERWORK

C. Woodfield

Two small pieces of wall plaster are noted.

SECTION Q: STRUCTURAL METALWORK

C. and P. Woodfield

Figure 151

The use of ironworking in medieval structures is clarified, ironwork occurring here as stonework ties from the fall of the tower, and also lead poured into dowel holes to prevent masonry moving. Pintles, decorative studs and straps of iron from doors, cupboard hinges, latch keys and saddle bars to support glazing also survived.

The iron nail clusters suggest that the chapels in the nave were divided by timber screens, and hint also at the survival of the *pulpitum* and the Rood screen throughout the school occupation. Drawn nails suggest the looting of coffins.

In 1560 the Corporation petitioned Queen Mary for the lead covering of the Whitefriars Church. One recognisable piece of roof lead survives, plus a few indeterminate fragments. Presumably other buildings were tiled.

SECTION R: THE POTTERY

S. Ratkai, J. Hurst and C. Woodfield

Figures 152-157

This assemblage of late medieval and early post-medieval pottery is of particular importance as a guide to the ceramic chronology of the West Midlands in these periods, because of its association with clear and often closely dated building phases. It includes Chilvers Coton Wares, Sandy Glazed Wares, Coventry Tripod Pitcher Ware, Brill, Potterspury, Developed Stamford Wares, Late Red Wares, Tin-glazed Enamels, Tudor Green, Midland Purple, Cistercian/Blackwares, Yellow Wares, and Rhenish Stonewares from Raeren, Siegburg and Cologne and Bartmann (Frechen) wares. Martincamp wares from Neufchâtel-en-Bray, and a Malling jug also occur.

The pottery includes a rare imported Hispano-Moresque (Late Andalusian) lustreware dish of the late 15th century, Fig. 152.21, found in a grave, with parallels at Glastonbury Abbey; also a Late Andalusian albarello, Fig. 152.21a, of which only about a dozen are known in England; the finding of two vessels of these types together on one site is unparalleled; there is also a South Netherlands Maiolica altar vase, Fig. 152.22 of the first half of the 16th century, paralleled at the Boston Blackfriars.

Some 110 vessels are illustrated. There is detailed discussion of the numbers and sequence of forms. These include 14th-century bird whistles and alembic distilling bases. Post Dissolution pottery includes a pedestal salt, a Yellow Ware figurine or jug, a chafing dish fragment with parallels to the Rainbow portrait of Elizabeth I at Hatfield House, and a Frechen drinking jug with the arms of Amsterdam. A transfer printed Pearlware teapot in the Greek taste from the last and previously unrealised gentry phase of the Whitefriars, just before the coming of the Workhouse in 1800, depicts a fighting Amazon and a victorious Amazon.

SECTION S: THE VESSEL GLASS

H. Willmott

Figure 158

Fragments of high quality early 16th-century Venetian glass came from the resonance passages, presumably residual from the period of the Friary occupation. Two were from goblets decorated with coloured filligrana canes, these being occasionally found on high status sites, such as the Augustinian Priory at Canons Ashby, Northants. There was also a possible goblet in coloured millefiori glass, a very rare archaeological find. A further lattimo glass flask? is paralleled at the Carmelite house at Maldon. A blue Venetian pedestal bowl was also represented. English forest glass included pedestal beakers, flasks, a small dish and hanging lamps. These last appeared to relate to the Grammar School.

SECTION T: THE SMALL FINDS

G. Egan et al.

Figures 159-165

This section is a supplement to Charmian Woodfield's 1981 paper. There is a terminus *ante quem* of *c.*1560. but some material appears to be residual. Monastic finds include a ?15th-century high quality blue-enamelled gilded-bronze roundel with silver-outlined cloisons from the base of a Hungarian chalice? A spigot tap, a clapper bell and a candle-holder appear to relate to the friary, as does the convent seal and pins, bone styli, a hone, a tomb brass fragment, a Canterbury pilgrim's badge, a badge with the Madonna and Child, thimbles and sewing rings related to shrouds (both English and Nuremberg imports); also jet, amber and quartz beads, from rosaries. A Jew's harp may be of monastic origin. In the Grammar School phase pins, including rare fine ruff pins, and lace chapes, occurred in large numbers. There were book cover accessories, and a rare spectacle frame; also lead cloth seals, one from Valenciennes, and musket and pistol balls, presumably for shooting pigeons? A calibrated scale in 16th-century Arabic numerals possibly related to distilling, is unparalleled.

Local metal working is attested from friary (slight) and dissolution contexts. Pin making (over 1,700 examples) and chapes (over 450) and the casting of tokens is attested, as on other monastic sites. There was also evidence for bone working for beads, and pinners' bones. Black-coated copper alloy dress accessories were recovered, as also twisted wire loops, a toy sword, bone dice, tile quoits and slate counters, and unusually stone and ceramic marbles. A pre-medieval copper alloy pin, a possible Roman weight, and prehistoric flints also occurred, presumably picked up as curiosities.

SECTION U: WOUND WIRE-HEADED PINS
C. Caple

This report covers dating, typology, metrology, alloy composition changes (with parallels in brasses and jettons), manufacturing sources and imports from North-west Europe. Coventry pinners are also discussed.

SECTION V: NUMISMATICA
P. Woodfield

Two coins of Richard II of the 1380s relate to the construction of the choir and the E chapel in the N transept. A penny of Henry VI of *c.*1434 relates to the fall of the tower.

Residual medieval coins from the resonance passage and presbytery run from the time of King John to James III of Scotland, this last being an extremely rare Crosraguel penny. The occurrence of rarely found Irish coins (two Dublin pennies of Edward IV) was particularly interesting, indicating Irish travellers to London seeking hospitality from the friars. There were five coins of the Grammar School Period, four of Edward VI, and one of Charles V (Spanish Netherlands).

112 jettons were recorded. A jetton of the French Derivative type (later 15th century) was found in the construction trench of the seventh N nave arcade pier from the E, dating the finishing of the nave. The Grammar School presumably used the numerous later jettons for teaching the casting of accounts, and, probably, games.

SECTION W: HUMAN SKELETAL ANALYSIS
P. Kiberd

Figures 166-167

Vandalism was particularly directed at graves, and so graves discovered before 1965, after their position was recorded, were left for the period after the removal of 'Coventry's worse problem families' from the adjacent Workhouse site. Unfortunately the arrangements made for their excavation were not adhered to. The Woodfields 1968 return from Sarawak coincided with the road construction machinery ploughing through areas not previously thought at risk. A part record was then possible for a 15th-century elaborate (the robbing produced eight fleur terminals) double stone-lined grave of a clearly wealthy benefactor's family: 68 12 (robbed) 13, 14 and, surprisingly, an empty southern half (68 15). The lowest burial (68 14) in a pine coffin, was of an adult male of 30+, who suffered from Diffuse Idiopathic Skeletal Hyperostosis, a frightening condition. The body above, also in a pine coffin (68 13), was of a female of 40+ with notably poor dentition; a juvenile (68 12) burial inserted into the same grave was severely damaged by robbing and machining, Fig. 166.

Another double stone family tomb, 68 16 and 17, occurred again in the western area of the choir, badly damaged by road works. Grave 16 appeared to be that of a male of 50 years, and grave 17 a female of 30+ years with considerable tooth loss, Fig. 166.

Burial 60.1, Fig. 42, at the entrance to the choir was identified before vandalism as a young male 14± years; this was a simple shroud burial, Fig. 167, in a part stoned-line grave, Fig. 61a.

The 1977 presbytery graves show post-excavation damage and loss of skeletal material. Grave 77 2 was again a stone-built tomb of the late 14th/early 15th century of an elderly person (sex uncertain) with serious bone damage including spinal collapse; a rare inscribed stone pillow was discovered within this grave, Figs 43 and 71 No 1123.

77 6 was a 14th-century stone grave, of a middle aged ?male, the severe caries being again notable.

Two earth graves, Fig. 167, of young women in front of the High Altar were notable; 77 4, was a burial of a young woman 'with a narrow slender face' in an oak coffin, as was also 77 5, a youngish woman with severe caries.

Despite the presumed wealthy background, the poor dental condition of burials was notable. The amount of pathologies were considerable despite that assumed wealth.

SECTION X: THE ANIMAL BONE

J. Rackham

Unfortunately there have been post-excavation losses of material. There is a little evidence of the diet of the friars, mutton, pork and beef, but their domestic areas were destroyed virtually without record in the 1970s.

There is a little more evidence from the early 14th-century Pre-friary period, this relating to light industrial workers. Mutton, beef and chicken were eaten, with occasional occurrences of rabbit. red deer and goose.

Workshop?

The later industrial workers (later 1530s to earlier 1540s) ate principally mutton, beef, pork and chicken; goose, duck, and squabs occur in small quantities; there are single occurrences of rabbit, heron, woodcock, and pigeon; cod, conger eel, pike (from the fishpond?), oysters and mussels were also eaten. However, it is not impossible that some of this material came from the friary kitchen in a late monastic period.

Grammar School c.1545 to 1558.

A very varied diet was represented.

Meat included mutton, beef, pork, rabbit and possibly hare, and to a much lesser extent red and fallow deer. Poultry included chicken, duck, mallard, teal, goose, turkey, possibly peacock, grey herons perhaps from the friary fish pond, mute or whooper swans, grey partridge, woodcock, snipe, pigeon and thrush.

Non-game birds apparently resident in the church, with its broken windows, included kites, crows, jackdaws, and rooks. A sparrowhawk may have been used for hawking as a hawking bell was recovered from the same deposit; shooting also occurred.

Apart from the pike, presumably from the fishpond, fish are marine species and cod, conger eel, skate and thornback ray occur, indicating a supply of dry or salted fish. Shell fish included oysters, mussels and cockles.

Other animal bones included cats and dogs in small numbers, and the bones of presumably scavenging animals, rats, mice, and badgers.

The exceptionally varied diet suggests the richer schoolboys brought their own food from home, while food may have been provided at the School (cooked in the Big House?) for the poorer boys. Cockerel spurred tarso metatarsi raise the question of whether the boys indulged in cock fighting. Also the geese were probably not only eaten but provided a supply of quill feathers.

In the Destruction phase, pork, mutton and beef were part of the picnic of those smashing up a fine chantry tomb (Grave 64 19) and destroying the burial.

SECTION Y: WOOD AND CHARCOAL ANALYSIS

G. Morgan

The timber from two burials was identified as oak (14th century), and from two others as pine (15th century), see Section W, *Human Skeletal Analysis*. The charcoal derived from Grammar School heating or cooking deposits, presumably from a brazier, was oak, poplar and hazel.

SECTION B

THE WHITEFRIARS IN COVENTRY - HISTORICAL BACKGROUND

C. Woodfield

Chill tell thee by my Vazen,
That zometimes che have knowne
A vair and goodly Abbey
Stand here of Bricke and Stone:
And many a holy Vrier
As ich may say to thee
Within these goodly Cloysters
Che did full often zee.

The Noise was passing trim
To heare the Vriers zinging
As we did enter in:
And then to see the Rood-loft
Zo bravely set with zaints:-
But now to zee them wandring
My heart wih zorrow vaints.

A Pleasant Dialogue between Plaine Truth and Blind Ignorance
(Elizabethan ballad: Thomas Deloney (1543?-1600))

HISTORICAL BACKGROUND

There has been neither funding, nor, any longer, time, available for the undertaking of substantial original research into the historical background of the Coventry Whitefriars, and what follows is a compilation of material, largely from existing publications (see separate bibliography at end of this section), but particularly from W. G. Fretton's 1872 paper. The exception is material from work undertaken by the late Dr A. and Mrs E. Gooder, which has produced some important new evidence, included here.

The Order of Our Lady of Mount Carmel, the Carmelites, or Whitefriars, originated as a group of hermits on Mount Carmel in Israel, owing allegiance to the prophet Elijah, (known in Greek as Elias), as long ago as the 9th century BC. They practised poverty, fasting and chastity, and are referred to in the Book of Kings (Kings, I, XVIII, XIX). At a later period we know of another cave-dwelling hermit group, the Essenes of the 2nd and 1st century BC, and the book of Micah refers to them 'as those that dwell alone in the forests in the midst of Carmel'. The Carmelites claimed descent from these cave-dwelling hermits and this was to be the basis of many a later medieval dispute on the subject of precedence. A church building was certainly in existence in the 12th century AD, with a fully formalised Order being established there by Pope Honorius III in 1226. The Saracens attacked this establishment in 1238 and the Crusaders' wars made their continued existence there impossible. In 1240 the first members of the Mount Carmel hermits were brought over to England by Richard, Earl of Cornwall, brother to Henry III, an early benefactor, and set about establishing the Carmelite Order here.

Briefly Christian Monasticism began in the 3rd century AD and was formalised by St Benedict in the sixth century. The friars, as evangelising and teaching orders, as opposed to the enclaustered older orders, first appeared in the early 13th century. St Francis of Assisi founded the Franciscan or Greyfriars in 1210, and St Dominic the Blackfriars in 1216. They were joined by the Carmelites or Whitefriars in 1240, and the Augustines or Austin friars in 1244. The claims of the Carmelite friars that Elijah was their true founder gave them, (despite their appearance being to western European eyes a millenium and a half late on the monastic scene), an opportunity to assert that the Carmelites were the true founders of all Christian monastic life. The first Carmelite 'hermitages' in England were established away from towns, at Hulne, Northumberland in 1242, where much remains, and at Aylesford, Kent also in 1242, still a practising Carmelite friary, but the movement into towns followed shortly with the London foundation being in 1247, Figs 3 and 4. The new rule of this year provided for a strengthening of community life in the convent, and the development of pastoral care by giving sermons and receiving confessions, and for common ownership.

Opposition against embracing the *vita activa* was expressed in the early days of the Carmelites, but it could not prevent their transformation from hermits into a mendicant order. However, the ideal of their former life in isolation and strict asceticism was kept alive. As early as the 13th century the Carmelites had successfully expanded to cover the whole of Occidental Christianity (about 150 convents). During the second Council of Lyon (1274) the order avoided dissolution which was demanded not only by many town clergy but also by Dominicans and Franciscans. In 1286 the order was finally confirmed by Pope Honorius II and in 1326 it was granted all the privileges of the older mendicant Orders.

The friars came into existence because the main monastic orders had tended to become wealthy, worldly and part of the establishment. Friars owned nothing, relied on gifts to survive, embraced poverty, and thus established a relationship to the poor. Their activities included prayers and masses, being particularly active as evangelists and public preachers. They buried (and fed) both the poor and those who died of the plague that others feared to touch; they also buried the nobility in choir and chapter house, for the Carmelites obtained patronage from royalty, nobility and the affluent laity, and at Coventry formed links with the City Guilds.

The friars ran colleges, and became noted scholars in theology, philosophy, logic and grammar - William of Coventry also studied 'poetry, dialectics, rhetoric and the best histories' - Carmelite glass surviving at Cambridge shows ten Carmelites in Doctor's caps. The friars were originators of the universities, and active in the promotion of sciences, including the science of architecture, and it was the Franciscan Roger Bacon who wrote down the first European recipe for gunpowder, in code. However, they were not allowed to take a degree 'for vanity's sake'. Hakluyt records a friar, Nicholas of Lynn, apparently a Carmelite, visiting in 1360 the circumpolar islands with his astrolabe, and recording a magnetic rock 13 miles in circumference under the north pole. Friar Nicholas is mentioned in Chaucer's Prologue to his *Treatise on the Astrolabe*. The Franciscan friary of La Rabida sheltered and encouraged Christopher Columbus, and Carmelite friars were with explorers of the New World, and it was their identifying a resemblance between an American mountain and Mt Carmel in Palestine, which gave the Californian town of Carmel its name.

The friars took the Confessions of kings and paupers alike (both doubtless alarmed at the approach of the Day of Judgement), Fig. 54. Their message was that covetousness and greed can well destroy every generous impulse, and abstinence, fasting, poverty, humility, charity and control of anger were urged. Especially through their contacts with guilds, and the cultivation of the cult of Mary (Fig. 55, hence they were often dubbed 'women's brothers'), they gained great significance in Europe in the later Middle Ages, and the brothers were sent far and wide to European centres of study and intellectual culture, Fig. 7. Due to their high level of education they were often called on to become Bishops. In England they also played a political role as advisors and confessors to the King's Court, and were often involved in political missions. The Carmelites did not remain untouched by the decay of discipline in the Orders, starting in the second half of the 14th century. A relaxation of the rule granted by Eugen IV (1434/35) took account of the new situation, but from the beginning of the 15th century efforts at reform were made within the Order, aimed at establishing stricter observance of the rule and at reviving the ideals of hermitage. Parallels to the reformed congregations of, e.g. Mantua and Albi, are not attested in Britain, and the formation of the Discalced Carmelites at the end of the 16th century came too late for the English Province. New questions are now being asked about the Dissolution in England - such as was greed or reform the real motive, and were the real causes economic and political, not religious. There has been a reluctant taking on board of the immense loss of artistic treasure.

Though many will have benefited from the presence of the friars, it should be noted that they had their detractors. In the Prologue to Chaucer's *Summoners Tale*, the summoner recounts a story of twenty thousand friars in hell, hidden under Satan's tail. The Carmelites were constantly attacked by the wealthy beneficed clergy in particular, and preached against them in turn. There were also controversies with other orders of friars, some certainly not of high intellectual or moral quality. There was a dispute with the Dominican friars of Cambridge in 1369 who held it 'more honour to be named after a man than a mountain'. There was also an objection to the (White)friars calling themselves 'the brothers of the blessed Virgin' in whose honour they wore the white garments, and then, 'by consequence, we all know whose uncles they pretend to be.'

HISTORY OF THE COVENTRY HOUSE

'as confessors particularly and as buriers of the dead, the friars popularity amongst townspeople had brought them the wealth that had set up for example, an establishment as magnificent as the Carmelite house at Coventry' (Platt 1978, 72, fig. 49)

The appearance of the phrase 'The friars did not possess the magnificent buildings of the traditional monastic orders' (McAleavy, 55) as late as 1996 shows how well established this belief still is, and how incorrect in many cases.

Historical sequence

The monastic buildings

Coventry was the 34th Carmelite house to be founded in Britain, there being eventually some 40 houses in all. Its central position in the country must have added to its importance. The founder was Sir John Poulteney, one of the greatest citizens of medieval London, a Draper and four times mayor of London; he was the first merchant to be knighted (in 1338, by the Black Prince) and was highly favoured by King Edward III. He founded the college of St Lawrence Poulteney, London, and gave many legacies for the poor. He was also the builder of Penshurst Place, one of the surviving great houses of Kent, but his family came from Misterton in Leicestershire, some 15 miles N of Coventry, Poulteney being a hamlet of that village, now reduced to two farmhouses which still bear his name.

It is clear that the founder's family maintained an interest in the Coventry House for in 1472 a descendant of the founder, John Poulteney, directed that his body should be buried in the church, and again in 1505-6 Sir Thomas Poulteney a member of the Corpus Christi Guild of the city likewise directed that his body be buried in the chancel and appointed that at his funeral twenty-four torches, each having his arms thereon, should be borne by twenty-four poor men, every one having a gown with the libberds head behind and before. A Founder's Chamber survived to the Dissolution.

It is known that William de Ingleton and Nicholas Sproton, priests, obtained a licence from the King, and gave to the provincial prior of the Order of Mt Carmel in England one messuage and 10 acres of land in Coventry. This licence of 1342 was for a church to be built '...in honour of the Virgin Mary' and a habitation. The Benedictine Priory seems, rather unusually perhaps, to have welcomed the Carmelites, and in 1343 the Benedictine Prior of Coventry gave to the Prior and brethren of the Order of Mount Carmel some land in Coventry. A note in the City MS annals gives a list of twelve men who purchased the freedom of the city four years before there was any mayor i.e. 1344, and 'then the White Fryers was builded', which indicates considerable building activity in two years, for John Ward, the first mayor, held office in 1348. It is presumably the standing E cloister range which is of this early date. In 1344 they gained another grant of land from the Crown, and in 1352 paid 6s 8d to the Crown for a licence to acquire two messuages adjoining their own manse, probably for the purpose of enlargement. William Luffe, third mayor of Coventry 1352, and John Box (could this be the master mason believed to be involved in the construction of the surviving cloister range?, see Section C) were parties to this transaction which in addition comprised the third part of two other messuages and one toft for a way in from Much Park Street.

The City Wall

In 1344, two years after the establishment of the Whitefriars, Edward III granted a charter of incorporation, and in 1356 the first stone of the city wall was laid at Newgate (the London Road) close to the Carmelite house. The Carmelites assisted largely in the expense of its construction where it joined their property, that is from Newgate E to the Mill on the river Sherbourne and then N to Gosford Gate, Figs 2 and 37, and the Whitefriars provided land in this section for both wall and ditch, a man to get stone for two years at the quarry, two masons, one carter, and one cart with four horses, etc. They also had to provide half the lime and all the stone for the line of the wall from Newgate to the Mill. The friars were granted a postern gate and a window towards the S, on condition of their blocking it with stone in two days if necessary, and citizens had to be allowed to take refuge in the precinct if required; a bridge was allowed over the ditch to provide passage for friars and others to and from that precinct.

The cost of this must surely have slowed down the construction of the church, and the building of the Wall seems to have continued into at least the friary's Rebuild phase (the late 1420s) that is in a period when they were having to cope with the attested 'ruin' of the church. The waiving of the Carmelites' right to freedom from contributions to the expense of the walling as religious men seems very unusual.

It has for many years been accepted that Lord Bassett of Drayton's will of 1383 leaving £300, a very large sum, 'for the enlargement of their church' to the Carmelite House was the springboard for the completion of the transepts and the construction of six bays of the nave, and the archaeological evidence fits well with this view. The connection between Bassett and the Coventry Carmelites was thought to be related to the connection between Bassett and John of Gaunt, a patron of the Order. However, a recent paper by John Hunt raises doubts as to the Coventry Carmelites receipt of money from this source, as Lord Bassett lived to make another will in 1389-90 in which the Coventry Whitefriars was not mentioned. However, we do not know whether a benefaction was made by Bassett, or indeed others, in the intervening years, of which we have no record; there seems clearly in any case to have been an intention in the early 1380s to 'enlarge the church'.

In 1413-4 King Henry V granted a licence to William Botoner of Withybrook (Warwicks.) to give the Carmelites a piece of ground in Coventry 141ft in length by 45ft in breadth for the enlargement of their habitation. It is possible that this refers to the construction of the NW corner of the cloister at this period. But additionally in Fretton's account 'he' bequeathed £20 to 'the making of the chamber in the house where he used to lie', and 'he' bequeathed to the Whitefriars his gown of crimson with the fur to make a vestment. It is not clear from this whether Fretton's pronoun refers to the King or William Botoner, and it has not been possible to trace all his sources to clarify this. Henry V was probably in the Midlands at this time, engaged in combating Lollardry, and as Botoner's dwelling place was only some half dozen miles from Coventry, it is not clear why he required 'a chamber' in that city.

Life in the Coventry Whitefriars

From the beginning the Coventry Whitefriars was a house of studies (*studium*) as the episcopal records show. The students of the Winchester Carmelite house, after receiving the minor orders, proceeded to Coventry, where in nearly every case they were ordained in major orders. This means that Coventry was kept for the study of Theology, and Winchester Philosophy. Coventry also had close links with the Oxford Carmelite house with its School of Philosophy. There were international connections as well, as it is known that in the second half of the 14th century William of Coventry, a historical and theological writer with an elegant and ornate style, and a studier of poetry, was also a lecturer at Paris. At the same period there was William Lubbenham, who went from Coventry to the Oxford House where he graduated as a Doctor of Theology at Oxford, and was a Provincial of the English Province in 1353; he also wrote on the subject of Philosophy. Lubbenham died at Coventry in 1361 and was buried in front of the entrance to the Chapter House. The friary would also have had its own school for the education of novices and local clergy, with suitably qualified brethren giving lectures which were also open to the public. The rather delayed structure of the nave presumably did not interfere with these studies, which would have taken place in other parts of the friary.

It looks, in any case, as if six bays of the nave were probably in existence by the beginning of the 15th century, Fig. 38. The reason for the three bay extension of the later fifteenth century must mean that six bays were not enough to accommodate those who wished to attend.

As well as the church and its probable three chapels known from excavation there are additional records of a separate square building apparently dating from the 1420s, known as the Lady's Tower or the Salutation Tower (although there are suggestions that this was a rebuild of an earlier chapel and its strange relationship to the City Wall does suggest it predates it, Fig. 37). The only physical records of it are as part of the City Wall however. Fretton comments 'In Dugdale's autograph copy of his History of Warwickshire is this additional unpublished account of the Lady Tower "This Chappell is in y't tower of the Cittye Wall w'th out Newgate, close by ye roadway leading towards London. On the outside thereof was a picture of the Blessed Virgin richly paynted, and within it an image and her altar, whereat most travellers wh'ch passd by did offer more or lesse, out of confidence that their journey would be the better blest."' To this image many pilgrimages were said to come and many offerings were made by religious devotees. There was however opposition, for in 1485 several persons were put to penance for refusing to honour the statue; subsequently the MS Annals record '1490, John Wygston, Mayor. This Mayor did stryve against our Lady place of the Wt. Friers' In 1499 contention arose again between the Carmelites and the then mayor, William Hopkins, 'who strove greatly against this tower of our Lady.' This is presumably an expression of the Lollardry for which the city was well known.

The Lady Tower chapel appeared to have not only its own altar but its own bell, for the City Accounts record '1539 It, for covering the bell at o'r Ladie of ye Tower iiij', and '1541 Costs mae'd on the leads at o'r ladie of the Towre.' These entries sound as if the tower and bell might have survived the Reformation for other civic purposes, and were being repaired, but the phrasing is ambiguous. Archaeology cannot now help here, for the site is unlikely to have survived the massive, unrecorded, roadworks of the 1980s.

There are two records, not known to Fretton and earlier antiquaries (which again raise questions about the usability of the nave, whose size suggests much activity) that in 1423 a plan was proposed for financing the repair of the church that had existed for 80 years and was now subject to ruin '*olim octuaginta annis jamfere elapsis ruinae subacta extitit...*' The plan called for the arrangement to last for 60 years, or until the church had been repaired (Egan in Fitzgerald-Lombard 1992, quoting *Bullarium Carmelitanum*, I, 174). Copsey (1992, Appendix I, 218) comments '1423 Martin V allows the Carmelites to apply the revenues from two benefices to the repair of the conventual church in Coventry'. The damage, to require such provisions, must have been severe and may have been caused by the fall of the new tower, but it is curious that the first Provincial Chapter to meet at Coventry was in 1431, only eight years later, for the MS Annals of the City record 'Then was the firste chapter of the White friers.' Is it possible that the nave was repaired and reasonably complete by then, even including the three western bays?, Figs 31 and 38. Or was the church still unfinished nearly a century after the foundation date? Certainly the rebuilding of the tower could take place within a decade or so.

More trouble was to come, for the MS Annals of the City record in 1446 'Then fell ye new worke at the White Friars' It is believed that it was the central tower which fell again, despite the buttressing which had taken place, the subsequent, secondary buttressing, suggesting this fall was to the NE.

The City Annals for 1471 recorded the use of the by now presumably fully completed nave for gaining Sanctuary. 'This yeare, one Gryffyth, a sergeant of Coventrie, arrested a man in the Church of the White Friars on All Hallows eve, and the Freres rescued the party and took the sergeant's mace from him'.

The relationship of the Carmelite house with the City Guilds is recorded from the 15th century on. There are records of the Carpenters, Pinners and Tylers (these last also were accustomed to offer at High Mass before their election, and went annually to the Whitefriars on St Stephen's day (26th December)); the Smiths, among others, held feasts at their House, and John Bird, the Provincial of the English House in the 1530s, was a member of the Smith's Company, and was also the Carmelites only known link to the important Trinity

Guild, of which he was a member. There are also records for the Cappers (1522) and the Carpenters with 'Item payd to þe ffrerys for synging iiij d' listed for their collation held at the Whitefriars in 1477, when 35 gallons of ale were consumed, (but not the wine of the Coventry Carthusians' feasts held just down the road). The food items for the Carpenters' feast were primarily mutton, but veal, geese and pork, garlic, onions and spices also occurred. The Carpenters in fact held their feasts for about a century at the Whitefriars. In 1507 the friars' butler was paid 4d by them for 'washing the cloths'. In 1515, at a great dinner of the Smith's company 'the cooke of the Whyte frer's assisted'. Although the feasts hardly represent abstinence, they were annual feasts. We have no record of what was eaten everyday at the Whitefriars, although we know there was a Brewhouse. There are also records for the Cappers (1522) and the Carpenters (1534) paying for masses and dirges at the Whitefriars.

Other provincial chapters met at Coventry, in 1490 and 1505. In 1494 Lawrence Burelli, Provincial of Narbonne, and deputy General of the International Order visited the White Friars in his progress through England, which provided the occasion for Latin poetical contests between the visitor and the students, for Burelli was famed for his epigrams and extempore versifying (Sheppard 1943, 32). In 1504 Peter Terrasse, Prior General of the Order, visited England, and is known to have been at Coventry on 7th December 1504 and again on 25th April 1505, for a Convocation of Priors for electing a new Provincial; this was Robert Love, who had studied at Cambridge where he obtained a doctorate in Theology. Both of these must have been spectacular occasions, with the church at its most splendid, but Father Copsey (*op. cit.*)comments that at this time the Province had 'lost much of its vigour' and states that 'Terrasse did little to stimulate reform within the order or to raise the level of religious observance.' The combination of splendid buildings and loss of way is a well known phenomenon.

In 1506 Thomas Bonde of Coventry bequeathed 'to the White Friars, towards the finishing of their cloister, 20 marks and that I have done before' Archaeology showed that the doubling of the western range of the cloister was in fact never finished, Fig. 47.

The surviving indication of carrells (small boarded enclosures erected to serve as studies for the brothers) are reminders that much of an ordinary day was spent in writing, illustration, reading and study, and the advent of printing must have created a lacuna in the monastic day. A printed letter of Fraternity survives from 1512, Fig. 55, granted from the convent at Coventry by the Prior Provincial in favour of Sir Henry Willoughby and his wife Helen (Dept of MSS and Special Collections, University of Nottingham, Middleton M5, MiF 1/7). The printed document has a border representing the Virgin Mary with the Infant Christ in her arms, and the names are inserted by hand in ink. As this is the only pre-Dissolution document surviving from the Coventry House it seems worth a translation from the Latin. (Robert Love had been elected Provincial at the Coventry house seven years before.)

> 'Brother Robert (Love), Prior Provincial and servant of the friars of the Order of Blessed Mary, Mother of God and of Mount Carmel, by which title our Order is in a special manner blessed, dwelling in England, to our beloved in Christ Sir Henry Willoughby and Lady Helen his wife, salvation and through the suffrages of our prayers, eternal happiness.
>
> Being well aware of the sincere devotion which you, in your reverence for Christ and His glorious Virgin Mother, Mary, have shown towards our Order, we are anxious to repay you by commending you to the Lord for the same, in so far as we may have influence at the throne of God, especially in the things most necessary to salvation.
>
> Be it known to all the faithful in Christ that our most holy fathers and lords in Christ, Adrian II, Stephen V, Sergius III, John X, John XI, Servius V and Innocent IV, by Divine Providence , have, in recompense for devotion to the Blessed and Glorious Virgin Mary, special protectrix and patroness of the Carmelite Order, mercifully granted to all the faithful in Christ who are truly penitent, who have confessed and are contrite, and who shall have received the Letters of Fraternity of the said Order, the remission of a third part of all their sins. Again Julius II confirmed, approved, and renewed, all the indulgences granted by his predecessors, the Roman Pontiffs, to our said Order, and in addition granted to all the faithful, truly penitent, confessed, and contrite, who have received the same Letters of Fraternity, an Indulgence of thirty years and thirty quarantines.
>
> We, therefore, by these present Letters of Fraternity, in consideration of your singular piety, grant you participation for ever, as well in life as in death, in all the Masses, prayers, fastings, vigils, preachings, abstinences, indulgences, labours and all the other good works, which the mercy of our Saviour may cause to be performed by our brethren in the said province.
>
> To this we add, conceding it as a special favour, that, when you are deceased, your memory shall be recalled in our Provincial Chapter, and the same will be done for you as it is customary to do for the deceased brethren of our Order.
>
> In testimony of which we attach our provincial seal to the present Letters of Fraternity.
>
> Given in the Convent of Coventry, in the year of

our Lord one thousand five hundred and twelve
By me, BROTHER TH. VICARS.'

(Thomas Vicars occurs again in the Surrender document, and in the 'Bishop's Palace' document of 1538-39, when he is still living 'within the precinct of the said late house of the Friars').

'The sum of the indulgences granted by the different Roman Pontiffs to the confratres, consorores and benefactors of our holy Order of Carmel amount to 5023 years and 80 days.' It must be said that the sale of Indulgences provoked much Protestant anger.

Sir Henry Willougby, Knight of the Sepulchre, was born in *c.*1451 and died in 1528, (when he bequeathed one mark to the Coventry Whitefriars for an obit) and was one of the wealthiest men in England in that period. His connections with Coventry were principally his holding of the manor of Wyken, with its coal mines, now in the eastern suburbs of the city. These mines brought him in £33 1s 9d in 1523-4. He was also commissioned, when in his 70s, with Sir Edward Ferrers (might the Whitefriars Ferrers shield, Figs 60a and 71, be of this date?) to repress a riot in Coventry in 1525.

It is of interest that he was the father of Hugh the Navigator, the first of our Arctic explorers, commander in chief of the famous expedition of the 'Mystery Company and Fellowship of Merchant Adventurers for the Discovery of Unknown Lands' to find the NE route to China. He was frozen to death with his crew of 70 on the eastern coast of Lapland in 1554.

Fig. 1a is an example of the quality that could have been expected from earlier documents produced at the Coventry house. It emanates from the London Carmelite house.

The 1534 *Valor Ecclesiasticus* gives the annual value of the house as £7.13s.8d. Rents of certain tenements standing on the site allotted to them for their church and buildings yielded £3.6s.8d, whilst the offerings in the Lady Chapel averaged £5.18s a year. However this presumably will bear little resemblance to the income in earlier periods.

Fretton's 'pleasant site' - still pleasant in 1872 and earlier, Figs 23, 44 and 56, - has suffered much from the second half of the 20th century, Figs 26 and 57. In place of today's traffic noise from close-set elevated highways, and the pollution, litter, and general air of squalor and dereliction, a visitor should attempt to visualise not only the great buildings in their magnificence, Fig. 31, but the gardens, orchards, dovecote and fishponds on the slopes leading down to the brook and mill. Formal gardens are to be expected; that of the Augustinian friary in Hull being a rectangle, divided into four by paths forming a cross, with narrow trenches apparently for box hedges defining smaller rectangles, with some containing wider trenches for planting.

The Dissolution

Concern was expressed by the city of Coventry, before the Suppression, for the survival of the House, as this letter, from the Mayor and Alderman of Coventry to Thomas Cromwell, of 20th September, 1538, shows. 'It is reported that the Grey and White Friars of Coventry are to be suppressed. Their churches can ill be spared; for in time of plague sick people resort to them to hear divine service. There are but two parish churches in the town, and no small number of Christian people belong to them. If in time of plague sick people resorted to the parish churches they would infect the whole city. We beg you therefore to intercede with the king that those two churches of friars remain, the religious persons thereof to be reformed at the King's pleasure.'

This is a confirmation of the courageous part played by the friars in time of plague (although they were not alone in this) and a support of recent scholarly re-assessment of the view that the Pre-Reformation church was all high living and low morals. Unfortunately the details of good behaviour are usually not those which survive or arouse interest, but it is noteworthy that Coventry, thought of as a centre of Lollardry, had no wish to dispose of its friary churches. It is however true that they had a special problem with their extraordinarily small number of parish churches, only two, when other cities like Norwich might have them in the forties. The Coventry position is presumably due to its division into the Earl of Chester's 'half' and the Benedictine Priory's 'half'.

The Surrender dates from 1st October 1538, and has the signatures of fourteen brethren, listed by Fretton as: Hugo Burnby, Thomas Fysher, Richard Wodcocke (Prior), Thomas Vicars (who remained living on the premises), William Walkar, William Harryson, John Pasty, John Hurst, Richard Cowper, William Madden, John Newbold, John Edyson, Richard Cowper and William Kynge. Their poverty giving them no claim to compensation they were turned adrift without pension (unlike the Carthusians only a matter of yards distant; their Surrender document of 16th January, 1539 allocated pensions of £5.6s.8d rising to £6.13s.4d for the 'old and blind'.) Is this difference because the Carmelites resisted?

The city's September letter clearly had no effect, for a further letter from the Mayor and Aldermen to Cromwell, dated 20th October, 1538, states 'The King's Commissioner, Dr London, is now at Coventry to suppress the two houses of friars for their demerits; and though we have asked him to forbear till we should hear from your Lordship about leaving the churches, or at least one of them, standing, we find him very hard. For all we can do, he has defaced the church of the Grey Friars and begun to do the like with the White Friars, but by very great entreaty we have got him to stay as to the latter till we have sent to your Lordship for help. We beg you to intercede with the King that we may obtain the same, with the houses and gardens, else it will be a danger and decay to the city.' A rental of the houses and gardens to the Whitefriars of Coventry is appended to this letter, viz., of thirty-one houses and eleven gardens specified by tenants' names or otherwise. The total sum was £5s.15s.8d. We have no means of knowing where these houses were situated, though some appear likely to have been within the precinct.

A letter of 22nd October 1538 from Doctor John London to Cromwell seems to imply that in fact Dr London and the Corporation were now on the same side as to the survival of the Whitefriars. 'Here I have laid down the idolatry of two chapels where offering was to an Image of Our Lady and to a rood [It is believed that these are the two chapels in the easternmost bay of the nave, and the associated decorated floor tiles suggest the N chapel to be that of the Holy Rood, and the S chapel that of Our Lady]. In all Coventry be but two parish churches which stand with the Priory as it were in one church-yard in the heart of the city. When the pestilence reigns, the curates of both churches collect the corpses at the great church door of the priory in the cemetery, and there leave them till after dirige or mass in the parish church... If the town could obtain the White Friars church and churchyard it would be a more wholesome burial ground for it lies out of the heart of the city'.

A letter of 31st October 1538 from John Hales to a Mr Hanby shows not only Hales' early interest (for he was not to buy the Whitefriars for more than six years) but indicates that the threat to the church had not gone away. 'The soil of the church, churchyard, and choir of the late White Friars in Coventry is worth yearly, after the buildings are defaced and the ground made clean - 6s 8d.'

The legal position of the land on which the church stood has always remained unclear. Fretton states 'Their church not having been built on their own land, a sum of 2s per annum was payable as a ground-rent to the heirs of Robert Norwood, and to this rent charge it will afterwards appear that the subsequent demolition of that building is due'. It is not clear how this relates to the entry for 24 February 1342 relating to the alienation in mortmain of the messuage and 10 acres, although this document did appear to specify 'habitation for a prior and some friars'. However, the amount of land would certainly seem to allow for the construction of a church.

In 1536-1539 there appears to have been a period, unparalleled as far as is known to the writer, of the leasing of the Whitefriars by the Crown as a 'Bishop's Palace', for some eight or nine years (*c.*1536-1544), to John Bird, the Coventry-born renegade last Provincial of the English Carmelites, and in 1537 Suffragan Bishop of Penrith, providing lodging, stabling and accommodation for the Bishop, his deputies and servants, particularly useful when making the long journey from almost the Scottish borders to and from the capital. This was the period when Bird, having acquired favour with Henry VIII by supporting his divorce from Catherine of Aragon and by preaching a sermon in his presence against the Papal Supremacy in 1531, was granted the offices of Protestant Suffragan Bishop of Penrith (1537-1539), then Bishop of Bangor (1539-1541), and finally Bishop of Chester 1541-1544, after which he would have had no use for, nor presumably access to, the Coventry buildings.. He returned to the Catholic faith under Queen Mary *c.*1554/5, and died in 1556. The Bishopric of Penrith, one of the six new Bishoprics created by Thomas Cromwell, did not survive Bird's tenure.

This document, Fig. 53, previously unknown to Coventry historians, had been brought to the writer's attention by Eileen Gooder. It supplies new information about the little known area S of the standing cloister which was the subject of an incomplete and unresolved excavation in 1977/78; it confirms the currently assumed position of the Prior's House, and provides a context as a new workshop or forge for the features listed below, over the filled-in site of the reredorter. It introduces the new concept of the Founder's Chamber and mentions a totally unknown structure, that of St John's Hall, (the remains presumably now destroyed by the 1980s ring road, Fig. 57, whose position on the site plan can only be an estimate; this hall may have lain S of the moved doorway in the SE cloister walk, i.e. E of its position shown on Figs 37 and 38). This Hall is referred to as having a 'western aisle' which implies that it ran N-S. St John is presumably John the Baptist, seen as a successor to Elijah by the Carmelites. It also appears that there were monastic dwelling houses in the garden E of the prior's house, and the document also confirms the presence of chapels, apparently related to the Bell-tower area.

PRO Sheet 6, (E318/19/967) FARM (*Firma*), Fig. 53

[*Firma* (Farm) is a fixed rent holding good for the terms of the lease, i.e. the life of the Bishop.E.G.]

'The farm of the Chamber within the precinct of the said late house of the Friars, called the Priours Chambre, with that new workshop/forge [*Fabrica* means workshop or forge, usually the latter in medieval Latin] joined on, and the Chamber called the Founders Chambre, with the small kitchen belonging to the same. And with all the buildings and easements belonging to the aforesaid Chambers; (which Chamber, indeed, with the aforesaid building, is situated at the southern aisle (*ad australem plagam*) of the Cloister of the said house of Carmelites, and the chamber called the Founders Chambre, which is the upper part of the same), with a garden (and house (*domus*) for fuel) which extends to the wall of the City on the east, having a yard (*ortus*) which Thos Vicars inhabits at the west of the dwelling-house (*mansio*) called the Garrett; but the kitchen is situated at (*ad*) the western aisle of the hall called St John's, and the 'office' (*officina*) of the Brewery [i.e. the Brewhouse] at the north. And also [the farm] of one stable next the entry of the place, adjoining the lane called the White Frere lane, between the aforesaid lane and the Cemetery of the convent [does this imply that this was the Friars' and not the Lay cemetery?] of the said late house (which are) leased to John Byrde, Bishop of Penrethe by indenture, under the Common Seal and the seal of the Official of the said late house, dated the 16th day of the month of July, in the 28th year of Hy VIII. [This last date is presumably an error, as 1536 was before the surrender of the Carmelite house, and before Bird became Bishop of Penrith. The lease to the Bishop is presumably from the Crown.] To have and hold the aforesaid chambers and their appurtenances to the aforesaid John during his natural life, [he died in 1556, but it is unlikely that the lease remained valid after he ceased being Bishop of Chester in 1544, by which time the lease was in the possession of Sir Ralph Sadleir]. A clause lays down that 'the said John and his assigns and all his servants and deputies should have freedom of entry to the aforesaid houses and buildings...' [this implies an expectation of accommodation for a considerable number of the bishop's entourage].

Sheet 7
'The Rent of the rest of all and singular buildings ..... remain in the hands of the lord King, not leased, the Church, Chancel, Belltower with the aisles and the chapels in them and the Cemetery being excepted and reserved is worth 6s 8d.....'

'... Memorandum: the Church, the Bellfrey, with the chappells and the Iles of the same, the Queare, Vestre, Churchyard with the ways and pathes to the same belonging, to be reservyed to the kinges majesties Use, Whereof the partyclers ar delivered to the Mayour and Cytezens of th Cyty of Coventre to be boughte and purchased to the use of the said Cytie...'

'Mem: to Reserve the leade, bells, and bell metal, Yron, stone and Glasse, etc.'

'20 June 36 year [of Hy 8th] [1544] for Thos Cotton. The Scite of the late Howse of Whyte Freres at Covntre: £7.7s.2d which rated at ix yeres purchace dothe amounte to the Some of lxvj li iijs (£66.3s).

'Memorandum: The Kyng must discharge the ?house of all incombrances except leases...

The Thomas Vicars mentioned is presumably the Thomas Vicars who signed the Letter of Confraternity, and the Surrender of the House. It appears he was permitted to continue to lodge on the Whitefriars premises. The mention of the glass raises the interesting question as to whether any of it may survive beyond the 21,000 excavated pieces that have been reported on (see Section J and Figs 95-134).

In 1543 the Coventry Treasurers Accounts state 'It' pd to Mr Flamake for the Whit freers xlii.; It' pd to Mr Pollard for the same xxli.; It' paid for the p'ticlers of the priorie and Whit frears xiijs'. Pollard appears to have been a member of the King's household, Flammock a 'despoiler' from Kenilworth. This appears to relate to the church, churchyard, and cemetery only.

The site's subsequent history is complicated. Letters patent were granted by the King (August 27 1544) to Sir Ralph Sadleir - a distinguished and wealthy statesman in the time of Henry VIII and the three succeeding reigns, principal Secretary of State in 1540, a member of the Privy Council for more than 40 years, a frequent ambassador for the king, and a member of the Council of the North. He was important enough to be included in Fuller's *Worthies of England*, and to have his life written by Sir Walter Scott. The Letters Patent granted his request to purchase the farm of the land and possessions of the late house (not the church and churchyard); the lists of the property include *inter alia* barns, a dovecote, fishponds, gardens, a granary, orchards and ponds; these seem to be the only references surviving to the monastic dovecote, fishponds, barns and granary. Reserved to the king were *inter alia* the bell tower and chapels in the church, and chancel, and the glass from the church. This is the second mention of the glass. Does this imply that the church was kept secure at this time?

Sadleir's ownership of the site, seems to have been for five months from August 1544 to 16th Dec. 1544, when Hales purchased it from him for the sum of £83.12s.6d. It is not clear why Hales did not purchase it earlier for he had expressed interest in the property as long back as 1538. The nature of the relationship between Sadleir and Hales is not clear, but seems to have been more than that of buyer and seller. They seem to have shared the Office of Clerk of the Hanaper, though this is disputed in some quarters. They both represented Preston in Lancashire in Parliament, Hales apparently in 1547 and Sadleir in 1544-45.

Sadleir was granted the manor of Standon, Herts, also in 1544, which may have caused him to lose interest in the Whitefriars. The arrangement with Bishop John Bird presumably survived into this period, as the deed dealing with his lease appears to be attached to Sadleirs deeds for this estate. It was there, in the event, that Sadleir built his great house, Standon Lordship. The size and splendour of that house raises the question, never apparently addressed, as to the nature and quality of John Hales' new building at the Whitefriars, where splendour could also have been expected.

Our knowledge is almost entirely of the conversion of the

cloister, and we know almost nothing about the purely Elizabethan work here, although there are hints in Figs 15, 23, 25 (left hand background) and 28-30, all rather surprisingly low-key. Yet Hales Place could have been expected to be a parallel to some extent to Standon Lordship, and to be a great Elizabethan house. It should be remembered, however, that we have no knowledge of the appearance of the southern block, presumably replacing the Prior's Hall, and that Hales Place was deemed fit, and indeed used, to entertain monarchs. The site has been largely destroyed in the last quarter of the 20th century.

Elizabeth I visited Hales at the Whitefriars on the 17th and 18th August 1566, when the Mayor and Council dined with her, and she was entertained with 'shows and pageants' some doubtless at the Whitefriars. She also visited Hales' School at St John's. The large surviving oriel window in the former dorter, Fig. 13, is recorded by Fretton as 'known as Queen Elizabeth's window'. A letter survives of 30th November from Elizabeth to the Earls of Shrewsbury and Huntingdon - 'we perceive that you brought the Scottish Queen to Coventry ... We directed you to bring her to that city ... we fynd strange that she should be placed in an inn ... considering we know how commodious a house that is there **where we ourselves did lodge**' (an unusually well attested case among the many tales of where Queen Elizabeth was reported in folklore to have slept) - commonly called 'the Frears. Our pleasure is that she be removed either to the Freary or to some other convenient house'. James I also stayed here, on September 2nd/3rd 1617.

Hales's patron seems to have been Sir Nicholas Bacon, who was building Renaissance Gorhambury at about the same time, and Hales was also a supporter of Somerset who built the magnificent Somerset House in the Strand.

John Hales was described by Anthony Wood (quoted in Fretton) as being 'commonly called "'Club-foot Hales" because in his younger days he had got that deformity by a wound from his own dagger at the bottom of his foot. Being very much addicted to letters from his childhood he was sent to the ministry and having a happy memory accompanied with incredible industry, became admirably well skilled in the Latin Greek and Hebrew tongues, and at length in the municipal laws and [interestingly] in antiquities, which made him admired of all ingenious men of his time.' His monument in the church of Peter le Poor in London, which does not survive, referred *inter alia* to that interest in antiquities. He was an enigmatic character, for he not only invested in monastic property, purchasing the Coventry Benedictine Priory and the Hospital of St John the Baptist as well as the Whitefriars, but was not just a speculator, for as well as being learned, he was a man of humanity, who made efforts to assist the poor by opposing enclosures and introducing parliamentary Bills such as that for the rebuilding of decayed dwelling houses. It is possible that he wrote the *Discourse of the Common Weal*, which concerned itself largely with the evils caused by the debasement of the coinage, as well as those caused by the enclosures. However, it also concerns itself with a history of Grammar Schools in late medieval and early Renaissance England, clearly a subject dear to Hales. It seems that Hales was also involved with the Marprelate controversy, involving a series of Puritan tracts; these were a Puritan attack on the episcopal structure of the Church of England, being a collection of anonymous, ribald and outspoken tracts under the pseudonym of 'Martin Marprelate', which appear to have been printed at the Whitefriars during Hales' absence at Frankfurt in the reign of Mary Tudor, for he had gone into exile on the execution of Somerset, and he is said to have been interred in the Tower of London and fined because of this association, but again there are disagreements among historians. He does seem to have been the author of *The preceptes of the excellent Clerke and grave philosopher Plutarche for the preservation of good healthe*.

The Corporation remained anxious to obtain possession of the church for the use of the City and in the Treasurer's accounts we find for 1545 'It' paid to Mr Burgoyne for the surveying of the Whit freres xxs'.

On 23rd July 1545 Hales obtained a licence from the crown to found a perpetual Free school, the annual endowment being 200 marks, in the western choir of the great Whitefriars church. Unusually for the day he had a commitment to the teaching of music, for this was the only School at the time in which a Music School was maintained alongside and in close connection with a Grammar School. Hales wrote *Introductiones ad Grammaticam* and *Highway to Nobility* in the 1540s for educational purposes, but despite his interest in education he remained a bachelor with neither wife nor child.

It seems that the School should have passed into the control of the Corporation under the founding charter, and indeed at about this time the church, with the School in it, was possibly intended to come into the City's possession, for there is a Coventry Treasurer's account for 1547 'It' pd for removying and settyng upp the high aulter in the Whit'frers xvijs'. This last may relate to an attempt to adapt the nave for public worship by moving the altar from the E end/presbytery, which the archaeology suggests became a workshop about this time, into the eastern nave, the western choir being occupied by the Grammar School. It seems odd that John Hales did not pay for this re-arrangement if no other party was involved.

However a 1553 or 4 entry states 'It' pd for drawing and engrossing of a supplicac'on to the Queen for the Whit'freers vd', so the Corporation were still actively engaged at that time in attempting to obtain the church six or seven years later than the moving of the altar.

This confusing dispute with the citizens seems to be based on their belief that the other monastic properties, including St John's Hospital, acquired by Hales, again in 1545, had been granted to him with the intention of his founding a school elsewhere than in the White Friars church which the Corporation wanted to be made parochial. However, there was clearly a general feeling of ill will towards Hales, perhaps because he was an outsider who had obtained a good deal of once monastic land within the city. This is epitomised by Leland's comment when writing of St John's Hospital, later to house Hales' Free School - 'This Hales with the clubbe foot hath gotten an Interest in this Colledge (St John's Hospital) and none but the Devell can get him out.'

There certainly was a shortage not only of churches but of schools, the Reformation having destroyed the Benedictine Priory Grammar School, founded in 1303, besides the School at the Charterhouse, and the novices school at the Whitefriars (see Woodfield 1981 for a further discussion of this matter and an account of the only School excavated in this country). The wording of the Free Grammar School Charter of 1545 'in our City of Coventry...no care has hitherto been taken for the promotion of piety and virtue in boys' is therefore not sustainable.

The Corporation, being proprietors of the land on which the church stood, did eventually compel Hales to move the School out in *c.*1557-58 to St John's Hospital, conveying there the stalls 'and other fittings', Figs 82-93, much of which remain in that now semi-derelict building. It appears, according to Sharp (1871), that they petitioned the Crown to have the Whitefriars church designated as a parish church. For reasons which are not clear, although a desire to remove the School from the Whitefriars church is supposed to have been the basis for the move to St John's, and the City had battled to obtain this church for some 20 years, after its accomplishment nothing further seems to have been done to put the church in order or in use.

Having obtained the building, there seems to have been a silence for a year or so on the subject of this intended parochial use of the church for the people. The subsequent records then show a very different intention. In 1559 and 1560 the Corporation petitioned the Queen for a grant of two bells (it is not known if these are additional to the bell from the Lady tower referred to above and/or to the Great Bell) and the covering of lead of the Church of the Whitefriars, 'and these were given them' (this last is confirmed as virtually no roofing lead was found on the site). There was clearly a delay in the removal of the Great Bell from the site perhaps for as long as fourteen years, but surprisingly this was eventually done apparently before the fall of the tower which might have facilitated this (assuming that the tower was the original position of the Great Bell). In the churchwardens books of Trinity parish is a record of the purchase from the Mayor and Corporation of a great bell from the Church of the Whitefriars: '1573 Item payd for drawing the bell from the fryers ijs Item paied for mendynge the church wall where the bell was broughte in xijd' Clearly the bell was too large to pass through the W door of Holy Trinity. The bell, or rather the bell metal, presumably surviving after various recastings, is now in the cathedral of Christchurch, New Zealand (Pickford 1987, 465 and 468). The indications seem to be that the Whitefriars church might have had four bells?

The City Annals record '1572-3, Mayoralty of Thomas Wyght. This year the magistrates plucked down the Whiteffriers church of Coventry'. The Gild and Chantry Accounts record '1573, Charges upon the takyng down of the Whytt fryers church ixl iiis'. The materials were sold to build a mansion at Cawston in Warwickshire, which does not survive. The demolition seems to have left a weakened tower and spire, for in 1574 the fall of the steeple is recorded, completing the destruction of the church: '1574 Symon Coton Mayor. This year Whit ffriers steple was let fall downe'. The churchyard may have remained as a burying ground, for there is a later reference to 'Lady Hales' church yard' and a find of a post medieval coffin handle, Fig. 165 No 135.

As for Hales Place, the name given to the mansion constructed by John Hales, it remained in the Hales family until 1717, when it was purchased by the Duke of Montague. It was sold five years later to Samuel Hill of Shenstone Park in Staffordshire, and during this period it appears to have been occupied by combers and weavers. It was subsequently sold to the Rev. W. Smith of Aspley, Bedfordshire; the high quality of the pottery found during excavation, Fig. 155, and the construction of an 18th-century garden wall with a great gate on the site of the S nave wall, both suggest a return to gentry use. Fretton in 1872 was aware that a gate was built 'in the centre of the northern cloisters which remained until recently'. He believed this to have been built by Hales, but it is most likely the undoubtedly 18th-century gate found during excavation, Fig. 42 and Fig. 23 (at the left).

Hales' nephew, also John, built a contemporary Elizabethan mansion of great splendour, The New House, near the then village of Radford, now part of Coventry. This was demolished in 1779. A reverse trend would be welcomed for the Whitefriars E cloister/Hales Place. A quarter of a century of neglect should not be allowed to continue.

In 1801 Hales Place was sold to the Directors of the Poor. It was the hatred of the population for 'the workhouse' and a strong desire for its destruction that the writer fought, with others, particularly the architect Jimmy Brown, in the 1960s, leading to its extensive restoration in the second half of that decade.

One of the two portraits of John Hales was destroyed during World War II; the other, presented by Dame Anne Hales in 1704 to the Grammar School at St John's Hospital, is now housed in the Mercers' room at the Council House, and is not normally accessible to the public.

SECTION B: BIBLIOGRAPHY

Bacon, Roger. (British Library Sloan MS 2156).

Bird, John. 1531. *Treatise in Favour of Divorce of Henry VIII and Catherine of Aragon* (PRO S.P. 1/62).

Bliss Burbage, F. 1950. *Old Coventry and Lady Godiva.*

Butler, L .A .S. 1987. 'Medieval Urban Religious Houses' in Schofield, J. and Leech, R. (eds.) *Urban Archaeology in Britain* (CBA Research Report **61**: London).

Cameron, A. C. 1970. 'Sir Henry Willoughby of Wollaton', *Trans Thoroton Society of Nottinghamshire*, 10-20.

Chaucer, G. 'A Treatise on the Astrolabe', and 'The Somnour's Tale' 396-418, and 587-8 in Skeat, W. W. (ed.) 1942. *The Complete works of Geoffrey Chaucer* (Oxford University Press).

Clark, J. (ed.) 2002. *The Religious Orders of Pre-Reformation England* (Boydell and Brewer).

Coppack, C. 1990. *Abbeys and Priories* (B. T. Batsford/English Heritage).

Copsey, Fr. R. 1992. 'The visit of the Prior General, Peter Terrasse, to England in 1504-5', 180-186 in Fitzgerald-Lombard, P. (ed.) 1992.

Coss, P. R. *The early records of Medieval Coventry* (British Academy).

Cox. J. 1908. 'The Carmelite Friars of Coventry', *History of Warwickshire, Victoria County History* **ii**, 104-5.

Deloney, T. See Mann 1912.

Dewar, M. (ed.) 1969. *A Discourse of the Commonweal of This Realm of England Attributed to Sir Thomas Smith* (Charlottesville).

Dixon, R. W. 1975. 'Hayles, John', *Compact Edition of the Dictionary of National Biography* (Oxford).

Duffy, F. 1992. *The Strippping of the Altars* (Yale University Press; Newhaven and London).

Dugdale, W. 1656. *The Antiquities of Warwickshire*, II (2nd ed. ed. W, Thomas 1730: London).

Dugdale, W. 1765. *The Antiquities of Coventry: Illustrated from Records, Ledgers, Manuscripts, Charters, Evidences, Tombes and Armes, beautified with many Curious Copper-plate Cuts* (Jones; Coventry).

Evans, Joan, 1949. *English Art, 1307-1461* (Oxford; Clarendon Press).

FitzGerald-Lombard, Patrick, O. Carm. 1992, *Carmel in Britain. Essays on the Medieval English Carmelite Province: Vol. 1, People and Places* (Institutum Carmelitanum; Rome).

Foxe, J. 1563. *Actes and Monuments (The Book of Martyrs* **9**).

Fretton, W. G. 1872. 'Memorials of the Whitefriars, Coventry', *Birmingham and Midland Institute, Archaeological Section Trans* **I**, 63-78.

Gooder, E., Woodfield, C. and Chapman, R.,E.1966. 'The Walls of Coventry', *Trans Birmingham Archaeol. Soc.* **81**, 88-138.

Harris, M. D.(ed.) 1907-1913. *The Coventry Leet Book or Mayors Register. (*Original series no. 135-6; Early English Text Society, London).

Hunt, J. 2000. 'Ralph VIII, Lord Bassett of Drayton and the Coventry Whitefriars', *Trans. Birmingham and Warwickshire Archaeol. Soc.*, **104**, 93-99.

Kingsford, C. L. 1915. *The Greyfriars of London.*

Knowles, D. and Hadcock, R. N. 1971. *Medieval Religious Houses; England and Wales.*

Lexikon des Mittelalters, V. 1991 (Artemis Verlag: Munich and Zurich)

Lines, C. 1989. 'Architectural Heritage. A Tale of Brave Survival. The Coventry Whitefriars', *Warwickshire and Worcestershire Life,* July 1989, 22-23.

McCaffrey, P. R. and Carm, O. 1926. *The Whitefriars. An Outline Carmelite History* (M.H. Gill and Son: Dublin).

McAleavy, T. 1996. *Life in a Medieval Abbey* (English Heritage).

Mackie, J. D. 1988. 'The Earlier Tudors', *Oxford History of England (*Clarendon Press; Oxford).

Mann, F. O. 1912. *The Works of Thomas Deloney* (Clarendon Press; Oxford).

Marson, G., Burton, A. and Metcalf, F. 1945. *King Henry VIII School, 1545-1945.*

Martin, M. T.(ed.) 1911. *The Percy Chartulary* (London).

Monsignano, E. and Ximenix, J. (ed.) 1715-68 *Bullarium Carmelitanum.* (Rome).

Nicholls, J. 1823. *The Progresses and Public Processions of Queen Elizabeth* (Soc. Antiquaries of London)

Pevsner, N., and Cherry, B. 2000. *The Buildings of England: Hertfordshire* (Penguin: London).

Phythian Adams, C. 1972. 'Ceremony and the Citizen: The communal year at Coventry, 1450-1550' in Clark P., and Slack, P. (eds.) *Crisis and Order in English Towns 1500-1700.*

Platt, C. 1978. *Medieval England Social History and Archaeology from the Conquest to 1600* (Routledge and Kegan Paul).

Poole, B. 1870. *The History and Antiquities of Coventry.*

Poskitt, M. 1992. 'The English Carmelites, Houses of Study and Educational Methods'. *Carmel in Britain, Essays on the Medieval English Carmelite Province*, Vol. 1, 155-165.

Reader, W. 1823. *New Coventry Guide.*

Rickert, M. 1952. *The Reconstructed Carmelite Missal* (University of Chicago).

Sadleir, Thomas U. 1905. 'Sir Ralph Sadleir', *East Herts Archaeol. Soc. Trans.* **III.1**, 79-94.

Sharp, T. 1871. *History and Antiquities of Coventry.*

Sheppard, L. C. 1943. *The English Carmelites* (Burns Oates: London).

Smith, J. T. 1992. *English Houses 1200-1800: The Hertfordshire Evidence* (RCHME: London, HMSO).

Soden, I. 1995. *Excavations at St. Anne's Charterhouse, Coventry, 1968-87* (Coventry City Council).

Toulmin-Smith, L. 1907-10. *The Itinerary of John Leland in or about 1535-43,* Vol 4, fol. 190 (London).

Vernor, Hood and Sharpe, (Publishers). 1810. *Beauties of England and Wales* (London).

Victoria County History, Warwickshire **VIII**, 132-4 and **II**, 104-5.

Willoughby, C. (Stevenson, W. H. ed.) 1911. *Manuscripts Report on the Historical Manuscripts of Lord Middleton preserved at Wollaton Hall, Nottinghamshire.*

Wilson, J. Dover. 1909. 'The Marprelate Controversy', *The Cambridge History of English Literature*, Vol. III, Ch. XVII (Cambridge).

Woodfield, C., 1981. 'Finds from the Free Grammar School at the Whitefriars Coventry, *c.*1545-c.1557-58'. *Post Medieval Archaeol.* **15**, 81-159.

Zimmerman, B. 1899. 'The Carmelite Monastery at Coventry', *Carmelite Review* **vii no. 3**.

Zimmerman, B. 1903-4. 'L'ancien couvent des Carmes de Coventry (Angleterre)', *Chroniques du Carmel* **16** 148-152.

Serial Works

Calendar of State Papers 1525, no. 1568 and 1743.

Churchwardens' Books of Trinity parish 1573-75.

Coventry Cappers Company's Accounts 1522.

Coventry Carpenter's Company's Accounts 1477 (also II CRO Acc 3/2f 7v), 1507.

Coventry City Accounts 1528 1539 1541 1553-54 1559 1573-74 1587 1599.

Coventry City Annals 1344 1431 1446 1471 1490 1499 1572-4.

Coventry City Leet Book 1429.

Coventry Gild and Chantry Accounts 1573.

Coventry Smiths Company's Accounts 1515.

Coventry Treasurer's Accounts 1543 1545 1547 1553/4.

CPR 1340-43, 387; 1343-5, 209; 1350-4 259.

Eighth Report of the Deputy Keeper of the Public Records, (London 1842) appendix ii, 18. Surrender document.

Inquis. ad quod damn. 15 Edward III, no. 23; 17 Edward III, no. 43.

PRO SP1/137 (Augmentation Office) Rental/PRO E318/Box19/967. Sheets 6 and 7.

Rot.Pat. 16 Edward III, p.1, m.32; 18 Edward III, p 1, m. 36; 1 Henry V, p.3., m.44; 37 Henry VIII, m.2.

Figure 1a Dedication of a Carmelite church, with Christ blessing above.

Initial T (terribilis) for the introit). The Bishop would knock on the door with his crozier and say 'Aperite portas principes vestras'. Note the acolyte with a gold cross, two tonsured choristers, a prior in a red cope, a bishop in blue coat and a gold mitre, and five laymen. The devil has been driven out of the church onto the roof. Late 14th century.

This Carmelite Missal derives from the London Whitefriars, with its close connections with Coventry. *c.*1390 (BM Additional MS 29704, fol. 68vo; Rickert 1952, 102).

Figure 1b Early 15th-century Coventry glass roundel commemorating the distribution by a woolstapler of food and drink to a begging Carmelite friar, a pilgrim and the lame and blind (reproduced by courtesy of the Victoria and Albert Museum).

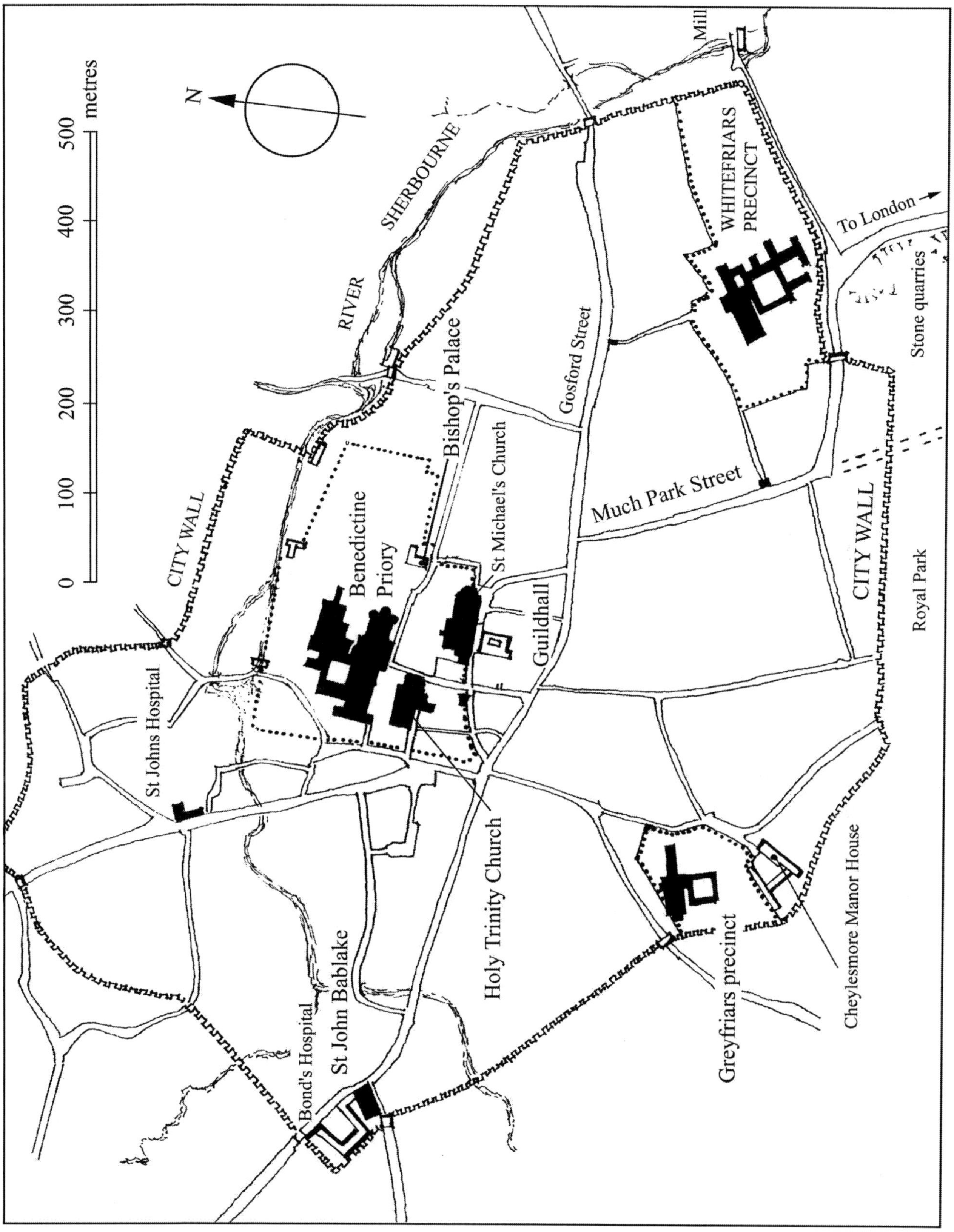

Figure 2 Map showing medieval Coventry and the position of the Whitefriars, St John's Hospital, the Greyfriars, the Benedictine Priory and the City's two parish churches.

Figure 3 Map of Carmelite Houses in the British Isles showing foundation dates and related houses in France.

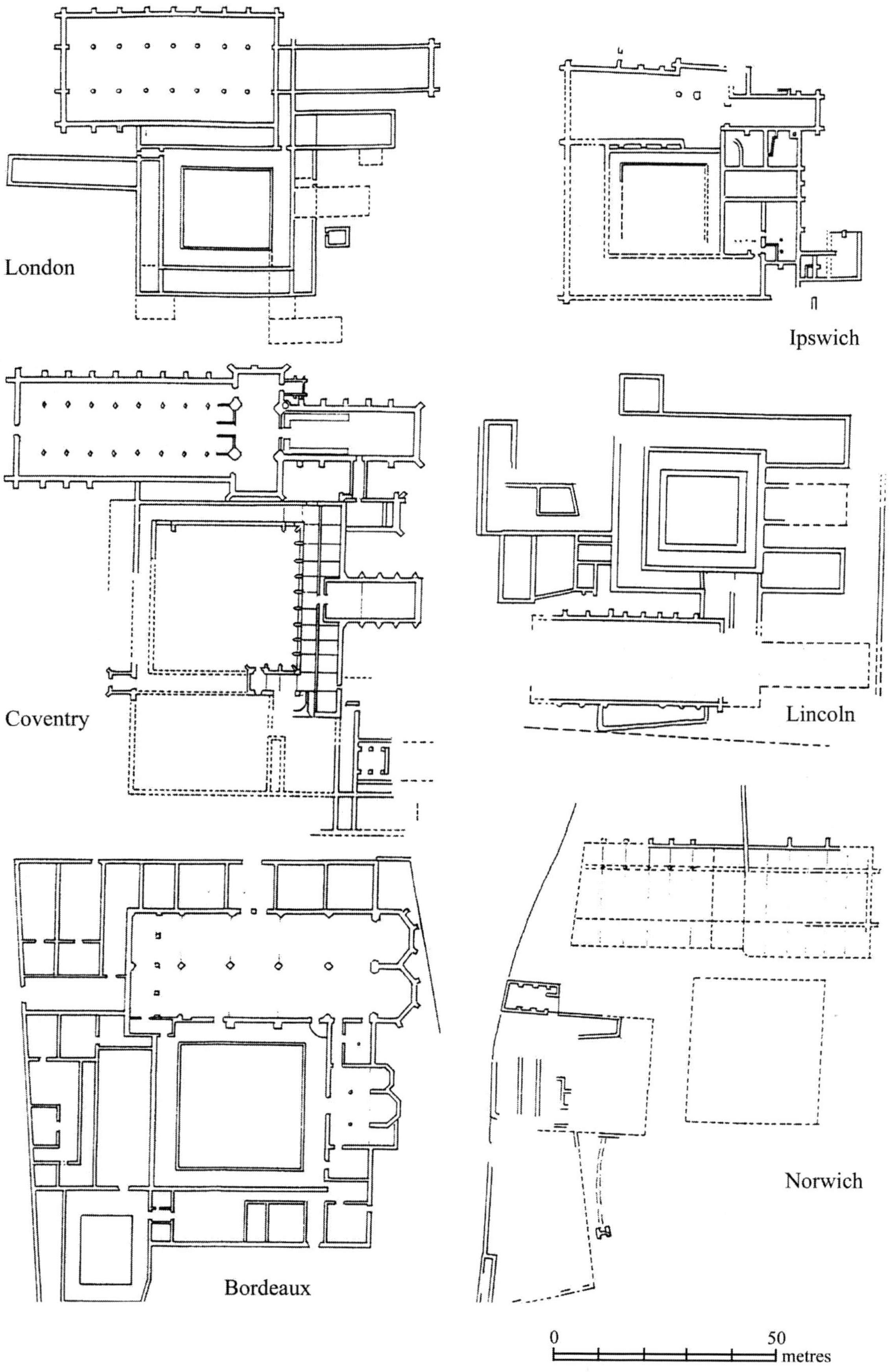

Figure 4 Comparative Carmelite plans - the larger friaries: England and France.

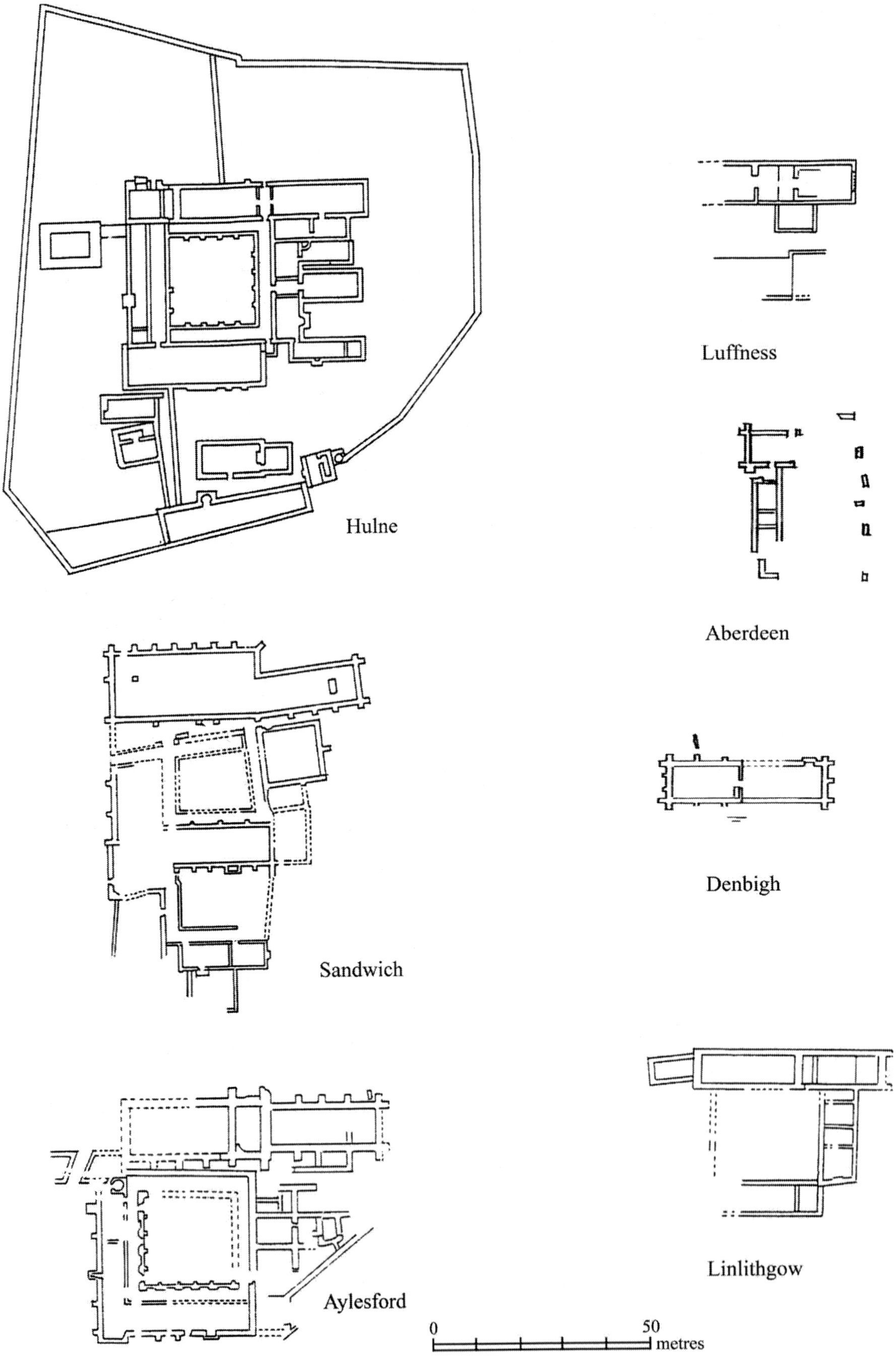

Figure 5 Comparative Carmelite plans - the smaller friaries: Scotland and England.

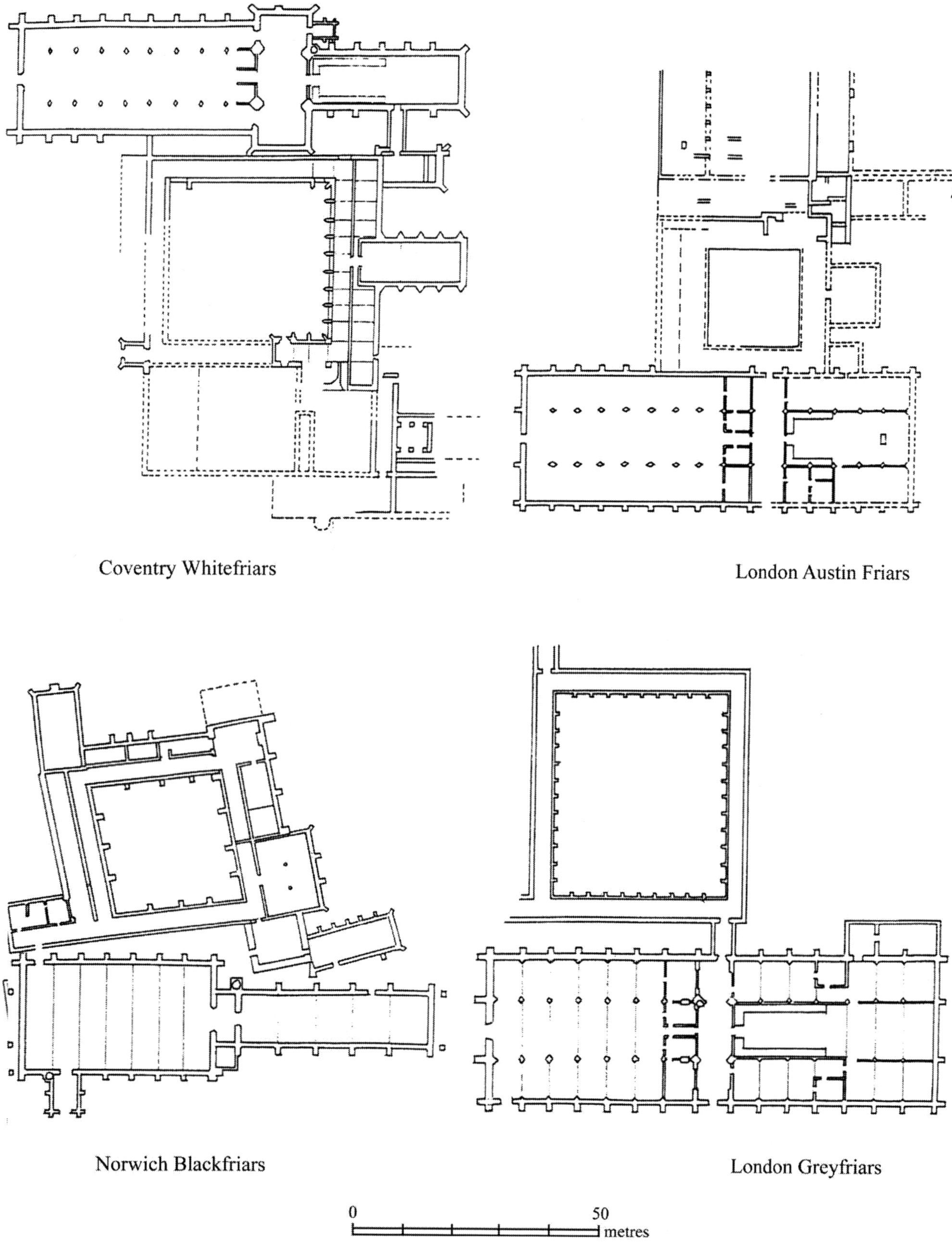

Figure 6 Coventry Whitefriars, and comparative plans of the larger friaries of the Austin, Blackfriars and Greyfriars orders.

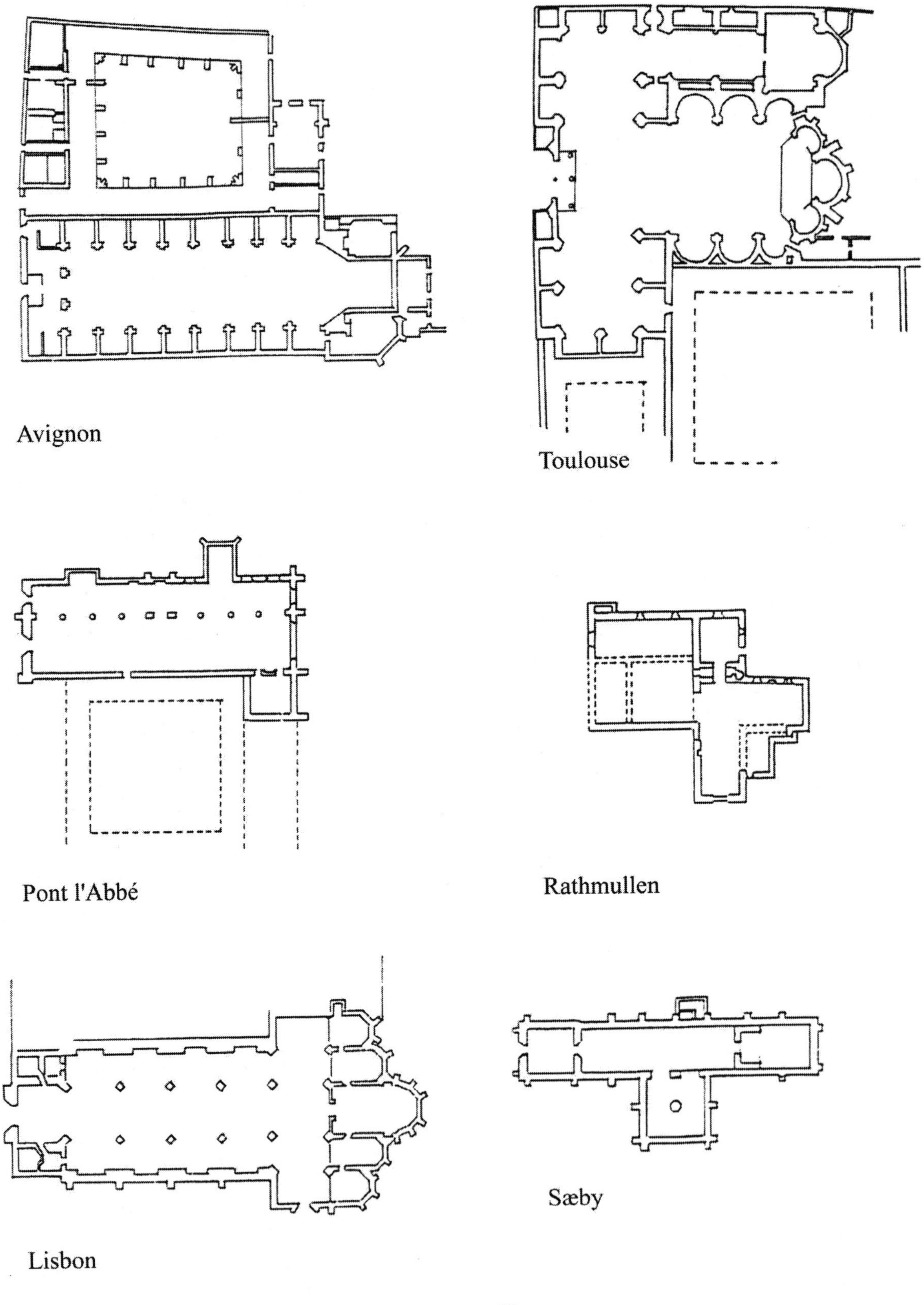

Figure 7 Comparative Carmelite plans: overseas friaries: France, Ireland, Portugal and Denmark.

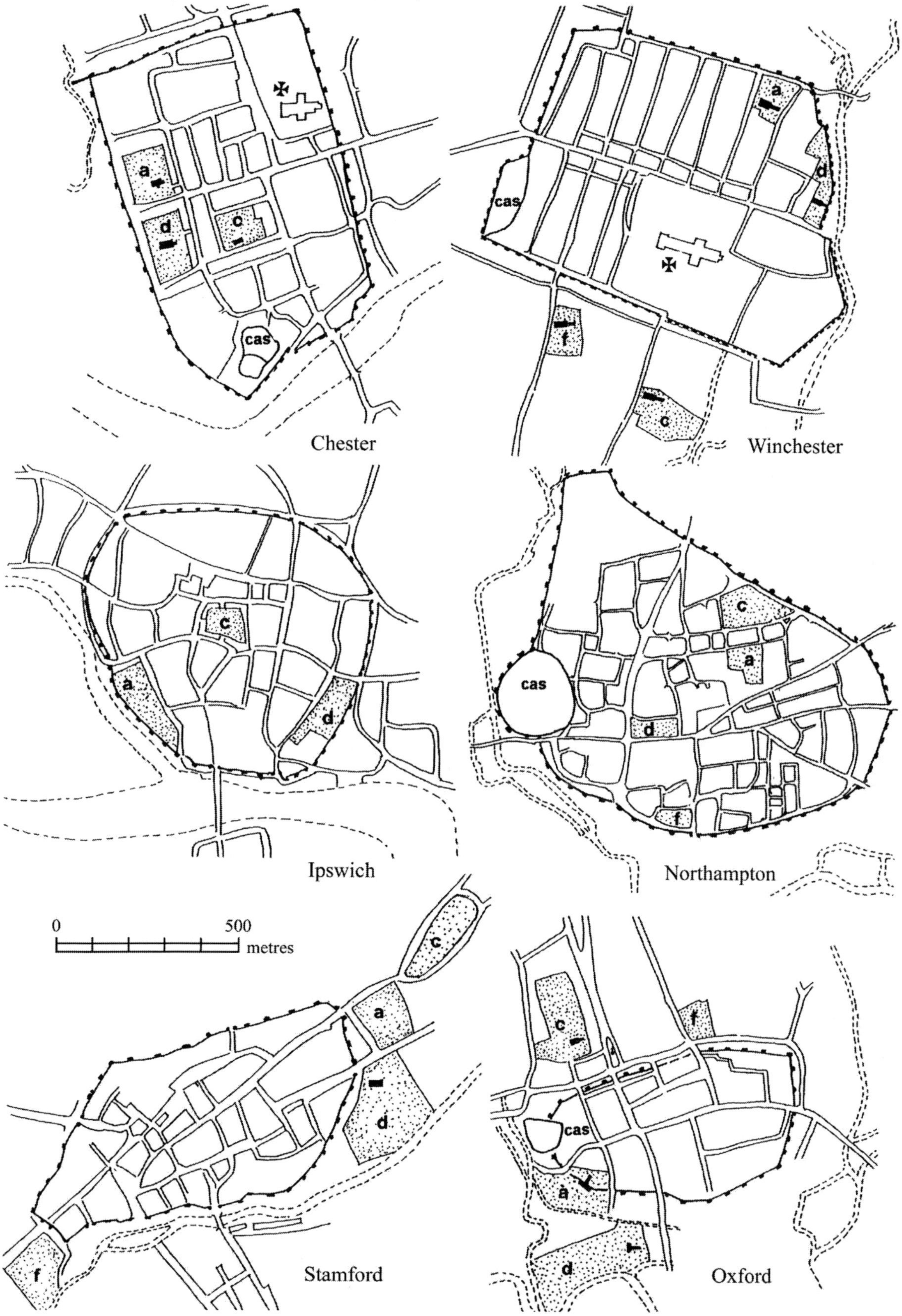

Figure 8 Plans of six medieval English towns showing the extent of land occupied by precincts of the four orders of friars. c is Carmelite, d Dominican, f Franciscan, a Augustinian.

SECTION C

THE STANDING BUILDING WITH A DETAILED ANALYSIS OF THE EAST CLOISTER RANGE

J. Cattell with a contribution by P. Woodfield

This section of the report is based on an investigation of the Coventry Whitefriars E cloister range undertaken by John Cattell for the Royal Commission on Historical Monuments of England (RCHME) in 1996-7. Paul Woodfield assisted with the interpretation of the building. The analysis of the building was accompanied by measured surveys of the ground and first floor plans by Nigel Fradgley and Mike Williams for RCHME and the resulting drawings are illustrated with this report. The results of recent (2002) dendrochronological analysis of the roofs have also been included. The full RCHME report can be consulted at the National Monuments Record Centre, Great Western Village, Kemble Drive, Swindon, SN2 2GZ.

Of the extensive medieval friary, only the two storey E range of the cloister to the S of the church, with the attached stub ends of the N and S cloister walks now survive, the building having been incorporated first in John Hales' great house after the Dissolution, and later forming part of the workhouse of the Coventry Poor Union in 1800, Figs 9-11. However, the outer gate from Much Park Street (see Section D 2 and Fig. 33) survives to the present day, albeit in a much altered state; and the route into the friary precinct has survived as a right of way. The inner gate on the SW corner of the cloister, which had the most spectacular of all the vaulting, survived in a ruinous state up to the 1950s. It had a star-vaulted gateway and chamber over and projected in a westerly direction at the southern end of the W walk providing direct access into the S walk of the cloister, Figs 12, 30 and 38. The founder's arms were emblazoned on the outward-facing façade, emblematic of his importance to the house. This gate was later used by John Hales as the principal entrance to his house.

ANALYSIS OF THE SURVIVING EAST RANGE

Figures 9-11, 13-30, 38, 45-46.48-49, 66-67, 133, 136 and 149

Pre-Reformation phases

The convent of the Whitefriars at Coventry was founded in 1342 by Sir William de Poulteney, four times Lord Mayor of London between 1331 and 1337, merchant, financier and draper, one of the most wealthy and influential men of business in the country. He had established a chantry in St Paul's and set up a college at St Lawrence Poulteney in London, and was at the time building his own house at Penshurst Place in Kent. The remaining structure of his Carmelite friary at Coventry is one of the most significant and substantial surviving remains of any mendicant house in Great Britain.

The E range of the cloister was almost certainly the first part of the complex to be built, probably in a continuous phase from the foundation in 1342 to *c*.1380, within which three sub-phases within the standing building have been identified. These main sub-phases are the equivalent of the archaeological phases termed Friary and Friary 1. The first sub-phase, labelled **1a** on the plans, Fig. 11, is a transitional period between the advent of the Perpendicular in 1332 (Bony 1979, 58; Coldstream 1994) and the demise of the Decorated by *c*.1350. Here the style of the E range is late Decorated, with ogees used extensively over doors and windows. By the 1340s the ogee had been in use for five decades and its employment at Coventry is comfortably within an architectural style now well established.

The identity of the master-mason architect at Coventry is not known, although Harvey has surmised on the basis of style, and a statement by Stow, quoted by Harvey (Harvey 1987, 244) that Penshurst was the work of William Ramsey III (Harvey 1984, 244). This he based on the assumed identity of the Early Perpendicular work of the 1330s in the choir of Gloucester Abbey (Cathedral), an assumption that has more recently been challenged (Wilson 1989), taking further Bony's reservation as to whether he was the same man. Be that as it may, the elaborate design of the Coventry Whitefriars, and the high quality of its construction remains remarkable. The use of vaults over the cloister walks in friaries appears to have been another rare occurrence of architectural ambition within the mendicant orders, and could possibly relate to the 1326 order received by the Carmelites that awarded them privileges equal to that of the Franciscans and Dominicans. The earliest Franciscan cloister known to have been vaulted, that at Yarmouth, is approximately contemporary with Coventry Whitefriars (Martin 1937, 35).

Phasing

The early phasing of the E range is extremely complex and there is a great deal of contradictory evidence to be reconciled. The sub-phases **1a** to **1c** discussed in detail below accord with the Friary phase of the excavation report. As stated above, an attempt has been made to identify three separate sub-phases dating from before *c*.1380 and to some extent to tentatively attribute these to different master masons. Red sandstone was used exclusively for walling for these early sub-phases and has in places suffered from extensive weathering, further hampering interpretation. Greenish-coloured sandstone appears to have been used extensively from the 15th century. As the E range was largely constructed in the 14th century, alterations in green sandstone can for the most part be safely attributed to the late medieval period, and to John Hales or his descendants.

Phase 1a (1342-1349)

Figure 11

The Ground Floor

It appears that the shell of the E range was built during the years leading up to the Black Death which claimed the lives of the patron Poulteney, and presumably many of the workmen employed on the work. It was a two-storey building of the same dimensions as the present structure, and was probably partitioned on a temporary basis to provide for the basic needs of the friars. At the same time, at least the two easternmost bays of the N range were built, along with the two or more of the eastern bays of the S range. Surviving from this sub-phase are the N, S, E and W walls up to the level of the eaves, Fig. 13. The internal features have largely been lost in later modifications.

Externally, apart, probably, from the tripartite windows looking onto the garth, the nature of the original fenestration is not known, for the ground-floor openings were replaced in the second building sub-phase. The first-floor windows are lancets with shallow ogee heads. The sills and lintels of these are invariably wider than the glazed sections of the window. Excavation evidence suggests that the roof was originally tiled with plain green-glazed tiles and decorated ridges, Fig. 149 Nos 9, 10, 12 and 14-15.

Facing onto the garth are 'cut-water' buttresses. These are of most unusual form for a religious house, although there are precedents for their use at Kenilworth Castle Great Hall and on a few West of England parish churches of the early 14th century (for example, St Andrew's Church, Wanborough, Wilts.). These buttresses are part of the first sub-phase of construction and on plan have pointed rather than the normal square ends. There is no structural evidence to suggest that triangular sections forming the pointed ends of the buttresses were added at a later date. The triangular sections are carried up to first-floor height where they terminate in pyramidal copings. At that point the buttresses become square on plan and are continued to eaves level in the usual fashion. Scarring in the re-entrant angles between the E and the N and S ranges provides evidence for internal angle buttresses. The foundation of the northernmost angle buttress indicates that they were also of cut-water form.

It is assumed at this stage that the ground floor provided a walkway along the W with rooms opening off it to the E. The latter probably included a temporary frater to the S and a parlour and sacristy to the N. The positions of the two original fireplace openings, subsequently blocked to varying degrees, in the E wall of the range may suggest the former existence of a central transverse wall, dividing the ground floor into two large heated chambers of approximately equal size, each half having its fireplace approximately in the centre of its E wall. In order to retain the heat in these two rooms they must have been closed off from the unglazed walk by a longitudinal partition, probably on the line of the present axial wall.

The other requirement in this provisional arrangement was for domestic services. These were probably contained in the one-bay southerly projection beyond the line of the S wall of the S walk, Fig. 37. At the southern end of the E walk is a pair of elaborately moulded doorways probably dating from the first sub-phase. Each has a two-centred head with a broad double-ogee or bracket moulding with a beaked and lobed hood mould springing from corbelled heads, now much eroded, Figs 14 and 66a-b. These openings are probably the remains of a set of three service doors, the outer two leading to buttery and pantry and that in the centre to a passage leading to an external detached kitchen further to the S (suggested by P. Woodfield, pers. comm.). The westernmost service room may have contained a temporary day stair replaced in sub-phase **1c** by a stone-vaulted newel stair. The kitchen passage remains but the cross wall incorporating the door to the E service room was removed, probably during the sub-phase **1b** alterations.

The Upper Floor

Figure 11

The upper floor of the range is always likely to have contained the friary dorter, but, initially at least, it may also have housed the *studium* and library. The present roof structure shown on Fig. 22, has been shown from a dendrochronological investigation undertaken by Dan Miles to be rebuilt in the later last quarter of the 15th century (Miles 2002; Miles and Worthington 2002). This re-roofing is discussed in more detail below.

Nearly all internal evidence for the arrangement of the dorter in the earlier Middle Ages has been removed. Based on comparisons with other friaries, it would originally have had had an open timber roof, probably of the trussed collar-rafter type, such as survives in the Gloucester Blackfriars dorter. The space was probably partially divided into separate chambers or cells by timber partitions: the dorter at the Carmelite house at

Hulne, Northumberland, for instance, was subdivided in this manner. There was a chamber over the sacristy attached to the E face of the range at Coventry and the doorway that communicated with it (now blocked) survives in the E wall near the N end of the dorter. The function of this chamber is unknown although it may have served as a library or possibly the prior's private chamber until separate lodgings were built for this purpose in the inner court, Fig. 38. Some evidence for the subdivision of the dorter can be seen in the original fenestration. There was a large two-centred arched window lighting the S end of the dorter range and this is shown, partially blocked in an Aylesford Collection watercolour, Fig. 15. The present window is a 19th-century replacement, inserted into the original opening. The same can be said for the large window at the N end, Figs 21, 25 and 26. Apart from these large windows, nearly all of the others at first-floor level were narrow lancets under shallow ogee heads. There are five windows of this type positioned at regular intervals in the area of the E wall, N of the chapter house, Fig. 20. The jambs on the N sides of these windows are straight whilst their other sides are splayed. This may indicate that there were stub partitions on the line of each of the straight jambs dividing this area into five separate carrels (places for preparing and illuminating manuscripts) similar to those in the exceptionally well-preserved *studium* at the Gloucester Blackfriars. There are windows with identical jambs in the N wall to each side of the large window opening, possibly an indication that carrels were also built against the N wall prior to the insertion of the night stair. At the N end the equal splays of the lancet window have been altered from wide to narrow. This suggests that the N end bay, with its door to a chamber over the sacristy, did not initially have a materially different function, and thus the chamber was directly and intimately concerned with the *studium,* possibly a book store or library, although the window was altered somewhat later perhaps to relate to the night stair.

The other narrow windows lighting the dorter had both jambs equally splayed and were probably associated with bed cubicles which did not need the steady N light required by the carrels. Three windows with two splayed jambs survive at the southern end of the range. The W wall of the dorter was lit by similar lancet windows; possibly one positioned between each buttress although the splays of the jambs cannot now be seen. There is clear evidence of the existence of such windows in the northern and southernmost bays and one was also positioned in the third bay from the S. Mullioned windows inserted by Hales have removed much of the evidence for the positioning of the other windows. These narrow windows under ogee heads are also evident in the truncated N and S walls of the N claustral range at first-floor level. There is some evidence for the existence of a larger window in the centre of the W wall of the dorter in the form of a jamb and half of the head of what may have been an ogee visible from both inside and outside the building in the walling to the N of an oriel inserted by Hales. The construction of the latter presumably necessitated the blocking of the earlier window.

Thus, initially the northern half of the first floor of the E range is likely to have contained the *studium* and library, with the dorter contained in the southern half behind a partition. By 1375-80 the growth in the number of brethren seems to have led to the removal of the *studium* to an unknown location elsewhere on the site and the freeing-up of the entire upper floor of the range to form a single large dorter. This would explain the introduction of a permanent night stair at the NE corner of the range at that time. The position of the earlier temporary night stair in the 1340s is unknown, although presumably it would have been sited close to the sacristy or the temporary church. It may have been located in the easternmost bay of the N range where there is an otherwise unexplained relieving arch in the S wall. This temporary stair would have been relocated elsewhere or rebuilt following the insertion of vaulting in this area as part of phase **1b**.

Phase 1b (*c*.1351-1356)

It is impossible to assess the extent to which the building programme was disrupted by the Black Death. However, even if it is assumed that its impact on the friars and the workforce was slight, the death of the founder, and of Ramsey, if indeed he were responsible for the first sub-phase, must have created something of a hiatus in the building programme. The documentary reference to John Box in 1352 would seem to provide some evidence for his appointment as the new supervising master mason in that year or possibly slightly earlier. If so, it is not clear whether he continued to work from the original designs assuming a 'master plan' existed and was available to him, or whether he simply picked up where the previous master mason, Ramsey or whoever he was, left off and continued the work to his own designs as funds allowed.

The most important alteration associated with this sub-phase was the construction of the vaults over the E walk, Figs 16, 17 and 39, and ground-floor chambers. The lierne based stellar vaults of the E walk and the plainer quadripartite ribbed vaults of the chambers to the E are positioned in alignment to either side of a very thin (37cm thick) wall, structurally feasible only because the transverse thrust of one vault is countered by the other. This means that the two vaults and the thin axial wall are coeval. The pair of elaborately moulded doors in the southernmost bay of the E walk must pre-date the E walk vaulting since the vault and the axial wall appear to have been built up against the E jamb of the easternmost door, largely obscuring it, Fig. 14. There is no joint visible on the E side of the axial wall at this point as any evidence for this was obscured by the subsequent thickening of the wall in this area by John Hales. The rib-vaulted area on the E side of the axial wall may have been subdivided or left as a long chamber of eleven bays, perhaps with a central partition. The vaulted bays in this area appear to be later than the fireplace openings in the E wall as the latter are not central to the bays. Where no earlier openings existed, new two-light windows with Y-tracery were inserted in central positions, respecting the construction of the vaults. There is disturbance to the line of the vaults where they meet with the E wall, suggesting, possibly, that they were modified to take the heads of the new windows. Scarring under the E wall vault ribs is probably an indication that the vaults had to be modified during construction in order to fit with the E wall, assuming the vaults were constructed across from W to E off the spine wall. Further evidence for the insertion of the vaults exists in the northernmost bay of the northern E chamber where a doorway leading to the sacristy or temporary church of the first sub-phase was blocked up and replaced by a wider doorway with moulded surrounds set somewhat further to the N. The new door is aligned with a two-centred arched door with deeply cut double-ogee moulded surrounds in the axial wall to the W. The space between the two doors may thus have been partitioned off in this sub-phase to form a passage at the N end of the E chamber connecting the E walk with the sacristy; on a measured survey of 1800 a thick masonry wall in this position was drawn as belonging to the pre-Reformation period, Fig. 30.

The use of lierne based vaults at Coventry marks the building out as being part of the mid 14th-century obsession with new designs omitting main diagonal ribs and playing with lozenge and diamond shapes to create a centralised stellar pattern. This concern with innovative designs for vaults is particularly notable in the west country at this time, a very similar design appearing in the transept of Ottery St Mary (Cherry and Pevsner 1989), although such innovations were also taking place elsewhere. Linda Monckton points out (in correspondence) that similar experimentation was also taking place in Kent, and is seen in the tomb of Archbishop John Stratford at Canterbury Cathedral, who died in 1348, the design of which is attributed by Harvey to John Box (Harvey 1984, 31) although he may here have only taken a supervisory role.

The southern rib-vaulted chamber on the E side of the axial wall was extended to the S by one bay following the demolition of the transverse section of wall which originally separated the provisional frater from the buttery or pantry in this position. The partial demolition of this transverse wall seems likely to have occurred at the same time as the construction of the vaults rather than as part of the alterations associated with the insertion of the chapter house in sub-phase **1c**. This helps to explain why the southernmost bay of the new chamber is 0.53m longer than those to the N and it also accounts for the existence of what appear to have been two internal doors, positioned close to each other in the E wall but to either side of the former buttery/pantry N wall. The more northerly of the two doorways has a two-centred arched head and plain-chamfered surrounds, whilst the S door has been blocked. The doors probably led to a chamber attached to the E side of the range. On the S side of the more southerly blocked door are the remains of a jamb, which appears to be contemporary with the construction of the main E wall. This jamb, which survived to the springing until removed during recent landscaping works, is chamfered on its S side providing evidence for a building to the N. There is a ragged joint in the masonry immediately to the N of the more northerly door probably indicating the position of the N wall of the chamber. This ragged joint extends through one and one half storeys, an indication that the chamber probably had an upper floor, but at lower level than the primary lancet window above. The chamber appears to have pre-dated the insertion of the vaults, and its function is unknown, although there is a possibility that it is an early reredorter.

In the E wall of the kitchen passage, in line with the blocked S doorway, is a narrow doorway with plain-chamfered jambs and shallow ogee head, which was later blocked by the thickening of the axial wall. This, taken with the blocked doorway just discussed, may have formed a S cross passage in the E chamber, opening into a passage known from excavation, and eventually, leading to the friars' cemetery and infirmary E of the E range; a similar passage is thought to have existed at Hulne (St John Hope 1890, 119). It was not possible to inspect or measure the area around the putative S door in the E wall at the time of the RCHME survey.

The E cloister walk comprises eleven bays, each with a lierne vault containing a four-pointed star enclosing a diamond-set square panel with quatrefoil cusping, Figs 16-17 and 39. Main diagonal ribs have been omitted, leaving only two ribs to spring from the corners. The narrow ribs have deep plain chamfers. Each bay is lit by a three-light window, originally unglazed, and set on a low wall. Resting on the wall and dividing each window into three, are two pairs of linked, hexagonal, moulded bases each supporting shafts composed of four filleted rolls. The latter culminate in ogee-moulded trefoil-headed arches under ogival hood moulds. Resting on the latter is a moulded string-course running the length of the walk. On the W side the vaults spring from the moulded string over the apices of blind ogee arches in the positions of the buttresses between each window bay. On the E side the vaults are carried on triple-shafted responds, which are in turn supported by corbelled heads. These heads are all heavily eroded but some are cowled and may therefore be representations of important Carmelites or lay benefactors, Fig. 66a-c.

The garth windows seem to form part of the same scheme as the E walk vaulting. There are two possibilities, one, that the garth windows formed part of the first sub-phase, or, more radically, that the garth windows were later cut into the primary walling between the buttresses making them contemporary with the insertion of the vaults and possibly the work of Box. The former possibility seems the more likely since the insertion of the windows would have been a major undertaking and there is no evidence of the considerable refacing of the stonework that would have been required in the area around the openings. One might also expect to find some evidence of earlier windows, of which there is none, unless they were contained within the area occupied by the present tripartite openings.

Similar vaulting in the N and S stub ranges was cut away by Hales to allow for the insertion of flat ceilings in these areas, but the form of the vaults is clear from scars in the masonry. The fenestration in the first bays of the N and S ranges was identical to that in the E, but a slightly different form was employed in the second bay of the S walk. Here, small uncarved blocks were placed over the centre of each ogee head and appear to support the moulded string. There is no logical explanation for the change unless the second bay which may belong to a later phase was left unfinished. Extensive disturbance to the stonework has obscured any obvious sign of a break in construction between the first and second bays.

At the N end of the E walk there is a large opening with a semicircular head. This appears to be contemporary with the E walk vaulting but it does not fit neatly under the N wall vault rib and is architecturally anomalous. There is an inner arch, the projecting jambs of which are formed of a bracket moulding of *c*.1350 resting on what were probably moulded bases, now heavily eroded. There are no rebates for glazing or doors, or indication that it formed a large doorway in the 14th century. Perhaps it was a 16th century remodelling to create an impressive opening to the cloister from the N. The inner surrounds were rebuilt, partly in green sandstone, after the Dissolution. Late 18th-century views show this opening to have been blocked, Figs 21 and 26, and the three-light mullioned window between the original bracket moulding and the outer face of the N wall must date from the early 19th century. Originally there was a step up to the opening from the inside, and the sill was cut down, probably in the early 19th century to facilitate access to a narrow door that must have existed in this position prior to the insertion of the mullioned window. The jambs of the opening on the N side of the wall are very slight and judging by the disturbance to the stone work around the opening they are most probably a later replacement.

Phase 1c (*c*.1375-1380)

This sub-phase sees the creation of a new chapter house, the construction of a new day stair at the southern end of the E range, and the addition of an elaborate night stair at the NE corner of the latter to link the dorter with the choir.

A place set aside in which the friars would have met daily to discuss the temporal as well as religious affairs of the house must have been included somewhere in the early building but its location cannot now be determined. A new purpose-built chapter house was constructed in this sub-phase, and connected to the E walk by a narrow vestibule, Fig. 18. It is separated from the middle bay of the E walk by a stone arch originally containing regular and ogival trefoiled tracery supported on a central pillar or trumeau. Most of the tracery and the pillar were removed prior to the late 18th century leaving the springings from which the form of the tracery has been reconstructed, Fig. 67. This entrance arch appears to have been a more elaborate interpretation of the cusped Y-tracery evident in the ground-floor E windows. Rebates on the E side of the inner chapter house opening indicate that small doors were provided to form the necessary ceremonial barrier without disrupting much of the view from the E walk. At each side of the entry arch are curious opposed passages entered via low, shouldered-arched openings with wave-moulded surrounds and shallow ogee heads, Fig. 19. These connect with the private chambers to the N and S of the chapter house. Wall passages are common in castle design, and indeed in larger churches, but the use of wall passages here in Coventry Whitefriars are thought to be unique and their precise function is undocumented. They seem to have been created with the express purpose of allowing the friars to move between the heated N and S chambers without entering the E walk or disturbing proceedings in the chapter house. There are rebates for chapter house doors on the W side of the entrances to the passages. The only other way of getting from one chamber to the other was through a narrow door, subsequently reset, opening off the E walk into the centre of the N chamber and a similar opening in the kitchen passage at the southern end of the walk. This would have involved a long journey along the cold E walk and some retracing of steps. The elaborate appearance of the passage entrances was dictated by their positioning at the entrance to the liturgically important chapter house since the doors to thc chambers at the end of the passages are extremely plain. The passages are very narrow and low, and to avoid the obstruction caused by the open doors, recesses were provided to accommodate the door in the open position. The existence of these passages infers a strong functional relationship between the N and S chambers. Unfortunately there is no conclusive evidence for the original use of the chambers and one must look to other mendicant houses for clues.

Only one bay of the chapter house survives, the rest having been demolished by the early 18th century and a new wall inserted on the line of the E wall of the range, Figs 18 and 48. The precise dimensions of the chapter house are not certainly known. Excavations indicate that it comprised three bays each of approximately 8m in length, and a diagonal net-vaulted ceiling carried on triple-shafted responds and mask corbels very similar to the earlier net-vault on the Exeter pulpitum and a reconstruction of one at Wells is suggested. It is likely to have had a large window at the E end and, from the surviving foundations, there is evidence that the N and S side walls were lit by narrow windows set in the thin sections of wall between large triangular buttresses. The 0.85m thick sections of wall between the buttresses sit on a 1.5m thick foundation suggesting, possibly, that the chapter house may have been built in two phases (see Section D for a discussion of the Reconstruction). A tentative reconstruction is shown at Fig. 34. Rough areas of stone on the floor near the side walls in the surviving bay are probably the remains of stone benches.

On the upper floor, above the chapter house itself, there was a room which opened off the dorter. The evidence for this is provided by the continuation of the splayed buttresses in the external angle up to eaves level and the thinner, replacement section of walling in this area blocking the opening on the upper floor. This blocking is of indeterminate date but clearly built after the demolition of the chapter house. The opening being the same width as the chapter house would seem to be an indication that this room was fully open to the main dorter, or perhaps partitioned off by a wooden screen and may well relate to the change of plan in the dorter referred to earlier. A room over the chapter house seems to be a fairly rare feature in friaries, but examples have been identified at Rhuddlan Blackfriars and Richmond (Yorkshire) Greyfriars (Martin 1937, 33, 37). The room over the chapter house at the Richmond Greyfriars was possibly the room close to the dormitory referred to in documentary sources as 'The Studies'. This was an area reserved for private study and it is possible that the room over the chapter house at Coventry was similarly used for this purpose, although a room serving that purpose could just as easily have been located alongside the dorter at the E end of the N range on the first floor. The existence of the elaborate vault at this upper level suggests that the inclusion of an upper chamber may have been only a temporary expedient, perhaps as an apartment for the prior, until a more commodious house for him was built.

The evidence for the dating of the chapter house and the associated passages is contradictory. On the one hand the surviving side walls of the chapter house, and the passages, appear to be of the same build as the E wall of the range. Furthermore, the splayed buttresses in the outer angles between the main E wall of the range and the truncated N and S walls of the chapter house would also appear to be coeval as there are no discernible joints in the masonry. Conversely, the side walls interrupt the regular pattern of vaulting E of the central axial wall, giving the firm impression of being a later insertion, and the wall ribs of the E side of the chambers to the N and S show signs of having been altered to meet with the side walls of the chapter house. The northernmost splayed buttress was adjusted to respect the jamb of a primary first-floor window. Also, the shouldered heads to the passage doors, their wave-moulded surrounds and the unusual continuation through the passage of the shoulders of the arches in the form of a continuous corbelled cornice (described as a 'torus cornice' by Fretton 1872), are very similar to those of the night stair on the first floor, which is definitely a later insertion, possibly as late as *c*.1380, as it was intended to connect with a passage leading to the new choir, Figs 45-46.

The triangular buttresses of the chapter house are identical in scale to those of the Great Hall and flanking towers at Kenilworth Castle built by the mason Robert Skillyngton for John of Gaunt *c*.1391. This has given rise to a suggestion by Dr R K Morris (1988) that Skillyngton may have been involved at Coventry Whitefriars. John of Gaunt was an important supporter of the Carmelites taking members of the order as confessors and founding a house for them at Doncaster. If Skillyngton was indeed responsible for the chapter house, and also the night stair and passage from the sacristy to the choir, then this would point to a probable date for these features of no earlier than *c*.1373 when, according to Harvey (1984, 275), he is thought to have first become active in the Coventry area. There is little doubt that the mouldings and shouldered arches of the chapter house passages and the night stair are by a different hand than the masons responsible for the earlier works to the E range. If Skillyngton was the master mason responsible for this third sub-phase, it seems that he was experimenting with the use of triangular buttressing at Whitefriars before going on to use the same feature some 15 years later at Kenilworth. Indeed it may be that their form was suggested to him by the triangular ends of the earlier cut-water buttresses in the garth.

On balance, therefore, the chapter house seems to be a later addition and this would have necessitated careful refacing and knitting in of new stonework in the area around the entrance to the chapter house, and, externally, at the point where its side walls met with the original outer face of the E wall of the range. This may account for the absence of the construction joints in the masonry that one would expect to find in these areas as evidence of the insertion.

The functions of the chambers created by the insertion of the chapter house are unknown and reference to similar rooms in other Carmelite houses is not particularly revealing. At London Whitefriars similar chambers were described in a grant of 1541 as the northern and southern dormitory (Clapham 1910, 28). This description, however, would seem to be based on the application of the function of the first floor to the ground-floor divisions and thus it cannot be taken as an accurate guide to the use of N and S chambers at Coventry. It has been suggested at Hulne (St John Hope 1890, 118) that one of the two rooms may have been the prior's chamber; however at Coventry the prior was originally more likely to have occupied a chamber on the first floor. Based on comparisons with other mendicant houses, the N chamber could have functioned as an inner parlour where the friars would have assembled before proceeding to the choir or chapter house. The S chamber may have been used as a schoolroom for novices, as at London Blackfriars. Using the chapter house passages the novices could have moved quickly between the two chambers before and after services.

The N chamber was entered from the W by means of the

arched opening at the very N end of the walk and a narrow ogee-headed doorway, blocked and reset, near the centre. The fireplace in the thickness of the E wall has been widened at its southern end and given a curved jamb. This feature should be investigated in more detail following the removal of the sundry archaeological finds that are currently partly obscuring it.

The S chamber is of five bays and is lit by three two-light windows similar to those in the N chamber, one on the S and two on the E between which are the remains of a small original fireplace. The N jamb and the northern half of the fireplace bressumer survive *in situ*, but the other half has been rebuilt and the opening blocked. The flue was carried up within the thickness of the wall. The N jamb of the lancet inserted immediately to the S of the fireplace, probably as part of sub-phase **1c**, is splayed to respect the earlier flue.

To the S is another low opening, chamfered with a shallow ogee head. The surrounds are regularly coursed into the adjacent stonework and the opening is probably therefore original. The low height of the opening, and the fact that from the W side its sill is some 60cm above floor level would seem to indicate that it was originally an aumbry or recess which was later made into a doorway. The lower part of the opening was obscured at the time of the RCHME survey making it difficult to interpret the precise sequence of development in this area. The opening is drawn as a recess in a Troughton sketch (Coventry Record Office 1/10/14). Externally, the stonework around the blocked former door opening is of poor quality, the N jamb and N part of the sill being fairly unconvincing. Internally, there are no rebates for doors suggesting that it formed some sort of open recess used for the storage of books. This feature together with the fireplace is consistent with the possible use of the chamber as a writing or schoolroom.

This sub-phase probably also included the construction of a day stair of high quality presumably to replace a temporary structure in the small service room on the W side of the kitchen passage. The new stone-vaulted stair rose in a clockwise direction and was of the newel type. The precise arrangement of the vaulting is difficult to reconstruct. The ribs appear to be supported by pendants and at the 90 degree point in the curve of the stair there are the remains of a large moulded arch the N end of which was presumably supported by the newel. The small window lighting the stair at ground-floor level is probably a sub-phase **1c** opening but the present semicircular head is an early-19th century replacement. Part of a splayed jamb and a sill are evidence for the existence of a larger window in the area between the ground and first floors which was subsequently removed by the insertion by Hales of a projecting bay containing a mullioned and transomed window. The original stair was set further back from the E walk door than the present modern stair and rose more steeply, thus passing under the small window. Scarring caused by the removal of the treads of the original stair can be seen under the existing structure.

The S range of the cloister may also have been completed as part of this sub-phase as the star vault of the adjoining cloister gate is unlikely to be very much later than the walk vaults of which it is a more elaborate version.

One of the architecturally most interesting features associated with the dorter was the night stair, of which only the upper entrance and top three steps survive. The friars used this stair early in the morning to make their way from the dorter to the choir for Matins, the first service of the day. There is little doubt, from the awkward way in which the side of the entrance to the stair is built into the thickness of the E wall of the dorter on an angle, that the Coventry night stair is secondary to the rest of the range. The entrance doorway has the same shouldered-arched head and torus cornices as the passages in the chapter house. The foot of the stair most probably connected with the passage, probably of the same date, which linked the sacristy with the choir.

The night stair was demolished in the early 19th century, but its appearance can be deduced with some accuracy from late 18th-century antiquarian watercolours and pen and ink sketches, Figs 21 and 44, and for internal views Figs 45-46. It consisted of a straight flight descending to the N and culminating in a landing lit by two, two-light trefoil-headed windows. The stair then returned in an easterly direction beyond the line of the E wall of the E range before terminating in another shouldered-arched doorway connecting with the sacristy passage. The stair had its own hipped and gabled roof clad with what were probably stone slates.

With the completion of the choir, the temporary church, which may have existed at the N end of the E range, would have been demolished leaving a yard enclosed by the E wall of the S transept, the choir and the sacristy passage. There is archaeological evidence for three burials in this area but it is not known if these were formerly incorporated within a temporary church or whether they date from after its demolition. If the latter, this may be an indication that the yard was used for a time as the friars' cemetery, Fig. 38.

The blocked moulded opening in the S wall of the S walk was in all probability associated with further works that followed the donation of land in 1413-4 by William Botener for the enlargement of the friars' habitation. For a description of the moulding to this door, see Woodfield, P., Section F, *The Architectural Stonework.* This doorway was blocked during the workhouse period by the insertion in this position of a 16th-century fireplace surround moved from elsewhere on the site. This is built into the S side of the opening and is now exposed as an external feature following the demolition of part of the workhouse kitchen. There is some disturbance in the walling to the inner face of the northern jamb of this door, suggesting it is a later insertion. It seems to have served as a formal entry to new buildings around the S court, or indeed to St John's Hall if it lay this far E. The dendrochronological dating suggests that the main cloister roof is all pre-Dissolution and of the Rebuild phase, having been constructed in the last quarter of the 15th century, the southern end having been remodelled by John Hales, Fig. 22.

Later Medieval Phase (c.1475 – c.1544)

The surviving masonry and architectural detail gives no clear evidence for later building phases in the mediaeval period. It had generally been assumed that the roof was a new structure put on the building by John Hales as part of his refurbishment campaign of the mid sixteenth century, although there had been occasional unfounded speculation that the roof had been brought in from elsewhere.

The style of the roof is consistent throughout its length, all the trusses having a tie-beam and two tiers of collars supported on three queen struts between the tie and lower collar, and two slightly raked struts between the two collars, Fig. 22. There are two ranks of side purlins both with curved windbraces. The upper purlins are clasped between the collars and the principals which are diminished at this level, whilst the lower ones are tenoned. The northern and southernmost trusses were built against the N and S gable end walls. This has partially obscured the large N window. The centre of the tie-beam of the truss against the S wall is supported on posts placed to either side of the large central window in order to prevent it and the collars cutting across the opening.

Given the lack of precisely dateable features in late medieval and early post-medieval roofs, a scientific study of the roof timbers was commissioned by English Heritage for the Royal Commission, and undertaken by the Oxford Dendrochronological Laboratory (Miles 2002; Miles and Worthington 2002). Satisfactory results were obtained from twenty timbers taken from various parts of the E range roof, giving a felling date range of 1474-1481, with two yielding the precise felling date of spring 1475 AD. Timbers from the middle bays of the E range, between bays 6 and 9 numbered from the N, also gave precise felling dates of winter 1491-2, spring 1493, and winter 1493-4. Two longitudinal beams in bay 11, the southernmost bay of the E range provided a date of 1531-63 and 1534-66 respectively and are likely to relate to Hales' ceiling in this part of the roof. A timber from bay 7 provided a felling date range of 1492-1500. This evidence suggests that there was a late 15th-century campaign of re-roofing of the E range of the cloister, beginning at the N end in *c.*1475 and completed in a second phase of *c.*1493-4. The completion of the re-roofing may have coincided with a visit on the 16th September 1494 of Lawrence Burrell, deputy master-general of the Carmelite order, as part of his progress through England (Fretton 1872, 65). The re-roofing was probably necessitated by a failure of the original roof. The study also shows fairly conclusively that the principal surviving interventions by Hales are confined to the ceiling of the southern end bay of the former dorter, the timber-framed first floor of the S range and the stub of the SW range of the service court.

Post-Reformation phases – 'Hales Place' (1545-c.1800)

The low number of brethren recorded as living at Whitefriars at the surrender of the house in 1538 and the lease of parts of the site to John Bird in 1536-37 are strong indications that the brethren were quite aware of the change taking place in the political climate and were gradually being dispersed prior to the actual deed of surrender. It seems likely that the house was being gradually run down from perhaps as early as 1530, and little maintenance to the buildings would have been carried out after that time. Some demolition began in 1538 as in that year the mayor and aldermen of Coventry pleaded with Thomas Cromwell to halt works underway there (McCaffrey 1926, 251). Thus, upon acquiring the house at the end of 1544 John Hales was most probably faced with a backlog of repairs, a factor to be balanced against his intention to turn parts of the complex into a fashionable house for himself. He seems to have made an early decision to retain the entire E range of the cloister and to convert this into the principal part of his mansion. In some respects this comes as no surprise since the double-width E range with its vaulted ground-floor chambers and elaborate stairs was the largest and architecturally most impressive part of the cloister. It also communicated with the choir, which was converted by Hales into a free grammar school. A study of the fate of Austin canons' houses at the Dissolution has revealed that the retention and conversion to domestic use of the entire eastern range of the cloister was a very rare occurrence (Dickinson 1968, 72). This was most probably due to the fact that this range usually provided more accommodation than was required for secular purposes, and possibly the determination of commissioners to destroy for ideological reasons what were the principal rooms of the religious house. In this context Hales' decision to convert the E range of Whitefriars can be seen as very bold and as reflecting his not inconsiderable social standing and political ambitions.

There is no way of precisely ascertaining the nature and extent of Hales' alterations to the friary buildings, as distinct from modifications made by his descendants, because the only reliable information on the appearance of the house prior to its conversion to a workhouse dates from the very end of the 18th century. However, much of the work must have been completed within the first twenty years in order for the house to be in a fit state to receive Elizabeth I and her retinue on the 17th-19th August, 1566 (Nicholls 1823, **I**, 197; Fretton 1872, 69).

From a letter written by her in 1569 to the Earls of Shrewsbury and Huntingdon she was evidently much impressed with the standard of the accommodation (McCaffrey 1926, 254). Complaining about the quartering of Mary Queen of Scots in an inn in Coventry, the Queen wrote 'we fynd strange that she should be placed in an inn very unconveniently even for names sake; and what might be the cause we cannot guess, considering we know how commodious a house that is there where we ourselves did lodge, commonly called "the Frears"…' (*ibid.*). It is thus reasonable to assume that Hales Place was the largest and probably the finest house in Coventry at that time.

The setting of Hales Place
Hales demolished the six westernmost bays of the S range and all but the easternmost one and one half bays of the N range, building, probably with reused stone, new gable ends to the truncated ranges, Figs 23-24, 38 and 44. He also demolished most of the buildings making up the inner court and built new ranges in approximately the same position to form what was probably a service courtyard. The roof of the surviving stub end of the SW range of the service court has been dated by dendrochronological analysis to 1547-8, confirming Hales' rebuilding of this part of the building at that time (Miles 2002; Miles and Worthington 2002). The cloister gate was retained as the principal entrance to the house and the more southerly of two walled gardens created by Hales on the W side of the E range. A lane led, through another area of garden, due W from the gatehouse to what was probably a new access road called Bachelors Walk connecting the westerly arm of Whitefriars Lane to the N with the London Road and Newgate to the S. The W wall of the W walk was partially retained and rebuilt to form the western boundary of the more northerly and larger of the two gardens, probably a privy garden, Fig. 37. The remains of the vaults of the W walk in the S end of the W wall are shown as minute dots on an Aylesford Collection plan, Fig. 30. The N garden was bounded by the S wall of the nave to the N, by the E range to the E, and by a new S wall aligned approximately with the N wall of the gatehouse and the truncated S range to the S, Fig. 30.

Alterations to the East range

Ground floor
The main entrance to the principal rooms of the new house was through a particularly resplendent doorway reset on the N side of the westernmost bay of the former truncated S walk, Fig. 24. This door is set within a single-storey projection built up against the W face of one of the original buttresses. The upper half of this two-centred arched doorway has elaborately moulded surrounds and would appear to date from the end of the 14th or the beginning of the 15th century. The door was removed by Hales perhaps from the prior's lodging in the inner court, or, possibly, from the public side of St. John's Hall or an equally imposing position in the demolished claustral ranges and relocated in its present position. The mouldings consist of three half-rounds with fillets, between which are wider recessed bands of floral enrichment. There is a hood mould terminating in corbels now weathered beyond recognition. A Troughton sketch, probably based on an earlier painting of *c.*1800, appears to show two mythical animals, one possibly a dog, one possibly crowned (Coventry Record Office 1/10/3), Fig. 81.

The reset door was in line with the inserted moulded door in the S wall of the walk, Fig. 38, thus creating an impressive passageway between the N and S walled gardens. By 1800 a wall had been inserted across the S walk on the E side of the opposed doors to form a passage, the only means of access between the two gardens.

Two further entrances to the E range were created by removing the mullions and the plinth from the garth windows in the second bay from the N and S ends of the E walk, Fig. 56. This provided convenient entrances to each end of the walk, which had become in effect a decorative low-level long gallery. In the summer one could obtain easy access to the gardens and in the winter the walk could be used to take exercise whilst enjoying views of the gardens. The garth windows were probably glazed at that time. There are hints of possible 16th-century glazing in the cloisters (see Fig. 133 and Section J, *Medieval Window Glass from the Church and Cloister*). The linear arrangement of the ground floor of the E range meant that the walk served as an important axial corridor linking and providing access to the apartments in this area. Given its proximity to the putative kitchen in the remains of the S walk, the S chamber most probably became the dining room. A new main entrance to the chamber, in the shape of a four-centred arched door, was created near its N end. At the same time the axial wall separating the chamber from the E walk was thickened presumably in order to help support new works on the first floor.

The discovery in the early 1970s (by CW) of an 18th-century sherd under flagging respecting the triangular buttresses suggests that the chapter house survived in some form until the early 18th century. At that time all but the westernmost bay of the chapter house was demolished and a new section of wall was built in line with the main E wall, thus turning the space into a small vaulted chamber between the larger chambers to the N and S, Fig. 20. The passages and at least part of the arch at the entrance to the chapter house were retained. The mutilation of the latter took place prior to the late 18th century. The survival of the chapter house after the Dissolution means that its upper chamber, if it still existed at this date, would have opened off a large room created by Hales on the floor above.

The function of the chamber N of the former chapter house in Hales' time is unknown, however it would have made an impressive and well-lit heated room. A new entrance with a four-centred arched head was created opening off the E walk in the centre of the chamber. It was subsequently walled up. This opening forms part of a larger area of wall extending from the northernmost respond of the walk to the transverse rib separating the third and fourth vault bays from the N, which has been rebuilt using a lighter-coloured sandstone in the area between the bottom two courses and original courses above the level of the vault springing. It is not clear why such a large section of wall should have been rebuilt in this way. The bottom of this section of replacement walling and the openings created by Hales in the E walk are approximately 30cm higher than the present floor level indicating that the floor was raised by Hales and subsequently in the 20th century returned to a point closer to its original level. The floor heights in the two ground-floor chambers are still at the higher level.

At the N end of the N chamber was a partition wall containing a door and forming a passage from the walk to a building referred to on the 1800 plan, Fig. 30, as 'Hales' Chapel' in the position of the sacristy, Figs 20 and 25; see also Fig. 38. From excavations carried out by Charmian Woodfield and from structural evidence in this vicinity, it appears that the S and N walls of the vestry/sacristy were rebuilt on top of the earlier wider footings, and the E wall was rebuilt further W, thereby shortening the building, Fig. 43. This new building may also have had a stone vaulted ceiling as the sole surviving vault rib, which is built into the E wall of the range, is in green sandstone. The new building had a four-light Perpendicular window and angle buttresses at its E end, and two, 2-light square-headed windows in its S side wall, Fig. 20. This work seemed to the excavator to be of the *Rebuild* phase, that is, a late building by the friars, and this building which is referred to as the 'Vestry' in Dissolution documents is probably what was later known as 'Hales' Chapel'. The chapel may relate either to the ground floor or to the timber-framed upper storey, seen on antiquarian drawings, Figs 20 and 25; this is likely to be the work of John Hales.

First floor
There is evidence for the insertion of ceilings in the two southernmost bays and in the northernmost five bays of the former dorter. This takes the form of grooves and mortices in the faces of the tie-beams in these areas, enabling ceiling beams to be morticed in at one end and slid into grooves at the other. Joists could then be fitted between the beams, and the new ceiling underdrawn with plaster. Only the southernmost bay has *in situ* inserted beams with the date range of 1531-63 and 1534-66 (Miles 2002; Miles and Worthington 2002) suggesting that they form part of the ceiling of the former dorter by John Hales, Figs 22 and 27.

That the first floor was later partitioned is apparent from a late 18th-century interior view, Fig. 27, and structural evidence. There was a panelled wooden screen inserted on the line of the truss between the second and third bays from the S. The screen had two doors suggesting the presence of an axial partition, which divided the second bay from the S in two and met with a timber and plaster partition between the first and second bays. A door in the easternmost lobby led through to the first floor of the range forming the E side of the S court, and another in the W lobby presumably connected with the first-floor stair landing. The former day stair at the S continued to form the principal means of access to the first floor and a shallow projection containing a mullioned window was built in the S wall of the range to provide it with more light.

On the N side of the panelled screen was in effect a four-bay first-floor chamber extending from and including the third to the sixth bays from the S. The tie-beams and lower collars of the trusses in this area were removed and a plastered wagon-ceiling inserted in the space below the upper collar; large mortices which originally received the tenons of the lower collars are clear evidence of the removal of the lower parts of these trusses. Small mortices in the top face of the second and sixth trusses from the S show that the section of wall above the ties at each end of the chamber was plastered. This room and its ceiling were illustrated in the late 18th century at which time they were in poor condition, indicative of an extended period out of domestic use, Fig. 27. The N end of the room was closed off by the insertion of a partition below the truss separating the sixth and seventh bays from the S. A recess to take the E end of this partition survives in the area of wall rebuilt following the removal of the chamber over the chapter house. The eastern two-thirds of this partition may have been of more open construction as only this section of the tie-beam is chamfered.

The wagon-ceiling post-dates Hales' involvement and the removal of the chamber over the chapter house, as the partition supporting its northern end would have cut across the entrance to the chapter house chamber, and been without adequate support at its E end. It is possible that the end of the partition was supported on an earlier load-bearing wall screening off the hall from the chapter house chamber, but this seems unlikely bearing in mind the awkward juxtaposition that would have resulted. The more likely sequence is that Hales created a large room consisting of at least five bays with a flat ceiling, and that the wagon-ceiling was inserted in the early 18th century following the demolition of the chapter house. The extent of Hales' ceiled first-floor chamber is difficult to determine, but in all likelihood it incorporated much or possibly all of the former dorter, forming, in effect, a kind of early long gallery heated by a large fireplace, Fig. 28, created in the area just to the S of the former entrance to the chapter house. There is certainly no structural evidence for former partitions except for those associated with the later insertion of the wagon-ceiling. An oriel window, in the W wall near the centre of the putative gallery is likely to form part of Hales' modifications. This is referred to as 'Queen Elizabeth's window' by

Fretton (1872, 68). There is no doubt that this is an insertion since it cuts across the arched jamb of an earlier window opening (see below for a description of the oriel).

The lateral stack of the first-floor fireplace is corbelled out over the ground floor partly cutting across the head of one of the two-light windows lighting the S ground-floor chamber. In the late 18th century the stack supported a square brick chimney but this was replaced, probably in the late 19th century, by a wide rectangular chimney in stone with a cap formed of two offsets and trefoil perforations in panels below. The stone fireplace opening is 3.1m (10ft) wide and has a four-centred arched head, set within a square opening, with moulded jambs and sunk spandrels, Fig. 28. The lower halves of the jambs are straight-chamfered with shaped stops. Above the cambered lintel is a large stone relieving arch, and above that, small square openings, now blocked. The latter may be the remains of fixings for an overmantel. Originally the room may have been panelled but there is no indication of this in the late 18th-century view, Fig. 27. At that time the walls were plastered and there was a moulded cornice.

Four new mullioned windows with square heads were inserted in the E wall of the chamber, one of three lights on the N side of the stack in the new section of wall, one of two lights with double straight-chamfered surrounds just to the S of the fireplace, and three- and four-light windows to the S of that in the position of two of the original ogee-headed lancets. By the late 18th century the N and two S windows had been replaced by new mullioned window frames with lower heads set within the surrounds of the earlier windows, the area between the heads of the replacements and the lintels of the earlier surrounds being infilled with brick. All of these windows were subsequently blocked or replaced.

The W wall of the chamber was provided with three new mullioned window openings, the most impressive of these being an oriel in the centre of the W wall, with canted sides, each of one light, and a four-light window in the wide area between. Each light is divided in two by a central transom, Figs 13 and 27. The jambs of the entrance to the oriel have straight chamfers and pyramidal stops at the base. The hollow-chamfered mouldings in the oriel are very crisp indicating that the original window frame was replaced in the late 19th century. Externally, the centre of the oriel is supported by one of the original buttresses which has been cut down, with moulded corbelling to each side. The profile of the latter is also very crisp, an indication that it too has been rebuilt. The buttress to the S of that supporting the oriel was cut down to make room for a five-light mullioned window whilst to the S of that was a four-light mullioned window. Both windows were inserted in the same position as original ogee-headed lights and both were subsequently replaced by six-light windows with king-mullions.

The function of the five bays to the N of the chamber with the inserted wagon ceiling is unknown, but this area was certainly divided into a series of smaller rooms by the late 18th century. There is no evidence of heating in this space unless a fireplace was built into an axial wall, subsequently removed, or in a substantial transverse wall enclosing the chamber on its N side. Both possibilities seem unlikely and it may be that heat was borrowed from the large lateral stack in the adjoining chamber through the partly open partition. An 18th-century view looking S up the night stair shows a corridor along the E wall in the three northernmost bays of the range with a door at its S end communicating with the four-bay chamber beyond. The corridor would have provided access from the chamber to a good room above Hales' chapel, perhaps a library or bed chamber, and to the NE external stair. The room over the chapel, Fig. 20 and 25, was of timber-framed construction with close-studded walls and a mid-rail with two full-height upswinging braces in its E gable-end wall. There were three four-light mullioned windows positioned at regular intervals above the mid-rail on the S side of the room and two three-light mullioned windows in the N wall. The chapel and the room above survived until the end of the 18th century. Little is known about the area on the W side of the corridor and the first-floor of the truncated N range. The northernmost of the three four-light windows on the W side of the E range was replaced by a three-light window, and in the bay to the N of this an external stair was created leading down from a door inserted beneath the upper half of an original, partially blocked, ogee window. This stair ran down across the cut-back angle buttress in the NE corner of the cloister before reaching ground level in the first bay of the N range where it partially blocked an original tripartite window of the N walk. This stair was removed in the early 19th century and a door with a semicircular head was inserted in the position formerly occupied by the foot of the stair.

The flooring inserted by Hales in the truncated N range in place of the N walk vaulting has been removed and there is a modern stair filling this area. In the late 18th century there were fireplaces probably at both ground and first-floor levels in the N wall of the range, the stack being accommodated within the thickness of the wall. There is an oval recess lined with thin bricks, probably a bread oven, at upper ground-floor level close to the former position of this stack. Disturbance to the walling around the mouth of the opening suggests that it is a Post-Reformation feature. Both rooms in the N range were lit by large windows in the rebuilt gable end, which have in turn been largely replaced. The functions of these rooms in Hales' time are unknown but the large mullioned windows overlooking the walled garden and the presence of heating would indicate that initially both were probably of high status. The outer face of the western half of the N wall of the N range was probably rebuilt by Hales as this section has slightly neater coursing and reset ogee-headed windows.

The first-floor room of the S range has a fireplace with plain-chamfered surrounds which was inserted in the thickened buttress on the E side of the present main entrance. This fireplace was centred in the N wall of the room, its original E wall being the timber-framed partition at the top of the small flight of steps leading up from the first-floor landing. The fireplace and timber-framing is the work of Hales. The partition to the W of this transverse wall is a modern insertion. The S wall of this chamber has been rebuilt in timber-framing following the removal of adjoining workhouse ranges in the 1960s, as has most of the northern stub of the range forming the W side of the S court, which is entered at first-floor level from the small lobby leading to the present first-floor office over the main entrance.

The South court

The southernmost garden on the W side of the house provided for vehicular access via the cloister gate to what was probably a new service court built by Hales, Figs 15 and 23. It is possible that he reused parts of the foundations of the friary buildings although there is no way of establishing this for certain without undertaking archaeological investigations in the vicinity. These have in fact taken place in the 1990s, but no details of the results are available. The only evidence we have for the appearance of these ranges is a handful of late 18th-century views, Figs 15, 23, 25, and plans Figs 30 and 38; Whitefriars is also shown in miniature in a 17th-century engraving by W. Hollar after Speed's 1610 plan of Coventry, however its accuracy cannot be relied on. These views, the irregular spacing and detailing of the windows and the overall form of the ranges, would suggest a mid-16th-century date, and it is reasonable to assume that most of these buildings were probably erected by Hales fairly shortly after he purchased the property, rather than by his descendants, an interpretation confirmed by the recent dendrochronological analysis of the remnant of the SW range of the court. A measured survey of the ground floor made in 1800 before the sale of the property to the Coventry Union shows these ranges in outline only and provides no other information on their plans, Fig. 30.

The entrance to the S court was from the W by means of a large square-headed opening in the ground floor of a narrow range forming its W side. A view of the courtyard in the Aylesford Collection would seem to indicate that this W range was of timber-frame and plaster construction, Fig. 15. There was a stair up to the first floor just to the N of the entranceway. The function of the range is unknown, although judging by the existence of small windows in its W wall at first-floor level (shown in late 18th-century watercolour views, Fig. 23), it was probably a service range, possibly communicating with a kitchen created in the two easternmost bays of the main S claustral range. There were larger windows and a W-facing gable over a long thin room on the ground floor in the southern half of the range. This may be an indication of better rooms on this part of the first-floor, perhaps guests' lodgings. The room below could only be reached from the courtyard and it probably fulfilled some sort of service function. The much-restored timber-framed stub of the northern end of the W range survives on the S side of the present building, Fig. 29. It had a queen-post roof with a single tier of clasped purlins and curved windbraces.

The range forming the S side of the courtyard occupied the site of the former prior's hall parts of which survived the Surrender, as the medieval tiled floor, Figs 49 and 136, is patched with what appears to be 18th-century brick. The range was aligned E-W and measured approximately 22.5m (74ft) long by 9.1m (30ft) wide. It was much wider than the adjoining W range and had a gabled roof which at its W end, at least, extended down over the first floor. No illustrations of this range exist except for a partial view of the W gable end, which projected beyond the W wall of the W service range, Fig. 23.

The E range of the courtyard measured approximately 15.8m (52ft) long by 12.2m (40ft) wide, Figs 15 and 25. It was a two-storeyed, gabled range aligned N-S. From this late 18th-century view of the courtyard it appears that the ground floor may have been of stone whilst the first-floor, which was jettied out over it, was of timber-frame construction. At the N end of the W side of the range on the ground floor there was a four-centred arched door with moulded surrounds which led through the ground floor of a small separately-roofed block in the angle between the E wall of the E range and the N wall of the E range of the courtyard, to the rear of the house. To the S of this doorway in the courtyard was a large, partially walled-up window with a later mullioned window inserted into the upper part of it. This is evidence of the later alteration of the E side of the courtyard, or, possibly, of the re-use of parts of the earlier friary buildings. The W wall of the range, Fig. 23, was interpreted as Pre-Reformation in the 1800 survey, Fig. 30. The first-floor rooms were lit on the W side by large mullioned and transomed windows, probably enclosing casements. This level probably communicated with the E end of the former dorter by means of an original doorway at its southern end and the block in the angle between the two ranges. The first floor of the E courtyard range may therefore have contained a suite of good rooms associated with those on the first-floor of the main E range. The N gable end of the E courtyard range can be seen in the background of a late 18th-century view of Hales Place from the NE, Fig. 25. This shows that the range probably had an attic floor as there is a window positioned high up in the N gable over three first-floor windows spaced at regular intervals.

It may be borne in mind that Hales also purchased the site of the Whitefriars Grange in Radford from Sir Ralph Sadleir in 1548. This land passed to Hales' nephew who erected there a large fashionable mansion called New House, built in the 1580s, in what is now a northern suburb of Coventry. This presumably curtailed spending on Hales Place. Sadly this fine Elizabethan great house is no longer extant.

Later Alterations
The subsequent history of the building, through the later gentry period and its subsequent use by the Poor Law Union as a workhouse is covered by the RCHME report, held in archive and this along with other material relating to the site can be consulted at the National Monuments Record Centre, Swindon.

ACKNOWLEDGEMENTS

I wish to thank Mr Paul Woodfield for his assistance in interpreting the surviving E range of the former friary, and Mrs Charmian Woodfield for so generously sharing with me information on the Carmelites and their house in Coventry. I am also grateful to Linda Monckton for reading this Section and making many helpful suggestions, most of which have been incorporated. Thanks also to Mrs Margaret Rylatt and Myk Flitcroft for providing access to the building, and to Mr Nicholas Kingsley of the Archives Department of Birmingham Central Library for allowing Aylesford Collection watercolours of Whitefriars to be copied. Mr Michael Jones, and Dr Andrew Brown of English Heritage facilitated RCHME involvement in the survey of the site. The RCHME measured survey drawings were produced by Nigel Fadgley and Mike Williams, and the photographs by Peter Williams and Mike Hesketh-Roberts.

JC

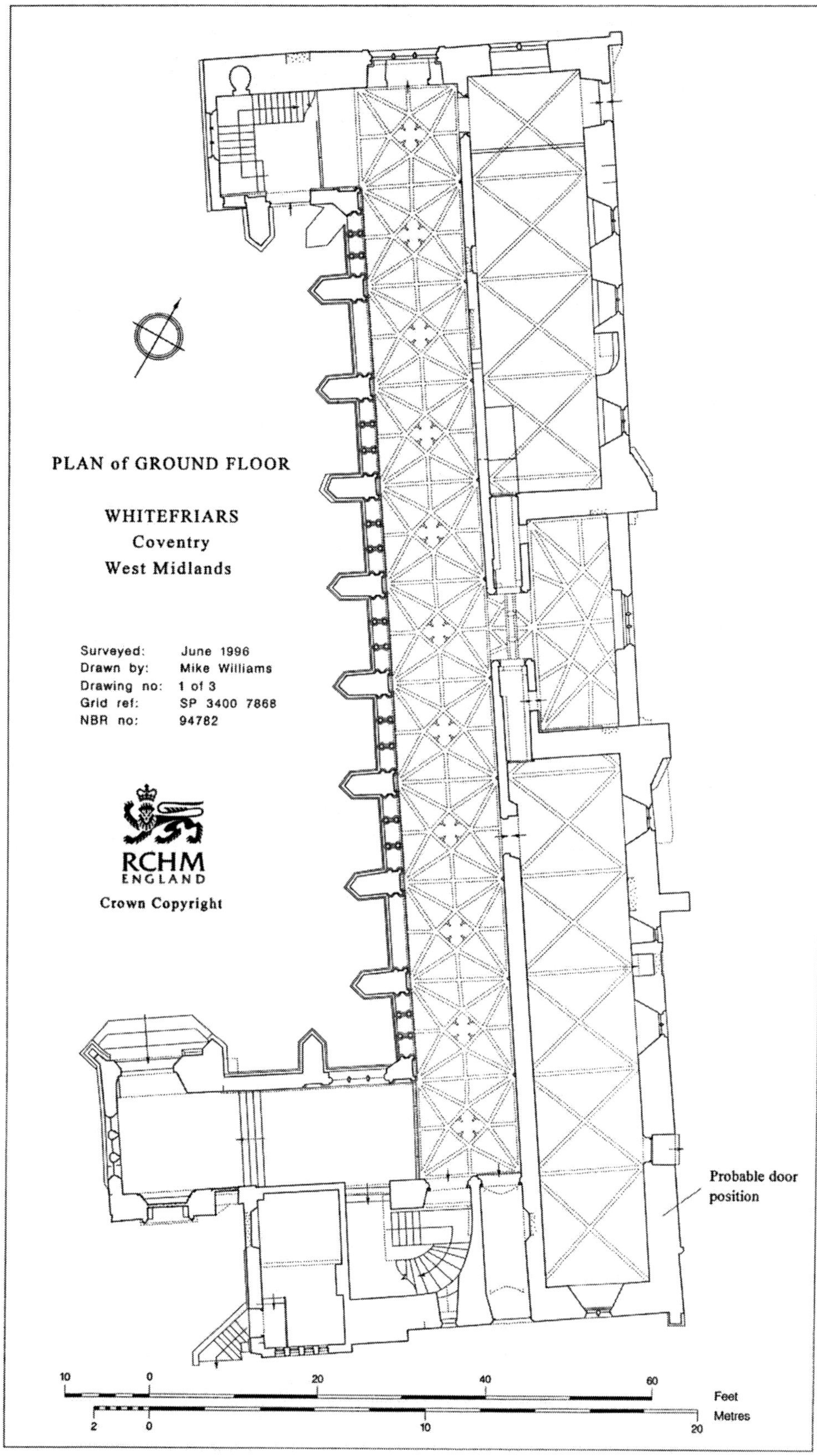

Figure 9 RCHME measured survey of the ground floor of the standing E cloister of Coventry Whitefriars, 1996. Crown copyright, NMR.

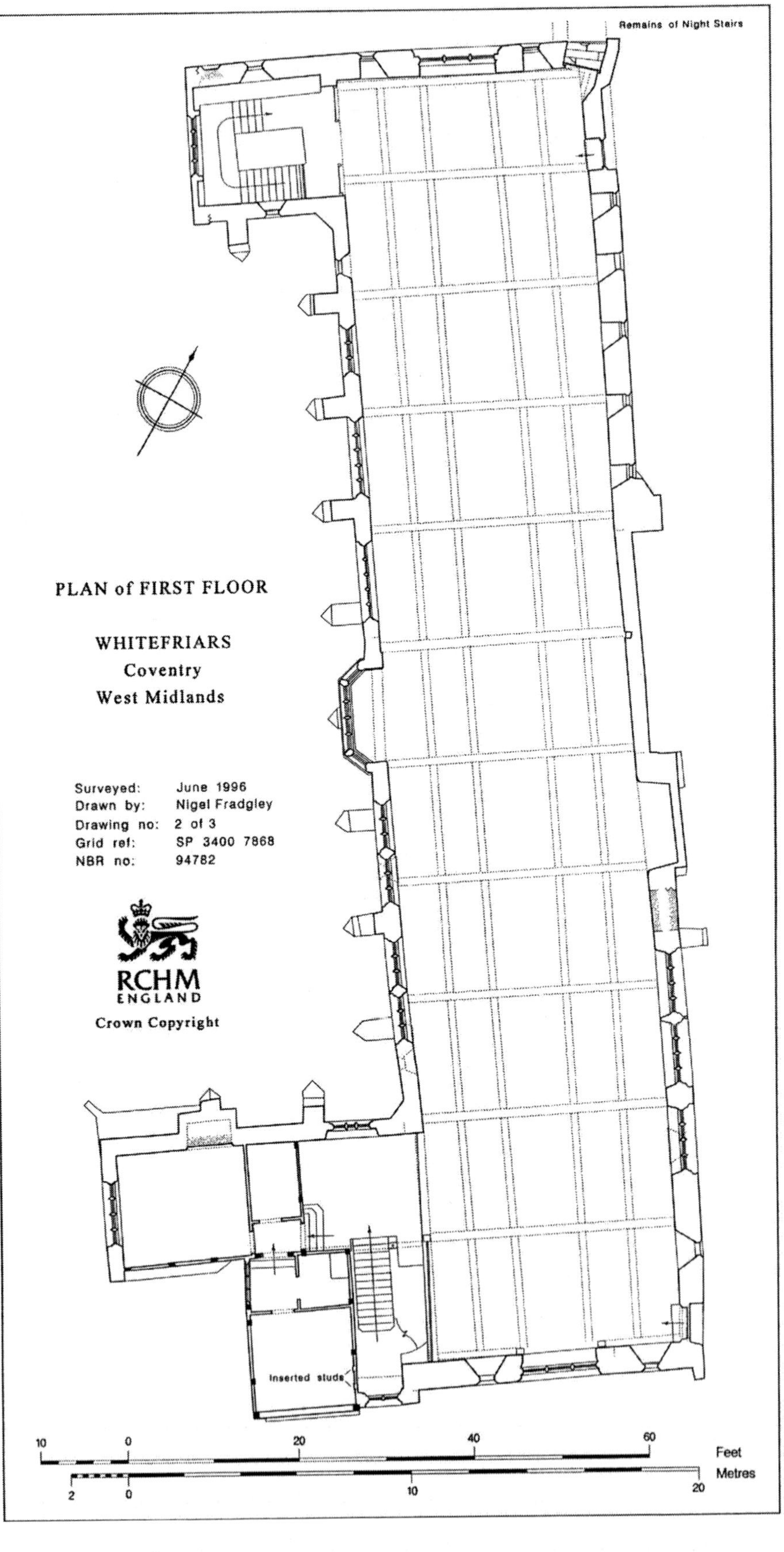

Figure 10 RCHME measured survey of the first floor plan of the standing E cloister of Coventry Whitefriars, 1996. Crown copyright, NMR.

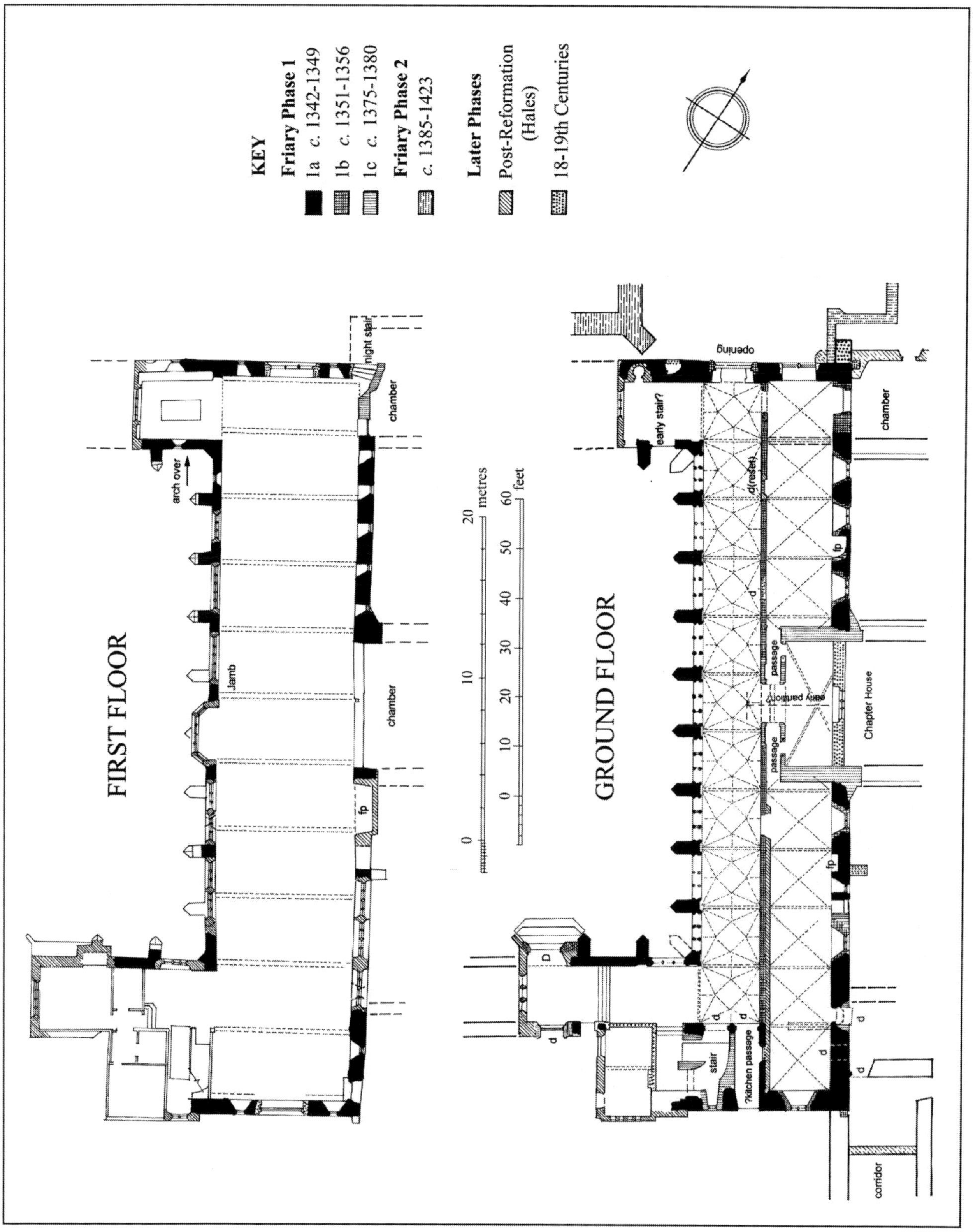

Figure 11 Phased plans of the standing E cloister of Coventry Whitefriars. Crown copyright, NMR and Paul Woodfield (for elaborate cloister and chapter house vaults see Fig. 9).
The 1a, 1b and 1c phases are the standing building's sub-division of the archaeological Friary 1 Phase.

Figure 12 Eighteenth century pencil drawing of the now demolished inner cloister gate, viewed from the W. Note the star vault. Reproduced by permission of the University of Warwick, Troughton drawing X 19.

Figure 13 West elevation of the Whitefriars 14th-century E cloister range viewed from the SW. The oriel window was inserted by John Hales. It is the window from which Queen Elizabeth I addressed 'Ye men of Coventry' adding 'what fools ye be'. Photograph Crown copyright, NMR (BB97/4371).

Figure 14 Former 14th-century service doorways at the southern end of E cloister walk, view from N. Photograph Crown copyright, NMR (BB97/398).

Figure 15 Late 18th-century view of the S (inner) now demolished court of Whitefriars (Hales Place), probably 16th century in the main. The upper part of the large window lighting the dorter was replaced in the Gothic style in the 19th-century. See Fig 29.
Reproduced by permission of Birmingham City Archives, Aylesford Collection (BB97/6270). Photograph Crown copyright, NMR.

Figure 16 Fourteenth-century E cloister walk, view from S.
Photograph Crown copyright, NMR (BB97/401).

Figure 17 Detail of 14th-century vault, E cloister walk.
Photograph Crown copyright, NMR (BB97/417).

Figure 18 Remains of the 14th-century entrance to the former chapter house, from the E walk.
The window is 19th century. Photograph Crown copyright, NMR (BB97/4381).

Figure 19 View looking N from within the S chapter house passage. The doorways are a unique feature.
Photograph Crown copyright, NMR (BB97/410).

Figure 20 Late 18th-century watercolour of the E elevation of the E range, view from E.
The slight remains of the chapter house side walls can be seen near the centre of the illustration, while to the right is the now demolished 'Hales' Chapel' with its timber-framed upper chamber built by Hales on the walls of the friary sacristy. Reproduced by permission of Birmingham City Archives, Aylesford Collection (BB97/6268). Photograph Crown copyright, NMR.

Figure 21 Late 18th-century illustration of the N end of the E range, view from NE, showing the now demolished night stair. Reproduced by permission of the Birmingham City Archives, Aylesford Collection (BB97/6251). Photograph Crown copyright, NMR.

Figure 22 General view of the former late (last quarter) 15th-century dendrochronologically dated former dorter roof, from the S. The two longitudinal beams in the foreground are associated with the ceiling-in of the dorter by John Hales. Photograph Crown copyright, NMR (BB97/431).

Figure 23 Late 18th-century illustration of the E range and gardens, view from W. The upper floor of the S range of the now demolished service (inner well) court (assumed to be 16th century) is visible to the right of the picture. Reproduced by permission of Birmingham City Council, Aylesford collection (BB97/6271). Photograph Crown copyright. NMR.

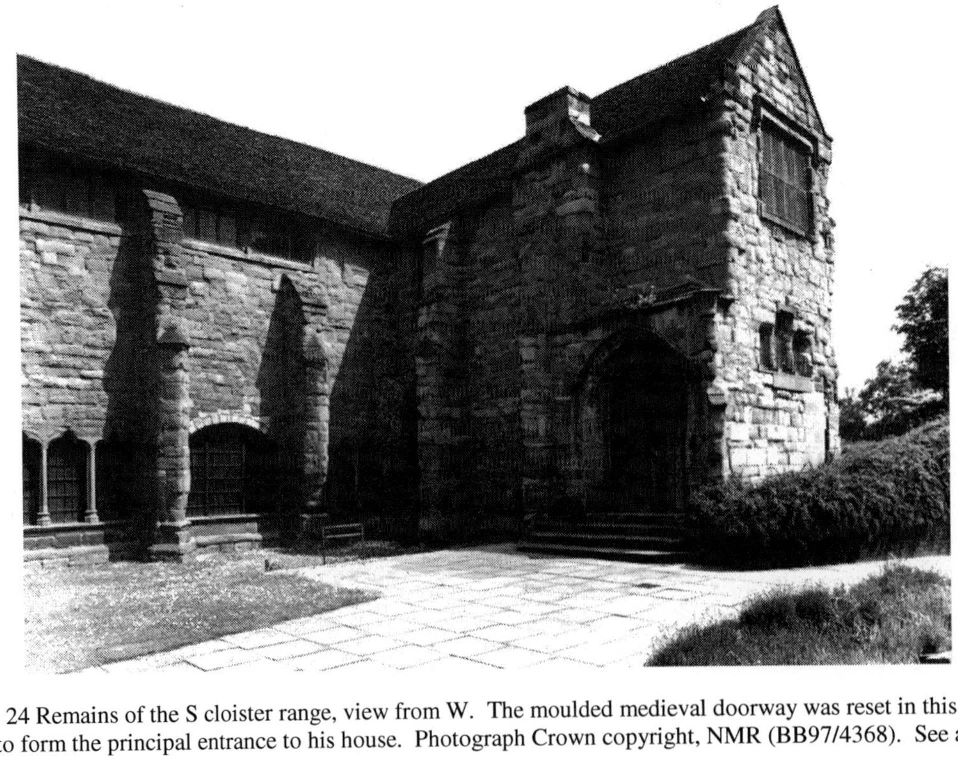

Figure 24 Remains of the S cloister range, view from W. The moulded medieval doorway was reset in this position by Hales to form the principal entrance to his house. Photograph Crown copyright, NMR (BB97/4368). See also Fig. 56.

Figure 25 Late 18th-century watercolour of Whitefriars, view from NE. The building forming the E range of Hales' service (inner well) court is visible to the left of the picture. To its S can be seen that part of the Elizabethan house (Hales Place), about which little is known. Reproduced by permission of Birmingham City Council, Aylesford collection (BB97/6257). Photograph Crown copyright, NMR.

Figure 26 General view of the E elevation of the E range, viewed from NE. The foundations of the eastern bays of the choir, the passage between choir and presbytery, and the N wall of the sacristy can be seen in the foregound. The mounting-block is a modern intrusion. Photograph Crown copyright, NMR (BB97/4356).

Figure 27 Late 18th-century illustration of the first-floor chamber (in the former dorter) with inserted wagon-ceiling, view from N. Reproduced by permission of Birmingham City Council, Aylesford Collection (BB97/6266). Photograph Crown copyright, NMR.

Figure 28 Detail of the 16th-century fireplace inserted by Hales in the former dorter. Photograph Crown copyright, NMR. (BB97/433).

Figure 29 The stub of the NW range of Hales' service (inner well) court, view from S. Photograph Crown copyright, NMR (BB97/4365). The upper part of the S. window to the former dorter is a 19th-century rebuild.

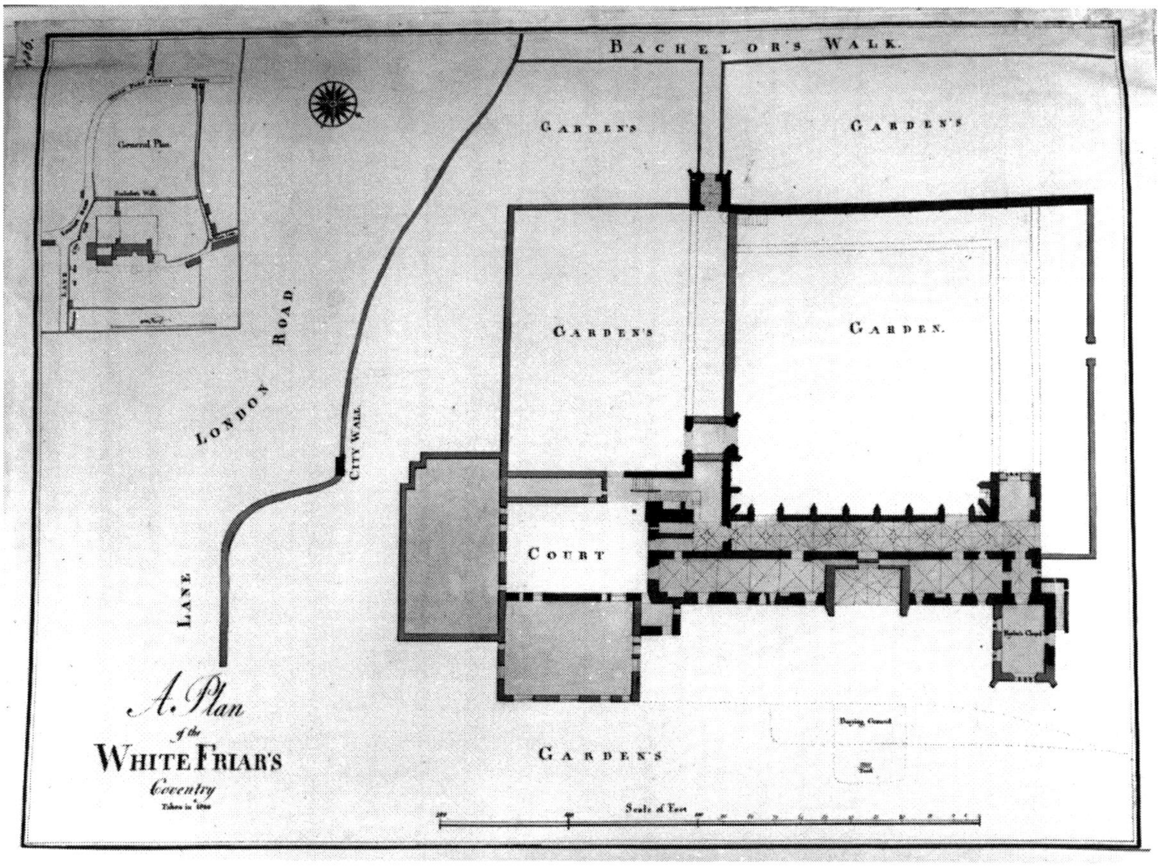

Figure 30 Ground plan of Whitefriars, 1800. The black line represents medieval structures. This confirms burials at the E of the chapter house, and provides a plan of the night stair, Hales Chapel, Hales Place and the cloister gate. The N garden wall and gate are 18th century. Reproduced by permission of Birmingham City Council, Aylesford Collection (BB977/6247) Photograph Crown copyright, NMR.

SECTION D 1
THE RECONSTRUCTION OF THE FRIARY BUILDINGS

P. Woodfield

Figure 31

Fig. 31 is an attempt to illustrate the Coventry Whitefriars complex as it might have been in around 1440, as seen from the SE. The other monastic establishments are seen in the background, from left to right, the Greyfriars, St Michaels's parish church, Holy Trinity, and the Benedictine Abbey. The Carmelite site sits in an angle of the newly constructed town wall, near the London Road gate, called the New Gate. This led to Much Park Street, where we find the gatehouse range to the Whitefriars, an addition, in its present form, of the mid 15th century. The church of the friars itself has the second, square tower, as roughly sketched by William Smith, Fig. 32, carrying a steeple of green sandstone without an octagonal drum, although this may have been present. The six-bay chancel has a fine 5-light E window with Decorated intersecting tracery containing the Tree of Jesse glass, and windows to each side bay, those three bays at its western end having raised sills to accommodate the canopies of the choir stalls. The short transepts rise to the same height as the chancel, also the same height of the nave, all having approximately the same span. Their angled buttresses suggest that they were independently roofed, rather than by an extension of the lean-to nave aisle roofs, as at Norwich Blackfriars.

By *c.*1440, the central tower was giving further cause for concern, it having been rebuilt since the first movement in around 1420. The underlying filled-in quarries were the continuing problem, and possibly the reason for the original change from a narrow steeple raised on a rectangular 'walking space' to the more stable form of a square tower. This opportunity to change the plan re-established the approximate 5.2m spacing of the choir bays, and carried it through to the W end of the church, perhaps a hint that the project was under the control of a master architect-mason. The nave, elevated on a plan that seems to have been established at the time of the change to a square tower, is by contrast to the Norwich Blackfriars church, shown with high roofed aisles each side, leaving only sufficient wall space for small clerestory windows in the nave wall, perhaps in the form of paired oculi, as at Great Walsingham. The greater interest in increased openness and manipulation of space became a feature of some friary churches and would be well served by tall aisles as at the London Blackfriars church, where the nave piers are of a similar profile and slenderness as Coventry, or at Winchelsea parish church choir. The lack of buttresses at the western end of the arcades indicates a more holistic approach to the design of nave and aisles, resulting in a consciously unifying treatment of the western façade. The absence of any significant quantity of roof tile indicates that the roofs of the nave, transepts and chancel were covered with lead, and consequently probably of a low pitch. Internally, the tower arch was probably similar to that at the contemporary St John's Bablake in Coventry, with equilateral arches on all four sides.

An earlier reconstruction floated the idea that the Coventry Whitefriars was a hall church, the nave and aisles roofed as one and the W end façade treated as one large composition. This was suggested as there is no evidence of capitals to the nave piers; it is unknown whether the arcades were buttressed at the W end.

The conventual buildings to the S of the church are shown around the known cloister and E range. The sacristy is shown in its Phase 1a form, with angle buttresses of two storeys, accommodating the night stair from the dorter to a single storey corridor into the choir of the church. This is followed on the E side of the E range by the rebuilt chapter house, discussed separately (Section D 4), probably something of a showpiece of architectural innovation of the later 14th century. S of this, a narrow two storey pentice provided access on the upper floor to the reredorter, and continuing to the prior's hall and founder's chamber; these are of the earlier Phase 1.

The reredorter is shown as raised on low arcades at ground level, somewhat in the manner of the extant but curtailed reredorter at Muchelney Abbey, Somerset. It was no doubt lit by simple lancet type windows, but with a high-set window in the E wall. Beneath, the nightsoil would accumulate and be washed down by rainwater from the roofs to a central channel, leading away to the E.

The prior's hall range, set apart from the conventual buildings by the inner court, contained both his private accommodation and that for important guests. There is a record of a vice stair against the S wall, and probably a fireplace. This building may well have been lengthened after 1440.

The position of the frater of the friary remains unproved, but it is suggested that it lay along the S range of the cloister, having, of course, direct access to it. This would bring the roofed height of frater and embedded cloister walk to the same as the E range, leaving the space above the cloister walk vault as an access way to the upper gallery of St John's hall. The kitchens are therefore shown at right angles to the frater, extending to the S, and furnished with a large louvre.

The question also remains open as to the position of St John's Hall, which features in a surviving record, Fig. 53, and was doubtless a major facility that the friars could offer to the various guilds of the town. It would probably need to have access for secular use set apart from the everyday frater, and from devotional activities within the cloister, yet it would probably have made use of the same kitchens. It is therefore suggested in the reconstruction that it lay at the western end of the S range, where access could be obtained from the outer precinct, or even from outside the town wall through the Whitefriars own gate.

SECTION D 2

THE MUCH PARK STREET GATE

P. Woodfield

SUMMARY

Land was acquired in Much Park Street in 1352, ten years after the foundation, to supplement the original access to the Carmelites' land through a postern gate on the N side of the site from Jordan Well. This route would provide better access to the precinct particularly needed for the construction of the convent. The present gatehouse itself was probably only built after the completion of the major part of the church, in the mid 15th century, a typological date offered by the roof construction and archway mouldings. Of this date are, it is suggested, the front and back walls, the internal timber framing, and in all probability, the two internal splayed openings on the first floor front representing the original windows.

The ground floor fireplaces may be original but are more probably remodellings or additions of the 16th century. Those on the first floor are of brick, with curved backs, probably added in the 17th century. The fire beams are not chamfered, and there is little indication of their date.

CONSTRUCTION

Figures 33 and 37

The gatehouse is built of red sandstone, with green sandstone used decoratively for banding on the front elevation only. There are suggestions that it may also have been used for later modifications to the original design. The construction of the gable end walls is much less clear. The N gable end wall is now of 9-in brick, rendered externally and plastered internally. The tie beam is partly embedded in the rebuilt brick wall, and the soffit is not fully visible although it appears to have no mortices or other features. The fact that the wall was replaced in 9-in brick suggests that it was not of stone, but of timber framing, although there is no positive evidence.

To the S, the end truss tie beam is visible, and this shows that the gable wall is quite independent of the adjoining timber-framed building, whose tie beam is at attic floor level of the gatehouse. The tie beam is grooved on its top face for wattle and daub, although the collar, as far as can be seen, does not have the corresponding anchor holes. Under the tie beam, there are drilled holes at 450mm centres, but no mortices for major constructional studs. The outer face of the tie beam is not significantly weathered. The evidence seems to suggest that the gatehouse may have extended to the S, although the late medieval jettied timber-framed building that was there until August 2001, was an entirely independent construction.

The flanking walls of the through carriageway were probably both originally constructed with timber framing and wattle and daub infilling; only that on the N side now survives, infilled with brick probably in the 19th century, whilst the S wall is entirely of brickwork. This framing on the N side of the carriageway, has the joints numbered on the horizontal members with a small chisel, beginning with I at the first stud behind the front masonry, and continuing to IIIII on the fifth; the last vertical stud only has a trace of what may be a sixth number. Although damaged by later alterations, there are no peg holes or mortices to suggest that on this side at least, the wall had any provision for an almonry, as might be anticipated in this position.

Internally, setting aside for a moment the possibility that the gatehouse was part of a continuous range, the accommodation is divided by the carriageway into two apartments, the upper floor similarly divided approximately equally between them above the arch. Each unit has a narrow door opening to the street immediately adjacent to the jamb quoins of the carriageway arch (the head of that on the S has now been replaced in modern stone). The inner arrises of the timber lintels over these doors are chamfered. An item of special note is the impression of a pointed arch on the inner reveal of both doorways – this must have been a purely decorative feature as the height of the springing would not allow a man to pass through in comfort. The opposite side of each, in the door passage, has in both cases been altered or rebuilt, and any corresponding arch on the other side of the entrance passage has been lost.

The original form of the fenestration of the ground floor is indicated by a narrow chamfered window head on the S side of the front elevation, above the present 19th-century sash window. Projected, this indicates an original window width of *c.*700mm. It seems likely that a similar sized window would have been placed in the northern half of the building. Internally, the opening has heavy rounded corbels edged with a simple chamfer,

reminiscent of the corbel course associated with the later chapter house and the former night stair attached to the N end of the standing building, dated by J Cattell to *c.*1375-80 (see Section C).
The ground floor of each side is divided into a larger front apartment, and a smaller rear apartment by a stone stack with a fireplace to the front bay. Both fireplaces have an uncomfortable relationship to the building, suggesting they are probably later insertions and neither has even a chamfered fire beam. The outer jamb of the fireplace on the N side is now the rebuilt external brick wall. On the first floor the fireplaces here are clearly additions to the stacks.

The first floor is now lower than the apex of the carriageway arches, and it is possible that it was always so, as the first floor dividing partition relates to the present floor level. The framing of the central section thus appears below the apex of the carriage arches. To raise this 3m wide central section so that it would not appear in the arches would leave raised narrow unlit spaces. However, the modern approach to planning and convenience often does not apply, and the centre section would only need to be about 750mm higher, involving 2-3 steps, and could be used for storage. The alternative explanation is that the whole floor of the building was originally high enough to clear the carriage arches, thus bringing the original window embrasures of the upper front windows in better relationship to the floor level, but reducing the clear height under the central tie beam to 1.9m. This raises certain complications with the cross-wall framing which relates better to the floors in the present position. The character of the timber framing appearing below the head of the carriage arches sheds no light on the problem as this appears to be later replacements. John Cattell (Section C) draws attention to Fretton's comment regarding the carriageway that 'Its groined archway has disappeared, it has been much curtailed in its elevation, and presents the appearance of neglect and decay'. In the present structure there is no evidence for a groining but this comment by a trained observer may be borne in mind.

Each first-floor chamber was apparently lit by a window to the front with approximately square internal embrasures, their sills 1.1m above the present floor, and the splayed jambs narrowing to the same estimated width of 700mm as the window below. If the whole floor were originally 750mm higher, these windows would be uncomfortably, but not impossibly, close to the floor. Each has rebates on the internal angle, probably for shutters, although in both cases the opening has been cut about. Four external superimposed red stones are probably a surviving part of the S window jamb. This position is further evidenced by an internal projecting (by 130 mm) horizontal 'hood' course directly under the wall plate and now appearing above the attic floor level. These are chamfered at 45° on their undersides, but otherwise are unmoulded (a drip would obviously not be required internally), but the purpose of such a string above the window positions cannot be otherwise explained. Windows in this rather eccentric position within the rooms would clearly have given an unbalanced distribution of light.
Externally, at the centre, the two red sandstone voussoirs forming the apex of the front carriage arch are noticeably larger and have a horizontal top. This, taken with a noticeable irregularity in alignment of the surrounding green stonework, suggests the former presence of a niche for a devotional figure, in this case probably Our Lady to whom the convent was dedicated, placed directly above the arch. It is unlikely to represent a further window as it would be divided by the internal timber framed partition. The founder, Sir John Poultney, was commemorated in a similar position and more appropriately on the inner gate.

At the rear, the ground floor of the S side has a small doorway in a position corresponding to the front doorway, the head of which has a well-formed pointed arch. The evidence is more confused on the N side, but nothing rules out the former presence of a similar doorway, now blocked up with stone. However, a series of irregular corbels on the inside may indicate the former existence of a spiral stair here and perhaps access to the upper floor was directly from the doorways at the rear of the building.

If, on balance, the rear doors were simply for access to the ground floor from within the monastic curtilege, each apartment would appear to have had what amounts to a through passage immediately behind the walls of the carriageway, and probably a small rear window lighting the ground floor room.

Above, there is virtually no evidence for the original fenestration at the rear, as the various openings that now exist are the result of many periods of alteration. There is, however, a large window with a high sill level on the first floor divided by the timber-framed cross wall, but its jambs are roughly formed, and it is more probably a later insertion.

The attic floor accommodation now also consists of two rooms, divided approximately equally by the central truss corresponding to the room division below. Each room is now accessed by the continuation of the small dog-leg stairs in the outer rear corners each side, and the rooms are lit by dormer windows in the rear elevation. These are of 20th-century date, and it is unlikely the attic space originally had any natural light from above wall plate level, and was thus used simply for storage. The observations that the attic floor is carried on timber rails pegged to the framed partitions, together with the window head moulding appearing above the present attic floor level seem to indicate strongly that there was originally no attic floor, the first floor rooms remaining open to the roof.

The roof is carried on three trusses, one central and one at each gable end, of identical form, consisting of heavy tie beams (170 x 210mm) with little camber, supporting raking queen struts to clasped cambered collar purlins, and principal rafters, not apparently diminished above the notch for the purlins. The rooms are ceiled at collar level and there is no means of inspecting the apices. Large curved windbraces (190 x 65mm) stiffen the angle between the principals and the purlins. On the S side, which is the only side available for any kind of inspection, there appears to be no windbrace mortices corresponding to the internal windbraces, to provide material evidence for further structure towards the S. The type of roof structure is, by its simple but competent construction, consistent with a 15th-century date, although a more precise date may well be obtained from the tie beams by dendrochronology.

It has been suggested that the gatehouse would have originally been crenellated (anon. (academic) pers. comm. to Mr R Morgan, the owner of this building), Fig. 33. There is in the standing building no actual evidence for this assertion, although nothing there that specifically precludes it; further, there is pictorial and drawing evidence that the inner gate at the Whitefriars was crenellated. It would have given a somewhat presumptuous aspect not entirely consistent with the original mendicant philosophy, although given the splendour of the church and conventual buildings, it seems quite likely that this could be the case. Where the evidence survives most friary gatehouses are of the 15th century and are indeed crenellated.

The 4-centred carriageway arch of the front elevations is moulded; a wide shallow hollow moulding defined by 50mm bowtells, which die away into the part-octagonal imposts. This is a very simple form of carriageway mouldings, the large and wide shallow great-casement occurring in a series such as at St John's College, Cambridge, after 1500 (pers. ob.), and flanked by bowtells as at Yatton, Somerset (Forrester 1972, No 150), late 15th century, and, with sharply defined bowtells, as the S door of Grantchester Church (Paley 1902, 14, pl. IX). The arch voussoirs at the front are overlain with a second arched course, probably carrying a projecting hood moulding, which may have risen at the centre to surround the central feature. The carriageway arch to the rear has only a simple chamfer.

USES

The primary purpose of a monastic gatehouse is to monitor and control the visitors to the religious house. This would require at least one gatekeeper to be in regular attendance, and he would probably be provided with overnight accommodation even if the gate were to remain firmly closed in hours of darkness, as was usually the case. It would be essential that he accessed the ground floor 'guard' rooms from within the walled monastic property, and it might be expected he would have a window to monitor the carriageway, although there is, in what little survives, no evidence for this. Further, it would be usual, in the 15th century, to expect some provision for heating, and the ground floor of both stacks may be medieval, despite their curious alignments. The upper floor was not heated.

In addition a monastic gatehouse is often associated with providing lodgings for guests, although in an urban context this will obviously not be on anything like the scale required by convents in more remote situations. Gatehouses are therefore often extended laterally along the boundaries of the precinct by suites of lodgings. In the case of the Much Park Street Gate, which was intruded into an already developed street frontage, this opportunity did not exist to the same extent, and the friary appears not to have ever owned the land immediately S of the gatehouse. On the N side, the fact that John Hales is recorded as being owner of the adjoining plot after the Dissolution suggests that he might have acquired it together with the conventual buildings in 1544, as part of the former possessions of the Carmelites. If this is the case, then the lack of a medieval end wall below the N truss suggests that the gatehouse continued for at least one bay, over the present car park, and provided at least some limited hostel accommodation, as was expected of religious houses. The argument for an extension to the gatehouse to the N may be supported by the lack of any distinctive quoining at the present ends of the front elevation. The fish and chip shop, which occupied this site until recent times, had two vaulted cellars parallel to the street, accessed from the rear, the stone barrel vaults springing from brick walls. These are not uncommon in Coventry and cannot be taken to be supporting evidence. On the S, the evidence for a continuation of the building in this direction is somewhat stronger, although the adjoining medieval three-storeyed jettied building which survived until August 2001, and had been later incorporated into the 3-storey brick-fronted Coach and Horses Inn, was of entirely independent construction. Following demolition of this building, it was clear that there was no substantial gable wall to the gatehouse this side and the rear wall clearly continued to the S without quoining (photographed on September 10 2001 by Ron Morgan). Whether this adjoining and apparently contemporary structure was indeed part of the gatehouse accommodation cannot now be demonstrated. A wing of independent construction, although belonging to the same building, was, for instance, noted on the mid 15th manor house at Sawbridge, Warwickshire (Alcock and Woodfield 1996, 51-72.).

PARALLELS

There must once have been many examples of gatehouses within built-up street frontages, particularly of friaries which are more likely than other orders to be located in such positions, but the fact of their being within urban settings has allowed very few to survive the many later alterations and rebuildings to which such sites are subject. Carmelite gatehouses occur at Aylesford (Kent), where the three-storey single carriageway outer gate is of the 15th century, much modified in 1590 (pers. ob.); at

King's Lynn (Norfolk), at the end of Bridge Street (Pevsner 1962, 236); at Stamford (Lincs.), in a semi-rural setting on the edge of the town, a single carriage arch flanked by buttresses, with a niche and crenel over of *c.*1350 (Pevsner and Harris 1973, 666); at Burnham Norton (Norfolk), a small gabled gatehouse of the early 14th century in what is now in effect a rural setting (pers. ob.), and again in a very rural setting; at the small early convent at Hulne (Northumberland), there a three-storey tower (pers. ob.).

At Buckden, Huntingdonshire (Cambs), the outer gatehouse for the episcopal palace has both a single carriageway and a separate pedestrian arch, the range extending each side to provide accommodation for visitors to the peripatetic episcopate (RCHM 1926 *Huntingdonshire*, 37-38). Even large domestic houses, like Northborough, (Cambs, ex Soke of Peterborough), have fine gatehouse ranges presumably serving much the same function (Pevsner 1968, 297-8).

THE DRAWING

Figure 33

The gatehouse fronting Much Park Street was measured up by P. Woodfield as a contribution to an overall understanding of the friary in Coventry.

On the drawing the red and green stones are marked 'r' and 'g' respectively on the elevation drawing, whilst newly inserted stone for repair and replacement is marked with a small cross 'x'.

A suggested reconstruction is also shown on Fig. 33.

Sincere thanks are due to Mr Ron Morgan, the owner, for allowing this survey to take place, and for his entertaining hospitality on the various visits made to complete the drawing and these notes. Thanks are also due to John Cattell of the RCHME for his comments and observations on this text.

SECTION D 3

THE INNER CLOISTER GATE

P. Woodfield

Figures 35 and 12, 30, 37

The last remains of the gatehouse leading into the SW corner of the cloister were still standing in 1956, when they were excavated by Ms Priscilla Telford for Coventry Museum, and the upstanding remains recorded by the Ancient Monuments Branch of the Ministry of Works. By then only the N side of the gate remained standing, but the foundations were exposed by excavation of part of the S side wall. The original ground level is not recorded, nor were the mouldings accurately drawn, probably due to excessive weathering, although a much-eroded profile of the cornice string was drawn (in archive).

Documentary records of the building consist of: a plan, Fig. 30, and a watercolour of c.1800, plus a drawing reproduced here as Fig. 12, all in the Aylesford Collection at Birmingham Central Library (plan BB 97/6237, watercolour BB 97/6242); a series of pencil drawings by Dr Troughton, now in Coventry City Archives; the illustration of October 1825 in the Architectural Papers of the Revd John Parker, in the National Library of Wales, and the excavation drawings and report, which have unfortunately been lost.

The drawing of the W side of the gatehouse, Fig. 12, shows an access path to Hales Place gardens from Batchelor's Walk, Fig. 37, passing through the gate. The outer wall of the cloister W range was then still standing, showing rather faintly the springing of vaults, at approximately 4m centres on the plan, Fig 30. A later wall extends from the gate to the blocked-off end of the S range, which still stood. Another wall on the N side of this walk encloses this pathway, which appears to be more in the nature of a raised terrace overlooking the southern garden than an access to the building, Fig. 23.

The watercolour and the pencil drawing (Fig. 12) show both front and back elevations of the gatehouse, by then in a decrepit state. They appear to show that the inner garden N of the path/terrace was still cultivated as an elegant adjunct to the house, but that the southern garden and terrace had been abandoned, although still called 'gardens' on the 1800 plan, Fig. 30. These watercolours are not dated but are presumably contemporary with the plan. The House of Industry, which occupied the E range and some of the surviving domestic buildings of the friary, was commenced about 1800, although the ranges which were to impinge on the gatehouse were probably erected later. The watercolour and drawing illustrate certain oddities; there is a raking cornice to the outer front elevation, whereas the return side is crenellated, returning as a plain coped parapet on the inner side where of course it was part of the cloister range. This arrangement is confirmed in the Troughton sketches. The wall arcade arch on corbels on the inner face of the gatehouse seems to be a continuation of that of the W range, and stops at the corner where the S range once started. Set in the E facing parapet is a panel, presumably once inscribed, which it would be impossible to see when the cloister stood. This suggests strongly that the parapet and western gable were part of a 17th-century refurbishment of the building when it became the entrance to the gardens. If all the parapets are of this date, it is quite possible that the gatehouse was originally of two storeys and was reduced in height at this period. Also shown by dotted lines, on the *c.*1800 plan and in the watercolour of the internal rear front is a supporting half-arch for a stair from the W range giving access to what must be the roof. This also seems to be a later addition and it presumably functioned as a means of access from the garden to a belvedere on the roof. It breaks crudely through the parapet, as is clearly illustrated in Dr Troughton's drawing (not illustrated). It might be noted that the masonry of the SE corner of the gatehouse is carried up as if was the remains of an internal vice stair, but this was not recorded in the foundations seen in 1956.

The drawing of the W front, Fig. 12, show a slightly depressed moulded arch rising from triple capitals, with what is probably an outer hood moulding. This arch is set between two small buttresses of questionable function and they may be additions. Above the arch is a major niche which carried a figure on a projecting moulded corbel, presumably that of the Virgin, and flanking, are two smaller canopied niches framed with colonettes rising to smaller pinnacles. Ivy growth over the ruined walling above the central niche obscures the Poultney arms, recorded by Dugdale as being set there. The inner arch was recorded in 1956 as being similar in size to the outer, and one jamb had similar mouldings and a door rebate, but the antiquarian illustrations show it as a simple smaller unmoulded arch, again perhaps a post-medieval modification.

As indicated above, the other main record is a series of pencil drawings by Dr Troughton, also made in the early 19th century, showing the building in much the same condition as the watercolours. Unfortunately, the fine pencil work of Dr Troughton's drawings is very delicate and only one could be satisfactorily reproduced here It is not obvious whether his drawings are made before or after the paintings and they could well be contemporary, differing only because of his rather more precise observations. He shows the pathway outside the gatehouse flanked by overgrown low walls on both sides (Troughton X.19) and observes the cornice mouldings rather better, but he confuses the outer arch mouldings with the internal arches, producing a tunnel-like effect, with a vault at the end. His drawing of the interior (Troughton X.20), however, makes it clear that it is a lierne vault, with a central hexagonal boss and, curiously, bosses at the junction of the ridge ribs with the wall arcades. The ribs are simply chamfered as in the E cloister range. The *c.*1800 plan, Fig. 30, confirms the form. Thus, the vault seems architecturally related to that of the Chapter House, dating the gatehouse to the cloister to Friary Phase 1c (*c.*1375-1380), Fig. 11. This would accord with the external decoration of framed statue niches which appear in the later 14th century and remain popular until the Suppression, and may also be the work of Robert Skillyngton (see Cattell and Woodfield, Section C, above). The W walk of the cloister is shown by Troughton (Troughton X.21) as having a regularly spaced wall arcade on stilted corbelled wall shafts, the southernmost encompassing the inner arch of the gate. This logical arrangement does not coincide with the corbels shown faintly at 4m centres on the *c.*1800 plan, Fig. 30, which begin further to the N leaving an odd bay inside the inner door. The spacing of the wall shafts on the plan is also at variance with the 3.5-3.8m known spacing of the garth buttresses of this range, thus for the purposes of the reconstruction drawing, the Troughton record (Troughton X.21) is taken as being the more correct. The stair to the roof too is shown on the 1800 plan as larger than would seem to be necessary.

The Ministry of Works archive records shows the foundations of the impost of the inner arch of the gatehouse. This also has a rebate for double doors opening into the cloister. The mouldings, roughly recorded, indicate a roll and flanking fillet, in the late Decorated manner. A similar arrangement may have been present in the outer arch but they are imprecisely drawn. The mouldings of the raking cornice, as sketched by Troughton, appear to be a hollow top chamfer, fillet and ovolo.

After a degrading time in the 19th century, when the building was used as a hen house, and an engine house, it suffered further neglect. In the enthusiasm for redevelopment after the Second World War, it was demolished, in 1956, on the assertion, all too frequently used, that it had been damaged during the blitz on Coventry. It was at this time the Ministry of Works was apparently called in and photographed and recorded what survived in September-October of that year. The excavation records of Ms Priscilla Telford made at about this time have been lost.

The reconstruction, Fig. 35, is an attempt to reconcile the illustrations to the unpublished Ministry of Works plan.

SECTION D 4

THE CHAPTER HOUSE RECONSTRUCTION

P. Woodfield

Figures 30, 34, 37-8 and 48

The chapter house is, as putatively reconstructed, a tour-de-force of architectural achievement of the 14th century architect/mason. Although little clarity was achieved by the 1977 excavations, it is clear from analysis of the standing building that it results from an early alteration to the E range, dated to *c.*1375-1380 by Cattell (1997), a rebuild of an earlier structure as William of Lubbenham, provincial master in 1353 was buried in the chapter house in 1361 (see Section B, *The Whitefirars in Coventry - Historical Background*). This alteration appears to have been carried out not long after completion of the E range, although long enough to demonstrate a change of mind. It perhaps replaced one of the E chambers which had served a dual use including the meetings of the chapter up to that date. The vault is clearly related to that of the cloister, being what Bony describes as an Angevin derived system of net type, not dissimilar to those of Tewkesbury of *c.*1340 (Bony 1979, 48; Pevsner and Verey 1970, 363) and Wells Cathedral. The entrance is indeed ingenious in the way it has resolved the unusual and clearly conflicting needs of providing an entrance of great dignity, and the clearly expressed need to provide direct access through the lobby from the E chambers without having to pass through the open cloister walk.

The surviving section of the internal vault of the chapter house determines the size of the bays. The excavation revealed a range of closely spaced triangular buttresses on each side confirming the bay spacing, but it did not extend beyond the fourth buttress beyond the E range walls, although there is some evidence that the N wall masonry had continued further to the E, beyond the limit of the excavation. It is inconceivable that this highly designed and fashionable building would end abruptly in a half-bay, thus the reconstruction, Fig. 34, shows an uncommonly long chamber of three square bays covering the total width, without any intermediate support in the form of obstructive columns. Indeed the presence of Graves 2a and 3 confirms that none existed at the relevant position, Fig. 48. At the E end of the excavation, there was apparently a thick cross wall with an offset foundation. The W facing of this wall was clear, and there is some evidence of an E face at the N end, making a wall 1.6m wide. This is now interpreted as a raised platform or sanctuary at the E end, on which the Altar stood, although it could represent a subsequent shortening of the building. It does however appear from photographs to be properly bonded to the N wall of the chapter house, rather supporting the raised E end theory. A small offset of the N internal wall foundation extending 1.2m from the E wall remains unexplained other than to indicate that the E wall is of a different build.

The external walls of the building, once clear of the E range, are notably thinner at 1.9m above the foundation offsets, 200mm on the outside, 70mm inside, and probably further narrowed above a water table or plinth. This, combined with the massive character of the triangular buttresses, indicates that this is a building of exceptional design, the weight being carried almost entirely on the buttresses with, presumably, the intervening space fully glazed. The use here of buttresses, triangular in plan, reflects those of the E range facing into the cloister garth, although they both project about the same (1.45m) the pointed splay of the chapter house buttresses continues back to the face of the wall. The curious design perhaps indicates that the same mason was retained for this, a second stage of the ambitious works. A distant parallel for glazing occupying the full wall width between buttresses occurs in the first form of the octagonal chapter house at Elgin Cathedral, of late 13th-century date, where the buttresses themselves are deeply chamfered above the lowest offset although not actually achieving a triangular form. This was modified to have smaller windows in the late 15th century (Fawcett 1999). Triangular buttresses are a significant feature of John of Gaunt's work at Kenilworth castle, designed *c.*1360 (pers. ob.), and appear also in a small church at Longborough, appropriated to Hailes Abbey *c.*1325, just within Gloucestershire (pers. ob.); interestingly enough, this church possesses some decorated floor tiles that are closely paralleled at Coventry Whitefriars (Section L, *Sixteen-tile pattern as laid*). They also appear later in the uppermost stage of the buttresses of the nave of Gloucester Cathedral, introduced in the remodelling by Abbott Morwent after 1421 and extensively renewed in the 19th century by Waller (Wellander 1991). The thin wall foundations between the buttresses, 900mm before any above ground offsets, clearly are seen as spandrel panels below windows, and it is suggested that the integrity of the structure would demand strengthening at wall top level between the buttresses and below the eaves. If this were expressed in such a manner as at Mayfield Palace hall (early-mid 14th century) or the great hall of Penshurst Place, *c.*1341, Sir John Poultney's own mansion, this would also do duty as a relieving arch (pers. ob.). Poultney died in 1349. The length of the Coventry chapter house in relation to its width finds a parallel at the Bristol Greyfriars, where the chapter house was lengthened from a simple 1:2 ratio (8 x 14m) to 8 x

22m, a ratio of 1:3.4 (Webster and Cherry 1974, 189-190).

The entrance from off the cloister and below the dorter appears to have dictated the height of the vault, for the first bay apex is at 4.73m above floor level, as is the cloister vault, and the springing just perceptible outside does not suggest the second central bay is any different in height. This is confirmed by the external relieving arch seen in the 18th-century print, Fig. 20, and still clearly visible now. The angled buttress at the N and S junctions of the remaining chapter house wall still however extends to eaves level on the present building. On the E wall face of the building, what may just be a door head can be seen. These fragments of evidence lead to the presumption that the chapter house structure is two storeys high, the lower occupied by the chapter itself, and the upper a chamber at right angles to the dorter and with direct access therefrom. What function this room had cannot now be told, but being in a prestigious position, it may have been a prior's chamber similar in function to the Abbot's Camera found at Valle Crucis abbey (Evans 1995, 40).

The reconstruction, Fig. 34, is an attempt to indicate the appearance of the building for which the triangular buttresses and bay spacing are the only surviving evidence. The bulk of the buttresses would undoubtedly be diminished by offsets at a number of stages and possibly returned to the square above the internal vault at first floor level, rising ultimately as diagonally-set pinnacles. The roof, in the mid-later 14th century, is likely to be pitched and given the buttressing, set behind a parapet which itself is more likely to be solid or pierced rather than the more frequent crenellated form of the 15th and 16th centuries. The windows may take a variety of forms, and it is quite probable an attempt would be made to bring together the upper and lower windows in one composition as for instance in the choir of Gloucester Cathedral (pers. ob.). The lower windows lighting the chapter house proper are likely to be twin lights, there being insufficient width for three and the height being too low for one. The window heads may reflect the depressed cusped ogees of the cloister and elsewhere in the building. The upper window is more problematical, and may have Y-tracery, reticulated tracery or some more exotic form. It is possible a circular wheel window or a spheric triangular form may have been used (shown in outline on the end bay). No moulded or cut stones were retrieved that can now be identified from the various excavations of the chapter house, thus we have no other guidance. It seems clear that the adoption of the triangular buttresses, of which there cannot be any doubt, opens a whole world of experimental and plastic forms.

SECTION D 5

RECONSTUCTION OF THE REREDORTER

P. Woodfield

Figures 31, 36-8, 49 and 52

The position of the reredorter of the Whitefriars is determined by the excavations of the 1970s, at the E of the SE corner of the standing cloister range, Fig. 49. This was at the time interpreted as a 'novices cloister', or alternatively as a slaughter house, but it was clear from the excavation records that there were two arcades of substantial piers at 3m centres, heading in an easterly direction. The area between and around the arcades was paved with heavy stone flags, which continued out beyond the piers on each side, the whole being laid to falls. In the late monastic period it was clear, first that the building had been substantially shortened, and then later demolished, Fig 52 Section J. The area had then been utilised as a heavy metal workshop, necessitating the erection of various partitions to enclose the activity and the building of a hearth at the end. The piers represented the open undercroft of a building attached at right angles to the dormitory range. There seems little doubt, given the heavy structure, the drained floor with an axial drain, and its position within the traditional monastic layout, that it is a reredorter.

The number of choir stalls, with their front benches, suggests that the maximum number that could be accommodated in the choir was 92, a number that presumably included resident friars, novices, students, and guests. Assuming that other provision was made for guests, the number the reredorter would need to cater for was about 80. Given the regularity of the monastic schedule and a standardised diet, there would be certain restricted times within which the majority would need to avail themselves of the facilities. The seating within a reredorter is usually aligned along the outer walls, where a clear drop could be devised within the ground floor arcades. Assuming there would be some sort of low partitioning (for decency) between individual openings in the continuous seat, an allowance of 850mm is made in the reconstruction for each emplacement, including the thickness of a timber partition. To accommodate 80 then, allowing for both sides of the building to be used without interruption, and in a given half-hour for each seat to be used twice (i.e. two 'sittings') a total length of (40 x 850mm/2) some 17m plus an end wall thickness, say 500mm, would be required for the reredorter.

The piers shown on excavation are at approximately 3m centres, providing fairly narrow structural bays, thus the substructure of the reredorter to provide this amount of accommodation would be of five bays of plain low arches, with an opening over the main axial drain on the gable end. There would of course be a need for ventilation on the upper floor but the windows need only be simple lancets and the necessary lighting could be obtained from a high level window in the eastern gable end. The western end, abutting the two-storey access corridor, may have been built up as a gable thus providing a western window, or the roof could have been hipped into the E range roof, the added width of the reredorter allowing for a small ventilator opening in the apex. It is assumed that the building is purely utilitarian, without raised gables or any other embellishments, although timber gutters and water spouts would have concentrated the rainwater to spouts, thus providing a more effective wash-down arrangement of the pavings than would have been possible with free-fall eaves. A similar arrangement of pavings can still be seen in the yard at Raglan Castle (pers. ob.).

Figure 31 Reconstruction of the Carmelite House *c.*1440.

Figure 32 Coventry in the 1570s looking NE from Greyfriars Green. The disintegrating Whitefriars' tower and spire is shown at the E. The slender Greyfriars' spire has been lost against the background of the Holy Trinity and St Michael's spires. Sketch by William Smyth, herald to Queen Elizabeth in the 1570s (Reproduced in Bliss 1950).

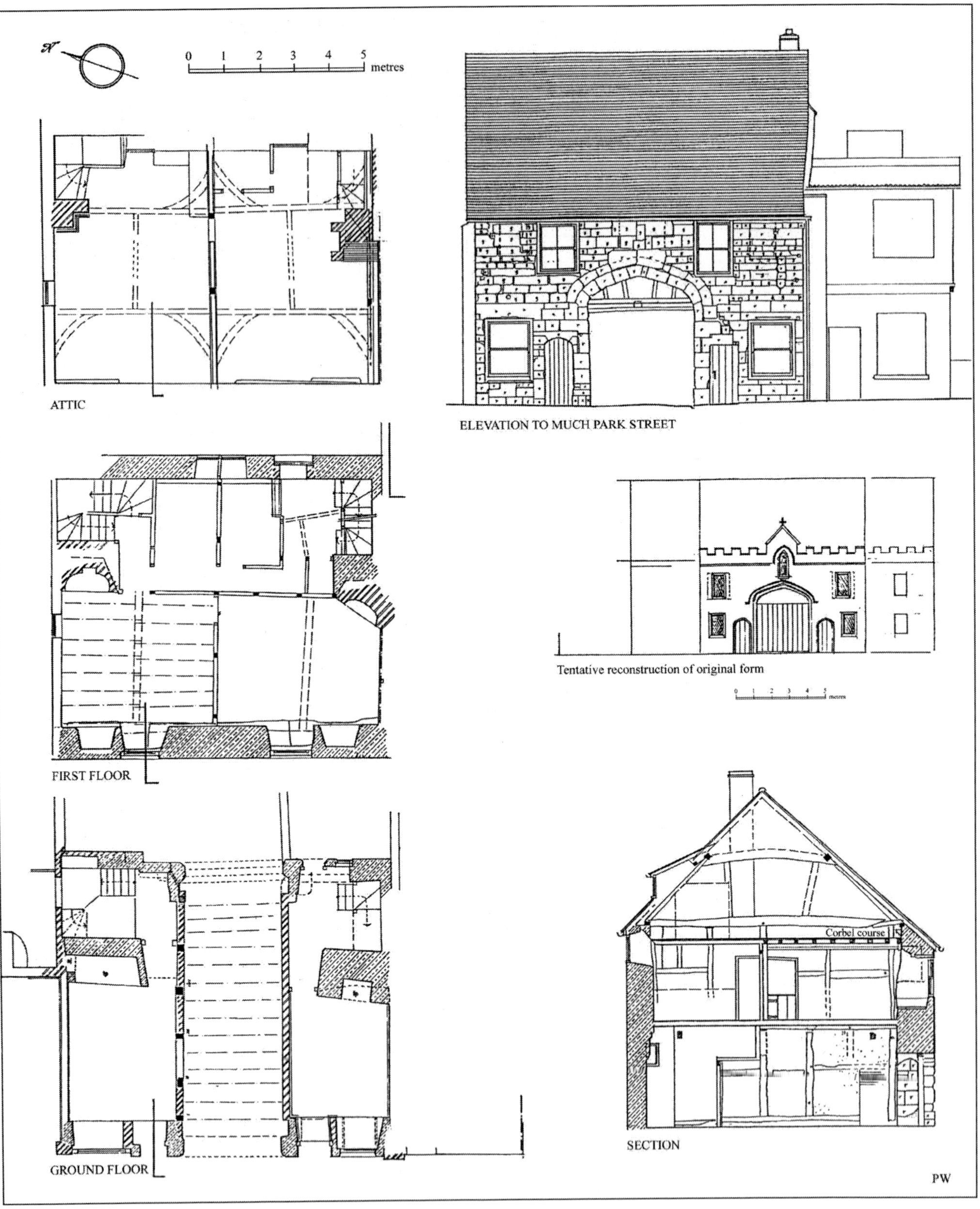

Figure 33 Recording and reconstruction of the 15th-century (plus alterations) Much Park Street gate (r for red sandstone, g for green sandstone, x for recent repair).

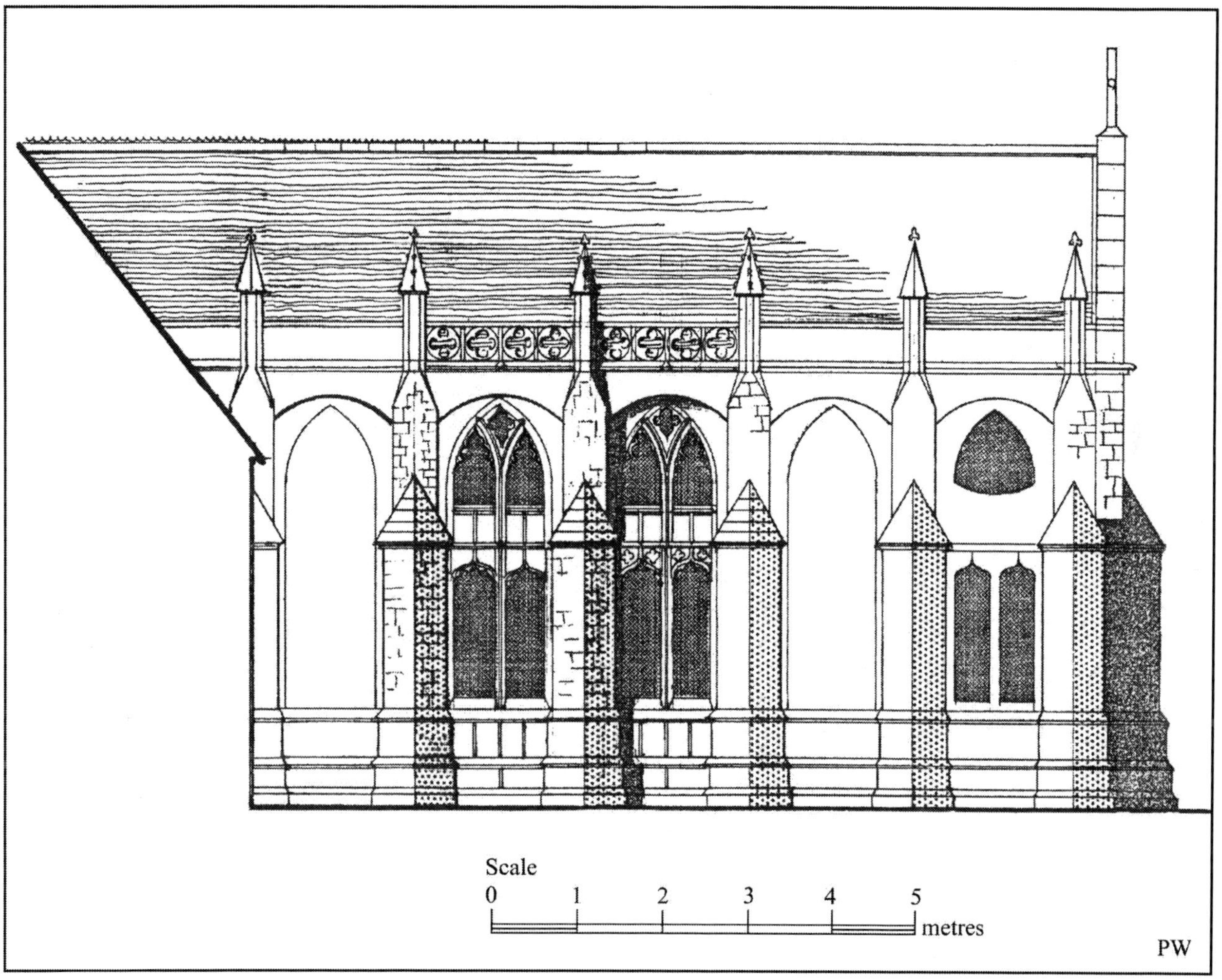

Figure 34 Reconstruction of the S face of the 14th-century chapter house.

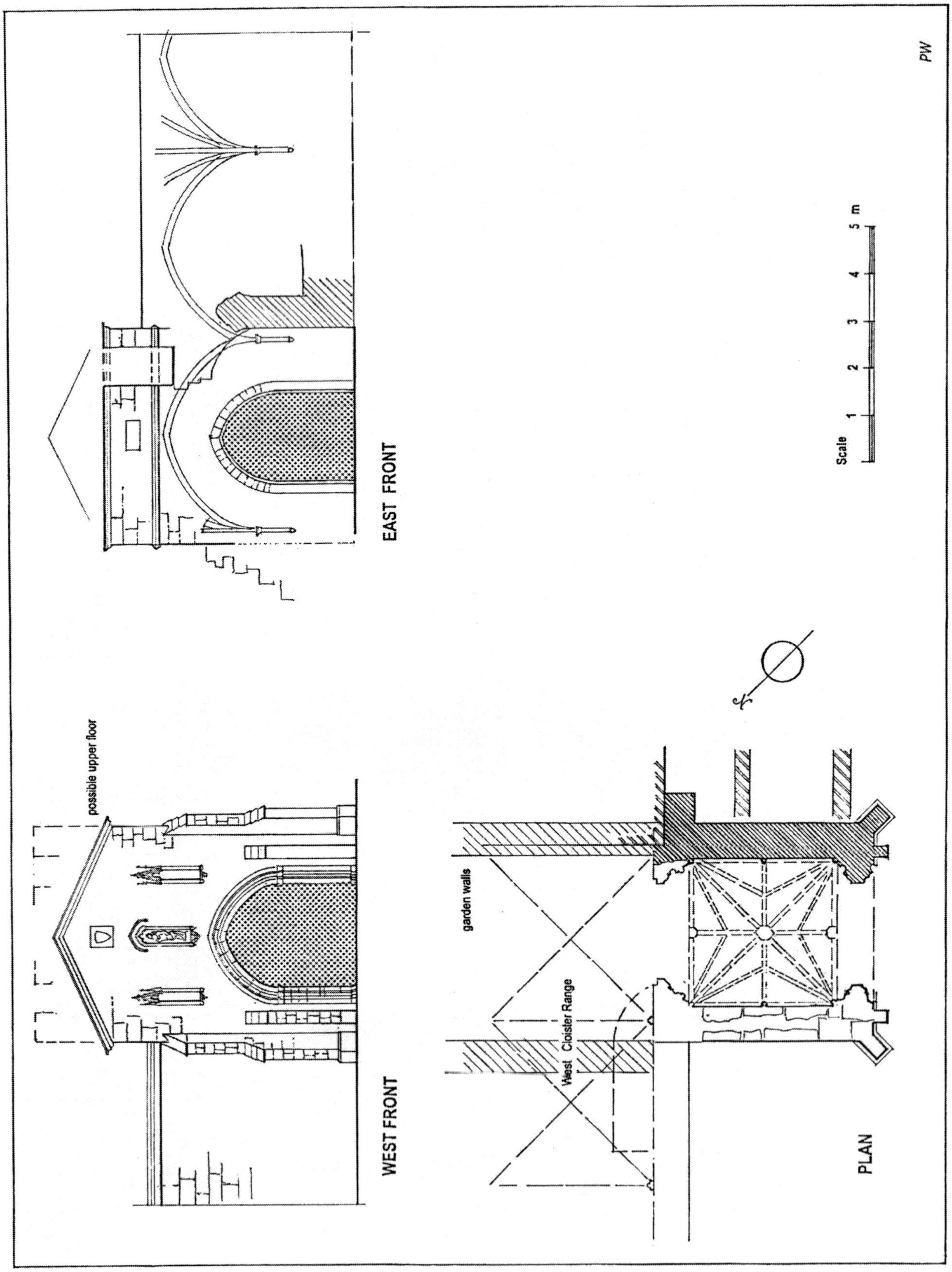

Figure 35 Reconstruction of the 14th-century inner cloister gate.

Figure 36 Reconstruction of the (originally 14th-century) reredorter, as shortened form five bays to two in the earlier 16th century, pre-Reformation. The floor of inward sloping stone flags continued for 1m outside the arcade, to bring in rainwater from water spouts? The original 5 bays would have provided some 80 seats. The section on Fig 52 and plan on Fig 49 record its conversion to a workshop shortly before the Reformation. (Scale 1:200).

SECTION E

ACCOUNT OF THE EXCAVATIONS AT THE THE CHURCH OF THE WHITEFRIARS, COVENTRY

C. Woodfield

1 THE REASONS FOR THE EXCAVATIONS

The Whitefriars, Coventry, lay in the SE sector of the medieval city and was, and still is, rather outlying to the centre, Fig. 2 The surviving cloister buildings shown on plan, Figs 9-11, were intended to lie outside the new late 1960s inner ring road, which itself passed across the site diagonally, covering most of what is now known to be the NW cloister area, the crossing, the E nave, and the W choir of the church. In view of this threat, and following a small trial excavation in the autumn of 1960, which made it clear that the remains of a very large church appeared to survive, excavations were undertaken for three seasons, 1961, 1962, and 1964. These excavations were financed jointly by the Herbert Art Gallery and Museum (HAGM), Coventry, and the Ministry of Public Buildings and Works (MPBW). The greater part of the nave and W end were sited in areas not readily available for excavation, and much of the site carried ruins, foundations and standing buildings of the Coventry Union Workhouse. There was also a considerable network of services underground, and there had been extensive stone robbing, apparently dating in the main from the 18th century. In spite of this it was possible to recover a considerable portion of the plan of this exceptionally large and important friary church, Fig. 38, not only in British but in European terms, Figs 3-7, about which previously nothing had been known. Details of the S wall of the choir, and the assumed night stair, and any other conventual buildings that could be assumed to lie to the E and S of the cloister were not under threat from the original ring road. In 1968 and 1969 rescue endeavours by the writer with Paul Woodfield and Bob Thompson, funded by the MPBW, recovered more information on the western part of the choir, not originally under threat from the primary road scheme, and the vestry, which had been considerably damaged in 1967 without record, by the making of a roadway for vans, etc.

In 1977/78 clearance of 'Victorian levels' in advance of landscaping was undertaken by Coventry Museum and revealed more of the chapter house, where limited Museum work had taken place in 1973 and 1975, and of structures to the SE of the standing cloister. A further change in road planning in the 1980s to construct an elevated highway, Fig. 57, destroyed, without archaeological record, the remainder of the nave with its burials, the lay cemetery to its N, much of the N, W and S walks of the cloister, together apparently with the frater, kitchen, brewery and possibly St John's Hall, lying S of the S cloister walk. It also seriously damaged the setting of the standing E range of the cloister in the fashion of the time (Fig. 58; Lancaster 1949, 46-7), once illustrated in 1810 as one of the 'Beauties of England and Wales' (Britton and Brayley 1810).

2 THE SITE

Figures 2, 30-32, 37-38 and 57

At the W of the church, and including the area of most of the nave, there is a slight rise in level (for ease of reference it is assumed that the church lies due W-E). The land is fairly flat to the N and S of the church, but drops quite sharply to the E to the river Sherbourne, some 250m away from the rear of the standing buildings, where it forms the eastern boundary of the medieval city. The friary was in existence before the City Wall, but the line of this had probably always followed the friars' boundary on the S as well as the SE sides. Presumably the NW boundary lay along Whitefriars Lane (where 'the King's stable' lay, though this term is possibly just post-Reformation) and then probably turned S some 45m W of the 19th-century Whitefriars Street (there is uncertainty about the boundary in this area, and indeed NE of the church). Cemeteries are known to have existed N of the nave and E of the choir, but their precise nature and extent is unclear, although the eastern cemetery is most likely to be monastic, and the northern lay. The eastern cemetery was damaged in the 1990s by landscaping work for Coventry University, but no records are available.

Once S of the area of the vestry, the friars' land extended all the way to the river Sherbourne, where they are known to have had a mill. A dovecote, a granary, barns, gardens and orchards, fishponds and other ponds are also known to have existed, presumably in this area, and some houses. The whole of the double E range, 12 bays at ground floor level, about 3 bays of the double S range, and slightly over 2 bays of the single N range of the cloister, survive with later alterations. Unfortunately the frater, and probably 'St John's Hall' known from documents to lie S of the S walk of the cloister, were, as stated above, inexplicably destroyed, without record, in the 1980s. Parts of what recent analysis has shown to be a shortened reredorter, a workshop/forge, and the prior's house were revealed during clearances of 'the Victorian overburden' for landscaping, *c.*1978-9. The fuel house, dwelling house, kitchen, and yard also apparently in this area, Fig. 53, have not been identified, nor has the infirmary been looked for to the E, and their survival is uncertain.

The site must have presented many difficulties to the builders as it seems to have been a mass of quarry pits with soft fill. Foundations up to 10ft (3.05m) deep and still continuing into pit fill were noted.

3 THE DATES OF THE VARIOUS EXCAVATIONS/CLEARANCES

The main periods of excavation (Woodfield), plus recording following clearance in advance of landscaping (Bateman) are as described above.

A list of the known main interventions are given below.

1956. Priscilla Telford for Coventry Museum. Excavation of the Inner Cloister Gate, during its demolition by the City Council. Some finds but no records survive.

1960-1964. Charmian Woodfield for the Ministry of Public Buildings and Works and Coventry Museum, under the aegis of Dr Graham Webster. Excavation of the church, NW cloister, and test pits in the cloister E range, Figs 37-38, 40-43, 47, 50, 51, 52b and 59-65. Some finds loss, but records kept by excavator. In 1965 Mrs Woodfield left her post as the Museum Field Archaeologist.

1968-1969. Charmian Woodfield (on her return from Sarawak), with Paul Woodfield and Bob Thompson, funded by MoPBW. Rescue excavations in the choir, sacristy and western cloister, Figs 41-43, 47, 50, 51, 53 and 61b. Some finds loss, records kept by excavators.

1973. Brian Hobley for Coventry Museum. Chapter House and E range of cloister. No finds nor records survive.

1975. Margaret Rylatt for Coventry Museum. Chapter House. No records survive.

1977-1978. John Bateman for Coventry Museum. Clearance pre-landscaping. E sacristy, E inner court wall, reredorter, tile floor in Prior's House, at which point recorded clearance ceased. Useful but unphased plans of features of all dates, much 19th century, now redrawn. E choir and chapter house planned, Figs 43, 48, 49 and 52.

The report on an important excavation seen at the S of the standing building in the late 1990s cannot be traced. Neither are any details available for the reputed human bone found in quantity in the area NE of the church during landscape work for the University of Coventry at that time.

THE STRUCTURAL REMAINS OF THE CHURCH

4 THE PHASING

Keys to main plan, Fig. 38 and to Figs 41-43 and 47

The following convention is used on plans. A continuous hard line ——— indicates that the dressed course is either standing, or known with certainty by firm-sided robbing trenches undoubtedly equating with the ashlar, or clear indications in surviving mortar. Foundations are not normally shown where the evidence for the dressed wall is clear. A dotted hard line ---------- by itself indicates the assumed lines of walls, etc. Where the dotted line occurs inside trenches it is based either on the lines of rough robbing trenches, or on the basis of some partially surviving feature, or by analogy with better preserved features elsewhere. Where the evidence for the assumed line of the standing dressed course is based on the existence of a foundation (but with no surviving indications as to the precise position and form of the dressed stonework) these foundations are shown on the plan.

Because of the extreme vandalism and variation of accessibility trenches were often filled in and then redug later over larger areas with different numbering, Figs 41-43. This has been simplified in the published plan. The Woodfield site notebooks and full size drawings will be lodged with the Royal Commission of Historic Monuments archive at Swindon.

COVENTRY WHITEFRIARS: STRUCTURAL PHASING

Figure 38

The phasing is shown differentially on Fig. 38. It is not shown on the (already overcrowded) detailed plans, Figs 41-43 and 47-48.

STRUCTURES	DATING EVIDENCE
PRE-FRIARY Quarries and clay pit. No structures .	13th-14th century or earlier. Jetton of *c.*1318. Pottery.
FRIARY, Phase 1 Priors house?, 1st reredorter, cloister, 1st chapter house, 1st sacristy, choir, 1st NE porch (in part), 1st ?lantern tower.	*c.*1342 to *c.*1380/85. Richard II penny of 1380s. Pottery. Red sandstone, pink mortar, architectural detail.
FRIARY 1, Phase 1a 2nd chapter house, night stair passage, N and E wall of sacristy, N wall of NE porch, part of NE transept, parts of E and S transept. Cloister gate, S and W cloister walls.	*c.*1385. Pottery. Structural breaks, straight joints.
FRIARY 2, Phase 2 New square tower, finishing of N and S transepts, nave chapels and rood screen and work on first six bays of nave and six eastern arcade piers. NW inner wall of cloister garth.	*c.*1385-1423. Pottery. Structural breaks. Green sandstone appears sparsely. Whitish mortar. Anticipated bequest of £300. 1413 grant. Still expanding.
FRIARY 2a, Phase 2a Sub-phase with construction trenches, and green sand trample. W three bays of nave at S (some overlap at E with phase Pre-rebuild).	Mid 1420s Green stone. First use of green stone at St. Mary's Hall, *c.*1410-20.
PRE-REBUILD, Phase 3 Strengthening of three of the tower piers, and NW transept. Construction of W three bays of nave, W door, and four W arcade piers. Buttress added in lane.	*c.*1423 to mid/later 15th century. Church 'in ruins'? in 1423 from fall of tower?. Financing for building arranged for 60 years.Green sandstone trench-built walls, mortar yellow in tower strengthening, pink in nave. Phase continues to later 15th century? 1431/32 Provincial Chapter meet in finished building.
REBUILD, Phase 4 Tower presumably rebuilt, with further strengthening (not. visible at footings level). NE chapel goes out of use as a result, wall is still rebuilt. Sacristy rebuilt, presumably after structural failure. Work (unfinished) in NW cloister.	Mid/later 15th - early 16th century. Fall of 'new work', tower again but its N presumably, in 1477. Worn coin of Henry VI of 1434 from makeup following fall of tower. New tower vault *c.* 1450+. Pottery. 1490 and 1505 Provincial Chapters meet in Coventry.

16th CENTURY REBUILD 2, Phase 5 Building of ? yard wall against N wall of N porch/chapel. Shortening of reredorter.	Pre-reformation 16th century (1520-*c.*1542). Pottery.
PRE-REFORMATION, Phase 5a (based on documents) Construction of workshop over shortened reredorter. Use of prior's house, stables, kitchens and gates, etc., as Bishop's Palace by the Suffragan Bishop of Penrith, John Bird, renegade last Provincial of the English Carmelite order.	*c.*1536-*c.*1544. Evidence largely documentary. Some pottery.
HALES? SCHOOL, Phase 6 (post-Dissolution) Use of choir as Grammar School under John Hales. Screen to separate off presbytery, which becomes workshop.	*c.*1545 to 1558. Groat and penny of Edward VI. 1547-9 and penny of 1550-2. Pottery and copious small finds.
and	
HALES CONVERSION, Phase 6 Demolition of most of three sides of the cloister. Rebuild of W cloister wall. Re-siting of door at SE corner of cloister. Opening of cloister walk arcade at N and S to provide arches for entrance. Reworking of prior's house and adjacent court as John Hales' mansion. Conversion of dorter into Elizabethan Long Gallery.	1540s to 1571. Pottery and documentary evidence. Royal visits.
DESTRUCTION, Phase 7 Largely of church, and final collapse of tower, brought about by Corporation. Levels producing building materials, architectural mouldings, sculpture, window glass, floor tiles, roof tiles, crests and finials, Stockingford shale, brick, The choir stalls are moved to St. John's Hospital and largely survive. No new structures.	1570s to 1574. Pottery and documents. Jetton of post 1570.

5 THE CHOIR STRUCTURES

Figures 31, 38, 42-43, 51 and 59-62

Before perusing the description of the surviving remains, the reader is asked to attempt to visualise the processional approach to the choir, from the crossing through the pulpitum - the great screen which closed the W end of that choir, with the loft above, and almost certainly a 'great organ' as at the Chester Whitefriars (there supplemented by four lesser organs). The pulpitum would be adorned with statues or paintings designed to inspire imitation in beholders, that is prophets, apostles, pious kings and saints. Of all this colour we have only a fragment of wall painting surviving on the S face of the later NE tower pier, which (too damaged to illustrate) appeared to depict a red curtain with black border, presumably framing that pulpitum.

Moving into the choir, the eye would be caught by the great vines and figures of the Tree of Jesse window at the E end, Figs 95-114, culminating in the image of Christ, and also the figures of saints, kings and prophets, in their frames of golden pinnacles in the international Gothic style, in the choir side walls, Figs 115-122. To one's immediate right and left there would be the high quality, largely surviving, choir-stalls, with (hierarchical) seating for some 90 friars and novices, their carved heraldic and figural miserecords awaiting examination, Figs 83-93. Of the high altar and its backing timber reredos and the sculptured figures, usually a carving in stone or alabaster of the crucifixion, we have only hints such as fragments of alabaster, with glimpses on the altar of rich velvets and elaborate Venetian glass goblets, Fig. 158, imported lustreware albarelli and maiolica altar vases from Spain and Holland, Fig. 152, and a gold, silver and blue enamelled Hungarian chalice, Figs 159.19 and 160. The choir, and particularly near the altar, would be the most valued place for burial, and there would have been elaborate graves with brasses.

The floors were tiled with elaborate patterns depicting

roses, fleurs-de-lys, acorns and oak leaves, vines, stags and birds, crowns and ostrich feathers, kings, dancers, grotesque figures, hearts, catherine wheels, heraldry, and lettering, Figs 136-46.

One should visualise singing, (doubtless enhanced by the metre deep acoustic chambers/resonance passages beneath the choir-stalls), the ringing of the great bell, processions and spectacular funerals, and prayers with amber and jet rosaries, remembering that these prayers were thought to be more powerful when undertaken in the choir. As the Barnwell Observances put it 'There is the true body of Our Lord Jesus Christ and the frequent presence of the holy angels' (Clark 1897). The choir is therefore the heart of the institution.

Pre-Friary and Pre-building Phase

Figure 51

Natural red sandstone occurred some 5ft 6in (1.68m) down as seen in the 1960 section at the extreme W of the choir ('ns' on section E, Fig. 51) and sandstone was exposed again throughout the floor of the N resonance passage. The sandstone was normally covered with a red sandy clay deposit of varying thickness. No trenches were dug deep enough E of the resonance passages to encounter bedrock.

A quarry was attested S of the chancel wall, running back to the cloister in 1960, Q on section E, Fig. 51. It reached a depth of a minimum of 1.25m but was not followed further. 1977 photographs of an unplanned section to the E of the S transept show cuts in natural rock, probably an extension of this. The quarry fill was red sand and small stone quarry waste, with a very occasional piece of roof tile.

Pre-church ground surfaces contained red sand, some stone, and scraps of mortar, tile and green 'slate' (Stockingford Shale, Fig. 150), presumably trodden in from the 14th-century building work. This level was reached in the 1960-1 western trenches in the choir, Figs 42 and 51, but the 1962 policy of concentrating on the church plan excluded this in the eastern trenches. No such level is described in 1977-78.

The glimpse of a dark silt layer (Fig. 43, 62 II (5)), E of grave 77.6, underlying the standard red sand make-up for the floor, made it clear that earlier features than the church existed but this could not then be allowed to divert the workforce of three from the priority of recovering the church plan and its extent. Piecing together odd sightings of additional early dark levels evidenced in the 1977 clearances of the presbytery prior to conservation of the masonry, the evidence suggests an area, at least 7-8m wide from W to E and 6.7m wide from N to S, of dark fill with charcoal flecks, about 1m or at least 0.75m deep, measured from the floor make-up level, and apparently cut by graves 77.4, and 77.5, and other unspecified 1977 'graves'. The base of this feature seemed to rise to a much shallower depth to the W. Further a 'brown layer under clay' (presumably the red sandy clay of the floor make-up) to the E of graves 77.1 and 77.2 produced a jetton of Edward I of 1318 to the 1320s (see Section V, *Numismatica*). The presence of this soft fill, into which the two parallel walls at the E of the choir were laid, is perhaps the reason both for the existence of the possible reredos footing or support and the apparently deep footings of both reredos and the E wall (see Fig. 51, 1977 Sections H and I, drawn from photographs). This does not, however, explain why the reredos is not parallel with that E wall. The dark charcoal-rich material presumably represents the fill of a large, not now precisely definable, bowl-shaped ?clay pit, unrecognised in 1977, lying N of centre under the easternmost bay of the choir and apparently running W under the next bay and out beyond the church to the E. 1977 references to copper alloy wire and a bone tool (now lost) apparently from this deposit suggest light industrial activity.

Friary Phase: 1342 to *c.*1385

Figures 42 and 43

The choir was six bays in length, the distance from buttress centre to buttress centre averaging 16ft (4.9m), the total length being 97ft (29.5m) and the width 30ft (9.5m), all measured from the internal wall faces. The N and S walls were 4ft 4in to 5in wide (1.5m) at dressed course level, but it is known that the wall reduced externally a further 4½in (11cm), the second external dressed course (but not the internal) being chamfered back. The E wall was a little wider, some 4ft 8in (1.42m). The offsets from the dressed course to the rough foundation were some 4-6in (10-15cm) on both sides of the wall. The buttresses were about 4ft 8in (1.42m) in length, and some 3ft 8½in (1.13m) wide, laid on a wide foundation of flags which projected up to 10in (25cm) all round the free sides of the buttress. The choir was the most homogenous in character of the remains of the different parts of the church. It was built of red sandstone, with the core of the walls partly mortared and partly small rubble set in red sand. The mortar was a distinct pinkish red throughout, and the foundation was undressed red sandstone set in red sandy clay. There was no apparent change of level between the crossing and the choir.

A Richard II halfpenny, probably of the 1380s, appears to have been found 'against' the internal face of the S wall of the choir in 1977, in the fourth bay from the W (see Section V, *Numismatica* No B19). This may have come from a construction trench, although this was an apparently unknown conception at the time of excavation.

The N chancel wall survived in Trench 62 I, Fig. 43, to the height of a first dressed course above floor level.

This was whitewashed, presumably before the putting in place of the choir-stalls.

Although the S acoustic chamber/resonance passage was cut right down into natural, the adjoining S choir wall had been founded rather surprisingly on a sand surface with pieces of building material (stone, slate, mortar and tile) overlying it - this was, however, only some 40cm or less above natural, Fig. 51 Section E.

It should be noted that, at the end of this phase, the midnight journeys from the dorter to the church for matins and lauds are straight into the centre of the choir, via the passage from the vestry, and not, as usual, via the S transept and crossing, the normal route.

Friary 1 Phase

The Resonance passages/acoustic chambers

Figures 42-43 and 51E-F

These passages, which ran under the choir-stalls, were cut into natural rock, below the medieval floor level. The N passage appears to have been just over one metre square in section, the S passage a little smaller. The walls of the passages, which, of course, were not visible in use, were very irregular both in plan and elevation. At the bottom of both passages was natural sandstone, and in the S resonance passage a soft patch occurring in the natural rock had been packed with six worn floor tiles of a later phase, Fig. 141, implying re-working (see Section L, *Late 14th and 15th Century Stamped Floor Tile,* Figs 139.22 and 144.99). No trace of stone-lined 'acoustic boxes' nor of acoustic pots survived, and neither was there any recognisable sign of seating for joists to support the stalls, but the top courses were damaged.

A metre length of what little had been left unrobbed of the S resonance passage at its E end was revealed in 1977. There is no written description and no context number for this. Photographs suggest that the stones incompletely recorded at the N corner of that passage were in fact a masonry foundation, possibly for a secondary lectern for cantors (the main four-sided lectern on which the antiphonarium rested would have been centrally placed). It is presumably of this phase.

The robbing of the S resonance passage permitted a clear view of its 5-7cm wide construction trench. Their building presumably took place later than the construction of the choir as they would have constituted an obvious hazard, and indeed the wall behind the stalls on the N of the choir had been whitewashed, as mentioned above, and this must have preceded the fitting of the stalls. The insertion of the secondary, Rebuild phase, strengthening to the NE tower pier was visible in the N resonance passage wall where it turned to the S. This must have meant removal of some of the choir-stalls, and is presumably the period when the worn floor tiles were introduced into the soft patch in the chamber rock floor, Figs 42 and 141.

The normal medieval archaeological level encountered in this phase was red clayey sand floor make-up, though often with later material from the destruction of the church trodden into its top surface exposed after the robbing of floor tiles. This level occurred throughout in the 1960s, but was little recorded in 1977, although photographs show it patchily present.

However, the medieval floors which should have lain directly on this level did not normally survive *in situ*, and no floor tiles nor floor matrix were recorded in position in the choir in the 1960s. Tiles did occur at the junction of the passage coming N from the vestry into the choir, Fig. 43, but these were a later re-lay. A tile of type 3, the 16-tile holly leaf pattern, Fig. 137, was represented, certainly original to the choir. Some small patches of floor mortar were recorded in 1977 against the S wall of the presbytery, (but no tile impressions as found for example in the crossing).

Friary 2 Sub-phase or Rebuild

Figures 42-43 and 51H-I

The interpretation of the unmortared and uncoursed rubble footing of rough but substantial stones running more or less parallel to the internal face of the E wall of the chancel, about 0.75m deep, and 0.85m wide, remains problematical, especially in the absence of written records. Its E face was hard against the chancel E wall at its S end (recorded at the bottom of the ?piscina drain (62 III 5)), but it then apparently moved westwards, leaving a gap of some 38cm at the N. It is not known whether this wall continued outside and to the N of the church, for there are no records for this area; at the S, the 16th-century external ground level (62 III 4) was not completely removed, masking what lay below. However, it remains likely that this ?reredos feature only existed within the church, and did not precede it.

The 1962 trench and 1977 photographs show clearly that this footing was covered by the usual red sand make-up for the chancel floor and there is no suggestion that it ever carried a mortared superstructure. It might, however, in some way have related to the support of a timber screen. Photographs of a section (no drawing survives) made across this in September 1977 (which removed a 2.75m unplanned central section of this footing, but its stones were visible in the background of photographs so could be drawn in) show a very dark fill (no description) between the stone base and the church E wall, which might be some sort of decayed timber support for a wooden reredos. We may be looking at some sort of reinforced construction trench for such a feature.

The apparent ditch recorded on plan to the W of this

feature at the N is here interpreted, in the absence of written records, as an arbitrary cut to display the reredos base, Fig. 51 Section I. It does not go deep enough to be a construction trench.

A pit in the SE corner of the presbytery with a rubble base was interpreted in 1962 as a possible piscina drain, Fig. 43, Phase Rebuild?. Two large stones were set one above the other in, and over, clean red sand in the extreme SE corner of the presbytery, i.e. the top stone and part of the one below had projected above estimated medieval floor level which the pit also cut. This top stone carried brick mortar and had later been used for some structure connected with the workhouse. There had been an intermediate use as a 16th-century pit, for to the N of the two large stones was a dark filling with 16th-century school finds (62 III 5) which overlay other, lower, large stones, covered to the S by the red floor make-up; in 1977 the removal of the floor make-up showed these to be part of a footing related to the now presumed reredos.

'Hales' Phase 6 and 16th-century Destruction

The levels representing this phase basically consisted of stripped-off red sand disturbed floor make-up, with red sandstone; the presence of smashed window glass was very noticeable, as also floor and roof tile fragments, and nails. These levels occurred throughout, except in the NE area where there had been erosion. There was only one small record of this level in 1977, adjacent to grave 1.

16th-Century Resonance Passage fill

Figures 42 and 51

Contexts: Trenches 60 II, 61 X, 61 XI, 61 XII, and 62 I. There was no context for anything recovered from the passage in 1977. This deposit had a high charcoal content, the wood represented including, oak, poplar/willow, hawthorn, rowan and hazel/alder, all being small-scale firewood; coal was also present, as was decayed vegetation, presumably from floor coverings. This is most likely to relate to heating the Grammar School, and there is a problem in that this black deposit may well include now undifferentiated losses from the friary, as the black decayed matter in general extended to the bottom of the passages.

There were also similar deposits from W of the N-S arm of the N resonance passage, and lying against the NE tower pier and to its S (61 XI A b, 61 XI C c, and 61 XI D j) here tipping down from a higher level over the passage W wall. It appears that School sweepings were dumped here before being actually tipped into the resonance passage. The numerous finds from here are of particular interest and are described in Section T, *Observations on some of the Small Finds*.

The top fill of the N resonance passage was red sand (61 XI A g, Fig. 51) in some 7.5m of the eastern arm (i.e. not the section running N-S), still continuing as red sand W to Trench 61 XII, see Fig. 42. This has become a red clay seal 'with much window glass' by trench 62 I - that is in the eastern 3m or so of the passage; there is a gap in between where the rubble sits directly on brown sand. The reason for these differences is not clear.

Rubble overburden is recorded in 60 II, 61 X 1, 61 XI A and 62 I, i.e. throughout, see Fig. 51 Sections F and E.

Tudor light industry levels?

Figure 43

A gully ran in a strip parallel with the NE wall of the presbytery (62 II 1a), its W end having been destroyed by a modern sewer. It was at least 0.9m wide at the E end of the trench and 55cm wide at the W end, and ran for a distance of some 4m. Its S side lay under the 1962 baulk. The fill was brown sand, and it contained a groat of Henry VIII of 1549 (Section V, *Numismatica* No A14) together with scrap metal, pins, jettons, tiles, plaster and window glass, and also food bone, apparently representing a workshop deposit, running contemporaneously with the School. It was deeper at the E end and may have been going to turn into quite a large feature (but was destroyed in 1977 without record, although its existence was known). It was cut into the red sandy clay of the floor packing and was some 12cm deep, deepening at the E end to about 17cm. There was a similar gully, 62 III 7, partly recorded running parallel with the E end at the S, with similar contents, which suffered a similar fate in 1977. The two gullies may have been a single continuous feature.

16th-century? screen between Grammar School in the Choir, and workshops in the Presbytery?

Some 1.25m to the E of the ending of the resonance passages was a 45cm wide strip of white plaster/mortar with broken fragments of roof tile and the occasional small stone built in. It is not clear whether it ran continuously from the N to the S wall of the chancel as 1.10m of its northern end and 1.9m of its southern end had been destroyed by modern disturbances. Its depth and its relation to other features is not known. This feature was not drawn by the Museum (it does not appear on the Museum's 1977 September plans), but was recorded by Paul Woodfield on a day visit in July 1977, and published, with some caveats as to its date and function, as a probable Grammar School partition screen (Woodfield 1981, 85 and fig. 2) which would have been in this position (the screen itself partly surviving in St John's Hospital, Coventry). Despite this and its comparative frailty (steps in the nave were not built with roof tile fragments) noted by the writer in 1978, and no apparent change of floor level between the choir and the presbytery, as would be normal in a friary church, it has been 'reconstructed' on site as a substantial brick step.

Photographs show that the buttress to the N of this feature had continued as a solid masonry wall to the N, outside the church, but its date and function must remain uncertain. It was not planned in 1977.

16th-century collapse, rubble with architectural mouldings

This layer (Fig. 51 Section F) is particularly thick at the W, and even thicker in the NW corner of the chancel, and along the N wall, where there was a major 'green stone' collapse with 'massive squared stones' into at least the second bay from the W. 'Massive squared stones' come also from the centre of the choir and its internal SW corner. Mouldings were still thick in the 3rd bay of the choir from the W, and rubble from the church collapse was still present in the easternmost bay of the choir where many mouldings were still to be noted, with much window glass mixed in. Five of the 1977 painted mouldings are recorded from 'Area 3' which seems to be the 2nd and 3rd bays of the choir from the E, but there is the usual uncertainty. See Section F, *The Architectural Stonework*, Figs 68-71 and 74. This includes painted and gilded material

18th-century and Later Features

The stone flagging recorded in three places in 1977, S of the choir, appears most likely to be of 18th-century date. It is described as overlying rubble (presumably from the collapse of the church) and lying below the ashy floor levels of the workhouse. It includes flagging S of the choir wall, and much of the associated pot was 18th century . The stone flagging adjacent to the chapter house had 18th-century pottery underlying it in June 1995 (pers. ob.) and it seems likely that there was a programme of flag laying round the standing building at this time, perhaps related to the construction of the 18th-century garden wall, Figs 23 at left, 30 at N and 42. The S side of the handsome 18th-century garden entrance should be noted on Fig. 23.

Postholes

The five earth-filled postholes identified in the choir in 1962 all cut 16th-century destruction levels, and were thought at the time to be well post-medieval. The 1977 clearances did not detect these postholes, but added four other certain postholes, three of them stone- and one clay-packed. As no details are given of what surfaces they cut they cannot be dated, and they are omitted from the plan. Of interest was one certain, and one possible, clay-packed posthole of some substance, which seems likely to relate to a gate closing off the N end of the passage running N from the vestry, known to have continued in existence to about 1800 despite the disappearance of the church. There is a schedule of these postholes in archive.

Unrecorded

Photographs show that digging took place externally to the choir, to both N and S, but there are no other records.

6 THE CHOIR BURIALS

The sites of 46 burials throughout the site were planned in the 1960s, but the destruction and dispersal of graves in 1960/1 (Figs 42 and 51 Section E) under the entrance to the choir, and in 1961/2, (Figs 42 and 51 Section D) and the impetus the presence of skeletons gave to all-over vandalism, meant that they were left for a later investigation. Unfortunately the plan for this work to be undertaken after the removal of 'Coventry's worse problem families' from the site was annulled.

The choir was the most desirable area in which to be buried, particularly near altars and important relics. A list survives of the choir burials at the London Franciscan Friars, probably the only friary church in Britain more magnificent than the Coventry Whitefriars. This included archbishops, bishops and friar-confessors to royalty. Also Queens, duchesses, countesses, earls, barons and knights and their wives, and mayors. The only friars recorded are the royal confessor, the baron of Lisle and five Provincials (heads) of the Order (Shepherd 1902, 266-287).

The burials recorded from the choir should not be taken as a complete record. In the 1960s the areas of the choir excavated were cleared consistently to the red sand floor makeup, but not examined in fine detail to establish whether or not this represented a primary or a secondary spread over graves, with a tiled-floor taken over. Graves with stone structures which had risen above the floor were noted. Additionally in 1977 there was no coherent clearing down to any particular layer, and graves are very likely to have been missed. There are no records for burials in the central two bays of the choir, where they must have, and indeed may still, exist.

Burials in the western two bays of the choir

Stone-lined graves

The first grave excavated in 1960, Trench II, Grave 1960.1, Figs 42, 51 Section E, and 167, lay in the centre of the western entrance to the choir, between the two resonance passages, but eccentric, offset to just S of the centre line. It was set in the primary red sand with sandstone packing, and is presumably an early Friary Phase grave. There was a red sandstone lining with four courses of consistent rough facing on the E, and it was also lined intermittently on the W. It was presumably a shroud burial as no coffin or coffin nails were noted. The body was extended, with the arms and hands by its side and the legs straight. The length of the grave was 1.57m (5ft 2in). Mr T. Sargent, orthopaedic surgeon with the Coventry and Warwickshire hospital, identified the burial, verbally on site, as that of a youth probably in his mid-teens, his height thought to be about 1.53m (5ft). Before further excavation and removal of the skeleton could take place, it was totally vandalised, putting an end to further study. A novice seems unlikely to be buried in this important position, and it is presumably the child of a benefactor.

Graves 61/68 G.12 to G.17 were recorded but not excavated at the time of their discovery in 1961 as they were not under threat from the then line of the ring road. They were snatched in 1968 from under the nose of a mechanical excavator, Figs 42 and 166.

Graves 68 12-15

Figures 42 and 166
These were sited in the W chancel, in the first bay from the W, S of the central line. This multiple grave must have lain in front of the first form of the choir-stalls to both its W and S, possibly in front of the prior's seat. Its position suggests important burials, presumably of a benefactor family, and the phase seems to be Pre-Rebuild. The complex was covered with some 12cm of red sand and was therefore presumably tiled or slabbed over, a necessity in order to avoid blocking circulation in the choir.

The green sandstones of the double grave structure walling were set as a facing against cut natural. At its N side there had possibly been a third, juvenile, interment, 68 G.12, at high level. There had been active grave robbing here at the Reformation, leaving a grave-shaped area with a robbing fill of mouldings, some painted, window glass, slag, much worn floor tile and 16th-century sherds to a depth and width of over 45cm, suggesting the removal of a small body under 1.57m (5ft) in height. Some high level coffin nails and coffin wood, a fragment of apparently immature vertebrae referred to in 1968 (now lost) supported this possibility, and the 1998 Kibberd *Human Skeletal Analysis* (Section W) identified a right juvenile parietal bone from the NW end of the grave.

The stone-lined grave was thinly plastered internally, but over the joints and fractures in the stonework only. The use of pink mortar in combination with the use of the 'later' green stone suggests a date in the 15th century, Pre-Rebuild Phase, but earlier rather than later. Several of the stones carried mason's marks, see Section F, *The Architectural Stonework*, Fig. 79 and also Fig. 166. The stone was tooled back *in situ* on the third course of the N grave to the correct straight-sided alignment. A break across a stone in the second course had been mortared over; work of a similar nature was also visible in the S grave and clearly the preparation was more careful than usual.

Grave 68.13
This underlay Grave 12 and contained the burial of an apparent female, probably 40+ years of age, in a softwood coffin, probably pine (identification Dr Graham Morgan, University of Leicester) 45cm (18in) wide at the head, square with slightly rounded corners, but with indications of a square-cornered lid. Nails were noted at frequent intervals round the coffin, but they were lying in all directions. They had a 6-8cm (2.5-3in) long, square shank and a semi-square head. The stain of the wood was observed to a depth of 40cm (16in) and its thickness was generally 3cm (1.25in). The coffin, length 1.9m (6ft 3in) tapered to a rounded foot only some 33cm (13in) wide at the ankle position.

The body was lying in an extended position, but on its right side with the head forced up against the top of the coffin into a vertical position. The arms were straight with the hands placed in the pubic region. The fill included roof tile, and a floor tile (Section L, *Late 14th and 15th Century Stamped Floor Tile*, Fig. 140 No 46, a large fleur-de-lys set diagonally) lay under the body but it seemed too worn to be placed intentionally at a burial when a new tile could be expected.

Grave 68.14
This contained a burial of a male aged some 30 years, Figs 61b and 166. The stature, based on femur length, is given as 1.78m, (5ft 9in). The body underlay Grave 13, with the traces of a coffin with noticeably squared-corners appearing immediately under the remains of the upper interment. The end timber was 2cm (0.75in) thick, and showed cross grain. The coffin nails were square-shanked, 6cm (2.25in) to 7cm (2½in) long. The partial outline of this pine coffin (wood identification Dr Graham Morgan) with its nails was first seen at a depth of 75cm (2ft 6in) plus. Part of the left upper side of the pelvis protruded through the fill, which contained a triangular floor tile, and a score of pieces of roof tile much with obvious mortar on both sides, therefore from use as levelling courses, indicating contemporary building alterations rather than a leaking roof. This may suggest a later phase, e.g. Rebuild, for these graves.

The feet of this individual were apparently standing vertically as they were removed at an intermediate level during excavation. The left hand lay over the right illium and the right hand over the head of the right femur. There was an unusually large attachment for the deltoid muscle on the left humerus, indicating a left handed individual.

The spine showed a run of bone, like candle-wax,

particularly on vertebrae 10 and 11, which would have made movement there impossible, and an orthopaedic surgeon from Coventry hospital, identified this as ankylosing spondylitis, or spondylitis deformans. This individual had been reburied at the Aylesford friary and was no longer available for examination, but Kibberd (*Human Skeletal Analysis,* Section W) voices the opinion, based on photographs and notes, that the disease is more likely to have been DISH (Diffuse Idiopathic Skeletal Hyperostosis). This would have been very painful, producing a semi-invalid condition.

The upper burials are presumably his widow and child.

Grave 68.15

Figures 166 and 79 'b' and 'e'

Very curiously although almost twice the size of the adjoining N grave (G.14), this was empty. It was cut into natural rock, and the stonework showed a mason's mark 'e' reproduced four times and a mason's mark 'b' produced once, Figs 79 and 166 (see also Section F, *The Architectural Stonework*). A shallow robbing attempt had been made at the W end where there was much window glass. The main fill was the usual red sand, with slate/roof tile, this having again been previously used as a levelling course with mortar on both sides, as the fill on the N side. Presumably after construction, and the first use of the N side, both sides were filled up to floor level. There was one calcaneum and an ankle bone in a good state of preservation, presumably from an earlier disturbed grave, but no other bone was present.

Graves 68.16/17

Figures 42 and 166

This was again a late, presumably late 15th century, Pre-Rebuild Phase, green sandstone, double, stone-lined grave, Fig. 42, set in the second bay of the choir from the W, just S of the central line. It was not under any threat in the earlier 1960s, but was being destroyed by contractors' machinery in 1968; some bones were rescued at considerable risk from G 68.16, and have been identified by Kibberd (*Human Skeletal Analysis,* Section W) as indicating a male of some 50 plus years.

Grave 68.17

Figures 42 and 166

The better preserved southern part of this double grave contained a female of some 30 years in age, with a stature estimated at 1.62m (5ft 4in). The conditions were such that it was not clear whether there had been a coffin. Some undisturbed red sand fill contained a sherd from an Andalusian lustre ware dish (Section R, *The Medieval and Later Pottery,* No 21, Fig. 152) of the mid to late 15th century 'used to show off imported Mediterranean fruits', and here presumably to decorate the choir; this is a rare vessel with parallels at Glastonbury Abbey. The grave had been robbed at the Reformation, and some two dozen 16th-century sherds were noted (seven survive). The impression was that of picnicking grave robbers, perhaps the Grammar School boys?

The discovery of a fragment of a tomb brass in the adjacent resonance passage (Section T, *Observations on Some of the Small Finds*, No 20, Fig. 159) may relate to the covering of these stone-built graves.

There were two earth graves to the S of stone graves 68.16/17, and some bones were salvaged during the continuing machining. Grave 68.42, a male aged 40-50, appeared to have been placed above grave 68.43, a sub-adult of uncertain sex but possibly male. No coffins or details were observable in the chaotic conditions, and it was clear that other graves were destroyed.

It should be noted that there is a gap with no records of graves in the central two bays of the choir. They will exist, and not at great depth. It is to be hoped that they will escape destruction.

The more complete of the 1968 skeletal material was reburied at the Carmelite Friary at Aylesford, out of respect.

1977 burials in the eastern two bays of the choir

The records are unclear, but these appear to have been partly excavated by the Coventry and District Archaeological Society. Surviving human bone is considered in Section W, *Human Skeletal Analysis.*

Stone-lined graves in the presbytery

Figure 43

Double grave 77.3/6

Grave 3 at the N appears to have been part of a double grave with Grave 6, and there is a part plan of the upper western stone course, but no written information. It appears to have been badly damaged by a 19th-century structure. If any skeletal material was recovered none survives.

Grave 6 is recorded on an unfinished plan (not published) which shows some stonework, but no coffin and only a sketchy indication of the skeleton. However, parts of the upper skeleton survive, suggesting a male of 40-45+ years with a damaged spine, possibly the result of tuberculosis. There is no dating evidence. A possible shroud fastener from the feet area of Grave 6 is illustrated as No 6 in Section T, *Observations on Some of the Small Finds*, Fig. 159 (although this may come from the industrial levels below). However, there was another similar object from adjacent Grave 5. The double grave must make this that of a benefactor/patron, with provision for family burial.

Grave 77.2
This is a single stone-lined grave. There is no plan except that of the upper level of the stonework, and therefore no illustration in this paper. There was a single large flagstone at the head end of the structure. The stonework is red with pink mortar and is presumably of the first Friary phase.

There was, very unusually, an inscribed red sandstone 'pillow', but this was actually found under the shoulders and neck, not the head. The body was extended, the head straight, the hands in the pubic region. No coffin nails or wood were apparent but they could have been excavated away - there is an occasional stain suggestive of a coffin visible on photographs. The skeleton is now very fragmentary, but is thought to represent an individual aged 35 to 50+, which could not impossibly be female. There is severe pathology of the lower spine, possibly of tubercular origin, and a fracture of the left fibula.

The stone pillow is discussed and illustrated in Section F, *The Architectural Stonework* (Fig. 71, No 1123) and appears to be inscribed 'ihs con.' This must represent 'Jesus Hominum Salvator', Jesus the Saviour of Men, and 'con' could represent either Coventry or Convent. The author is grateful to Father Bertram and John Cherry for their comments on this. The significance in this context is not clear.

Graves 77.4 and 77.5

These, are both of young women and were excavated in front of the High Altar, a very prestigious position, perhaps related to an image of Our Lady?

Grave 77.4
This was a well preserved almost complete skeleton, Fig. 167. There was a plan but no written records, and the date cannot be determined. It is now known that the body was certainly that of a young woman between 18 and 25 years of age, with a narrow slender face and a height of 1.64m (5ft 4in). She was buried in an oak coffin. The body was extended with the left hand on top of the femur and the right hand in the pubic region. Finds seem to have included three copper alloy objects, including a 'pendant clasp', now lost.

Grave 77.5
An incomplete plan of body and coffin survives, Fig. 167. This was the burial of another young woman, aged 18-25 years, the date again unknown. Kibberd's (*Human Skeletal Analysis,* Section W) comments are incomplete, being based on a damaged and fragmented skeleton, which had been vandalised, presumably in the 1970s. The only surviving find with her is described as 'a hooked bronze pin', which may be a shroud fastener, No 7 in Section T, *Observations on Some of the Small Finds.* These were also present in grave 77.6. A piece of shroud fabric was said to have survived, but could not be located.

These two burials arouse speculation as to the social background of these young women, in view of the high prestige of their location. Kibberd (*Human Skeletal Analysis,* Section W) additionally comments on the low level of severe (occupational) pathologies, and the high level of tooth decay, thought to be due to the consumption of sugar-rich products, both relating to wealth. There can be little doubt that these were young women of high status, related to wealthy benefactors, anomalous perhaps in an establishment dedicated to poverty.

External burials, presumably the friars cemetery to the east of the church

Figure 43

The skulls only from two earth burials were recorded, graves 77.7 and 77.8. Only the skulls were uncovered, and these were not removed.

CROSSING, CHAPELS AND NAVE

Figures 38, 41-2, 62a and 64a

7 THE CROSSING/WALKWAY

In the first period, Friary Phase, the N wall of the choir, Fig. 42, (and presumably the S wall before extensive robbing) terminated in a more or less triangular-shaped pier, hardly more than a thickening on both faces of the junction of the N chancel wall with the E wall of the N transept. The first, moulded, dressed course on this pier was covered by later work, the drawing, Fig. 42, representing, therefore, a plan of the base for the second course. This pier duplicates, on its W face, mouldings of the later of the two SW tower piers (and presumably the earlier pier as well for which no mouldings evidence survived). Despite this they cannot be of the same actual building period, being of Friary 2 Phase, but are presumably of the same intended building period, creating the phasing problem for this site of whether one is phasing according to intention or to actual construction.

This second SW tower pier in turn relates in form to the nave arcade piers, Figs 41-2, and it seems that in spite of alterations and interruptions the church is basically a one period building, at least as an intention at foundation level. The external junction of the N chancel and NE transept wall was not a straight right angle as it appears to have been at the S, but, S of the surviving stub of the S wall of the chapel, the corner was thickened externally by about 1.5m (5ft) giving in a sense a large sub-rectangular pier of 3.8m (12ft 6in) at its maximum dimension. This is quite out of proportion to what is known of the three other first period tower piers, and this presumably carried a stair to the loft above the pulpitum, and presumably also to the tower, though if so it would have been a narrow one; there was, however, no direct surviving evidence in the ground to suggest stairs. At its southernmost point the pier appeared to be rebated, presumably to take a timber screen; there would be a gap between this screen and the assumed position of the back of the choir-stalls of about 30cm (lft), which presents interpretation difficulties.

It should be noted that the tower is some 18.5m (60ft) W of what would be the normal expected position in relation to the cloister.

8 CHAPEL TO EAST OF NORTH TRANSEPT (FORMERLY THE 'NORTH PORCH')

Pre-friary

Red sandy clay natural was recorded between the construction trench for the late Rebuild Phase green stone, triangular, buttress, at its SE end, and an apparent quarry, which cut it. The quarry fill was noted some 3.65m (12ft) to the N and for at least as far to the E-NE. Its shape and extent is not known.

Figures 37-38, 42, 51D-E, 62b and 63a

Chapel west wall and step

Friary, Friary 1 and Rebuild Phases

There was a doorway in the E wall of the N transept, a very unusual position, thought originally to relate to access from the town to the church, which must originally have been from Gosford Street (Figs 2 and 37-8.) and the N-S arm of Whitefriars Lane, and which presumably continued as an approach after the friars obtained their way-through from Much Park Street in or after 1352. The doorway was recessed, Fig. 42, 60cm (2ft) on the inside of the church, the diagonal sides of the recess carrying a simple moulding. It appeared from the position of the surviving hinge on the S side of the doorway that the doors opened outwards, and, when first discovered, the doors were assumed to lead out into a porch. The complications of the N wall of the chapel are discussed below. The original arrangements for access through the door are now unclear, but apparently at the fourth stage of the tower in the Rebuild Phase (below) the door was blocked, or perhaps the threshold merely raised, probably with the idea of improving structural stability. What was presumably the old threshold of the doorway, which perhaps acted as a substantial base to prevent subsidence (levels do not indicate that steps from church to porch would have been necessary), seems then to have been removed subsequent to that blocking, and a base, presumably for an altar to replace that lost in the abandoned chapel, was constructed over a reduced area within the transept. An altar would of course have been normal in this area, and part of the processional sequence. The new internal face to the previous blocking wall was very roughly mortared, and obviously not intended to be visible, presumably being concealed by that altar. The gap left, however, between the new, dressed, N edge of this apparent altar base and the old N door jamb was filled with three courses of carefully dressed masonry, not the rough rubble and mortar finish of the rest of the blocking. The stone used was green, and the mortar was rather yellow in colour, indicating that this work was contemporary with other tower strengthening works. The E side of the blocked doorway was occupied by one apparently continuous green stone, though somewhat splintered by later pick-axing. A piece of green sandstone 38cm (1ft 3in) wide projected eastwards from the blocking, just N of centre, to a surviving length of some 70cm (2ft 4in), and had obviously continued further. The purpose of this is not clear.

South wall of Chapel

Friary Phase

The S side of the doorway was confirmed in the 1968 rescue work to continue eastwards as a wall for some 4.9m (16ft), mortar patterns indicating that it was buttressed at its E end, showing that this was a two bay not a single bay structure. This wall had been largely destroyed and covered over by later work, and only some two or three stones survived at the point where it joined the E wall, and little of it was visible. It was apparently 75cm (2ft 6in) wide at first dressed course level, adequate for a single storey structure. The builders' trample associated with it, or possibly with the E wall (or even with the *in situ* base of the 'slot', which ran parallel with the E wall to its immediate W, and overlay natural) produced a fairly fresh Richard II York penny of the 1380s.

The position and dimensions of the fragmentary buttress at the E end of the S wall relate oddly to the choir buttress immediately to its S, but the mouldings of the first NE tower pier indicate a primary intention for a S chapel wall, although of course its actual construction could have been later, to parallel the other chapel walls; the crucial junction would have been destroyed by the later green triangular buttress.

North wall of Chapel

Friary 1 and Rebuild Phases

To the N of the doorway a robbing trench showed that there had been a wall in a similar position, but apparently of later date. The N edge of this wall at foundation level seemed fairly clear, and a turn in it to the N was thought to have been the remains of a buttress. The 1968 rescue work established the presence of that buttress, and also of a wall with a footing of some 1.05m (3ft 6in) to 1.20m (4ft) wide, offsetting to some 85cm (2ft 9in) as shown by the mortar lines of the missing ashlar (i.e. the same width as the E wall). It revealed that this wall also had an external length of 4.88m (16ft), ending in a buttress running to the N. Both buttresses, which survive largely at low level, have a width of some 90cm (3ft) and a length of 1.22cm (4ft). The surviving chamfered buttress stone, with an ashlar course below (the chamfered stone was kept and re-used further S in the rebuild) only projected some 60cm (2ft) from the original ashlar wall, however, its foundation being therefore double its standing length. The green sandstone used in the chamfered buttress stone is normally a feature of 15th-century work elsewhere on the site, confirming the suggestion from the earlier 1960s work that the two sides of the doorway were of different dates, and the N wall having two phases.

The internal measurement of this structure was 4.26m (14ft), and the intermediate buttress on the N wall, clarified in 1968, divided it into two equal bays of just over 2.14m (7ft). The width of the building was some 2.45m (8ft).

A strip 1.37m (4ft 6in) long and 15cm (6in) wide projecting from and parallel to the N outer face of N wall 2, was filled with what appeared to be secondary stone packing subsequent to removal of ?a threshold stone. This suggested that a stone step had possibly originally existed here, for a doorway subsequently obliterated when rebuilding. An external band of green sand trample overlying natural, thicker in its centre, in the same position, seemed to indicate external builders' trample through such a doorway. This again indicates that the N wall was built after the green sandstone quarry came into use, probably in the first half of the 15th century. If so the absence of the normal 16th-century ground surface in this area suggests that the use of a door continued after rebuilding as a boundary wall.

East wall of Chapel

Friary and Friary 1 Phases

This survived at foundation level, but mortar indicated a thickness again for this wall of 76cm (2ft 6in). There were no indications of a doorway at the E, understandable if the access was from the N. It shared a short buttress at its S end with the E wall, its length curtailed by the existing buttress to the choir. There was another buttress at the N making a pair to that of the N wall.

A 90cm (3ft) wide 23cm (9in) deep 'slot', with a flat bottom and a 45 degree sloping edge, ran N-S, and was parallel with the full length of the internal face of the E wall, partly overlying its footings. It was robbed in the 16th century, and filled at its N end for 1.07m (3ft 6in) with a tip consisting entirely of roof tile (except for two Cistercian ware sherds). Might that have been the robbing of an altar, (it seems too wide for a stone bench) confirming the identification of this structure as a chapel at some point in time?

Structural Anomalies

Friary 1 Phase

Figures 38 and 42

It was noted in the earlier 1960s excavations that the pink mortar, so much a feature of the choir up to and including the S side of the doorway, changed N of the doorway to a white-when-dry, yellow-when-wet mortar, more resembling that of the nave. Additionally the doorway was not central to the first transept, but to the second, as narrowed by the rebuilding or strengthening, again using yellow mortar, of the NE tower pier (discussed below under 'Third stage of tower'). All this seemed to mean that the two sides of the same doorway belonged to different periods, the first period relating to the construction of the chancel, and the second to the construction of the eastern part of the N transept; the strengthening of the NE tower pier being a yet later phase. The 1968 work confirmed this hypothesis.

Interior of the Chapel and floor surfaces

Very little of the interior was excavated under the difficult circumstances in 1968, with the contractors' machinery only feet away, and it had in any case largely been destroyed by the insertion of the later green sandstone triangular buttress. No evidence for original flooring was recovered. Any tiled floor was in any case presumably removed when the chapel was demolished.

The general sequence of layers over the area was that of green sandstone rubble at the top, overlying a red clayey level with roof tile, over a reddish brown sand level representing destruction, over another brown sand level representing a buried surface later than the demolition of the yard walls, all 16th century, and all over the earlier medieval rubbish dumps. There were locally anomalous small patches, i.e. two on the drawn section - red clay 128, and rubble 126 (Figs 42 and 51 Section G), and a buried surface did not survive outside the putative door in the N wall of the chapel, where the green trample occurred immediately over natural. A deep deposit of rubbish to the E and NE of the chapel again suggesting the presence of an earlier quarry, tipping away to the N.

The green triangular buttress destroying the chapel is discussed under the Fifth Phase of the tower, below.

Later walls

The second N chapel wall seems to have been of the Rebuild Phase (Fig. 51 Section E, fragmentary wall 2) presumably related to destruction caused by the assumed second tower fall in 1447. Rebuilding of the whole chapel is unlikely to follow the insertion of the green sandstone triangular buttress, which would surely have made that chapel unusable, and this rebuilding, which seems to have immediately followed the construction of that buttress, is unlikely to have been a serious structural wall at under 60cm (2ft) wide. Some sort of yard or boundary wall seems likely. This second N chapel wall, had been built parallel and immediately adjacent to the first wall, just overlapping its northern edge. Its internal face lay 45cm (18in) N of the first N chapel wall's wide footings, which had been removed to build it, the resultant robbing trench, which had presumably removed more of the old wall than was necessary, having then been repacked, between the green sandstone triangular buttress and the area of the chamfered buttress stone, with over fifty pieces of what had presumably been the chapel's 15th-century vault, destroyed by the tower collapse, layer 60 III 6, Fig. 51, Section E; these pieces were a smaller version of Standard moulding A, see Section F, *The Architectural Stonework*, Fig. 69 Std B (4 in no). Much of this material was lime-washed green sandstone, and the fill of its robbing trench was green, a late indication, as were the traces of a construction trench some 30cm (lft) wide, Fig. 51, Section E. The rebuilt wall had a 16th-century level overlying its remains, and is late, but still pre Reformation, work.

This rebuilt wall 2 was later extended eastwards by wall 3 (Fig. 51 Section G), a little narrower at 54cm (1ft 9in) wide and of different, largely monoblock, build, to a position beyond the chapel by a distance equivalent to slightly more than a chapel bay, presumably fortuitous. The partly monoblock nature of its construction (paralleled by the wall bounding the reredorter paving at the N) indicates a late, but again not necessarily a post-monastic date, Fig. 42. It was inserted into what might be termed a hollow rather than a pit, which was filled with industrial (iron slag) and other rubbish up to 1.5m (5ft) deep (IIIE 127) and cut into red sand and sandstone (which is more likely to have been quarry fill than natural) to the N of the wall, with a cleaner, but still at least 1.05m (3ft 6in) deep deposit on the S (128). Industrial rubbish deposits (127 and possibly 107, which included slag and pins) apparently preceded all the wall 3 structure, including its return to the N, where there were suggestions of a doorway to the E. Unfortunately it was not possible in the 1968 debacle to retrieve any more of the plan of this structure. If layer 107 was contemporary with wall 3, it seems to lie outside any associated building, and it cannot be argued that wall 3 represents part of a workshop on the evidence.

The industrial rubbish deposit to the N (127) was immediately overlain by a level (IIIE 26, Fig. 51 Section G) of stone rubble and roof tile, presumably a destruction level, but the usual underlying buried ground surface was here absent. All earlier ground levels had been removed. Layer 127 contained slag, charcoal, much food bone and late 15th and early 16th-century pottery, presumably relating to the putative late workshop of the 16th-century Rebuild Phase. However, to the S of the wall a 16th-century buried ground surface, 124, did occur, and became thicker as it spread to the E, and in fact overlay the remains of wall 3 on its N-S course, showing that it had been demolished during the 16th century. At the particular point where the section was drawn, red clay deposit 128 had preceded it, overlying the footings of, and butting up against, wall 3. The reason for this is not clear. It only extended for a foot to the E and its extent to the W is unknown.

Wall 3, where it turned N was 23cm (9in) wider at 70cm (2ft 6in) and was laid over a footing of 1.20m (4ft) width or more. It's footings were also noted to be at a different and higher level - almost 30cm (1ft) -than the W-E wall, but there was not a butt joint at the corner. These differences suggested that a doorway might have existed just to the N of the excavated area, and the footings suggested that some feature had projected to the E. This was a wall with two faces, not monoblock. It again is 16th century, for level 124 with its earlier 16th-century pottery, overlapped the footings of wall 3. It was destroyed in that century, possibly by the third fall of the tower in the early 1570s.

These various rebuilds all seem to represent boundary or yard walls. Their purlieus had been used as a dump in the 16th century for building materials, sculpture, architectural mouldings, plain and decorated floor tiles and much glazed roof (mainly green, but much ginger-brown, a little cream) and some ridge tile, nails, and also Tudor brick; the deposits also included slag, and domestic and probably school rubbish, attested by a chipped tile disc. There had also been a roof tile tip (including a finial) in the robbed remains of the ?altar (the 'slot') at the chapel's E end.

These late N walls had been cleared away level and had been covered with a red clayey deposit with the ubiquitous roof tile apparently during the 16th-century destruction of the church.

About one third of the area inside the porch was unexcavated.

In 1968 a costumed wodewose in three fragments, and a

dog's head spout, were recovered apparently from the 1570s collapse of the tower at the external angle of wall 3. In 1969 a further water spout representing Samson was recovered from a contractors' trench some 9m to the NE and 7m to the E of the chapel. What appeared to be rubble from the fall of the tower indicated the use of green sandstone in its construction, but the sculpture was of red sandstone. For detailed descriptions see Section G, *The Architectural Sculpture* Nos 1072-3, 1076-7 and 1079, Fig. 80.

A well (68 IIIE 130) was discovered and emptied by the contractors to the NE of this area towards Gosford Street, its precise position being unknown. It produced pottery of 16-17th-century date and a stamped iron tool, probably a blacksmith's hardy, Section T, *Observations on some of the Small Finds* No 104, Fig. 163).

9 THE NORTH AND SOUTH TRANSEPTS

North Transept (construction)

Friary 1 Phase

Figures 51, 63b and 64a

The diagonal buttress on the NE corner of the N transept was certainly of choir type and its foundations may have been laid early, but the complications of the chapel area indicate that it was unlikely to have been built above footings level in the primary phase, whatever the original intention, but in the Friary 1 Phase (Fig. 51 Section D) where there is evidence again for a quarry requiring deep footings. Some 6.10m (20ft) to the W of this buttress what appeared to have been a pilaster buttress had been constructed, apparently 1.65m (5ft 6in) wide by 53cm (1ft 9in). The W side of this buttress continued at a slight diagonal across the N transept wall, and the NW wall of the transept butted against it, and was clearly later work. It appeared, therefore, that this sub-phase of the first period of construction had come to an end at this point. This pilaster buttress had been built opposite the first period NW tower pier which lay some 5.5m (18ft) to the S. Of the foundations of this pier very little survived later disturbance - some irregular red sandstone set in red sandy clay, and traces of pink mortar survived among the top stones. It was at first thought that the lack of demolition material and the fact that the floor make-up 15cm (6in) in depth, continued clean and hard and apparently undisturbed right across and beyond the foundation may have meant that construction stopped at this (foundation) point, but the mortar rather indicated further work had existed, and the subsequent discovery of a timber beam slot running N from the equivalent SW tower pier also under later floor make-up indicates that both these piers had been standing to some height at least above ground level, and had been linked by some sort of timber screen or wall. The floor make-up was not removed beyond the immediate area of the NE tower pier foundation and so this feature was not noted in 1962. It should, however, probably be assumed to have existed.

Small areas of floor tile matrix and worn re-used floor tiles survived in the N transept, but none in their original positions.

The crossing would have been where two processional groups which had come eastward down the nave aisles met, presumably both having passed an altar on the E side of both transepts, and, before passing through into the choir, would have viewed the pulpitum screen with its organ and many statues or paintings of prophets, saints, apostles, kings and doctors of the church

South Transept

Friary 1 Phase

Figures 62a and 64a

The first period south-east tower pier was presumably similar to the NE tower pier, although there was no direct evidence for its form. The suggested reconstruction is based on the NE tower pier, but no evidence at all survived to suggest its shape. It was robbed entirely out down to a flag foundation set in sand, about 60cm (2ft) below the floor level. This foundation was perhaps a levelling course, and had been covered with a thin layer of hard sandy clay 5-7cm (2-3in), which had hidden it from the stone robbers. All the undressed stone and clay foundation which presumably existed above this had been robbed.

A very short length of the SE transept wall ran S from the area of the pier foundation at a higher level, and then came to a halt, on the edge of a quarry. It was the normal red-sandstone-set in sandy-clay first period foundation. The continuation of the transept wall, of different construction, wider, and deeper, with yellow gravelly mortar, clearly later work, butted against it at the S. It is assumed that the first period of construction ended at this point. An altar would be expected here, against the E wall of the S transept, but only a small stony deposit survived as a possible hint of this.

The first SW tower pier survived also very fragmentarily, cut about by later disturbances. From under the graves which cut through the N side of the pier emerged a line of clay packing carrying a beam slot, presumably for a screen, which ran N for 1.37m (4ft 6in), then continued under the baulk (not examined further). At this point the slot was also observed to turn and run E for 45cm (1ft 6in), again continuing beyond the baulk. The surviving timber in the slot was 16cm wide (6½in), set in a clay-packed trench 35cm wide (1ft 2in). The remains of both pier and beam slot were covered over by an average of 15-20cm (6-8in) of red sand floor make-up, which was carried right over the foundation without indications of any demolition. Presumably the demolition of the piers, and the removal of the timber beam and any associated walling were completed before the levelling off of the site and the placing of the make-up for the subsequent tiled floor.

The area now built, choir and four tower piers (height unknown) was presumably temporarily enclosed, of which this beam slot running N from the first SW tower pier, is our only evidence. The make-up for the floor was normally not removed on the site owing to difficulties of time and labour, and further beam slots, etc., may well have existed/been destroyed. The chancel was presumably roofed, tiled, glazed, and provided with choir-stalls (Section H, *The Choir-Stalls*, Figs 82-93), with a chancel arch of some 7.5m (24ft 6in) width, leading into a rectangular 'walking place' space at its W end, temporarily closed off by some sort of timber screen, presumably shutting off the spaces between the tower piers. We have no means of knowing how much of the octagonal lantern intended to crown the walking space was constructed. There would be presumably no windows to glaze, and we have no evidence for flooring within this area.

North Transept

Friary 2 Phase

Figures 42, 63b and 64a

When building work recommenced it was apparently decided to replace the rectangular based tower of the usual friary type, presumably carrying a partly constructed (or intended to carry) slight octagonal lantern (based on centres approximately 10.65 x 7.60m (35 x 25ft) with a tower based on a square of approximately 10.65m (35ft) centres. As tower piers apparently of the same type were used it looks as if this decision was made on grounds other than inherent structural ones, i.e. not lack of confidence in their original form, and the reason may be fashion, e.g. the rebuilt tower of the London Austin Friars, Fig. 6. The existing western tower piers must have been completely cleared away down to foundation. The N wall of the N transept was continued to the W another 3.35m (11ft), and then returned 8.3m (6ft) to make the W wall of the very shallow transept. The diagonal buttress at the external NW corner of the transept was smaller than the NE buttress. Of the second NW tower pier which must have been built, virtually nothing remained. It is just possible that the elaborate moulding recorded in the 19th century as coming from the church (Troughton drawing no 1/10/37, University of Warwick) came from the Victorian excavation of the large workhouse rubbish pit which destroyed that pier.

Presumably the two westernmost tower piers were preceded by the footings for two arcade piers, but if so the northern one had been completely removed, and the southern one would have remained concealed under the surviving masonry of the second SW tower pier.

South Transept

Friary 1 (Phase 1a) and Friary 2 (Phase 2)

Figures 42, 62a and 64a

All the walls of the S transept were very massive at foundation level, from the point where the Friary 2 Phase foundation of the S wall of the nave widens out W of its junction with the cill wall (not a butt joint), to the point of junction where it butts onto the earlier stub of wall running S of the SE tower pier of the Friary 1 Phase, Fig. 42. This butt joint occurs on the edge of a quarry which probably underlies the whole of the S transept area. However, the start of a quarry cut is not normally the signal for a butt joint and this is most unlikely to be the only reason for its occurrence here, but rather a change of period. The S transept wall would seem to have been about 2.5m (8ft) deep, and therefore deeper than the N transept wall (Fig. 51 Section D), but no dressed masonry survived. However, it is likely that the standing wall of dressed stone was similar in thickness to that of the N transept, some 1.45m (4ft 9in). The evidence, however, for a diagonal buttress at the W was clear, and the foundation of this turned S, making a tail butting against the N wall of the cloister. It is likely that the buttress was normal in form above ground, as there was no trace of mortar on the face of the cloister wall here, and therefore masonry did not seem to have butted against it at a higher level. The S wall foundation was rather irregular and sinuous. At a point about 5.5m (18ft) along the S transept wall from the W, the wall foundation narrowed to barely 1.2m (4ft). This is less than the likely thickness of the dressed wall here, 1.42m (4ft 8in), and it seems probable that this thinner sector may represent some earlier, and surely necessary, entrance through from the cloister, central to (or possibly just E of centre to) the S transept. This would presumably lead into the fourth bay from the E of the N cloister walk. The swing to the N of the foundation in the eastern 3.5m (10ft) of the transept S wall appears to have been a setting out error, or perhaps an extra strengthening for the corner. The mortared core of the wall surviving here showed no trace of a butt joint. The mortar here was rather intermediate in type being white with a somewhat pinkish tinge. There was no direct evidence for an eastern diagonal buttress, except for tenuous indications (patches of rubble) of a possible robber trench overlying a massive foundation butting against the cloister wall (to which it was clearly secondary, the top two courses being laid against the cloister wall dressed face), and projecting 3.5m (10ft) N of it. This foundation overlay a quarry pit. To the NE the badly robbed S wall of the choir had terminated in the robbed base of the Friary Phase 1 SE tower pier. A short length of the SE transept wall foundation (Friary Phase 1) red sandstone in red clay, ran S from the robbed pier for about 1.05m (3ft 6in). The remaining 5.2m (17ft) of the wall was of a different build, with a very clear butt joint, the wall to the S clearly being later (Friary 2 Phase). This wall was also wider, up to 30cm (1ft), and a good part of it retained a yellow gravelly mortar with large core stones, not found surviving elsewhere on the site. The top foundation course was mortared, unlike the earlier wall, and the foundation was deeper.

10 THE TOWER

Relocation of the western tower piers and alterations of the accompanying transepts, Phases 3 and 4.

Pre-Rebuild Phase (Phase 3)

Figures 32, 38, 42, 62a-64a

It is assumed that the NE tower pier showed signs of failure (or indeed that the tower had actually fallen) and that a foundation some 3.95m (13ft) square was inserted round the standing pier, and apparently to a lower depth. The core of this second (Phase 3) pier overlay the mouldings of the first. This work was built largely of green sandstone with a green-mortared rubble core, but with the use of a distinctive yellow mortar; the core of the first pier having been sand and rubble. This new foundation was inserted into the resonance passage down to the natural rock at the bottom, and was mortared right down to the last course. On the S face of this later pier a 1.5m (5ft) length of dressed masonry survived above floor level for a few centimetres, carrying the remains of a wall painting, apparently representing the base of a scarlet robe or drapery of some sort, edged with black (this had been limewashed over and is too damaged to illustrate but is recorded in an archive photograph).

A slightly smaller 3.65m (12ft) square foundation for the NW tower pier indicates, despite heavy robbing, a more radical rebuild. Of the earlier pier that must have stood here of Phase 3 nothing remained, though the chapel wall to the W, and the door cill to the N, that must have been associated with it, did survive. Sufficient of the later foundation, set in yellow mortar right to its base, survived to indicate that the earlier pier had been entirely removed at the time of the construction of the later pier foundation, and this is presumably the site of the main structural failure. To accompany this pier a second door cill was built adjoining the earlier one to the E, but with a deeper foundation. It contained re-used mouldings. Apparently reconstructed at the same time was the internal E half of the W wall of the N transept, including a new arch respond.

It seems likely that the blocking of the door in the NE transept (described under *8, Chapel to East of North transept*, above) took place at this time, presumably for structural reasons.

The Tower

Rebuild Phase (Phase 4)

Figures 32, 42, 62b and 63a

The tower was subsequently further reinforced at its N by the addition of, originally faced, heavy masses of rubble and green mortar buttressing, between the external angles of the N transept, and the nave and choir walls respectively. This seems to have involved the removal of the western bay of the chapel N wall. The surviving triangular mass here presumably had a dressed course along the external diagonal face, but this had been robbed. This mass survived at a height of two dressed courses above foundation and may have run as a solid buttress more or less in this form right up this corner of the transept, hard against the tower, perhaps to a considerable height? The foundation was traced down in 1968 for a further 70cm (2ft 6in) with an offset of 30cm (1ft), of dressed stone, and a further irregular offset 23cm (9in) lower in rubble taking the wall out another foot (30cm). A construction trench for this green triangular buttress was partly excavated in 1968, N of the S wall of the porch. It contained pottery of the mid 15th century.

The S porch wall was destroyed, as well as part, at least, of the N porch wall, though some of the N wall may have been retained as buttressing, and indeed added to, as it appears to have seen some reconstruction in the Rebuild Phase. At the NW external angle of the N transept a similar reinforcement had been constructed. Its foundations were not examined, and are likely to have been larger than shown.

It is assumed that it was the tower that fell in 1447 (described as 'the new work') and that this was the second fall..

Glazing of the Transepts

The glass looks to be probably of *c.*1425 in the main, presumably of the Friary 2 Phase, the little surviving suggesting that it is cruder and later than the choir glass, with very little colour. The vicissitudes of the transepts must indicate later repair. See Section J, *Medieval Window Glass from the Church and Cloister*, Fig. 130.

Floor tile matrices

These survive particularly in the S transept, showing both diagonal and 'straight' laying patterns. No tiles survived *in situ* as originally laid, but there was a patch of random relaid tile apparently related to Grave 61.2, Figs 42 and 141.

11 THE RELATED CROSSING BURIALS

Referring again to the known graves in the London Greyfriars, Fig. 6 (Shepherd 1902, 266-287), one would expect 'in the passage between the quire and the altars' knights, esquires, doctors of law, merchants, rectors, wardens, friars and friary porters, and sisters and wives. Apart from the wall tomb, Grave 61.2, and stone-capped grave 23 (NE of the SW pier), there is little evidence for high status here. Where there is evidence for dating, the graves are mostly 15th century, probably because the crossing was not completed till then.

Previous comments about the difficulty of excavating graves in the presence of 'Coventry's worst problem families' apply.

North Transept graves

Figure 42

The most substantial of the graves, the wall tomb Grave 61.2, Fig. 51 Section D, was inserted into the wall of the NE transept, some 2m to the NW of the new altar, and seems likely to have been that of an important benefactor. The space above the tomb was presumably arched, and faced with elegant tracery, as surviving at, e.g., the Irish friary of Kilconnell, County Galway, of the same later 15th-century date (pers. ob.). It was partly excavated and then vandalised. The interior of the tomb had roughly mortared-up faces, with a plaster over it of 0.75cm thickness. A quarter round inserted whitewashed moulding fronted the tomb, its green colour implying a 15th-century date. The apparently related disturbed area in the adjacent floor had been patched up (see above, *Floor tile matrices* and Fig. 141).

The grave had been disturbed at the Reformation; it was excavated to a depth of 75cm (2ft 6in), when it was totally vandalised. It is unknown if the Reformation activity had left skeletal or coffin remains in position. There is therefore no bone report.

In view of the vandalism, graves were noted but not excavated. A short account of what was noted is given below. A fuller list is preserved in archive.

Grave 61.3 lay close to wall-grave 61.2 in the N transept wall, but N of that wall, and is evidence for the ?lay cemetery to the N of the church.

Six graves were noted more or less in line running between the NE tower pier and the N transept wall. Five of these are certainly 15th century or later, and presumably relate to the altar of that date now suggested to have been set against the E wall of the N transept. The distance from that altar suggests the presence of railings. Six other graves were noted in the N transept, 15th century in the main. One earlier grave was stone-lined with slabs 60cm (2ft) long, otherwise these were earth burials. They were not excavated. There was considerable intercutting.

Grave 64.23, NE of the 2nd tower pier, in the S crossing, Fig. 42, exceptionally had a stone-capping and was again probably 15th century. Seven other graves were noted in this area, one again with remains of stone-capping, the rest apparently earth graves. None were excavated. There will, of course, have been many other burials in the crossing.

12 THE WESTERN AND EASTERN NAVE

Figures 41-2

Phases Friary 2, Friary 2a Sub-phase and Pre-Rebuild

It had always been assumed that the brick boundary wall of the workhouse at the W, Fig, 59a, marked the ultimate possible length of the nave at eight bays, as the London Whitefriars, Fig. 4, but a trench in 1960 against that wall (60 V), Fig. 41, suggested a nave of seven bays as at the Norwich Blackfriars, Fig. 6. However, Trench 62 IX, which involved an unofficial excursion beyond that brick wall into the yard of International Computers Ltd., established the length of the nave at 9 bays, confirmed by Trench 64 XXVI, an excursion into the area of a road used by the Ancient Order of Druids' beer lorries, which revealed the W Door.

A nine bay nave is paralleled in the London Austin Friars, Fig. 6 (destroyed by a land mine in 1942), there with an aisled six bay choir. The London Greyfriars, a church of similar length to the Coventry Whitefriars, apparently again had a nine bay nave with a five bay aisled choir,

Fig. 6. The E bay of the London Greyfriars nave had chapels, as the Coventry Whitefriars, of the Holy Rood and St Mary (there were two additional chapels at the Greyfriars).

Nave: Chapels and eastern two bays

Figure 42

The two Chapels in the first bay of the Nave

Pre-Rebuild, Phase 3

The N chapel was apparently the Chapel of Our Lady (see Maria monogram floor tile, Fig. 144.86 and Section B for a letter of 1538 from Dr John London to Thomas Cromwell referring to such a chapel). The slightly truncated door cill running N from the destroyed second NW tower pier and the wall of the little chapel to the W of that pier did survive, with different coloured mortar and shallower foundations than the later work. The N wall of the northern chapel was only 35cm (1ft 2in) wide at the W, but 10cm (4in) wider at the E) and these little walls perhaps carried a light stone or timber screen of no great height. There were only very tenuous indications of a stone screen running S from this pier, and its foundation seems to have been, at least in part, only some 13cm (7in) below a later floor level, and it cannot have been a substantial structure. However, the course of the S wall to this little chapel was quite clear, and it had been continued westward, after a small gap, for a minimum of 2.5m (8ft 3in) by a slight timber screen of which the beam slot survived. It is assumed that the area enclosed by these two slender walls represented a small chapel some 3.58m (11ft 9in) N to S by some 2.75m (9ft) E to W, for use by the laity. The floor level was at least 20cm (8in) higher in the chapel than in the nave, and there was presumably a step up. The altar position is assumed. There was no evidence for it.

An elaborate Renaissance sculpted fragment found in this chapel, indicated the presence of an elaborate screen, or possibly tomb (Section F, *The Architectural Stonework* No 1114, Fig. 73).

The S chapel was apparently that of the Holy Rood (see Section B for letter of 1538 from Dr John London to Thomas Cromwell referring to a Rood chapel). The N wall of this chapel had been as slim as 30cm (1ft) at its western end. The foundation of the main screen wall forming the back of the chapel was some 1.75m (5ft 9in) wide. This is wider than would seem to be needed for a stone screen, and it appears likely that the western part of the foundation carried an altar. Part of a polished slab of Purbeck marble was found nearby, though this might just be from a tomb chest. The wide foundation came to an end 1.06m (3ft 6in) N of the standing face of the S chapel wall, leaving a rather odd space in this corner of the chapel. There were definite indications of a wall face running N from the second SW tower pier incorporated in that pier's dressed masonry. If this face projecting from the pier had continued due N, it would give a screen wall of about 53cm (1ft 9in) width, as indicated on Fig. 42. The floor level in the chapel had again originally been at least 17cm (7in) higher than in the nave or crossing, again implying an original step. Two floor tiles of the same 4-tile pattern, and as originally laid, were an unusual survival, Section L, *Late 14th and 15th Century Stamped Floor Tile* No 11, Fig. 136-7.

The Passage between the two Chapels

This was of interest as a wear gully had formed in the sand makeup, clearly indicating that the passage was in use for some time before tiling took place; presumably the nave and crossing were also in use untiled. It seems that mosaic floor tiles were used only in this passage, Section L, *Late 14th and 15th Century Stamped Floor Tile* Nos 122a-d, Fig. 145.

The Rood Screen

Figure 42

Of the assumed Rood Screen with its great crucifix and the attendant figures of the Virgin Mary and St John, nothing remains, except perhaps the burnt wood surviving to the N of the N nave chapel. However, the original purpose of the neat circular pit, 64,XVIa(3), some 1.5m in diameter, and 0.5m deep, lying centrally just to the W of the two chapels, with its post-reformation fill of uprooted mosaic tiles and human bone, is unclear. Could it have some connection with a free-standing Rood?

Piscinae

The areas marked 'pd' on Fig. 42 were pits filled with large-scale rubble and silt, and were thought to have been piscina drains.

13 THE EASTERN NAVE BURIALS

These included Grave 64.31, in the NE nave, Fig. 42, plan of tile grave cover Fig. 141 and Section L, *Late 14th and 15th Century Stamped Floor Tile,* Nos 36-8, Fig. 139. This was an earth grave, the sinking of whose fill had preserved its unique, apparently specially commissioned, tile cover, as these tiles did not appear elsewhere. They are paralleled at Dudley Castle. The date is 15th century. Not excavated.

Six other graves, 20, 21, 22, 23, 32 and 33 (details in

archive), were noted but not excavated in the area of the N chapel. Four were earth graves 20, 21, 22 and 23, of which two, 20 and 21 (which cut 20) had been robbed and had tiles and mortar in the fill. Grave 21 additionally contained stone mouldings. The natures of graves 32 and 33 is unknown.

Four tiles of the tile cover of Grave 22 remained *in situ*, but were very worn. Grave 23 exceptionally had a stone capping of which six flag stones survived up to .4m in length . None of the above were excavated.

Grave 64.19, in the second bay of the nave from the W, Fig. 42, was of particular interest. It was a canopied, perhaps chantry tomb, with a vaulted grave below. It was heavily robbed. The stones recovered from this robbing included a small fragment, with an asymmetrical hollow painted red, ending in a roll, painted black, Section F, *The Architectural Stonework* No 197, Fig. 77. The elaborate colouring suggests it is part of a decorative feature, probably the tomb itself. There is insufficient to suggest what element it may be in that context, perhaps part of a hood/canopy.

Additional to this is item 2450, Section F, *The Architectural Stonework* Fig. 75. This is described as being in green stone, and identified 'as the jamb of an opening, a hollow chamfer flanked by rolls. The inner face is painted with a series of black diagonal streaks. It is rebated behind this. It would seem feasible that this is the support end pier for the canopy of an open tomb, perhaps mounted above the vault. The mouldings suggest a 15th-century date.'

Well dressed 30cm wide ashlar blocks faced the interior of the tomb. Part of the burial vault remained in position in the NE corner, at a steeper than 45 degrees angle. The tomb had been robbed at the Reformation. There is a parallel for its position in the church of the Bonshommes at Edington, Wilts., there a monastic burial (pers. ob.).

Bones from Reformation grave robbing of an infant of 3-4 years and a sub-adult of 7-17 years occurred in some quantity in the mosaic tile pit, Fig. 42, presumably from child burials in the eastern bays of the nave.

The Whitefriars Churchyard

It is possible that burials continued after the destruction of the church for 'Lady Hales' churchyard' is shown N of the church on a *c.*1800 map in the Aylesford Collection (BB97/6254), Birmingham Central Library. A ?17th-century iron coffin handle was found in the NE transept area, Section T, *Observations on some of the Small Finds* No 135, Fig. 165). This practice is common in the churchyards of ruined friaries in Ireland, e.g. at the Quin Franciscan Friary, County Clare (pers. ob.).

14 THE COMPLETE NAVE

Figures 41-2, 50 and 65ab

The S chapel wall and screen wall running N are shown by the dressed masonry to have been all of one piece with the second SW tower pier. The W face of the pier duplicates the arcade piers, and they are presumably all part of one overall plan. The NE and E faces of the pier, however, duplicate the equivalent faces of the first NE tower pier, and one must assume also represent the original scheme being continued, despite the fundamental decision to alter the design of the tower. A cill, still covered with some of the original sand and clay floor make-up ran southwards, joining what appeared to be the foundation of an arch respond on the internal angle of the S nave wall, and the foundation of the W wall of the transept.

The nave, Figs 41-2 and 50 Sections A-C, was nine bays and 44.79m (147ft) long, the bay width averaging 4.98m (16ft 4in) from centre to centre of the arcade piers. The internal width of the nave with aisles was 20.5m to 20.57m (67ft 3 to 6in,) the aisles being some (5.03) 16ft 6in wide, the aisle bays, therefore, being virtually square. The width of the nave alone was 10.5m (34ft 6in). All measurements are taken from arcade pier centres or from the internal faces of walls. The width of the N and S walls appears to have been 1.02m (3ft 4in) at first dressed course level, about 30cm (1ft) less, therefore, than the earlier period choir walls. The core seems to have been set entirely in hard mortar. The mortar colour in the nave was mainly rather whitish (though more varied than the choir with its distinct pink/red mortar) tending to be yellowish when wet (but patches of strongly coloured pinkish mortar occurred, especially on the N wall towards the W end).

The normal buttress seems to have been 1.12m (3ft 8in) wide, and 1.42m (4ft 8in) long, like the choir buttresses, but their foundations were reduced to a normal 15cm (6in offset), as the foundation for all the nave wall i.e. they lacked the wide flag foundation of the choir buttresses. The abnormal length of the buttress 4 footing on the N wall was apparently due to a pre-church pit in this area, and it was probably quite normal above ground. There was no evidence for a N porch in this area. Some of the buttresses were mortared in their top foundation courses, again a feature not present in the choir, and a confirmation of a different building period.

The S wall of the nave at the E was robbed, but there were indications that the dressed wall had been the generally standard width of 1.1m (3ft 4in). However, there was considerable width variation in the S wall, due partly to equivalent variations in the sub-surface from the presence of quarries. Firstly, the wall at the E, at foundation level, with the usual nave wall thickness at this point of 1.22m (4ft), widened to 1.62m (5ft 4in), at a point 1.2-1.52m (4-5ft) W of the junction with the screen and transept walls. There was no trace of buttress 1, Fig. 42, and it had clearly never been built. Buttress 2 is a little shorter than the norm, being 1.42m (4ft 8in) at foundation level, reducing presumably to 1.27m (4ft 2in) or thereabouts at first dressed course level; it was an addition, with a straight joint with green sand builders' trample with late 15th-16th-century pottery, and was apparently part of the Rebuild Phase concern with stability.

The Friary 2 Sub-phase is represented by the appearance of construction trenches (walls being normally trench-built) in bays 5 to 8 at the S. There are also signs of widening of the nave S wall again in bays 5 and 6, and by bay 6 the width of the foundation was 1.9m (6ft 3in), half as wide again as the nave foundation elsewhere. There was no evidence that the nave wall was rebuilt here, but an underlying quarry is known in bay 6 (see Fig. 50 Sections B and C), and the extra width is presumably to secure stability. Part of buttress 6 (Fig. 50 Section B) seems to have lain on natural rock quarry edge, and part in the quarry, and the rock was sufficiently near the surface here at the W for the nave wall to have been also laid in part directly on natural rock, from whence stone robbing activities had partly removed it. A void had formed due to subsidence of quarry fill, large enough for a small child to have been found hiding under buttress 6 in 1962. However Section B, Fig. 50, indicated a standing wall at this point, just clear of the quarry, of the normal 1.1m (3ft 4in) nave width, and the western three bays were also presumably clear of quarries.

The use of construction trenches was unexpected in the early 1960s, but was confirmed again in the 1968 rescue operation. These sometimes projected beyond the wall by as much as 60cm to 76cm (2ft to 2ft 6in), and were visible mainly S of the nave wall (the N face of this wall was difficult to examine because of the presence of a 19th-century brick wall), see Fig. 50 Sections B and C and plan, Fig. 41. A late Rebuild phase of building was noted elsewhere to relate to the use of construction trenches, though none were of this width. There are other possibilities, e.g. a miscutting for a trench-built wall, or, if the presence of a quarry was known in the adjacent bay to the W, this may alternatively have been a test trench to establish its extent.

In bays 1 to 4 to the E there was no sign of such a construction trench and the builders' trample was the earlier red sand in bays 1 and 2; the nave wall here was of a different build, apparently of the main Friary 2 Phase. Both red and green sandstone were, however, used in the walls in this intermediate phase.

A green sand builders' trample further confirmed Friary 2 Sub-phase, for this part of the wall bays 5-8/9. It overlay a dump of apparent quarry waste immediately external to the S nave wall in bays 5 and 6 at a level that seemed unlikely to relate to its initial construction but might relate to the repair of the ashlar stage of that wall in a green stone, Fig. 50 Section C. However, this late green sandy spread occurred all over Trench XXVIII extending S into the area of the cloister walk as well as the intended double W range of the cloister, Figs 38 and 52b, and it may well relate to work on that cloister and not to the nave. It seems unlikely that work would commence, as clearly it did, to extend the cloister W range if there were still five bays of the nave to construct and possibly the cloister walk itself to finish, and it is not thought that this area was part of the latest work on the nave.

The cloister wall coming up from the S (underlying the Hales' garden wall) occupies the position of one nave wall buttress. Additionally there was no buttress to the S wall of the nave in the expected position to its W. This may be because of an intention to build a double cloister range here, which was not to be carried out. However, to extend the outer wall of that intended range N against the church would not actually have put such a wall in the correct buttress position, and in any case there was no trace of any remains of an intended wall running N from the cloister area here. The reason for the buttress's absence remains unclear. Perhaps the presence of an undisturbed rock base was thought sufficient support.

This cloister wall butted onto the nave (cutting through the construction trench) so the nave must have been pre-existing; both are however thought to be of Friary 2 Phase. Additionally the overlying Hales' wall butted against the nave wall, which it seems that he retained for his garden boundary and this could be an early example of the Gothick ruin as a garden feature? It should be noted that the substantial green sandstone garden wall consolidated in part on site is 18th century, not 16th century. Its gate was built over the by then demolished S nave wall at the E, Fig. 42. It is visible, with its 18th-century gate pier on the left of Fig. 23.

The W wall of the nave is estimated as standing at some 1.52m (5ft) wide, very slightly wider perhaps than the E end wall 1.42m (4ft 8in). Despite its curious position in relation to angled buttress 9 at the N, the W and N walls of the nave at their junction were clearly of one build, at least at mortared core level.

The West Door appears to have been 1.9m (6ft 6in) wide, recessed internally, apparently with two doors opening internally and steps leading up out of the church, the ground level being apparently at least 45cm (18in) higher outside to the W than the church floor level. Not sufficient survived or was accessible to determine the external form of the doorway. It appears that the wall thickness was reduced by 35cm (1ft 2in) internally, traces remaining at the N of the doorway of a dressed face at this point. A secondary, rather flimsy, and small, inner entrance had been constructed at some date (quite possibly post-Reformation) making an entrance some 75cm (2ft 6in) wide very close inside the earlier door. This was only partly inside the trench, and its extent remained unknown.

A letter from Cyril Scott, Museum Curator, to C. Woodfield, of 14th February 1968 referred to 'notes left (by C.W.) of excavations still to be carried out at the Whitefriars'. Scott referred to the 'eventual excavation of the W end' together with the comment 'consideration must be given to exposing it permanently'. Unfortunately this was not carried out.

So far, from the evidence of the eastern bay of the nave and the S wall, the construction of the nave appears to have been in the main of Phase Friary 2, basically the eastern 6 bays of the nave, and the later Friary 2 Sub-phase work involving the S wall in bays 7 to 9 with an overlap of these two phases in bays 5 and 6 again of the nave S wall.

Unfortunately, for the main central sector of the nave, evidence is slight, because of the unwillingness of the Antelope Motorcycle Club to allow access. Nevertheless the initial construction of a six bay nave seems likely, though no evidence was recovered for a temporary W end.

Evidence from the North Nave wall

Figures 41 and 50 Section A

Excavation in bays 6 and 7 of the N nave wall revealed, after the removal with pneumatic drills of the reinforced concrete floor of an Air Raid Precaution shelter, Fig. 65a, a trench-built wall at dressed stone level, of apparently a wider width at 1.2m (3ft 11in) than that of the nave wall at the S; there were one, or sometimes two, offset courses of footings, giving a foundation trench at its widest of 30cm (1ft), but this was only revealed on the S side. This implies a wall at foundation level of some 1.70m (5ft 7in), this again being wider than the usual measurement for the S wall. A sewer cut through the wall revealed footings continuing down at a depth of 1.2m (4ft).

The S face, in green sandstone, was whitewashed. The course below was red sandstone set in pink mortar, the mixture indicating uncompleted wall building of Friary 2 Sub-phase or perhaps even earlier.

Buttress 6 was abnormally long 2.43m (8ft) at foundation level. It was cut into what seemed to be a cess pit which contained 14th-century potsherds; its built length above foundation level is not known.

There was clearly no doorway present in bay 7 or bay 8.

North wall of Nave with the turn for the west end

This trench, dug unofficially in International Computers Ltd's yard, revealed a wide W wall of 1.65m (5ft 5in) width at foundation level, a buttress continuation of the N wall 2.13m (7ft) long, and a curiously placed buttress, basically a continuation of the W wall, but offset to the E. This was 1.1m (3ft 8in) wide, wider than the other buttress which continued the N wall to the W. Despite these anomalies the various structures appeared to be all of one build.

A curious feature (62 IX 2) occurred in the internal NW corner of the nave at this point; this was a collection of tiles of mixed date, Fig. 141, erratically laid in mortar, with indications of having had a square or rectangular-based object, with rounded corners, set into mortar laid over the faces of the tiles. This may have been the base of a holy water stoup. The tiles represented included numbers 11, 12, 15, 24, 29, 34, 62a, 65, 66a, 71, 79a and 97 (see discussion in Section L, *Late 14th and 15th Century Stamped Floor Tile*).

The Arcade Piers

Five piers were excavated, at the S only the heavily robbed pier 1 at the E, but at the N the two eastern piers 1 and 2, and the two western piers 7 and 8 were excavated. They were identical, indicating presumably an intention to continue the nave westwards to the early design. However, the evidence from the N and S nave walls indicated different methods of construction, particularly at the W, and so presumably also of intermittent phases of building activity. The dating of pier 7 at the N to the later 15th century means that the nave did not have a preliminary layout at foundation level with a nine bay nave; it is possible that a nave with only six bays was the primary intention, and such a nave indeed seems to have been largely constructed in the Friary 2 Phase.

The piers presumably carried a similar 11cm (4½in) chamfer to that surviving on the NW side of the second SW tower pier, which in fact duplicates exactly the shape of the arcade piers. The form of the pier bases at the next level is known from the recovery of a complete section, Section F, *The Architectural Stonework* Nos 1246-7, Fig. 76. The dimension of these piers below any such chamfer, but 5cm (2in) above medieval floor level, was 1.22m x 84cm (4ft x 2ft 9in). The standing column, as reduced above the base mouldings, would have been slender, probably rising to a small or indeed absent capital, presumably with a view to allowing the largest number of people possible a clear view of the pulpit in this large preaching nave.

Pier 1 at the N retained a setting-out mark, two lines at right angles, as did pier 7, again at the N, with here a cross at the N, and simple lines at the W and E, and the mortar impression of an X from the stone above, Figs 41-42. This pier survived 5cm (2in) above floor level and was whitewashed. A later 15th-century jetton of group A2 of the French Derivative type was recovered from the minuscule 'construction trench' of this pier, confirming that the nave piers had not been all constructed as foundations in the Friary 2 Phase.

Window Glass

Very little was recovered from the nave, and that virtually all clear, with a limited amount of yellow staining. See Section J, *Medieval Window Glass from the Church and Cloister*, Fig. 131 for the W end and the upper section of Fig. 132 for the E end of the nave.

Burials

No burials were recorded for the main body of the nave, but they must have existed; these will have been destroyed by the 1980s road works (pers. comm. by road engineers and M. Redknap). What is known of the burials in the easternmost bay of the nave is detailed above.

15 NIGHT STAIR AND SACRISTY

Figures 21, 30 and 43-46

The night stair, Figs 43 and 21, was located at the NE corner of the surviving E cloister range. This was to take the friars into the church for nocturnal prayers. It survived into the late 18th-earlier 19th centuries. The 1800 survey in the Aylesford Collection, Fig. 30, shows an L-shaped construction, with the short leg emerging in a northerly direction from the traditional position of a monastic dorter at the NE corner of the E claustral range. It proceeds down a short flight of some half dozen steps, to an elegant windowed landing, Fig. 46, from whence it descends to the E by a flight of some dozen steps, debouching originally into the passage that linked the sacristy with the chancel, immediately to the W of the doorway that led into that passage from the sacristy N wall; recent damage had removed detail at footings level, Fig. 43.
The passage walls are not shown on the 1800 survey, the E wall having presumably been demolished at the same time as the church (in 1969 its E wall was shown to be overlain with 16th-century cobbling) although its line certainly survived as a cobbled path into the late 18th century, and pottery from the overlying deposit (69 XXIX 8a) indicates that this was an 18th-century gentry occupation deposit (Section R, *The Medieval and Later Pottery* Nos 76-86, Fig. 155). There are also indications of a Gothick porch in the area in, e.g. Storer's engraving of the Whitefriars for the *Beauties of England and Wales* (Britton and Brayley 1810).

The use of the northern third of the 'dorter' in actual fact as a *studium generale*, as attested by the form of its windows, apparently constructed to light carrels, may mean either that this was in fact not only a night, but also a day stair from an upper floor working area.
The western part of the stair structure would not appear in the archaeological record, as it was corbelled out. It was noted in 1969 that the footings that survive in the ground of the eastern sector of the night stair are secondary to the cloister, to a buttress to that cloister at its NE corner, to the N wall of the sacristy and to the passage between the sacristy and the chancel, and indeed they stop short of that passage's W wall. This stair may also be a later medieval attempt to respect the privacy of use of the building that replaced the earlier sacristy, through which it is possible that a descent from the dorter area to the chancel was previously made.

A first night stair may be suggested by the position of the first floor doorway leading into the upper part of the sacristy, but this could well have had another use. It seems a little curious for a night stair to lead into the presbytery, but the position of the tower so much further W than normal presumably gave little choice.

Sacristy/Hales Chapel

This account is based on firstly the rescue recording of 1969 by C and P Woodfield for MPBW after damage to the N wall by machining, and secondly a clearance in 1977 previous to landscaping by the Herbert Art Gallery and Museum of the E sacristy area.
Figures 20, 25, 30, 38 and 43

This building was some 5m (16ft 6in) wide in both phases Friary and Friary 1, and 10.5m (34ft 6in) long internally in its first, Friary, phase, measured from the present external wall of the cloister to the estimated inner face of the easternmost E wall.

It would be natural to assume that the primary diagonal buttresses found in 1977 were the same as the diagonal buttresses attested on the 1800 survey, Fig. 30, but the measurement given in the 1800 survey for the length of this building corresponds with the inner fragment of the eastern wall found in 1969, Fig. 43, which in any case appeared then to be part of the later narrower sacristy phase, and this last was noted in addition to appear to have been added to the primary footings of the N wall, and to have contained green sandstone, not ever present in primary work, but thought to date from the later 15th-earlier 16th century.

The sequence then appears to have been that of a longer primary sacristy, with originally diagonal buttresses supporting both eastern corners. The two eastern buttresses do not appear to have been built at the same time, for they are set at disparate angles, assuming there has been no fault in the 1977 planning (there is no photographic cover of the NE buttresses). A buttress seems to have been added to the N cloister wall at the E at this stage, for there was a straight joint at this point. Presumably there were already signs of structural failure.

There seems to have been a break in building, this then continuing with the north-eastern section of the sacristy wall, later buttresses at right angles reinforcing the diagonal buttress at the NE corner. The northern sacristy wall appeared to be of one build with these diagonal buttresses and with the eastern wall of the passage. The existence of the buttress added to the N cloister wall seems to have fixed the position of the N wall of the sacristy, which is rather oddly offset to the N, though this may be in part to allow for the stairs.

This first sacristy had wide footings to the S and E with foundations 2m, (6ft 6in) wide, and the standing walls at 1.15m (3ft 9in) were also of unusual width. The fact that this structure was coeval with the cloister is shown by the fact that the original southern wall of the sacristy was bonded into that structure.

In the Rebuild Phase the sacristy was rebuilt, Fig. 20, with narrower walls, a four-light E window, and two two-light windows to the S, but no windows to the N, and diagonal stepped buttresses to the ground floor only. Fig. 25 shows what may well have been the remains of the diagonal SE buttress to this second phase. The equivalent NE buttress would have been cut about by a sewer trench, but traces of what might have been its footings were recorded in 1969, and again partially in 1977. If these were the buttress footings they seem likely to have formed a polygonal or rectangular platform for that NE diagonal buttress.

Fig. 25 further attests the existence of a close-framed upper storey, with two four-light timber windows, and another apparently of two lights, all at the first floor timbered level on the S wall, and a small two-light window on the E face at the NE corner. There is nothing apparent on this drawing to prevent this structure being of late medieval date, and it is likely to be coeval with the rebuilt night stair. The very wide first N wall of the vestry at the W is presumably because it was related to the descending staircase in some manner. Fig. 25 also records the N aspect with a door into the sacristy and an upper storey with apparently two three-light windows.

Both the 1800 survey and the 1969 work give an internal length for this rebuilding as 8.23-8.53m (27-28ft). The Woodfield survey indicates some 8.07m (26ft 6in) to the inner of the two eastern walls as does the Museum HAGM survey; offsets would of course add a further few millimetres. The width remained the same, as the new walls were on the internal faces of the old.

It was noted in 1969 that the foundations in this area attest generally to the usual structural problems caused by quarrying on this site. The thickness of the N wall of the sacristy W of the passage (though this might relate to the stairs), and the presence of an additional polygonal buttress (possibly post-Reformation for its packing contained lead calmes) W of the night stair footing, the recording of natural rock at high level just within the NE corner of the sacristy but not elsewhere on the actual sacristy site, all attest the usual quarry problems. The considerable width of the original wall footings (2m) must relate to a perceived instability problem.

The surviving scar on the standing building shows that the sacristy consisted of two storeys in stone in its original form. It is not possible to be certain why the decision was taken to rebuild it, but it is not impossible that it partially, or even totally, collapsed. The thin replacement walls, 0.8m (2ft 9in) wide at ashlar level with their green stone and the use of timber framing for the first floor storey, suggest both that the reduction of weight was an important consideration, and that the date was late in the Middle Ages. A post-Dissolution date is ruled out for the ground floor by the tracery, attested in Figs 20 and 25.

The narrower rebuild noted in 1969 was particularly clear on the S wall, involving the use of green sandstone, here with a coarse pebbly mortar, and including work to the better surviving S face of the doorway in the N wall.

The rebuilding of the N wall clearly involved rebuilding that doorway (and reflooring, of which activity a fragment survived the June 1969 machining). The doorway position is likely to have been original, however, and is so attested by surviving details on its N face. The apparent blocking stones recorded at the same time may have been merely to raise the level of the walk, for the doorway survived to appear in the 1800 survey.

The unexpected June 1969 destruction of the interior of the building without record makes interpretation difficult for its precise use.

Various stone and timber features were recorded in July in a thin surviving strip against the internal face of the N wall. There seemed to be red clay deposits probably associated with an early floor, and a green floor makeup of the later medieval period.

Passage from Sacristy to Presbytery

Figure 43

This seems again to be of the same (slightly later) phase, Friary 1, as the northern wall of the sacristy, for it was again noted in 1969 that there was a partial butt joint between the N wall of the presbytery and the W wall of the passage. That sacristy N door and passage are of the same date is indicated by the similarity of door and splay mouldings. Presumably these are time differences within basically the same construction phase.

The W passage wall does in fact relate rather oddly to the chancel buttress spacing, but this is perhaps merely caused by the necessity for the passage entrance into the chancel not to conflict with the position of the choir-stalls. (It is assumed that the large stones planned in 1977 in the missing buttress position are paving, but unfortunately there is no description of this area.)
This doorway into the presbytery again showed signs of later altering on its eastern side.

The passage walls showed signs of having been rebuilt by Hales, and parts of his sandstone cobbling flooring survived in 1969.

Well 2 and the well yard

Figure 43

A 1977 plan survives and a note that F.18 was a 'red plastic clay surround' to the well (the F.18, presumably fill of a construction trench, pottery suggests a 16th-century date, apparently Hales Phase.). It does not appear that the well was emptied.

The yard to the W of the passage is a curious feature, Fig. 43. Finds indicate a pot scatter and metalworking in the yard in the Friary 1 period, making the presence of Grave 46, with its implication of consecrated ground, surprising, this being identified in 1969 after being damaged by the builders. There was no trace of a coffin, and the bone material recovered has been subsequently lost. Another burial was referred to by HAGM but there are no details, and there is no other record from the clearing undertaken in this area. There was much 16th-century activity, or at least rubbish dumping. Pit 11 contained 16th and 17th-century tankards and cups continuing that tradition, as did the *c.*1800 gentry pot scatter (Section R, *The Medieval and Later Pottery* Nos 72-74a and 76-86, Fig. 155).

18th-century garden wall

Figures 23 and 42

This turned back to the cloister wall at the point shown on Fig. 42, E of the SE transept, presumably defining the end of the 'polite' garden. The form of its associated gate is partially shown on Fig. 23 (extreme left). This was a high quality ashlar wall in green sandstone.

16 THE CHAPTER HOUSE

Figures 18, 38, 48 and 34 (reconstruction)

The Records: 1973 and 1975

No written records survive from 1973 (the western section of the chapter house) or 1975 (the eastern section), except for a conventionalised draw-up of the not used western section of the chapter house, dating possibly from 1973.

The photographs for 1973 (none in 1975, for the photographs and some slides so labelled are in fact of the Benedictine Priory chapter house) are almost entirely of graves and not of structure; little can be said about either.

Skeletal material survives labelled 1975, 1978 and 'uncertain'. Grave 75.3, apparently a disturbed relic of the 73.3 grave, Fig. 48, from under the baulk, appeared to be that of a young male but only part of the cranium, eroded tibiae and the right femur survived excavation. As in the eastern range of the cloister, where burials are known to have existed, though unplanned, these are likely to be burials of friars, presumably of greater seniority if buried in the chapter house. Male patrons are likely in the W of the chapter house.

No graves appear to have been excavated in 1977, but it is not apparent that any were looked for. It seems unlikely that burials would stop neatly on the eastern line of the 1973 baulk, and indeed the 1800 drawing referred to below makes it clear that burials existed in this area.

The remains of burials apparently from three earth graves were found in the 1990s in a box marked 'Chapter House 1978' and described as from 'underneath the ?18th-century blocking at the W end' of that structure. There are no other records or plans of these graves, and little could be said by Kibberd (Section W, *Human Skeletal Analysis*) about their largely lost contents. An important grave is known to have been in this area, for William Lubbenham, Provincial of the English Carmelite province, is recorded as being buried in front of the entrance to the chapter house in 1361 (McCaffrey 1926, 244).

The lack of professional competence displayed by the above account should not have been acceptable in the excavation of a major building of European importance in a major English medieval city.

Archaeological features?

In 1977 the whole chapter house was re-excavated in advance of consolidation. Two features/layers were recorded. The recording runs currently with the choir, which explains the spacing of the 'feature' numbers.

F.38 was a canoe-shaped strip some 0.6m (2ft) wide, 4m (13ft) long, tapering to a point at the E end and squared off at the W. The fill of stone rubble, clay and mortar flecks suggests it had been dug through the floor. Its depth was not recorded, but its form, and the stepping apparently within this feature rather mitigates against its having any archaeological meaning. It ran roughly parallel within the N wall, at a distance to its S of half a metre, between the area of buttresses 2 and 3, as numbered from the W. Might it have been a *sondage* of the 26 Junior Leaders in 1975? (It has been omitted from the plan.).

F.73 (double numbered with grave 3 in the choir) seems to have been a small area of ?16th-century destruction towards the E of the site (no plan).

The 1977 drawn-up plan is more informative than the 1973 plan, which conflated the two phases of the building into one. Additionally the 1973 drawing seems to record a drainage hole in the centre of one of the northern buttresses (which would be of importance as a parallel with the work of John of Gaunt at Kenilworth). However, the 1977 drawing, and the only 1973 photograph of structure, show this to be eccentric, and to cut the later paving, and it has been omitted.

USE AND STRUCTURE

Figures 9, 20, 30, 34, 38 and 48

Fig. 48 is based on a combination of surviving drawings, photographs, the exposed remains, and the evidence of historical documents.

The chapter house was used for the daily chapter, confessions, business matters and punishments. It was the place where the Visitor conducted his enquiries into the running of the friary. It was here that the Confraternity would have been conferred on Sir Henry Willoughby, Fig. 55, and where he would have been allocated a seat. The western four bays would give an equal amount of seating to that provided by the choir-stalls, with a raised eastern bay for the prior's seat, and a western vestibule.

As surviving, and as recorded in 1977, the chapter house in its second (Friary 1a) phase was a structure of just under some 19.5m (63ft 9in) long, with 5 bays of 3.9m (12ft 9in), the westernmost bay being inserted into the pre-existing cloister, providing the vestibule, which may have been used as a small library, as at Fountains Abbey. A sixth, raised, bay is now suggested at the E, partly on account of the requirements of logic in the vaulting, and because a Troughton drawing, Fig. 30, of *c.*1800, indicates the rectangular remains of such an extension in this sixth bay position. This was not realised at the time (1977) to be an extension of the chapter house; on the *c.*1800 drawing the western part is labelled 'Burying Ground' and the eastern part 'tomb', this latter, not taken on board, apparently being a burial of some structural solidity in front of the altar; presumably a prior's grave.

The existing E wall to the ruins of the chapter house is, of course, post-Reformation. There are no records of this area being examined during any excavation, despite the 1990s appearance here of the 1978 burials mentioned above, apparently from below this blocking wall, which was in place in the late 18th century; the gothic window set in it is of 19th-century date, Fig. 26. The width of the building is double that of the bay measurement, at 7.8m (25ft 7in).

There are difficulties in establishing the details of the earlier building, as there was no consistent exposure of footings to any one phase, and the records do not make it clear when one is, or is not, looking at offset ashlar set in mortar, or the wider undressed footings set in clay (the norm on this site as recorded since 1960). An attempt was made to show masonry surviving at a higher level, but this is unfortunately not helpful in this instance. In addition the photographic cover of structure is quite inadequate.

However, it does appear that the walls of the second phase building are narrower than the 14th-century norm at 0.8m (2ft 7in) - (the E wall of the cloister stands at some 1.25m (4ft 1in)). An earlier, apparently ashlar, wall beneath the N and S walls of the chapter house of 1.2-1.3m (3ft 11in-4ft 3in) is discernible in places, and this wall is visible at the E with its own footings taking its width up to 1.95m (6ft 5in). This last is now interpreted as a raised sanctuary, providing a seat for the prior at the E end, as would be expected, and which would make more sense than a wall of this exceptional width. There are further complications where the N and S walls butt on to the standing structure. This, and the unusual triangular buttresses, with their John of Gaunt and Kenilworth connections, are discussed by Paul Woodfield (Section D 4, *The Chapter House Reconstruction*). The buttresses suggest a date of the later 14th century for this structure, as does the surviving vault.

Seating

No traces of seating against the long sides of the chapter house were recorded, but there are still slight indications that these existed.

Window glass

Some cusped tracery window glass survives from that

found in the Whitefriars Chapter House, and is illustrated on Fig. 132.23-30 (Section J, *Medieval Window Glass from the Church and Cloister).* Researchers should be aware that some window glass labelled Whitefriars is actually from the chapter house of the Benedictine Priory.

Floor tiles

Considerable amounts of presumably medieval floor mortar survived in 1973, but if there was a visible matrix, there is no plan, and there is no record of the floor tiles that survived *in situ* in 1975.

Several different patterns of floor tiles are, however, recorded from the chapter house, and the provenance here seems reliable due to the tiles being marked. The main category represented was large early tiles of the 'endless repeating' patterns, Nos 30, 32a and 34-5 (Section L, *Late 14th and 15th Century Stamped Floor Tile*, Fig. 139) representing seventeen tiles in all, eleven being of type 30. Tiles 34 and 35 were recorded only in the chapter house. It is possible that these tiles, particularly 30, were used as a grave cover and were those that survived *in situ* due to subsidence, see grave 31 in the NE nave. Large early four-tile patterns, Figs 138-40, included 20a, 20b and 26, also 44 - a single pattern tile - of which 4 survived, this being a pattern that only occurred in the chapter house. The impression is of an original floor of sophisticated floral and leaf patterns. Small later tiles, Fig. 145, show the introduction of heraldry, 104, 108, 109, 112, and 113, and another version of the 'endless repeating' tile No 120 with a grotesque mask. There were also two examples of a small border tile 127 again with foliage, Fig. 146.

The stone paving outside the chapter house at the North

A sherd of 18th-century pottery was visible in a red sandy matrix beneath the stone paving against the N wall in 1995, presumably the date of that paving.

17 THE AREA SE OF THE CLOISTER

Figures 49 and 52A Sections J and K

A corridor range from the cloister running S, forming the E side of the inner court and leading to the shortened reredorter (replaced just pre Reformation by a workshop) and on to the prior's house with the founder's chamber above occurred here.

This area was 'cleared of obviously Victorian overburden' by the Herbert Art Gallery and Museum in 1977-78 (John Bateman *in litt.* 1992) 'with no examination below floor surfaces' with incomplete recording and no attempt at establishing sequences or dating, with unacceptable interpretations (slaughter house and/or novices court for the reredorter), i.e. it was not an excavation as normally understood. It has presented very considerable difficulties of interpretation.

Some elements remain certain. There is a N-S corridor range some 26m (85ft 6in) long, represented by walls 61, 89 and 100, of the Friary Phase. There are hints of southern, eastern and western extensions, indicated by dotted lines on plan, presumably of this phase, representing the Prior's House. These walls presumably enclose the decorated medieval tile floor of the prior's hall (Section L, *Late 14th and 15th Century Stamped Floor Tile*, tile patterns 3-10, Figs 136-7) which confirms the suggested primary date. The evidence for the prior's house and Founders chamber is presented in *The Whitefriars in Coventry – Historical Background (Section B).* Further confirmation for this corridor range being medieval, and additionally two storied, is confirmed by there being a surviving door coming out into that upper storey from the S end of the standing Friary Phase cloister building. It is assumed that it is primary, as the removal of its (much altered) two-storey N wall has left a scar on the standing building, which it is unlikely to have done if an addition had been removed. The upper floor is presumably open or semi-open as the E wall (F.89) is narrower, presumably carrying less weight. This N-S range is too narrow for living space, and is clearly a corridor.

F.105 is a (partly planned) stub of a wall which from its width and apparent character (no straight joint at the W) should be medieval and from this first phase, running E from the N-S range, apparently of coeval build, just S of the reredorter. Its existence implies other medieval buildings S of the reredorter, perhaps a cross wing to the Prior's House. The decorated tile floor (Section L, *Late 14th and 15th Century Stamped Floor Tile*, Figs 136-7) from its tile size, type and layout is of primary Friary Phase date, but there is later patching, including brick, up indeed to the 17th or 18th century, judging by the photographic evidence (the floor was not lifted, but it is not certain if it survives machining for landscaping). The boundary of the tile floor to the N is not known, nor is its precise position (but two separate calculations for this, using photographic evidence, made by C. and P. Woodfield, produced two positions within 45cm (18in) of each other, and any error in positioning should be slight). There are indications that the tile floor was paved over with large paving slabs, presumably in the 18th century, at a level about 30cm (1ft) above the level of that medieval floor.

There are no records suggesting how the rest of the N-S range might have been floored in the medieval period.

The documentary evidence (Section B, *The Whitefriars in Coventry – Historical Background*) indicates strongly that a two-storied Prior's House stood hereabouts, with a Founder's Chamber above, and the tiled-floor is most likely to have been in the prior's hall.

A medieval drain F.119 seems to have run through a doorway (as is normal), presumably serving the prior's house, or it may have turned and helped to flush the early reredorter. In the absence of full records and analysis both these are possible.

Shortened Reredorter

Just over half way down the corridor, on its eastern side, lay a (now reduced) two-storied reredorter, clearly curtailed in a later period. Its original size is not known. On its ground floor it had double arched arcades at some 3m (10ft) centres on its long N and S sides. From parallels these will be low arches not much more than 1.15m (3ft 9in) high, and are to enable access for cleaning out, i.e. they are unlikely to have architectural embellishments. These appeared to be of one build with the E wall of the N-S corridor, (although it is true that the junctions were not well preserved). It is also true that the obvious parallels, Muchelney, and Vale Crucis (pers. ob.), are post 14th century, but there seems no reason to doubt the primary nature of the pier bases. It is quite clear that a church supplied with choir-stalls for seating 90 persons would not originally have had a reredorter of this small size, and we cannot be looking at a plan of the whole building; however the pier bases seemed to be all that was left of the first period of the reredorter.

No excavation took place under the reredorter floor, so there is no evidence for earlier drainage systems, nor the primary paving. It should be noted that Section J, Fig. 52A, does not proceed downwards below this later paved surface, and we have no idea what underlay it or whether it survived the landscaping.

Reredorter

Sixteenth-Century Rebuild 2, (Pre-Reformation 1): c.1520 to c.1535

There was an ingenious arrangement of what must have been secondary pitched paving for sluicing purposes, with a projecting apron to the N and S (largely destroyed at the S) catching water from two ground drains (F.84, and probably F.118 although this last is only planned at the W) coming through perhaps from a prior's kitchen in the inner court, and probably from the water spouts on the reredorter roof, (and perhaps from adjacent roofs to the N-S range, which would help further to explain the apron formed by the paving). The use of rainwater spouts in this way is attested at Raglan Castle's pitched yard (there 16th century, but with a 15th century predecessor; pers. ob.). Such a structure in this position and of this form is most unlikely to be anything but a monastic reredorter. This paving must be secondary, as it is in green sandstone, which does not come into use until the later 15th century and afterwards in the church, where it is most conspicuously related to late buttressing of the tower. The paving showed signs of being shattered by frost, particularly at its eastern end, presumably the most exposed. Clearly it was not in use in an enclosed building.

The presence of a very large drain 1.56m (5ft 3in) wide (later narrowed to 30cm (1ft) in the Pre-reformation 2 period) with its accompanying rebuilt wall forming the new reredorter E wall, confirms the reredorter function. The area E of the E reredorter wall was not recorded, and it is unclear what happened to the reredorter drain as it left that structure. The photographic evidence suggests disturbance at this point, probably related to the insertion of a wall of the workhouse period which ran parallel to the E wall of the reredorter.

Wall 88 which bounds the reredorter paving to the N, also resembles very late 16th-century work in the church (e.g. the narrow, part single stone, boundary wall attached to the N porch). It is not clear if it was contemporary or added, but appears to be the first, which is the reason for the date suggested.

There was a door between NE pier F.96 and wall F.88, attested by an iron pin still in its structure to its S, and a small rebate to its N, presumably to give access for cleaning the reredorter paving.

Wall F.99 is not only not primary, but itself of two phases (firstly as the E wall of the shortened reredorter, and secondly presumably as the wall of the later workshop/fabrica, below).

Dr Glyn Coppack comments 'I have no difficulties with a prior's lodging adjacent to the reredorter block. It was an idea first championed by the Cistercians and can still be seen at Fountains and Rievaulx. It would not surprise me if the prior also had access to the friar's dormitory through their latrine, because it provides an element of supervision or control. Because most reredorters were water-flushed, smell was not a problem'.

Workshop/Fabrica

Pre-Reformation 2: c.1535

Figures 49 and 52A

Subsequently the floor of the reredorter was levelled off

(Fig. 52A Section J) with layer 92c with its demolition material producing 16th-century pottery (and food bone including small birds) to date this activity; this was one of less than half a dozen groups of stratified material from the whole of this area. It was then overlaid with a yellow mortar floor of which little appeared on section, but was just visible in photographs. Over this a 'grey level' is recorded (most of these levels are not in the notebook/context sheets), 'grey' elsewhere being ash. The 'chimney breast', Fig. 49, 104a and 104 b, must be inserted, as this is not going to occur in a reredorter basement (and it looks to be inserted on photographs). The thin-handmade-brick ash pit, Fig. 49, F.112, with coal that appears to go with the chimney breast (there was coal in the Grammar School deposits so its presence is no problem) was also inserted. The levelling of the reredorter and the ash spread, Fig. 52A Section J, suggests an industrial use, and this interpretation is confirmed by evidence of a hearth and ashpit.

Photographs indicate that wall F.108 was lined with very thin bricks on its N face, presumably now, forming some sort of working feature in the SE corner of the workshop, wall 105 having been previously demolished, Fig. 52A Section J. Wall F.108, Fig. 49, does not appear to be coeval with wall 109, the S continuation of the E reredorter wall - it could post date it. The blocking of the big drain apparently involved its own small drain of some 40cm (16in) width internal to the wall, but again draining out to the E (there are virtually no details of this). This period of the blocking of the E reredorter wall, distinguished by 'monolithic offsets', continues to the S (not on plan) for at least 6m (19ft 8in) according to the photographic record, indicating that the hearth (126) area is part of the workshop - again the evidence is from photographs. All this is likely to relate to the documented mid 16th-century, recently built, fabrica/workshop (see Fig. 53 and Section B, *The Whitefriars in Coventry – Historical Background*).

There are some hints of this unplanned, and with only a four word description (including here no photographic record) 'hearth of upright tiles' F.126 some 3m (10ft) or so to the SE of the reredorter. Size again mitigates against this area being a kitchen, and it is more likely a spin off from the workshop, especially with the use of brick.

Division of the main range/corridor into rooms, apparently relating to the workshop

Walls 85, 101 and 102 appear to be inserted into the N-S range at this time (they are narrower than the monastic walls but the same thickness as each other as far as one can tell and appear to have straight joints to the medieval wall). This created two small rooms or stores (the southern one seems likely to have been unlit), and are possibly related to the workshop. The northern one appears to have contained a rectangular working platform of some sort, cut about by a later drain, and there were stakeholes, just possibly a bellows-setting or something similar, but not planned. There were apparently conspicuous charcoal and burnt deposits in this room, as well as food dumps, which may well relate to the fabrica, workshops being frequently food strewn. There seems to be no dating evidence surviving.

Little is known of the southern room, for the entry for F.111, for the area between cross-walls 101 and 102, comments that there are several layers, but tails out at 'a) brown soil prob...'

The northern wall of the whole N-S range was heavily altered and rebuilt. The N doorway in wall 61 stood several courses high, preserving chamfers and stops, which did not prevent its demolition in 1978. An external water tank F.59, 1.2m (4ft) deep - presumably for some industrial purpose - and a drain (Fig. 52A Section K and Fig. 49) were added at this time or thereabouts, material from the latter's fill suggesting a 16th-century date.

It seems likely that wall 87 was of the Fabrica period, and formed a passage to the N of that workshop. Another possibility is that this feature is related in some way to some form of latrine replacing the now defunct main reredorter, for the deposits on pottery from drain 24/34 suggested this. This drain apparently had three rows of brick running longitudinally as its base, as also a brick arch which would equate with this late date.

Post-16th-century walls, drains, etc.

The W-E wall at the N of the site, Fig. 49 presumably Elizabethan and part of Hales' house, whose numbering seems to be F.55, 56, 58 and 63 carried brick and was thought to be that shown in the 1800 survey, Fig. 30, but it does not fall in the position there depicted. It appears to have been constructed at a higher level than other walls present. The very slender walls 106 and 107, apparently brick, S of the reredorter area, may be later garden walls. It is unfortunate that the length of occupation of the main range/corridor is unclear; it seems to have gone by 1800.

A pair of drains (F.83) running E, and a drain of similar construction (F.33) seem post medieval.

The unplanned plaster floor at the extreme SE of this area, Fig. 49, mentioned in the written records but not planned, seems likely from the height at which it appears on photographs to be fairly late, perhaps 18th century.

Paving is attested in photographs of the area N of the ? Prior's House tiled-floor, running N past earlier drain F.118 and some fragments are planned.

Walking over the site in July 1995, 18th-century pottery was observed in red sand under the paving N of the chapter house, and it is likely that the paving in this range was of the same date.

Other parts of the site

Undated

There are no records of what was found W of the N-S corridor range, although it is known that the trench extended to its W for a metre or more. It was presumably then that the well marked on Fig. 49, subsequently rebuilt in the 1980s on unknown evidence and now vandalised, was found. There are no records for this well.

What appeared to be the remains of two stone walls (and unrecognised robber trenches) F.136-7, 139 and 140 (not indicated on plan, as the record is rough sketches only) continued the line of wall 89, the E wall of the N-S range, to the S. It is assumed that one of these was medieval and formed a boundary to the ? Prior's House tiled-floor. Walls 134 and 135 at right angles to this were also sketched.

18 THE CLOISTER

Figures 47, 50 and 52B

Examination was made of the NW corner of the cloister garth, in 1964 and again in 1968, primarily to see if the cloister had been completed and whether there had been a double range of buildings here at the W. It was also under threat from the intended road works. The form of the cloister gate (Figs 12, 30 and 35; demolished in 1956 by the Corporation, not, as currently maintained, by the Luftwaffe) had suggested that the W range of the cloister was certainly not double at its southern end. The internal NW corner of the cloister survived as a red sandstone base foundation, overlaid with some 5-7cm (2-3in) of hard red sandy clay which had concealed it from the stone robbers. The lack of evidence for the cut water buttresses of the cloister E range (the spacing of the buttresses remained the same with centres of 3.65m (12ft)) suggested a later phase than that E range, which is to be expected, as the urgency of supplying praying, living or working accommodation would be unlikely in this area. The fact that the surviving cloister bay spacing does not match on the N and S ranges is also an indication that this structure is multi-period. The 1964 buttresses were not standing at ashlar level, but were clearly not long enough to carry cut water buttresses similar to those on the standing building.

The cloister was, therefore, as might have been expected, square internally, the dimension being *c.*50.6m (102ft 6in). The foundation found at the internal NW corner of the garth was some 1.15m (3ft 9in) to 1.22m (4ft) wide, a little narrower on the W wall than on the northern wall, but apparently of the same phase. The front arcaded wall of the standing cloister is about 60cm (2ft) wide. There was no diagonal buttress on this internal corner as there had been on the NE internal corner (this has been subsequently removed, but the writer has checked its foundation by excavation) but there was what appeared from wear to be a door cill. The small stones shown on plan on the W side of the doorway were set vertically and resembled post-hole packing. This certainly implies a built wall and working doorway, and therefore presumably a constructed cloister walk here.

The 1968 rescue work sectioned this trench-built (and therefore presumably not later than the Friary 2 Phase) W wall again near the NW corner of the garth, Wall III, Fig. 52B Section L, where four courses survived with a width of some 88cm (2ft 11in), its foundations slenderer and shallower by two courses than the external cloister walk wall. The cloister walk itself was 2.75m (9ft) wide.

No floor or obvious floor makeup survived in the cloister walk. Any tile floor would presumably have been removed at the same time as Wall III was demolished in the 16th century, and floor tiles occurred thinly in 16th-century levels. It is not impossible that it was never floored but more likely that all traces were removed during works for Hales's privy garden.

The expected site of the external cloister walk wall turned out to be occupied by a massive, well-built, deep-foundationed, 16th-century wall, containing in its foundation many arcade pig-nosed mouldings similar to those in the standing cloister wall arcade (raising the question whether the same moulding was used at a later phase to produce a uniform cloister) and was presumably constructed as a garden boundary wall by John Hales during his conversion of the monastic remains to a house, after his demolition of two thirds of the cloister (21 out of the 32 bays.) It was buttressed on its western, external, side, at centres of 6.4m (21ft), with quite substantial 2.1m (4ft 3in) square buttresses at ashlar level. The construction trenches of the 16th-century wall were emptied out to some depth, but there was no clear evidence for the N wall of the N cloister walk in its expected position, though there were slight indications, seen only at the base of the eastern construction trench of Hales' wall some 90cm (3ft) S of its expected position, of a deep structure of uncertain character, consisting of 3 courses of a somewhat sparse spread of thin stones at 1.83m (6ft) depth. Its S edge lay some 60cm (2ft) to the S of the intended N cloister wall to the W.

The 1968 trench (Fig. 52B Section L and Fig. 47) also sectioned Hales' Wall, and found that it had been erected on the remains, only one or two courses deep, of the wall of the external cloister walk. Troughton drawings show this standing with some remnants of vaulting near the cloister gate so it must have been built at the S. This is Wall II on Fig. 52B Section L and has 1.57m (5ft) wide footings, wider, and therefore presumably intended to be higher, than the internal cloister garth wall. However, the fact that it has construction trenches, not normal in early work, and cuts level 10, a spread of green sandstone chippings, and 16, a post 15th-century layer on the pottery evidence, which overlies the unbuilt outer late cloister wall, implies that it is a late medieval footing. A layer of green sandstone fragments were cut for Hales' wall also in trench XXIII, and as there is no evidence in the standing building that he used the green stone, some late medieval building work seems certain to have taken place in this area.

An obvious question is whether the lower portions of Hales' wall are in fact certainly those of the medieval cloister wall. The sequences of layers under Hales's wall in Trench XXVIII, Fig. 50 Section C1, which seem at first glance to be hardly that of a wall, are explicable if it is remembered how little of that wall was itself available for inspection in that trench. The 25cm (10in) wide construction trench cut into natural rock obviously indicates wall construction, and the strip of 'red sand with brown sand including clay with slate and medieval plaster' is explicable if a rough foundation stone course was set slightly back here. The overlay of a band of red clay then equates with the wall construction noted in the NW corner of the cloister garth in 1964, here with one surviving mortared stone course above, with Hales' offset footing above that. The cloister wall butted onto the nave (cutting through the nave wall's wide 'construction' or perhaps false trench) which must have been pre-existing.

If a standing medieval cloister walk existed at the W (as the Troughton drawings and Fig. 30 – here just visible - confirm that it did, why did Hales feel the need to rebuild its outer wall at the N? It seems likely that it was in poor order, and that he needed a strong retaining wall (implied by the buttresses) doubtless to support an internal bank providing a raised walk from which to admire the formal privy gardens which must have occupied the space in front of this part of Hales' Place. Even if he had retained the wall, as he did at the S, the broken remains of the cloister walk vault would not presumably have been acceptable, or 'romantic', in the 16th century, and would have needed to have been covered by earth.

The postulated existence of a standing western double cloister range to match the E cloister range was eliminated in 1968. The area to the W of John Hales' wall revealed, in 1964, Fig. 47, what appeared to be a late medieval ground level under a demolition level of green stone chips, both cut by Hales' construction trench. This ran uphill to the W and was certainly not a floor level. However work had to finish before the trench was taken far enough down to be absolutely conclusive, but the suggestion was that there had been no standing building at this point.

This was confirmed by the 1968 rescue work, which revealed in three trenches, lengths, as recorded from N to S, of the intended outer wall of the double range of 1.57m (5ft 6in) of its W-E course, a 1.1m (3ft 7in) length of wall on its N-S course, and a 7m (23ft) further length of that N-S course. An analysis of the finds from a section, Fig. 52B Section L, suggested a 15th or perhaps early 16th-century date (there was 15th-century pottery in its 15cm (6in) wide construction trench) overlaid by 15th and 16th-century layers and tips. These footings would have given an external cloister range of 3.65m (12ft) width. They were seen to continue to the S for at least 1.52cm (5ft), where they were shortly lost in a deep disturbance at a depth of 2.45m (8ft) to 2.75m (9ft) with tips of large stones that had destroyed all trace of the footings. There was no indication of any robbing trench nor demolition levels, and any intention of constructing a double W cloister range must have been abandoned at this point and the footings had become covered in earth. The (archive) MPBW 1956 plan and drawing of the N elevation of the then surviving remains of the Cloister Gateway also show that this wall had not been constructed at the SW corner of the cloister. The deeper, wider, footings, imply that a two storey range was intended.

At the N this outer wall of the intended range was faced on its E side suggesting the intention of a door. There was a 60cm (2ft) gap between that wall and the rough uncompleted remnants of the wall's return to the E, a space which, although narrow, furnished with the usual offsets at ashlar level, could still have provided a small postern. At the S the wall was fully recorded for a length of 1.2m (4ft in the N of trench XXVII and its eastern face traced for a further 5.8m (19ft)).

Does the Bond money of 1506 for finishing the cloister relate to the construction of these footings or to the fact that they were known to have been abandoned and the money was bequeathed in the hope of completing the work?

A level of what appeared to be red sandstone quarry waste, Fig. 52B Section L layer 1, occurred throughout all the 1968 trenches in this area..

Section L – detail (Fig. 52B)

Trench XXVII sectioned the W range of the cloister from an apparent quarry outlying the intended double range at the W to a few feet into the cloister garth. The first activity on the site is assumed to be the construction of the foundation of the garth wall, trench-built through deposits of red clayey sand with variable amounts of small red sandstone rubble. No ashlar course survived and it seems that any floor would have been at a higher level, now destroyed. The green demolition level overlying it (10) seems to be spread from the demolition of the outer wall of the cloister walk wall II, and the construction of Hales' wall.

The second activity is the construction of the footings only of the unbuilt outer wall, its depth, width and block size implying a double storey intention; its construction trench (4) produced 15th-century pottery. This wall was overlaid by an earthy sand deposit (16) which produced slate roof and floor tile suggesting a date of the 15th century or later. The third activity was the making of a construction trench for the W wall of the cloister garth, a dump from work on this wall (19) containing material from the use of green sandstone. The immediately overlying level of what looked like red stone quarry spoil (1) is of late 15th or 16th-century date, overlain by rubbish layers (2) and (15) also of 16th-century date, (2) producing a chipped tile disc or quoit, normally a sign of School occupation, and layers 5 and 13 must be of this date as they are cut by Hales' wall. Layer 5 appeared to be a ground surface. A date late in the 15th century at the earliest is implied for both outer cloister walls. The green and red sandstone spread (14) presumably relates to demolition of these walls, preceding Hales' garden works.

No burials were found in these examinations. Surviving oblique photographs (Brian Hobley) show what are clearly grave pits of burials which were found in the E cloister range (but not apparently in the cloister walk) in 1973? There are no other records or finds from this activity.

The arrangements made for further examination of the cloister garth, particularly for a check for the existence of a central fountain or other feature, unfortunately came to no fruition, and later much more extensive road works have destroyed the SW area of the cloister and related buildings, including the S walk and presumably the refectory, St John's Hall, kitchens, and probably a provision for studies, without record.

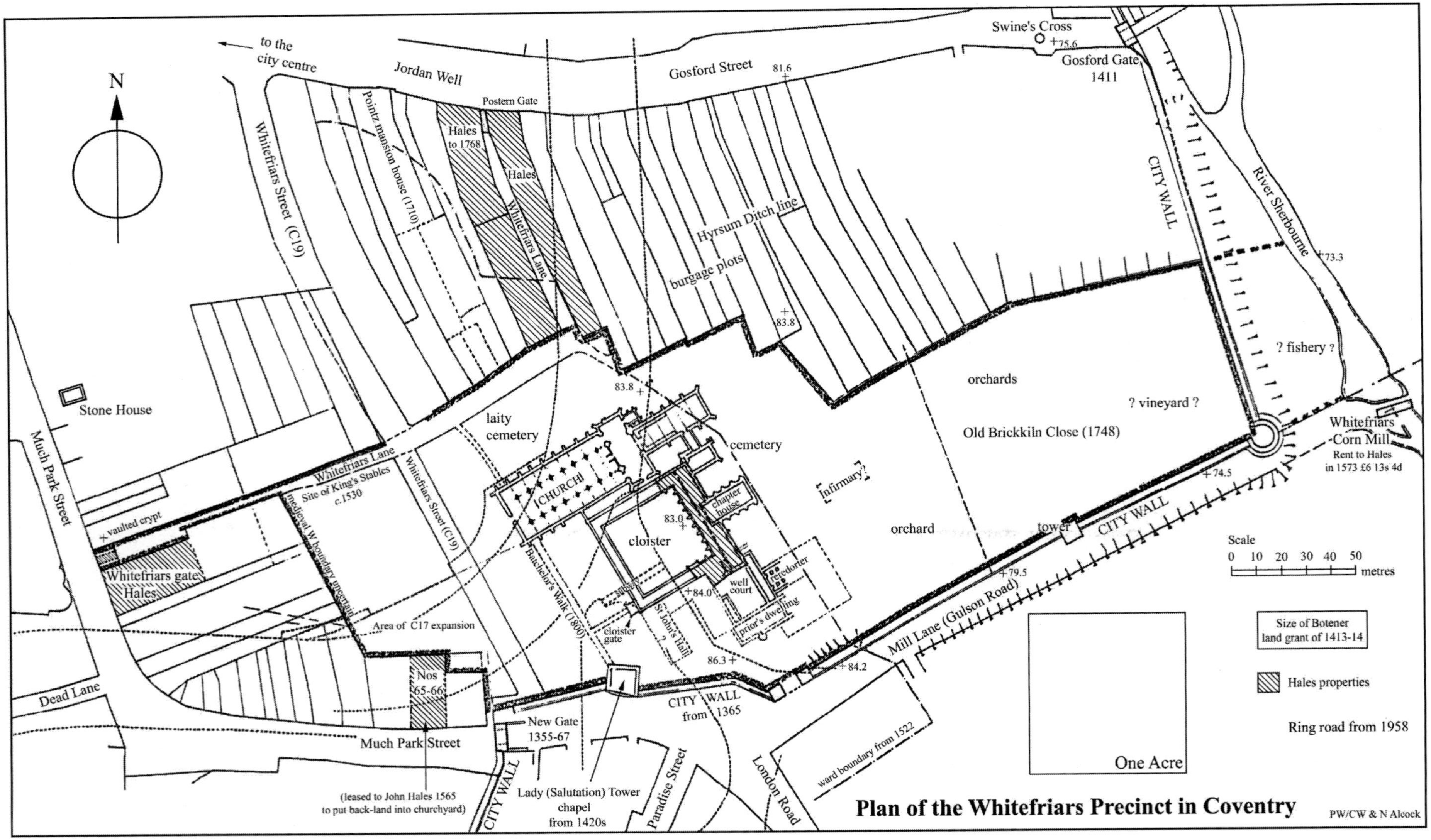

Figure 37 Plan of the Whitefriars Precinct in Coventry, showing access routes from Gosford Street and Much Park Street, and its relation to the later city wall. Dotted lines indicate, at the W the late 1950s/60s ring road, and on the E the then suggested area for landscaping.

Figure 39 Existing 14th-century E cloister walk, looking S. Copyright Warwick University (Troughton XII).

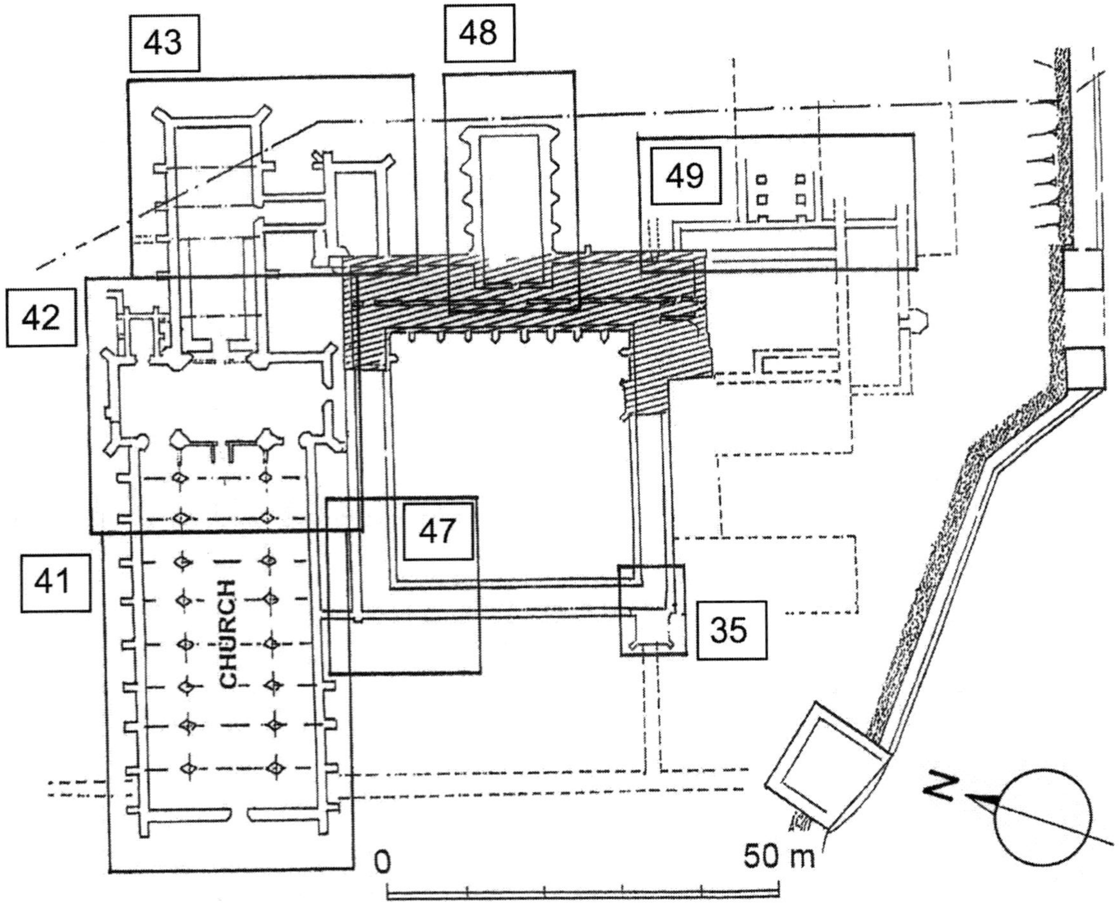

WHITEFRIARS: Key to letters used on the large plans and sections

A	Altar, probable position
D	Door, probable position
F	Feature (+ no), foundation.
G(+no)	Grave, with its number
Q	Quarry-excavation in natural
S	step
Bl	blocked/blocking
bs	beam slot
ct	construction trench
gs	green sand (builder's trample)
gst	green stone used in construction
mt	mortar bedding for tile flooring
nr	natural rock
ns	natural sand
p	pit
pp	scaffold stanchion hole
pd	piscina drain
pm	pit with mosaic tile
ph	post hole
rb	robbed wall or feature
rd	rubble deposit
rs	red sand
rst	red stone used in construction
sj	straight joint in construction
sp	stone pit
t	tile
tm	tile matrix, mortar with imprint of tiles
w	burnt wood
y	yellow mortar

Figure 40 Plan of Whitefriars showing the position of detailed plans and a key showing conventions used on larger scale plans and sections.

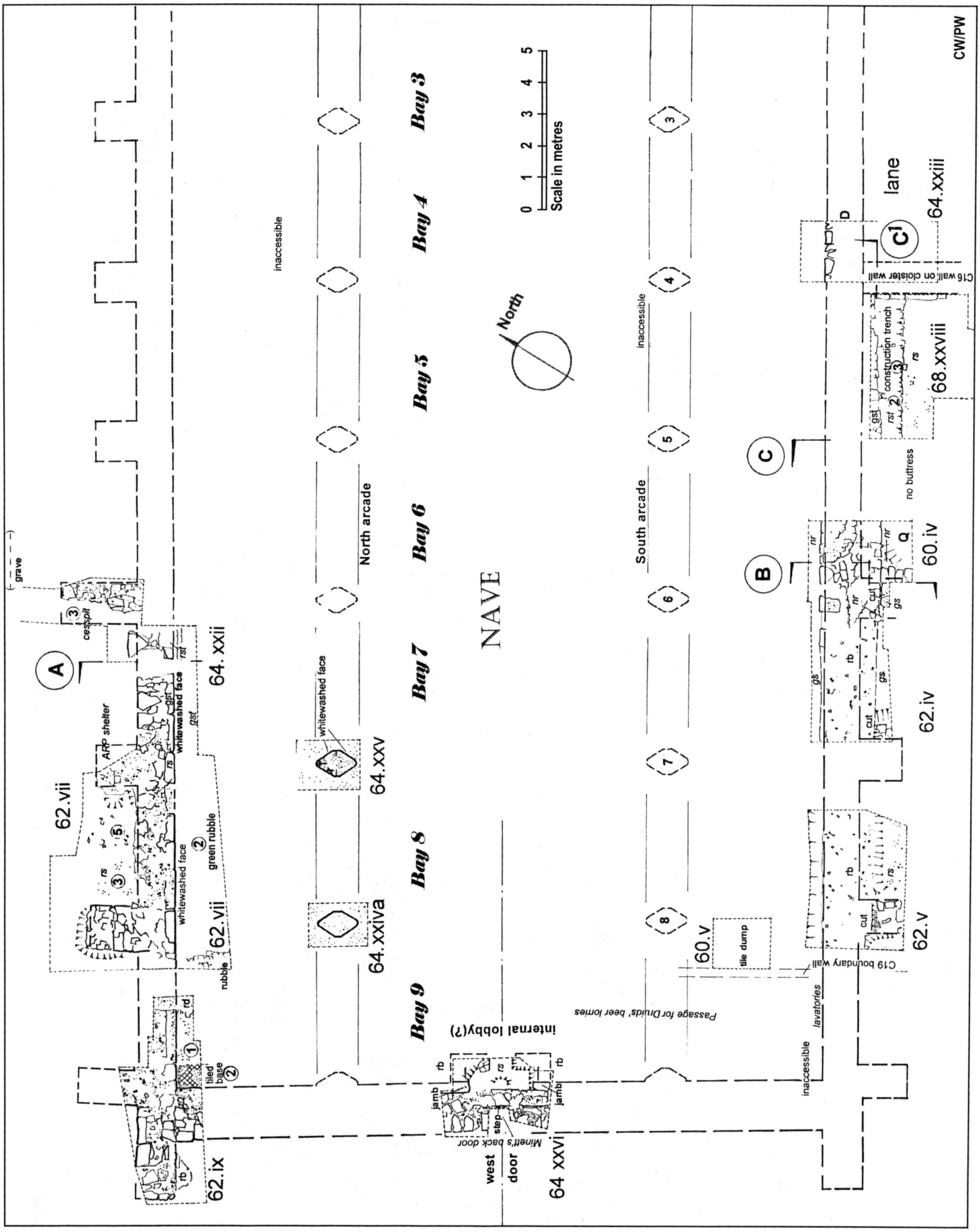

Figure 41 The seven western bays of the nave. Phase 2, *c.*1385-*c.*1423, and Phase 3, *c.*1423 to late 15th century.

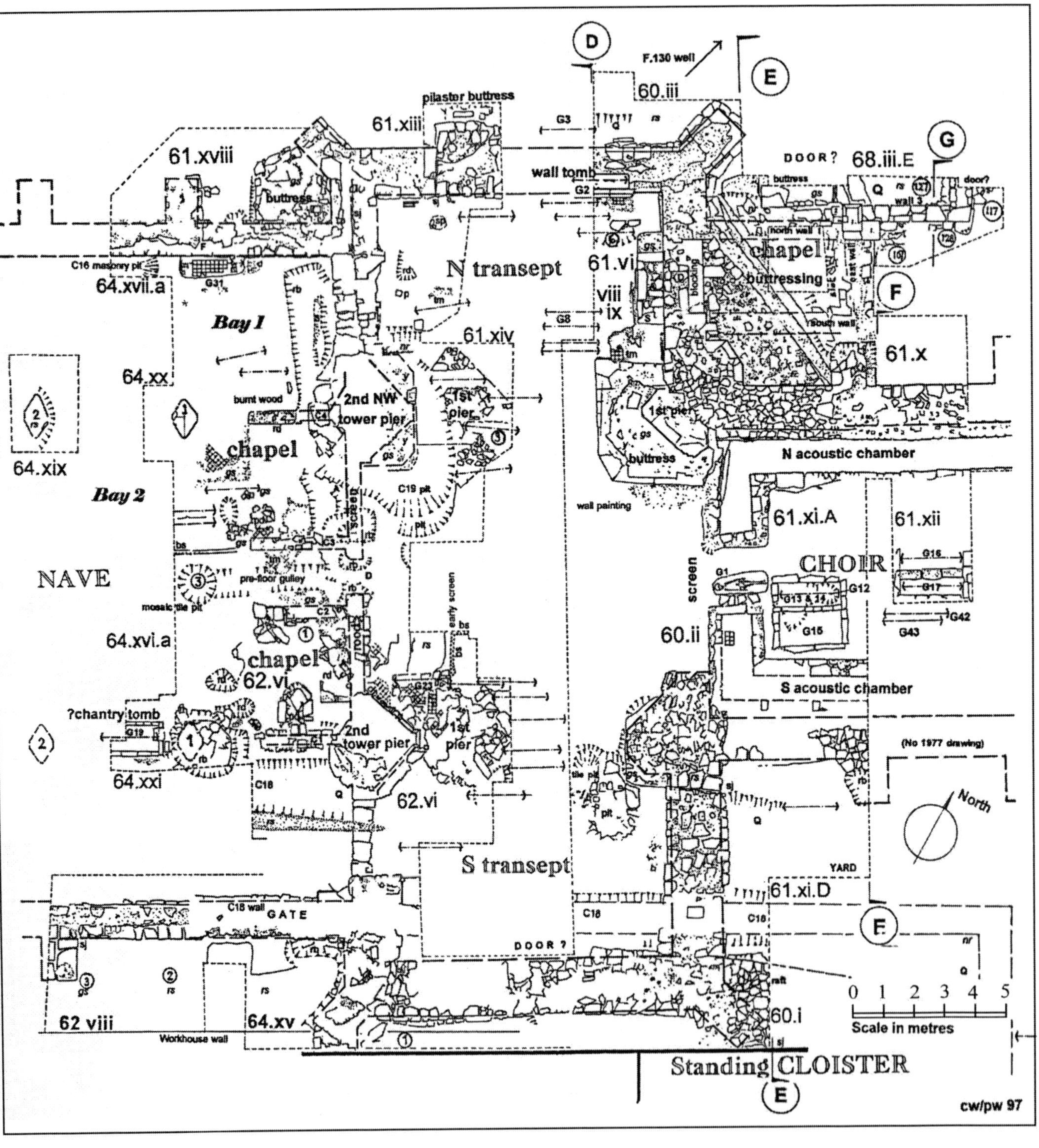

Figure 42 The two eastern bays of the nave, with chapels of Our Lady (N) and the Holy Rood (S). The crossing, with transepts, and remains of the friary lantern, replaced by a tower, and a chapel E of the N transept. Note buttressing to failing tower. Two western bays of choir, with acoustic chambers (resonance passages). Phases 1-6, 1342 to post-Dissolution are represented. See also plan 142.

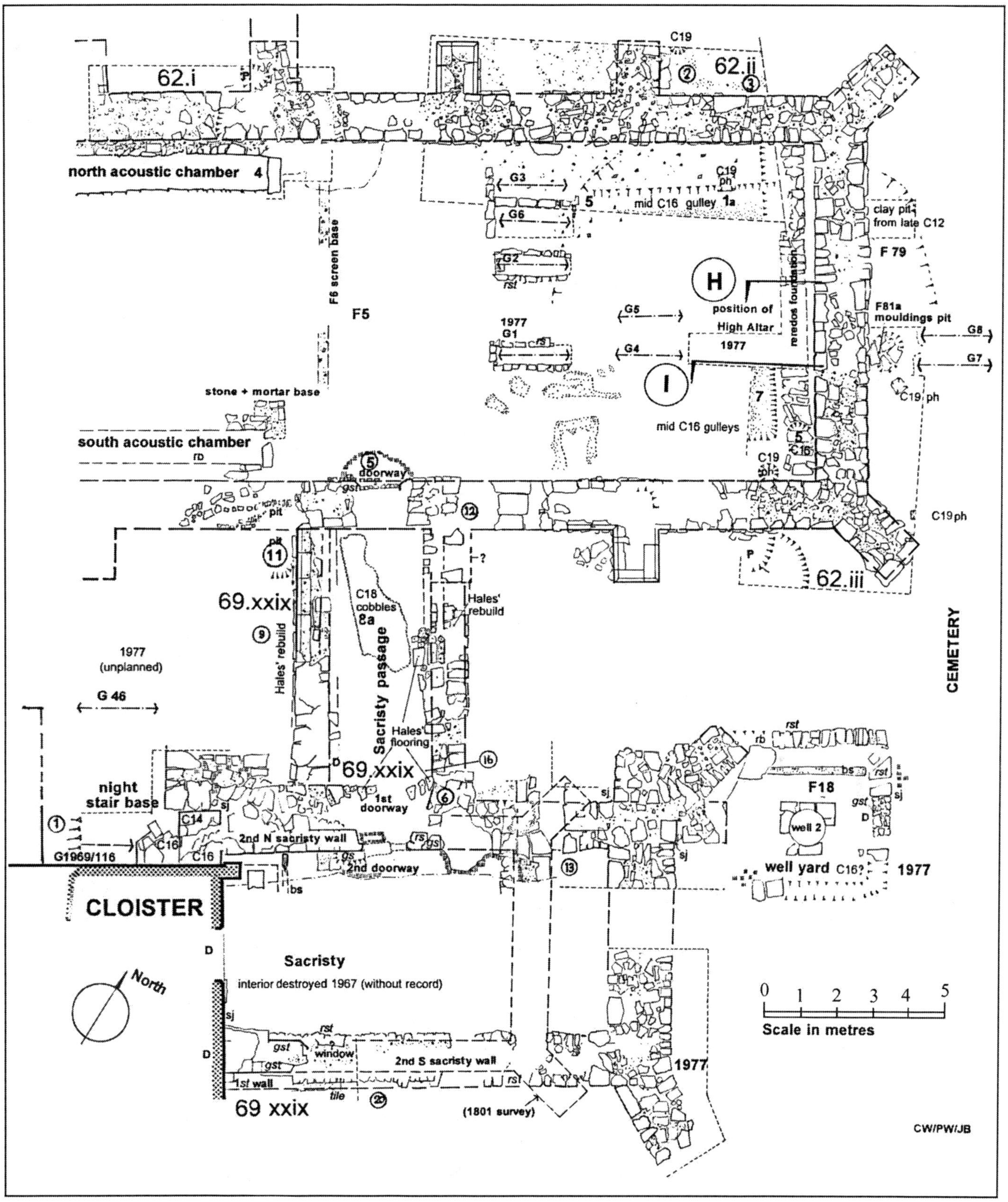

Figure 43 The four eastern bays of the choir. Passage to sacristy, base of night stair and 'yard' with burials to its W. Sacristy and passage rebuilt in the 16th century. Well yard (?16th century) to its E. Screen dividing 16th-century school from ?industrial workshop in E choir. Industrial gullies. Phases 1, 1342-1485; 1a, *c.*1385; 4, late 15th to early 16th century; and Hales, mid 16th century, are represented.

Figure 44 Eighteenth-centry view of NE end of cloister showing night stair, view from W. Reproduced by permission of Birmingham City Council, Aylesford collection (BB97/6236). Photograph Crown copyright, NMR.

Figure 45 View of landing of night stair (*c.*1385), from S. The spires of Holy Trinity, St Michael's and the Greyfriars can be seen. Reproduced by permission of Birmingham City Council, Aylesford Collection (BB97/6255). Photograph Crown copyright, NMR.

Figure 46 View from top landing of night stair (of *c.*1385) leading to entrance to dorter, with unusual 'Caernarvon' type mouldings, looking S. Reproduced by permission of Birmingham City Council, Aylesford Collection (BB97/6256). Photograph Crown copyright, NMR.

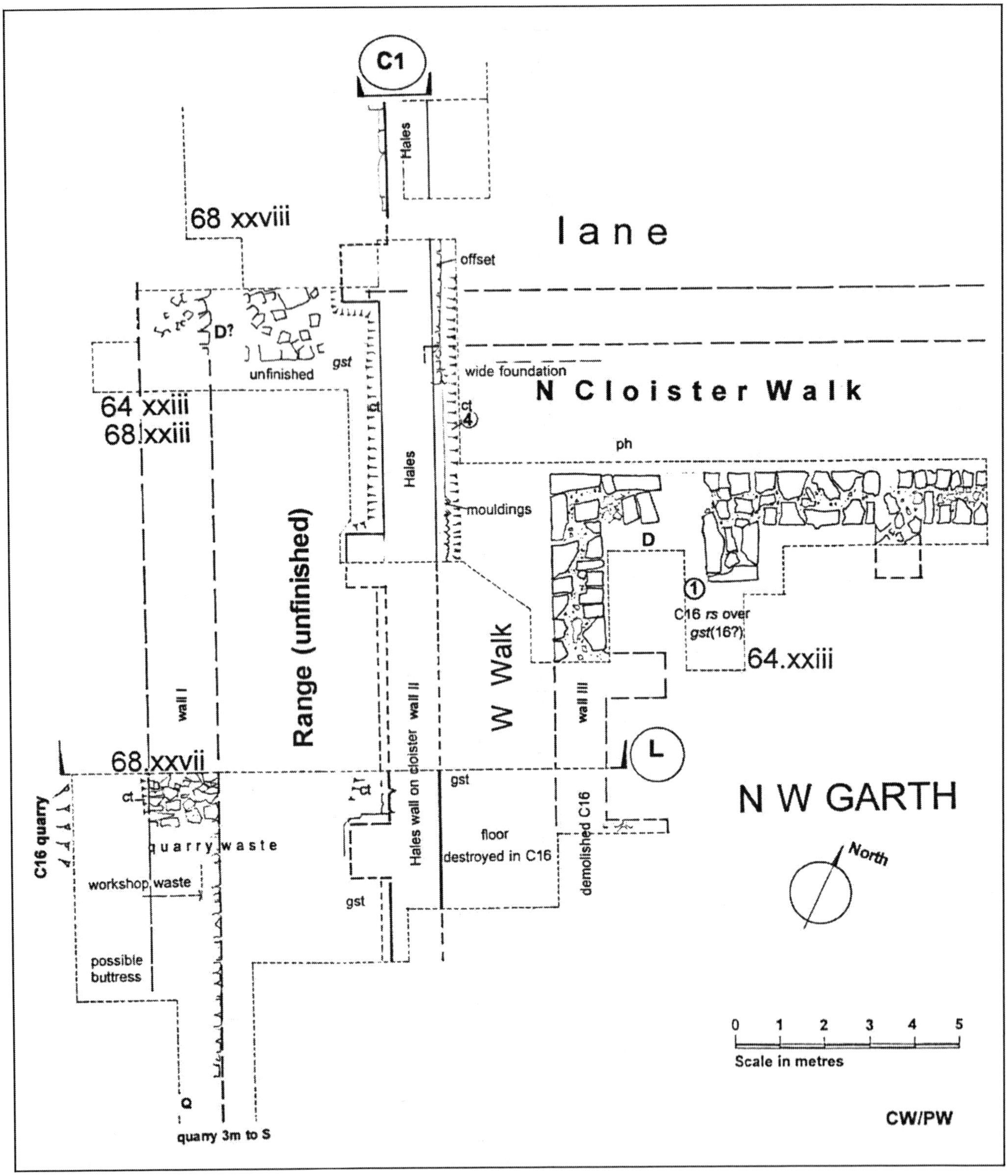

Figure 47 NW area of the late 14th- to early 15th-century cloister. An attempt to make a double cloister range was abandoned in the early 16th century. The external wall to the cloister walk was demolished, and then rebuilt by John Hales as a garden wall . Phase 2, *c.*1385 to 1423; Phase 4, late 15th to early 16th century; and Phase 6, post-Dissolution, are represented.

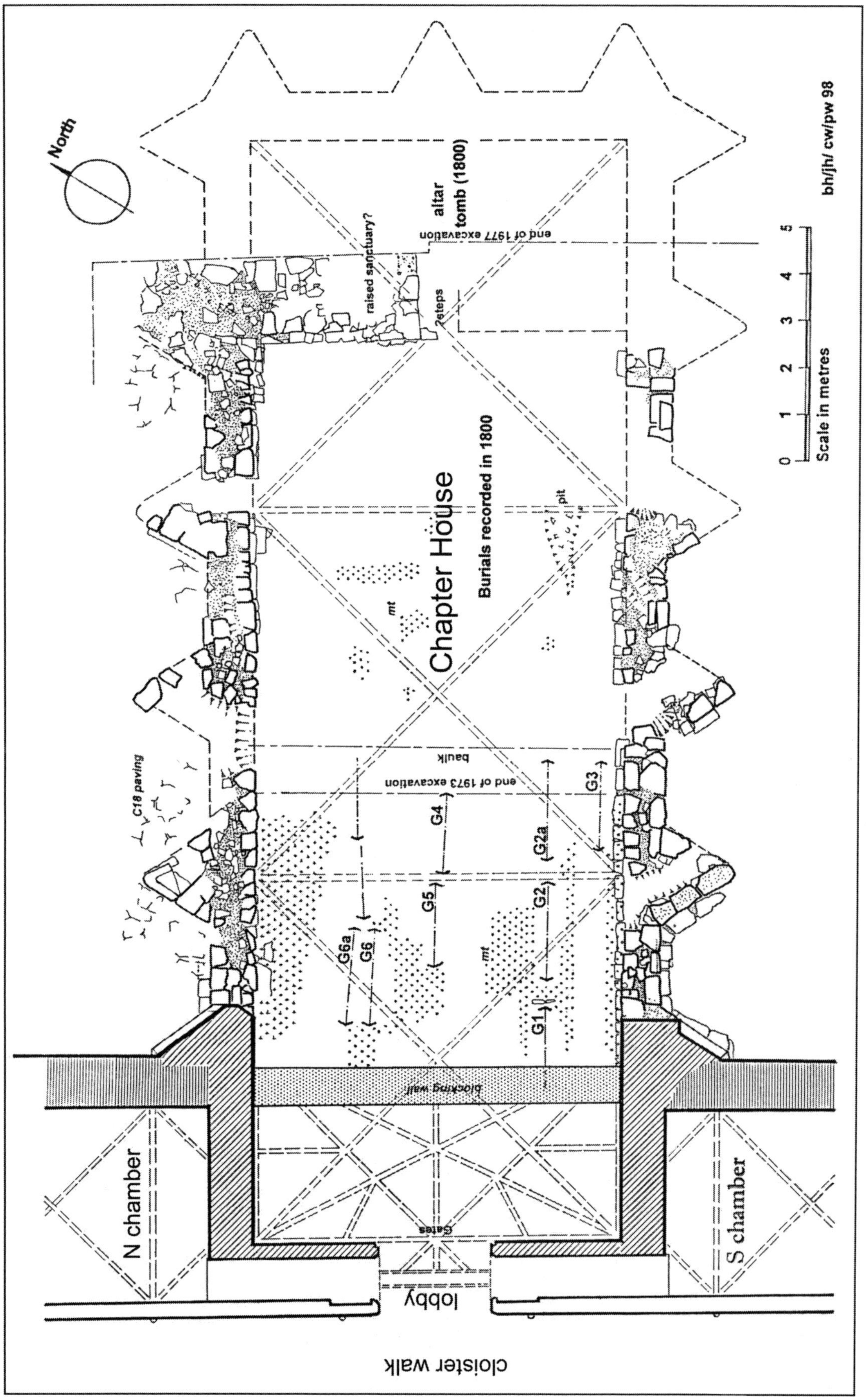

Figure 48 The 14th-century chapter house. The triangular buttresses are paralleled at Kenilworth Castle. The 1800 plan (Fig. 30) suggests unexcavated burials in the E. Chapter house, together with an altar tomb? some 20m to the E of the standing building. Phases 1 and 1a, 1342-1385 are represented.

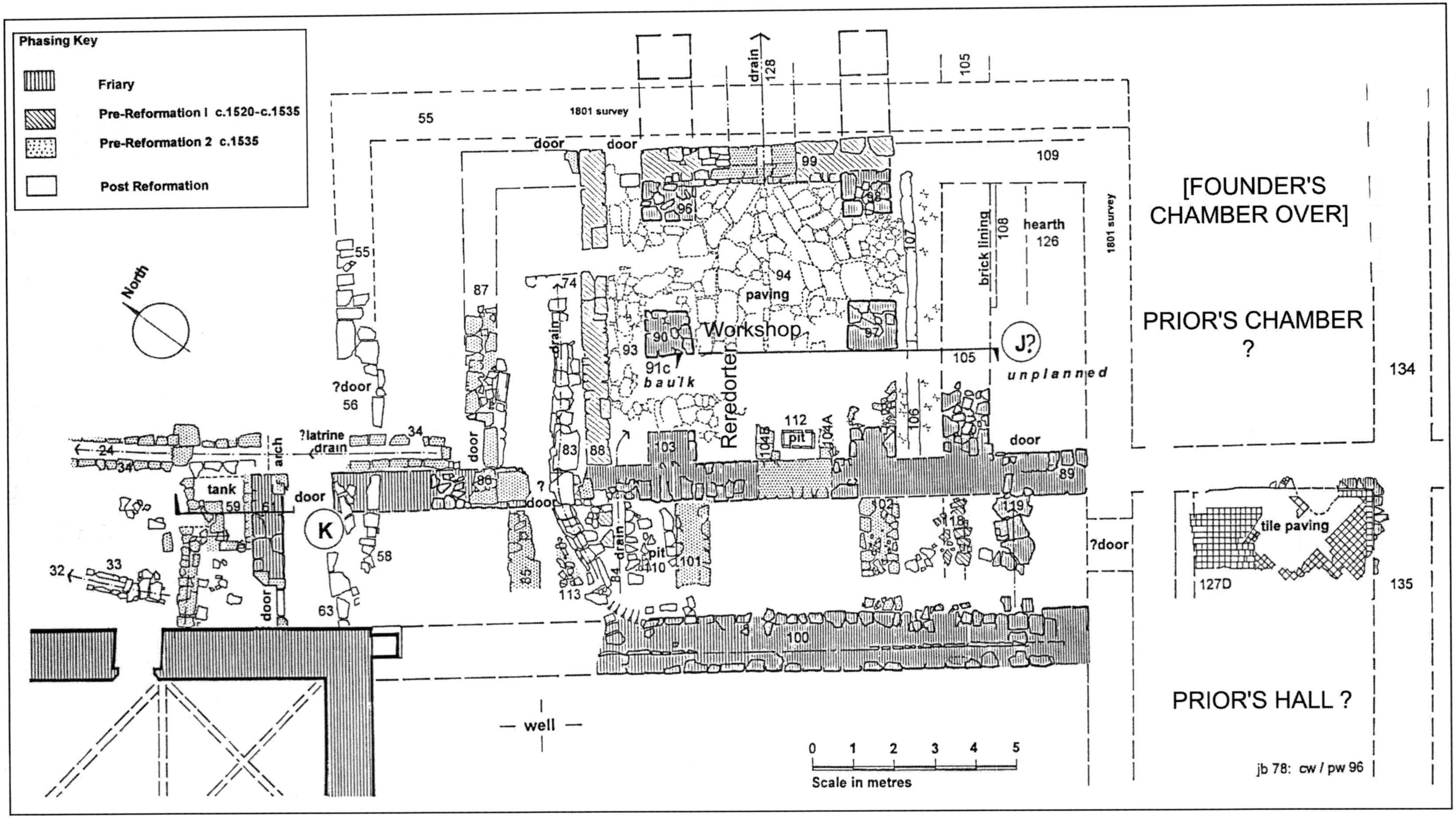

Figure 49 Area S of standing cloister. E range of inner well court, apparently with Prior's Chamber and Hall to the S, the last with a partly surviving medieval tiled-floor, Fig. 136. The arcaded reredorter with pitched paving was replaced by a workshop *c.*1535. This area was partially 'cleared' in 1977-78, and lacks precise stratigraphy.

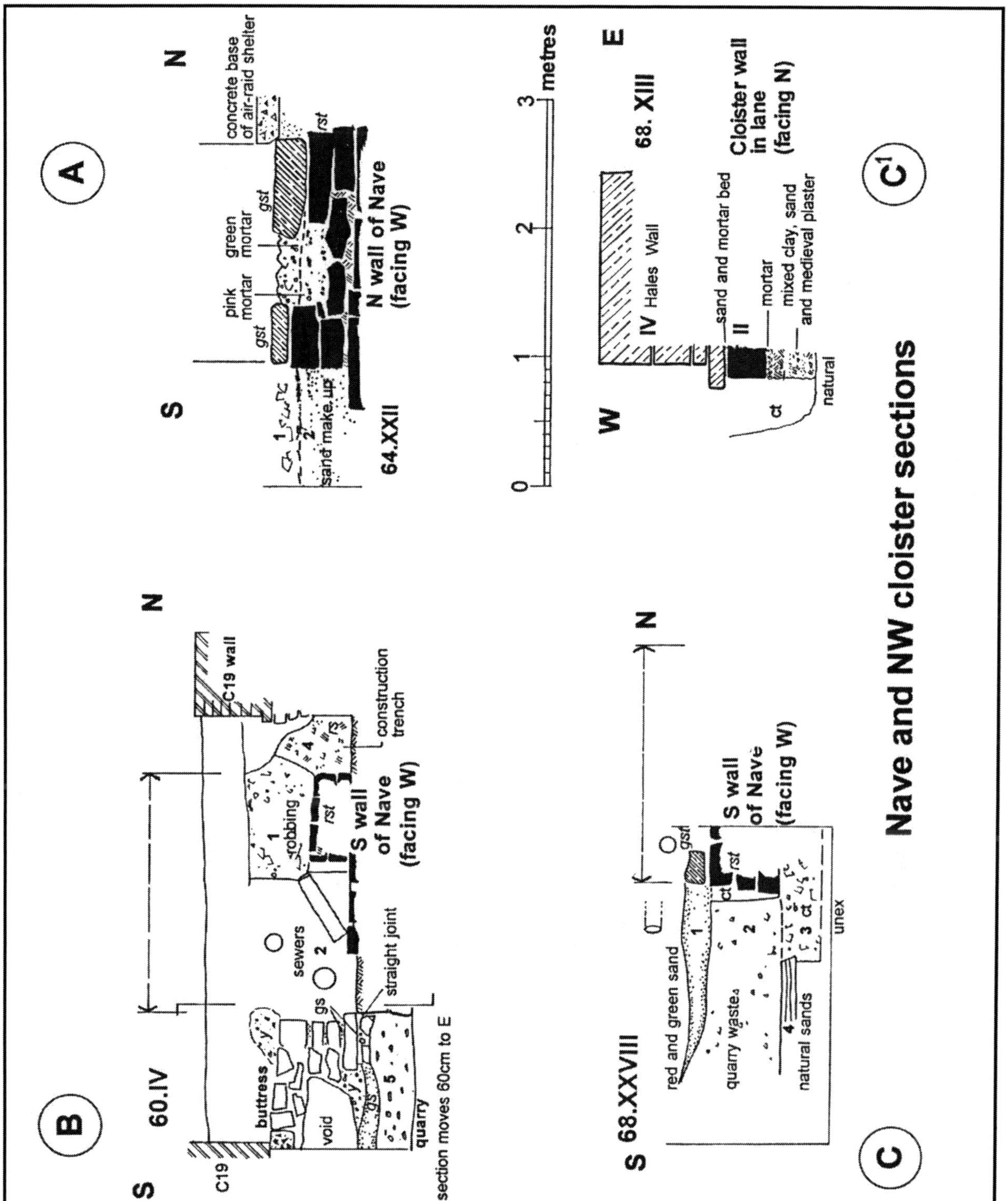

Figure 50 Nave sections A, B, C, and C1, see also Fig. 41. The western nave bays use green sandstone as well as red; the S nave wall and the NW cloister wall are built with construction trenches.
NB 'Facing' indicates that the viewer is facing the specified direction.

Section A: N wall, 3rd bay of nave from W. Green and red sandstone, green and pink mortar. Phase Pre-Rebuild.
Section B: S wall, 3rd/4th bay of nave from W. Green sand spread and construction trench.
Sinkage of added buttress during construction, forming a void. Quarry.
Phases Friary 2 and Friary 2 sub-phase.
Section C: S wall. 5th/6th bay of nave from W. Green and red sandstone. Construction trench of two widths. Quarry. Phase Friary 2 sub-phase.
Section C1: NW cloister. W wall II of W cloister walk with construction trench, and mortar foundation. Phase Friary 2 sub phase.
Post-Reformation wall over.

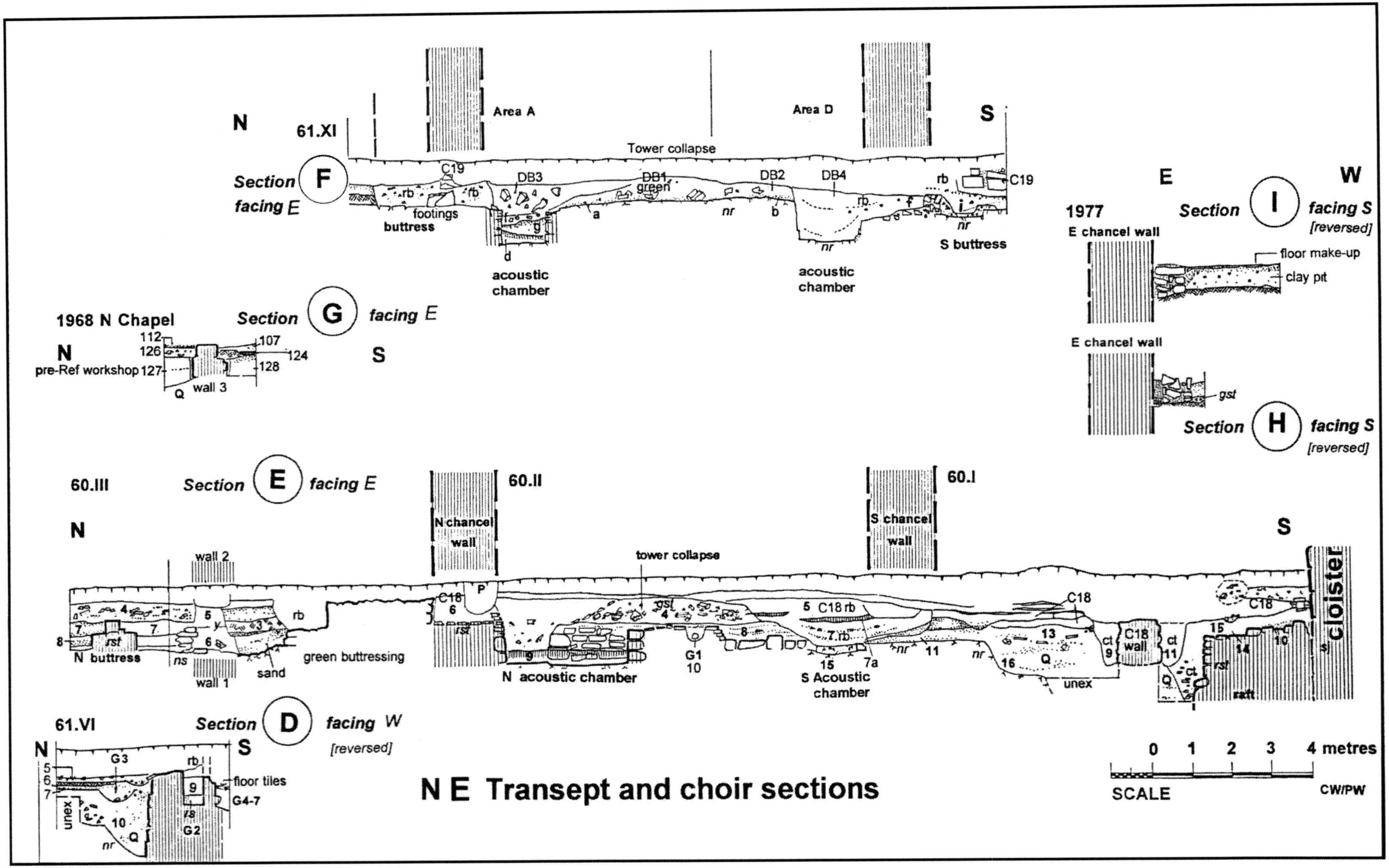

Figure 51 NE transept and choir sections D-I, see also Figs 42 and 43. NB 'Facing' indicates that the viewer is facing the specified direction.

Section D: NE transept - inserted 15th-century wall tomb (1961 G.2) with moulding and relaid tiles; earth graves internal and external to church, construction levels, and a pre-existing quarry. Phases Friary 1 and Rebuild.

Section E: N transept buttress, original and rebuilt robbed walls of N porch/chapel, tower buttressing. W. choir - N acoustic chamber (resonance passage) with School and Destruction levels. Grave 1960 1; floor make-up, raft buttressing cloister, and stone quarry, Q. Phases Friary, Friary 1, Friary 2, Rebuild, 16th-century Rebuild.

Section F: Second bay of choir from W. Buttress, resonance/acoustic passage, with fills: School A(d), destruction A(g), collapse rubble A(f) with location of mouldings (DB) from tower collapse.

Section G: Section through ?pre-Reformation ?workshop wall 3, associated with industrial spreads, and inserted into earlier friars' industrial and rebuilding levels. Phase 16th-century Rebuild.

Section H: Section through ?reredos wall, showing, gap between reredos and E chancel wall, and use of late green sandstone.

Section I: Section through ?reredos wall hard against E chancel wall, inserted into Prefriary clay pit. Phases Prefriary, Friary and ?Rebuild.

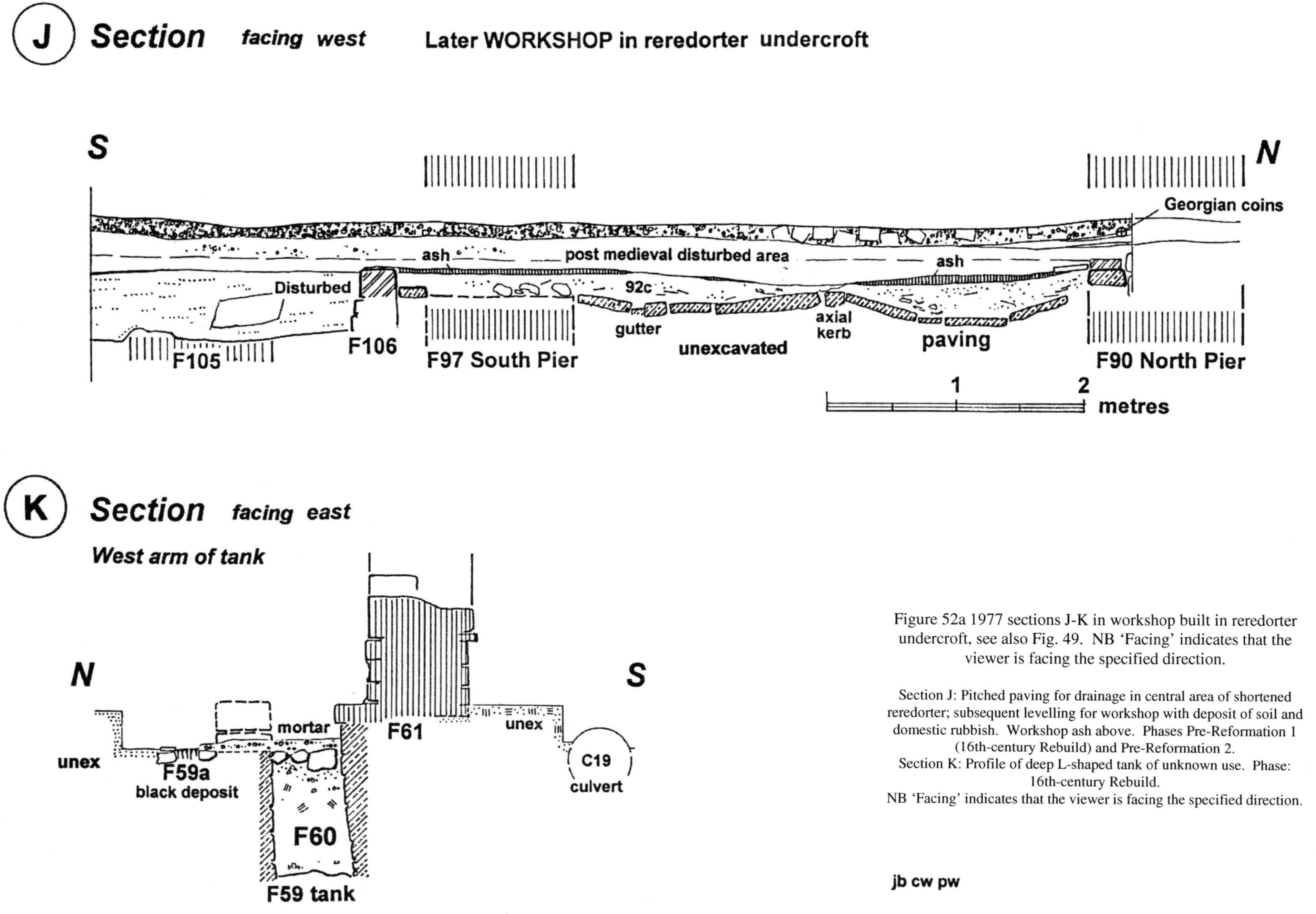

Figure 52a 1977 sections J-K in workshop built in reredorter undercroft, see also Fig. 49. NB 'Facing' indicates that the viewer is facing the specified direction.

Section J: Pitched paving for drainage in central area of shortened reredorter; subsequent levelling for workshop with deposit of soil and domestic rubbish. Workshop ash above. Phases Pre-Reformation 1 (16th-century Rebuild) and Pre-Reformation 2.
Section K: Profile of deep L-shaped tank of unknown use. Phase: 16th-century Rebuild.
NB 'Facing' indicates that the viewer is facing the specified direction.

jb cw pw

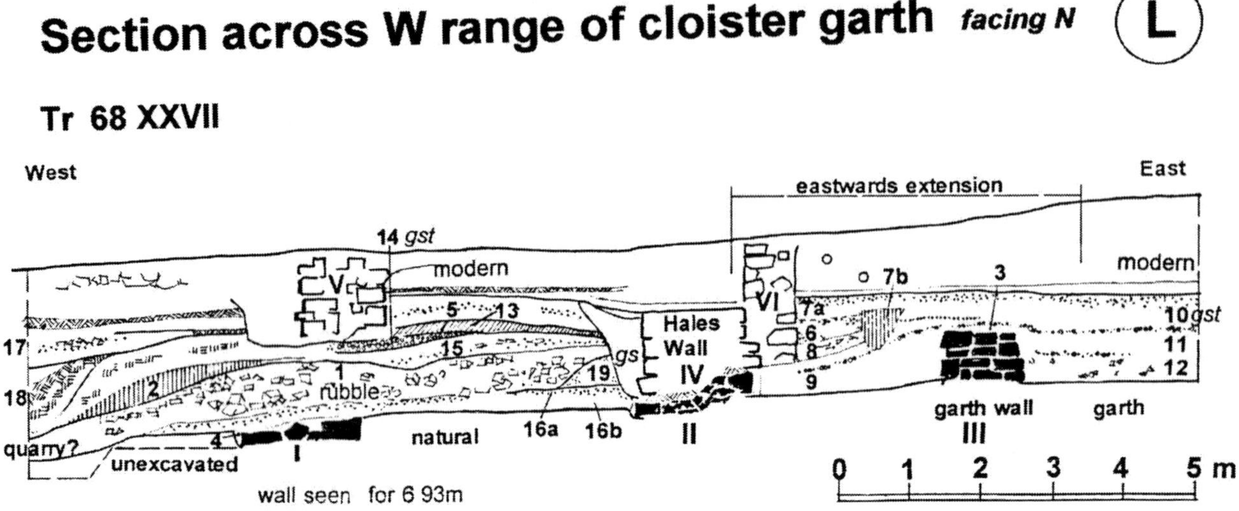

Figure 52b Section L, through W range of cloister, see also Fig. 47. Wall I, unfinished footing for a double cloister W range, Phase 16th-century Rebuild. Wall II, external cloister walk, Phases Friary 1a/2; 16th-century quarry waste, with domestic and metal working wastage above. Demolition of Wall II followed by its rebuild by Hales.

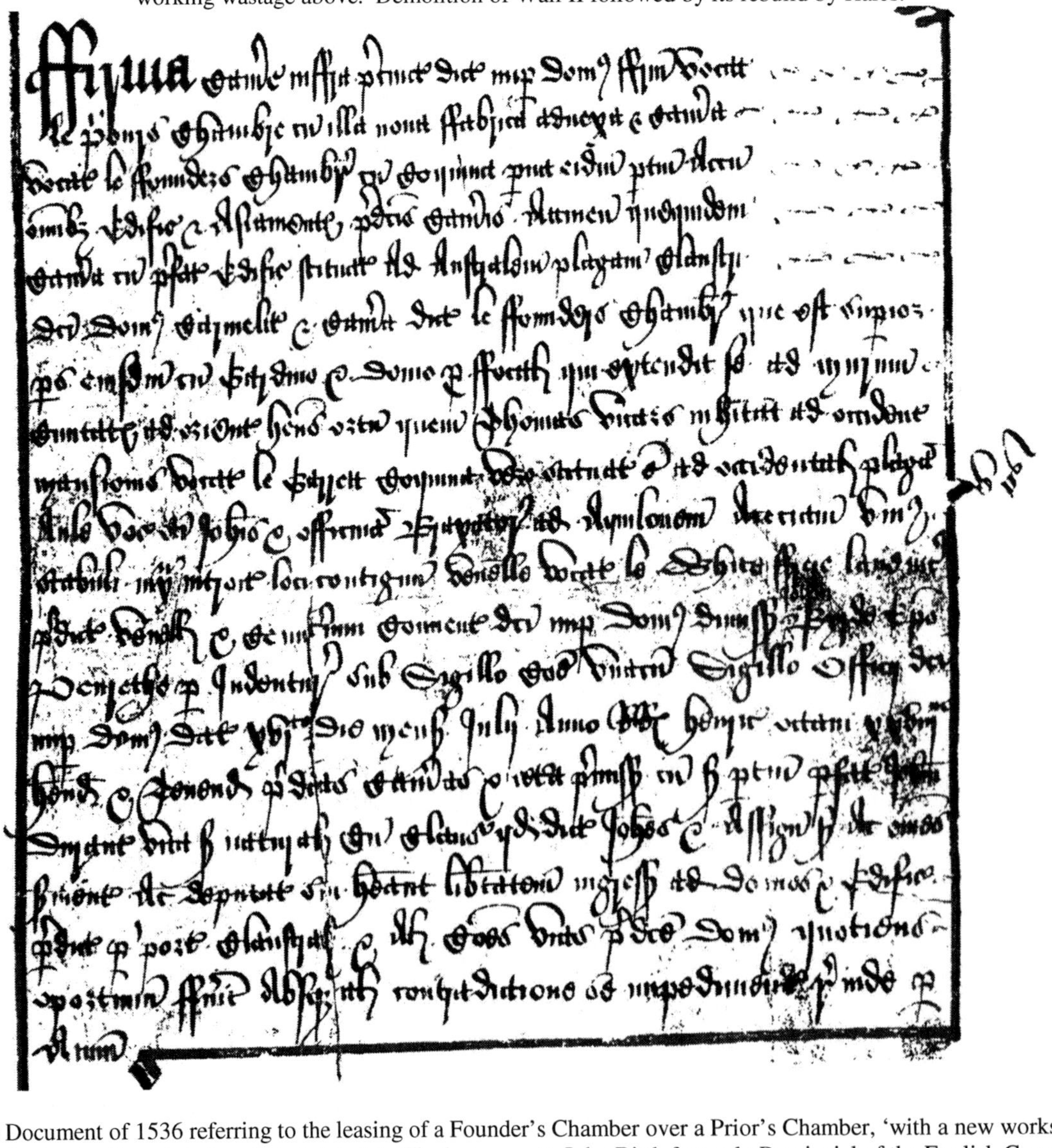

Figure 53 Document of 1536 referring to the leasing of a Founder's Chamber over a Prior's Chamber, 'with a new workshop/forge (officina) joined on'. Also, 'a hall called St John's'. The lease was to John Bird, formerly Provincial of the English Carmelite Order, then Bishop of Penrith. Reproduced by permission of the Public Record Office, E.318/19/967.

Figure 54 Life in a Carmelite Friary: hearing confessions, here of a nobleman, threatened by the Devil and the fires of hell (from a volume of the works of Richard Rolle, English, *c.*1400. Lincoln Cathedral Library, ms 218, f.89).

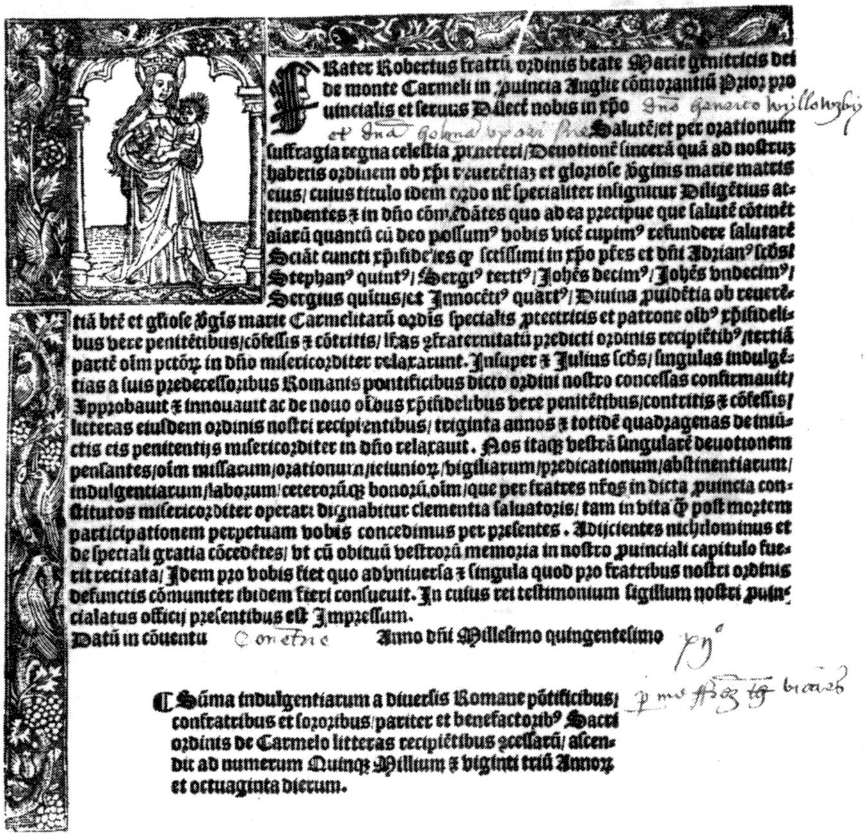

Figure 55 Printed letter of confraternity issued at the Coventry Whitefriars to Sir Henry Willoughby, and Lady Helen his wife, in 1512. This granted remission of sins to confessed penitents. Willoughby owned the manor of Wyken, now within the City of Coventry. This is the only document to survive from the working life of the friary (Department of MSS and Special Collections, University of Nottingham. MiF 1/7).

Figure 56 View in the late 18th century, a period of Romantic elegance, from the SE cloister walk to the 15th-century reset gate in the S walk, and the upper floor of the inner cloister gate. Reproduced by permission of Birmingham City Council, Aylesford Collection (BB97/6233). Photograph Crown copyright, NMR. See Fig. 57 for the damage that was to come.

Figure 57 Late 20th-century view of the cloister and purlieus. This second stage of the Inner Ring Road obliterated the northern, western and southern cloisters, St John's Hall, the frater and kitchen, the Prior's House, Hales Place, the Lay Cemetery, the western choir, the crossing, the nave and their burials. Photograph Crown copyright, NMR (RCHM 1998 18 177/02).

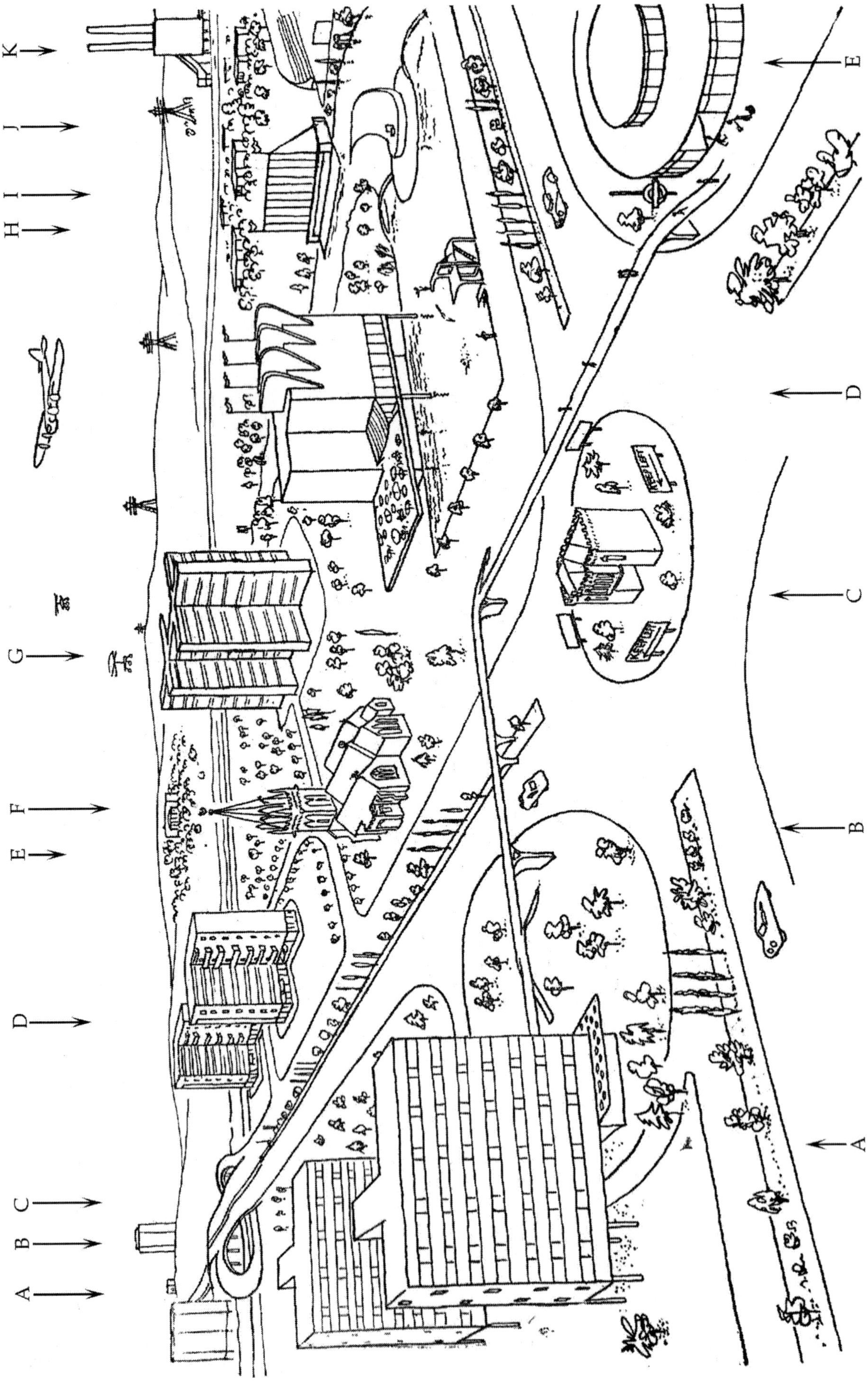

Figure 58 The ethos of post World War II urban planning. 'The Drayneflete of tomorrow' as seen in 1949. Note the fate of the 'cultural monument' on the roundabout in the foreground, and the 'clover leaf crossing and bridge' in the top left hand corner (reproduced from Lancaster 1949, 47).

Figure 59a View from the choir's second bay from E, to crossing, N and S transepts, and S wall of nave at W. The nave continued 6.7m beyond the boundary wall to the position marked by the white stars. 1962. Copyright C. Woodfield. For phasing and scale of Figs 59a to 65b see Fig. 38.

Figure 59b The E end of the presbytery looking NW from the SE corner diagonal buttress, with its Phase 1 red sandstone. The removal of the piscina drain filling shows the footings of the base of the ?reredos later wall. 1962. Copyright C. Woodfield.

Figure 60a Red sandstone boss with the arms of Ferrers, vermilion and gold.
Find place uncertain, but probably W central choir? 1978? Copyright C. Woodfield.

Figure 60b N resonance passage/acoustic chamber with its rock base and masonry sides, looking W to the inserted second N tower pier. 1961/62.
Phases 1 and 4. Copyright C. Woodfield. For choir stalls see Figs 82-93.

Figure 61a Looking NE across the western choir, with return of both resonance/acoustic passages. Shroud burial of grave 1960.1, with red sandstone lining. Phase 4 stone double graves 1968.13-15, with partial robbing. Tower collapse in section. Red sand make-up for once tiled floor. 1960/61. Copyright C. Woodfield.

Figure 61b Fifteenth-century double family tomb, graves 1968.12-15, from the 1968 rescue excavation, presumably a benefactor with wife and child. The larger tomb had not been used. The lower interment was a male in a ? pine coffin. Copyright C. Woodfield. See Fig. 166.

Figure 62a S chancel wall, looking W, Phase 1. Robbed-out SE tower pier, Phases 1 and 4. Straight joint to E wall of S transept, between Phases 1 and 2. 1961. Copyright C. Woodfield.

Figure. 62b Looking NE at turn of N resonance passage/acoustic chamber.
Phase 4 green sandstone reinforcing tower pier (with traces of wall painting on its southern face) enclosing Phase 1 red sandstone pier. Complex of successive strengthening works to failing tower, Phases 1, 2 and 3 to 6. 1961. Copyright C. Woodfield.

Figure 63a Phase 4 green stone blocking to red stone Phase 1 doorway of porch/chapel, E of NE transept.
New green altar base to W. Porch obliterated by green triangular buttressing to failing tower.
Acoustic passage (resonance chamber) and the reinforced tower pier behind.
Phases 1, 4 and 5. 1961. Copyright C. Woodfield.

Figure 63b NW transept with Phase 3 diagonal buttress and Phase 5 strengthening.
NW first bay of Phase 3 nave, with tiles of grave 31. The two-period door sills,
Phases 3 and 4, running S to robbed out NW tower pier. Phases 3 to 5. 1964. Copyright C. Woodfield.

Figure 64a The full width of the W crossing, looking N from the 18th-century gateway, across western tower piers and door sills, the eastern bay of the nave, nave chapels of the Holy Rood and Our Lady (walls marked by ranging poles), to the N nave and transept. Phases 3-5. 1964. Copyright C. Woodfield.

Figure 64b NW internal corner of cloister garth, looking E to standing cloister. Doorway and buttress to S. Phase 3. 1964. Copyright C. Woodfield.

Figure 65a N wall of western nave, bay 8, looking, N. The S, dressed, face of the wall is lime washed. To the N are two robbed buttresses. The concrete line on the E was an Air Raid Precaution shelter. 1962. Copyright C. Woodfield.

Figure. 65b NW corner of nave, and part of buttress 9, oddly offset to the W wall, looking W. The re-used floor tile feature (see also Fig. 141) perhaps acted as a base to a holy water stoup? 1962. Copyright C. Woodfield.

SECTION F
THE ARCHITECTURAL STONEWORK

P. Woodfield

Figures 60a, 66-79. For details of scales see the note on the drawings at the end of this section.

The stonework recovered from Whitefriars is, taken together with the ground plan, the primary evidence for the pre-Reformation appearance of the church building, and the various stages of above-ground structural alteration to the building up to its conversion to other uses and partial demolition following the Dissolution.

The foundation date at Coventry of February 24th 1342 represents the first grant in the city to the brothers of the expanding Carmelite order. It consisted of one messuage with 10 acres of what is now known to be heavily quarried back land on the edge of the built-up area of the city. This grant, in the names of William de Ingleton and Nicholas Sproten, chaplains (McCaffrey 1926, 242-3) of the Benedictines' house in Coventry whose land it was, may have been seen as a counterbalance to the growing influence of the Franciscans. This order of preachers had already set up in Coventry in 1234 (Egan, 1992, 28-29) on a site a little to the NW, and now, a century later, had become firmly established and influential in the city.

It is reasonable to suppose that the first Carmelites to arrive would be accommodated either in temporary accommodation on the site, or lodged elsewhere in the city in property belonging to the founder, or with persons well disposed to the founder's purpose. The first friars would no doubt have been selected for being already acquainted with the problems of beginning a new convent, and probably for their knowledge of the design of Carmelite houses elsewhere, and they would no doubt have had some practical knowledge of setting up building contracts and the problems associated with building construction. The first task would be to refine the plans for housing the new community on the newly acquired site, to investigate the possibilities for water supply and disposal, to arrange levelling, and specifically at Coventry, the clearing of the site, and the levelling off of the fill of the old quarries on the site, assuming the friars were aware of their existence.

The plans which they evolved here would almost certainly be derived from a building layout already proved to be successful, and it would be modified or expanded to take into account the site conditions and the anticipated size of the future community in Coventry. This seminal plan cannot be readily identified, but the London Carmelite house must be a distinct possibility for a model, Fig. 4. Thus it can be anticipated that a comprehensive plan for the church and claustral ranges was established early on, perhaps within some months of the official foundation date, and very probably within the year, Fig. 37.

The priority for a newly founded community would be the domestic quarters in which to house and feed the main phalanx of the brotherhood as soon as possible, and it seems certain both from the evidence, and from a logical point of view, that a part of the E claustral range would be built first to provide the necessary domestic accommodation, Fig. 9, divided up on a temporary basis. This no doubt was commenced as soon as some Poulteney funds became available, and a contract with a master mason could be engrossed. A 'stone house' is referred to by McCaffrey (1926, 242).

However, the terms of the foundation, and the imperative of the new community would probably ensure that high priority was given to the more detailed design and construction of a useable church. Religious observances may have taken place in a temporary building in the interim period, although there is no evidence of substance for this. Any such interim arrangements would make no architectural demands that would be identifiable now.

Almost two years to the day after the foundation, in 1344, faculties were granted by Edward III to the Prior of the Benedictines in the City to provide the wherewithal to enable the Prior and Carmelite brothers to enlarge their house, and for making an access road to their site from Much Park Street (McCaffrey 1926, 243). The position of the first access is not known for certain, and there may have been a number of such points off the existing streets, as the town at this date was not as yet walled. The postern on Gosford Street, Fig. 37, the evidence for which was regrettably removed without record in the late 1960s, is one such point of access, and it is likely there was another from the direction of the road to London.

In architectural terms, work of the 1340s-50s is on the cusp of change. In London, in 1349, the Carmelites were already rebuilding their church on a more ambitious plan under royal patronage (McCaffrey 1926, 133-4). The appearance of this great London church is not known in detail (for plan, see Fig. 4), but the change from the Decorated style to Perpendicular can be said to begin in London under Master William Ramsey, the third of that name (*floruit* 1323-1349), who was working at St Paul's Chapter House in London in 1332 (Harvey 1984, 244). Whoever is responsible for the design of the new church for the Coventry Whitefriars, if not Ramsey III himself, was highly unlikely not to be aware of this development in style in the metropolis. This association is also reflected in the choir stalls design, Figs 82-93.

The advent of the Black Death in 1349-50, in which both Ramsey and the friars' patron and founder, Sir John

Poulteney died (Egan 1992, 30) is likely to have diverted the attention of the brothers from their building programme to their more pressing duties such as tending the sick and burying the dead, acts for which they were long after affectionately remembered in the city (McCaffrey, 1926, 253). However, the need to utilise the skills of those tradesmen who survived must have been the more urgent, even if their labour did cost more, and although the plague almost certainly would have caused a hitch in the programme, no great hiatus in the building programme might be expected or indeed, can be identified.

Thus, the initial work in Coventry of the 1350s, if not designed by William Ramsay III himself, was probably directly influenced by the metropolitan style rather than being provincial or derivative in character. In the decade 1340-50 it may still be expected to exhibit the legacy of the Decorated period in detail even if the overall concept and design had changed. The minor ogee arch, the wave moulding, Fig. 67a, the tight three-quarter hollow flanked by fillets of the later Decorated period in the Midlands, Fig. 67f, and the roll-and-fillet, Fig. 68 No 706) are distinctive of this period of change. The work in the surviving cloister range largely substantiates this view.

From 1365, the resources of the friars were, it seems, under fresh pressures, for in that year they received an order of distraint from the Mayor and bailiffs of the city on 'men of religion' for contributions towards the building of the city wall, the trace of which was adjusted on the SE side of the city to encompass the Carmelite precinct (Cal Close R. XII). Religious orders were not normally expected to contribute to such civic works, and it may be their special needs requiring realignment of the City Wall in this sector involved them in having to make a contribution, Fig. 37.

The Coventry Carmelites were probably aware of a promise of a further handsome legacy of £300 in the first will of 1384, by Lord Bassett of Drayton, Staffordshire, for the enlargement of their church (McCaffrey 1926, 243). The wording strongly acknowledges that a good start had been made on the building of the choir and tower of the permanent church itself, Fig. 38. Whether they were to receive this money when Lord Bassett eventually died is less sure, but the terms of the will, and his interest in the preaching orders, as demonstrated by his founding of the Austin Friars house at Atherstone, 10 miles to the N of Coventry (Knowles and Hadcock 1953) seems certain, and he may have provided earlier grants. Amongst the stonework found we must therefore anticipate a renewed campaign of building from 1385 to be represented (Fig. 11, Phase 2), and it is to this time, Friary 2, the change of plan, and the laying out of the revised crossing, with transepts, tower and the eastern six bays of the nave with its two chapels is dated. This, the age of master mason Henry Yeveley in terms of architectural design, is not easily distinguished in terms of mouldings from the earlier, but there is a tendency for the mouldings towards the later decades of the century to be less deeply defined or sharply cut, and to exhibit the introduction of the double-ogee and the fully developed symmetrical casement moulding.

In 1423 (Phase 3 Rebuild) the Whitefriars church is recorded in a Vatican document as being 'in ruins' but whether this means the church building itself, or the whole monastic complex, is not clear. It could be that what was observed was simply the uncompleted church, or even the unfinished claustral buildings, a situation that must have been all too common at all religious establishments throughout the medieval period, but the fact that it was remarked upon at all suggests that what was observed was out of the ordinary, perhaps the result of the first slippage and even a fall of the rectangular central tower and octagonal lantern, due in part to the weakness of the NE tower pier having had to accommodate a spiral stair, and to some extent due to a foundation subsidence. The fall clearly caused considerable damage in the NE direction and brought about a reappraisal of the use of the N transept chapel. The opportunity seems to have been grasped to redesign the whole crossing area and to carry it up as a more substantial square tower, capped now, or somewhat later with a spire. Such a feature was recorded by Sir William Smyth of Hill Hall just after the Dissolution, Fig. 32. The archaeological evidence shows the transepts were widened to the W and the layout of the nave adjusted accordingly. Work on the three W bays of the nave followed somewhat later, possibly aiming for the completion of the church in time for the meeting in Coventry of the Provincial Chapter of the Order in 1431-2.

In line with many other monastic houses, there was a further significant building phase in the three or four decades prior to the Dissolution. There were further alterations including the strengthening of the central tower, which must have still shown signs of weakness on the NE side, and a shortening of the reredorter was made at this time, Figs 38 and 49. In 1506 Thomas Bond left 20 marks for the completion of the cloister (McCaffrey 1926, 247-8). It may be that a doubling of the W range of the cloister was planned although it does not seem to have ever been carried out beyond the laying of the foundations, Fig. 52b.

In 1573 the great bell was removed by the Corporation of Coventry, who had acquired the lease of the Whitefriars church, and they sold it to Holy Trinity church (McCaffrey 1926, 247-8). This indicates that the steeple was then still standing, but was to fall, a year or so later when 'the Corporation let the steeple of the Whitefriars fall down' (Harris 1907-13, 15).

THE STANDING BUILDING

Figures 9-11, 13-14, 16-31, 38, 39, 56-57 and see also Figures 44-46

The initial reference point for investigating the stonework recovered from the various excavations must be the standing E claustral range, Figs 9-11. This is discussed in detail by J. Cattell in Section C, *The Standing Building* and is only reiterated here when it refers to the illustrated details.

The E Claustral range began, it is argued by Cattell, as a simple rectangular building running N-S, with a walk partitioned off along its W side, and with the temporary service arrangements for the community at its S end behind a stone wall with three service doorways in the standard medieval domestic manner. It probably had the first bays of the N and S cloister walks at the ends. What is less clear is the nature of the first openings to the future cloister, and what arrangements were made for a temporary church. Surviving details from this build, assigned to Friary Phase 1 on Fig. 11, are two of the steeply 2-centred arched internal doorways, at its S end, with asymmetrical bracket moulded jambs and lobed ogee hood moulds rising from large, vigorously carved head corbels, recorded by Dr Troughton in the nineteenth century, but now very eroded, Figs 14 and 66a-b. The work is suggested by Stow to be that of William de Ramsay III, the King's Chief Mason for all works S of the Trent who was advisor to Lichfield Cathedral in the same diocese (Harvey 1984). His associations with Coventry probably arose from his connections in London with Sir John Poulteney, Coventry's founder, for whom he had worked in St Paul's, and had advised on, if not actually designed, Poulteney's own great house at Penshurst, Kent (Harvey 1984).

Cloister Phase 1b, 1351- *c.*1356, is identified by the insertion of the slender stone spine wall designed to carry counterbalanced vaults both sides, Fig. 9. The vaults differ in detail. Those in the cloister walk are carried on corbels carved as cowled heads, carrying stilted triple shafts extending up to the springing line, Fig. 66c. The plain, deep-chamfered vaulting ribs themselves have longitudinal and cross ribs in each bay, which, together with intermediate tierceron ribs, stop short towards the centre of each bay to leave a diagonal square, furnished with minor cusps, Fig. 17. On the other side of the inserted wall, the long 11-bay E range has a simpler inserted vault of deeply chamfered ribs which descend to a point springing in the walls. A door towards the north end now has a more developed and symmetrical bracket moulding Fig. 66e.

A similarity in the design of the cloister vault with certain vaults in the West Country, has led Dr R. Morris to suggest that the master mason John Box could have been responsible for the design (pers. comm.). His name suggests a family origin in the village of that name near Bath, well known for its stone quarries. He was clearly already known to the king when he was called to London *c.*1351 whilst in the service of the prior at Canterbury. In London he undertook work at Westminster Palace from 1353, and at the Tower, and could well have taken over at Coventry after Ramsey died. Certainly a John Box appears in Coventry in a legal document dated 1352 whereby the Carmelites acquired their new access to Much Park Street 10 years after the initial foundation. As well as the vault, the openings to the cloister may well be of this period. There are nine bays of 3-light windows with trefoil heads under an ogee arch, which internally reaches up at the centre to meet a horizontal, slightly beaked, scrolled string, Fig. 66d. John Box departed to take charge of works in Calais in 1356 for two years, suggesting a break in the works at this time, returning to royal works in England in 1358 (Harvey 1984, 31).

A meeting place for the Chapter must have been required from the foundation date, and the position of the first purpose-built chapter house is probably indicated by the foundations of walls projecting eastwards from the centre of the original building, Fig. 38. There was certainly a chapter house at the Whitefriars in 1361 when the provincial master in 1353, William Lubbenham, is recorded as having been buried within it (McCaffrey 1926, 244) and indeed ten burials, now largely lost, were located in the 1977 excavations. One may well have been William Lubbenham himself. In this case there must have been a door opening directly out of the 11-bay E section of the E cloister range. This arrangement must have in time been found to be unsatisfactory, and, in what is identified as Phase 1c on Fig. 11, it was rebuilt in the same position to provide a more traditional and imposing entry from the cloister walk itself, setting the entrance back to allow for the continued N-S connection in the long E range of rooms. This is the first clear departure from the initial plan.

Fig. 67 illustrates details from Phase 1c, the period when the chapter house was clearly rebuilt, set into the pre-existing range, and occupying rather less than three claustral bays in width, cutting uncomfortably into the vaults of the main eastern range rooms. The entrance arch from the claustral walk still pronounces a mid-later fourteenth-century date by retaining a wave moulding, Fig. 67a,, one of the very few on site and a small arris moulding at the entrance, Fig. 66f. Low shouldered arches give access to narrow passages connecting what has become two chambers on the E side of the range, Figs 67c and 19. Details, particularly of what might be termed a continuous torus moulding extending the shoulders of the arches within the low and narrow passages, with the new day stair at the S end of the range, and a new night stair (now lost) attached at the N end indicate a contemporaneity of date, Figs 45 and 46. This latter element also confirms the chancel of the church was up and functioning at this time, a date suggested by the heraldry on the choir stalls, and the floor tiling.

The surviving western end of the new chapter house, of which less than half survives embedded within the existing range, is covered with a square-bay vault, Figs 11 and 18, the ribs springing from stilted corbels similar to those in the cloister walk, Fig. 67d-e, but is elaborated with subsidiary ribs, spanning the full 8m width. The elaborate arch at the entrance is purely decorative and carries unglazed tracery, moulded with double wave mouldings parted by a small hollow, Fig. 67f. A reconstruction of this arch, with its somewhat bizarre straight tracery elements, Fig. 67g, suggest that it either terminated in a pendant, or less likely, was supported by a central trumeau. Given the rebates for double doors into the chapter house, the entrance, even accounting for the ingenious if odd provision of the side passages, would have been most impressive, Fig. 18.

The clearances of the 1970s clearly showed that this second phase of the Chapter House had triangular buttresses, Figs 34, 38 and 48, such as were employed by the mason Robert Skyllington for John, the 2nd Duke of Lancaster, at his new Great Hall at Kenilworth Castle, built probably in the 1380s and still being worked on in 1391, after he was granted leave to impress labour to the rebuilding of the Great Hall ('Grant of the 8th July 1391', Cal Pat Rolls 1388-92; Harvey 1984, 275). The mason at the Whitefriars appears to have been developing the keeled buttress theme of the original build, and if he were Skyllington himself, went on to develop it further at Kenilworth. One hesitates to continue to ascribe the work at Coventry to the few known great master masons of the medieval period, but Robert Skyllington is recorded as having designed and worked on the fine tower of St Michael's Church, Coventry from 1373, and at St Mary's, Warwick from 1381 to 1396 (Harvey 1984, 275). On this basis, and acknowledging a basic change in plan with a different approach to the detailing, the chapter house, with the day and night stairs, is ascribed to the period 1375-1380, Fig. 11.

On the first floor of the surviving range, probably initially functioning as both *studium particulare* and dorter as, for instance, at Gloucester Blackfriars (water-colour reconstruction by Terry Ball in the writer's collection), there were narrow single-light transomed windows ranged along both sides, Fig. 10 the reveals unequally splayed on those in the N half of the building suggesting the presence of study carrels. Five of these windows survive on the E side, with evidence internally for others, Figs 20 and 26. Those on the W have been mostly replaced by mullioned and transomed windows inserted by John Hales during his post-medieval conversion of the building. These single light windows also have ogee heads and hood mouldings. The lowered doorway in the angle of the NE corner of the upper level and leading to the night stair, was inserted at the time of the rebuilding of the chapter house. It has only a simple chamfer. The other doorway on the upper floor gave access to the upper chamber over the sacristy, which was apparently first built in stone, but shortened and rebuilt in partial timber framing in the later medieval period, probably the sixteenth century. Below, on the ground floor, lay the vaulted sacristy chamber, which when the church was built, acted as an ante-room to the chancel, entered by an asymmetrical door from the four-bay chamber behind the cloister walk. This door was blocked and its N jamb removed when the present later medieval door with bracket mouldings was inserted.

THE ARCHAEOLOGICALLY RECOVERED STONEWORK

Materials

The freestone used for the architectural and banker work at the Whitefriars is of two main types, the dominant and earliest being the Lower Keuper Sandstone found not only locally in the Coventry area, but even on the site itself. A series of pits had formed part of a chain of quarries in use in the twelfth and thirteenth centuries, before the friary was founded (Demidowicz 1996). The quality varies, from massive easily worked freestone, to a coarse-grained variety, strongly bedded, and of lesser value for constructional purposes. The second main variety used, particularly in the later fifteenth century, is a finer-grained glauconitic sandstone of a greenish colour, also obtained from beds in the New Red Sandstones, perhaps those to the S of the city (thanks are due to Dr David Keene, Department of Geology, University of Coventry, for this observation). This finer stone, which appears in the vault of the entrance to St Mary's Guildhall, Coventry, pre 1412, also appears in a rib of the eastern cloister vault, but the small extent of this might owe its presence there to a later repair. It is undoubtedly better in sustaining fine detail than the Keuper Sandstone, but is more vulnerable to abrasion and weathering, and in some areas it has dissolved to a fine green sand. There is a small quantity of stone of fine pale red colour, probably from a similar source. The green stone was utilised in small quantities in the vault of the first period cloister, and there are indications that this was no longer used after the first quarter of the fifteenth century.

A further subsidiary stone, a laminated micaceous shale, probably from Stockingford, near Nuneaton, was utilised in the actual laying of the stone and for obtaining a very positive compression joint in the construction of vaults and for packing and levelling between courses, necessary at least during the curing process of the lime mortar, see *Slate*, Section O. This shale may be waste from the shaping of stone roof slates.

Masoncraft

The architectural elements show, in their preparation, a very high degree of competence in masoncraft and bankerwork, and clearly were worked to prepared drawings and profiles, as was customary at the time. The stones often retain setting out marks on their meeting faces, with centre lines scribed on axial roll mouldings and arcs on tracery; occasionally meeting faces, presumably those considered to be at risk from movement, are cross hatched to permit the better bonding of the mortar. Perhaps surprisingly, there are few masons' marks, and those recorded are discussed below, and illustrated on Fig. 79. The mortar was, as usual, a fine-grained sand lime mortar, presumably prepared on site well before use, with a finer-sieved lime putty mix used for setting ashlar work. The aggregate often includes numerous mixed dark coloured particles, presumably obtained locally from crushed stone, or from reclaimed mortars.

There was little sign of mechanical handling or fixing in the recovered stonework, and the conclusion is that the sections were handled manually with levers and ropes. The mason appears to have relied largely on compression in well-designed joints, and in his mortars to hold the building together. Some sections of vaulting have joggled shoulders, and the ribs are at times rebated at the back forming keys or elongated tenons (Fig. 69 Std A), again a standard practice by the fourteenth century. However, just occasionally their faith in well-tried traditional building practice was not absolute, and the occasional iron cramp and tie was found, see *Structural Metalwork*, Section Q. This must represent familiarity with such methods and their adoption when needed. Occasionally special measures were also employed in the construction of vaults and tracery. Joints in what has become to be called the standard 'A' vault ribs were on occasions packed with slate to obtain an early load-bearing capacity which would have expedited the work, and one tracery piece had a small hollow cut on the meeting faces, and a pebble inserted to act as a dowel. This appears to be an *ad-hoc* decision, as there is no evidence for regular use of the well-known practice of using a harder stone for dowels, although unassociated pebbles would not, of course, normally have been identified. In this particular case, its use must have been the result of a particular and justified concern that there was a distinct likelihood of lateral movement which could cause a structurally dangerous displacement. Mason's tools, other than masonry line pins 8-9cm long, made of iron or lead, were not found.

Mason's marks

Figure 79

Only eleven different and distinctive mason's marks were found. Two occurred a number of times in the walling ashlar of the empty southern double grave in the chancel (Grave 68.15, Fig. 166); one of these, Fig. 79e, is probably nothing more than a hurried execution of the double triangle mark (Fig. 79b, Graves 68.12-14) which otherwise occurs four times in the same grave, all on the S wall, Fig. 166. The contiguous N side triple burial had three examples of Fig. 79d, showing, fairly conclusively, it was not contemporary with the double grave to its immediate S.

Elsewhere, four marks occur on the standard 'A' work in red stone, Fig. 79a,, on the coloured face of blind 'Standard A' tracery, and as there is no attempt to conceal this large and well formed mark, it may be presumed that this stonework was in an elevated position where it could not be closely inspected, Fig. 69 No 1159.

This, and another mark from the N transept (Fig. 79g and stone catalogue No 1054, not separately illustrated) are the only ones where curves are employed, otherwise many of the others are based on two parallel lines. The simple cross, assuming it is a mason's mark and not a simple location marker, did occur both on the underside of the lowest course of the seventh N nave arcade pier (its impression left clearly in the mortar bed, Fig. 41), and on an unspecified buttress 'on the N side of the church', presumably of the chancel recorded in 1977. The general paucity of mason's marks in relation to the amount of stonework recovered suggests that the marking of masonry was generally not required, perhaps indicating that only one integrated and self-regulating team of masons was employed at any one time. The marks at Whitefriars are not paralleled by any of those noted at St Michael's, Coventry or St Mary's Guildhall. One piece of sculpture, No 1075, Fig. 81, had a V-shaped mark on the top jointing face (not illustrated). It is ill formed and indistinct, and is probably the result of casual or accidental marking during handling.

The construction of Graves 13 and 14, the double grave in the chancel is of some interest, Figs 61 and 166. Unusually, blocks of stone display mason's marks, Fig. 79b, of the same individual as on the S side, and two from another hand on the N side. This suggests that the stonework was contracted out and it was necessary in this case to keep a tally on the amount produced by individuals. The blocks of local green sandstone are large, and shaped up by a mason's axe, and rubbed to produce a good level finish without removing all the dressing marks. One, the largest is approximately 1.22 x 0.38 x 0,2m (4ft x 1ft 3in x 8in thick) and would weigh in the region of 113.5kg (250lbs). It was probably manipulated by at least two men and a pair of sheerlegs. After being laid on the bedrock, the walling was carried up in a lime mortar with fine joints, one stone out of alignment was cut back *in situ* with a chisel, and on reaching a suitable level the joints were 'buttered' to achieve a smooth flat finish internally. On completion of the sides, the median wall was apparently finished by standing blocks on end, this order of procedure presumably allowing for space on the outer walls. It subsequently bowed, suggesting the N side, the one containing the burials, was filled up whilst the south double grave remained empty. The use of green sandstone here indicates that it was dug through the chancel floor well after the building was finished.

Finishes

The internal stonework at the Whitefriars appears to have been generally limewashed, many substantial coats sometimes being apparent on some architectural elements indicating a frequent renewal of the coating over time. In Coventry the proper time for limewashing was annually at the feast of Corpus Christi, and/or midsummer (Harris 1907-13), but this may not have applied to religious houses. Generally no evidence of figurative wall-paintings, masoning, or decorated mouldings have been found on the structure except a small area of damaged plaster seen and photographed *in situ* at the base of the S wall of the second, mid-later fifteenth-century, NE tower pier, which had been coloured red and black and may have been part of painted dado curtaining. The one exception to the paucity of colour represented in the finds is the vaulting material, Figs 69 and 71, where a small percentage of the total amount found had been brightly coloured, the mouldings picked out in red and yellow (presumably gold), against a vivid blue background. However, in the case of special features like wall tombs, shrines or canopies, Figs 73-78, the full range of materials available to the medieval 'whytelymer' were employed, including yellow/gold and red ochre (rodel), a warm siena ochre, blue, green and black. Important elements of tombs and shrines and vaulting boss roses were gilded. In this context reference should be made to the oyster shell palette containing amongst a unique range of colours, a flesh colour and an azurite blue, similar to that on the stone, see Section K, *Scientific Examination of an Oyster-Shell Palette* and Fig. 135a-f.

Methodology

Amongst the stonework recovered from the excavations all cut and finished stone identified as having been used in an architectural setting was entered on a database. The stones were selected on the criterion of being freestone ashlar worked beyond a simple squared building block, and having a distinct shape, often with mouldings. Coventry Whitefriars is unusual in that an exceptionally large quantity of such pieces was recovered from the excavations of 1960 to 1965, and from later excavations, clearances, road works and landscaping in the vicinity of the Friary. Material from the 1960-1965 campaign was sorted so that the smaller and repetitive mouldings could be recorded, in notebooks, and then discarded; and the more informative pieces marked and set aside for future detailed study. This group was further worked through by others at a later date, during or after the Hobley and Rylatt excavations, and the majority discarded. Some 200 pieces, together with pieces from the Benedictine Priory, were taken to Coventry Charterhouse, where 105 were built as a monastic mélange in a landscaping wall, others being left piled at the back of the site, the markings now mostly illegible. As there is now confusion due to conflation with material from the Charterhouse and the Benedictine Priory, and the probability that some stones from the Whitefriars were recorded in notebooks before being moved to the Charterhouse, and thus are already included on the new database, this group has been discounted from further consideration.

The following report is based on the records made in 1965, augmented by the writer in 1969 in the museum store, and by examination in the chapter house of some material from the 1978 excavation, and such unmarked 1970s stonework that remains in the Whitefriars and in other museum stores, that can with a reasonable degree of confidence be assigned to the Whitefriars.

The records, and descriptions of the surviving stones were entered on a working database (in archive) recording: (A) the physical form, size, material, mouldings and finish of the stone, (B) the area location and layer, and (C) a tentative interpretation of its original purpose or function. A total of 2,436 stones appear on this list, very substantially more than has been recovered from any other friary in Britain (e.g. Northampton Greyfriars (Williams 1978), Gloucester Blackfriars (unpublished), Perth Whitefriars (Stones 1989), Ipswich Whitefriars (unpublished), Oxford Blackfriars (Lambrick and Woods, 1976)). With material salvaged from the later excavations and clearances not being marked, and subsequently mixed with that from other sites, a judgement has had to be made whether a particular piece is from the Whitefriars; this must inevitably result in an unfortunate but unavoidable bias against those pieces originating from the Whitefriars site, but which differ from the routine range. Also, with the moving around of the material from museum store to museum store, a stone recorded in the Whitefriars in 1968 and retained, may appear in a store elsewhere having lost its marks by handling, and thus be duplicated in the record. It is estimated that the rate of duplication would not exceed 2-3%, so that the impact on the overall conclusions is unlikely to be significant.

Three recorded historical events have some bearing on the occurrence of architectural masonry on site. Firstly is the known collapse of the 'new work' at an unspecified location, but probably the tower, in 1447, see Section B, *The Whitefriars in Coventry - Historical Background.* Secondly, the surrender of the house on October 1st 1538, with the church and site passing severally through various hands including those of Sir Ralph Sadleir (McCaffrey 1926, 248) in 1544 to, in December of that year, John Hales, and thirdly, the record in the Coventry Leet Book of 1572-4 quoting 'In that year the Corporation allowed the steeple of the Whitefriars to fall down' (Harris 1907-13 - the records vary between 1572 and 1574). It may be supposed that on each of these occasions the collapsed material would be thoroughly turned over and sifted through, the squared ashlar work salvaged for re-use elsewhere, but the more elaborately worked pieces, where not smashed by the fall, either left on site or used for hardcore or for lime mortar recovery. The use of the chancel for Hales' newly founded Grammar School and the adaptation of the eastern part of the S cloister range and the prior's house for his own dwelling house would also have occasioned some disturbance to what was to become the archaeological record.

DISTRIBUTION OF ARCHAEOLOGICALLY RECOVERED STONEWORK

With the problem of disturbance in the background, the stonework was reviewed area by area to elucidate any distinct pattern of distribution, and whether there is a concentration of an identifiable stonework type in any one area that might permit some deductions to be made about the superstructure. The total number of 2,436 stones were sorted under 47 area groups, the last being the material recovered from excavations after 1969, in the chancel, vestry, chapter house and south-eastern cloister-reredorter and the assumed Prior's House area, which were undifferentiated. No material is known to survive from the 1956, 1973, 1975 and 1979 excavations, or indeed from the small trenches cut by the City of Lincoln Archaeological Unit in 1996, over the SE range, although some architectural stonework was seen at the time on the site. Any report on this last excavation has not been obtainable.

Generally, much of the stonework recovered is from post-Reformation contexts, but some is from earlier demolition or collapse which was of such magnitude that it had not been thoroughly turned over.

The architectural material recovered from the 1960s excavations inside the chancel was differentiated into that recovered from the comprehensive excavations impinging on the central choir area, adjacent to the tower, with that from the more complicated NW corner, itself further subdivided to distinguish the material from the trench over the N wall further E along the resonance passage, Figs 42 and 61a. All these areas are heavily permeated with the 'Standard A' blind tracery from the supposed collapse of the tower.

In the subsequent text the individual mouldings discussed are given the illustration figure number, followed by the database number, which is also marked on the surviving pieces of stone.

Only three examples of true stone mouldings were found *in situ* in the church remains, two on masonry of the argued primary build, and one, in green sandstone, related to a wall-tomb (Grave 2, found in 1961 in the N transept), Figs 42 and 51 section D. The first and more informative is the suite of internal mouldings of the doorway leading from the N transept into the eastern chapel, which has an asymmetrical half-round hollow leading to a fillet and an attached demi-roll cut in a shallow angle in the 45° jamb of the door case, Fig. 72 No 499. This rather elementary arrangement, with the lack of symmetry in the hollow and with an inset roll retains some of the feeling of the Decorated period, but its rather elementary nature suggests movement towards the greater geometric simplicity of the late fourteenth to early fifteenth century. The second moulding *in situ* is a simple hollow chamfered plinth on the second south-western pier built for the later square tower, Fig. 75 No 1143, which, at its centre, is shaped for an attached quarter-roll shaft flanked by right-angled projections on the pier face. The third moulding *in situ* is that around the projecting base of the N transept wall tomb Grave 2, Fig. 42, inserted in the fifteenth century. It is a simple hollow chamfer.

The Standard A suite of mouldings

Figure 69

This is based on a standard rib in limewashed red sandstone, consisting of a 50mm radiused axial roll or bowtell, mounted over well-formed hollowed chamfers, in some cases with a roughly finished 'key' at the back 100mm wide, to key the piece in into a suspended position, as in a vault, Fig. 69 top. Further, many pieces, the full worked length of which usually varies between 312 and 317mm, exhibit a concave curve. These are interpreted as vaulting ribs although the striking radius cannot often be determined, and on many smaller pieces the shape is not apparent at all. However, in some cases, from the soffit (or inner face) of the roll of 'Standard A', it was possible to estimate a striking radius of 8.6m (27ft 2in), and on some of the larger sections, the rolls are curved in elevation. Others, set at an angle of approximately 163° suggest that they may have been multi-sided, the ribs curving upwards to a decagonal apex ring, rather in the manner of Hurley's octagonal timber octagon at Ely (Bony 1979). The hollow chamfers develop cusping each side of the axial roll, the cusps having bold triangular foliate terminations. Rolls meet at various angles, on two planes, and large elements of blind tracery recovered show a direct association with a second type of cusping with 'cylinder' terminals to the cusps, sometimes coloured.

A selection of samples from the 'Standard A' suite are illustrated on Fig. 69. They would appear to be part of an internal blind wall tracery system, which probably develops seamlessly into a vault, and from its location it seems eminently probable that it all once formed part of the internal lining to the square tower, raised on the modified crossing in Friary Phase 2 (*c*.1385-*c*.1423). In 1977, a remarkable group of stone with cusped blind tracery was recovered from Area 3a, the fourth and fifth bays of the chancel from the E, which was remarkably well preserved, showing some variety in the formation of the fleur terminals, with one cylinder terminal painted an orangy-red. Three have blue backgrounds, Fig. 69 Nos 502, and 1158-9. A smaller version of the same moulding executed in the green sandstone, is shown on Fig. 69 Nos 1199 and 1208-9. These will be discussed further.

Parallels for the simple roll over hollow chamfer base moulding in this assemblage are not hard to find, but more difficult to date as it seems to become a 'type immobilisé' for vaulting after *c*.1400. Early examples are Gloucester Cathedral cloister, of before 1377 (Morris 1979) where there are similar vaulting ribs on a much smaller scale, and at the convent's founder, Poulteney's own house, Penshurst Place in Kent, of *c*.1340 and before 1349 (pers. ob.). Its very simplicity, boldness and clarity speak more of the fifteenth century than they do of the 14th century, and at the Coventry Whitefriars it is very likely to be associated with work erected after the availability of Bassett money in 1385, if such was forthcoming. Towers were symbols, and were, like Beauvais, sometimes erected even before the nave was completed. At Coventry it is not inconceivable that the early erection of a tower was aimed to match or even to intimidate the rival Greyfriars, and there would be some practical advantage in that the scaffolding could be freely erected at the W. Curiously, nothing recovered in the mass of collapsed material in the excavations is indubitably from the exterior of a spire, but the large quantity of green sand from perished green sandstone, Fig. 61a, may indicate that the finer green sandstone was indeed used for the second spire. The rubble contained the majority of the iron cramps recovered from the various excavations, see Section Q, *Structural Metalwork*. A spire is known to have existed, for it is sketched by Sir Thomas Smythe in the mid sixteenth century showing the top of the spire broken, Fig. 32, and we also have the 1572-4 reference to a steeple, usually meaning tower and spire together, being allowed to fall.

The Chancel

Figures 61a, 62b, 68 and 69

The earliest building work, apart from the eastern arm of the cloister discussed above, is to be expected at the E end of the chancel, the western part being confused by what seems to have been a series of serious structural movements on at least two pre-Dissolution occasions, one accompanied by the probable collapse of the tower, followed by the major post-dissolution occasion in 1574 when the whole steeple fell from neglect (Harris 1907-13). Of the total of 17 pieces found in 1977 in pit F.81a, (and drawn in 1978) outside the presumed E window of the chancel, Fig. 68, sixteen consisted of lengths of a 174mm wide (7in) mullion with an estimate depth front to back of *c.*500mm. It has a simple chamfer outside, and a filleted roll on the inside developing from an ogee chamfer to form a bracket moulding, Fig. 68 Nos 706-7. Three sections, however, of similar section were 'waisted' outside the glazing groove, and in 1977 a complete length of tracery of similar 'waisted' section was recovered from the chancel area. This illustrates the full depth was 565mm front to back, Fig. 68 No 1161. The waisted sections are no doubt from a king mullion from the same suite, the added depth providing greater stability whilst the waisting reduces the visual impact.

From the N chapel area came a piece showing this same moulding section bifurcating into arched tracery, Fig. 68 No 222. The mouldings are of the same general type as used as the major element in the Bishop's Eye at Lincoln Cathedral (Morris 1979, 11c), there dated to *c.*1325.

Away from the pit at the E end, pieces of similar section were scattered over and outside the chancel, suggesting it may have been the standard section used for most if not all the chancel windows, although, in the western chancel area a very similar moulding, but with a more strongly formed ogee, formed in the green stone was found. Some pieces had been deliberately cut back on the inner face (e.g. Fig. 68 No 765) while a section of matching green window jamb came from the N cemetery area (No 793, not illustrated), recovered when the road drainage was being installed. Curiously, a detached piece, Fig. 68 No 408, appears to be the missing offcut.

Most pieces presented evidence that the internal, that is the fillet roll end, had regularly been limewashed up to the glazing groove. As with the majority of the architectural elements throughout the church there was no evidence of colour having ever been applied.

At the E end there was also a small section of a smaller chamfered mullion, 88mm in thickness, Fig. 68 No 324.

From the areas of the E end inside the chancel accessible to excavation in 1962 there were 45 pieces of architectural masonry, 19 stratified in destruction or collapse contexts. Eighteen pieces were identified as wall strings, their lack of curvature precluding hood moulds and the early date generally excluding labels. One type has a bold fillet with wavy upper face, some pieces showing signs of weathering, chamfered below, and grooved immediately below the face fillet, Fig. 68 Nos 960 and 964. As the short lengths recovered show no curvature this may be an external mid-wall string. Internally, there were six more delicately carved pieces also with a wavy top, but beaked and an ogee below, Fig. 68 Nos 979-82, etc. Perhaps this is the internal wall string. Two further pieces, Fig. 68 Nos 73-4, appear to be an ogee and fillet surround to a raised ashlar panel, and a further 254mm run of recessed quarter-round moulding complete the range specifically related to the E end of the church.

Other forms of window tracery were found in the eastern chancel. One piece from the E end, Fig. 68 No 1232, based on a small leading roll, displays the dividing of the mullion, without a supermullion, with glazed circular openings either side and in the cloison above. The seventeenth piece from this context was a cusp point. The mouldings indicate it cannot be from the same window, and the diameter of the feature, at approximately 400mm suggests either large semicircular cusps or small oculi as occur in the apsidal eastern windows of Lichfield Cathedral choir, (where, as mentioned earlier William Ramsey was an advisor), again of the second quarter of the fourteenth century (Bony 1979, pl. 223).

Amongst this E chancel group there were 10 pieces of 'Standard A' moulding, Fig. 69, a bold leading roll flanked by a simple hollow-chamfer, apparently a vaulting rib section flung far from the collapsing tower; numerous other examples are discussed with the W chancel deposits on Fig. 69. Unstratified, but from the general choir area is some tracery with a 45mm front fillet and including cusped ogee elements in the design, Fig. 68 Nos 639 and 642-3. These are probably the outer face of the 'Standard A' tracery, and the limewashed inner face is represented by others, Fig. 68 Nos 636-8, displaying a horizontal transom (supertransom) the soffit of which is cusped. Perhaps the nearest example is at Knowle Warwickshire where a chapel was founded in 1396 (Harvey 1978, pl. 43), but this element does appear earlier at, for instance, Edington, Wiltshire *c.*1352-61 (pers. ob.), and with cuspings on the soffit at Maxey, after 1367 (Harvey 1978, pl. 44), Walpole St Peter, *c.*1350-1400 (pers. ob.) and Melrose, 1385

(Harvey 1978, fig. 6.14 and map V).

From the 1977 unstratified groups come two drip or coping sections, Fig. 70 Nos 679 and 705, one clearly from an exposed position as it had grooves for running-in with lead, whilst the other is drilled vertically to a weathering groove, and is probably a drip originally built into a wall.

A part-octagonal moulded base, Fig. 68 No 650, for an attached wall shaft may illustrate internal wall articulation.

Areas related to the Chancel

Figures 68, 69 and 74

Outside the N side of the Chancel, the material amongst the 59 pieces recovered in the 1960s is different. As well as the 'Standard A' 174mm wide roll-and-fillet-nose rib, a smaller 120mm (5in) rib in green stone is represented by 8 pieces (13.5%), Fig. 69: Std 'B'. This seems to be part of the destroyed vault, developed out of the wall articulation of the N transept chapel. Again a sizeable proportion (25%) of the material is deposited from the collapse of the tower.

The occurrence outside the building on this side of a section of the painted ogee canopy from a tomb or sedilia or shrine, Fig. 74 Nos 1101-3, is indicative of the thoroughly mixed nature of the material. Although the N cemetery lay in this area, it is clear that this piece came from within the church, and other parts of the same structure were recovered from the resonance passage. Such elements as this, and probably much of the other moulded material would have been of rather less value to stone robbers than squared stone. It appears that at this spot just outside the building such pieces of no use to the robbers, like the sculpture, were jettisoned, reinforcing the 1960s idea that after the Dissolution a dump of unusable stone was established somewhere outside the N transept chapel.

Only one stone, Fig. 68 No 267, was recovered from the S side of the chancel; unusually this carried a very small wave moulding and is probably part of a larger series.

The Chancel Eastern end, west end and south side

Figures 68, 70 and 71

This zone represents the eastern end of the choir and the area immediately to its E on the N side. In the central chancel, where 84 stones were recovered, mullions are not strongly represented (three at 17.4cm wide standard) but one unusual piece, a complete waisted mullion section with the internal roll-and-fillet-nose, Fig. 68 No 1161, was recovered. One smaller (10cm wide) mullion appears for the first time. The lack of window material in this area suggests that side windows were small or even absent above the canopies of the choir stalls, with larger windows confined to the three eastern bays of the chancel. No windows in the western three bays however would be very unlikely, as it would produce an unparalleled external appearance. There is no hint whatsoever of clerestory windows, nor should any be expected from the plan. There is also no indication of distinctive elements from vaulting, and it may reasonably be concluded that the chancel had a timber ceiling or open roof.

One unusual stone was found in 1977. It had been placed as a pillow under the head of the deceased in Grave 77.2, Fig. 43, in the approximate centre of the presbytery. The stone is rectangular, 280 x 195mm, smoothed but otherwise unworked, but is rudely inscribed with a legend which appears to read IHC, legible, curiously, from the head end, Fig. 71 No 1123. John Cherry (British Museum) has suggested "the first letter might be a G or the abbreviation for 'Con' – there is clearly an abbreviation line above it." Con. could be for Conventus? Fr Jerome Bertram suggests IHC is for Jesus, and what looks like the standard contraction for CON, like a 9, with an e, which is what we seem to have, i.e. 'conne'. Perhaps it can be read as "Jesus converte" – Jesus turn and look? The stone appears to date from the late fourteenth or early fifteenth centuries.

Material from the 1977 excavation and clearances in the area of and around the central part of the chancel, extending from the centre to the W, and S to the E of the standing cloister range, were not subdivided and marked by area, other than to differentiate an area, labelled at the time Area 3, from the area E of the choir stalls. From these excavations came 184 pieces; some of which produced a further amplification of the earlier evidence. Of the total, only a small proportion (13%) was not some part of the 'Standard A' suite. Amongst the others was some interesting tracery with subsidiary (i.e. set back) pointed cusping, with trefoil cusps beneath a horizontal transom, Fig. 68 Nos 636-7. This had been glazed, and probably relates to stones Nos 642-3 which have cusps on ogee sections. A section of axial roll hood moulding, Fig. 68 No 647, with an estimated radius of 760mm (2ft 6in) may have been over a smaller feature such as a sedilia or piscina. The roll-and-fillet-nose mullion continues to appear in small numbers, much fragmented. There are also two pieces of chamfered drip moulding with a hollow-cut underside, Fig. 70 No 705; one is pierced vertically for no apparent reason. Again approximate parallels are numerous, such as at Edington, Wiltshire, dated 1352-1361 (Forrester 1972, 226). The 'Standard A' assemblage here exhibits some interesting features, blue coloured backgrounds to blind tracery, and a 90° junction of the axial roll, suggesting 'T' and 'X' junctions.

North West Chancel

Figures 42, 61a, 69 and 70

Of this large deposit, of 249 stones, 92% (226) are of the 'Standard A' suite, with some pieces of cusping or tracery, much of it smashed into fairly small pieces. This must represent the place of impact of the fall of the tower, with its wall panelling and vault. Only five of the total are of green sandstone, two of which are identical to the standard axial-roll section. The significance of this is not clear; it may be the vault was undergoing erection when the green stone source quarry opened, or that a later repair was undertaken in this material. Some 'Standard A' pieces exhibit features of the vault (Fig. 69 No 245 is a section of a complex cusped vault) where paired ribs or tiercerons meet a ridge rib at an angle of 40-50°, the ridge thereafter splitting in a 'Y' at 125°. Others have a 45° junction on one side of the axial roll only. Some sections of rib have 150mm keys at the back.

A number of pieces of ribbing are complete in their length between joints. This is surprisingly short, and not uniform; the stones varying between 178 and 330mm in length, averaging at 250mm and often made to a standard imperial dimension of 10 inches, and 1ft. This shortness of unit is perhaps due to the added difficulties of making larger lengths accurately to a curve, but as the presence of curvature is very difficult to ascertain in these short pieces, it may be that in practice short straight lengths were easier to assemble, and did not require detailed accurate setting out or specific allocation of each individual piece to large-radius curves, and they may equally be employed for straight lengths. Dr Morris suggests that the bigger pieces were however likely to have been carted off for re-use (pers. comm.).

Of the remaining 23 stones, there are 9 pieces cut to a large curve with wide terminal face or fillet, although not necessarily to an identical template. This moulding occurs mostly around the crossing area, and is interpreted as the intrados moulding of a large arch, such as would be required over the crossing between the tower piers. In one voussoir (Fig. 70 No 2448, and similar) the curvature could be approximately determined at a 3mm rise in 380, suggesting a radius of approximately 6.02m. With the width between piers of the chancel of 7.8m, the arch, struck from centres inset by 1.7m, would therefore rise 5.6m above the springing. The resultant proportions would be entirely acceptable in early Perpendicular work. Other pieces came from the same deposit and one from the S side of the choir (No 1275, not illustrated). The range of similar mouldings is shown on Fig. 70.

One stone is particularly odd. It appears to be a base for a 57mm shaft attached to a right-angled corner, with a large echinus type of moulding which is in regular rising form, Fig. 70 No 254. No useful suggestion as to its purpose can be made other than it might be part of some sort of sill or corbel.

Three of the remaining pieces (Nos 1985-1986 and 1994, not illustrated) are short lengths of a tapering column in green stone, two of which join, with an aggregate length of 118mm.

Chancel - West End

Figures 51, 61a, 69 and 70

At the W end of the chancel there was a remarkably rich deposit of architectural masonry, thickly packed, filling the resonance passages, and sealing the Grammar School deposits, which it could only do after the school moved to St John's, taking the choir stalls with them. This was subdivided into a general W chancel area, with 332 pieces, and, the NW side with 234 pieces (excluding the deposit in the resonance passage which was treated separately). A large group of 247 pieces came from a small trench a little to the E, also over the resonance passage, and the SW side, with a further 103 pieces, similarly excluding the southern resonance passage. The total number of architectural stones recovered from these four areas was 916, with a further 307 reclaimed from within the resonance passages. In practice they may all be seen as one deposit related to the major collapse of the central tower in 1574.

In the general W chancel area, of the 332 pieces recovered, 224 were stratified in 'collapsed tower' contexts, whilst a further 8 were recovered in 1968 from the robbing of Grave 12 (Figs 42 and 166), all curiously being standard fleur terminals. As might be expected from the distribution further to the E, all the zones in the western chancel are dominated by material from this 'Standard A' suite.

In the general W area, 328 (96%) were definitely of the 'Standard A' suite of blind tracery and vaulting including the related cylindrical cusps. Of the remaining 13, some were not specifically identifiable and others a miscellaneous few pieces of mullion and coping. It is this distribution that allows an assumption that 'Standard A' represents both vaulting and blind wall panelling within the tower, which was finally allowed to fall down in 1574. There were no clearly coloured pieces, only three smaller pieces showed some signs of colour, Fig. 69 Nos 502 and 1158-1159.

The NW choir area is where it seems the fall of the tower had its greatest impact. Here, 85% of the 234 stones are of the standard suite; of the others, there are 5 pieces of mullion and 2 of strings. More interesting are four or five sections carrying a large curve, possibly a moulding from a major arch, Fig. 70 Nos 1017-8 and 1046-7.

On the SW side of the choir there were many fewer stones, almost certainly the result of the extensive robbing on this side of the building. Nevertheless, of the 102 pieces found in the collapse stratification, only five were non-standard, one being a carving of a leaf coloured initially blue, but subsequently whitewashed over, Fig. 76 No 1082. Of the 'Standard A', there were a high number of unbroken lengths, varying considerably between 178mm to 343mm, but a number at precisely 229mm long. The implication is that the feature, probably a vault, during building required irregular lengths to fit in, and that these were made to a drawing.

Resonance Passages

Figures 74 and 42, 43 and, 51

The resonance passages or acoustic chambers in the western part of the chancel ran the full length of the choir stalls. The lower levels contained material related to the occupation of Hales' Grammar School, an entirely different picture to the upper fill, which was, as would be expected, largely full of mouldings from the tower collapse. The lowest deposits include some broken stone resulting from early iconoclastic damage, recorded as happening at or after the time the property was dissolved and passed to Sir Ralph Sadleir, for the mayor and aldermen complained to Cromwell that 'Dr London...has defaced the church of the Greyfriars and...begun to do the like with the Whitefriars' (McCaffrey 1926, 251), and further damage occurring during the tenancy of the school. After the removal of the choir stalls in *c.*1558 the passages would be open to the accumulation of stone displaced by general decay and unwanted rubbish before being covered dramatically with the tower collapse.

The N resonance passage was excavated almost in its entirety; the southern was, like the adjoining walls and piers, very heavily robbed.

The N passage produced 201 architectural stones.

The lower layers contained some gilded and painted stonework, mentioned earlier, broken away from tombs, shrines or similar richly adorned features within the church. Nine were from the earlier deposits, confirming the disrespect shown to fittings. These included pieces of a crocketed and gilded ogee arch, Fig. 74 No 1101, of which a piece was found outside the chancel on the N side.

The upper deposit included 14 fragments of the standard 178mm axial-nosed mullion, and a smaller 125/128mm mullion, with some tracery, indicated by the survival of five pieces of pointed cusping (Nos 9-11, 33 and 266, not illustrated), suggesting that the windows had survived the school's occupation, at least in structural form, if not the glass. One piece was of green stone, with diverging rolls, each 17mm radius, which had been gilded, also seemingly from a tomb. There were 14 pieces of string course or hood mouldings, the latter only differentiated if they were sufficiently long to display noticeable curves. Some damage had obviously occurred during the school's existence, for sections of string broken into short sections had been rubbed smooth and drilled for inkwells, with smaller drillings around presumably in which to stand quills (Woodfield 1981, 116-118, fig. 14, and other drawings in archive). The quantity, 12, suggests that this had become a regular practice. Some sections of shafting of unknown origin had been treated likewise. The strings were equally divided over three types, the short 22mm-filleted roll, the elongated roll-and-fillet-nose with a 48mm fillet, and the beaded roll-and-fillet, Fig. 74 Nos 92, etc., 391 and 498.

Of other stones, there was a small quantity of mouldings in the later green masonry, including some roll-and-fillet mullions, and a group of what are probably jamb mouldings in the same series, where limewash continued on the back for 75mm indicating that the outer demi-roll-and-fillet moulding projected. One piece, Fig. 74 No 1242, had a similar series of roll and hollow chamfer as the extant door jamb, Fig. 72 No 499, but differing in detail and dimensions. There were also fragments of an angular base, what may be a base torus, Fig. 72 No 725, and of a chamfered weathering course, Fig. 74 Nos 956-957.

The short length of the southern resonance passage available to controlled excavation in 1960-1965 had been very heavily robbed for stone in the eighteenth century. The 106 pieces found reflects that of the passage on the N, with two pieces of tomb or shrine (Fig. 74 Nos 1080 and a small gilded inset angle piece, No 1093 (not illustrated)), 2-4 pieces probably from a nave pier (Nos 185, 1952 and 1957, not illustrated), and two wall strings. There was one piece of pointed cusping. One unusual very slender chamfered-mitre mullion, Fig. 74 No 220, with an angled nose internally, has a 75mm joggled top joint; it is of a type that was not recorded further E in the church and may be an alien piece. Of special interest was a large boss portraying a flower (No 384 – now lost and not illustrated), presumably from a vault. Of the 106 pieces, 81 (76%) were from the 'Standard A' suite.

The large group of 'Standard A' found in this NW chancel area displays no additional clues to the comments above. No 2044 (not illustrated) has its meeting faces cross hatched.

The North Transept

Figures 70, 72 and 73

The deposit from the western areas of the chancel continued without a break into the N transept, where 149 architectural pieces were found. The distribution of stone types between the two areas is, however, rather different.

In the N transept 'Standard A' mouldings form only 10% of the total, contrasting with over 28% of mullion sections and jambs, mostly of the type with a leading roll internally. There were 36 sections of the standard 175-178mm wide-464mm (7in x 18½in) deep mullion with axial roll necked off a chamfered section (as Fig. 72 No 708 but larger), the other side simply chamfered with a 25mm fillet, and its corresponding jamb. Less clearly identifiable are pieces displaying a simple end fillet between chamfers; these may be the outer end of the same mullion, another type or indeed a vaulting rib. A smaller and thinner mullion of the same section was also represented, particularly strongly in the eastern side of the transept (25 lengths, of which four are in green stone). It is suggested that the occurrence here is related to the N transept Chapel where a minor vault using the same section as 'Standard A' was almost certainly employed.

Mullions are particularly significant, which need not cause surprise, as the transept would have windows on three sides, with perhaps additional gable lights on the N. Of 33 pieces, 29 are of the standard axial roll type, Fig. 69, discussed earlier, some pieces curving as within a major arch in a panelled tracery window-head (Nos 300 and 303, not illustrated). The dominance of this type perhaps suggests the upper levels of the transept, as opposed to the footings, are of one build, although there is no means of knowing whether the material recovered is equally representative of all windows and identical with the Great East Window. Tracery fragments with pointed cusps were also present.

Four small pieces of painted or gilded stone from a shrine or similar were found, possibly related to the wall tomb (Grave 61.2, Fig. 42) inserted into the N transept wall, Fig. 73 No 1184.

Two sections of a large roll-and-fillet moulding, the fillet being 165mm (6½in), were also found, Fig. 70 Nos 1043-4; these again may represent the intrados mouldings of a major arch, perhaps the main chancel arch. The fluidity of this moulding could indicate a date in the late fourteenth or early fifteenth century.

Strings are not common in the N transept deposits, amounting to 12 pieces in all. They fall into two groups, the long and short scrolled or ogee type with angled end fillet, there being an almost equal number of each. The short 'pig-nose' string 78mm deep is very similar to those found at the E end. There is one of angular section, Fig. 72 No 259, which is perhaps not a string at all, but an offset from a part-external octagonal feature such as a stair tower.

There were 11 pieces of string course, equally divided between both short and long nosed varieties, Fig. 72, as No 200 short, and No 953 long, not illustrated. The surviving lengths are not sufficient to distinguish any shaping or curving.

A few stones cannot be explained at all (Fig. 70 No 1238 - NW chancel) appears to be a flat panel, rising to a small edge fillet and framed with a small cyma, reading as an ogee in elevation. No 281, Fig. 70, is a small roll set in a 135° angle between worked faces. No 151, Fig. 72, has a similar sequence of mouldings to the *in situ* N transept E door jamb, but is not from the same feature but probably some other door. A door may have existed in the N wall of the N transept where there is a distinct change in build.

There were two pieces of the large intrados moulding, perhaps from a transept arch.

Apart from the one door jamb *in situ* in the E wall of the transept, there were no other distinguishable jamb mouldings.

North Transept: east side

Figure 69

The deposits from the NE side of the N transept were significant for the sudden concentration of the 'Standard B', Fig. 69, the smaller version of the roll over hollow chamfer rib, which formed over 16% of the total of 51 pieces, some being in the green stone. The largest quantity of this moulding was found just to the E of the transept, packed into a trench of the N wall of the N chapel/porch, built there at its later rebuilding. The use of the green stone here indicates a date, at least for the vaulting, of after 1400 AD, probably later in that century, Fig. 42 (and see, Section E, *The Church of the Whitefriars, Coventry*). The concentration here, including curved ribs in 'Standard B' green stone, suggests that the chapel was originally vaulted, and with the ribs carried down the walls as shafts to the small moulded bases. The rebuilding was probably occasioned by movement in the tower, and further buttressing eventually rendered the building unusable for its original purpose, and it was rebuilt in the sixteenth century as a workshop, continuing as such into the post-dissolution period. Unlike the 'Standard A', the axial roll of 'B' appears to have both bases and capitals belonging to wall shafting, Fig. 69 Nos 1199 and 1208-9. This suggests that there is in this area, a subsidiary vault reflecting that of the tower, but on a smaller scale, which almost certainly had been thrown over the eastern chapel to the transept. Conjoined merging rolls indicate that the vault was tapered down to a point stooling in the walls, presumably in a position intermediate between wall shafts. Pointed cusped tracery was again present with axial-roll mullions and glazing bars. The chapel was demolished to insert a large diagonal buttress to the tower in the mid to later fifteenth century.

A section of cinquefoil arcade, Fig. 77 No 1052, was also found, similar to a piece from the W door area, Fig. 77 No 221.

Crossing and the Southern Tower Piers

Figures 42, 75 and 76

Two stones recovered in the 1960s from the main area of the crossing, and which are not assignable to other areas, include a section of shafting built into the floor make-up against the SW tower pier, and a small piece of cusping.

The material from the robbing trenches of the western piers of the crossing was also differentiated. The first, earlier, NW tower pier provided 3 pieces, all being a 42mm-diameter half-roll on one face of a 68° acute angle, Fig. 75 No 170; a fourth being found in the 1st nave pier robbing on the N side. This is probably a vertical arris against a squint opening, and is probably unrelated to the pier itself. The second NW tower pier produced one stone, a lower part of a bead bound by a fillet, a smaller version of the bead bounding the polygonal intrados of the nave arcade, Fig. 76 No 161.

The SW tower pier had the hollow chamfered base mouldings still in position, mentioned above, Fig. 75 No 1143, indicating a central demi-shaft on the inner canted face of the pier, flanked by right-angles.

North East Transept Chapel, External

Figures 73 and 80-81

The N chapel, which at the early stages of the excavation was believed to be an entry porch from an access from Gosford Street, provided a total of 207 pieces of architectural masonry, some of particular interest and quality.

Five pieces of sculptural work illustrated on Fig. 80 from the general area NE of the chapel and outside the chancel wall were recovered in 1968 from the destruction and post-Friary levels, some being eighteenth century levels, see Section G, *Architectural Sculpture*, Figs 80-81. These included the hairy torso of a costumed wodewose (Sculpture No 1076), part of a head also found nearby probably belonging to the same piece (Sculpture No 1077), as also a left hand clasping a presumed torch (Sculpture No 1079); there was also a dog-head gargoyle spout (Sculpture No 1072). These were found together in a group immediately outside the N chapel wall at its E end (68 IIIE.117), Fig. 42. If these came from the chapel itself rather than from a dump of unwanted material then it speaks of a richness of embellishment. Some painted work was also found, including an arch with evidence of gilding, a 7-lobed terminal enriched with leaves, Fig. 73 No 1114, and what may be pieces of a tomb or shrine which had coloured pig-nose mouldings and a square corner with hollow chamfers, embellished with red, white and blue stripes 16mm wide, Fig. 73 No 1084.

Of the architecture, here was a good quantity (50 pieces) of a smaller version of 'Standard A' moulding for vaulting, often worked in the green stone. Most of these came from the Rebuild phase, although one or two pieces of 'Standard A' were also included, one clearly having been mortared in with a type 'B' moulding. Two pieces were monolithic with their bases suggesting that the vaulting had been carried down the walls as attached shafts, Fig. 73 No 1113, and No 1133, not illustrated. Shafts have also been separately identified. This material had been overlaid by an eighteenth-century layer of redeposited 'Standard A', totalling some 63 pieces.

Evidence for the windows is very slight. One window head, based on the smaller (120mm) mullion, was recovered from an eighteenth century level and is not at all conclusive, and a piece of 184mm mullion, halved lengthways, indicates a form of Perpendicular tracery, and was also found in eighteenth-century levels.

South Transept

Seven stones were recovered from the S Transept, with more from the eastern part of the transept, an area very heavily robbed. 'Standard A' is represented by three, possibly four pieces; amongst the other is one piece of the smaller standard mullion and one piece with a wide curve, believed to be an element in the major arcade or crossing arches.

South Claustral Range

Although extensive excavations took place in the 1970s, E of the standing building and between the sacristy and the S end of the claustral range, no architectural masonry was retrieved or is now extant. A small excavation carried out in 1995 by L. Donel for the City of Lincoln Archaeological Unit (unpublished) similarly did not retain the two or more pieces observed, including a mid-wall string and a chamfered piece of architectural work.

The Nave

The Eastern Nave

Figures 42, 70, 75, 76, 79(mason's marks) and 80 (sculpture)

The lozenge pier foundations of the nave arcade can with some confidence be reconstructed above ground by the fortunate recovery of a section of pier from a 1969 contractor's trench, ex context, but in the NE end of the Nave, Fig. 76 Nos 1246-7. This has a polygonal intrados moulding, flanked by beads, leading to a bold roll, 84mm radius (6½in diameter) terminating in a 53° projection. A curved section of what is interpreted as an arch intrados, Fig. 76 Nos 1239-41, suggests that the pier mouldings rose into the arcade arches without the interruption of a capital, but the shafts on the inner and outer faces of the nave walls would probably have risen to small capitals, perhaps co-terminus with corbels supporting wall posts for the roof trusses, thus articulating the nave and aisle wall surfaces.

Of the 60 fragments of architectural elements found in the whole eastern end of the nave, there were only 5 pieces of the 'Standard A' series, providing some confirmation that the tower fell in a NE direction.

Three pieces of the large roll-and-fillet moulding, Fig. 70 No 1045, etc., found W of the screen and near the SW tower pier, were perhaps from the crossing arch soffit moulding.

In the E nave there were two chapels defined by screen walls, one either side of a walkway into the crossing. The E side of the chapels is defined by a screen to the crossing. Stone robbing had been extensive in this area but a number of architectural stones exhibited quite a different range of detail from anything met further to the

E, and the small scale of some suggests that some architectural lavishness was expended on these chapels.

From the destruction contexts 64 XVI.1 and 64 XVIA.1 over the southern chapel, there were a total of 11 stones, with a further 3 from 62 VI.7a the context of the tower collapse. One small piece was a radiused corner painted with a red ground and gilded, and also from this context came the remarkable piece of sculpture carved in the round in an early Renaissance style showing confronting dolphins, Fig. 75 No 1099, a piece not earlier in date than the early sixteenth century and probably nearer 1530. Associated with this latter piece was a 90mm thick slab of Purbeck-like fossil limestone, Fig. 75 No 1197, perhaps part of an Altar table within the chapel for which the carved piece was a supporting leg. Other coloured pieces were found. Some feature in this area was octagonal or at least shaped with internal and external angles defined by beads (Fig. 76 No 183, Fig. 75 Nos 354-6 and No 184 not illustrated), one having a mason's mark, Fig. 79i. This may represent part of the nave screen.

There were also five pieces of a type which has tentatively been described as a major crossing arch, having a large curve turning out at the end to a 165mm fillet (Nos 1246-1247 and 1270-1272), as illustrated on Fig. 70 No 2448. These were in an eighteenth-century context. One stone stratified in a collapse context may just have been a door jamb.

No 1250, Fig. 75, is a small moulding in a coarse sandstone, possibly part of a series, unusual in its greater complexity.

The first eastern nave pier on the N side, context 64 XX.1 contained three pieces of architectural work one of which is unexplained, Fig. 75 No 1283. All have a half-round arris roll between fair faces meeting at an acute 68°.

Apart from elements from the nave arcade and the supporting piers, no great diversity of architectural elements might be expected from the great body of the nave, which was essentially a large and simple space.

Central Areas of the Nave

Figure 76

The central section of the nave was not directly threatened by road building in the 1960s therefore excavation was limited to that necessary to retrieve the plan of the building. Some sections were also not accessible. Trench 64 XIX, Fig. 42, on the N side second nave pier, in addition to confirming the buttress spacing provided, yielded three pieces, Fig. 76 Nos 1224-6 in whitewashed green sandstone, from an architectural element having an asymmetrical bulge, 28mm high between two faces meeting at approximately 112°. The purpose of this moulding or feature is not known. It may be significant that this moulding has also appeared in the crossing area, and is in the green stone associated with later work. A similar but larger moulding came from the W door area, Fig. 77 No 426.

Two stray pieces of the 'Standard A' series and one piece of long-nosed string were also recovered.

North-West Side

Only small sections of the central bays of the nave were accessible to the 1960-65 excavations, and the material recovered is not proportionate to the other more completely excavated areas. The only accessible part in 1961-1965 was a section along the N wall (62 VII, extended in 1964 as Trench XXII), Fig. 41. It was placed over the second and third bays from the W on the N wall. Stratified layers here began with a sixteenth-century level, below which a pre-rebuild level, dated to *c.*1430, was identified, overlying a pre-Reformation collapse. Of 10 pieces of architectural masonry, three might be identified as pieces of window mullions, of which one was the standard lead-roll mullion. One was a piece of wall string with a lower lobe, and what might, given that it displayed weathering on the upper chamfer, be a piece of wall coping. One piece was a 225mm length of the large-curve-and-fillet moulding of a type similar to the three from the central nave area.

The West End of the Nave

Figures 77 and 81

Again, only a relatively small area of the W end of the church, Fig. 41, was available for excavation in 1960-65 and this under abnormally difficult circumstances. Notwithstanding, the bountiful deposit of 85 pieces of architectural work found requires some explaining, and it seems probable that the W door remained the access to the area still defined by the outer walls after the Dissolution, with stone being carted away from the building through this door. Unwanted stone or pieces difficult to re-use, such as any heavily moulded pieces may then have been jettisoned by the door. Small excavations were also made to establish the presence of the nave piers on the N side, to confirm the presence of the N wall of the nave and the existence of the arcade piers, in order to confirm the church plan. The amount of green stone employed in this area is proportionally higher, at 20%, than generally noted on the site, with the exception of the door area, where 53 of the 55 pieces recovered are in red sandstone.

In the last but one N arcade pier trench at the W end (64 XXV) there was part of a simply chamfered window mullion. Similar chamfered stones with a 25mm face fillet in red stone were also present. Also, in the seventh N nave pier, Fig. 42, a short section of a wide fillet, flanked by a chamfer and leading to splayed hollow chamfers was found in a collapse context and is likely to be the soffit moulding of the arcade. A sharply angled piece, Fig. 77 No 228, roughly finished on top, is also of undecided purpose, and may be part of a series of offsets, or simply a rebate. No 1236 with 1115, Fig. 77, may be a corner of a monument plinth; a tiled depression in the floor indicates a heavy feature stood against the wall at the NW corner of the church, Fig. 41. Two pieces of sculpture, both mask label stops, were later handed in to Mrs Woodfield, reported at the time as coming from a former garden W of the W end. These appear in the sculpture report on Fig. 81 Nos 1074 and 1400.

In summary, the three western bays of the nave are believed to be of a later period (later fifteenth century) than the rest of the nave. The W end deposit, if originally related to the area, suggests the nave had simply chamfered mullioned windows, with the use of green stone.

West Door

Figures 77 and 78

The total of 55 architectural pieces from this small area suggests the existence of a post-reformation dump of unwanted stone and floor tile just inside the door. Perhaps salvage agreements involved carting out of the building all disturbed material as part of the recovery of useful squared ashlar.

Thirty-nine (70%) of the architectural pieces in this deposit were parts of windows, being mostly simply chamfered mullions, the axial fillet being of three sizes: 35-38mm, 30mm and 20-25mm, the first size dominating (15 of the larger; 5; and 5 respectively) [the 8in mullion]. The two types with the larger fillet are generally limewashed, whereas the smaller fillet is not. The survival of limewash is of course not necessarily consistent. One of the smaller has a return at 90°, and others, e.g. Nos 234 and 235 (not illustrated), have the springing of cusping on either side of the mullion. A further example, Fig. 77 No 2462, 450mm from inside to out, has the springing of a sub-arch on each side. It is probable that the wider fillet is internal, and the smaller external, with the intermediate size probably belonging to a subsidiary element like a supermullion.

There were two pieces of what are probably window sills, with the external face measuring 62mm, the other 38mm. One could be a vertical jamb.

Ten elements of hollow chamfered cusping are present showing that the cusping was pointed. The picture is that of subarcuated cusped traceried windows, and as the one type is dominant, they were probably lighting the nave from a W window over the door.

There were some six pieces where the axial fillet is straight and flanked by hollow chamfers, i.e. not cusping. One has an axial roll (broken off) and appears to be from the internal edge of a type of window element found at the E end.

One large limewashed piece, Fig. 77 No 426, has an asymmetrical curve, related to the three pieces, Fig. 76 Nos 1224-1226, from the N nave pier. It has a 75 x 42mm rebate in the face of the curve, perhaps a seating for a parclose screen inserted under a major arch.

One coloured piece, Fig. 77 No 1439, with a red-painted hollow chamfer, and a whitened 42mm diameter bead is probably from a tomb; perhaps this is also the interpretation of one small shaft, 45mm in diameter and tear-shaped in section (No 1427, not illustrated), similar to the larger nook shaft (No 153, not illustrated, and Fig. 78 No 1401).

Vestry Passage

Figures 43 and 68

Of the 23 pieces recovered, 16 were pieces of 'Standard A', the spread from the collapse of the tower, none adding to our knowledge. There were five pieces of what appears to be the standard lead-roll window mullion and tracery of the chancel. No 740 (not illustrated) showing the development of this mullion into recessed cusped tracery under the head arch of the window, and a curved section with a 16mm axial fillet having pointed cusping both sides, the cusps simply chamfered with a slight 3mm front fillet. Stone No 1064 (not illustrated) is a small section of shallow cut mouldings, perhaps from the door to a chantry tomb or similar feature. One piece of string with ogee top and inclined fillet, the lower bead missing (No 1072, not illustrated) is of the type usually associated with the chancel.

Chapter House

Unfortunately the bulk of the material from the two excavations in 1973 and 1977 has been lost, and there is now little evidence of how this remarkable structure might look. Four stones however survive, one, from 1973 is simply a piece of stone painted with vertical orange lines 20mm thick. Apart from this there is one nose from a chamfered mullion and a square corner moulding.

Cloisters

Figures 77 and 47 (plan)

In 1964, a small area at the NW corner of the cloister (64 XXIII, Fig. 47) was excavated in order to determine the location of the W range. This trench, which was later duplicated to the S (68 XXVII) produced a total of 24 pieces of worked stone. There was only one piece of the 'Standard A' range. Two sections with a polygonal keeled front and cavetto back appeared to be representative of a new type, Fig. 77 No 228, and jambs of a similar section, chamfered back and front (Nos 122 and 1041, not illustrated) appear to relate. The only other stone of this particular section was found in the N resonance passage.

Fragments of various other windows were also present, and other mouldings of unspecified use, including two pieces (No 172, not illustrated) bearing a half-round on one side of an acute (68°) arris such as occurred in the robbing of the first NW tower pier. One string moulding was present, of a curious downward facing roll-and-fillet design not recorded elsewhere, Fig. 77, 192. One bead, No 158 (not illustrated), is similar to that of the nave arcade piers.

The main significance here is the appearance of the polygonal-fronted shaft, No 228.

The mouldings of the standing building are represented by the base of the garth arcading built into John Hales' sixteenth century walling, Fig. 77 No 1150. The present highly decorative entrance arch to the building seems to be re-set in its present position, and its original location is not known. It cannot be alone, for the inner door opposite the entrance, Fig. 66g, is similar in character and a further section of an external arch with similar complex mouldings including a vine meander and quatrefoil flowers, twigs etc is held in the museum store (Fig. 66h, and No 2439 in store, not illustrated). These are so wholly unlike the general run of mouldings from the Whitefriars that they must be of a different period, perhaps the work of the fifteenth or early sixteenth centuries; Dr Richard Morris, and John Cattell (RCHME) both consider this type of elaborate and enriched moulding could, however, be as early as the fourteenth century (pers discussion).

Some moulded stones were recovered from a trial excavation in the grounds of Gulson Road Hospital, which may indicate the position of the expected Infirmary. Two moulded stones were also found in the small 1995 trench in the area S of the cloister, in the probable position of the Prior's House. These, one of which was a wall string, were unfortunately not retained for recording.

COLOURED AND GILDED STONEWORK

Figures 69, 71, 73-76 and 78

Altogether there were 78 pieces of stonework recovered from the site which bore traces of colour, 18 of which showed gilding. Most came from the chancel and its resonance passages, and from the E end of the nave.

The 'Standard A' series appears as blind tracery, where the background is coloured a rich blue with azurite, Fig. 69, and is generally of the variety with cylinder cusp terminals, themselves coloured red with vermilion, although often only the 'V' sinkings at the end of the cylinders retained the colour. One had globular terminals not seen elsewhere, Fig. 69 No 502.

There are 11 bosses, or parts thereof, bearing the device of a double rose of five and six crinkled and pointed petals, Fig. 71 No 1125, or a single rose of six or four petals with a centre boss, perhaps a daisy, although one has only three petals and a blue coloured central boss. Generally the flower centre is painted red, and the petals gilded, all set against a blue background, Fig. 71 No 1156. All these flower carvings appeared during the work of 1977 apparently found towards the E end of the chancel although the precise location and circumstances of recovery are not now known, but it seems likely that they were in the W part of the presbytery opposite the entry passage, Fig. 43. It is clear that some, including the larger ones, are bosses over the intersection of vaulting ribs, and the form, particularly of the double rose, suggests a late fifteenth or sixteenth century date, probably from the rebuilt tower, although this design had already appeared long before, in the fourteenth century. There are no bosses over the vault intersections in the standing cloister and their absence could indicate an early date, although the omission of bosses does occur in early Perpendicular designs; it is possible the group of bosses, being from one particular area, may relate to a separate and later inserted vault, perhaps in the presbytery itself. The roof of the first presbytery, probably ceiled in timber, may have had to be replaced. Red stone was used for its stronger load bearing properties. One stone, said to have been found under the rubble of the tower was a carved boss in the form of a shield bearing the generic arms of Ferrers (vair, or and gu.) and was probably also a vault boss, Fig. 71 No 1124 and Fig. 60a. As a coin of the 1380s was found in the builder's trample of the NW corner of the choir it is unlikely that the actual person represented here was Robert, 2nd Baron Ferrers of Chartley (d. 1350), or John, the 3rd Baron Ferrers (d. in 1367), and the 4th Baron Ferrers, Robert (d. 1413) is more likely to be the person represented by these arms, if in fact they do refer to a specific family member. A branch of the Ferrers held an estate in Stivechall in Coventry from the thirteenth century up to 1573, with ancillary lands in Pinley and Whitley (DNB 1973, 1246-1252, and Coventry Leet Book). Ferrers de Groby was involved in a money raising procedure with the Prior of the Benedictine House in Coventry in 1430 (Harris 1907-1913) and Dugdale (1730, 54) records the Ferrers arms in glass of the collegiate church of St John's church, Bablake, built in 1342-1400.

Some of the decorated stonework represents coloured architectural elements, such as the crocketed ogee canopies (No 807, not illustrated, and Fig. 74 Nos 1080 and 1101-3) of a form which probably covered a piscina or sedilia, although its richness may well be more appropriate to a tomb. These come from the chancel or resonance passages. Two additional small fragments produce further evidence: a very small red sandstone fragment from the destruction in the area of the S nave chapel (64 XVIa.1) bore a scarlet paint, and gilding, and a further fragment with a charcoal grey paint of a greenish tinge came from the second bay of the choir from the W (61 XII.8) It had apparently been painted over a fine pinkish lime ground laid over the green stone.

The deposits at the E end did produce a number of pieces from elaborate tombs or shrines. A finial displaying early renaissance elements, Fig. 75 No 1099, has been discussed separately by Helen List and the writer (see Section G, *Architectural Sculpture*) and associated with this is a piece of a fossil limestone slab, approximately 300 x 240mm and 90mm thick, with the edges vertically tooled, and probably part of a ledger slab of a tomb, Fig. 75 No 1197. A further small piece was recovered from the N resonance passage. Two further pieces from the area of the tomb are coloured, one, has a roll coloured black, with an adjacent hollow moulding in red, a 4-way double-ogee moulded shaft with its base, Fig. 77 No 197, and there is another section of a beaded moulding, complete at 400mm long and found in the robbing debris of the first pier of the S arcade (No 157, not illustrated). Stone No 726, Fig. 73, also found here is probably the support for a canopy of the tomb or part of a stone screen. It is scored underneath to provide a stronger key. A tomb (Grave 64.19) or possibly a small chantry, Fig. 42, 64 XXI, is similarly placed to the Cheney chantry-tomb of *c.*1401 at Edington, Wiltshire (pers. ob.). Of strings, there are a few pieces of the long-nosed string, as Fig. 72 No 200).

GRAVES 13 AND 14: DOUBLE STONE GRAVE IN CHANCEL

Figures 42, 61b, 79 and 166

Comment on the construction:

Unusually, the blocks of stone display mason's marks, four of the same individual on the S side, two from another hand on the N. This suggests that stonework was contracted out, and it was necessary to keep a tally on the amount produced by specific individuals. The blocks of local red sandstone are large, and shaped up by a mason's axe and rubbed to produce a good level finish without removing all the marks of dressing. One, the largest, is approximately 1.22 x 0.38 x 0,2m (4ft x 1ft 3in x 8in thick)., and would weigh in the region of 113.25kg (250lb), and was probably manipulated by at least two men and a pair of sheerlegs. After being laid on the bed rock and carried up in a lime mortar with fine joints, one stone out of alignment was cut back *in situ* with a chisel, and on reaching a reasonably level wall the joints were 'buttered' to achive a smooth flat finish internally. On the completion of the sides, the median wall was apparently finished by standing blocks on end, this order of procedure presumably to allow for working space on the outer walls. It subsequently bowed, suggesting the N side, the one containing the burials, was filled up whilst the S double grave remained empty. The stone is green implying an earlier 15th-century date.

SUMMARY

The areas of recovery of the 'Standard A' profile strongly suggest that this range of mouldings came from the fall of the central tower. All pieces of this moulding are heavily limewashed, indicating the tower had internal blind wall tracery which rose to develop into a bold tierceron type vault, rather than a fan, but having some liernes forming a star shape at the centre. No terminal central trap ring was recognised, but probably existed as the church is recorded as having bells. Some sections of the vault were brightly coloured; these may have been around the crown of the vault.

The nave arcade appears to have had attached wall shafts rising to a high level string or corbels for posts of the roof trusses. There is no distinction between the nave face and the aisle face of the piers, which might just suggest that the building was of a hall church type, the aisles of equal height to the nave and no clerestory, although this idea is perhaps more difficult to sustain with the significantly lesser width of the aisles, despite window elements being scarce in the nave. The arcade face of the piers has a moulding which is seen also on a curve, suggesting that the mouldings ran seamlessly into the arches. A distinctive ogee moulding with a flat soffit is perhaps representative of the four great cardinal arches at the base of the tower, the radius being approximately 6 metres, but at the early fifteenth century it would be unwise to rely on simple compass-struck arches as they might well be four-centred or stilted. The nave is known to have had at least one tomb in the eastern bay of the S arcade, similar to that surviving at the semi-friary of Bons Hommes at Edington, Wiltshire. This was, from the pieces found, brightly coloured and perhaps gilded in places.

The Chancel had an unusually extensive range of choir stalls (see Section H, *The Choir Stalls*) in the first three structural bays from the W, with canopy work over some, fixed back to the plain walls, either window-less or similar to those further E but with higher sills. Also, remarkably, two ranges of low benches for novices on each side. Beyond the arched doorway from the vestry passage, it would appear that there were three bays of large windows rising from an internal wall string, and having early perpendicular tracery with supra-arches, based on a roll-and-fillet moulding, holding exceptionally fine glass depicting a range of saints and other devotional symbols in full colour, Figs 115-129. The E window appears to be of the same type, although the sill may well have been raised above a reredos, with tracery containing a Tree of Jesse in glass, see Section J, *Medieval Window Glass from the Church and Cloister*, Figs 95-114. It is probable that there was an ogee-headed and crocketed sedilia on the S wall, Fig. 74, represented by the red and black painted fragments. There may also have been other wall tombs with freely standing canopies, or tombs raised over the stone vaults, for a number of finely wrought fragments of small square shafting, and painted pinnacles were found swept into the cavity under the choir stalls, and later sealed by the collapse of the tower.

The N Transept has a complex history, the first period building presumably having an arched opening on the E wall leading into a small, probably vaulted, chapel. It was subsequently altered, probably necessitated by serious structural movement of the tower, which necessitated the insertion of a large triangular buttress. This appears to have rendered the chapel unusable for its original purpose, and the door was blocked, the Altar being brought forward into the transept and set on a plinth. Perhaps shortly after, the chapel's N wall was rebuilt, perhaps for an external purpose, and provided with a door, later becoming something of a workshop directly accessible from the pathway from Gosford Street. The chapel before these unfortunate events, may well have been richly fitted out, with wall shafting rising to simple capitals and apparently supporting a handsome vault based on a scaled down version of that of the tower, over its two bays, Fig. 69. The reason for a chapel in this position is interesting, and it may have served as a dedicated chantry for the founder or for a craft gild.

The W door remains mysterious, largely due to the difficulty of obtaining access for broader excavation. The mouldings seem to be in a simple range, with sharply angled members, and unelaborated axial-rolls. The presence of green stone in quantity confirms that it had been built at a later date than the main nave. It was provided with an internal lobby.

THE DRAWINGS

With such a large quantity of stone, the drawings were necessarily prepared at a reduced scale, 1:4 for the early drawings, 1:5 for recent drawings, with detail of small elements drawn to 1:2. An exception is made for variations on the 'Standard A' tracery, which were prepared at 1:8. These scales are those of the drawings on Figs 66-78 except where a drawn scale is shown on the figure. All stone mouldings are in red sandstone, except where the letter 'G' on the drawing indicates that the green stone is used. They are drawn specifically to represent the intention of the mason, thus do not show imperfect right angles, slight errors of setting out and unintentional asymmetry, all of which adds nothing to the general understanding of the building. Different types of elements have been grouped together, initially in function groups, and where this is not ascertainable, in groups having common moulding elements. The numbers shown are those of the new database, which will be lodged at the Coventry Record Office, and are the same numbers painted on those stones that do survive the various museum culls. Thus, not all illustrated pieces are specifically discussed in the text.

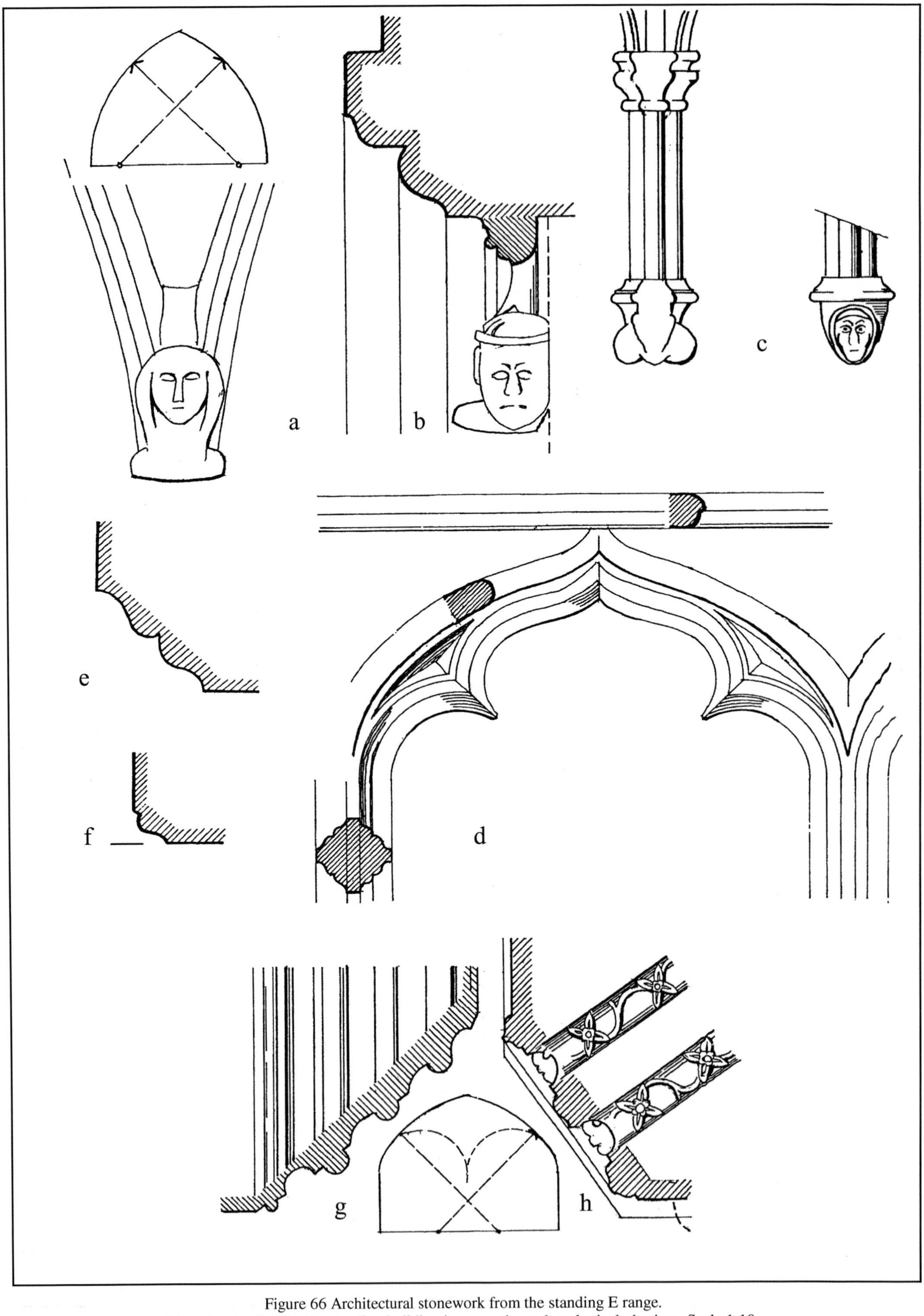

Figure 66 Architectural stonework from the standing E range.
Note the phasing for the standing building is not as the archaeological phasing. Scale 1:10.
Standing building Phase 1 (*c.*1342-1349), S end doorways: a) central corbel and arch, b) mouldings.
Standing building Phase 2 (*c.*1361-1356), cloister arcade and vaults: c) stilted corbels, d) walk arcade, e) N end doorway, f) ?
Standing building later works: g) S doorway to ? St John's Hall, h) external porchway (reset).

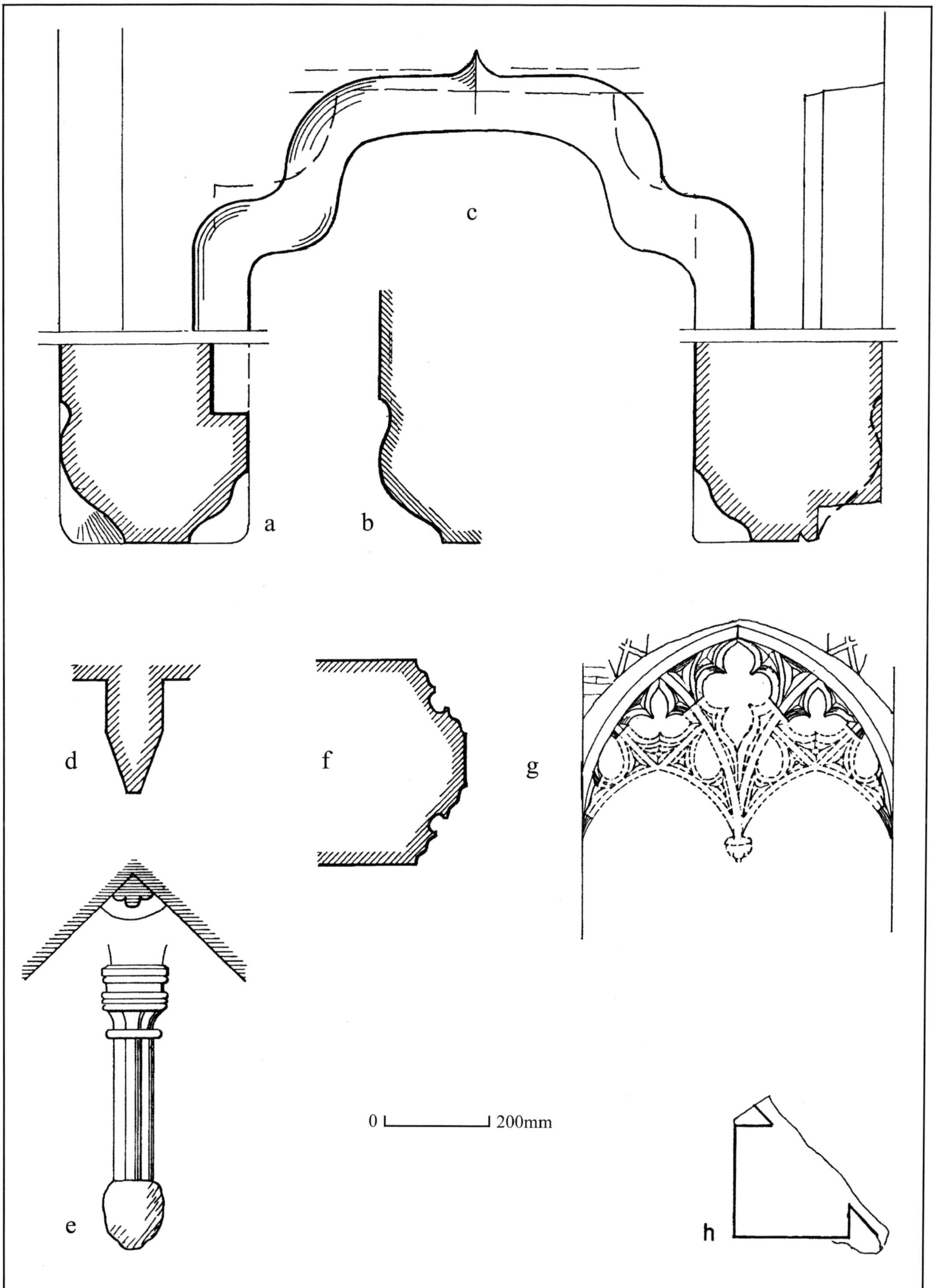

Figure 67 Stonework details from the chapter house: a) mouldings at entrance to the side passages, with entry arch (c), the right-hand jamb rebated for doors. b) impost moulding at entry from the cloister. d) vaulting rib of chapter house. e) corner corbel of chapter house vault. f) transverse arch over the entrance with moulding detail and g), a reconstruction drawing. h) moulding 703 recovered from the excavation of the chapter house. Scales 1:10 except reconstruction drawing, g, at 1:40.

Figure 68 Choir and E window: window tracery - probably from the Great East window, and other window stonework from the choir. Wall string mouldings. Nos. 222 and 763 from the N porch, but of identical sections. Scales 1:10 and 1:20 (bottom left).

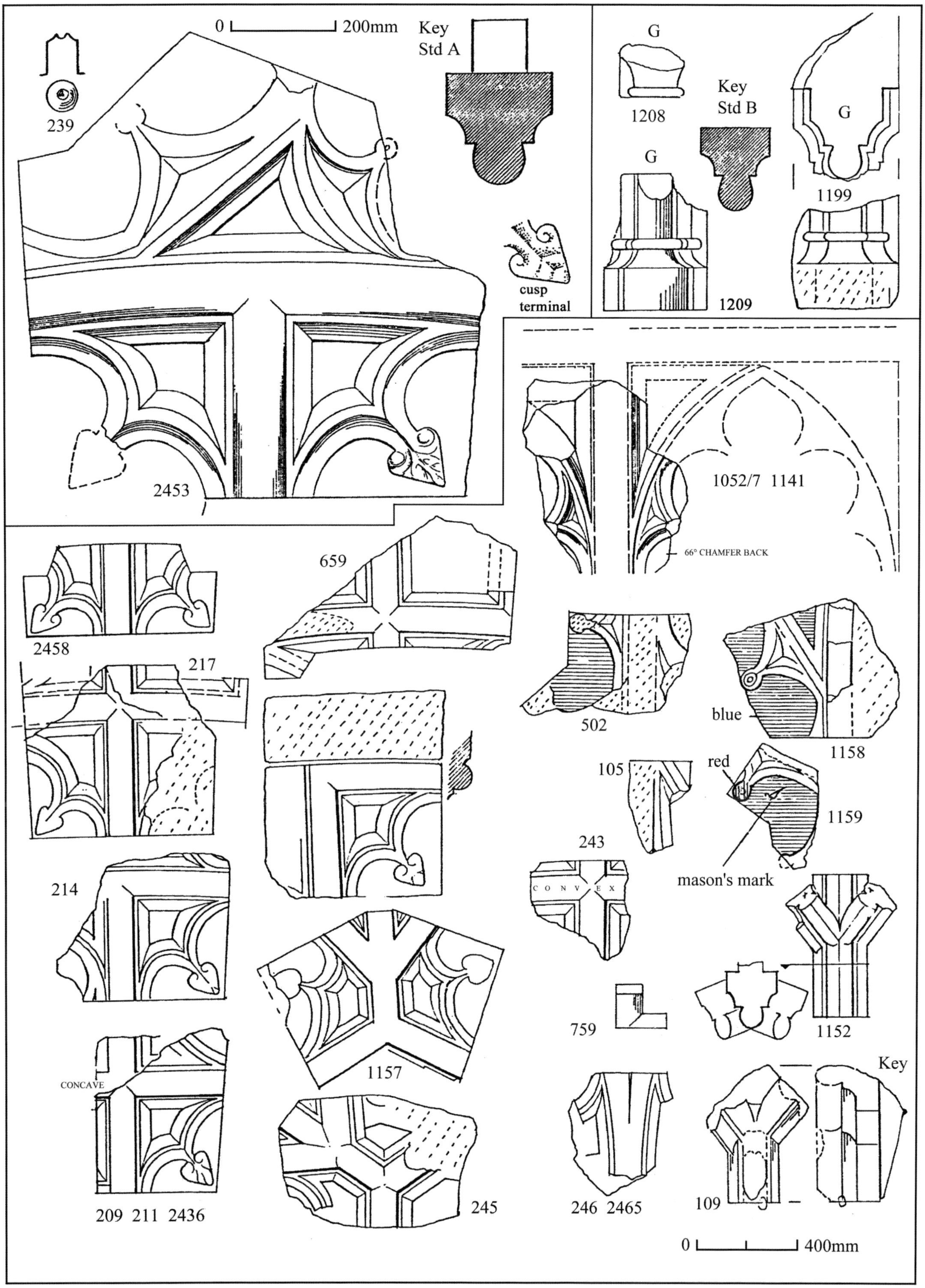

Figure 69 Standard A blind tracery (top left) with the range of variations below, including fleur and barrel cylinder terminals (No 239). Standard B detail (top right). Nos 109 and 105 are similar, but from the W. door area; 1052-7 and 1141 are from the N transept/porch. [G = green sandstone; coloured background indicated heraldically]. Scales 1:10 and 1:20 (below line).

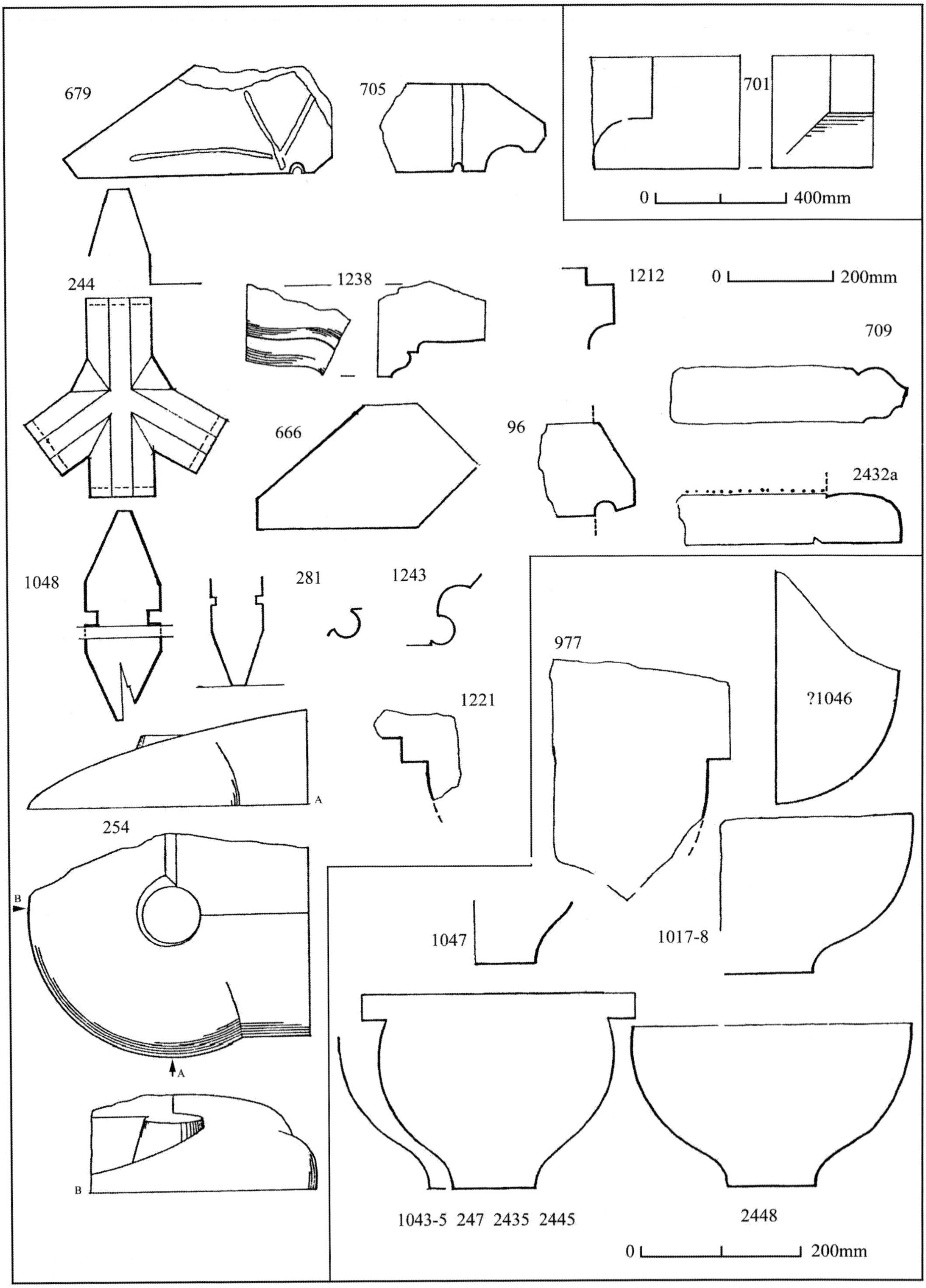

Figure 70 Stonework from the chancel, N and W areas. No 701 is a small moulded panel, and a group of similar large mouldings (box in bottom right corner) were found in the N chancel area entering the crossing, probably the intrados of a large arch. No 679 is a grooved sill with channels for running in lead. No 705 is an internal drip course with channel for water. Scales as shown.

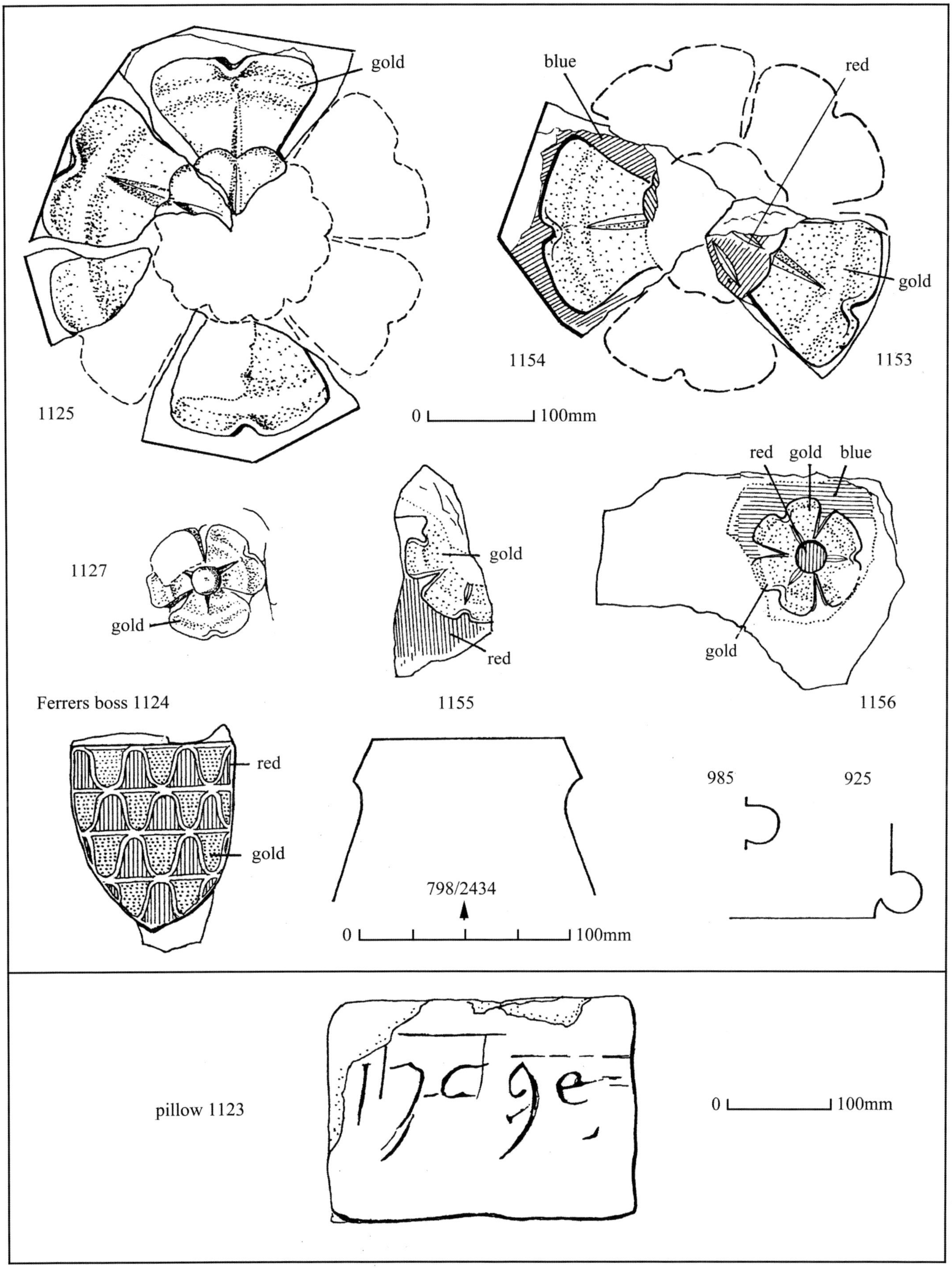

Figure 71 Vaulting bosses and similar elements from the W chancel area. No 798 is from the N porch area, and the arris mouldings from the W chancel. No 1123 is a pillow stone from a stone-lined grave, 77.2, in the presbytery. Colours indicated in heraldic conventions. Scales as shown except No 1124 at 1:10.

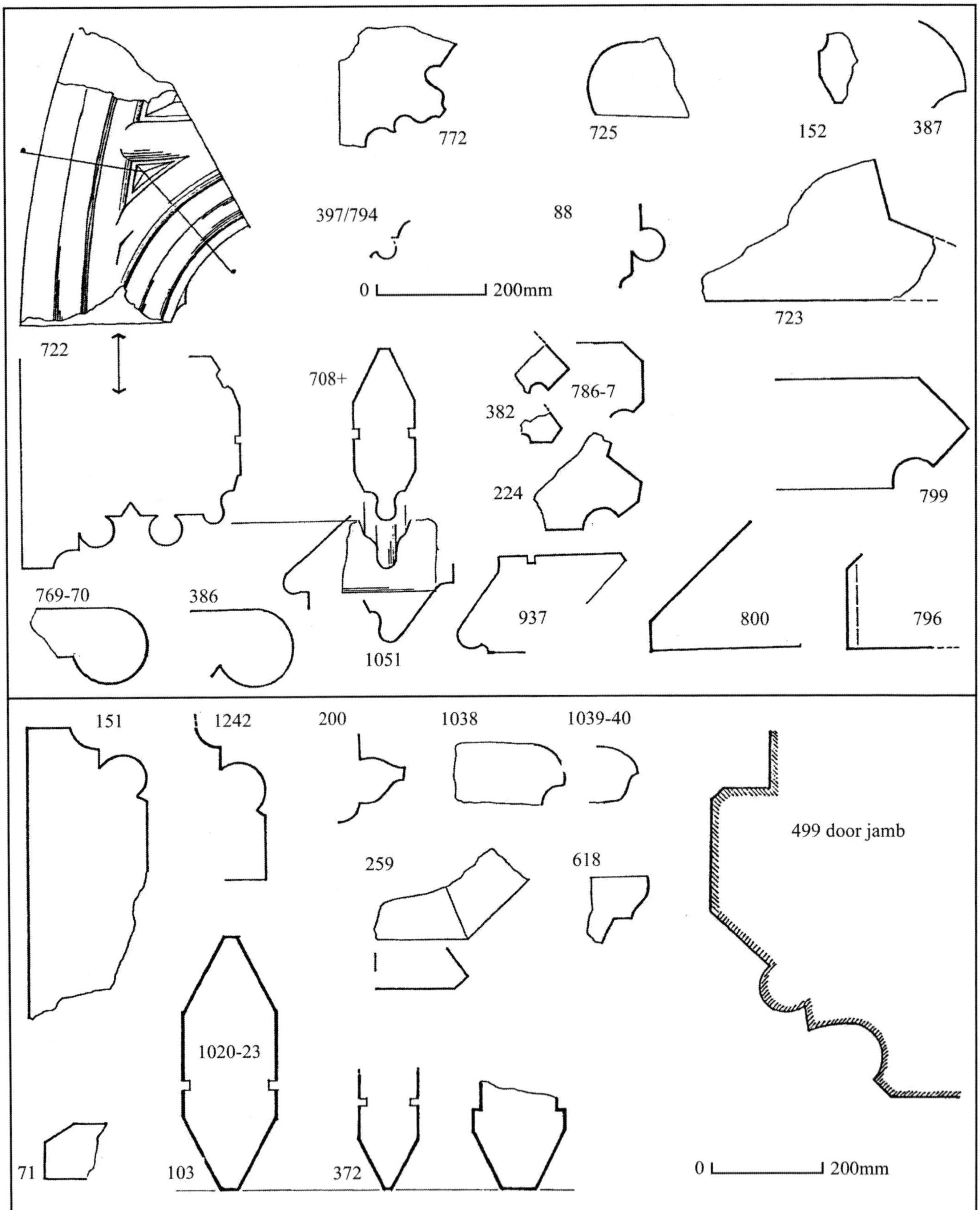

Figure 72 Stonework recovered from the area of the N transept and its eastern chapel, including window jamb and mullion, chamfer and string courses. Nos. 71, 937 and 1051 are similar mouldings from the N. resonance passage. Scale 1:10.

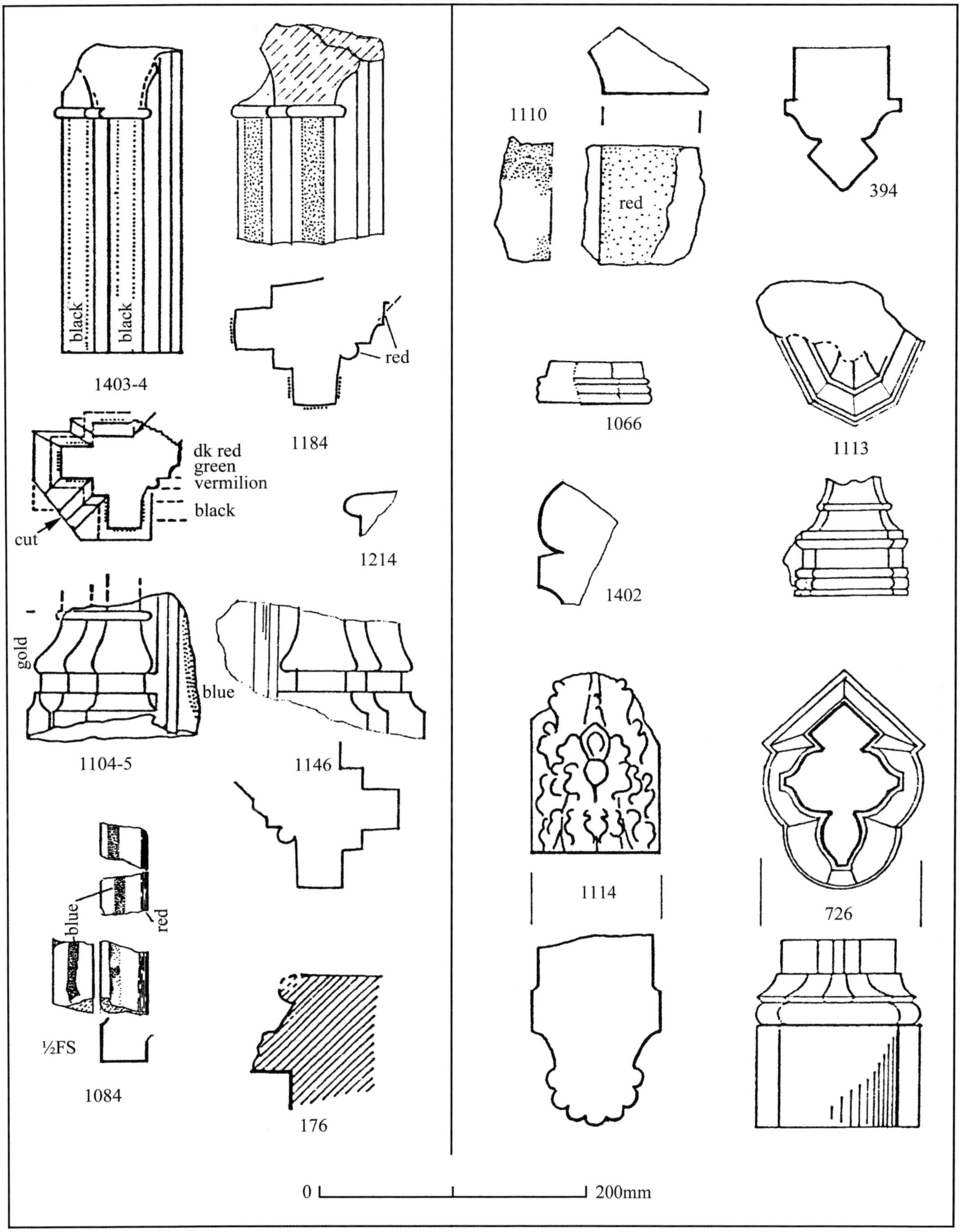

Figure 73 Decorative stonework, probably from tombs. The right panel shows pieces from the N chapel, except No 726 which is from the E end of the Nave. The left panel shows pieces from the N transept, except No 1104-5 which are from the NE end of the nave. Scale 1:4.

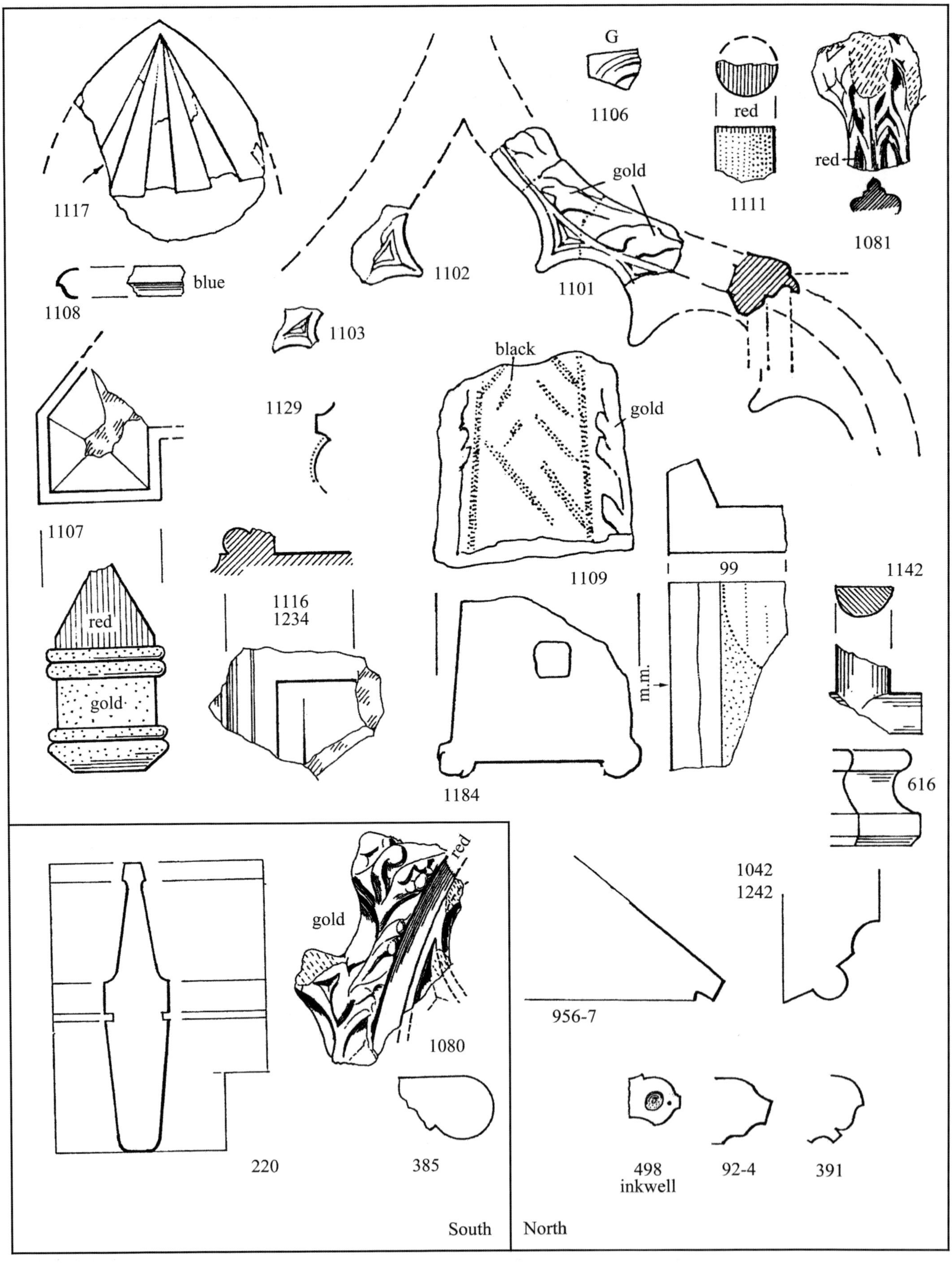

Figure 74 Stonework from architectural features recovered from the N resonance passage, and from the S resonance passage (inset at bottom left). No 1101 is a gilded ogee arch, as is No 1080, perhaps a tomb canopy. Nos 1107 and 1109 are elements from the corners of decorated tombs. No 1117 was possibly reworked for Hales' School, and No.498 a string course section reused as a School inkwell. Scale 1:5 except Nos 1080 and 1081 at 1:4

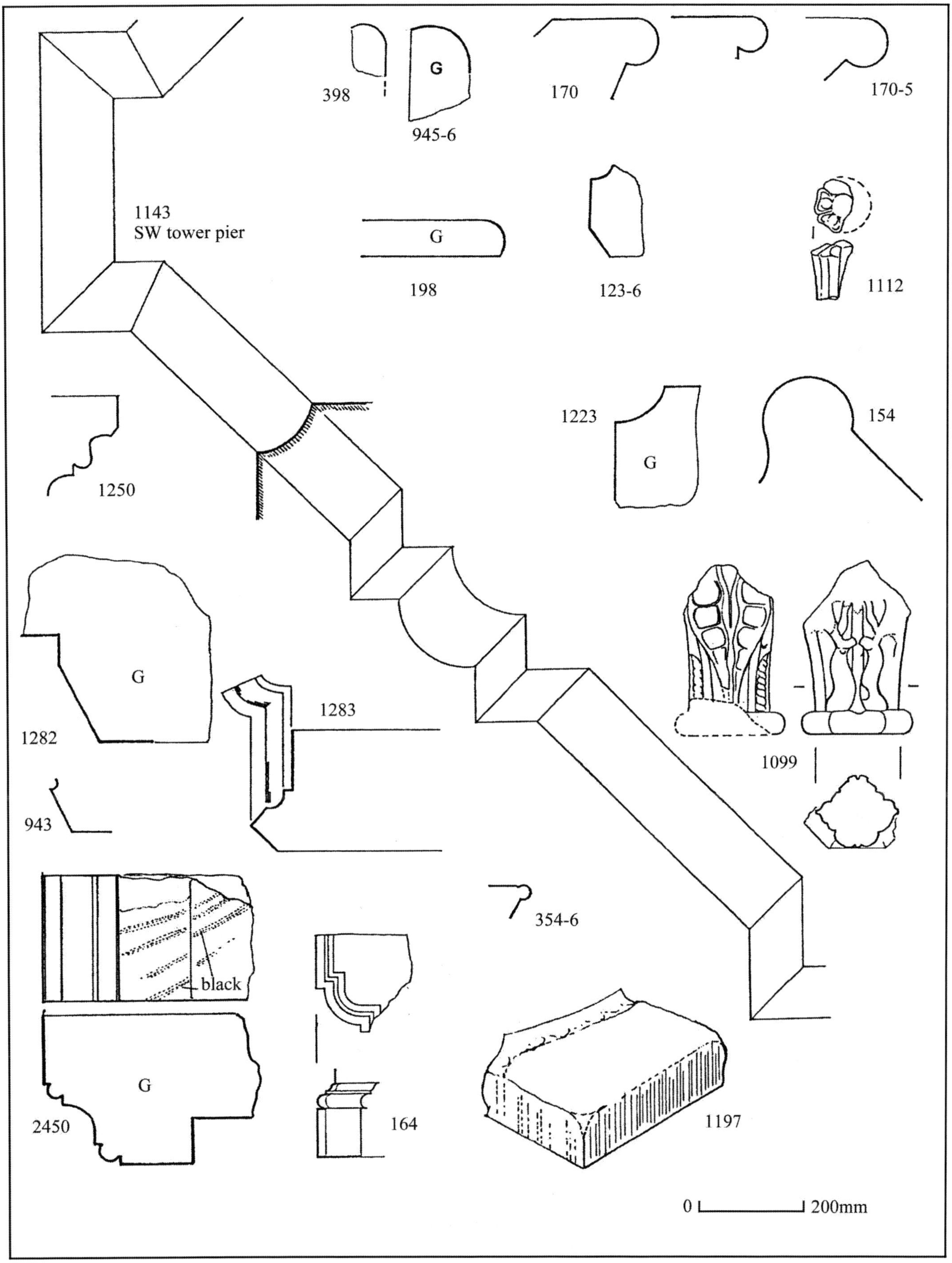

Figure 75 Stonework from the eastern bay of the nave, including the *in situ* SW tower pier (No 1143). No 1099 appears to be from a late tomb or feature with early Renaissance detail. No 2450 is painted. No 1197, 12 x 9.5in may be a small portable altar. Scale 1:10.

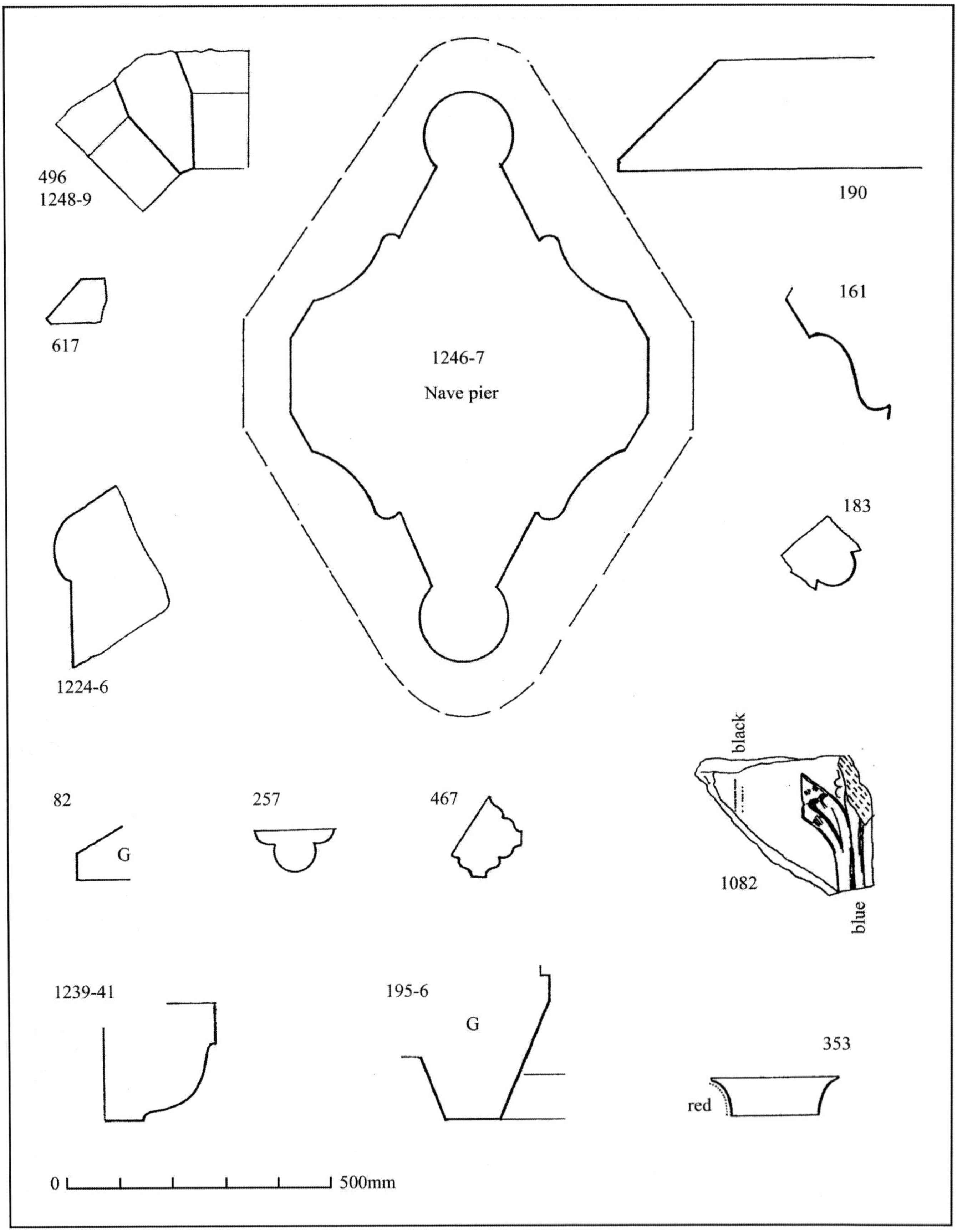

Figure 76 Stonework from the nave. No 1246 is a full section of a nave pier. The pieces on the left side are from the western end of the nave. No 1082 is a decorated piece, picked out in blue, and later overpainted with limewash, from the SW chancel. Scale 1:10.

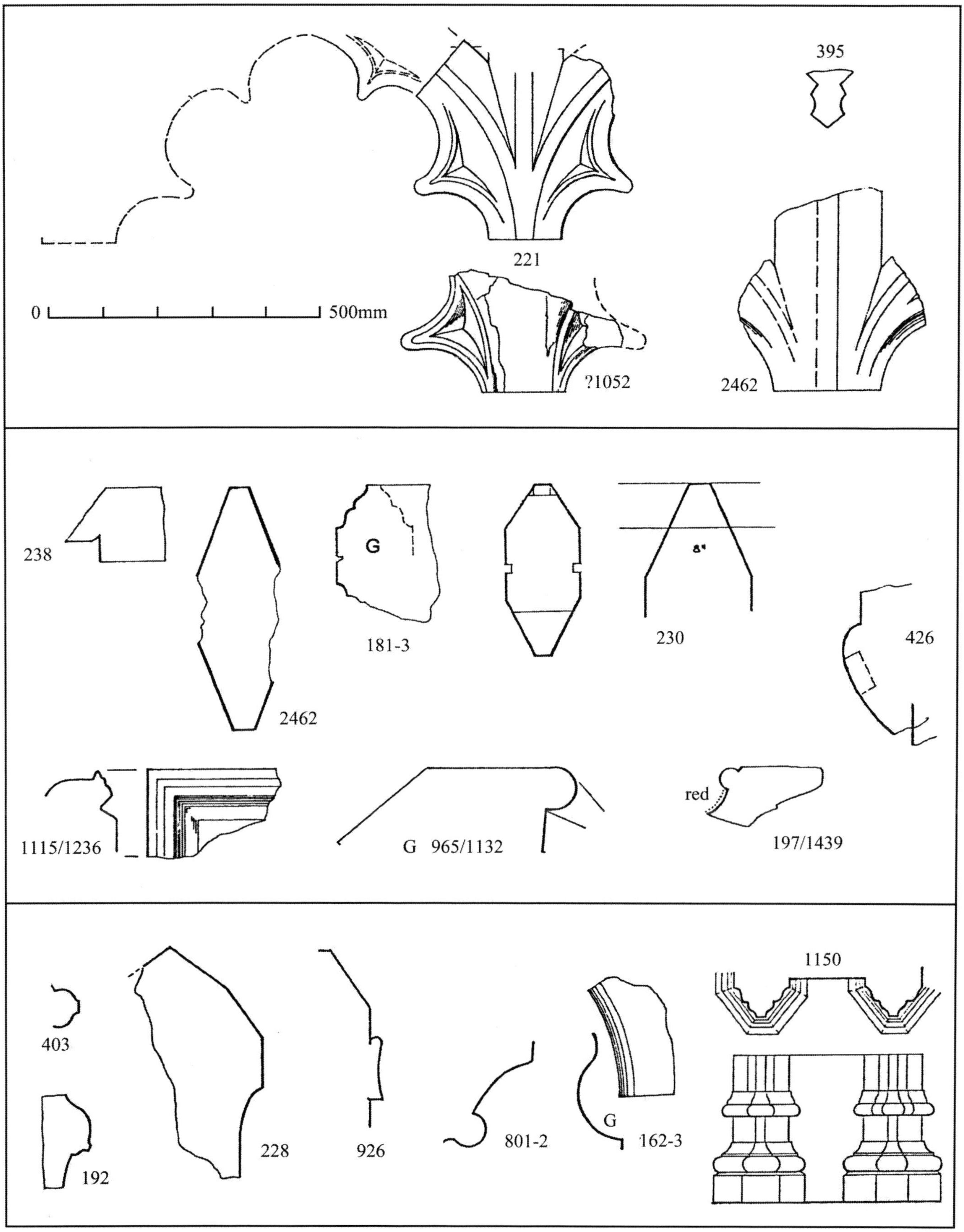

Figure 77 Stonework, tracery and mullions, from the area of the W door, and the W end of the nave (Nos 1115 and 1132 only). No 1052, from the N. transept, is almost identical. The bottom panel contains stonework from the cloister excavations. Scale 1:10.

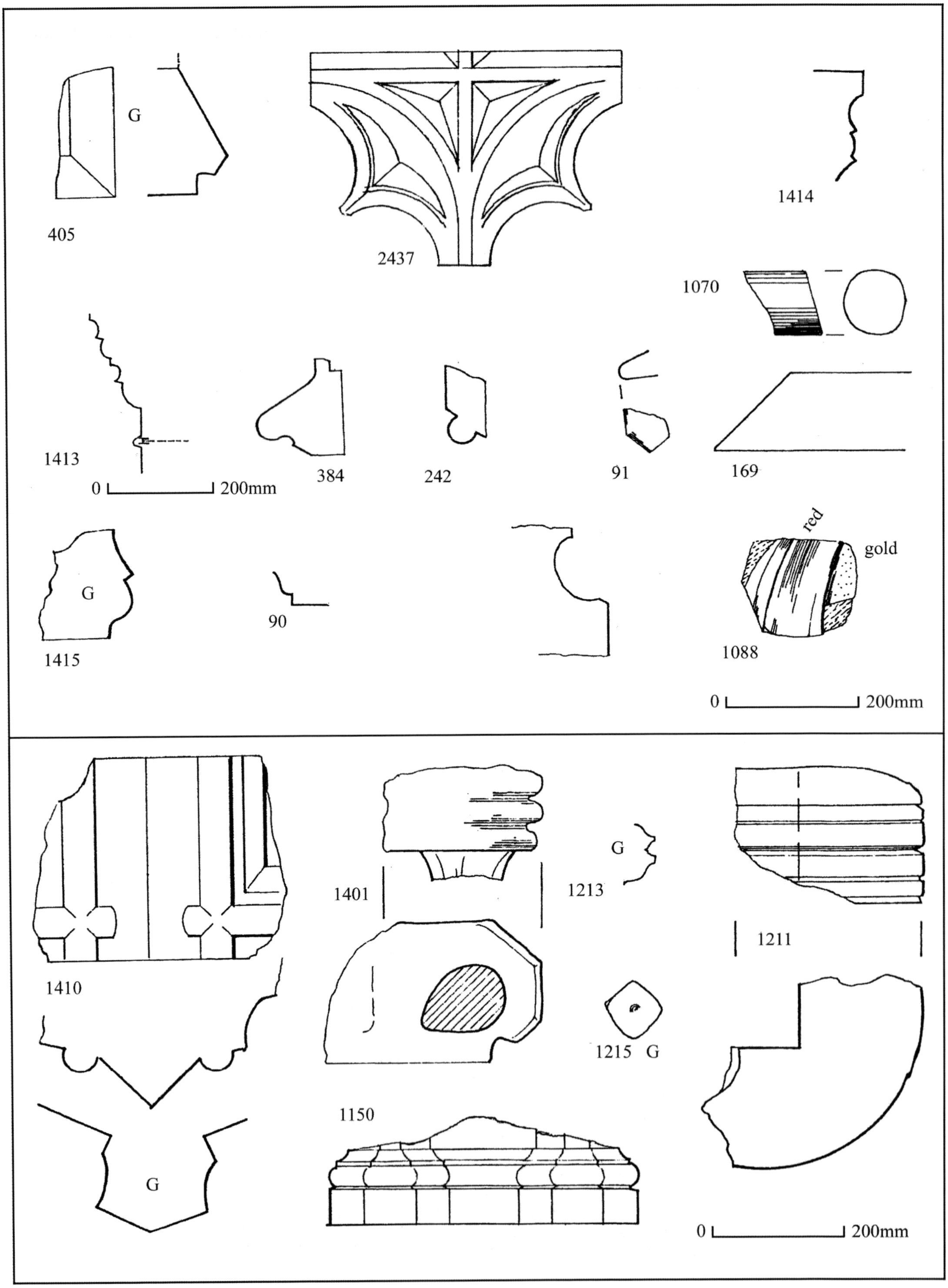

Figure 78 Stonework believed to be from the Whitefriars, without provenance, from Museum stores. The red and gold leaf decorated piece, No 1088, is, however, from the N transept chapel. Scales 1:10 and 1:8 as shown.

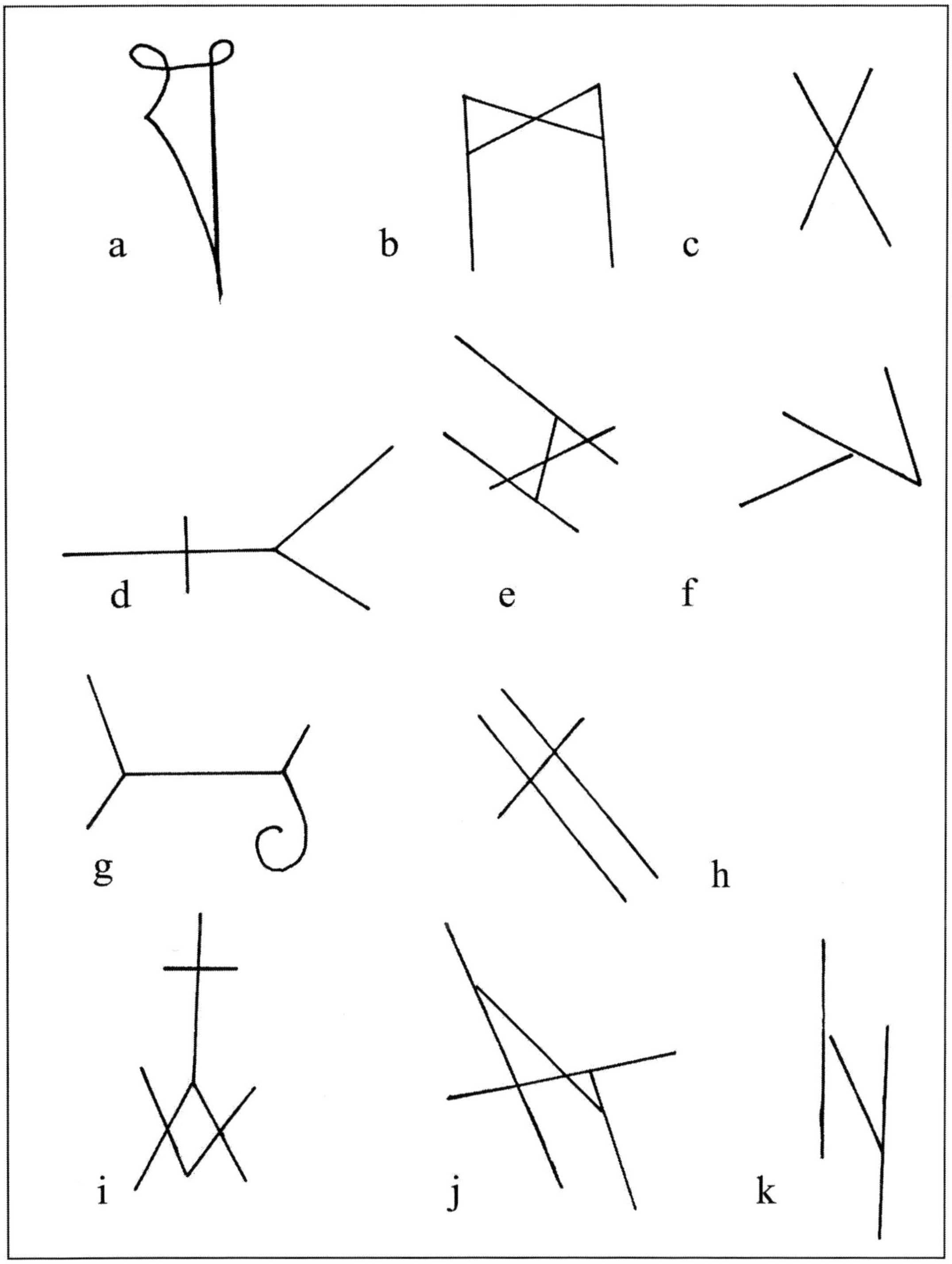

Figure 79 Masons' marks (not to scale):
a Stone 1159 (Fig. 69). On painted blind cusping Standard A, from W chancel;
b on chancel double grave S side (1968 XID 12-14);
c on seventh nave pier on N side, and buttress on N side of church (1977), however, this is not certainly a mason's mark;
d on chancel double grave, N side (1968 XID 16-17);
e on chancel double grave, S side, Grave 15;
f a shaped stone from the 1977 excavations;
g on Standard A blind cusped tracery (Stone 1054) from N transept, XVIII.1;
h on Standard A blind cusped tracery (Stone 1653) from W end of chancel, II.4;
i on an angled piece (Stone 99) from NE nave, XVIIA;
j on buttress at E end of church, S side;
k on interior stonework of the vestry passage (1971).

SECTION G
THE ARCHITECTURAL SCULPTURE

H. List
University of Warwick, (1997)

Revised and extended by P. Woodfield (2000)

Figures 80-81

GENERAL DISCUSSION

Amongst the group of sculptural pieces surviving from the Whitefriars there are two items of more than local importance, the gargoyle of Samson and the Lion, and the figure of an apparent wild man or wodewose.

The Samson theme is a subject well known through 12th-century English, French and German Romanesque sources, where it is encountered both in architectural sculpture and in metalwork (Réau 1956, **II** pt I, 240). The Whitefriars figure serves to draw attention to its persistence in the later medieval English sculptural repertoire, and this figure is perhaps the most substantive example of the subject that has come to light from the period. Here Samson's symbolic wrestling has apparently been chosen for its own sake, rather than being included in a wider, Old Testament cycle of images. Its detailed representation here is itself unusual for an item that was probably intended for what must have been a fairly high location on the building; in comparable examples of grotesque animals the approach is small and quite different, for example, a mid-13th century boss at Hailes Abbey, Gloucestershire, another, of much simpler form, on the N aisle corbel table at Salford Priors in S Warwickshire (*c.*1325-1350) and an earlier one in the vestibule to the Chapter House at Southwell Minster of *c.*1280 (Dr Phillip Lindley, pers, comm,).

The figure of the second piece, the wild man, is more difficult to understand as its original location cannot now be ascertained or even guessed at, other than it was very probably placed on the exterior of the building, and most likely on its N side. The initial introduction of this subject to the English scene had been in the early 14th century as an element of the chivalric culture of the aristocracy. There is a distinct sculptural group of them in Suffolk, on fonts and pinnacles to parvises, generally of the 15th-century-date. Notable early depictions are found amongst the marginalia of manuscripts aimed at the aristocracy, and here these grotesque figures are baited by dogs and fight one another, for example, in Queen Mary's Psalter (BL Royal Ms 2B VII. F. 173) and the Luttrell Psalter (BL Add Ms 42130, ff 70 and 157). They also occasionally appear in a heraldic situation, such as that on a seal of Hugh de Berwick in 1359 and 1375, where the wodewose is behind a shield supported by wingless wyverns (J. A. Goodall, pers. comm). The situation is one in which the wild men frequently found on 14th and 15th-century misericords, or indeed in architectural sculpture, have to be seen in the context of an influential cultural background, represented by the dramatic performance and masquerade, through which their meaning was gradually evolving (Halliwell 1841, quoting Dugdale 1656, 116), eventually emerging into the open in the 1503 translation and printed edition of the French romance *Valentine and Orson* where he possesses a distinctive character - that of the savage redeemed for civilized culture by the knightly valour and the courtly Christianity of his long lost brother (Valentine and Orson 1937, 67-70). The Whitefriars figure goes some way to support a dramatic interpretation in that his hands and feet appear to be uncovered by hair, which stops at what might be interpreted as cuff bands, one on the back of the hand, and the other below the knee, suggesting that it is in fact a man covered with a hairy pelt. An illustration of men dressed as wodewoses appears in a 15th-century illustration of the Bal des Ardents, described by Froissart, when the participants were burned by their pelts catching fire from their torches or *juddasys* (Ingram 1981), and a tapestry at Notre-Dame de Nantilly, Saumur (Bernheimer 1952, figs 19 and 23). The accounts for the Draper's Guild quote 'P for a torch yat wodhowsse had for ye juddasys xvjd'. Juddasys are large torches probably held in some sort of metal frame; there are also references to them in the Dyers (1468 and 1519) and the Smiths (1516) accounts (Ingram 1981, 467). The figure on a misericord at Holy Trinity, Coventry also appears to be wearing a hairy garment leaving the hands and legs exposed. It may be emphasized here that Coventry was particularly well known in the late medieval period for its pageants and plays performed annually by the various guilds, the text of some of the plays being still extant (J. A. Goodall, pers. comm.; Sharp 1816/1825, 67).

It is this capacity of the wild-man concept to change according to the expectations of its audience, which explains its popularity with 20th-century scholars. The extensive use of the theme in 15th and 16th-century European art is seen as a meeting of interpretations; the earlier medieval suspicion of the unknown and feared shadowy figure, colliding with the later humanist preoccupation with the innocent savage (Bernheimer 1952; White 1972 and Bartra 1994). English artistic traditions remain distinctive in this respect in that they concentrate on the wild man's capacity to fight and subdue ferocious beasts and ignore other preferred

Continental themes. Moore (1992, 135-144) raises the peculiarities of English iconography in a more sympathetic fashion, going so far as to suggest an amalgamation of hostile and positive intellectual traditions in such depictions. The later 14th-century misericord (Tracy 1997, pl. XXVIIC, Holy Trinity IX) from the Whitefriars church, and now in Holy Trinity church, Coventry, Fig. 90a, depicting the wild man is, for example, one of several such depictions which show him seated, with a lion upon a chain. Examples of 'tamed' lions have also been noted at Chester, Lincoln, and Norwich (Remnant 1969, 23, 89 and 106). There is a parallel here in the distinctive hairy figures found in the supporters of East Anglian fonts of the 15th century, and spandrels of church doorcases, wielding clubs and combating lions or dragons; in Suffolk for example they occur at Cratfield, Peasenhall and Yaxley, and in Norfolk at the de la Pole foundation of Cawston. Such a southern distribution indicates a Suffolk workshop, one which might also be the source of numerous, standardized fonts in that county also featuring wild men as shield bearers. The Suffolk figures are however a unique cluster, interestingly contrasting with the relative absence of wild men in the architectural sculpture of the midlands.

To pursue the pageant argument in the context of Coventry, Dugdale, in his great volume *The Antiquities of Warwickshire* (1656, 116) says 'before the suppression of the monasteries this cittye was very famous for the pageants that were played therein upon Corpus Christi Day. Their pageants were acted with mighty state and reverence in the streets by the fryers of this house, and contained the story of the New Testament which has composed into Old English rime'. Although Dugdale may be referring specifically to the Greyfriars here, who were the acknowledged custodians of the tradition, it is worth recalling that at this period many of the city guilds regularly held their corporate dinners at the Whitefriars, the Carpenters, for example, in 1462, 1463, 1465, 1474 and 1476, and the Smiths in 1473; the carpenters paid the friars good money (iiijd) for 'synging' in 1476 (Ingram 1981). Indeed some of the Whitefriars' more illustrious patrons, such as Sir John Poultney and Sir Henry Willoughby were Drapers themselves. The Willoughby's, whose principal seat was at Middleton Hall, 15 miles to the NW of Coventry on the Staffordshire border, held the manor of Wyken, just outside Coventry, from the late fifteenth century, and also had held property in, significantly, the Drapery in the city since at least 1432. Although a number of the medieval mystery plays have survived, it is most unfortunate that the play which was the particular responsibility of the Drapers, the Doom or Doomsday, is lost. Thomas Sharp (1816/1825) however details their accounts for the pageant, which includes 'hair 3lbs for the Demon's coat and Hose', and 'Itm pd for ij pound of heare for the demons cotts and hose mending'. The suits were usually of canvas into which tufts of wool were fixed, and they always wore black gloves and hose (Kay Stanisland, pers. comm.). The street performances lasted the whole of the day into darkness, and Sharp notes entries in the accounts for 'juddasys' – the large torches constructed with a metal frame which were carried in the procession, often before the Sacrament. The first reference to juddases is in the Dyers Accounts for 1468 (Ingram 1981). That they were carried by wodewoses is shown by the account 'P for a torch yat wodhouwsse had for ye juddasys ... xvjd' (Ingram 1981, 467). The Doom may well have been one of the last plays of the day to be performed and probably benefited, both practically and dramatically from great fiery torches borne by sub-human beings. These probably also account for the unfortunate event at the Bal des Ardents described by Froissart, when costumes caught fire.

Interesting parallels to the Coventry figure may be detected in the three medievalising figures which crown the parapet of the large bay window at Nevill Holt Hall, Leicestershire (by coincidence the childhood home of the excavator). They are of similar size, clad in hair and each carries a long curved staff-like object which may be torches. In this location no doubt weathering has removed significant upstanding detail, but it would not seem unlikely that the three wodewoses here were similarly engaged in lighting the path to Thomas Palmer's (d.1474) or his Nevill son-in-law's great hilltop house with what appears to be their flaming torches. It is interesting to note that the Nevill Holt figures are also carved in the round except that they stand with their backs to the supporting angle crenels of the parapet, and that two have their silky beards forked as the Coventry figure.

The Whitefriars figure and perhaps even more the ones at Nevill Holt, could also be seen as imports both of Continental iconography and style in their avoidance of native traditions. Despite the Suffolk fonts, serious deployment of wild men as heraldic accoutrements is more a Continental habit (see Bernheimer 1952, 176-185). In later 15th-century Spain for example, they feature prominently in the flamboyant sculptured reliefs in Burgos cathedral commemorating the Connestable, Fernandez de Velasco and on the façade of the church of San Gregorio in Valladolid, as jamb figures deployed in a programme incorporating the royal arms and those of the see of Toledo. These heraldic, and other Continental ideas would have been available to English artists and patrons through the extensive presence of wild men on imports of luxury goods; their important place in German and Swiss culture is indicated for example by their frequent occurrence in the 15th-century tapestry production of Strasbourg and Basel (Husband 1980, figs 14, 15, 30-31). In this respect the role of engravings in constituting one of the most fluid and convenient of currencies for the transmission of artistic ideas from the 15th century on is indicated by examples such as Martin Schöngauer's shield-bearing wild man vignettes of the 1480s and 1490s (Möller 1964, 260-264) and illustrations by Dürer. However, that the wild men were a popular feature in later 15th-century English art is indicated by no fewer than six depictions found in the misericords of St. George's chapel, Windsor, which are dated to between 1477 and 1483. Still in the field of misericords, the arrival of continental, rather than English iconography is also apparent on an example of the early 16th century from Henry VII's chapel at Westminster, which depicts the novel and essentially humanistic subject of the wild man as *paterfamilias* with a wild woman and children (Remnant 1969, 5-7) and Henry VII's chapel at Westminster (Remnant 1969, 98).

The limited quantity of figurative sculpture recovered by excavation at the Whitefriars site is probably from a stone dump E of the N Transept created by the demolition workers. Antiquarian sources can only supplement these survivals by indicating something of the quality of sculpture from the surviving cloisters before loss of detail by weathering and pollution in the 19th and 20th centuries. In particular two prominent, but now completely eroded label-stops, a lion and what appears to be a crowned animal. Fig. 81, on the reassembled present S entrance to the cloister could possibly be cited as 15th-century parallels for the extravagant Samson figure (Troughton collection Vol X. fol mss 4+6 (Coventry Record Office). Mention should also be made of three images formerly in St. Mary's Hall, Coventry, which reputedly came from the Coventry cross, a civic monument erected in 1541 and demolished in 1771 (Charmian Woodfield, pers. comm). These constitute two small 15th-century robed figures, probably of apostles, situated within the northern oriel window, and the figure of a king, supposedly Henry VI (1422-1471), recorded in pre-World War II descriptions of the building as having been situated in the entrance vestibule adjacent to the main staircase, but now no longer on display; these were also recorded by Fretton (1871, 223 and 217; 1891, 27). Their connection with Whitefriars is given in the comment attached to a newly commissioned engraving of the cross in the 1730 edition of Dugdale's *Antiquities of Warwickshire,* 'curiously Embellished and Furnished with Statues, some of them brought from ye WhiteFryers' . This in effect suggests that some of the figures on the cross came from the Whitefriars site. The editor of this edition, the Rev. W. Thomas, although meticulous and exact in his methods, was apparently willing to use oral testimony and this reference appears to be to an early 18th-century tradition, perhaps given credence by the prominence of the Whitefriars site, Figs 31-2, in relation to other monastic houses at Coventry (see Jenkins 1931, 9-13 on Thomas's approach to historical truth). The original contract for the cross, as transcribed by Dugdale himself refers only to re-use of monastic material without providing a provenance, of, to quote, 'six to eight old images if suitable to be repaired or incorporated' (Dugdale 1730, 143. A second copy of this contract, made by the antiquary Humphrey Wanley, *c.*1691-1695 is in the B M. Ms Harley 6466, f.35-36v). If from the Whitefriars, then they may be figures salvaged from the Rood screen, which would probably be the first to be hidden from the reformers.

'The noise was passing trim
To heare the Vriers zinging
As we did enter in:
And then to see the Rood-loft
Zo bravely set with zaints: -
But now to zee them wandring
My heart with zorrow vaints.'

A Pleasant Dialogue between Plaine Truth and Blind Ignorance
(Elizabethan ballad: Thomas Deloney (1543?-1600))

The wider significance of this problem is the indication of how little has survived from what should have been an expansive sculptural programme of an important 14th and 15th-century church. It seems the more surprising then that there is such a common theme of secularity running through this imagery. The Samson figure for example, although comparable with other misericord depictions in clothing the biblical hero in contemporary costume, gives him a prominent hunting horn, complete with an elaborately detailed harness, Fig. 80 No 1073. This attention to detail can also be seen in the depiction of the spaniel water spout, a very particular type of dog, Fig. 80, No 1072. The dog was regarded in the middle ages as the emblem of fidelity, hence the names *terrier, terri, tray* and *fido,* and the advice given in the Master of Game as to the proper use of spaniels does not reflect any aspersion on the animal. They were a precious beast, one able to retrieve fowl in their soft mouth, and can be trained to bring back prey unhurt (we are grateful to Pamela Tudor Craig (Lady Wedgwood) for these observations). Samson's lion-wrestling is also significant in being a subject that has close parallels with medieval English depictions of wild men as fighting with lions. Despite the serious theological intent contained in the Old Testament subject of Samson, it might be suggested that this was one likely to be chosen by a community whose predilections for heraldic and 'fantastic' imagery are evident in the earlier misericords surviving at the Whitefriars, and is, moreover, an excellent subject for a gargoyle.

CATALOGUE OF THE SCULPTURE

The numbers used in the main text, catalogue and drawings are those originally allocated by P. Woodfield to each piece when the architectural masonry was drawn and studied, the numbers then being painted permanently on each item. Thus the numbers have been retained here to avoid any confusion which might arise from re-numbering.

The location entered as Stony Stratford is the present location of pieces which will be returned to the Herbert Art Gallery and Museum, Coventry (henceforth HAGM) after publication.

All the items are in the local red sandstone which had been regularly exploited since the founding of the convent, and used generally for external work as being more resistant to weathering than the contrasting green sandstone from the same local geological source.

No 1072

Figures 80 and 42

DESCRIPTION
A gargoyle spout in the form of a dog's head, made up of three fragments in local red sandstone. It has lost most of the left ear, the right damaged in its lower sector, and there has been further damage or erosion to the forehead and around the spout, whilst a horizontal fracture has detached the muzzle and right ear. The eyes droop, and it has drooping ears. The whole sculpture is covered with a representation of wavy hair or fur, depicting the coat of a curly haired dog, apparently a breed of spaniel.

DATE
Both the realism and lack of stylisation in the treatment of an animal and the choice itself of a breed still known in 1405 as a continental introduction would indicate a later 15th-century date.

PROVENANCE
Although the location of this find, close to the debris associated with the fall of the tower, would appear to indicate a provenance from the lower stages of the second, post 1447 structure, it should also be stressed that the lead piping originally contained in this gargoyle would have made it the target of special attention on the part of the demolition teams. Therefore removal from a site elsewhere in the priory complex cannot be ruled out.

ICONOGRAPHY
Where dogs are a persistent element in misericords and in manuscript marginalia they are usually as part of hunting scenes, rather than depicted for their own sake: the dog alone carries no moral or theological message which would allow for its straightforward representation (Anderson 1938, 54). Although spaniels were prized amongst dogs in the medieval period for their fidelity and ability to retrieve game unharmed, they are not a common element in architectural sculpture, the only other surviving Warwickshire example being a bear-baiting scene at Ilmington parish church, originally supposed to have come from a secular building in the vicinity.

Whilst the Whitefriars gargoyle resembles a modern breed of spaniel, its prominent silhouetted ears and the heavy muzzle containing the water spout should be considered also as practical solutions to the decoration of a gargoyle from a low viewpoint. The early 15th-century Master of Game, the principal English authority on later medieval hunting practice, recognises the spaniel as a class of dog imported from the continent, most frequently from Spain, and employed only in hawking, for the retrieval of partridges, quail or waterfowl. The characteristics then associated with the better examples of the breed are, 'a greet heede and greet body and of faire hew or white or Tawne', and the point that such dogs 'shuld not be rough jough [throughout] but his taile shuld be rough' permits comparison to be made with this gargoyle, where the representation of fur is rather finer than on the other pieces of hairy sculpture. The fact that spaniels feature little in other 15th and 16th-century sources in comparison to hunting breeds can be attributed to the more menial status accorded to this dog who was better adapted to the important task of retrieving small fowls rather than being associated with the heroics of the chase.

MEASUREMENTS
263mm in height, 345mm width at centre and 243mm in depth.
CONTEXT
Unstratified.

EXCAVATION NO
1968, Area of III.E 117+ (NE corner of Chapel/Porch, but machine disturbed).

PRESENT LOCATION
HAGM (Whitefriars store).

No 1074

Figure 81

DESCRIPTION
A heavily eroded red sandstone hood mould terminal with an indeterminate combination of human and canine features which are best seen from below; a rotund face with nose and forehead carved in one section, prominent floppy ears, a recessed jaw, and hooded, almond shaped eyes, complete with the remains of incised pupils. There are indications of whitewash.

DATE
Difficult to judge from internal evidence, but a later 14th-century date would not be inappropriate on stylistic grounds. The western bays of the church were built after *c.*1420 at the earliest, so this will have come from elsewhere in the church.

PROVENANCE
The stylistic similarities with item No 1400, Fig. 81, suggest a provenance from a related sculptural programme. However, the quality of the sandstone blocks used varies greatly between the two heads, raising doubts as to their proximity.

ICONOGRAPHY
There is ample evidence both in marginally located sculpture and other art forms where the medieval onlookers are provided with entertainment through the deliberate representation of the ambiguities of composite creatures. If a specific source were required for this combination of the human and the canine then the cynocephali, a monstrous race of dog headed humans described in bestiary literature in the apocryphal acts of the apostles Andrew and Bartholomew, might be cited (Friedman 1981, 15, 67-9). This, however, would probably be an over-weighty interpretation for these two items which are neither prominent nor accomplished items of sculpture.

MEASUREMENTS
157mm in height, 156mm width at centre and 101mm depth.

CONTEXT
Possibly from the W end of the church; handed in at start of excavation. Said to have been found in a garden W of the Whitefriars church site.

EXCAVATION NO
1960.

PRESENT LOCATION
Stony Stratford.

No 1400

Figure 81

DESCRIPTION
A heavily eroded hood mould terminal which is carved in a darkened and prominently bedded sandstone. A rotund face with forehead and nose carved as one section, with the remains of rounded eyes and a recessed jaw. Presence of whitewash remains not recorded.

DATE
Possibly early 15th century, on the basis of a comparison with No 1074.

PROVENANCE
Stylistic similarities with No l074 suggest a provenance from a related sculptural programme. However the quality of the sandstone blocks used varies greatly between the two heads, raising doubts as to their original proximity.

MEASUREMENTS
122mm in height and 107mm width (drawn from an early measured sketch).

CONTEXT
Possibly from the W end of the church; handed in at start of excavation. Said to have been found with No 1074 in a garden to the W of the Whitefriars church site.

EXCAVATION NO
1960.

PRESENT LOCATION
HAGM (now lost).

No 1075

Figure 81

DESCRIPTION
A roughly rectangular masonry block in local sandstone with a hand carved in relief on the face clasping a narrow tapered circular neck at the top of an indeterminate object which bells out immediately below the heel of the hand. Despite the breaking away of the face of the stone, the treatment of the hand, the expression of the phalanges, taken with the projection of its relief, indicate that it was produced by a fully competent sculptor. The block itself is the top left hand corner of a larger piece, the two surviving faces are axe dressed to a well-finished face at right angles, the left return face having the stooling for an approximately circular horizontal member or shaft. There is some evidence for it having been whitewashed.

DATE
A date on the basis of internal evidence is difficult to suggest. The find spot for the piece near the resonance passage suggests it came from a nearby structure, although it seems unlikely that it was an element in the original construction of the chancel for which there is no evidence of a sculptural programme. As other items of sculpture, it may relate to the postulated dump of stone, that was difficult to re-use, in this general area.

PROVENANCE
The small scale and delicacy of the hand suggests it was part of a more intimate programme of sculpture than that pertaining to the tower, and the whitewashing suggests an internal location. Given the position in which it was found, it is possible that it belongs to the decorative schema for the N chapel/porch where the scale was necessarily reduced, although it may of course still be another element emanating from the collapse of the central tower. These provenances both suggest a 15th-century date.

ICONOGRAPHY
A difficulty in interpretation arises as to whether the hand is held up, in which case the figure would have presented its back to the viewer, or whether it is held downwards, with the figure facing the onlooker. In either case the arm is apparently held away from the body, and the hand clutches a swelling vertical staff, which is possibly approaching its end with the tapered pointed section ending at the stone joint. This latter observation gives a slight preference to the first interpretation. Given the extent of the surface damage and the curious pose, a precise identification is virtually impossible. Emphasis could be laid however on a subject-matter calling for the demonstrative use of hand gestures. The mid 14th-century frieze of musician figures on the tower of Adderbury in Oxfordshire, for example, provides models of hand-bell ringing, which could be seen as parallels, although hand-bells are not normally held in the manner indicated on the Whitefriars piece. Musical angels, as demonstrated at Coventry in the wood carvings of the 1390s on the roof of St. Mary's Hall, and at Warwick in the stained glass of *c* 1447-49 in the Beauchamp chapel, would not be an unlikely subject.

MEASUREMENTS
The block measures 190mm high by 287mm across and 140.5mm in depth, with the hand itself 60mm in width, and surviving to *c.*100mm in length.

CONTEXT
From disturbed material outside the third bay of the choir from the E of the chancel, later filling the N resonance passage, Fig. 43.

EXCAVATION NO
1962.I.4+.

PRESENT LOCATION
Stony Stratford.

No 1076 (see also Nos 1077 and 1079)

Figure 80

DESCRIPTION
A torso carved in the round in local red sandstone, of which the head (No 1077), arms (No 1079) and legs have been broken off. The body is covered in regularly carved tufts of wavy hair, which extends around both sides and the rear, also extending down over the top part of the legs. The representation of hair extends around the back diminishing in relief towards the centre, which is flat as if the figure was set against a wall or pillar, rather in the manner of the parapet figures of the bay window of Nevill Holt, Leicestershire, there dated 1471 or after. It is not possible to ascertain what pose was adopted by the arms, but it appears that the left leg is set slightly forward of the other, giving the figure a posture of slightly bending forwards. His right leg appears, just above the break, to end at a cuff. Of surprise and particular significance is that, despite the hair, the figure is furnished with a 'fig-leaf'. This is large and lobed, more probably an oak leaf symbolic of his origin in the wildwood, with the curved mid-rib pointing upwards, and

although crinkled in the normal way appears to be flat and empty of any masculine content. It may, however, represent a costume with a codpiece, and relate to the Draper's play.

DATE, PROVENANCE AND ICONOGRAPHY
See below.

MEASUREMENTS
460mm in height by 310mm across.

CONTEXT
16th-century destruction level outside the NE corner of the N Chapel/Porch.

EXCAVATION NO
1968, 111.E 117.

PRESENT LOCATION
HAGM (Whitefriars Store, now in two pieces).

No 1077

Figures 80-81

DESCRIPTION
The lower section of a badly damaged face in local red sandstone; drooping eyes, a mouth with possible indications of teeth, an extravagant forked beard and hair on the surviving left cheek, presumably related to No 1076.

DATE, PROVENANCE and ICONOGRAPHY
See below.

MEASUREMENTS
166mm in height, 181mm wide at the base and 91mm deep.

CONTEXT
16th-century destruction level outside the NE corner of the N Chapel/Porch.

EXCAVATION NO
1968, 111.E 117.

PRESENT LOCATION
HAGM (display).

No 1079

Figures 80-81

DESCRIPTION
Three fingers and the thumb of the back of a hand clasping a ribbed circular section shaft or staff, the ribs apparently running longitudinally. The wrist, as far as can be gauged from a photograph, has three wisps of long wavy hair above a slight swelling, probably representing the scaphoid process of the ulna. On the back of the hand the hair ends at a line apparently representing a cuff, or less likely, something akin to the garter or hose on the leg. The stone was originally part of a larger composition, as depicted on Fig. 80.

DATE, PROVENANCE and ICONOGRAPHY
See below.

MEASUREMENTS
Not available for study, but judging from the 1968 photographs, approximately 200mm from wrist to the end of the bended fingers, presumably relating to No 1076.

CONTEXT
16th-century destruction level outside the NE corner of the N Chapel/Porch.

EXCAVATION NO
1968, III.E 117.

PRESENT LOCATION
HAGM (now lost).

The three pieces last described, the torso (1076), the head (1077) and the hand-with-staff (1079), were found very close together in the same stratified deposit, and are now discussed together.

DATE
The figure or figures (see Iconography below) have the hall marks of a provincial essay in the late medieval style, perhaps with a hint of the coming Renaissance. The strong bulging torso and head seem to indicate fuller more naturalistic classical proportions, rather than the more attenuated Gothic presentation of figure sculpture, which tends towards elongated arms and legs. In addition the presence of a leaf would be a piece of prudery absent from truly medieval English examples of the subject, although it appears in the 15th century and quickly gains in popularity, becoming the exaggerated cod-piece of later periods. It is possible that it is a practical solution to dressing in such costume, where there might well be a flap extension of the garment at the rear bringing up between the legs and secured at the front, but if so, then the sculptor has failed to observe the actual fixing device, unless of course it was simply pinned. Certainly a different treatment of such a piece would be desirable as to have the fur running upwards would presumably not be visually acceptable.

These three pieces then, assuming that they are from one piece of sculpture, should be dated to not before the last quarter of the 15th century, or more probably to the decades immediately prior to the Reformation, in spite of the use of the red sandstone normally associated with 14th-century work at this site.

PROVENANCE
Given their location amongst the debris from the tower and their style, these pieces could be suggested archaeologically as coming from the second tower programme of post 1447. However, the presentation of the subject and the hint of Renaissance influence, even as part of an armorial display, recommend a rather late addition to the structure.

ICONOGRAPHY
Each of these three segments can be identified with a wild man, wodewose or wodehouse, the hairy, club-bearing, personification of untamed humanity popular in medieval art and marginalia. Wild men were often employed in later medieval armorial display as supporters of arms or as shield bearing figures; although the most distinctive English examples are the three wild men, each bearing a torch or symbolic weapon, standing at a higher level than the griffins on the exterior parapet of the late 15th-century bay window at Nevill Holt Hall, Leicestershire. If the Whitefriars torso has a slightly oblique stance, as observed by List, this would be appropriate to a subsidiary shield-bearing figure. Although the three fragments cannot actually be proved to be from the same piece of sculpture, their close provenance and comparable scale recommend their association. The thin band on the back of the

hand and something similar at the top of the calf, suggests the figure is in fact a man dressed as a wodewose as in neither case do the features seem strong enough to be as convincing as his chains or bonds, as on the much smaller example of a chained wodewose at the foot of Sir Robert Whittingham on his tomb at Aldbury, Herts. The wodewose holding a chained lion portrayed on another misericord, now in Holy Trinity Church, Coventry (it should be noted that Dr Tracy dates this rather earlier, i.e. 14th century (Tracy 1997, pl. XXVIIC)) does have naked lower arms and legs and this is consistent with other representations of men dressed as wild men when taking part in a masque or dramatic performance. Such performances as the Mystery Plays performed by the guilds of the city were a great feature of later medieval Coventry and demons dressed in hairy pelts appear in the records, particularly those of the Drapers who were charged with presenting the Doom play. The section of staff in his right hand could well be part of the judases or flaming torches which appear in the records, and which were clearly required in various performances. These may well have had long shafts which in some cases could be supported on the ground and carry a basket of flaming oil or other material at a high level, although they might have been shorter and more like the now eroded objects carried by the Nevill Holt figures, where they probably symbolized the lighting of the approach to the great house. If however the Whitefriars figure did bear or support heraldic arms, as has been suggested, it might reasonably be supposed that they were the arms of a previous benefactor of the convent, and, in this case, they could be a rebus of the skinner William Woodhouse, Lord Mayor of London in 1377, making a punning reference to his name. The wild man armed with a club, accompanied by a chained lion on one of the misericords from Whitefriars, was so attributed by Mary Dormer Harris. The numbers of coats of arms of Lord Mayors of London and Coventry merchants displayed on the early 15th-century Whitefriars misericords are an indication of the community's willingness to acknowledge such benefactors (Harris 1927, 251-60; Tracy 1997). The unusual but explicit appearance here of a *cache-sexe* on this figure may also be seen as symbolic of his origin in the wildwood, even though, as a costume the need for such sensitivity would seem to be obviated. That it is so prominent is a definite statement, as if deliberately masking his more primitive side. The codpiece and fig leaf, for that is what it eventually resolved into, is indeed a mark of the increasing prudery which first took hold in the 16th century and increased as time passed. It was not present in the true Middle Ages, thus is an indicator that the representation of the Coventry figure is influenced by Mannerist ideas developing within the influence of the church. In N Europe, Dürer had used a bramble leaf for Adam and a vine or fig for Eve in his Adam and Eve engraving of 1504 although the subjects here obviously required special attention to the concealment of sex.

No 1073

Figure 80

DESCRIPTION

A large gargoyle in the form of a male figure carrying a lion over his right shoulder, the mouth of which is being forced apart to form the water spout. His face has impassive rather than grotesque features and is bearded and moustached, with prominent eyes and his hair is pulled back off his forehead and secured by a band. He wears a close jerkin with a hunting horn suspended by a ring from a strap over his right shoulder, and he has a close drawn belt into which is tucked his slightly curved hunting knife or dagger at the front, presumably in a sheath. At his side, a defaced swelling probably indicates a water bottle. His left arm is folded across his breast, with the folds in his jerkin indicated, and the hand is engaged in pulling at the lower rim of the lion's mouth. The other arm is badly damaged at the wrist, with the hand missing, but it seems clear that this too was forcing open the other side of the animal's mouth. The animal is represented with bulging lentoid eyes and a long mane down its front, but its front legs have been broken away, as has his torso on the right side. Its grotesque features and curiously scrolled ears are designed to be viewed from the outer projecting end of the gargoyle, together with the top of his head.

On the top of the gargoyle there is a deep and crudely cut round-bottomed channel for a lead pipe which runs the length of the piece until passing through the animal's head.

In terms of quality the concept of the double figure is confidently handled, and details such as the folded back ends of the shoulder strap, and the supporting leather band of the horn, are clearly shown. If the torso and arms appear somewhat formless, the slim figure is clearly quite good enough for the position for which it was carved. The whole, which is in the local red sandstone, has also suffered some erosion consistent with lengthy use on an exterior site.

PROVENANCE

A position alongside a projecting roof segment rather than jutting out in itself, is suggested by the damaged and unfinished nature of the right hand side, as opposed to the stronger detailed sculpture of the left. This view is supported by the little use that is made of a strong silhouette. The detailed composition of two juxtapositioned heads, finely drawn rather than coarse and emphatic, suggested (to List) it was intended to be seen from a close view point, such as a single story location, rather than one higher up. Although the lead it contained would have made it attractive to the salvage teams, it is heavy and unlikely to have been moved very far from its find spot, a position likely to relate to the fall of the tower, known to have been in the NE direction.

DATE

The tight fitting tunic, low belt and stylized hair of the figure are all elements associated with the fashions of the 1340s to the 1360s, the 'Age of the Black Prince', and also the period of the successive epidemics of the black death' (Newton 1980). The reluctance in the later 14th-century architectural programmes to employ this type of prominent sculptural detail is a further factor in suggesting a mid century date. P. Woodfield, however, would suggest a mid-later 15th-century date and a higher location, such as a tall, perhaps two-storey porch on the basis of examples such as those on the S porch of St Mary, Launceston (Cornwall) and St Mary Magdalen, Stony Stratford (Bucks).

ICONOGRAPHY

The subject appears to be that of Samson struggling with the lion (Judges 14 vi.) commonly depicted in medieval representations in the action of forcing the animal's jaw apart with his hands. The well developed beard and moustache would be inappropriate for the youthful David, and he wears a belt of strength more characteristic of Samson. Samson's struggle is held to pre-figure that of Christ ascending into limbo, with the act of rending apart the lion's jaw being symbolic of his breaking of the gates (Réau 1956, 240-1). Confusion with the similar subject of the young David wrestling with the lion to rescue his sheep (1 Samuel 17 xxxiv-v) is absent here, in that there is no sign of the rescued lamb and also that a mature figure is shown with emphasised hair. The Samson and the Lion subject matter is encountered in architectural and furnishing sculpture as a popular subject amongst the iconography of the Old Testament. It is employed for example as a corbel in work of the 1320s - 30s in the chancel of Heckington, on Humberside, (Sekules 1990 pl. lxxxii), on roof bosses in the 13th-century Hailes Abbey, and the early 14th-century choir and Bishop Grandisson's nave at Exeter cathedral (Prideaux 1909 nos.67, 185 and 219) and found on 14th-century misericords at Ely, Worcester and Nantwich, Cheshire (Remnant 1969, 18, 27 and 170).

MEASUREMENTS
1090mm in height, by 455mm across and 315mm deep at the upper section of the figure.

CONTEXT
Found by chance by a workman employed on the Woodfield 1969 excavation, off duty whilst walking, in a position 7m E of the E wall of the N Chapel/porch, and 9m N of the chancel wall at the third bay from the crossing, in the area of the supposed N Cemetery. It should be borne in mind for the future that other sculpture may well survive N of the surviving three western bays of the choir.

EXCAVATION NO
1968, IIIE 131 (unstratified).

PRESENT LOCATION
HAGM (Whitefriars Store).

No 1099

Figures 75 and 42

DESCRIPTION
A much eroded oval portion of local red sandstone, rising from a broken, but roughly hexagonal base and beginning to splay gradually out at the point at which two diagonal breaks intervene. It is carved on all four sides, one face with a symmetrical design either side of a central vertical rod, the other with what might be termed two symmetrical 'open pea-pod' motifs.

DATE
Judging from comparisons made below with other Warwickshire grotesques a later 15th or 16th-century date might be suggested, perhaps related to one of the donations of funds made by Thomas Bond, he apparently being in the habit of funding work at the friary. Even so, it is a precocious piece to appear before the Reformation, and perhaps illustrates the urbane connections of the early 16th-century friars.

PROVENANCE
Despite the suggestion of a branching 'Y'- support in the splayed form, this fragment lacks the strength and geometrical rigour needed to be part of the fabric of the church. It appears to derive from liturgical furnishings within the screen chapel, near where it was found, but further identification remains tenuous. The closest parallel is with a decorative crocketted finial on screen work, for which this could be a base, but an unusual one in being carved on both sides, rather than on the side facing the viewer.

ICONOGRAPHY
This piece fits into the stylistic context of a group of later 15th-century clerestories in Warwickshire churches decorated with a highly distinctive series of corbels, gargoyles and label stops, using grotesques employing both abstract, insect and animal forms, most notably spiders and bats. The restored motifs on the chancel of Holy Trinity, Stratford-upon-Avon form the most distinctive example, but clustered in the W of the county; the nave grotesques of Wootton Wawen, Henley in Arden and Lapworth parish churches also indicate the prevalence of this workshop (List). P. Woodfield suggests that this is a particularly interesting example of the early use of Renaissance motifs in sculpture, where various decorative features are deployed symmetrically either side of a central stem; here on one side two S-shaped dolphin like features are parted by the central rod, and on the other, an open pea-pod motif with vertical twisted ropework at the angles. If this is a feasible interpretation of this heavily eroded piece, then it more likely belongs to the second or third decades of the 16th century, and be a part of a very late addition to the church such as a stone screen or a tomb. What was clearly a vaulted tomb, probably of some importance, lay between the arcade piers some 5m to the SW of its findplace (Fig. 42, Grave 19).

MEASUREMENTS
Standing approximately 36cm long on a base of 20cm wide.

CONTEXT
Found in the S Nave chapel, against the N wall, with part of a Purbeck marble grave slab.

EXCAVATION NO
1964, XVIa. 1.

PRESENT LOCATION
Unknown.

Nos 225, 1124-1125, 1127-1128, 1145, 1153-1156, 1164 and 1202.

Figures 71 and 43 (fragments not illustrated)

DESCRIPTION
Eleven complete and fragmentary pieces of decorative bosses in red sandstone, in the form of single and double flowers (heraldic roses). Most retain some colouring and some are gilded. The larger bosses (1125 (Fig. 71) and 1128 (not illustrated)) are in the form of double or superimposed heraldic roses, each flower of 6 petals, without sepals, the petals themselves crinkled, although two related pieces Nos 1153 and 1154 reconstruct as the more conventional five-petalled double flower. The background stonework where it survives, is painted blue.

The smaller flowers, No 1127 and Nos 1153-6 (four illustrated on Fig. 71) have their three crinkled petals gilded, with the central boss, in the case of No 1156, seeded red. No 1155 is set against a red field, and No 1156 on a blue field, and the mid rib of the petals coloured red, or possibly a decayed green.

DATE
Heraldic bosses of double-rose type are usually considered to be late 15th or early 16th century, a badge of the Tudor dynasty, a conclusion that is supported by the bold and rather mechanical repetitive approach to the subject.

PROVENANCE
It seems reasonable to assume that both sizes of bosses represent related major and minor decoration within one architectural scheme. Although they superficially resemble the bosses of vaulting ribs, there is no evidence at all for their being attached to such vaulting ribs. The background to the bosses is

worked smooth and painted and was clearly set flush with the stonework panel face, and the edges of the block are worked back to a joint face at irregular angles, so that the bosses were set, almost as a key, in a vault. In one, No 1156, the blue background stonework is in two distinct planes. It is therefore concluded that they must have been set flush in the panels between the ribs of the vault, as for instance in Wolsey's heraldic vault under Tom Tower, Oxford.

The scale and boldness of the treatment suggests that this belongs to a major element of the building, and intended to be seen at a distance. The location of the find grouped in the tumbled masonry in the chancel area indicates strongly that this was the lower vault of the tower, or, less likely, from some location within the chancel, (for which there is no other evidence for its rebuilding) and not to a minor element such as the N chapel.

The Ferrers shield, Fig. 71, No 1124 and Fig. 60a, on the other hand, found apparently at the same time and in a similar location below the rubble of the tumbled tower, does have plain chamfered ribs.

For a consideration of the paints see Section K, *Scientific Examination of an Oyster-Shell Palette*

Most of the stonework was apparently removed by stone robbers before the collapse of the tower in 1574.

MEASUREMENTS
Two standard sizes can be ascertained, two larger flower bosses of diameter *c.*640mm and 720mm, and a small size boss of *c.*220mm diameter. All are in red sandstone, and none has any indication that it was mounted on vaulting ribs.

CONTEXT
This area of the chancel was cleared in 1977. Few details remain of this work, and the flowers were entered in the finds notebook together, on one day. It is not clear whether they were actually found close together.

EXCAVATION NOS
1977, Area 3, unstratified, in the chancel, probably the fourth bay from the W.

PRESENT LOCATION
Some in HAGM (Whitefriars Store).

SCULPTURAL ELEMENTS IN THE STANDING BUILDING

Hood mould terminals of arches at south end of the east claustral walk

Figures 66a and b, and Figures 9 and 14

The two surviving doors at the S end of the E cloister walk have hood mouldings which end in prominent terminals, which have clear evidence of having been carved. They are now so eroded that only their salient features are recognisable, but fortunately they were drawn in the eighteenth century.

There are two terminals, one at the W end, and one in the centre. An assumed terminal at the E end was removed when the spine wall of the E range was replaced in stone.

DESCRIPTION
The W terminal, Fig. 66b, is in the form of head and shoulders of a male figure, with lentoid eyes and brow ridges, and a slightly down-turned mouth. He appears to have a 'pudding basin' hair style, and wears a head band or circlet which, on the inner side, splits into two strands and may represent braided hair. No drapery is evident on the shoulders, one of which is partly obscured by the modern glazed screen.

The central terminal (Fig. 66a) is somewhat larger, terminating both adjoining hood moulds, and is set lower than the surviving western terminal. It takes the form of an oval female face with a rather pointed chin, a long neck and narrow shoulders. Each side of the face is long loose-hanging hair, or a veil. The features are not at all clear and little can be said.

DATE
Cattell (1997 and Section C, Phase 1b, above) has argued that the spine wall was inserted in the first claustral range in the first modifications which took place in the later 14th century.

ICONOGRAPHY
Hood and label mould terminal stops in the form of masks of human form are a regular feature of the architectural embellishment of openings since Norman times, continuing right through the medieval period, although in later work, mouldings were more likely to end in simple out-turns, scrolls or heraldic shapes or shields. The degree of erosion, which must have accelerated greatly since they were observed in the eighteenth century, allows little to be deduced as to the sculptural quality of the heads, nor indeed about whether any particular representation was intended. As they are rather large, and are placed in a position where they would be seen at close quarters on a daily basis, it would not be surprising if they were intended to represent some virtue, or indeed some individual, but the depreciations of time have denied us further enlightenment.

Small corbels below the stilted springing of the cloister eastern alley vault

Figures 66 and 16

The vault of the E range of the cloister was, it is suggested (Cattell 1997 and Section C, above) inserted in an early phase of alterations to the first building, in *c.*1351-1356, at the time the central spine wall was built, replacing an assumed timber predecessor.

The vault springs from a series of simple capitals, each extended down the wall as triple shafts to a moulded base, itself supported on small corbels in the form of face masks. There were twelve of these, those surviving all seriously decayed due to salt migration and surface pore blocking by atmospheric pollutants, a process which is still continuing at an alarming rate, and a further two in the W corners of the remaining bay of the chapter house which are in equally poor condition.

Numbered from the N, the twelve faces appear to fall into the following categories:

Figure 66
a. Head with head-dress, with wide lumpy shoulders; these numbered from N to S occur as , Nos 3, 4, 5, 8 and 9 (Fig. 66b);
b. Probable head of triangular form, absorbing

shoulders, Nos 7 and 10 (Fig, 66c);
c. A cowled head, No 11 (Fig. 66c).

No 1, in the NE corner, is absent and probably never existed, and No 2 has been cut away, whilst No 12 is also absent due to its clash with the earlier hood mould of the S doors. No 6 to the left of the Chapter House is too worn even to ascertain to which category it belongs, although in this position it may have partnered No 7 and be part of the alterations which appear to have taken place to the chapter house in 1375-1380.

It is clear that No 11, Fig. 66c, was always intended to be different, with a close fitting cowl or habit, with the usual underband across the forehead. The reason why this corbel was selected for special treatment cannot be ascertained.

Hood mould terminals, south entrance doorway to the cloister

Figure 81 (bottom)

The ceremonial doorway in its secondary position as the entrance to the S range return of the cloister, has hood mould terminals of exceptionally large size and interest, but very severely eroded. Little can be gained by discussing the iconography without recourse to the antiquarian drawing prepared by Dr Troughton (Troughton set 1. x. No 6. in Coventry Record Office). He draws an angled sketched view of the doorway as it was in the 1830s when it had been less exposed to the polluted atmosphere of the industrial city, and shows each terminal as a large animal facing inwards, that on the right a long-bodied creature (foreshortened in the drawing) with a curious round head and muzzle and its tail over the back with a trefoiled terminal; the head has now disappeared and little can be made of what survives. On the left terminal the animal, which has now lost much of its rear quarters and its head, turns to face the onlooker, with drilled eyes and apparently small upstanding rounded ears. Troughton's drawing indicates something on the head, perhaps a crown, and pawed feet. The animals are even now remarkable for their size, although insufficient remains for the eroded blocks to be convincingly reconciled with Troughton's drawing.

ACKNOWLEDGEMENTS

The original text was prepared by Helen List as part of her PhD thesis at Warwick University, under the guidance of Dr Richard Morris. Various people have made later suggestions and contributions, including: John Goodall, Martin Henig, Kate Stanisland,, Lady Pamela Wedgwood, and Charmian and Paul Woodfield. The text has been kindly read by Dr Phillip Lindley, University of Leicester, and his erudite comments and observations have been incorporated into the texts.

The drawings were prepared by Paul Woodfield, except for Nos 1072, 1073 and 1079, which are by David Watts.

Thanks are due also to Paul Thompson, for making the sculpture available at various times for further study.

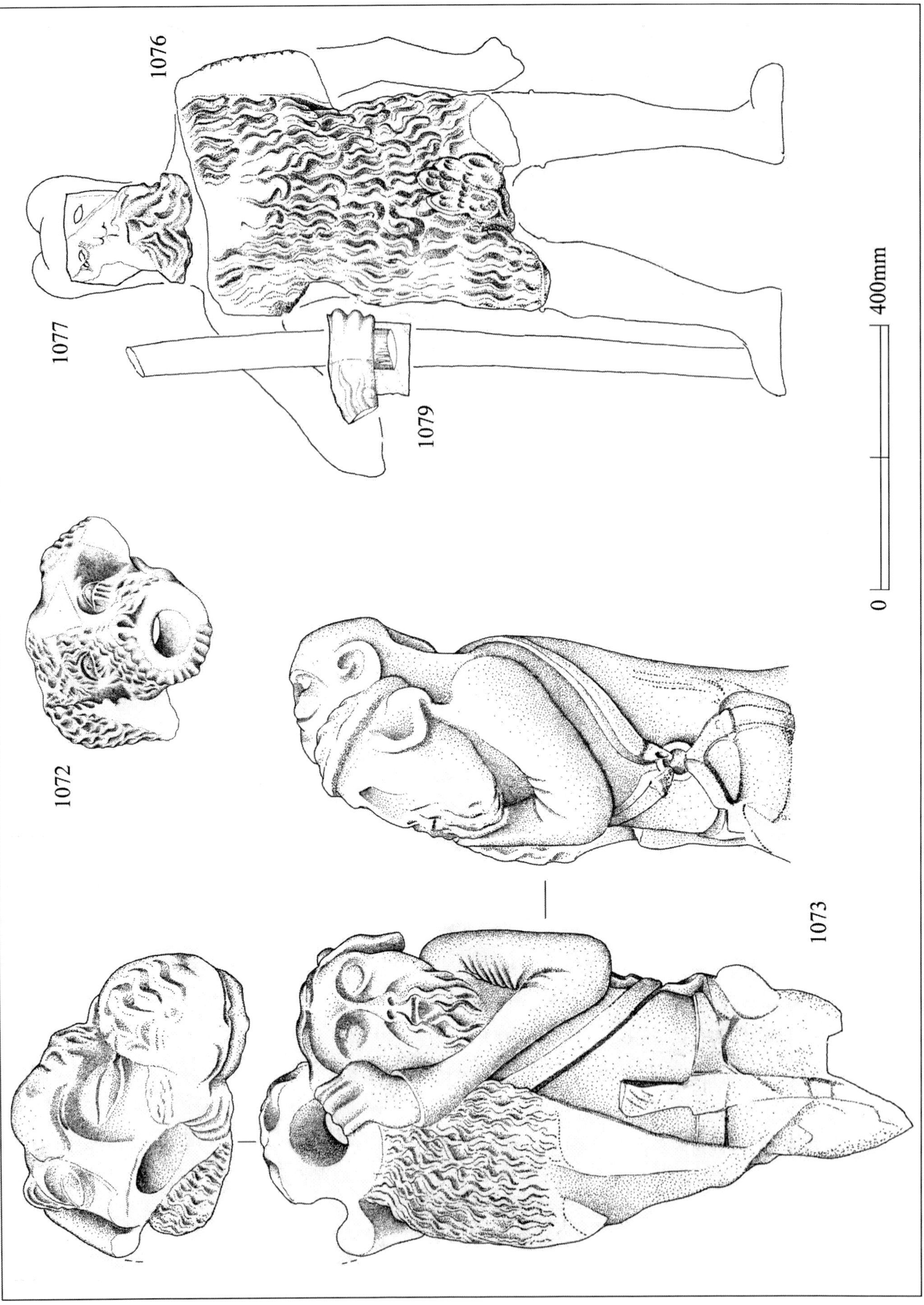

Figure 80 Architectural sculpture, Samson and the lion, and an actor? dressed as a wildman/wodewose carrying a torch. No 1073 found in 1969, 9m N of the chancel wall, third bay E of crossing.

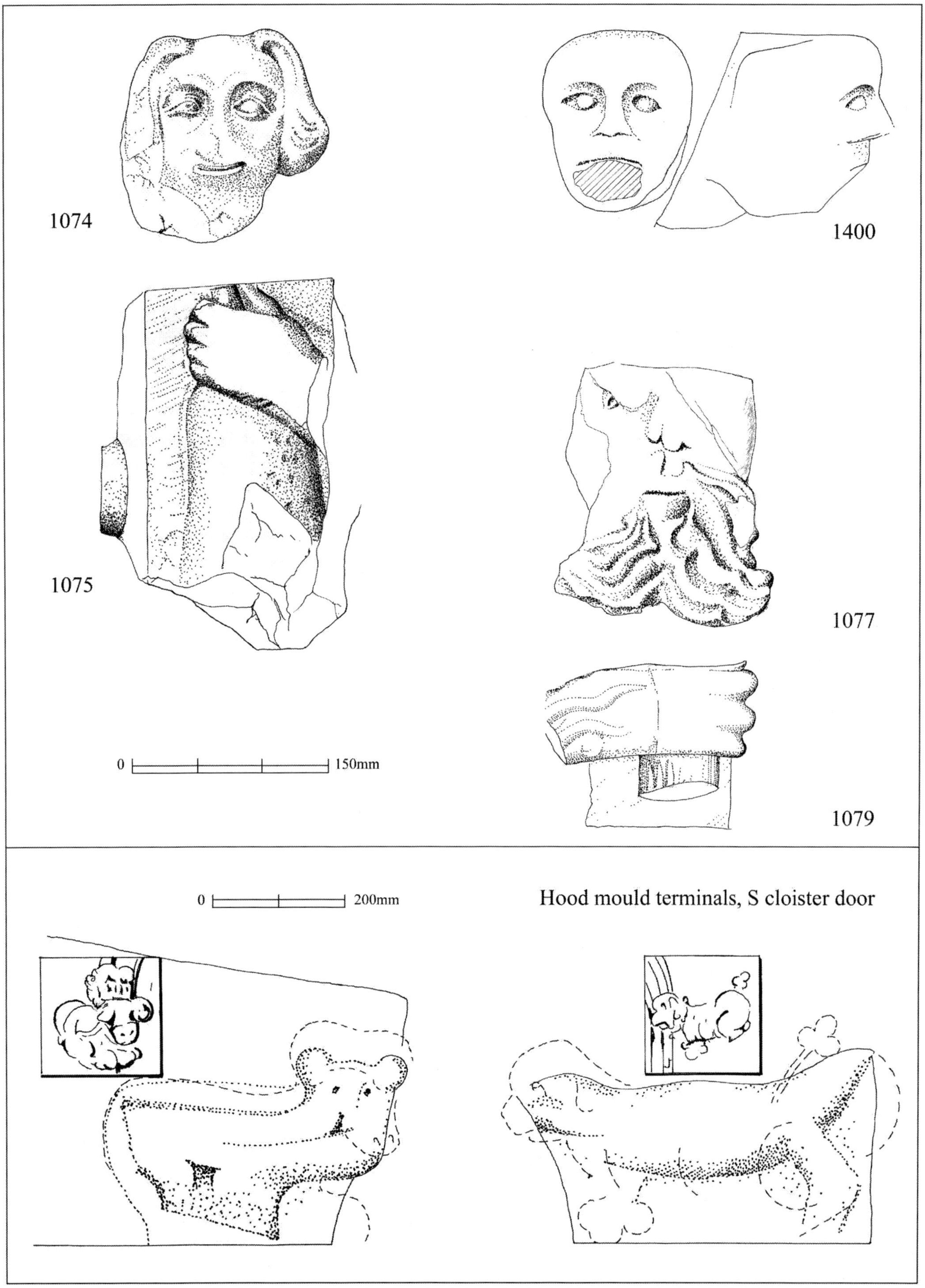

Figure 81 Architectural sculpture from NE of the N transept of the church – Nos 1077 and 1079 - detail of wodewose fragments. Nos 1074 (spaniel) and 1400 from beyond the W end of the church. No 1075, hand holding a bell?, from third bay of choir E of the chancel. Hood mould terminals from reset door at S corner of cloister (bottom section).

SECTION H

THE CHOIR-STALLS

C. Tracy

Figures 82-93

*The study carried out on the choir-stalls was originally undertaken by Dr Charles Tracy specifically for this report, but with the unwillingness of English Heritage to fund publication in full, and their eventual withdrawal of all funding for the project, Dr Tracy proceeded to publication separately, and the article 'The Choir-Stalls from the 14*th *century Whitefriars Church in Coventry' appeared in the Journal of the British Archaeological Association, CL.(1997). The following is an abridged version, included here for completeness. Two figures and seven photographs are the same as accompanied the original article, but eleven additional photographs of misericords are now included, together with an illustration of the rare 1801 E. Percy penny showing the missing front benches, Fig.84a.*

The Coventry choir-stalls are a surprising survival from the very chequered Post-Reformation history of monastic church furniture, and still remain little known. They were overlooked by Francis Bond in his seminal study of English Choir-stalls (Bond 1910), having been cut down and put to use by Coventry's Free Grammar School for 327 years, based first in the choir of the Whitefriars, then in the chapel of the medieval hospital of St John in Coventry. They are one of only three sets of probable friary choir-stalls to survive, the others being from the Austin friary of Clare, now in Belchamp St Paul's church, Suffolk (Bottomley 1981, 206), and from the Franciscan house of Llanfaes, now in Beaumaris Church, Anglesea (Charmian Woodfield pers. comm.). The future safety of the important Coventry set, the finest of all three, remains in doubt.

Sir John Pulteney, founder of the Carmelite house at Coventry, died in 1349, seven years after its foundation. Archaeological evidence suggests that the choir of the Carmelite house at Coventry was not finished before *c.*1385, although the building of the church to the W continued until the later 15th century. The misericords at Coventry were studied by Mary Dormer Harris in 1927. She concluded that they could be dated to the late 14th or early 15th century. The 1997 thorough-going study of the joinery together with its surviving decorative carving has facilitated a more detailed analysis of the stalls as a whole assemblage, and shows that the choir-stalls, with their thirty-two surviving misericords, twenty-seven from the original Whitefriars set, are an important addition to the known corpus of 14th-century English stalls (Tracy 1987). Moreover, their joinery, carvings and heraldry provide some insight to the patronage of this major Carmelite house.

In 1554, twelve years after its Dissolution, the church was granted to the eminent scholar, writer and influential politician, John Hales (DNB). He had been granted a licence to found a free school in 1545, which commenced in the choir of the church until he acquired the 13th-century St John's Hospital as a more permanent base, and to where he transferred the school in 1557-8, together with the furniture including many of the stalls. The school, which had such eminent pupils as Sir William Dugdale, the antiquarian, became a grammar school in 1572, and continues to this day, though not on this site.

At St John's, the stalls are an amalgam of two or more different sets of furniture, and their unecclesiastical layout in the chapel conceals an original piscina, and denies the original purpose of the building. This layout was observed by Charmian Woodfield in 1981 as typical of a Tudor grammar school, with the master's desk at the centre of the E side of a 'U'-plan (Woodfield 1981, 84). Their long use by generations of schoolboys is signified by the carvings of initials and channels, possibly 16th century, in which to run marbles on the desktops(Section I, Fig. 94), and were not abandoned until a purpose-built school was finally erected in Coventry in 1885.

There is evidence that the Whitefriars stalls were roughly treated when moved and re-assembled at St John's, where they were badly joined together, with the seat capping damaged or sliced off. Later damage includes depredations to the elbows and particularly to the royal heads at the angle junctions. There is also slight evidence of some substantial post-medieval structure in the area of the reading desks. Large mortices have been cut through the surviving desks (on the N side the mortice is 825mm square), and rectangular ones on the benches in front, with holes at the top of the centre plank at the back of the seats. The stalls have not been treated well in the 20th century, and are still languishing in damp and uncared for conditions in an unused building with an uncertain future.

THE MISERICORDS

M. D. Harris published thirty-five misericords including a supporter bearing a shield (Harris 1927, 246-260). Although all the Holy Trinity Whitefriars misericords are still *in situ*, only two of those moved to the new grammar school are there now (Harris, GS VIII and GS XV), the remainder being placed in the Herbert Art Gallery and Museum. The single supported fragment is lost (Harris, GS XIII) as is a foliate misericord (GS IX). The present

Holy Trinity stalls, installed by G. G. Scott in the late 19th century, incorporate three ancient seat standards at the W end of the S side. They are of the 14th century, of equal thinness as those originating at the Whitefriars, but they have the same archlet chamfer under the seat capping, like the seats in St John's. They cannot however have come from St John's as their scantling is too thin, and must originate from another, unidentified, set of choir-stalls, possibly from the Benedictine Priory. Seven of Harris's published misericords are not from the Whitefriars, including her GS XIV and XV, which are about 9cm wider than the others and the style of carving is cruder. They represent the astrological signs and Labours of the Months and share some of the vitality and spontaneity of the set in Worcester Cathedral, dated to *c.*1390. They are too wide to have come from the St John's stalls. Harris's GS VIII, depicting a pair of angels carrying a shield, is also alien in its carving style and shape of the seat. A further four, HT 1-IV, are in an early 15th-century style, with distinctly different moulding profiles, and must be excluded from consideration with the Whitefriars stalls. Other local sources might be the Greyfriars and, less likely, the Charterhouse in Coventry. It is also possible that some may represent a repair at the Whitefriars itself after the fall of the tower in 1447.

In addition to the twenty-seven extant carvings published from Whitefriars, we know of another five (NS 1-V). Four were sketched by Dr Nathaniel Troughton (1794-1868), a local antiquary, amongst his invaluable and generally accurate drawings recording the town (Coventry Record Office, 1/X.45 b-1). Two of these are heraldic, and must belong to the Whitefriars group (NS I and II, Tracy 1997 pls XXIIC and XXIIIA), the first completing a truncated misericord recorded by Harris (GS XIII), whilst the other two depict animals consonant in style with the rest. One with lions (NS III) and the other a grotesque bird-like creature with bats wings, chained by its legs, is presumably a devil (NS IV, Tracy 1997, pl. XXIIIB). We cannot be absolutely sure of their provenance as the group described as being from the Whitefriars clearly include some from St Michael's. These apparently depict three of the Seven Corporal Works of Mercy – Tending the Sick, Clothing the Naked, and Burying the Dead and seem to be the only carvings of this series to survive into modern times, until lost in the last war.

Another Troughton drawing we can be certain about, because the central part survives in the museum (NS V, Tracy 1997, pl. XXIIID) shows an owl with floral supporters. Owls are often taken to symbolise the Jews as it was believed they both preferred darkness to light. It is a rare theme, Remnant (1969, 260-262) only recording ten examples, and the sole depiction of an owl earlier than that at Coventry is on an early 14th-century stall in Winchester Cathedral, possibly related in view of the close Coventry Whitefriars connections with the Winchester Carmelite house. Two more fragments have survived, a crossed shield decorated with scallops, and a supporter of 4-petalled flowers (Tracy 1997, pls XXIIB and XXIIIF). The first is the central part of one of Troughton's heraldic misericords (NS I), belonging with Harris's lost piece (GS XIII), the second is one of the supporters of the owl misericord, (NS V). In all, therefore, we appear to have a reliable record of thirty-two of the fifty-two original misericords from Whitefriars. Apart from the ten heraldic misericords, most of the carvings are either purely foliage or secular in their subject matter. Amongst these are images of a wodewose and a green man (Figs 89b and 90a), three human (Figs 88ab and 89a) and one angel head (Fig. 93b), heraldic animals, particularly lions (Figs 85a and 86b - thirteen including supporters - Figs 91b and 92a), and grotesque creatures – a griffin (Fig. 90b), also two bats (Fig. 91a) and an owl. The only obviously biblical allusion is the misericord showing the closed door of Mary's virginity (Fig. 93a).

THE HERALDRY

Harris made great play of the heraldry in her published article. She identified arms of noble and gentle families, such as the Arundels, possible descendents of the Earls of Chester (once lords of Coventry), and de Vesci, founder of the first English Carmelite house at Hulne. Also identified was the Coventry merchant's mark of John Onley, and more noteworthy still, the arms of leading London victualler mayors of the generation following Pulteney, the founder of the Coventry house: Philipot, Brembre and Walworth. Harris goes on to recount the quarrel between Richard II and his uncle John of Gaunt, representing various factional interests of the victualler producers against the consumers, and recalls Gaunt with his brother, Thomas of Woodstock, joining the Trinity Guild in Coventry, perhaps using Coventry as a counterweight to London.

It would be remarkable if such drama were to be represented in heraldry in a set of choir-stalls at Coventry. Harris's identification of a connection at Coventry with the Arundels and de Vesci is perhaps uncertain, as demonstrated by her attempts to attribute no fewer than three families to the one misericord (HT XI, John Goodall pers. comm.; Fig. 87b), and the reference to Pulteney's 'libberds' is fanciful as lions' masks were ubiquitous in heraldry and decorative sculpture at the time. However, the inclusion of de Vesci as founder of the Carmelite order in England is likely, and John, Lord Arundel, and Eleanor Maltravers his wife were received into the Coventry Trinity guild on the 4th November 1379 (Harris 1927, 254, n 1). The link with Sir Nicholas Brembre, a leader of the anti-Gaunt faction, is adduced because his arms are shown in some antiquarian sketches of the misericords in the British Library (Lansdowne MS 209), and a Coventry source from anywhere other than the Whitefriars is unlikely in the case of a London mayor's arms. This is important as Brembre was mayor in 1383, 1384 and 1385. He was hanged for treason in 1388 so his inclusion must surely precede this date, supporting a mid 1380s date suggested by the archaeological evidence. This 18th-century source is entitled 'Coats of Arms under ye Benches in Coventry Free School' (Harris 1927, pls XXVII-XXX), but the drawings are sometimes careless, and we cannot always take them as reliable.

Four merchant families can definitely be confirmed as memorialised in the Whitefriars stalls. These are Adam Francis, mayor in 1352 (HT XV, Fig. 85a), John Stodye, mayor in 1357 (GS XI, Fig. 85b)) Sir William Walworth, mayor in 1381 (HT XX, Fig. 86a and GS XI, Fig. 85b), and John Lovekin, Mayor in 1348, 1358 and 1366 (also HT XX, Fig. 86a). In addition the Lansdowne MS heraldry suggests Philipot, mayor in 1378-9, also a victualler. Richard Dodenhale, mayor of Coventry in 1383 is also represented, but we cannot be sure the illustration is one of the Whitefriars misericords, and Coventry mayors are not otherwise attested in the Whitefriars set. Reference on other misericords to the Coggeshalls of Essex (NS I) and the Norreys of Speke (NS II) cannot be explained in a Warwickshire context, although a John Coggeshale was ordained deacon and priest at the Malden Whitefriars (less than 10 miles S of Coggeshall) in 1366. This may give us a tenuous connection (Simpson 1986, information pers. comm. to C. Woodfield).

In summary Harris's interpretation of the heraldry to support a connection between the London victuallers and the Coventry Whitefriars although significant, remains unproven.

NUMBER AND ARRANGEMENT OF THE ORIGINAL CHOIR-STALLS

The forty seat standards now at St John's belong to the Whitefriars, as does another now in the Herbert Art Gallery and Museum. Taking this, with the evidence of the seat cappings, there can have been originally no less than forty-four seats. The suggested layout, based on the excavated plan of the chancel proposes a grand total of fifty-two, Fig. 82. The standards from the friary have their mouldings cut off under the seat capping, whilst those from St John's stop at small archlets within a square in the same position. Also the width of the Whitefriars's seat standards is narrower, and the seats are narrower too. The mouldings and the treatment of the elbows are also distinctive.

There are two 19th-century drawings of the interior of St John's, one, a watercolour entitled 'Interior of the Free School, Coventry', is in the Aylesford Collection in the Birmingham City Archives (Large vol. f.23). Here two sets of desking with matching benches are shown, with three access-ways each side, excluding the one in the foreground. Two short sections of benching are also visible at the E end, with another access-way at the centre. There probably would have been other access points in the corners. Twenty-one back stalls are shown each side and in addition there were probably four sets of quasi-sub stalls inserted at the E end of the lateral stalls and on the returns instead of desks. The excavation of the Whitefriars chancel revealed a single trench only, under the backstalls, so we know there never were any real sub-stalls in the church. The 1801 Philemon Holland penny, Fig. 84a, confirms the presence of front stalls, still surviving at that date.

Apart from the four unaltered desks shown in the 19th-century drawings, there is an abbreviated skeletal desk in the museum. This could have been part of the return desks from the Whitefriars, allowing for two return desks in front of the return stalls flanking the W entrance to the chancel, and two fronting each side of the lateral stalls.

Of particular interest is the original benching shown on the early drawings, for this rarely if ever survives. This would have seated the novices and choir boys as well as tertiaries and visiting friars. Four of the ends of these benches have been preserved in St John's, set against the ends of the desks.

An isometric reconstruction of the installation of the stalls in the church, Fig. 83, shows that the present elevated setting of the benches at St John's is far from authentic, where they have been raised well off the ground presumably to satisfy the needs for visibility required by teaching methods of the day. Normally, the bench ends rested directly on the ground, as they had done in St Katherine's-by-the-Tower (Tracy 1987, pls 165, 168), and still do at St Margaret's, King's Lynn. The latter carry the arms of Henry Dispenser, bishop of Norwich by 1370, and Edward the Black Prince, who died in 1376. The Lincoln Cathedral stalls were probably one of the forerunners of the trend to elevate the desks on plinths, and stone was usually used to form the base. It seems that, in the later 19th century, the free-standing benches at St John's, with their quatrefoil cusping below, were tucked under the desks. It is a tribute to the Victorian respect for antiquity that the bench ends were retained at all.

In attempting a reconstruction of the original layout at Whitefriars within the revealed plan, there have been a number of problems. A plan of the furniture prepared by T. W. Whitley in 1870 shows all nine St John's stalls placed either side of the NW door. The four W of the door have now been removed to the museum. It cannot be taken as an exact representation of the layout as it only shows six at the E end, which is impossible, and it is ambiguous on the N side (Tracy 1997, fig. 1).

Mortices on top of the seat cappings of the Whitefriars furniture indicate that the W return stalls, and the first three seats of the lateral stalls each side originally carried a double-screen superstructure. Such a reservation of canopywork to the W end of the set of choir-stalls is remarkably unusual in medieval England, the only other example so far discovered being the lateral stalls of *c.*1530 at Kings College, Cambridge. This perhaps emphasises how little is known about mendicant stalls as a whole.

The piece of traceried panel at St John's, carved out of a single plank of oak, re-used as the front of the masters desk, is part of the 19th century re-ordering of the E end, already mentioned, which took place in the later 19th century. It may have come from a screen or even the doorhead of the screen at the entrance to the chancel. It may however not be from the Whitefriars at all, Fig. 93c.

THE FOUNDATIONS

Woodfield has referred to the foundation trenches either side of the W end of the chancel as 'resonance passages', Fig. 84b, stating that they were approximately 1.067m (3ft 6in) square, constructed of the natural rock with rubble sandstone walls, the natural rock being actually cut back in places. They did not have acoustic boxes or pots let into the walls. There was a patch of six worn encaustic tiles inserted at one point, seemingly to 'harden up' a soft clayey patch in the rock base. The extensive wear on these mainly 15th-century tiles indicates that access under the stalls must have been achieved at some point in the late medieval period, possibly following damage from the fall of the tower in 1447. The walls were not rendered, and it seems little doubt that the intention was to provide a resonance chamber under the whole length of the stalls. Since classical times the use of cavities or jars set in the fabric of a building is a well attested practice designed to improve the sound quality, and foundation trenches do occur under most sets of North European, including English, choir-stalls. As at Whitefriars they are usually substantially larger than would have been required for simple ventilation purposes. The *Chronicle of the Celestins of Metz,* of 1432, records the instruction from the prior that pots should be put into the choir of the church (cited by Minns 1872, 95). A post-medieval writer was certainly aware of the improvement to sound quality to be achieved when he wrote, in 1662, 'Of fifty singing men that the public maintain in such a house, there are sometimes not more than six present at the service; the choirs are fitted with jars in the vaults and in the walls that six voices there make as much noise as forty elsewhere' (Meliton 1662, quoted by Hills 1881-82). It was commonplace to place horse skulls under floorboards of public rooms in inns in the Middle Ages and later, although our later age has cast doubt on the efficacy of the use of acoustic pots. Jars were inserted into the back walls of the foundation trenches at Fountains Abbey (Hills 1871, 294-5), and probably also at Ripon Minster. They have also been found at All Saints Church (Phipson 1866, 392), St Peter Mancroft and St Peter Mountergate (Minns 1872, 93-101), all in Norwich, and at St Nicholas, Ipswich (*Archaeol. J.*, **6** 1849, 76), and stone open-fronted 'boxes' have been recorded in the Beauchamp Chapel at St Mary's, Warwick (Chatwin 1928, 155; I am grateful to Charmian Woodfield for this reference). An alternative positioning is found at St Lawrence Ludlow, where they face outwards under the desks.

THE FUNCTION OF THE CHOIR

The survey of the seating at St John's (Tracy 1997, fig 1) brings the estimate of choir-stalls in the original Whitefriars church to twenty-one each side, the equivalent required to cover the resonance passages just discussed. Eight of the seats from the west end of the S side are lost, as are the centre two of the ten return stalls. There were also four desks, two the size of the two survivors in St John's, and the two the size of the desk at the W end of the chapel, which would have fitted laterally in the Whitefriars choir. The two shorter return desks would have been placed in front of the return stalls, as shown on the plan, Fig. 82.

The number of surviving stalls, and the adduced total, might seem excessive for a friary church, but the Coventry Carmelite house was no ordinary one. As shown elsewhere in this report, the church building was longer than any other mendicant one in England except for the London Greyfriars, which exceeded it in length by some 4.6m (15ft), and which would indeed have had a *c.*10m greater length of choir-stalls, Fig. 6. Indeed any fewer would have looked incongruous in churches of such scale and grandeur.

There is no contemporary record of the numbers of friars in Coventry in the 14th century, and it seems striking that a house ever needed fifty-two back stalls, even allowing for the wholesale defection of an institution's members, either to secular work or abroad. At the surrender in 1538, it only had a prior and thirteen friars, and like so many similar Dissolution figures elsewhere, the friars must have been severely depleted as the final closure approached. The largest Whitefriars community for which records survive, is at Oxford, where fifty-seven members are recorded in 1377 (Russell 1944, 177-212), swelled no doubt by foreign students. A similar situation probably obtained at Cambridge, and indeed also at Coventry which was a centre for the order's theological studies. York had 38-42 members in 1335-7 and Lincoln 34 in 1335, Fig. 4. Even the much smaller mother house at Aylesford, Fig. 5, had 20 friars in 1326. Unfortunately we do not know how many stalls there were in the London Austin Friars church, which had retained its woodwork until the 19th-century fire. Overseas, the Dominican church at Berne, Switzerland had 42 back stalls and the Franciscan church at Fribourg, 67.5m (221.5ft) long, had 36 back stalls, augmented by an additional 32 substalls. These substalls would have been suitable for the Friars Minor, and were probably fronted by benches similar to the ones at Coventry.

At Coventry, the total number of seats, including the front benches, would have been approximately 90. This is not excessive when it is borne in mind that the students of the Winchester house, having gained their minor orders, proceeded to the theology and philosophy school at Coventry to gain their major orders. William of Coventry, the celebrated friar-scholar may have studied there, and Zimmerman claimed that the paucity of the provincial chapters at Coventry must have been due to the preoccupation with teaching there (Zimmermann 1904, 149-151). We do know that Coventry had a substantial guest hall, St John's, which may have been used for visiting students; unfortunately the site was destroyed in the 1980s without record.

STYLE AND DATING

In many respects the misericords from Whitefriars exhibit close stylistic links to Lincoln, and there is also a similarity of proportion to the seat standards of New College Oxford, dated to 1386 (Tracy 1987, 56-59, and pls 188, 192, 195, 197 and 200-202).

However, the comparison most often made is between the profile head from the Whitefriars (HT VI, Fig. 88b) with the heads from St Katherine-by-the-Tower, founded by Queen Isabella, *c*.1365, and those from Lincoln and Chester. Although the subject is close in concept, the execution is very different, that at Coventry being the more sophisticated, with squared-up misericord supporters including the voluted 'trefoil' leaf foliage, characteristic features of Lincoln, Chester and elsewhere. Another feature in common between Lincoln and Coventry is the way that the leaf crockets or misericord supporters emerge from grooved plates of wood. St Katherine's does not match this in quality, although the lack of stop mouldings under the capping, and the plain moulded columns fronting the standards is quite similar. The junctions of the return ends and side backing stalls at Coventry probably had crowned royal heads, as do St Katherine's, Lincoln and Chester. Altogether the Coventry Whitefriars stalls are closer in spirit to Lincoln than to any other monument. The flatness of the foliage is similar in both places, even though the Coventry work is more naturalistic whilst the Lincoln carvings appear to be 'stuck on'. There are few close comparisons in the misericords; the Lincoln ones are more imaginative and iconographical, whilst the Coventry ones are more conventional, static and less ostentatious, without the witty masks and inhabited foliage. The heraldic carvings are very precise in Coventry. The wodewoses and green men in each place look very similar, and can be compared with the men fighting birds and lions at Lincoln. The 'house style' consistent at Lincoln is a phenomenon of medieval workshops, and the Coventry misericords produce the same feeling of central artistic direction. The elbows at Coventry, although much worn, are on a generous scale, and are of a pleasing plasticity. The lion elbow is similar to the ubiquitous lion masks of Lincoln (Tracy 1997. Pl. XXVIIF). The treatment of the foliage elbows too recalls the sensitive inclusion of detail such as stalks, fruit and flowers at Lincoln.

The Whitefriars misericords were compared by Crossley to those at Loversall which are supposed to come from either Roche Abbey, or from the parish church at Doncaster to which Lovershall was a chapel of ease. A close comparison can be drawn between the green men at both, where the foliage comes out of the mouth, and the oak leaf supporters. The two sets are clearly very close in date, and the similarity in style underlines the autonomy of the Midlands and North Country in ecclesiastical furniture making at the time.

Misericord HT XVIII at Coventry shows an angel with a square neck line, Fig. 93b. This can be paralleled at Lincoln, and was a fashion adopted in the 1360s and 1370s (Newton 1980, 96-97 and pls 33-34). There are several instances of the motif on tombs clustering in date around 1370, as at St Mary's Warwick on Thomas Beauchamp's monument. All these stylistic indicators therefore point to a period of 1370-1375 for the making of the Whitefriars choir-stalls.

The archaeological and heraldic evidence however, suggests that this date needs to be brought forward approximately ten years as the choir of the church cannot have been completed before *c*.1380-84. This date is supported by the inclusion of Sir William Walworth's arms (he died in 1385), and probably those of the Brembre family, and possibly also the Dodenhale families.

[Dr Tracy's 1997 article appends a detailed catalogue of the misericords, augmented by notes on the heraldry by John A Goodall, and a note by the latter on the Lansdowne MS. His article is illustrated by photographs of St John's and seven of the complete surviving misericords, with full descriptions of the heraldry not repeated here, with relevant comparative material].

Appendix
A note of the surviving elbow rests at St John's, Coventry

C. Woodfield

Briefly these group, in order of quantity as:

Plants, of which there are nine. These are mainly rosettes and sprays of oak (?). Two have voluted trefoil leaves, Tracy 1997, pl. XXVIIIA.

Heads, of which there are six. One is a head at a stall return, probably once a king, but now seriously damaged, Tracy 1997, pl. XXVIIB.

Angels, of which there are three.

Beasts, of which there are three. One is a corner lion, smiling with protruded tongue, Tracy 1997, pl. XXVIIF. Another is a winged beast with claws, and another a whale, Tracy 1997, pl. XXIVA.

Human Figures, of which there are two clerics, plus a recumbent human figure.

Birds. One perching bird with a leaf.

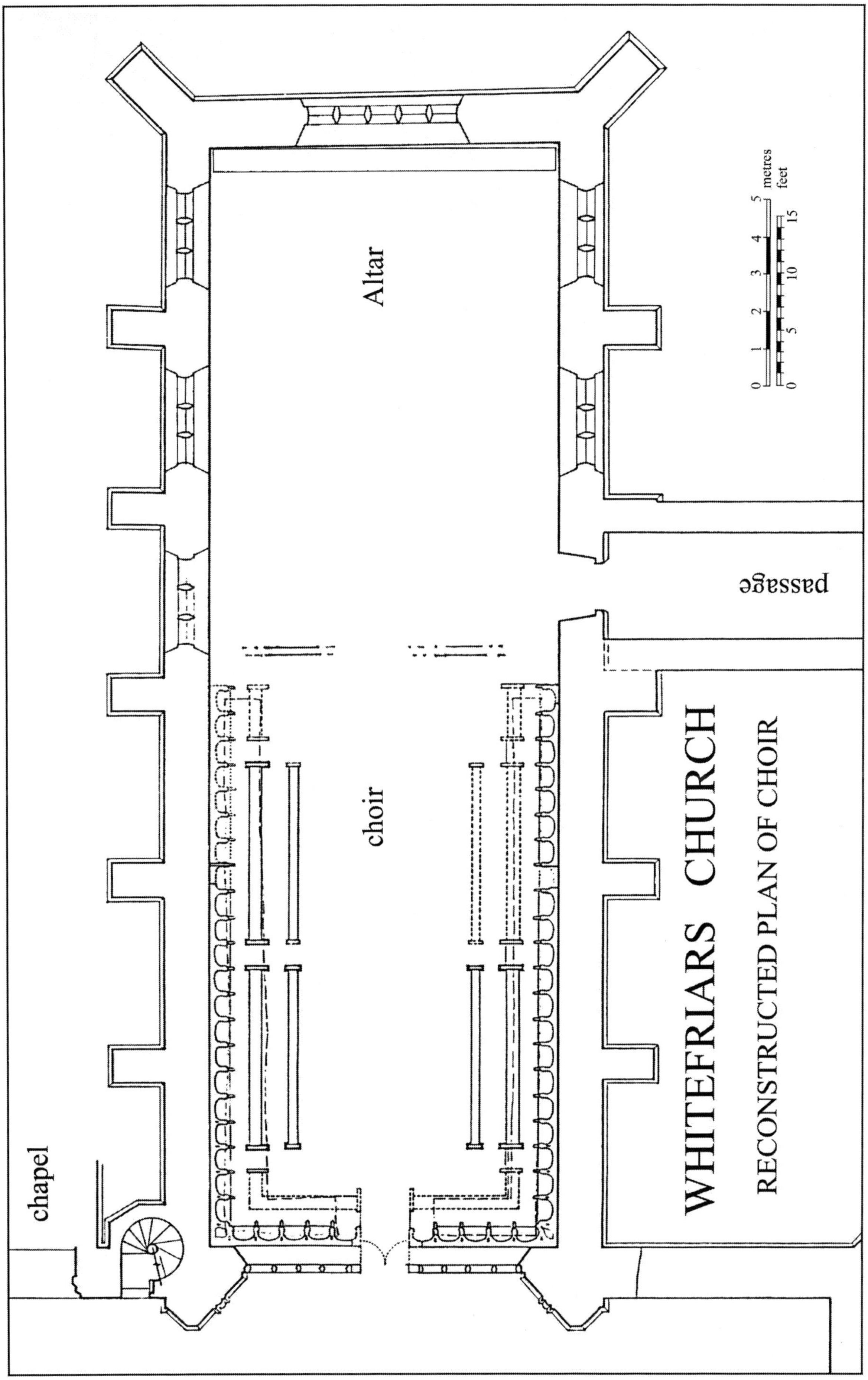

Figure 82 Reconstructed plan of the choir stalls as originally placed in the Whitefriars Church. The dividing screen at the E of the choir stalls relates to the Grammar School period.

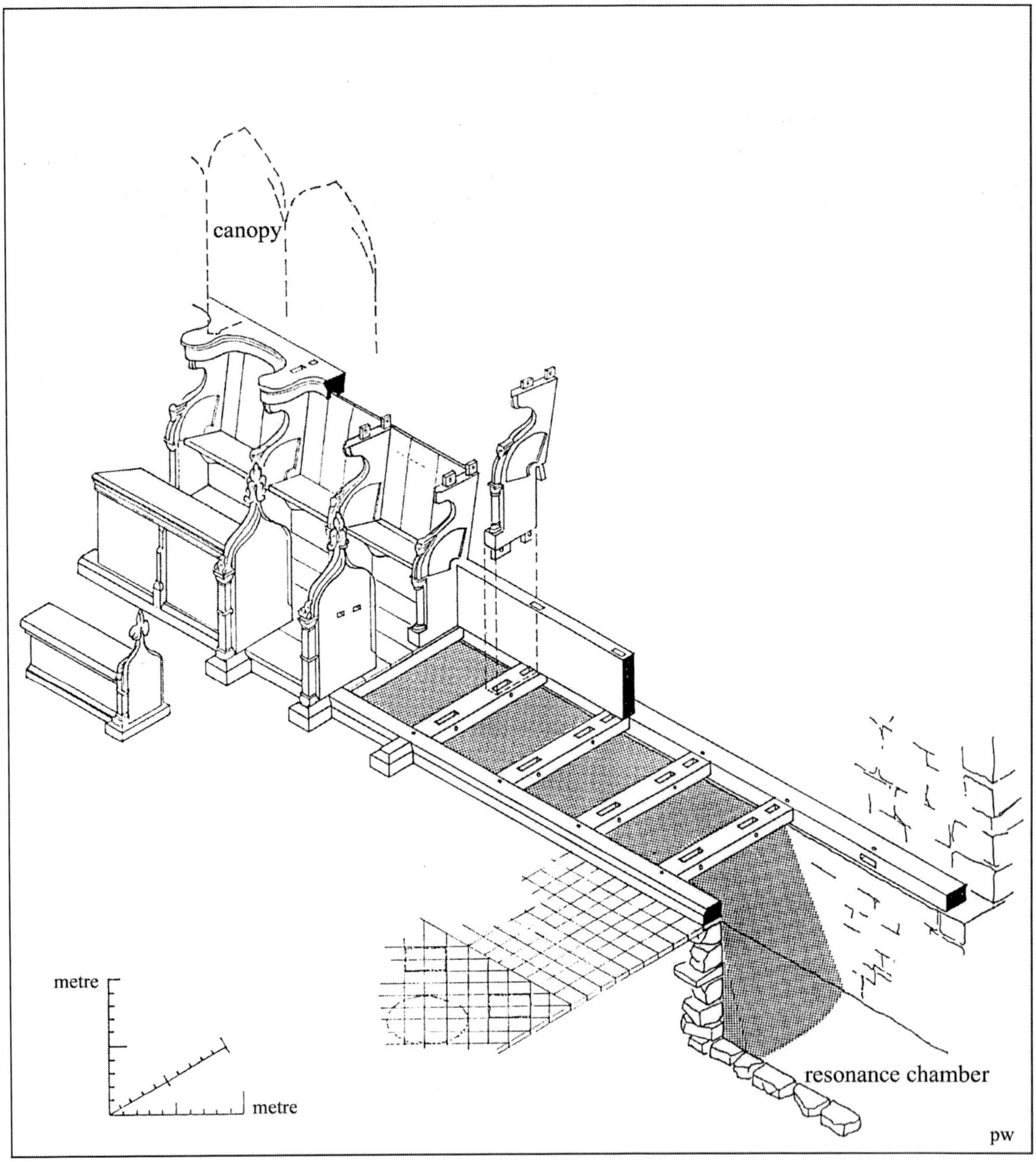

Figure 83 Isometric view of surviving choir stalls and acoustic/resonance passages as they would have been at the Whitefriars.

Figure 84 a) E. Percy 1801 penny. Reverse (R) showing choir stalls at St John's, with front benches now largely lost. Obverse (L) showing bust of Philemon Holland, translator of Pliny's *Natural History* and Camden's *Britannia*, headmaster of the School in 1628. Actual diameter 36mm.

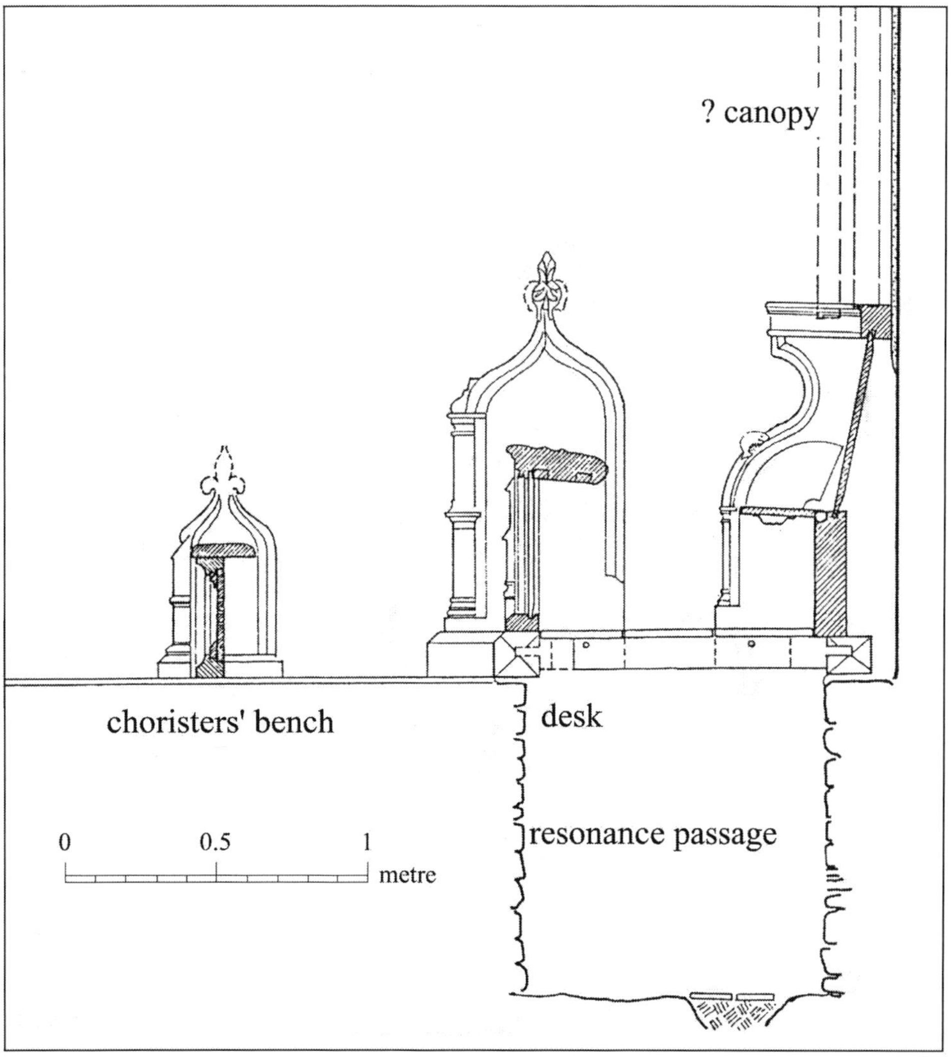

b) Reconstructed section of choir stalls and resonance passage to enhance singing at the Whitefriars; the increase in volume was thought to be some 60-70%.

Figure 85 a) Coventry misericord Harris (1927) Series HT XV. Arms of Adam Francis, mercer, mayor of London in 1352.
All misericord photographs are by courtesy of Christa Grossinger.

b) Coventry misericord Harris (1927) Series GS XI. Arms of John Stoyde, vintner, mayor of London in 1357.
The sinister figure is Sir William Walworth, the dexter unidentified.

Figure 86 a) Coventry misericord Harris (1927) Series HT XX. Arms of Sir William Walworth, fishmonger, mayor of London in 1381. He married Margaret daughter of John Lovekin, whose arms appear on the dexter supporter. Walworth was traditionally supposed to have killed Wat Tyler and his statue can be seen on Holborn Viaduct.

b) Coventry misericord Harris (1927) Series HT XVI. Harris (1927) suggested Fitzalan, Earl of Arundel, the sinister supporter representing Eleanor Maltravers, his wife, and pointed out that they were received into the Coventry Trinity Guild on November 4th 1379. Goodall (1997) suggested Hausted of Kent for the dexter supporter.

Figure 87 a) Coventry misericord Harris (1927) Series GS X. The shields commemorate Margery, sister and co-heiress of Giles de Badlesmere and her first two husbands, William de Ros (d. 1363) and Thomas de Arundel (d. 1350/4). They were presumably benefactors.

b) Coventry misericord Harris (1927) Series HT XI. Harris (1927) suggested John de Vesci of Alnwick, who brought the Whitefriars to England from Palestine, as a possibility for the dexter supporter, and Hugh de Patteshull, Bishop of Coventry and Lichfield, for the sinister supporter. The centre shield remains unidentified, though Harris suggested de Say, but Goodall (1997) has outlined problems with this interpretation.

Figure 88 a) Coventry misericord Harris (1927) Series GS VI. Woman's head with fleuron ornamented crimped veil, and the same perpendicular 4-leaved flower decoration as the angel misericord, Fig. 93b.

b) Coventry misericord Harris (1927) Series HT VI. Bearded man with close parallels to a misericord at St Katherine by-the-Tower.

Figure 89 a) Coventry misericord Harris (1927) Series GS V. Bearded man.

b) Coventry misericord Harris (1927) Series HT V. Head of green man.

Figure 90 a) Coventry misericord Harris (1927) Series HT IX. Wodwose, or rather man dressed as wodwose with cuff lines apparent at knee and ankle (see discussion in Section G, *The Architectural Sculpture*). He is also holding a club and a chain attached to a collar round a lion's neck, and appears to be sitting on a stool incorporating lion's feet.

b) Coventry misericord Harris (1927) Series HT XIII. Griffin, but not with the usual eagle's beak.

Figure 91 a) Coventry misericord Harris (1927) Series GS IV. Lion-faced winged demon.

b) Coventry misericord Harris (1927) Series GS III. Winged lion or lion springing.

Figure 92 a) Coventry misericord Harris (1927) Series HT VII. Centre and supporters, three lion masks. Not impossibly an echo of Pulteney's three libbards heads.

b) Coventry misericord Harris (1927) Series HT X. Voluted 'trefoil' leaf foliage.

Figure 93 a) Coventry misericord Harris (1927) Series HT VIII. A closed door with rose supporters. Note there are ogee arches on the tracery. Emblem of the virginity of the Virgin Mary. See Ezekiel xliv 'Then said the Lord unto me... This gate shall be shut .... and no man shall enter in by it'.

b) Coventry misericord Harris (1927) Series HT XVIII. Angel wearing a garment with square-cut neck, ornamented with fleurons (see also Fig. 88a).

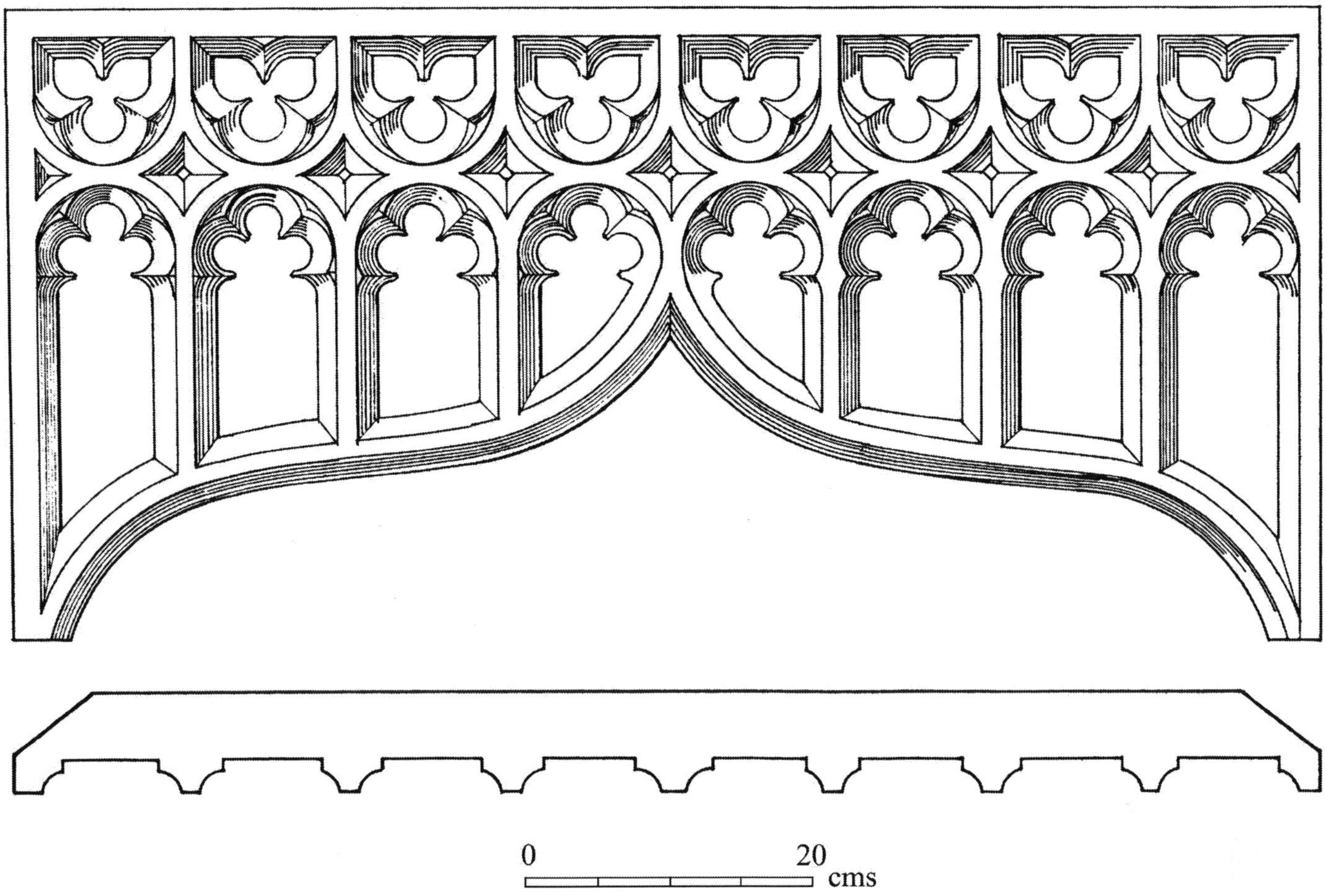

c) Panel from an oak screen or doorhead, probably originally from the Whitefriars Church and now in St John's, where it may have functioned as a master's lectern, removed here with the choir stalls. Late 14th century.

SECTION I
'MARBLES' GAMING BOARD

C. Woodfield

Figure 94

Unique 'marbles gaming board', 2.2m long and 0.45m deep, carved on one of the surviving Whitefriars choir-stall desk tops, and now on display in the Herbert Art Gallery and Museum, Coventry. As many as six mid 16th-century and later schoolboys could have sat along the bottom edge of the desk. The patterns of cutting seem to indicate that more than one generation of schoolboys was involved. The desk is now horizontal, but originally appears to have been set at a more upright angle. The shading on the drawing indicates hollows for a central channel, with subsidiary channels and scoring holes. The deeper the shading the deeper the channel or hole. The game was probably played by three to six players, who sat at the positions indicated on the drawing, Fig. 94. The deep holes on the sides could drop the 'marbles' back into the boys' laps or on to the floor; or, conversely, they may represent three points of entry (and/or exit?) to the 'gaming board'. The game may be more related to bagatelle than to modern marble games. Bagatelle was played originally on a board some 6ft (1.83m) x 1ft. 6in (46cm) (*Everyman's Encyclopaedia* 1961, vol. 1, 676).

The late 14th-century choir stalls were in use at St John's Hospital until 1885, but in view of the fact that this board is thought to be unique (G. Egan, pers. comm.) an early date is likely. Some dozen stone and ceramic marbles were recovered from Grammar School deposits in the early 1960s and are amongst the earliest known examples from Britain (Section T, Fig. 165 No 127; Woodfield 1981, 105, fig. 11).

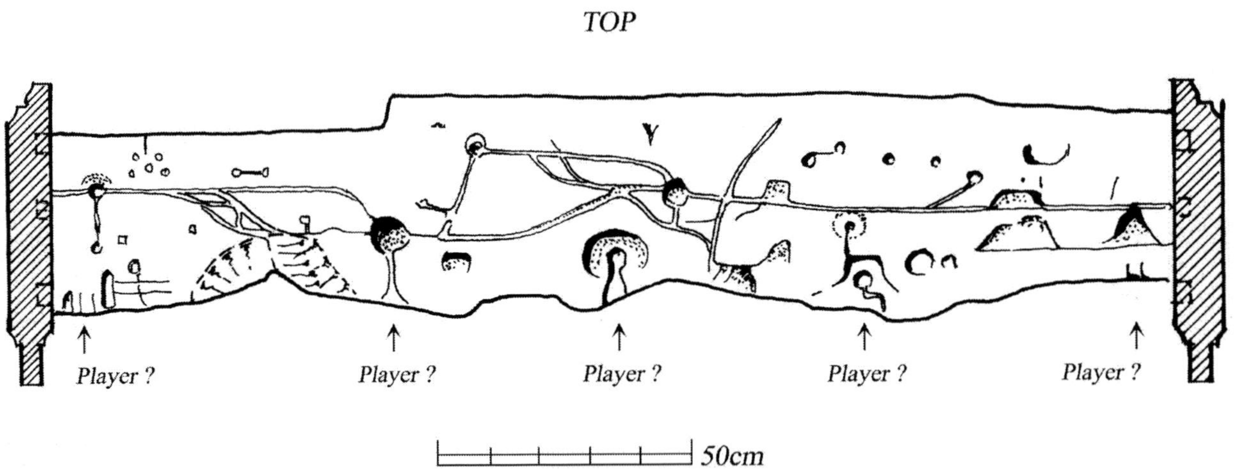

Figure 94 'Marbles Game', possibly mid 16th-century. Horizontal desk top showing what appears to be a 'board' for a marbles or bagatelle game with channels and scoring holes, an apparently unique survival. The now reset board would originally have been more upright. The board is some 2.2m long and could have seated some half-dozen boys. (Drawing E Watts and P Woodfield).

SECTION J

MEDIEVAL WINDOW GLASS FROM THE CHURCH AND CLOISTER

with a discussion on other medieval window glass in Coventry and other Carmelite and Franciscan glass

C. Woodfield

with contributions by Father Jerome Bertram and Richard Marks

With wide windows y-wroughte, and walls well high
That mote been portreid and paynt and pulched full clene,
With gaie glittering glass glowing as the sonne.

Pierce the Ploughman's Crede (Anon. *c.*1393-1401)
(Skeat 1867, lines 120-122)

The Coventry Whitefriars church is the second largest known medieval friary church in North Europe, after the London Greyfriars, and is of cathedral size. It was founded in 1342 by Sir John Pulteney, Mayor of London, and the surviving misericords suggest patronage by London Mayors until the end of the 14th century.

The site was excavated in the 1960s by Charmian Woodfield for the Ministry of Public Buildings and Works and Coventry Museum, and there was clearance work mostly in the SE cloister area by John Bateman for the Museum in 1977-1978.

Prof. Marks comments that this report covers important material for the history of medieval glass in England. Firstly it provides new evidence for glass painting in one of the major centres of the craft, and one with very little *in situ* remains; secondly it is from a mendicant context and very little window glass has survived from English friaries. Medieval Carmelite glass is however much more common on the Continent.

It should also be noted that it is very rare to have meaningful groups with excavated glass, and to be able, as here, to identify the subject matter of a window. Normally there is only a thin scatter of material.

LOCATION OF THE WINDOW GLASS ON SITE

The main body of the surviving glass was recovered from two areas - that from the destruction of the Great East Window in the 1550s or 1560s, lying where it fell, in the main (this includes small quantities of glass apparently from the eastern presbytery windows, where there was a slight overlap of the fallen material from these two sources); and secondly, glass swept into the Grammar School rubbish deposits in the N resonance passage in the western three bays of the choir (this including small quantities of glass from elsewhere, doubtless in part from being picked up by the schoolboys). Both deposits give evidence for the destruction of images probably largely in 1547, a period within the occupation of the choir by the Grammar School (Woodfield, 1981, 81-159). At this period the presbytery seems to have been occupied by small scale metal workers, largely pinners. It is not certain how much destruction took place in 1538, the period of the dissolution of the Carmelite house. The choir continued in use as a Grammar School until 1558, although to its E it seems that the presbytery was probably a light industrial workshop. The presence of musket balls in School deposits may account for some loss of the glass. The use of the nave is unknown.

QUANTITY

A total of some 15,000 pieces was estimated, when re-assessed for publication in 1996. The subsequent recounting of it (twice) elsewhere, under the instructions of English Heritage, for yet more assessments, caused much damage, resulting in a total of some 21,300 pieces, and much loss of information due to considerable further breakage of large meaningful patterned pieces. This is not a desirable methodology with this type of material.

A preliminary analysis of the glass (not all was available for viewing) was subsequently undertaken by Dr Pamela Graves in the same year, but there was no funding for the preparation of a report. The glass is now at Coventry Museum, accession no 20/7/ 1 to 51, i.e. there are 51 boxes.

CONSERVATION

Details of the conservation of this glass are given in *Coventry Whitefriars Medieval Window Glass. Conservation Report and Site Archive* (1998, Lincs. C.C. Education and Cultural Services Directorate, Conservation Department). This anonymous Report is now at Coventry Museum, the funding being by English Heritage.

METHOD OF PRESENTATION AND BACKGROUND TO ILLUSTRATIONS

The aim has been, as with the whole Report, to give some idea of the visual impact and one time splendour of much of the material, and, despite much decay and loss, this has been achieved to a degree hard to imagine from a casual inspection of the surviving largely blackened glass. Owing to the smashing of images, the impact of this material is largely of high quality painting of background detail and elaborate costume, often ignored in older studies of painted glass because of an understandably greater interest in figure painting. The glass also illustrates a point in history not often seen with clarity, that is the condition of windows in the mid 16th century, as they were left when attacked by iconoclasts, before the disposal and destruction of subsequent centuries.

The representation of colour has, however, presented a problem. With much of the blackened glass the colour is indistinguishable, but where known this is indicated. There seems to have been a good quantity of clear glass. The letters YS indicate that yellow stain is certainly present, but the details cannot be discerned. Where more precise yellow shading is shown in a drawing of the back of the glass this may, on occasions, be not entirely certain in its distribution. Back painting was rarely discernible, but is shown where possible. Grosing is indicated where surviving in good condition, but many edges had crumbled, and the absence of a grosing line cannot be taken to mean it had not existed.

The glass ranges in thickness from 2-4mm which is the norm, although it can reach 5-6mm, and is occasionally barely more than 1 mm. thick. The thickness does not appear to have any relationship to the chronology.

The scale of the drawings is 60 percent of life size; the explanation of the various shadings is given on Fig. 134.

The lead calmes are now held at Durham University and are not available for examination. Calme profiles are illustrated in Section T, *Observations on some of the Small Finds*, Nos 28-29, Fig. 161.

Some 380 calmes are recorded as being recovered in the Woodfield excavations. Large complex pieces survived, and there was considerable variation in the form of the calmes. The majority (some 330) were recovered from the choir and presbytery. Of these over 260 examples were recovered from the School deposits in the choir resonance passages; the conclusion that the Grammar School functioned in a partly windowless establishment is inescapable. Elsewhere only some 50 calmes were recovered, mostly from the N transept and N porch, and elsewhere in the church only in a very thin spread.

The sorting, classification and illustration of this amount of material was a massive task, involving an inspection of every piece by the writer, and the preparation of some 3,250 drawings, necessary because it is impossible to work directly with the damaged and illegible glass. The excavator is grateful to all the illustrators concerned, but particularly to Erica Jane Waters who accomplished a task thought by many to be impossible, and without whose, and indeed the author's, determination this report could not have been produced.

There are some 1640 drawings presented in this Report: 106 were drawn by Arthur Hillyer in the 1960s, funded by Coventry Museum; 470 by John English in the 1970s, funded by a Work Experience project; 101 by Paul Woodfield in the 1990s, funded by Woodfield Architectural and Archaeological Services; 92 by Anne Endean, and 42 by David Watts, both funded by English Heritage in the later 1990s. The remaining 836 are by Erica Jane Waters, funded by Woodfield Architectural and Archaeological Services in 2001. Of the additional 1624 drawings in archive, 1214 are by Erica Jane Waters.

With six illustrators there has been variation in the style of shading and washes. Illustration of colour, etc. presented problems in any case due not only to the decay but to the coatings of various preservative materials (best practice is actually to draw the glass between washing and treatment) and again the precise interpretation must remain to some extent fluid. The notion of leaving the writing up of material to 'posterity', as favoured as an escape route in our time, was not thought to be acceptable.

The task of sorting, editing, mounting and producing a comprehensible report from this mass of material was undertaken in 2001 by Charmian Woodfield, accepting the once traditional responsibility of the excavator for publication. It is a pity that much fine glass from other large scale monastic excavations, e.g. the Ipswich Whitefriars, has no chance of seeing the light of day.

The writer would like to thank Dr Richard Marks for acting as academic reader, Father Jerome Bertram for his valued help with the black letter script, and Woodfield Architectural and Archaeological Services for the considerable sum required to fund the production of this Report. Further financial help came from the Carmelite Friars.

It is regrettable that the nave of the church (as also the probable site of the frater, the Prior's House and perhaps St John's Hall, presumably all with fine glazing) were destroyed by road works in the 1970s and 1980s without any archaeological intervention whatsoever, and also that most of the chapter house glass has been lost. This report is therefore strongly biased towards glass of the choir.

DATING EVIDENCE

In view of the size of the building and the limited resources, most areas of the church were only cleared down to floor make-up level, and the vast bulk of the window glass was recovered from post Dissolution mid 16th-century levels. There are therefore only slight archaeological indications of dating, as follows.

The fragment of ?embroidery marked 'Friary 1' on Fig. 101.33 came from a level related to levelling-off the floor makeup for tiling in the E end of the choir. Likewise the *ex situ* fragment of vine stem on Fig. 96.12, also marked 'Friary 1', is from the make-up for the floor of the NE part of the S crossing; these suggest a date of *c.*1400 for the Great East Window and imply the glazing followed the installation of the choir stalls in the later 1380s or even 90s, but was probably contemporary with the laying of tiled floors with the larger type of decorated tile, *c.*1395-1400.

The glass with which the Great East Window material seems to have an immediate rapport is that of Thomas of Oxford with his *c.*1400 Tree of Jesse at Winchester College, with rose and lion roundels, see Fig. 106.1-18, interestingly very close to the site of the Winchester Carmelite Friary (Harvey and King 1971, 149-177). However, study of the detail of the two windows does not seem to show any matching close enough to indicate the same workshop. The resemblance may be just that of similar date and similar use of the International Gothic style.

The lettering fragment on Fig. 130.39 came from a Pre-rebuild level in the NE porch/W choir area which can only suggest that this lettering predates *c.*1423. It is paralleled by glass on Fig. 124 from the western choir. Likewise the pinnacle fragment, marked 'Pre-rebuild' on Fig. 130.1-2 is also paralleled in the adjacent western choir, Fig. 115. Similarly, the striped and cross-hatched border on Fig. 119.39, marked 'Pre-rebuild', comes from a floor makeup level over a grave of this phase in the western choir. It therefore seems likely that the western choir glass is of later date, by a decade or two, than that of the Great East Window (although there is a similarity between the two forms of diamond quarries showing roses, Figs 113 and 125.1-17). This glass is very unlikely to be later than 1423 when the church was reported to be in ruins.

The dating evidence for the site is discussed more fully elsewhere in this report: Tracy, C., *The Choir Stalls*, Section H; Woodfield, C., *Late 14th and 15th-Century Stamped Floor Tiles*, Section L; Woodfield, C. and Ratkai, S., *The Medieval and Later Pottery*, Section R;' and Woodfield, P. *Numismatica*, Section V. Richard Marks has commented that 15th-century glass fragments cannot be confined to a narrow time frame; however, there is archaeologically dated glass from this site.

Otherwise there are generally only very occasional small, unillustrated, fragments of glass from levels of the Rebuild phase. However, an exception is the fragment of ?door marked 'Rebuild' on Fig. 116.5, and this confirms a date of before the later 15th century for those pieces of higher quality among the western choir glass.

Rackham (1930-31, 110) refers to the 'declining skill of the local school of (Coventry) glass painters in the third quarter of the 15th century' and it is assumed that the coarse and wildly painted glass post dates 1423, when money was scarce, for this is a time of known financial and building problems. The glazing in the W end of the nave could well date from half a century later (see Cattell J. and Woodfield P., *The Standing Building with a detailed analysis of the East Cloister Range*, Section C; Woodfield, C. *The Whitefriars in Coventry – Historical Background*, Section B; and Woodfield, C., *Account of the Excavations at the Church of the Whitefriars, Coventry,* Section E, for the relevant evidence). This could give the glass a date post the 1447 fall of the tower.

CATALOGUE OF ILLUSTRATED WINDOW GLASS

Note that 'passage' or more usually, 'resonance passages' refers to the metre deep square-section chambers built for acoustic purposes under the choir stalls, and into which much glass was deposited between 1545 and 1558, Fig. 60b. A key to the detail on the illustrations of the glass is provided by Fig. 134.

Section 1: The Great East Window

Figures 95-114 are from the area of the Great East Window. On the few occasions where the provenances suggest that some material is more likely to be from the eastern presbytery windows this is indicated. The glass is from Destruction and Collapse levels of the mid 16th century, immediately adjoining both the western and eastern sides of the E wall of the choir. It is clear that the final Collapse phase follows earlier smashing and removal of 'images'. Despite this loss of figurative material, the original 1962 identification of the E window glass, by the writer, as depicting a Tree of Jesse has been confirmed.

A Tree of Jesse is a genealogical tree, or vine as in this case, showing the descent of Christ from the royal house of David, who was the son of Jesse, who is shown at the base of the window as a reclining figure. From Jesse's recumbent body the vine springs, its branches and leaves and grapes running upwards forming the basis of the design, and supporting images of Christ's (variable) royal ancestors, and prophets. The design is normally crowned by figures of the Virgin Mary and of Christ.

The Tree is an interpretation of the prophecy in Isaiah XI, Verse 1 'And there shall come forth a rod out of the stem of Jesse, and a branch shall grow out of his roots.' Verses 2 to 10 describe the nature and virtues of this 'rod'. Verse 10 again refers to Jesse – 'And in that day' (later interpreted as the coming of Christ) 'there shall be a rod of Jesse which shall stand as an ensign for the people'.

There are some 2,000 drawings of fragments of the Tree of Jesse window, of which over 900 are published here. Drawings in archive consist of much foliage and architectural panelling and some 45 additional drawings of hair and beards. Panelling occurred more frequently than foliage throughout the recovered assemblage.

Trees of Jesse are not known otherwise in Coventry window glass. However, a now destroyed misericord at St Michael's did depict one, but this was of later 15th-century date (Harris 1927, 263-4). The Tree of Jesse windows at Mancetter and Merevale in Warwickshire do not appear to be by the same hand as the Whitefriars glass.

Figure 95

Great East Window Tree of Jesse. Border designs with varying yellow stain; clear or occasionally green glass. c.1400?

The evidence was clear for a yellow stain 'diamond', within the quarry (more than 20 examples) and a stained indented rectangular frame (some 15 examples). There was, however, only slight evidence (2 examples) that the diamond did occur unstained, and rather more (6 examples), for an unstained frame. The central leaf motif appeared to be yellow-stained in only about 6 examples and was mostly clear, although green in one example, No 18. Colour standardisation does not seem to have been a priority. The cusping on these quarries implies a relationship to the border strips and arcading shown on Figs 111-112.
This design occurs in the Queen's College, Cambridge, Carmelite glass (Wayment 1994, fig. 9) there thought to date to the mid 15th century. As reset at Queen's the quarries alternate with small rectangular pieces of blue and red glass (Wayment 1994, 140 and fig. 11.1). This type of quarry has also been noted in the parish church of Haversham, Bucks. (pers. comm. Anne Endean, and observation by the writer). There is a version of it at Sempringham (Graves, 2000, fig. 226).

Versions of the main design, Nos 4, 9, 13, 16, 20 and 28, occurred only in ones and twos. A border quarry without the edge frame is also illustrated, Nos 13, 16 and 23, and here the diamond appears to be clear glass. This version is paralleled at York, there with a fleur-de-lys as a central motif (Lee, Seddon and Stevens, 1989, 43, section 10). This style also occurs as a closer match further N from the Whitefriars church, at Linlithgow, West Lothian, again in the E window (Stones 1989, 150-153, ill. 93).

Another version, No 17 shows a three petalled flower, and no cusping. There are also variant additional fragments with yellow-stained running scroll borders, e.g. No 24.

There are some 170 drawings of border designs in this main design in archive for the E end, and it is clear that this design relates to the Great East Window; its appearance in eastern presbytery windows, although unlikely, cannot be entirely ruled out. Seventeen examples, all small, were also recovered from the resonance passage Grammar School deposits dating to 1545-1558, and there will inevitably have been other movement of pieces of eye-catching glass by schoolboys.

The small size and percentage of fragments seems to rule out the appearance of the main design in the western choir.

Figure 96

Great East Window Tree of Jesse. Vine stems and leaves with elongated comma-shaped veins; clear glass with some yellow stain. c.1400?

The vine stems all seem to have had a central line with indications of curving, branching and tapering, Nos 1-16. The glass was clear, and had only shading in a large majority of cases. However yellow stain was observed in some seven cases, all these being on stems with a thinner central line.

There are some 70 drawings in archive of additional stems, together with 6 strays in the passage.

The vine leaves

In the Winchester College E window (Harvey and King 1971, 148-77) the leaves are in the upper range of lights. This is very likely the case here, as there is much architectural panelling for which space has to be found, and in the absence of pinnacles it must have been placed at the base of the windows?

The leaves occurred in some half dozen main designs, those, with 'commas', Nos 18-26 and 29, being one of the most numerous. There were variations within this classification, Nos 27-28 and 30.

The majority of the leaves are clear glass, but where the centre of the leaf survives there is a yellow stain ring in one example, No 18, but it only seems to be present in one other apparent central leaf fragment, No 21.

One drawing, No 30, shows a yellow-stained leaf, as do two drawings in archive, but these are the exception.

There are some 40 drawings of the 'comma' glass in archive, and two 'strays' were found in the resonance passage.

Figure 97

Great East Window Tree of Jesse. Blue and yellow-stained vine leaves with curved veins but no 'commas', and grapes (top); red and blue vine leaves with straight veins (bottom). c.1400?

These vine leaves do not have the comma shaped veins seen on Fig. 96, but the top leaf of the vine, Nos 6, 8 and 9, is again pointed. It seems likely that the leaves in the main are clear with small amounts of yellow stain (some 5 examples, not illustrated) apparently involving both leaves and stems, but the detail is uncertain. Four illustrated pieces, Nos 20-23, and two unpublished pieces, were in blue glass. There are some 30 drawings in archive, and 2 strays were from the resonance passage.

Grapes

These are under-represented by the numbers of the drawings, Nos 24-29, as there were apparent fragments too small to have been drawn. Some grapes appear to have been in clear glass, and some with yellow stain, and there was the odd hint of blue (not illustrated). There were 4 fragments apparently showing grapes from the passage, giving 2 more with yellow stain.

Vine leaves

Similar to Fig. 96, but with more pronounced veins, Nos 30-50. Colour was more evident with these, with the presence of red and blue leaves as depicted. However clear glass leaves with yellow stain were again present (not illustrated). There are some 10 drawings in archive, and 2 strays were from the resonance passage.

Figure 98

Great East Window Tree of Jesse/E presbytery. Vine leaves with thick veins and a tendency to large and irregular leaf indentations, Nos 1-17; leaf pattern with distinctive dots, with an internal oval (and possibly also a circular) frame, Nos 18 and 28; red and blue leaves with dots, and straight or curved borders with a single line, Nos 20-27 and 29-33. c.1400?

Eight of the vine leaf pieces had clearly carried yellow stain, unfortunately not all illustratable, and some three appeared to be partly clear glass, and one blue. There are some 25 additional drawings in archive.

The 'dot' pattern unfortunately has no certain clues as to the form of the extended pattern to the right of the oval, though No 28 may relate. One piece of glass was noted as 'clear' but there is no other information on colouring. There are some dozen drawings in archive. This pattern may have originally been in the eastern presbytery S window rather than the E window.

The 'dot' pattern appears again with a thin line and wider band border, both straight (ten examples) and curved (three examples). Both red and blue glass are recorded. There are some half dozen drawings in archive. This pattern may be from the eastern presbytery. There is one example only from the resonance passage.

The blue glass on the bottom line, Nos 29-33, may also have originated in eastern presbytery windows; however of two in archive, one is from the Great East Window.

Figure 99

Great East Window Tree of Jesse/E presbytery. Blue, red and yellow stain broad and narrow stripe borders, associated with leaf patterns; bordered roundels (or perhaps ovals) some red with leaf patterns. Terminals and unbordered leaf and flower patterns not previously represented. Fragments from very large leaf patterns. Plain terminals. c.1400?

The first, bordered, categories are certainly from the E window, Nos 1-14, 16-18, 21-22, 25, 27, 31 and 40; the colour range where surviving is clear (14 examples), and blue (7 examples). Some 35 drawings are in archive including 3 further blue examples, and 2 from the resonance passage. In addition there are 10 drawings in archive of the leaves with a 'bent bristle' effect, e.g. No 30, with one yellow-stained example from the passage. The red piece of glass, No 25, may come from an eastern presbytery window.

Of the glass in the upper 'roundel', No 32, two pieces are blue, and in the 'oval' below, Nos 33-36, two are red; the distribution suggests their appearance in both the eastern presbytery windows, and the E window, and from that last context come the apparent fragments from very large leaves, Nos 29-30 and 38-39, of which there are some dozen drawings in archive, of which 3 are yellow stain, 2 are blue, and 1 is red. They are, as far as can be told from fragments, as common in the resonance passage, and may therefore have occurred throughout the choir.

The group of three, Nos 24, 28 and 37, with smaller flowers and a leaf on a dark ground, are all yellow stain. The single line and leaf terminals, Nos 43-52, are apparently from the E window, but there is little evidence for colour. One piece of glass with foliage unusually has small areas of cross-hatching, No 36. In addition to the terminals shown, there are 3 single line V terminals, 1 of which one again is yellow-stained.

Figure 100

Great East Window Tree of Jesse. Background red, blue, green and yellow-stained 'seaweed'. Glass with foliage and 'cross-hatching', some red. Large flowered patterns some yellow-stained, from panelling and borders. c.1400?

'Seaweed', Nos 1-22, occurs in the following colours, red 2, emerald green 1, blue 1, yellow stain 2, and clear 1. There are 11 drawings in archive, 2 with yellow stain. 'Seaweed' is about three times as common in the resonance passage (not all was drawn, see Glass Box 50 in archive), but its occurrence in the E window as well seems certain.

The glass with cross-hatching, Nos 23-29, is paralleled to some extent by glass on Fig. 108 and this technique is overwhelmingly a western choir type. Of the panelling, Nos 30-45, 2 pieces are yellow-stained. This glass is certainly from the E window.

Figure 101

Great East Window Tree of Jesse. Possible fabrics, embroidery, and brooches, some blue, yellow and amber. Gold crowns and ermine, some on red, yellow and blue grounds. c.*1400? The ermine might be heraldic. The crowns confirm the expected kings and queens in a Tree of Jesse window*

There is a greater proportion of yellow stain than usual. The large blue piece, No 32, was damaged but originally had been very fine, with fern sprigs all over and signs of back painting.

The apparent 'ermine', Nos 48-56 appearing on coloured backgrounds (1 red, 1 blue and 2 yellow-stained backgrounds), may have heraldic significance, but as Prof. R. Marks notes (*in litt.*) might equally be from a garment worn by e.g. the Queen of Heaven, or one of the kings portrayed in a Tree of Jesse. There are two parallels with possible ermine tails on Fig. 122 (Nos 37 and 39) but otherwise there are no obvious parallels to the material on Fig. 101, from the W choir.

Figure 102

Great East Window Tree of Jesse. Possible green costume, chain mail, shoes. Eyes, possible ears and gold haloes, beards and hair, some yellow; hands and wounds of Christ. Hands indicating figures of at least two scales; hands holding a book and a staff. c.*1400?*

Richard Marks comments (*in litt.*) 'the eye, No 20, may have affinities with John Thornton of Coventry's work'. However, there is little resemblance in detail between, e.g., the Thornton Great East Window at York and the Whitefriars glass. The absence of faces, and so an ability to match the famous Thornton nose, is not helpful. Marks adds 'there are similarities between Thornton and Thomas of Oxford', and with the latter we do have greater affinities. See discussion in this paper on Coventry Glaziers.

The 'fabric' decorated with a grid and crosses, No 11, is paralleled by shoe leather in the Tree of Jesse window at Lowick, Northants. (pers. ob.), though the Lowick glass is much earlier. Note the shoe with the band at the bottom depicting an overlying garment, No 9.

From this glass one could expect a Virgin and Child and a Day of Judgement and apparently Christ showing wounds, though this would be unusual in a Tree of Jesse.

The damage and loss, presumably that of 1547 following Edward VI's Order in Council that 'all images whatsoever should be taken out of churches...so that no memory of them remain in.., windows' is very apparent. Richard Marks comments that the Edwardian prescriptions on images are much more complex than this Order in Council (see Marks 1993, Chapter 11, and Aston 1988 - the best treatment of the subject). This smashed glass would presumably have largely left the site, although some could have been expected to have been swept into the resonance passage, see Fig. 122, where fragments, perhaps the yellow hair, possibly from an image of the Virgin Mary, may have originated from the E window. Fig. 122 also has parallels to the apparent chain mail and a wound of Christ in a different style, suggesting another Crucifixion, although the life-sized Christ in the Great East Window could have been sitting in judgement showing His wounds, as at Winchester College (Harvey and King 1971,148-77).

The only colour is yellow stain, except for one green piece, No 10.

It is clear that life-size, half-size and one-third size figures are present. The half size figures are likely to be kings and prophets. The third size figures at Winchester College are the craftsmen (Harvey and King 1971, 148-77).

Figure 103

Great East Window Tree of Jesse. Angel's wings, some yellow; fine blue red and yellow scratchwork ?fabric; maniple? in clear and yellow glass with crosses and crosshatched borders. c.*1400*

Where discernible the wings are yellow stain, Nos 1-6, whereas the scratchwork, Nos 7-29, is blue, red and yellow stain, there being some 25 further drawings in archive, confirming the blue and adding another example of scratchwork on red glass; this scratchwork design seems too small scale for the arcs to indicate architecture.

The high quality ?maniple, Nos 30-35 is clear glass. Cruder possible ?maniples, Nos 36, 40-41, 45, 49 and 53, are yellow-stained, and the 10 drawings for these in archive indicate other versions with yellow stain crosses. It is possible that the golden feathers might represent costume for the bodies of angels, as in the Coventry Mystery plays (Rackham 1930-31, 97).

No angel wings nor ?maniples were recovered from the passage. However, one or two examples, presumably strays, of the scratchwork fabrics on Fig. 119 are in the same style as those shown here.

Figure 104

Great East Window Tree of Jesse. Red and yellow jewelled edgings. Folds in clothing? Furs, (or strange beasts?), hair and beards in clear and yellow glass. c.*1400?*

Yellow stain is apparent on five examples of the beading, plus one on the three archive drawings; it presumably represented gold; there is also one parallel from the resonance passage, Fig. 120. The ?clothing occurs in red once, and blue twice (not illustrated); the fur on the possible creature, which occurs only here, is yellow in seven cases; and there are some 45 archive hair, beard and fur drawings, giving 5 extra yellow stain examples.

Figure 105

Great East Window Tree of Jesse. Black letter with indications of scrolls, some yellow stain, and probable fragments of kings' and other appropriate names (e.g. Eliacim and Salathiel). 'Floor tiles': black and clear and black and yellow. Bells for suspension on the person? or architecture? c.*1400*

Borders indicating four different sets of lettering are present, and some half dozen pieces from the resonance passage fill might also be from the E window, see Fig. 124.

Father Jerome Bertram has listed the fragments with probable readings and these and his general Discussion are given here. This also applies to the Fig. 124 entry.

1 **&** ampersand.
2 terminal **s**.
3 **d**.
4 **ḷia**, as in Eliacim.
5 **B**, as in Booz.
6 **S**, as in Salmon, Salomon, Salathiel or Sadoc.
7 **ea,** as in Eleazar (or Micheas as at Winchester?, C.W.).
8 **ạc** (curved for scroll) as in Isaac or Jacob.
9 **ı**, (curved for scroll).
10 **d(omi)ni**.
11 **hy**, as in ? Ezechyas.
12 **ṣị**, as in Osias.
13 **d**.
14 **ạc**, as in Jacob or Isaac.
15 **III**.
16 **n**.
17 **P**, as in Phares.
18 **?en or em**, as in memento?
19 **iel**, as in Salathiel.
20 **ụ̣**.
17-20 on curving scroll.
21 **ı̣**.

No 10, with its apparent joining piece, forms the common abbreviation *d(omi)ni*, (of the Lord), probably from a date, *Anno Domini.*

No 18 seems to belong to a curving banderol or scroll, possibly a supplication memento *mei* 'remember me', which would be appropriate for a donor figure kneeling at the base of the window.

Several fragments can plausibly be matched with the names of Kings, though such tiny fragments cannot obviously be located with any certainty. No 4, Eliacim, and No 19, Salathiel, are the most convincing. The curious 'hy' on No 11 warns us that the spelling of Hebrew names may be very erratic, bearing in mind the parallel of the Dorchester Jesse (cf. Newton 1979, 83-4).

Seven of the lettering illustrations indicate yellow stain.

For comparative 'tiles' from the resonance passage see Fig. 118 Nos 33-39.

The bells may be architectural (cf. Fig. 116); there is no evidence for colour. Might they be hawking bells, or bell-shaped purses?

Figure 106

Great East Window Tree of Jesse. White and red rose, and lion roundels. c.*1400*

Four drawings combine to make the reconstructed 11cm diameter rose roundel, No 11, and there is evidence for another 5 large and 2 smaller rose roundels, Nos 1-10 and unillustrated. Evidence survives for yellow outer petals on two of these roundels, Nos 1 and 11, and there is also a hint at a red rose, No 7. The two rose roundels, Nos 8-9 and 10 are from the resonance passage, and it is therefore possible that smaller roundels occurred in the passage.

The reconstruction of the lion, No 18, as a roundel, which seems the most likely form, is based on Thomas of Oxford's roundel from Winchester College chapel, adjacent to the site of the Winchester Carmelite house. Here the E window, another Tree of Jesse, had roundels of roses and lions (Harvey and King 1971, 148-77). These also occur at e.g. York Minster (Gibson 1979, pl. 24). There is no evidence for lion roundels elsewhere at the Whitefriars.

Figure 107

Great East Window Tree of Jesse. Bull's eye windows, or a background pattern, one blue, and fine line background architecture; heavy line architectural detail, clear glass and yellow stain. c.*1400*

An origin in the choir is possible for the bull's eye blue window, No 2 (although it is possible that these bull's eye pieces (Nos 1 and 2) are a background pattern (Prof. R. Marks (*in litt.*)). The fine line architecture appears to have yellow shading, and here only some two-fifths of this type was from the E window, the remainder being found in the resonance passage. Cf. Fig. 118 for further fine line panelling.

The heavier 'rounded forms' (turrets) of architectural panelling, Nos 26-45, also have yellow shading, (10 examples).

It seems noteworthy to the writer that none of the arcading from the Great East Window area has Gothic pointed arches, but perhaps this is the norm.

There are some 55 drawings in archive, of which a dozen show additional yellow staining.

Figure 108

Great East Window Tree of Jesse. Continuation of 'rounded forms' architectural (turrets) panelling. Architectural panelling with cross- hatching - some possibly choir. Clear glass and yellow-stained glass. c.*1400*

Some 4 of the 'rounded form' category, Nos 1-21, have yellow stain. It should be noted that the amount of decay can make it difficult to distinguish between decayed shading, and decayed yellow stain. Seventeen drawings in archive appear to be mouldings, 4 of which show yellow stain; there are six others, 3 from the resonance passage.

'The rounded turrets area design was adopted by Thomas of Oxford *et al.* from earlier canopy designs' (Prof. R. Marks (*in litt.*)).

There are 11 examples in the cross-hatched category, Nos 37-46, of which 1 bore yellow stain. These are ten times as common in the resonance passage deposit, and these may be out of place.

Figure 109

Great East Window Tree of Jesse. Architectural Panelling with 'angular ' forms. Clear and yellow-stained glass. c.*1400?*

One, No 6, shows signs of fine cusping, establishing a link with Fig. 110 patterns. Some 14 examples preserved signs of yellow stain (as indicated). Of some 70 unpublished pieces, 9 show yellow stain. There are only 4 examples from the passage.

Figure 110

Great East Window Tree of Jesse/E presbytery. Architectural panelling with smaller quatrefoils, trefoils, and tracery, clear and yellow-stained glass. c.*1400?*

The 'very small quatrefoils', Nos 19-22, 35 and 41, material is possibly from the south-eastern window of the presbytery. There is only one piece of coloured glass, No 15, and yellow staining is as indicated. There are some 15 unpublished drawings of the larger architectural 'tracery' (as No 32), including 1 blue, and 1 yellow stain (with 3 examples from the resonance passage) and also some 10 unpublished drawings of the smaller tracery. Only one piece of glass, in a different style to this form of architectural panelling, occurred in the resonance passage, confirming the illustrated material as the norm. 'Some of the traceried window designs shown here look earlier than *c.*1400 and could be from virtually anywhere in the 14th century' (Prof. R. Marks (*in litt.*). However, the construction of the choir is likely to have continued to *c.*1390 at the earliest.

Figure 111

Great East Window Tree of Jesse. Architectural panelling with medium-sized quatrefoils and tracery, clear and yellow-stained glass. Blue border with white spheres and circles. c.*1400? or a little earlier.*

The 'tracery', Nos 1-17 (3 examples from the resonance passage), and the quatrefoils, Nos 26-46 (4 from the resonance passage), have some 5 examples each of yellow stain (including the dozen unpublished sherds of quatrefoils).

The 'rings and circles' border, Nos 18-25 and 47-50, has two examples of blue glass and two examples of yellow stain, including the half dozen unpublished examples.

Figure 112

Great East Window Tree of Jesse. Borders with larger quatrefoils, clear, yellow-stained and some blue glass. c.*1400? or a little earlier.*

There are 9 examples with yellow stain, but also 2 in blue glass. There are some 65 unpublished drawings, of which 9 showed yellow stain. Four pieces of this type occur in the resonance passage.

Figure 113

Great East Window Tree of Jesse. Bordered and unbordered diamond quarries with yellow stain flowers and margins. c.*1400? The quarry, No 16, is post 1400, however (pers. comm. Richard Marks).*

The reconstruction of the bordered quarry, No 11, is based on three pieces of glass. There are indications of some 7 other quarries, Nos 1-10, with slight variations; the flower and the border are yellow-stained. See Fig. 125 for parallels from the resonance passage.

Reconstruction of unbordered quarry No 16; there are indications of some six others, Nos 12-15 and two in archive. The flower is yellow-stained, and there is back painting behind the spoke, presumably also yellow stain, but not now discernible. See Fig. 125 for the resonance passage examples.

'All except No 16 are designs in vogue during the second half of the 14th century; No 16 is post 1400' (Prof. R. Marks (*in litt.*). It is unlikely that glazing started before 1385 at the earliest.

Figure 114

Great East Window Tree of Jesse. Non linear patterns made from shading, red, blue, green and yellow stain, Nos 1-17; patterns involving wavy lines, clear and yellow stain, Nos 18-29. Patterns involving bands of 'scribbling', clear and yellow stain, Nos 35-46. Red edge pieces and miscellaneous patterns, one (unstratified) piece with scratch marks, Nos 47-61. c.*1400?*

With decayed glass it is sometimes impossible to distinguish between shading and yellow stain, but this shading/yellow stain pattern category does appear to have five yellow-stained examples, Nos 3, 6, 9, 10 and 12; there is also shading on blue, Nos 1-2; red (1), No 11; and green (1), No 7, glass. There are 35 unpublished drawings. See also Fig. 125. Wavy lines, Nos 18-34, and 'scribbling', Nos 35-44, were used infrequently but are illustrated as part of the range of techniques. Much of the scribbling was associated with yellow stain, and seven examples are illustrated, Nos 35-40 and 46. Pieces of uncoloured glass up to 6 x 4cm, occurred with tight scribbling all over.

Eight red edge pieces are as shown, Nos 47-54. Unpublished, unpainted coloured glass consisting of 11 red, and 2 blue pieces occurred. 3cm wide clear glass edge pieces also occurred, usually with slight shading.

Miscellaneous patterns not otherwise represented, Nos 55-61.

Unclassified glass 110 drawings in archive, of which 14 show yellow stain, and 2 blue.

Additionally there are 30 drawings of 'arcs'/ panelling, etc. (2 yellow stain , 1 blue).

130 of 'striped borders'/panelling (35 yellow stain, 4 red, 1 blue).

100 of 'thicker black line'/ panelling (15 yellow stain, 2 red, 1 blue).

Section 2: the window glass from the N resonance passage in the W choir

'Level, level with the ground
The towers do lie
Which with their golden glittering tops
Pierced once to the sky'

The Wracke of Walsingham
(Bodleian Library MS Rawl. Poet. 291 fol. 16, perhaps Philip, Earl of Arundel, Sixteenth century)

The second large deposit of window glass is that swept into the N resonance passage in the W choir at the time of its use as a Grammar School, presumably in the main from some half dozen windows, and between 1545 and 1558. However, it is known that glass was reaching the passage from the E window, doubtless brought there by curious schoolboys, and some E choir glass may occur here. With this has been combined the small quantities from the S resonance passage, and various Destruction/Collapse levels in the western choir, from which levels very little glass was recovered. The virtual absence of foliage, apart from obvious strays, is most marked. It is possible that this glass is a decade or so later than that in the Great East Window? Certainly some of the glass, Figs 127-129, is so bizarre that it must surely represent later patching?

Figure 115

Resonance passage/W choir. Pinnacles and related structures. All in clear and yellow-stained glass. Presumably from International Gothic frames for figures. 15th century, perhaps early

The vines which formed a frame round the, now largely lost, figures in the E window are here replaced by the elongated architectural frames of the International Gothic style. Presumably there were simple linear structures carrying these pinnacles in the main, and these would not be recognisable from fragments. Yellow stain survives in 5 examples only, Nos 1-4 and 9. 12 drawings in archive.

Figure 116

Resonance passage/W choir. Architectural panelling. Columns, arched and curved architectural motifs and small scale angular patterns, clear glass and yellow stain. Architectural 'Bell'. Early 15th century?

The cusped tracery of Fig. 116 differs from that in Fig. 111. Other 'bells', e.g. as No 29, occur in Fig. 105, but these last did not appear to be architectural. Six are yellow-stained, Nos 7, 10, 17, 19, 21 and 35.

'Most of the architectural work in the upper half of the figure looks second half of 14th century' (Prof. R. Marks (*in litt.*).

Figure 117

Resonance passage/W choir. Architectural panelling. Columns, arched and curved architectural motifs (continued). Small scale 'angular' patterns. All clear glass and yellow-stained glass. Early 15th century?

A comparison with Figs 107-109 shows variations in the architectural panelling style between the E window and the W choir. But note that strays in the passage from the E window may not have been identified. There are 7 examples of yellow stain, Nos 8-9, 14, 21-22, 33 and 36.

Figs 116-117. 57 arched and curved architectural pieces in archive, 11 of which show yellow stain.

Figure 118

Resonance passage/W choir. Small scale patterns, patterns with trefoils and quatrefoils, fine line panelling, Nos 1-32. 'Floor tile', or heraldic motif, Nos 33-39. All clear and yellow-stained glass. Early 15th century?

The architectural glass has 6 examples of yellow stain, Nos 12, 15-17, 24 and 28, and the 'floor tile' 1 example, No 39.

There are 23 drawings of fine line panelling, no yellow stain, in archive, and 20 drawings in archive of miscellaneous architectural panelling, no yellow stain, of the types occurring on Figs 116-118. Also 20 drawings of miscellaneous architectural panelling, no yellow stain, as occurring again on Figs 116-118.

Figure 119

Resonance passage/W choir. Designs involving cross-hatching. All clear and yellow-stained glass. Early 15th century?

Seven drawings show yellow stain, Nos 2, 16, 45, 47, 49-50 and 52.

Additionally there are 42 examples in archive, of which 5 show yellow stain, and therefore these designs are ten times as common as in the E window deposits, Fig. 108, where they may be partly intrusive?

Figure 120

Resonance passage/W choir. Jewelled bands, Nos 1-5 and 7-11; fabrics and decorative motifs, Nos 6 and 12-36; red (Nos 46-48), pink (No 12), blue (Nos 27, 62 and 67-69), and yellow-stained (Nos 20, 29 and 35) glass; 'gems' (Nos 37-40) and scratchwork (Nos 42-45). The large leaf spray, No 65, is yellow stain on blue glass. 15th century?

No yellow stain occurred on the illustrated jewelled bands, nor indeed, except for Nos 20, 29 and 35, on other decorative items in Fig. 120. The red with black stars is notable, No 46. Much of the scratchwork designs at the bottom of the page, Nos 49-69 are on blue glass, including the leaf shown yellow-stained, No 65, which was also on blue glass. Six drawings in archive, mostly simple lines. Some 20 apparent clothing folds are in archive. They appear to be on clear glass.

Figure 121

Resonance passage/W choir. Floral designs, in red, blue and yellow stain; textiles and costume in clear glass with yellow stain, Nos 12, 14, 39 and 41. 15th century?

'Embrowdid was he as it were a mede,
Al full of fresshe floures, white and rede'

Chaucer's squire, *c.*1385 in *The Prologue to the Canterbury Tales* (OUP 1942 edition, lines 89-90)

Where surviving, the colour indication was yellow stain, Nos 12, 14, 39 and 41; blue, Nos 7-8; and red, No 2.

Some 25 drawings in archive. Two with yellow stain and two blue.

Figure 122

Resonance passage/W choir. Haloed head of Christ, No 4; face fragments and hands in clear and yellow glass, Nos 1-5, 7, 12-15, 21, 25 and 38; maiden with hand on breast, No 6. Yellow hair, perhaps of the Virgin Mary, Nos 23-24. Beards, other hair and ears, head of Christ? and the bearded head, Nos 16-22, 26-27 and 29-30. Haloes, Nos 8-11; Crown of Thorns, No 28; Wounds of Christ, Nos 32-34. Chain mail, No 31; ermine?, Nos 37 and 39; and a blue crown? or sceptre, No 35. 15th century?

The tripartite division of the halo confirms the identification of the small haloed head, No 4, as that of Christ. There is a partial second small head with an early 15th-century hair style, No 5. The early 15th-century dating of these two heads has been confirmed by Prof. R. Marks (*in litt.*). There are slight hints, only, at a John Thornton style. The long yellow hair, Nos 23-24, may imply the Virgin Mary, as may the blue crown-like object, No 35. The apparent chain mail, wounds and crown of thorns (1 example only) may imply a representation of the Crucifixion (the wounds being in a different style than those of the E window). Figures probably occurred at three scales. A face, a hand and three examples of hair show yellow stain, Nos 2-3 and 22-24.

Some 25 hair and beards in archive, 2 yellow-stained. Also 3 possible eye fragments, 2 possible haloes and 2 chain mail items.

Figure 123

Resonance passage/W choir. Foliage, Nos 1-8, including yellow stain leaf on blue glass, No 6. Blue, red, green and yellow stain 'seaweed', Nos 9-39. Terminals, and clear 'seaweed'. Early 15th century?

Foliage is virtually absent from the passage, and all are illustrated here. Blue, Nos 2, 6, 13-17, 20-23, 26-29, 33 and 37 and yellow stain, Nos 7, 34-35 and 38, are represented, and one leaf, exceptionally, is blue with yellow stain, No 6. There were 20 pieces of foliage which appeared to be strays from the E window (not illustrated).

'Seaweed' occurs most commonly in blue, 13 examples illustrated, red 7 illustrated, green 2, yellow stain 3; it also occurs in clear glass. Some 40 in archive, 1 blue;

plus 8 'seaweed' terminals, 2 blue. Prof. R Marks has suggested (*in litt.*) that the 'seaweed' ground dates to *c.*1390-1430/40.

Figure 124

Resonance passage/W choir. Lettering in clear glass and yellow stain referring to dates, donor inscriptions, and references to a Cruxifixion? Markings on glass, a possible Coventry glazier's signature. Early 15th century?

There seem to be some 10 different styles of lettering at the least, and some may refer to later patching. Three of those illustrated have yellow stain.

The identifications are by Father Jerome Bertram

1	**:** (stop or word-separator).	
2	**:.**	
3	**:I:** (? a numerical digit).	
4	**:I.**	
5	**:.**	
6	**ṛ.**	
7	**ı:ı.**	
8	**xḷ** (numerical, for 40?).	
9	**ṭio.**	
10	**suo.**	
11	**ı.**	
12	**[anim]ab(u)s**, terminal flourish?	
13	terminal **ṣ**, terminal flourish?	
14	**d ı.**	
15	**n̄s**, contraction for d(omi)n(u)s. Nos 13-15 probably go together.	
16	**ū ı**, (contraction mark for ...u(m)	
17	**[eccl]îe**, (with contraction mark for eccl(es)ie). Nos 14 to 17 may go together.	
18	**ıec.**	
19	**ııı.**	
20	**ṛa.**	
21	**ıı**, (curving scroll)	
22	**oru.**	
23	**ịṛ.**	
24	**lu.**	
25	**ọ.**	
26	**ịtụ.**	
27	**ọ.**	
28	**ọ.**	
29	**ped.**	} }These two fit togther to read *pedum*
30	**du.**	}
31	**la.**	
32	**&.**	ampersand
33	**çẹ.**	
34	**e.**	
35	**ṇ.**	
36	**a.**	
37	**th.**	
38	**ḥịṇ.**	
39	**ıh.**	
40	**ıtı.**	
41	**ııı.**	
42	**ııı.**	
43	**ııı.**	
44	**ı.**	
45	**tı.**	
46	**it.**	
47	terminal **s.**	
48	**o** or **d.**	
49	**s.**	
50	**ı.**	
51	**B.**	
52-53	Marks of uncertain significance (maker's marks?)	
54	(con)ny, Coventry?	
55	**ccc**, part of a date?	

Nine examples are in archive, representing i three times, ii three times. Also a?, i, n and r.

Father Jerome Bertram writes:

Nos 1-5 have large pierced lozenge stops used to separate words. Since the large capital I appears between sets of such stops, they could have been part of a date. No 8 is XL, almost certainly part of a date, so we have XL : I : I giving [14]42 (though other digits could be missing, leaving the possibilities of xliii, xliiii or even xlvi-xlviii). However, other evidence suggests a date for the glass of before 1440. Could this be a reference to the founding of the Friary in 1342?

No 12 is the common abbreviation *aiabz* for *a(n)i(m)ab(u)s*, as in the formula *Orate pro animabus* 'pray for the souls', or *quorum animabus propicietur deus* 'on whose souls may God have mercy', both common on donor inscriptions.

No 17 appears to be *eccl(es)ie*, 'of this church', as in a commemoratory inscription to a church official (not necessarily of *this* church). Nos 13 to 15 are rather rougher lettering, possibly from a different window or panel from the others.

Two pieces appear to join to make No 29 , possibly *pedu(m)* 'of the feet'. It could conceivably refer to the nailing of the feet in the Crucifixion, and there is evidence for a Crucifixion in other glass from this area, Fig. 122.

Of the marks one has the usual abbreviation for *con.*, looking like a 9, giving the implausible name *'conny'* for the painter, unless it is simply meant for 'Coventry'. No 55 could be part of a line of Cs out of a date, though these marks could be simply assembly guides.

Discussion

All the fragments are in late mediaeval Gothic minuscule bookhand, *textura quadrata*, known traditionally in

England as 'black letter'. The forms vary little between the 14th and 16th centuries, but a 15th-century-date is plausible for all these fragments, the archaeological evidence suggesting a date early in that century. The *quadrarta* hand is notable for its extreme illegibility, since virtually all letters are reduced to a series of vertical strokes ('minims') with the top and bottom of each stroke finished in a square foot (hence '*quadrata*') set diagonally. This makes even complete inscriptions difficult to read and phrases like *in nimium vinum minimum minium inicies* ('put a little cinnamon into a large quantity of wine') quite impossible. Many of the Coventry fragments consist of incomplete minims represented by the undotted i. The majority of the fragments are too small to yield any meaning. The few more enlightening ones are discussed under the respective Figures.

Figure 125

Resonance passage/W choir. Bordered and unbordered diamond quarries, late 14th century, clear glass and yellow stain. Patterns made from shading and yellow stain, in one case on blue glass. Various decorative patterns. Early 15th century?

The quarries, Nos 1-17, are in clear glass, with yellow stain borders, and yellow stain flowers and leaves where the evidence survives. There are 6 drawings in archive. There are equal numbers of these represented both here and at the E window, Fig. 113, and presumably they were used in both parts of the choir. Prof. Richard Marks comments that the 'flower quarries look like late 14th century and the remaining pieces on the figure 15th century' (*in litt.*).

The patterns made from shading, Nos 18-27, unusually have one blue example. The evidence for decayed yellow stain as against shading is, as before, Fig. 103, unclear. There are about a third the number of this type in the passage compared to the E window, and again they probably occurred throughout.

The decorative textures, Nos 28-46, are unrepresented elsewhere.

Figure 126

Resonance passage/W choir. Cross patty, blue grapes?, but classification largely uncertain. Early 15th century?

A cross patty, No 1, can be assumed, and perhaps blue grapes, No 2, but these are not the rounded grapes of the E window, Fig. 97. The 'ball of wool' effect, No 3, has not been identified. The various textured surfaces do not fall into previously established categories.

In archive there are 3 pieces of blue glass with vague trails and dotting.

The arched form, Nos 7-9, is paralleled by the Infant Christ's halo in the Winchester College Virgin and Child.

Figure 127

Resonance passage/W choir. Terminals; edge pieces in blue, red and green glass. Early 15th century? 'Broad line' patterns.

Three terminals are red, Nos 5-7, and one is green, No 8. There are additionally some dozen terminals in archive, 2 blue, and 3 yellow-stained. One of the terminals illustrated is a foliage point, No 3, but normally there is a single painted V-shaped line, No 4. Some half of these appear to be recut glass.

There are also 7 blue, 4 red and 1 yellow-stained edge strips in coloured glass, with 6 red, 2 blue and 2 emerald green in archive.

The anomalous 'broad line' pattern, Nos 21-39, seems to have been originally clear glass, with some yellow stain stripes, 3 examples illustrated; there are some half dozen of these in archive, 1 yellow stain. This pattern is probably later than the main body of the glass, and does not occur in the E window.

Figure 128

Resonance passage/W choir. Broad line 'wild' and unclassifiable patterns, clear glass and yellow stain. Presumably later repair? Third quarter of the 15th century?

These patterns do not occur in the E window, and are presumably later in date. They may relate to repairs to glass damaged by the instability and fall of the tower, which was causing trouble during the second quarter of the 15th century, suggesting a repair date of the third quarter?

The glass is usually clear, but yellow stain is discernible in 4 examples.

The archive contains some 30 drawings, only 1 with yellow stain.

Figure 129

Resonance passage/W choir. Broad line 'wild' and unclassifiable patterns in clear glass and yellow stain. Third quarter of the 15th century?

These patterns do not occur in the E window, and are presumably later in date. They may, as Fig. 128, relate to repairs. There are 7 examples of yellow stain. Nos 35-38 suggest giant architectural panelling.

There are some 340 drawings in archive of glass from the resonance passage.

Section 3: Glass from N transept, N porch/chapel, S transept W nave, E nave, sacristy, chapter house and cloister

As so little material was been recovered from these areas, virtually all has been illustrated, with only 30 drawings in archive.

The nave and the major parts of the northern, southern and western cloister ranges were destroyed without any post-1960s archaeological intervention on the road works of the 1970s and 80s.

Figure 130

1) N transept and N porch/chapel. Repaired multi-period windows? The large leaves are a new style, post 1423? or later in the 15th century. Colour is virtually absent

This material comes from Destruction and Collapse levels except for the Friary 2 and Pre-rebuild material mentioned below.

It is probable that the N transept window glass was originally of the same period as the earlier 'neater' glass from the choir, as 5 fragmentary but 'neat' pieces (unillustrated but including 'seaweed' and possible lettering) come from a green sand trample, Friary 2 Period, a building level dating from before the second decade of the 15th century, and therefore representing damage to pre-existing glass. This also implies that the 'wilder' painting styles probably date from after the end of the first quarter of the 15th century, after the completion of the W end, the drop in artistic standard possibly being due to a shortage of funds, attested in the Whitefriars 1423 Vatican document or to the'decline in skill of the local (Coventry) school of glass painters in the third quarter of the 15th century (Rackham 1930-31, 110).

One piece of unillustrated glass from a Friary 2 building level is part of a margin quarry (for type see Fig. 95) which might give strength to the suggestion that these may have been used throughout a primary choir and eastern transepts programme, and not just in the Great East Window. Presumably the church had a timber framed western end and narrow 'walk way' at this time. There are also grapes, No 23, and leaves, Nos 12-13, and lettering, No 39, with general parallels with the Great East Window Figs 97, 99 and 105 (4 examples).

The majority of this glass seems again likely to be from repaired multi-period windows, and compares with that already discussed from apparent mixed period window glass in the N resonance passage. There are some 20 general style parallels with glass from the resonance passage depicted on Figs 115, 117-118, 121, 125-126 and 128-129. It should be borne in mind that some of this, and the Great East Window fragments, may be a scatter of dropped pieces when moving lead and glass from elsewhere during the destruction processes.

The two pinnacle examples, Nos 1-2 (plus another example in archive), derive from 1960 IX (2), a Pre rebuild level again giving a date of pre 1423 for this glass (see Fig. 115 for other examples of this copious material). An illustrated fragment of 'angled' panelling, No 5, also comes from a deposit of similar date (cf. Fig. 115), and a fragment of lettering, apparently 'et', No 39.

The absence of coloured glass is marked. There is one example of yellow stain in the top section (and one recorded on the 18 archive drawings), and one in the lower section (none recorded on the 5 archive drawings).

2) S transept. As above with larger pieces apparently new types. Colour is virtually absent

This glass again seems to be from repaired multi period windows, as above. Some pieces here again may be strays, on their way to being carried out of the building with the lead, with some 6 general parallels of style with the E window types, viz, Figs 95, 109, 111, 116, and 120, and archive. However, there are an equal number of parallels of style with western choir glass, Figs 124, 127-129, and 131.

The lower rows indicate new patterns in the main; there is one example of yellow stain with this material, with no colour recorded on the six drawings in archive.

Figure 131

Nave, W end. Glass mostly of later types, ?post 1423 or later in the 15th century, from the western nave. Late yellow stain examples and a ?stray blue example

This material is from destruction levels; the border pieces Nos 1 and 4-6 are not paralleled elsewhere. There are style parallels from Figs 124-128, 130, and 132, and it seems unlikely that all this material represents strays. The impression is that the last stage of glazing involved the whole nave, the eastern transept and repairs to the choir.

Colour is again virtually absent, although there is one blue piece.

Yellow stain was apparent on the new type of borders and 2 other examples.

There are no drawings in archive.

Figure 132

Nave, E end, sacristy, chapter house. Early and later glass from: (1) the eastern nave, with yellow-stained examples. (2) NE Sacristy,(3) Chapter house (reading from top to bottom)

1) Eastern nave, Nos 1-21

The border design is a later variant of those shown on Fig. 95, the reduction in fine detail being notable. There are many style parallels with material from Figs 120-121, 123-125, 127 and 129-130, indicating a relationship with glass from the western choir and its repairs, the transepts and the W nave. The lettering appeared to be a 'p' and an 'iud', Nos 7-8.

No coloured glass was noted, but yellow stain was observed on 4 examples.

2) NE sacristy, No 22

The majority of the 1969 glass is now lost, and this piece, No 22, is the only surviving hint as to the glazing of this building, which was reconstructed in the late 15th century. There are no obvious parallels but it is more likely to be from the second structure, and therefore later 15th century?

3) Chapter House, Nos 23-30

The majority of the glass from the Hobley/Rylatt excavations of the 1970s is lost. The few surviving pieces from the 'floor level' indicate that the chapter house was glazed not much earlier than the Great East Window, with parallels to material on Figs 103 and 110.

This level also produced a damaged but very finely drawn scratchwork piece with leaves, No 28, and from a destruction level came some very fine cross-hatched fragments not otherwise paralleled, Nos 23-24.

Prof. R. Marks confirmed (*in litt.*) that these pieces from the Chapter House are of 14th-century date.

There was no evidence for colour.

4) Pieces on display at Coventry Museum but of uncertain provenance, Nos 31-37

This glass is from the 'Godiva's City' display at Coventry Museum. No site or layer provenances are there given, or recorded elsewhere. However, No 32 is, despite some loss and wear, clearly the same piece as No 1 from the E end of the nave/crossing; foliage Nos 33 and 36 resemble foliage from the E choir and crossing, and Nos 34 and 37 foliage are almost certainly from the Great East Window. No 31 occurs on a slide dated January 1978 of Whitefriars finds (no further information); its white glass and other features date it however to the 18th century (identification George Wigley, The Monastery Stained Glass). This is of particular interest because machining of the Prior's house area had taken place shortly before January 1978, and it implies that that building could have retained some medieval glazing, requiring repair - as did the medieval tile floor in that area, the bricks with which that is patched being also 18th century.

Figure 133

Cloisters: 1) Glass from the Cloisters area but apparently unrelated, Nos 1-8; 2) Late medieval or ?post medieval red, blue and yellow-stained glass of distinctly different style, from the E range of the Cloister, Nos 9-21.

1) Glass from Cloister area but apparently unrelated, Nos 1-8

A very thin scatter of medieval glass was recovered, mostly in levels that could be late monastic or relate to the E cloister range conversion to the Elizabethan Hales' Place. This glass seems to derive from elsewhere on site, with style parallels to Figs 95, 105, 107, 114 and 120, from the area of the E window, and Fig. 128 from the western choir. The two border pieces, however, Nos 7-8, are not paralleled from elsewhere on the site; the particularly finely painted border with ?formalised grapes came from the western cloister, and might just relate to the cloister gate demolished in 1956, no information on the glazing of this having survived. However, as it came from quarry fill, it might be from elsewhere in Coventry.

There is no structural indication that the cloister walk had ever been glazed in the medieval period, and the slightness of the glass finds would not support such a theory.

2) Late or Post medieval glass?, Nos 9-21.

There was a large percentage of undecorated quarries present in what certainly appeared likely to be 16th-century levels, (largely Cloister Bay 7, context 1 - the associated half dozen pottery sherds being of late 15th-16th-century date); a half dozen of these were in red glass, three in blue, and three in a greenish blue, one red, No 9, and two blue, Nos 10-11, being illustrated. There were also some seven uncoloured quarries, three illustrated, Nos 12-14, and a similar amount of ungrosed clear glass apparently from large cut pieces; some of these appeared largely to be of ?16th-century date, although the odd piece might have been re-used medieval material.

The painted glass in a very different style from all the other glass present on site, Nos 15-21, came certainly from the cloister, or in two cases from the lane between nave and cloister. Two of these pieces, Nos 15-16, were unstratifed strays. This material could therefore theoretically derive from John Hales' conversion of the dorter to a Long Gallery, but it would be curious to have so much discarded glass if this related to a Hales' rebuilding scheme, and it seems most likely that this was glass that was being removed from a late glazing of the dorter, related perhaps to the early 16th-century grant of Thomas Bond for 'finishing the cloister'(1506; *The*

Whitefriars in Coventry – Historical Background, Section B).

Two of the illustrated pieces showed yellow stain surviving on clear glass, Nos 16-17.

Additional late or post medieval glass with a similar painting technique to that illustrated

One piece occurred in an orange/amber colour, and another in pink, both painted with a wide stripe, as in the widest illustrated striped example, No 20.

Many pieces of glass showed traces of this 'broad brush' technique, and there was much shading on this type but generally with no further painted detail, and only one or two of these additional pieces carried a stripe. At least three additional pieces appeared to be Prussian blue in colour, some shaded.

THE NATURE OF THE GLAZED WINDOWS

P. Woodfield

The design of the windows and their tracery can only be very approximately determined from the surviving pieces of masonry from the excavations. These are discussed in *The Architectural Stonework*, Section F, some illustrated on Fig. 68.

The clearest indication is for the Great East window of the chancel. The width of the structure, at approximately 9.2m, cannot accurately predicate the size of the East window. The comparably sized East window of the mid 13th-century Lady Chapel of Chester Cathedral, has 5 stepped lancets, but the more contemporary fine curvilinear East window of the slightly narrower chancel of Selby Abbey, has seven lights. It seems fairly probable that, in contrast with Selby, the unaisled chancel of the Whitefriars East window was of five lights (or even four), this being adequate for the internal proportions without being ostentatious, Fig. 31. This window appears, from the fragments, to have had supermullions, and these very probably developed with subarcuate intersecting arches with transoms cusped on the soffit. This is consistent with progressive early Perpendicular work of the mid 14th century, i.e. predates the window glass by several decades. The side chancel windows cannot be identified amongst the mass of masonry, but being contemporary with the East window, are likely to be of two or three lights, perhaps the latter with intersecting heads and cusped ogee quatrefoils, perhaps under depressed 2-centred arches. The question whether the sills of the windows of the three western bays were raised to accommodate the canopies of the contemporary choir stalls remains open, but it is highly unlikely windows were totally omitted at the western end.

Precise evidence for the windows of the transepts is non-existent, both in the stonework remains or the glass itself. There were no doubt large end windows, which being only slightly narrower than the chancel, may well have been of four lights of a similar but simpler design than the East window, and the gables above them perhaps furnished with an oculus to achieve greater penetration of light to the crossing. The shortness of the transepts and the adjoining structures may have precluded E and W windows, or, if present, these would have been high and small.

The nave no doubt had a progression of fine large windows at its W end, such as survives in the Norwich Blackfriars church. These were probably of no more than three lights with transoms and reticulated head tracery appropriate for the later date. On the basis of the nave column form, the reconstruction, Fig. 31, shows the windows to be taller than usual, perhaps with segmental pointed heads, with the clerestory windows of the nave suppressed into 'spherical triangular' form or paired oculi as at Great Walsingham, all providing a well lit and distinctively mendicant church. This is however purely surmise. The windows along the length of the buttress-less wall facing on to the 'lane' would almost certainly have had high sills and smaller windows.

There is no evidence whatsoever for the windows of the W elevation. As the western three bays are of a later date, there may well have been a variation in the style of the window tracery, for which no evidence can be identified.

It is likely that some fifty windows were glazed in the church; forty-four windows are attested in the London Blackfriars church (Clapham, 1913, 257).

MEDIEVAL WINDOW GLASS FROM OTHER BUILDINGS IN COVENTRY

C. Woodfield

It should be remembered that Marks (1998, lxv, 179, 182) saw Coventry as a possible regional glass-painting centre in the 14th century, with outliers beyond that immediate area. The most famous and well-documented case is that of the York Great East Window, (French 1995, 5) where the contract between the Dean and Chapter and John Thornton of Coventry, glazier, survives. It is of interest that Thornton was given a three year term for the work, and was obliged to paint figures with his own hand. The window was completed in 1408, and is therefore of the same period as the Whitefriars Great East Window and the W choir glass. Unfortunately 'figures' scarcely survived the iconoclasts at the Whitefriars (see Figs 102 and 122 for those slight remains) so details such as the famous Thornton noses are not available for comparison. A careful study by the writer of French's volume, and the glass itself at York, does not support this attribution, although there are obvious similarities due to the International Gothic style.

Rackham (1930-31, 110) refers to the 'declining skill of the local school of (Coventry) glass painters in the third quarter of the 15th century'. This is the date of our Pre-rebuild and Rebuild phases, where reglazing at this time of the crossing and the eastern nave, due to the damage caused by the falls and rebuildings of the tower, means that the glass of about 1400, the finest glass from the site, would be restricted to the choir, Figs 95-126, probably excluding the westernmost bay where there are indications of late repairs to the choir stalls caused by structural collapse and serious damage which would have affected the glass. There is a conspicuous decline in the standard of the glass of this later period, Figs 127-131, from other parts of the church, thought to date from the third quarter of the 15th century in the main. Rackham's statement seems therefore to be borne out by the Whitefriars glass.

Surviving Coventry glass

Earlier glass than that from the Whitefriars included that from St Michael's, marked by the presence of much grisaille glass. Rackham (1930-31, 96 and pls xv and xvi), describes 'vast quantities' of later glass from the beginning of the 15th century, much in a fragmentary state, and much in the clerestory, of which little record existed as it was so high up. However, there were also two side windows in the chancel of which more is known, and there was apparently much canopy work (Rackham 1930-31, 97) and a Last Judgement window. Some of the St Michael's glass can be attributed to Thornton (Marks, 1993, 182 and fig. 147). There are no obvious resemblances to glass at the Whitefriars.

Much of the St Michael's glass that survived the war has vanished since it was briefly seen by the writer in the 1960s, but some early 15th-century glass survives, remounted in the S porch memorial chapel (Marks, 1993, fig. 147).

Some 1,500 pieces of window glass came from excavations at the Benedictine Priory Chapter House (Newton 1971, 107-111 and figs 9-12), where it is dated to *c.*1310-1330. There were figures of saints below canopies, with foliage trails with birds and animals in the borders. In February 2000 large amounts of glass were excavated from the W end of the Benedictine nave (pers. ob.) but at the time of writing there has been no publication.

A small quantity of glass (there has again been losses) of the same date as that of the Whitefriars choir came from excavations at the Charterhouse (Shepherd 1995 119-120 and fig. 30). The 110 surviving fragments were, however, so small that all that could be said is that they dated from post 1385 to the 15th century. There is no evidence to relate them to the Whitefriars material.

Glass from many periods, including glass coeval with that from the Whitefriars, and some apparently Thornton glass, survives in St Mary's Hall (Marks 1993, 89, 182, 191, fig. 159; Rackham, 1930-31 pls xv and xvii). The history of that glass is too complicated to go into here, but there are no obvious parallels to the Whitefriars glass in the surviving material. Rackham thought that the famous N window with the series of English kings of *c.*1451-61 was the work of London glaziers, and, in view of the Coventry Whitefriars founder being Sir John Pulteney, Lord Mayor of London, and the other connections with London mayors at the date of the 14th-century glass (see Tracy, *The Choir-Stalls*, Section H) a London glazier is a high possibility for the Coventry Whitefriars.

Rackham (1930-31, 99, pl. xvii) also thought that some of the glass in St Mary's Hall might be from the Coventry Greyfriars, that is one piece representing the Greyfriars escutcheon shield with five wounds of Christ and a heart. However, no possible Carmelite glass has been recognised there.

There is, however, a Coventry 15th-century roundel, Fig. 1b, first published in the *Gentleman's Magazine* by the Coventry antiquary Thomas Sharp in 1793 (397 and fig. 1) and later by Pierre Turpin,(1917, 214-218, fig. 1) and then again by Herbert Read (1926, pl. 42) - this being the best illustration as it is a Victoria and Albert Museum photograph, rather than a drawing. The roundel represents one of the Works of Mercy, 'Feeding the Poor' and depicts, *inter alia*, what appears to be a Carmelite friar. The central, distributing, figure is not a saint as there is no nimbus, and his dress suggests a wool stapler. Is he a founder or benefactor, and might this roundel have some connection with the Whitefriars? It is not unlike our later glass, Figs 128-130. The roundel is now in the Bodnant Collection of the Victoria and Albert Museum.

There is no surviving glass in the Collegiate church of St John the Baptist. Nor is there any apparent link with the fragmentary glass at Holy Trinity, in the NW chapel.

The Ford's Hospital glass is post 1509. Some surviving glass was rescued by the writer after having been crushed and dumped over a wide area in the 1960s; it was then restored by D. J. King and the author put it on display in Coventry Museum in the 1960s. It bears no resemblance to the Whitefriars glass.

At the Church of St Mary, Ecclesfield 'In the westernmost N window late medieval glass with an inscription referring to the Carthusian prior and monks of St Anne, Coventry, "*qui istam cancellam et fenestram fieri fecerunt*" (Pevsner 1989, 190). This glass, which is not referred to in the *Coventry Charterhouse Excavation Report* (Soden, 1995) does not appear to be a product of the same workshop as the Coventry Whitefriars glass, but could, under the circumstances, be another case of glass from a Coventry workshop.

Possible Whitefriars parallels with known Glaziers

Rackham (1930-31, 89) stated 'It is reasonable to infer ... that the work done at the beginning of the 15th century by Coventry glaziers... was of the first order.' One could argue that the Whitefriars choir glass bears this out. However, as stated above, it is possible that a London glazier was involved with the choir glass, as indeed were London glaziers later involved at St Mary's Hall and the Beauchamp Chapel at nearby Warwick, where Henry VI's glazier, John Prudde, worked from 1514 to 1547. Very little glass survives from London, and it would be hardly possible to look for Whitefriars parallels there.

If arguing for a more local glazier, the work of Thomas of Oxford seems to present the strongest parallels (e.g. the window at Thenford, *c.*1400, (Marks 1993, fig. 142). This window, showing St Anne teaching the Virgin to read, is 'possibly by Thomas the Glazier of Oxford'. There are also resemblances to the Tree of Jesse and other Thomas of Oxford glass at Winchester College Chapel, *c.*1393 (Marks 1993, fig. 31). The Winchester College Tree of Jesse, which is the same date as the Whitefriars Jesse window (Harvey and King, 1971, 149-177) is in a chapel that is virtually on the Winchester Carmelite site, which is thought-provoking. This glass is, however, again different in fine detail to that at the Whitefriars, although it presents a familiar world.

Also to be considered is the glass at Oxford New College chapel (Marks 1993, figs 141 and 144b) - the last now in York Minster, and also from the workshop of Thomas the Glazier of Oxford. The dating of the first of these (Marks fig. 141, New College) is *c.*1380-6, and it is not impossible that our suggested date of *c.*1400 for the Whitefriars choir glass could be a decade too late. The question does arise whether many of these windows bear resemblances to the Whitefriars glass merely because they are of the then current International Gothic Style? Nevertheless they remain the closest parallels.

There are other, earlier, 14th-century Trees of Jesse in Warwickshire. That at Merevale (Rackham 1930-31, 90-92, pl. xiv) almost certainly derives from the nearby, now ruined, Cistercian Abbey, and is of very high quality. This, though incomplete, has 15 figures, reminding us that the Whitefriars Tree would presumably have had some 20. The detail at Merevale presents little resemblance to the Whitefriars glass.

There is another, more fragmentary, Tree of Jesse window at Mancetter. This is also mainly 14th century, but generally earlier than the Merevale and Whitefriars examples, and there is again little detailed resemblance. Only three figures survive. (Rackham 1930-31, 92, pl. xiv).

Other Carmelite Glass

In view of the slight knowledge of Carmelite glass, it seems useful to make a summary of what is known from other Whitefriars sites.

Cambridge Whitefriars. Carmelite glass survives from the Cambridge Whitefriars, in the form of ten roundels depicting Carmelites wearing their Doctors' caps, and can be seen in the Library of Queen's College. It was published by Wayment in 1994. The Whitefriars choir standard border design pattern (Fig. 95, No 10, etc.) occurs also with this Cambridge glass, there interspaced with rectangles of 'blue or ruby' glass (Wayment 1994,.140, figs 9 and 11); it is there dated to the mid 15th century.

Denbigh Whitefriars. Sites and Monuments records indicate that armorial glass is known from this site.

Ipswich Whitefriars. It is known that 'much fine window glass' was recovered in the 1988-89 excavations, probably of the later 15th century. There is 'no intention to publish this site'. The writer holds a record of four scanned pieces.

Lincoln Whitefriars. Forty-eight pieces reported but not illustrated (City of Lincoln Archaeological Unit Report No 338, **2**, 11), from St Mark's, High St (which includes the Whitefriars); little useful can be said concerning the 48 pieces attested.

Maldon Whitefriars. Only four pieces of painted medieval window glass were recovered during excavations at the Maldon Whitefriars, but were too damaged to be illustrated (Andrews 1999(a), 92-93). This might indicate it was moved elsewhere?, though it was recovered from the cloister which was perhaps unglazed.

Newcastle Whitefriars. Good quality grisaille and yellow stain glass (the first is likely to relate to the Friars of the Sack, the previous occupiers of the building) were present; the Carmelites took over the site in 1307. The glass largely represents foliage (Harbottle 1968, 218-219 and fig. 17).

Oxford Whitefriars. It appears to this writer that the excavation (Poore and Wilkinson 2001) located a wall representing 5 bays of the buttressed N wall of the choir (there would have been six bays in all) together with the turn of that wall to form the E end. St John Street seems to fossilise the friary 'walkway' (crossing) as a surviving path, a common happening on friary sites. It looks as if there was probably a six bay nave, with a western porch of two bays of similar width. The glass (Cropper 2001, 46-54 and figs 16a and 16b) though disturbed, came from the above choir area, apparently clear of the remains of Beaumont Palace and so not glass from that source.

The division into styles one, two, and 'unattributable' makes the report rather difficult to follow. However, two main Friary glazing periods were identified, producing some 400 pieces of glass. The glass was thought to be of late 14th/early 15th-century and later 15th-century date, with a doubtful period in between. The vine leaves are thought-provoking, especially as they cluster against the E wall, (see Poore and Wilkinson 2001, 24, Section numbers, for provenance), but this cannot be more than a hint at another Tree of Jesse. Unfortunately vine stems can often be neither recognised nor drawn, as was the case with the earlier drawings for the Coventry Whitefriars; if present they could prove another Tree of Jesse. There are some resemblances to the Coventry Glass on fig. 16a, but no reason to suppose it is from the same workshop, although it is probably the same date. The ?later glass on fig. 16b bears little resemblance to Coventry material.

Of interest in England is other local excavated friary glass at the Northampton Greyfriars (Williams 1978, fig. 19). This glass, reported on by the late Peter Newton, is second half of the 15th century and is not by any glazier represented at the Whitefriars.

In Scotland there is a small amount of glass published by Stones (1989, 150-153, ill. 93). Curiously the border designs from the Linlithgow Whitefriars E window are paralleled at the Coventry E window (see Coventry entry under Fig. 95, No 10, etc). They are also represented in the Cambridge Carmelite glass.

At the Burrell Museum, Glasgow, there is glass showing a Carmelite, which is thought to be 'from the Midlands' (Wayment 1994, fig. 25).

The writer is not aware of any other surviving Carmelite glass in mainland Britain.

Two Franciscan friary excavations are worth mentioning in the context of the Whitefriars glass (Hunter 1987; Youngs, Clark and Barry 2996, 194-6). The find of a collapsed late 13th-century leaded window at the Carmarthen Franciscan Friars in 1983 (a very unusual occurrence in terms of excavated window glass), pointed up the impossibility, as at Coventry, of establishing heraldic glass in the absence of leads. The Carmarthen window represented, in deep blue, colourless, or flashed red glass, three winged birds of prey, probably eagles, with a red border, the eagles themselves being colourless, this apparently representing 'argent', i.e. silver birds on a red field. The central portion of the window was triangular in shape and represented a shield bearing a blue chevron accompanying these. None of this could have been recognised with the Coventry unleaded material.

It was also unusual to be from a location that was not the church, but apparently an infirmary south of a second, southern, cloister.

The Carmarthen friary was also temporarily a School at the Dissolution and had earlier 16th-century workshops 'in all areas of the site', as at Coventry Whitefriars.

It would be of interest, in a field where so little is known, if funding could be found for the 'very large number' of pieces of window glass, mainly from the second half of the 14th century (dated by Peter Newton), from the Cambridge Greyfriars excavations (Salway 1996, 20., pls. I and II and fig. 7) to be fully published, as these are from a friary nave, whereas the Coventry Whitefriars glass is largely from a friary choir. The fourteen drawings published by Salway, represent the Annunciation; the infant Christ in the arms of the Virgin Mary, the child holding a bird; the Crucifixion; a bearded prophet; the wings and feet of a seraph; a devil; a monkey with a tambourine; part of a tonsured head; a lion resembling Whitefriars Fig. 106, No 18; pinnacles and arches.

Figure 95 Great East Window Tree of Jesse. Border designs with varying yellow stain; clear or occasionally green glass. *c.*1400 (Scale 60 percent of life size).

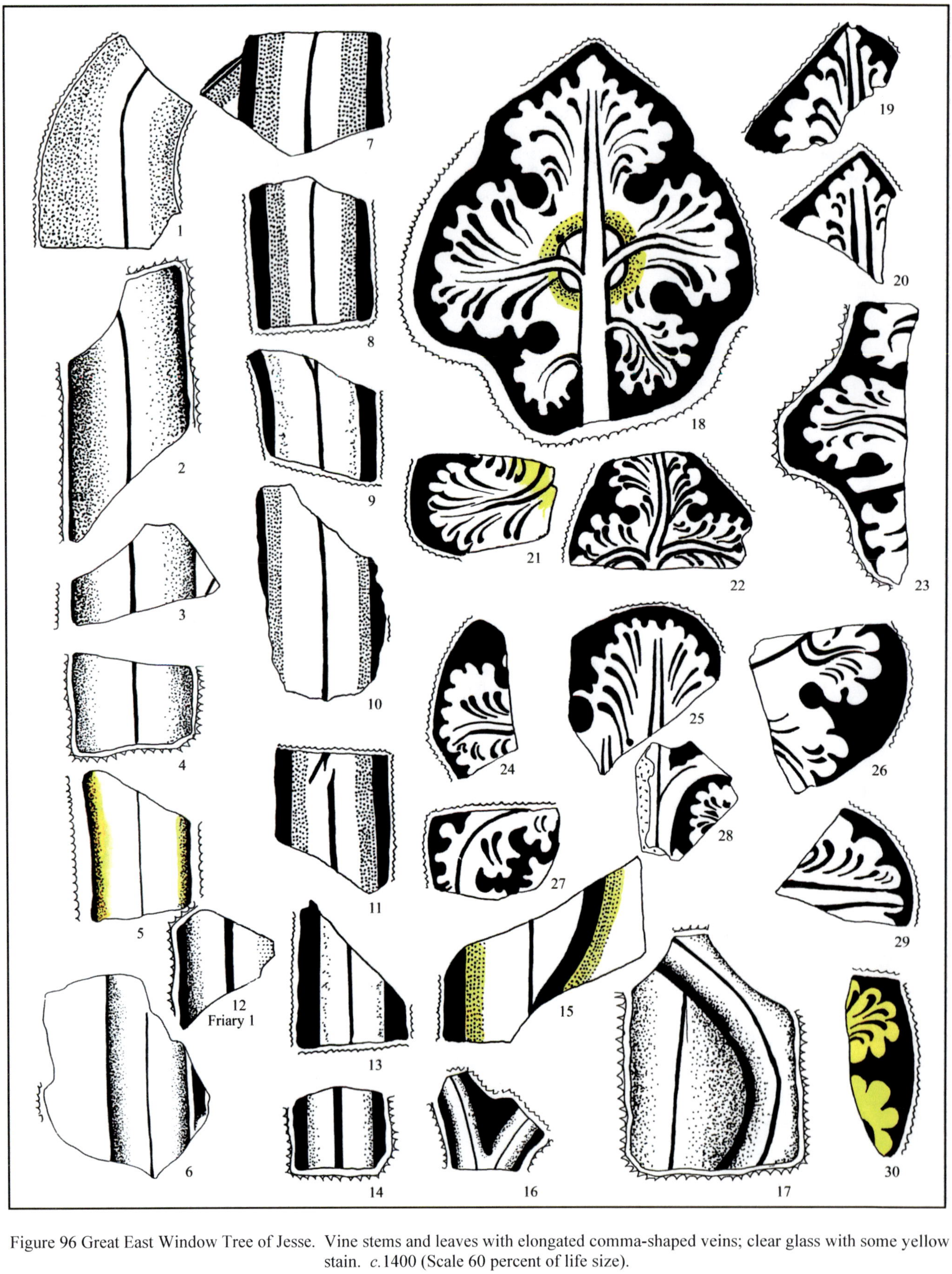

Figure 96 Great East Window Tree of Jesse. Vine stems and leaves with elongated comma-shaped veins; clear glass with some yellow stain. *c.*1400 (Scale 60 percent of life size).

Figure 97 Great East Window Tree of Jesse. Blue and yellow-stained vine leaves with curved veins but no 'commas' (top) and grapes; red and blue vine leaves with straight veins (bottom). *c.*1400 (Scale 60 percent of life size).

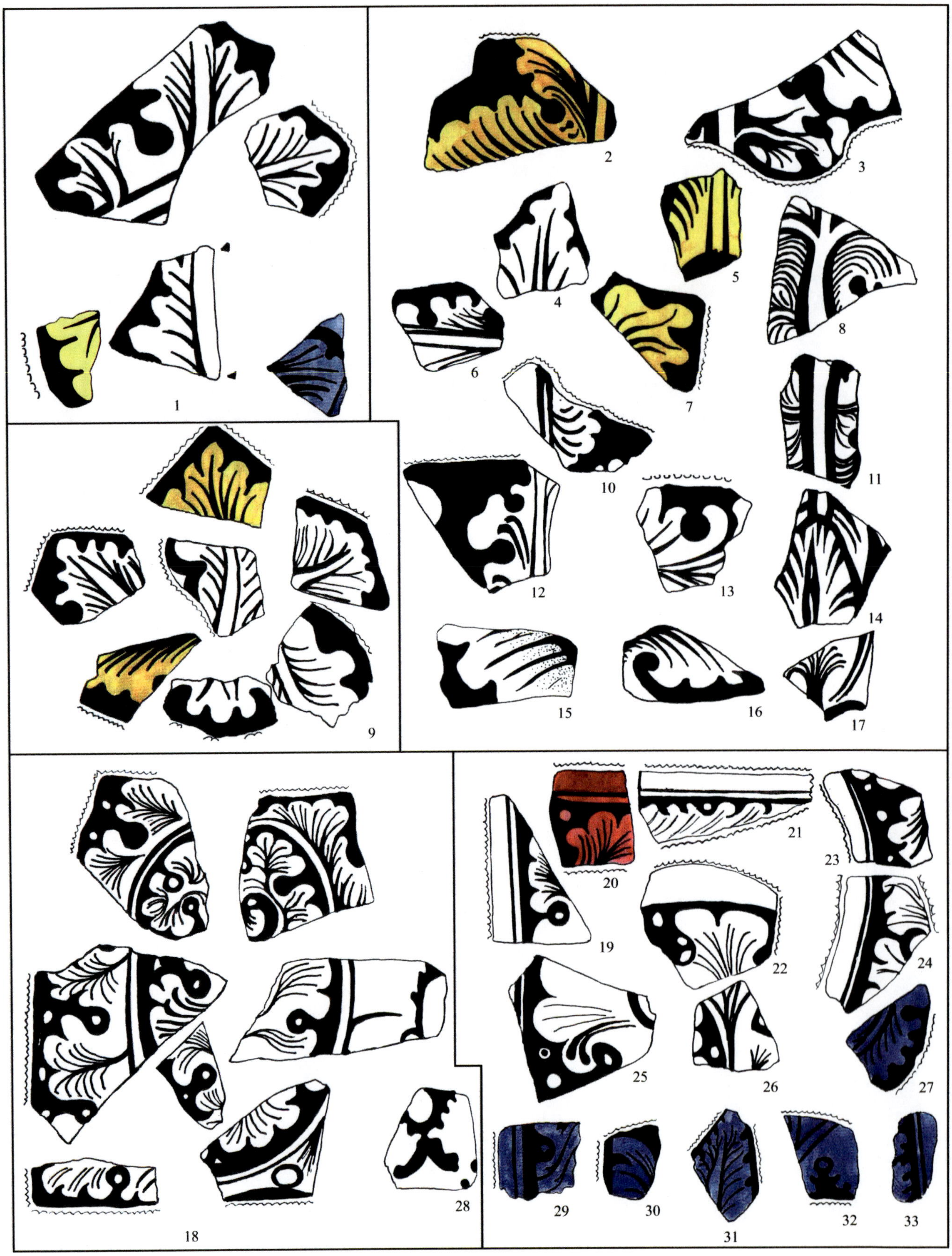

Figure 98 Great East Window Tree of Jesse/E presbytery. Vine leaves with thick veins and a tendency to large and irregular leaf indentations (top); leaf pattern with distinctive dots, with an internal oval (and possibly also a circular) frame (bottom left); red and blue leaves with dots, and straight or curved borders with a single line (bottom right). *c.*1400 (Scale 60 percent of life size).

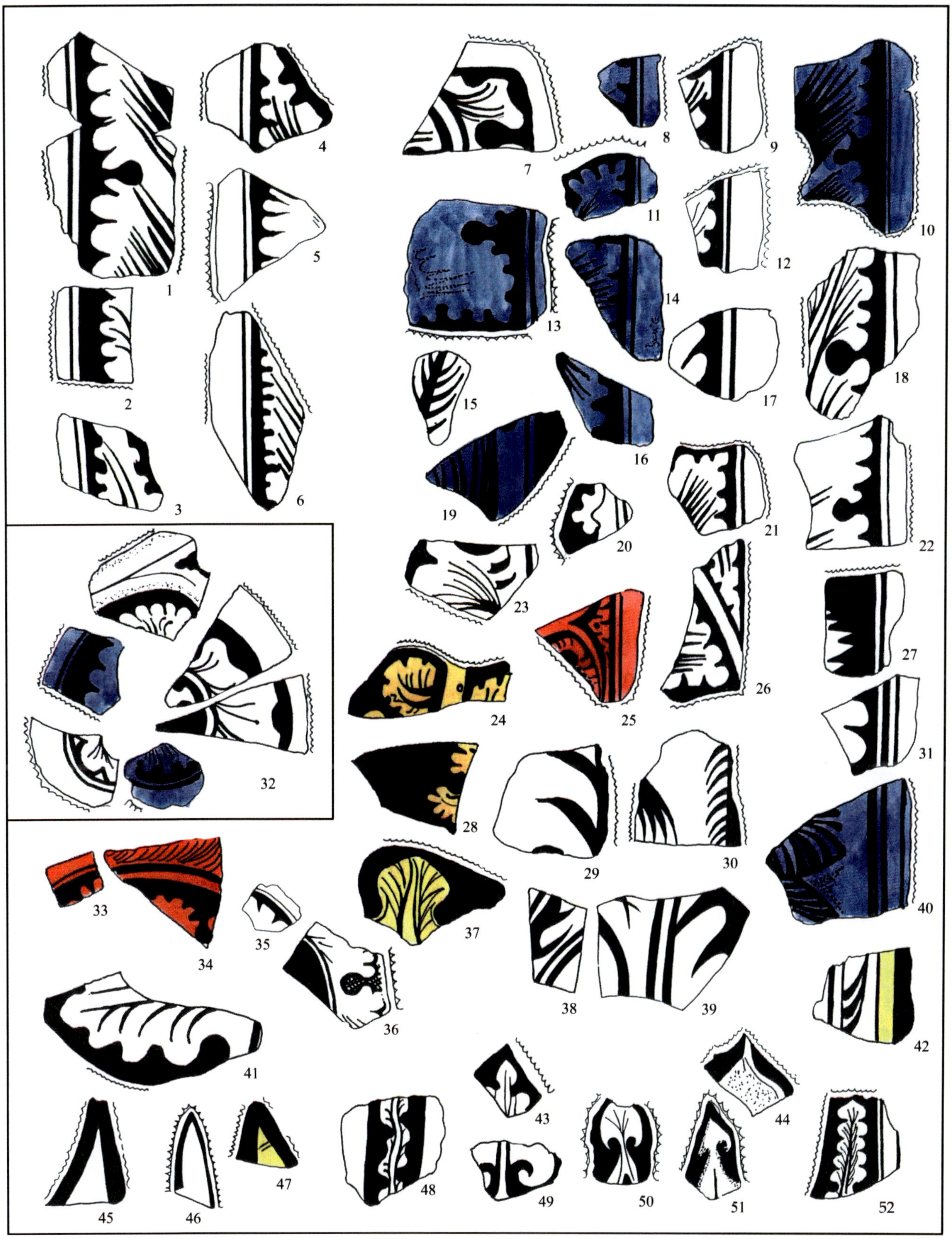

Figure 99 Great East Window Tree of Jesse/E presbytery. Blue, red and yellow stain, broad and narrow stripe borders, associated with leaf patterns; bordered roundels (or perhaps ovals) some red with leaf patterns. Terminals and unbordered leaf and flower patterns not previously represented. Fragments from very large leaf patterns. Plain terminals. *c.*1400 (Scale 60 percent of life size).

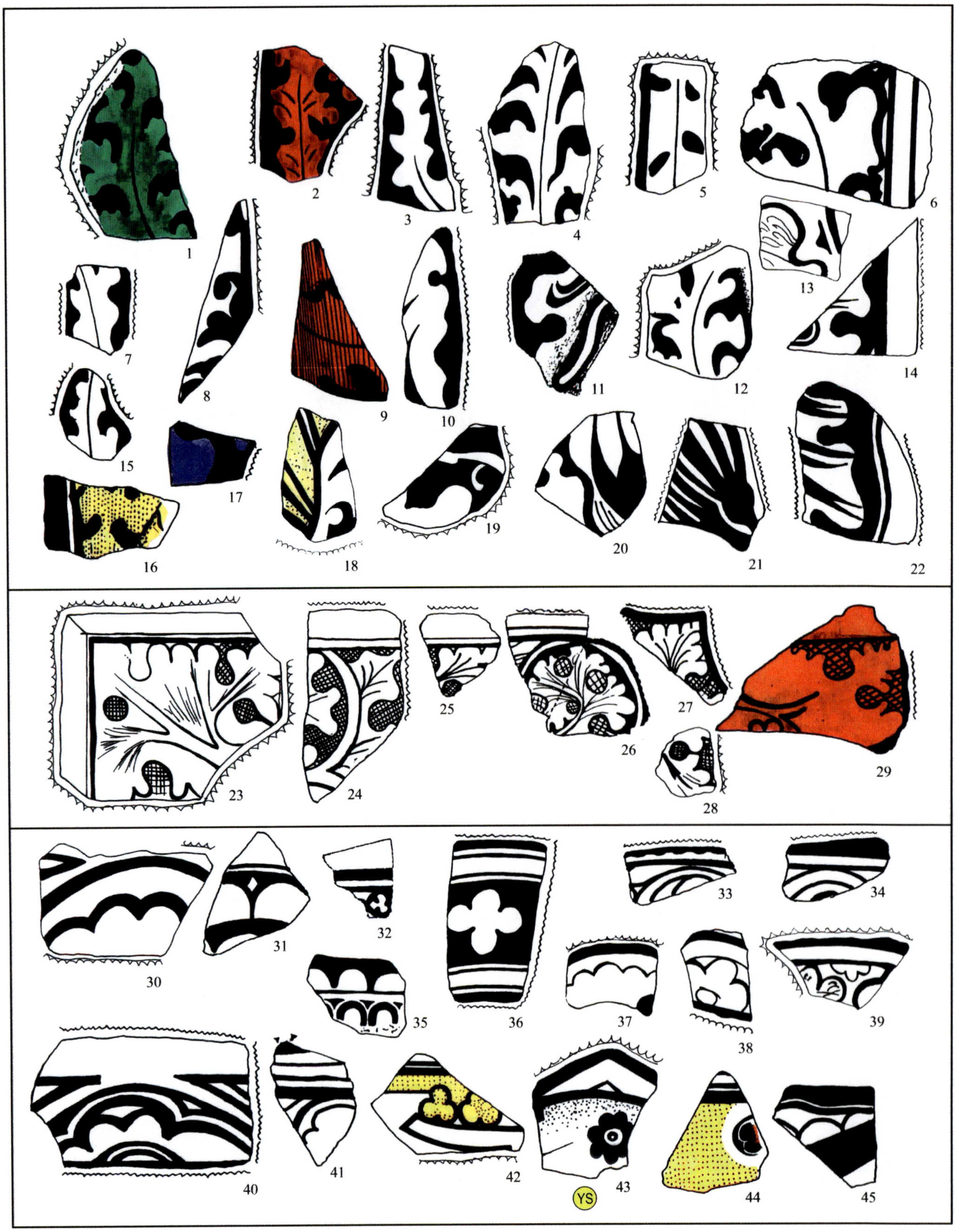

Figure 100 Great East Window Tree of Jesse. Background red, blue, green and yellow stain 'seaweed'. Glass with foliage and 'cross-hatching', some red. Large flowered patterns, some yellow-stained, from panelling and borders. *c.*1400 (Scale 60 percent of life size).

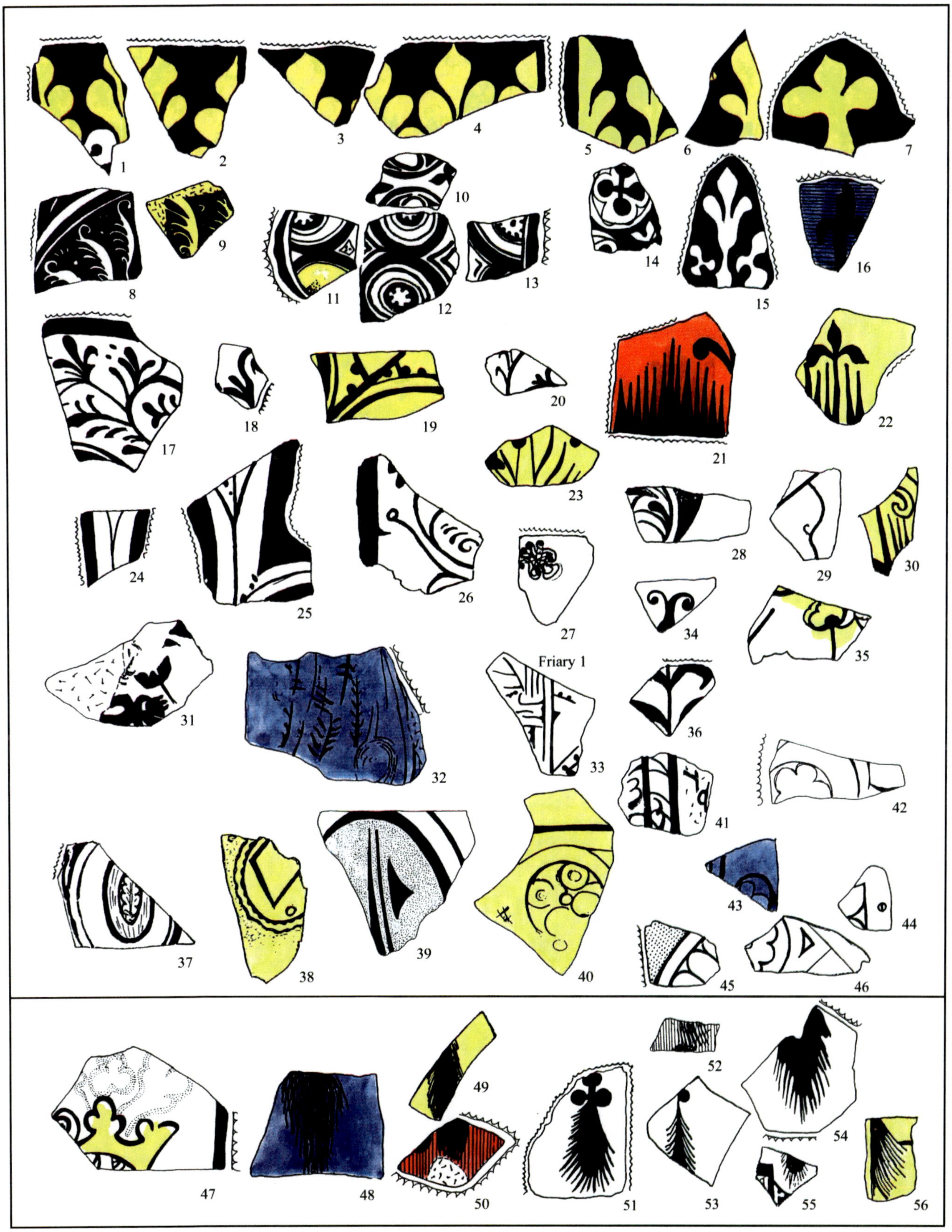

Figure 101 Great East Window Tree of Jesse. Possible fabrics, embroidery, and brooches, some blue, yellow and amber. Gold crowns and ermine, some on red, yellow and blue grounds. *c.*1400. The ermine might be heraldic. Kings and Queens of Heaven would be expected in a Jesse window (Scale 60 percent of life size).

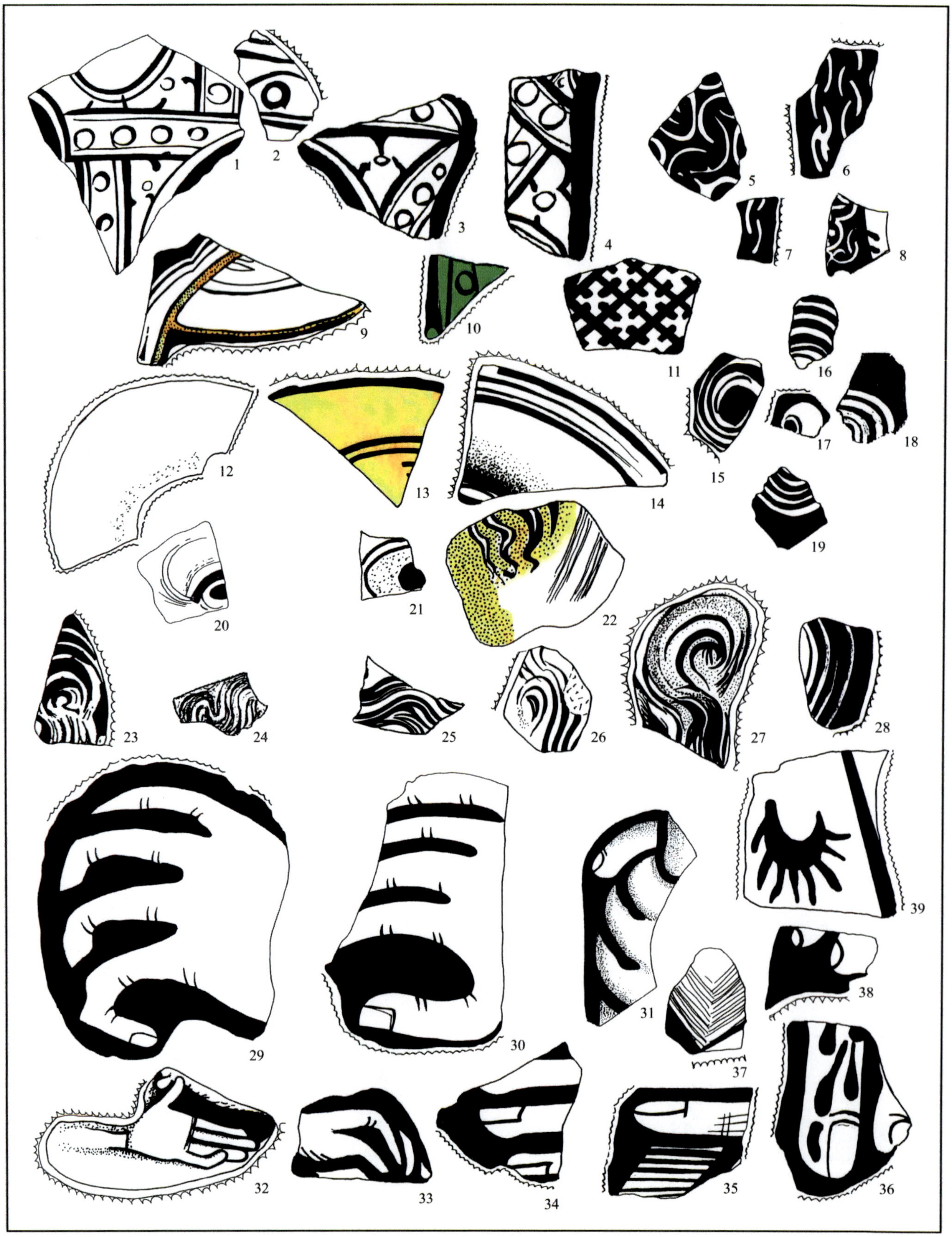

Figure 102 Great East Window Tree of Jesse. Possible green costume, chain mail, shoes. Eyes, possible ears and gold haloes, beards and hair, some yellow; hands and wounds of Christ. Hands indicating figures of at least two scales; hands holding a book and a staff. The eye may have affinities with John Thornton of Coventry's work, but in general there is little resemblance to Thornton glass. *c.*1400 (Scale 60 percent of life size).

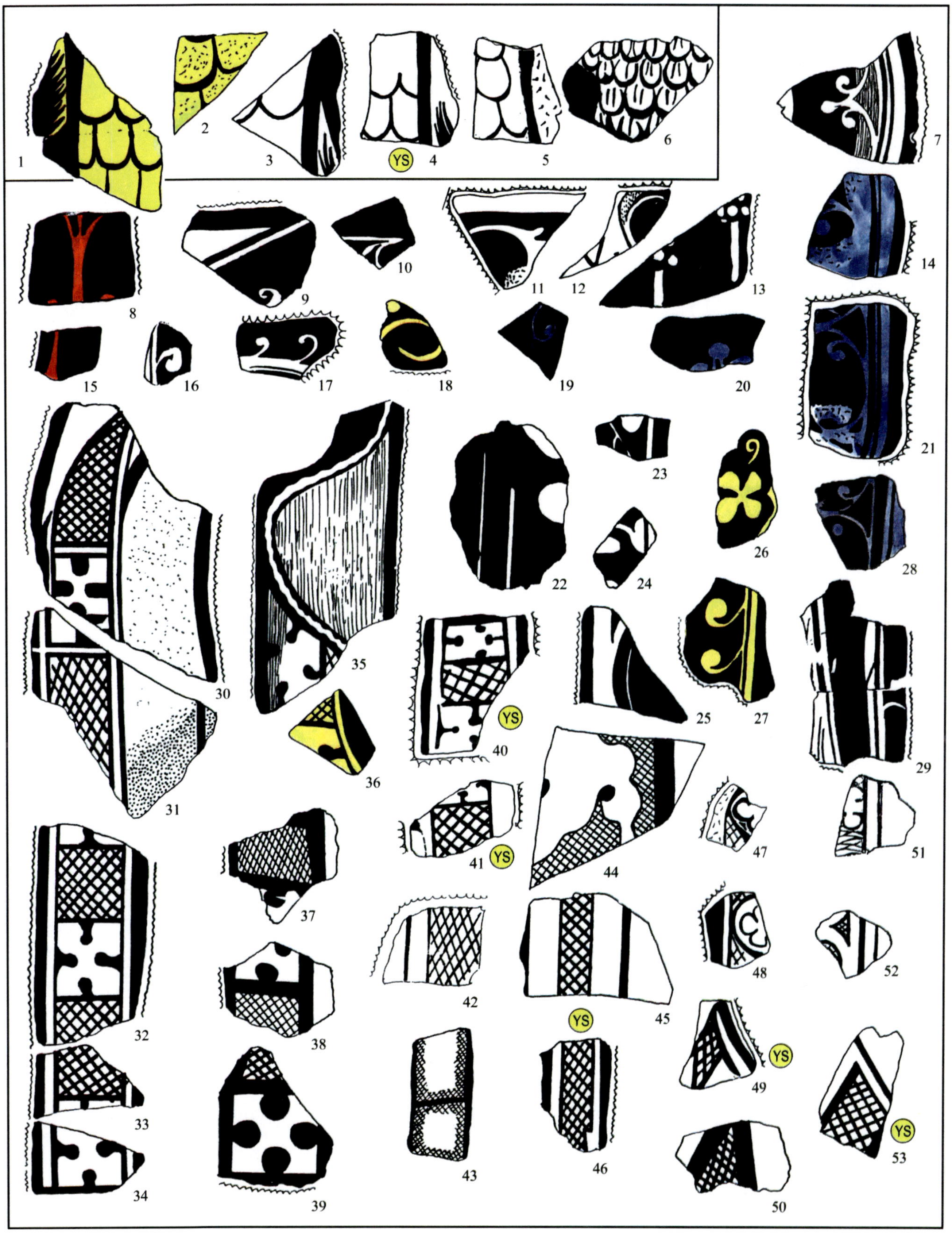

Figure 103 Great East Window Tree of Jesse. Angel's wings, some yellow; fine blue red and yellow scratchwork ?fabric; maniple? in clear and yellow glass with crosses and crosshatched borders *c.*1400 (Scale 60 percent of life size).

Figure 104 Great East Window Tree of Jesse. Red and yellow jewelled edgings. Folds in clothing? Furs (or strange beasts?), hair and beards in clear and yellow glass. *c.*1400 (Scale 60 percent of life size).

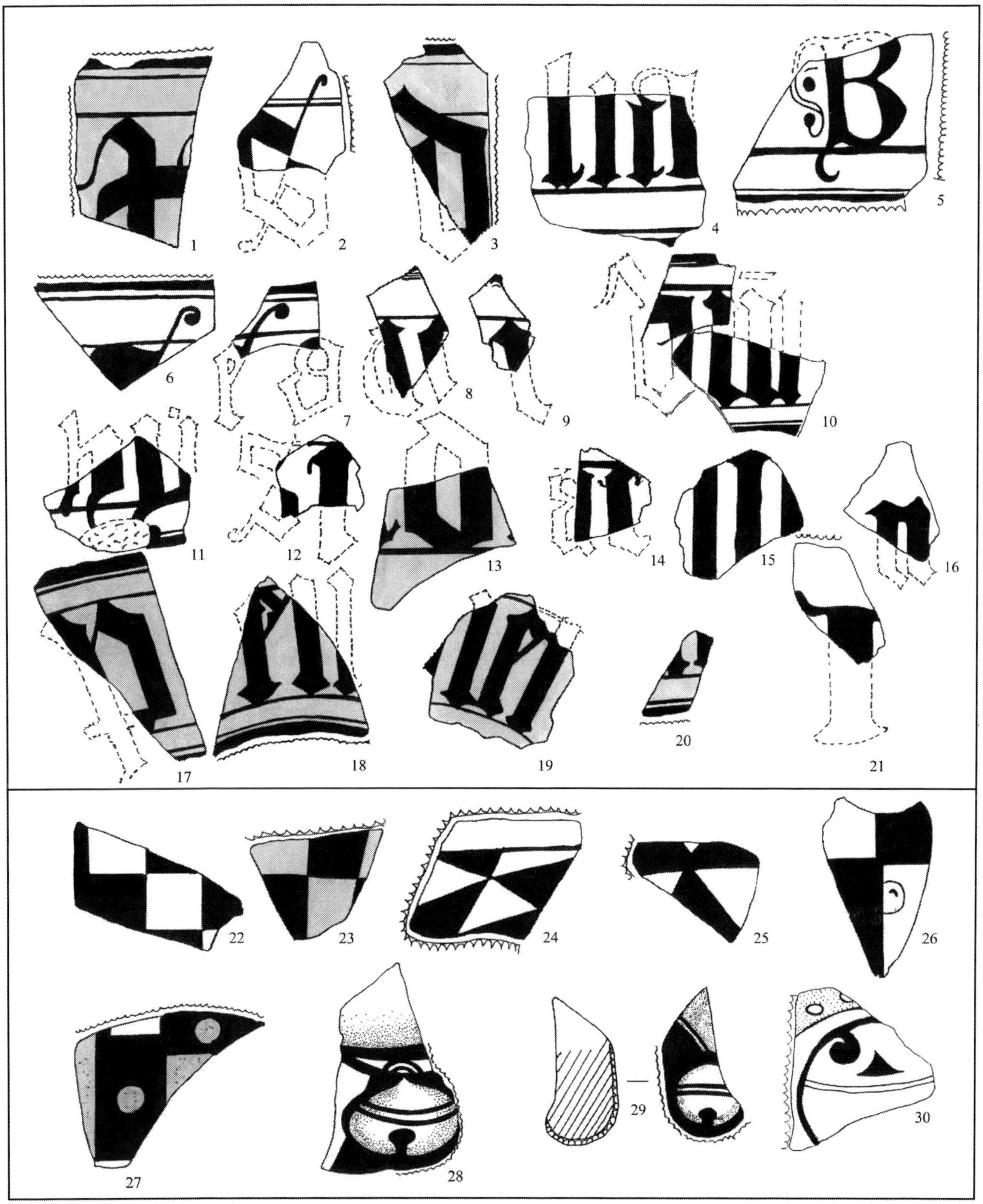

Figure 105 Great East Window Tree of Jesse. Black letter with indications of scrolls, some yellow stain, and probable fragments of kings' and other appropriate names (e.g. Eliacim and Salathiel). Floor tiles: black and clear and black and yellow. Bells for suspension on the person? or architecture? *c.*1400 (Scale 60 percent of life size).

Figure 106 Great East Window Tree of Jesse. White and yellow roses, red rose (7), and lion roundels. *c.*1400 (Scale 60 percent of life size).

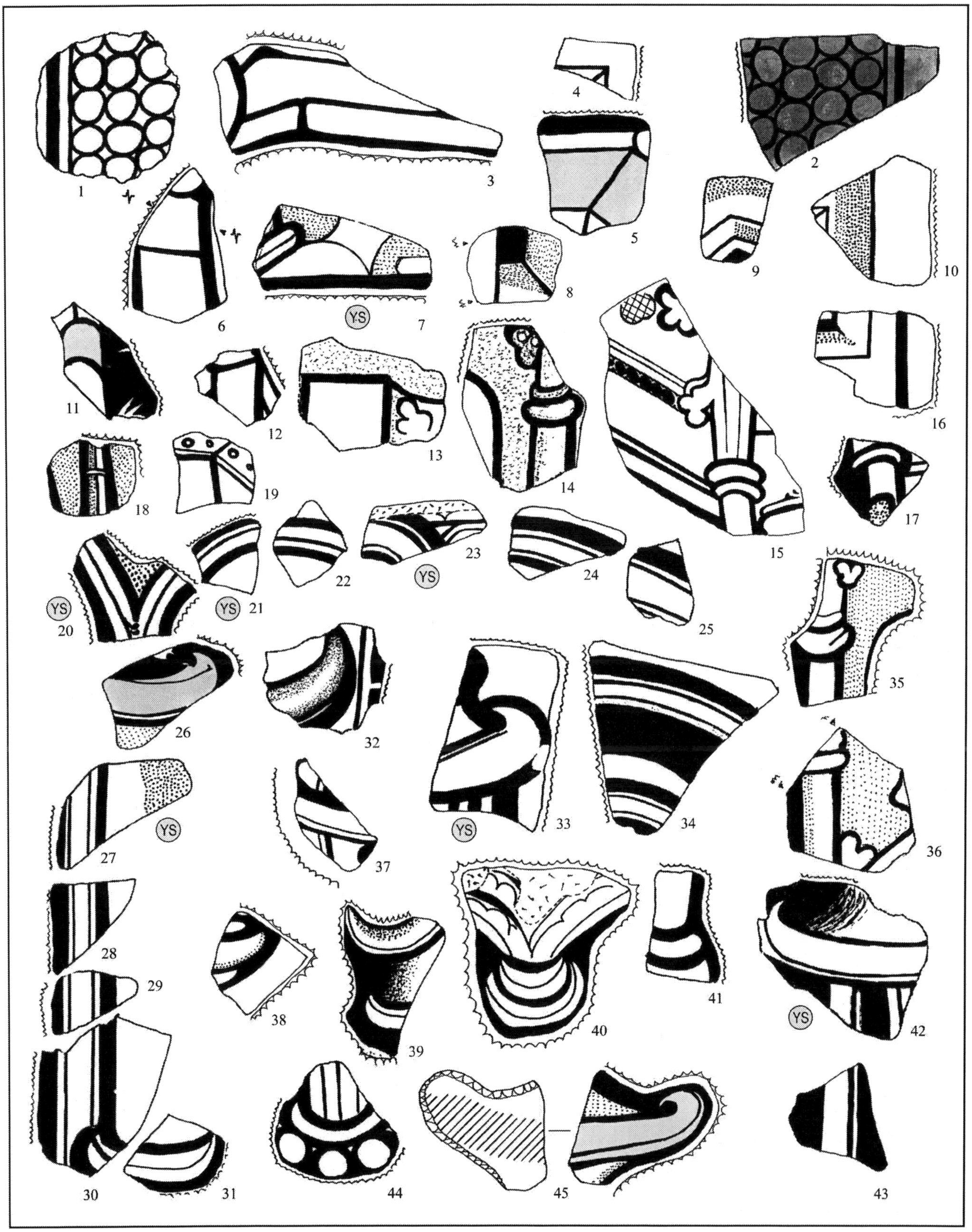

Figure 107 Great East Window Tree of Jesse. Bull's eye windows (on a background pattern?), one blue (2), and fine line background architecture; heavy line architectural detail, clear glass and yellow stain. *c.*1400 (Scale 60 percent of life size).

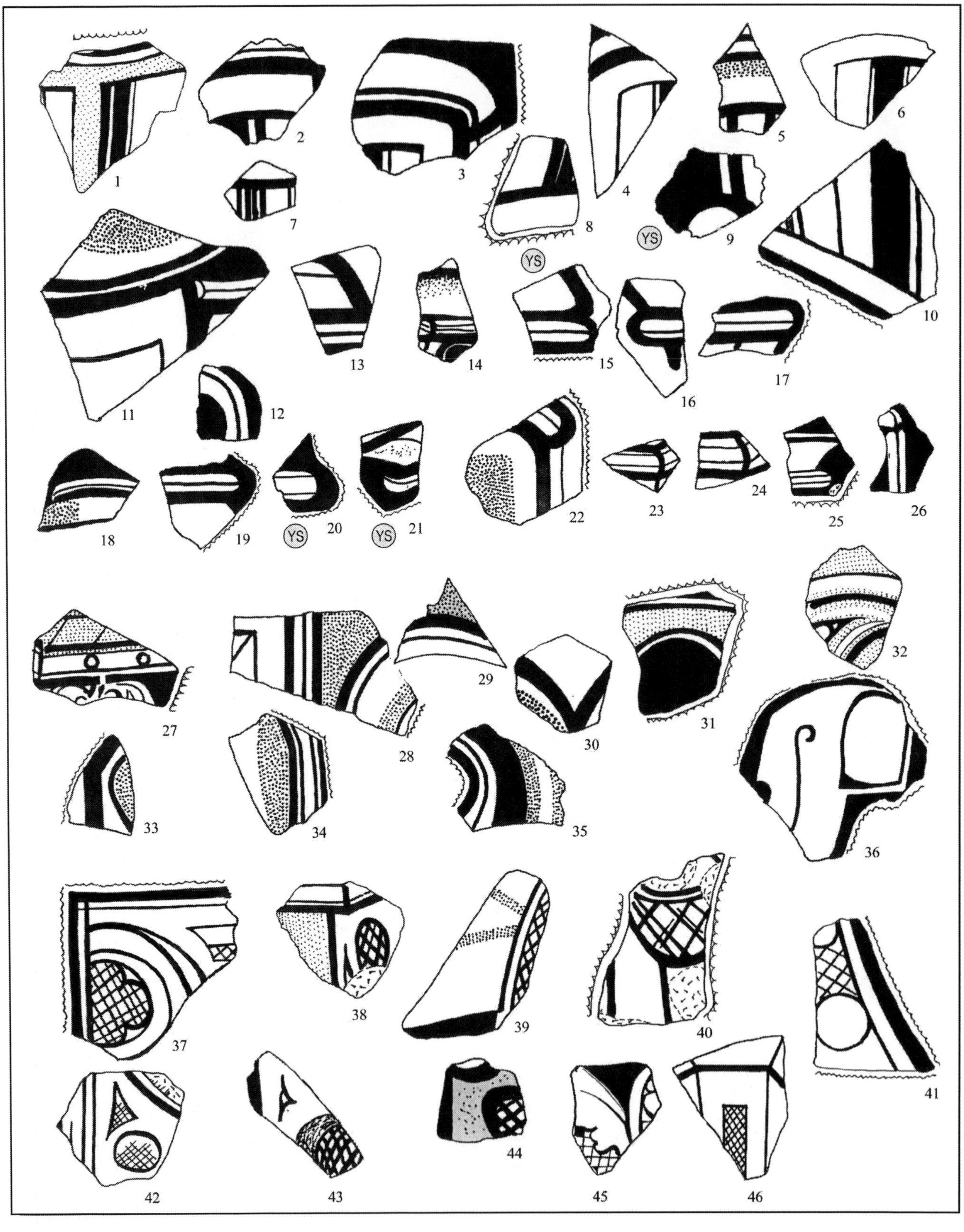

Figure 108 Great East Window Tree of Jesse. Continuation of 'rounded forms' architectural panelling. Architectural panelling with cross-hatching - some possibly from choir. Clear glass and yellow-stained glass. *c.*1400 (Scale 60 percent of life size).

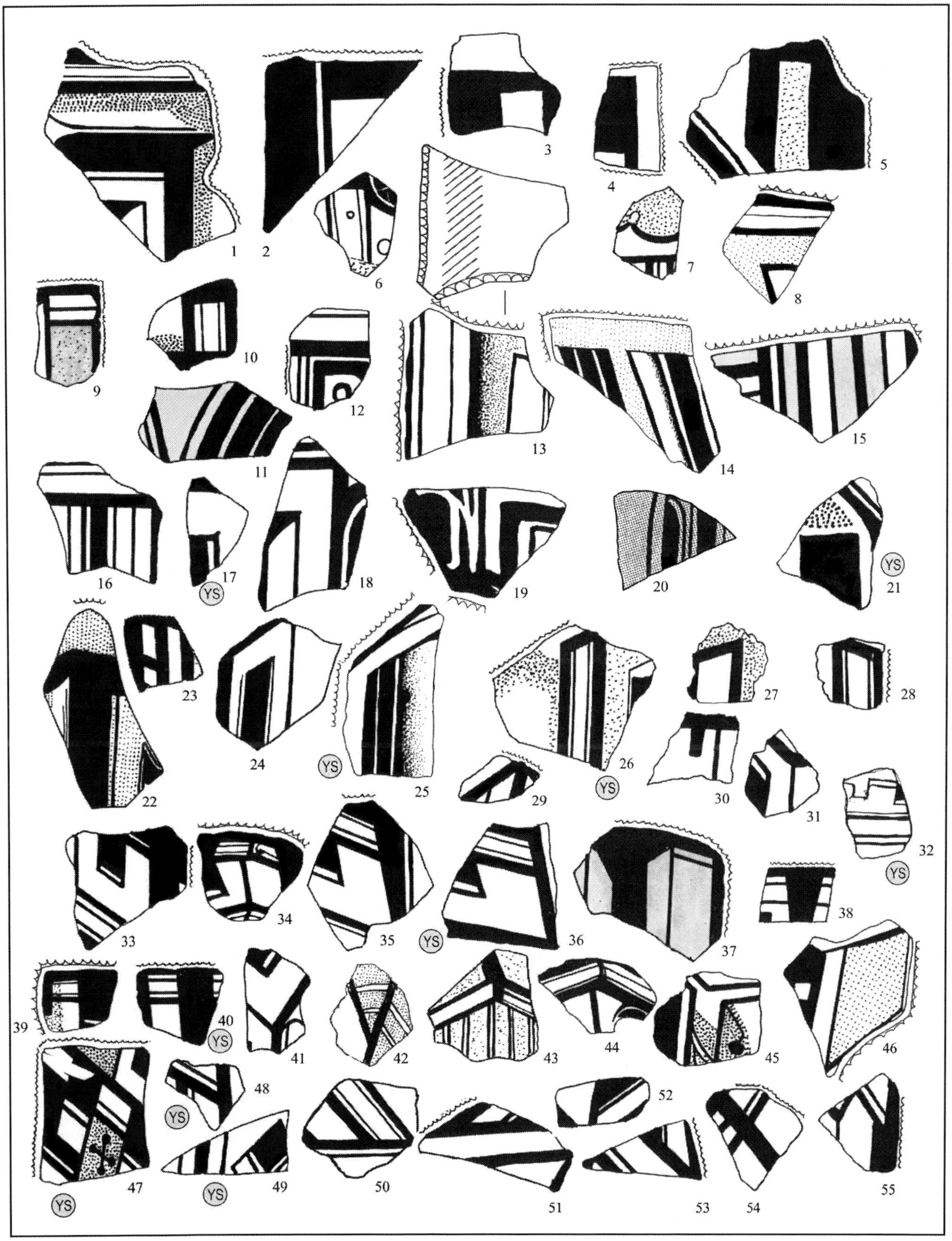

Figure 109 Great East Window Tree of Jesse. Architectural panelling with 'angular' forms. Clear and yellow-stained glass. *c.*1400 (Scale 60 percent of life size).

Figure 110 Great East Window Tree of Jesse/E presbytery. Architectural panelling with smaller quatrefoils, trefoils, and tracery, clear and yellow-stained glass. *c.*1400 (Scale 60 percent of life size). 15 is red.

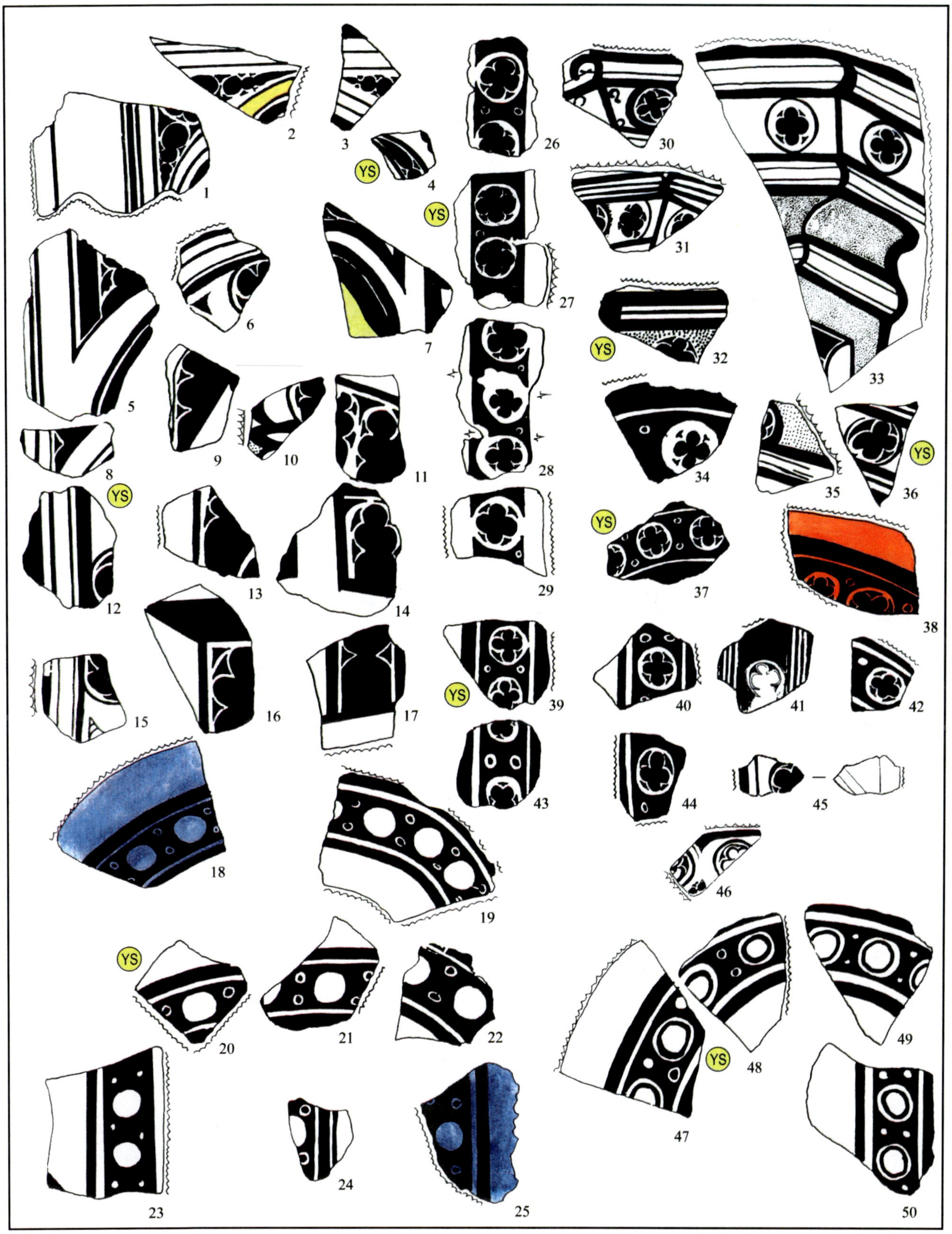

Figure 111 Great East Window Tree of Jesse. Architectural panelling with medium-sized quatrefoils and tracery, clear and yellow-stained glass. Blue border with dots and rings. *c.*1400 or a little earlier (Scale 60 percent of life size).

Figure 112 Great East Window Tree of Jesse. Borders with larger quatrefoils, clear, yellow-stained and some blue glass. *c.*1400 or a little earlier (Scale 60 percent of life size).

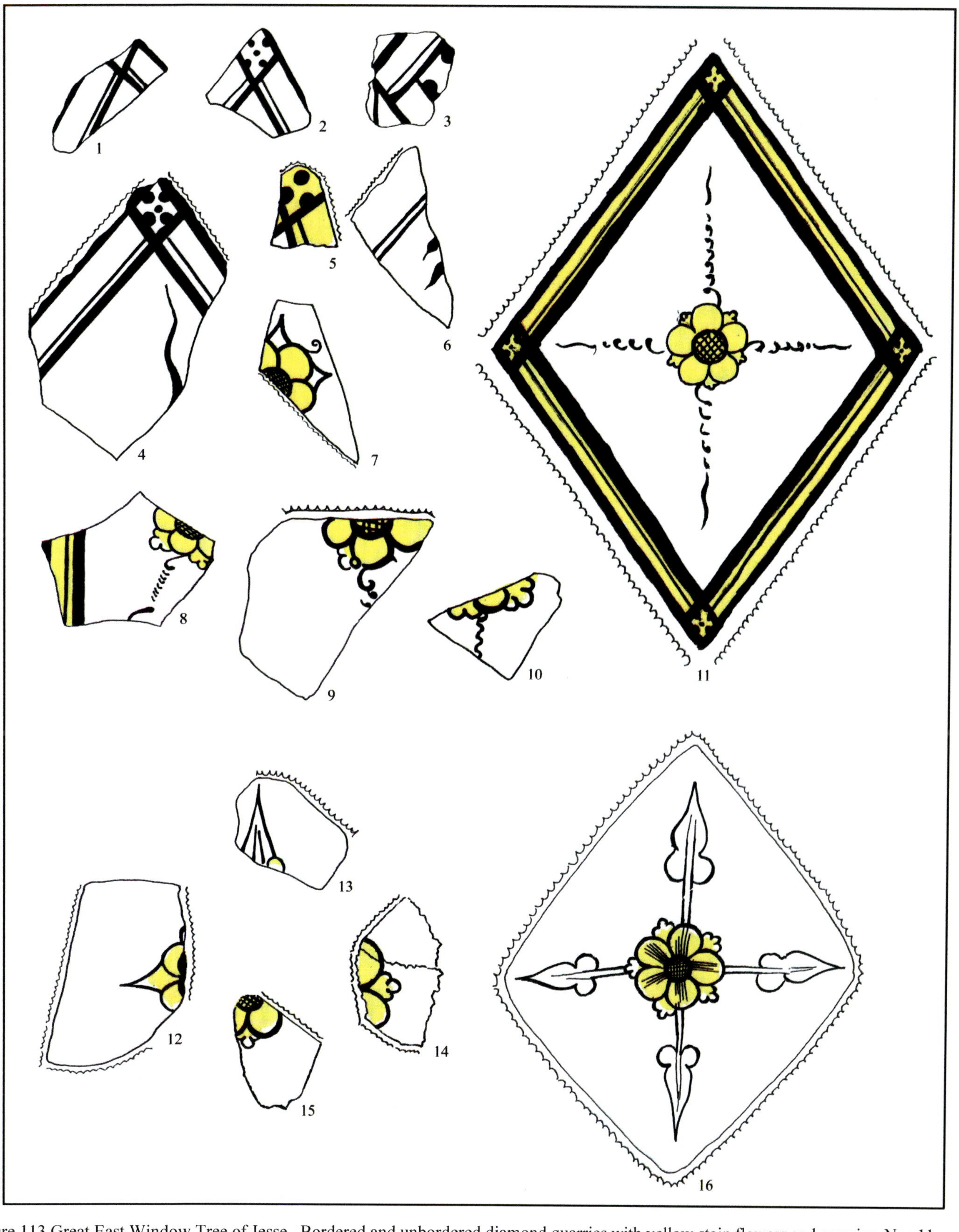

Figure 113 Great East Window Tree of Jesse. Bordered and unbordered diamond quarries with yellow stain flowers and margins, Nos 11 and 16 are reconstructed. *c.*1400 (Scale 60 percent of life size).

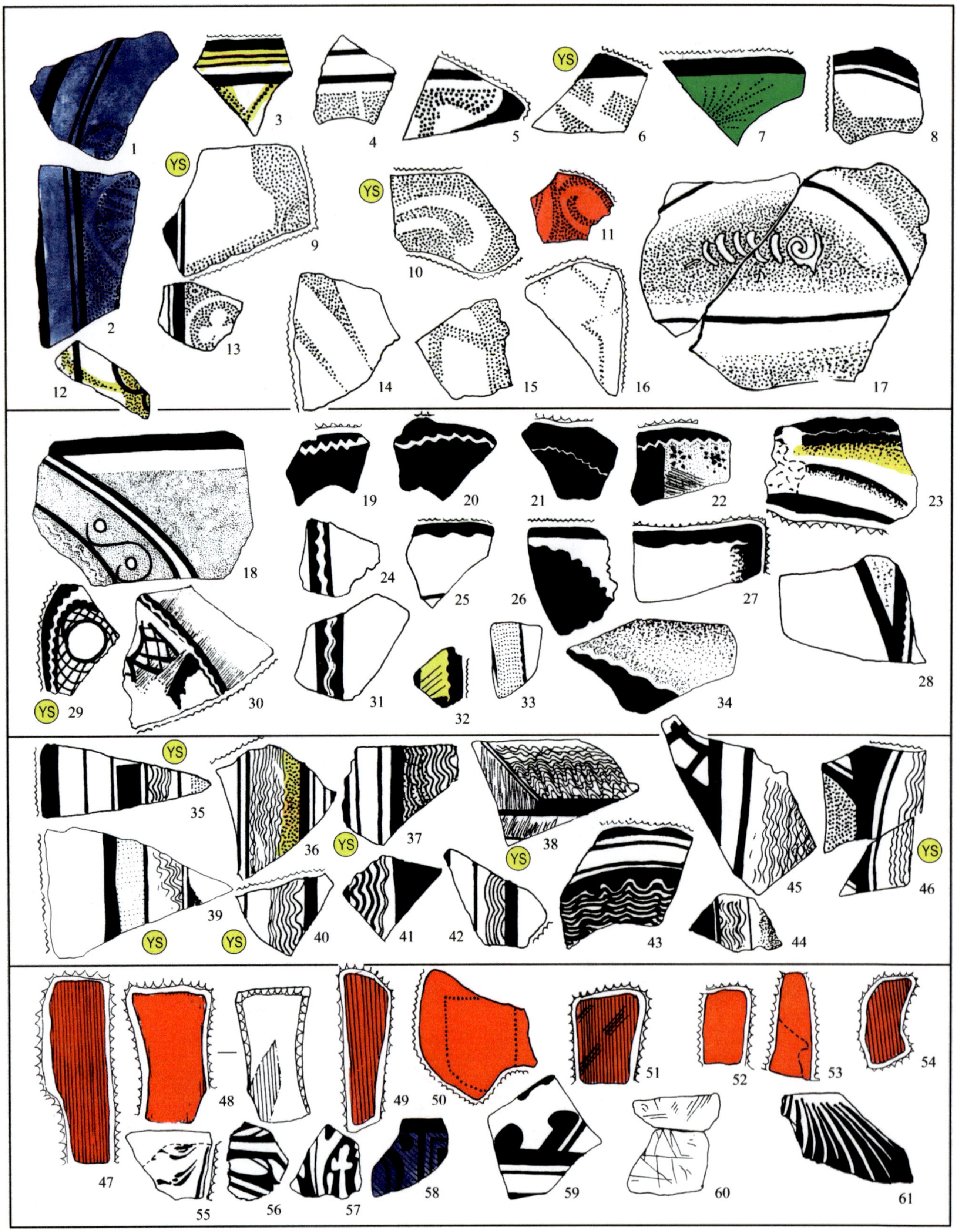

Figure 114 Great East Window Tree of Jesse. Non-linear patterns made from shading, red, blue green and yellow stain; patterns involving wavy lines, clear and yellow stain. Patterns involving bands of 'scribbling', clear and yellow stain. Red edge pieces and miscellaneous patterns, one (unstratified) piece with scratch marks (Scale 60 percent of life size).

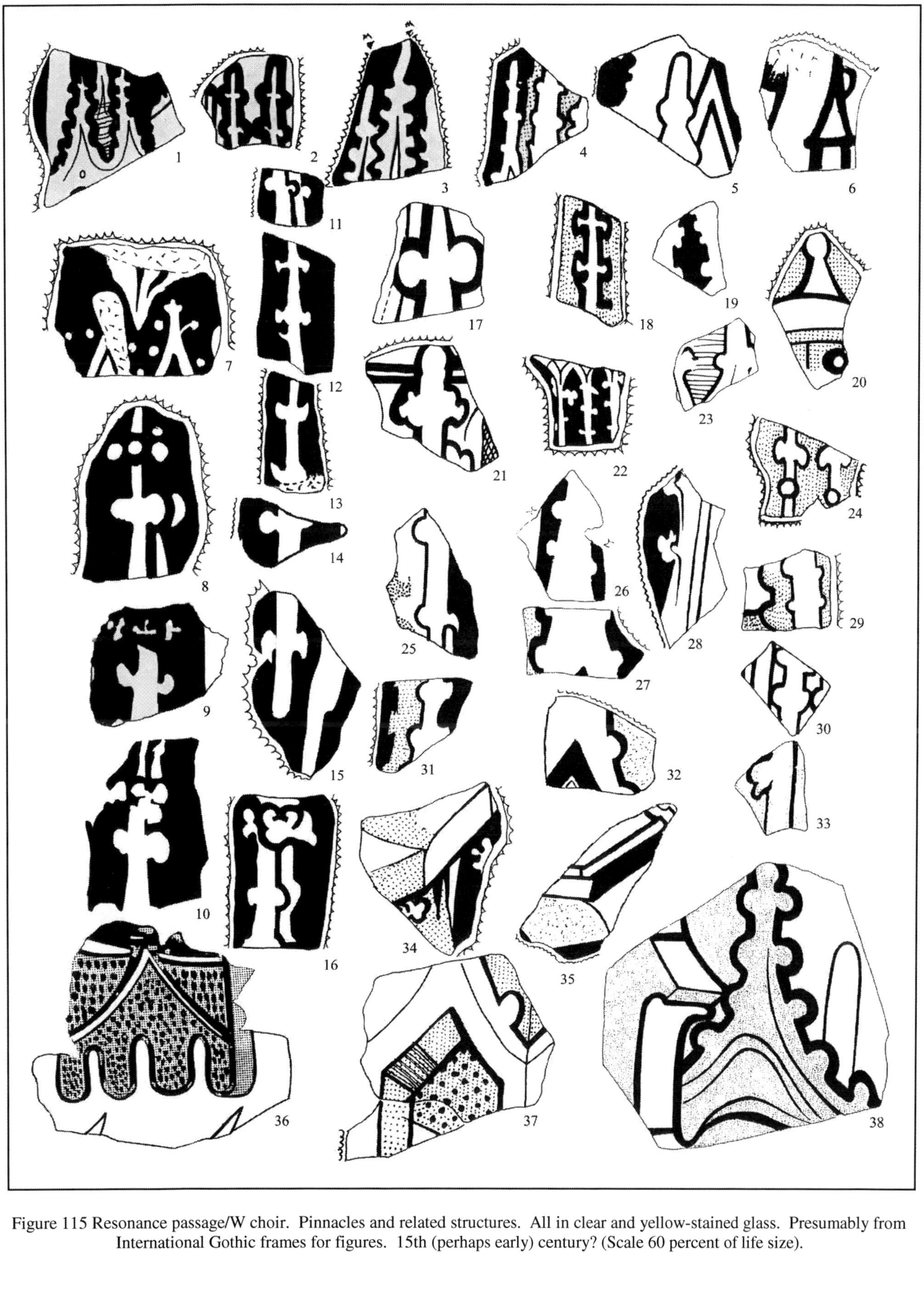

Figure 115 Resonance passage/W choir. Pinnacles and related structures. All in clear and yellow-stained glass. Presumably from International Gothic frames for figures. 15th (perhaps early) century? (Scale 60 percent of life size).

Figure 116 Resonance passage/W choir. Architectural panelling. Columns, arched and curved architectural motifs, clear glass and yellow stain. Architectural 'bell'? Early 15th or very late 14th century? (Scale 60 percent of life size).

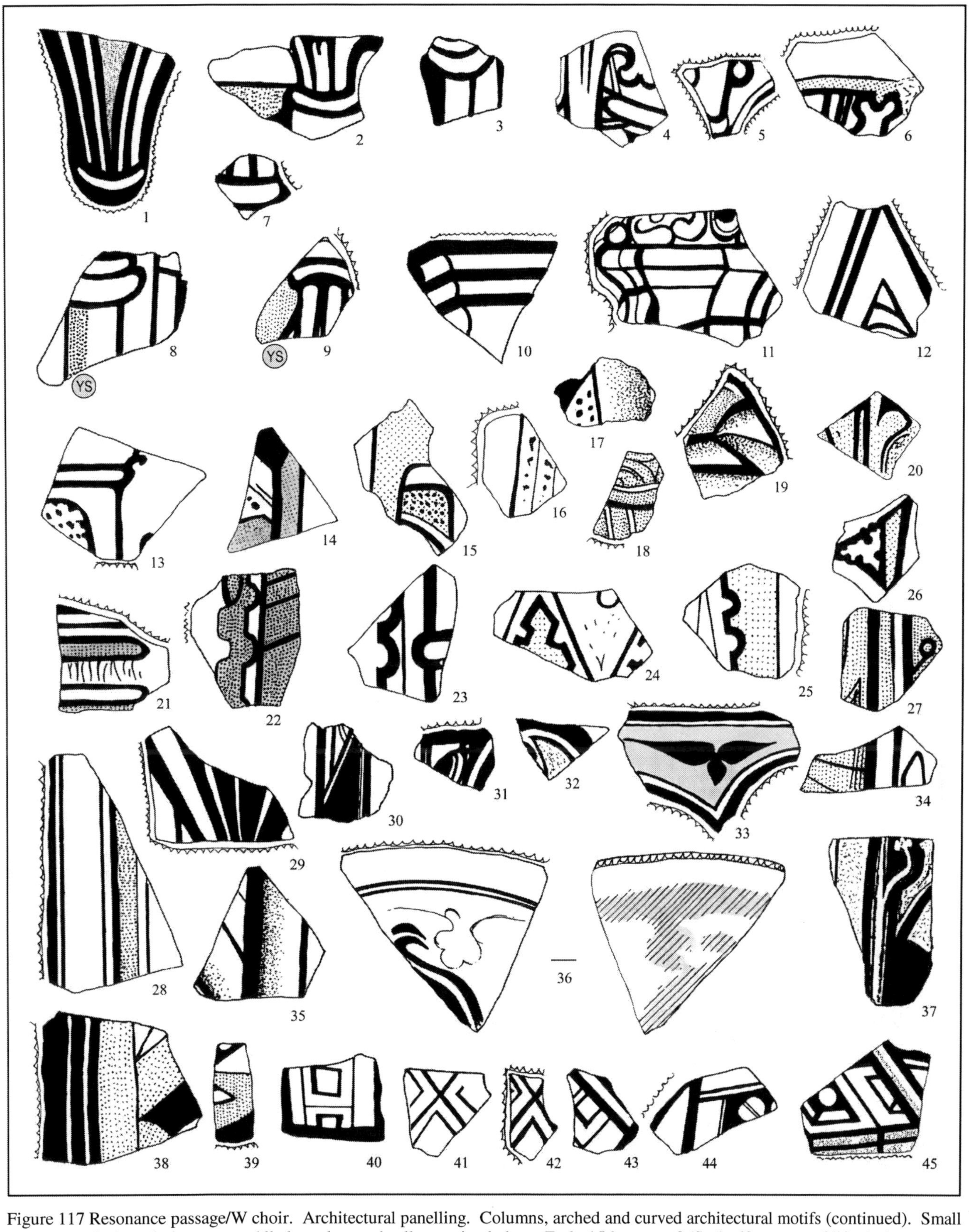

Figure 117 Resonance passage/W choir. Architectural panelling. Columns, arched and curved architectural motifs (continued). Small scale 'angular' patterns. All clear glass and yellow-stained glass. Early 15th century? (Scale 60 percent of life size).

Figure 118 Resonance passage/W choir. Small scale patterns, patterns with trefoils and quatrefoils, fine line panelling. Floor tile, or heraldic motifs. All clear and yellow-stained glass. Early 15th century? (Scale 60 percent of life size).

Figure 119 Resonance passage/W choir. Designs involving cross-hatching. All clear and yellow-stained glass. Early 15th century? (Scale 60 percent of life size).

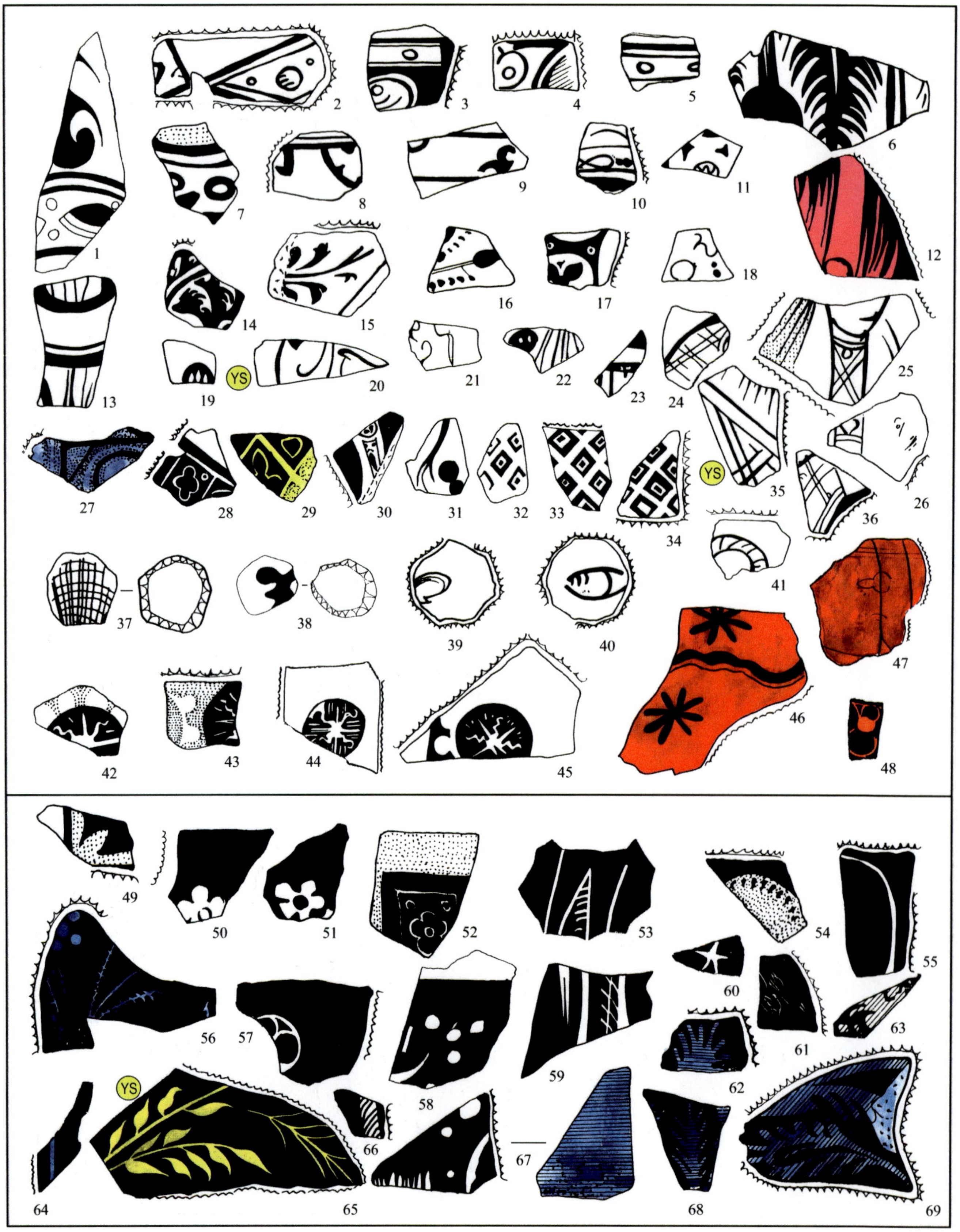

Figure 120 Resonance passage/W choir. Jewelled bands, fabrics and decorative motifs, red, pink, blue and yellow-stained glass. 'Gems' and scratchwork - the large leaf spray is yellow stain on blue glass. 15th century? (Scale 60 percent of life size).

Figure 121 Resonance passage/W choir. Floral designs in red (2), blue (7 and 8)and yellow stain; textiles and costume in clear glass with yellow stain. 15th century? (Scale 60 percent of life size).

Figure 122 Resonance passage/W choir. Small haloed head of Christ; face fragments and hands in clear and yellow glass; maiden with hand on breast. Yellow hair, perhaps of the Virgin Mary. Beards, other hair, ears, haloes. Crown of Thorns, Wounds of Christ, chain mail, ermine?, and a blue crown (35)? 15th century (?), but the head of Christ and the bearded-head look early 15th century (Scale 60 percent of life size).

Figure 123 Resonance passage/W choir. Foliage, including yellow stain leaf on blue glass. Blue, red, green and yellow stain seaweed. The seaweed grounds look *c.*1390-1430-40 (Scale 60 percent of life size).

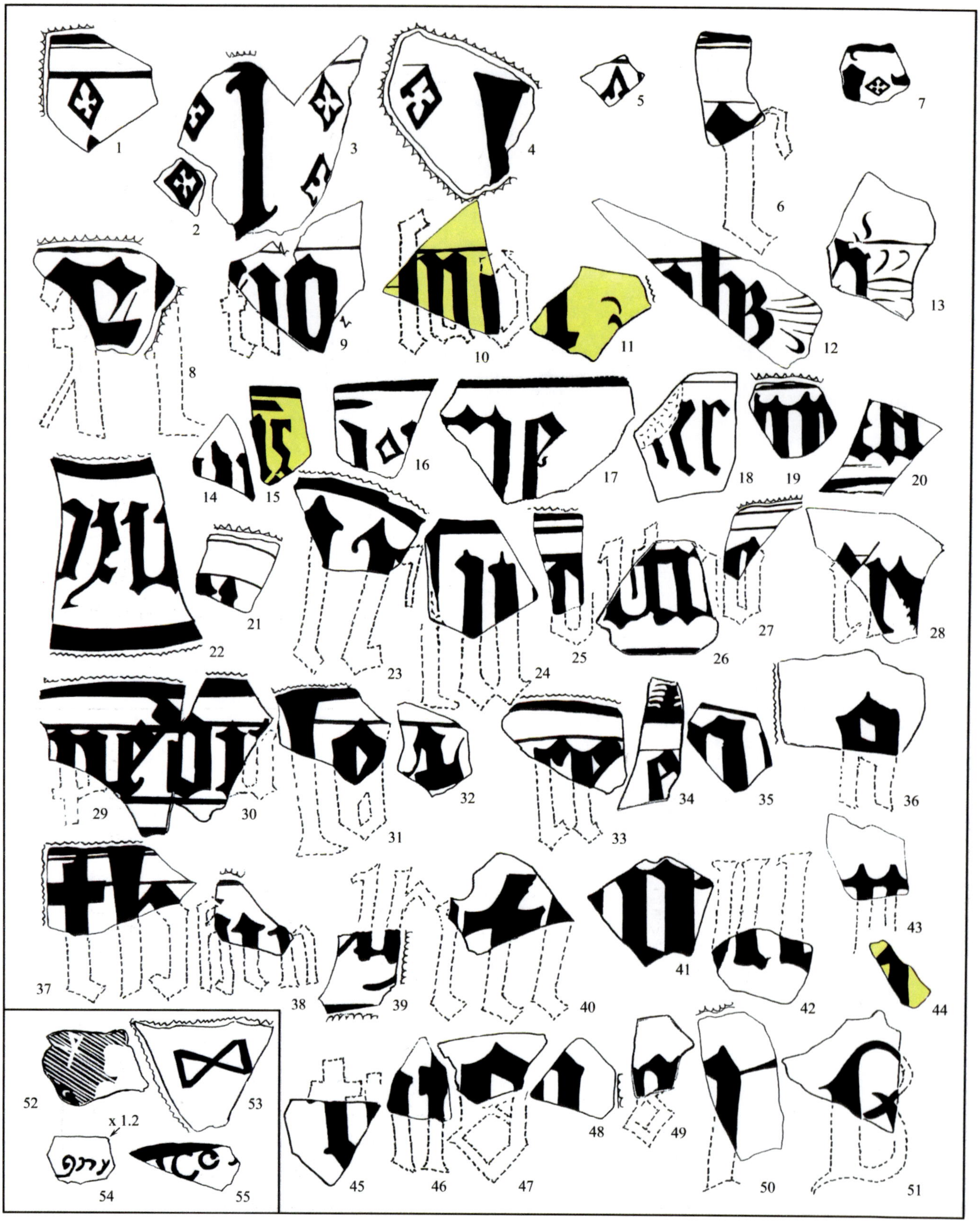

Figure 124 Resonance passage/W choir. Lettering in clear glass and yellow stain, referring to dates, donor inscriptions, and references to a Crucifixion? A possible Coventry glazier's signature (scale 2:1) Late 14th - early 15th century (Scale 60 percent of life size, except No 54 at 120 percent of life size).

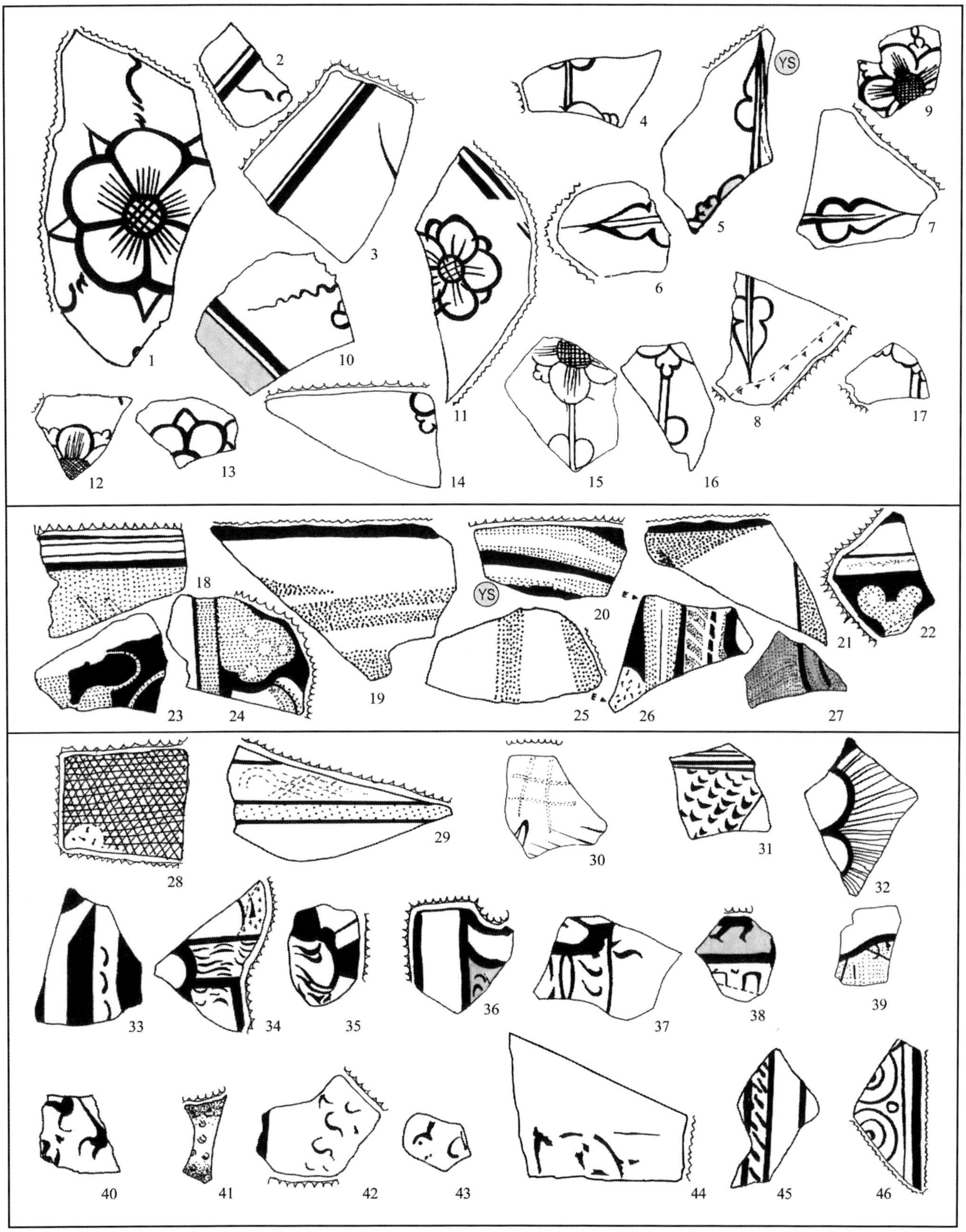

Figure 125 Resonance passage/W choir. Bordered and unbordered diamond quarries, clear glass and yellow stain. Patterns made from shading and yellow stain, in one case on blue glass (27). Various decorative patterns. Early 15th century? (Scale 60 percent of life size).

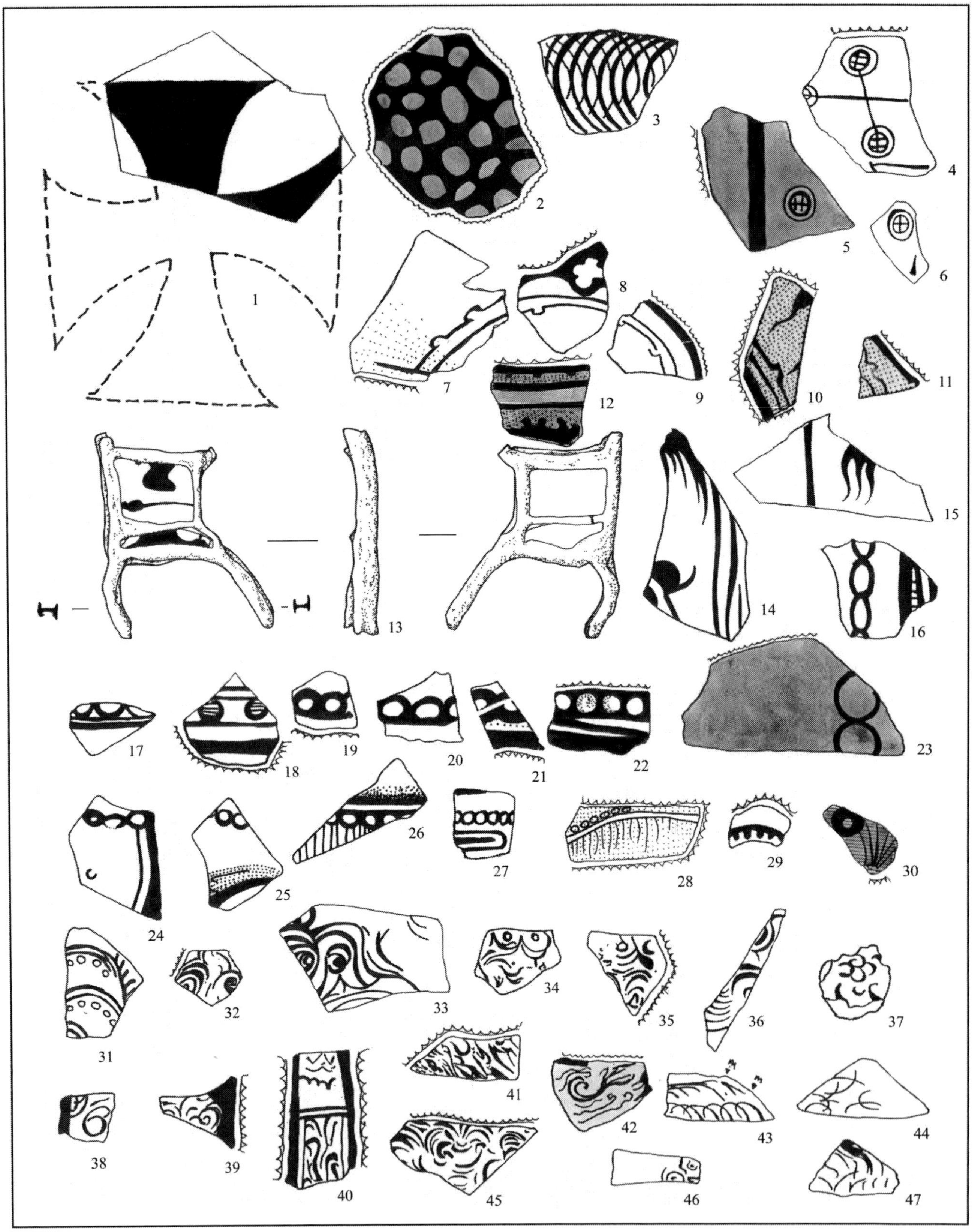

Figure 126 Resonance passage/W choir. Cross patty, blue grapes?, but classification largely uncertain. Early 15th century? (Scale 60 percent of life size). 2, 12, 23 and 30 are blue. 5 is green. 10, 11 and 42 are yellow stain.

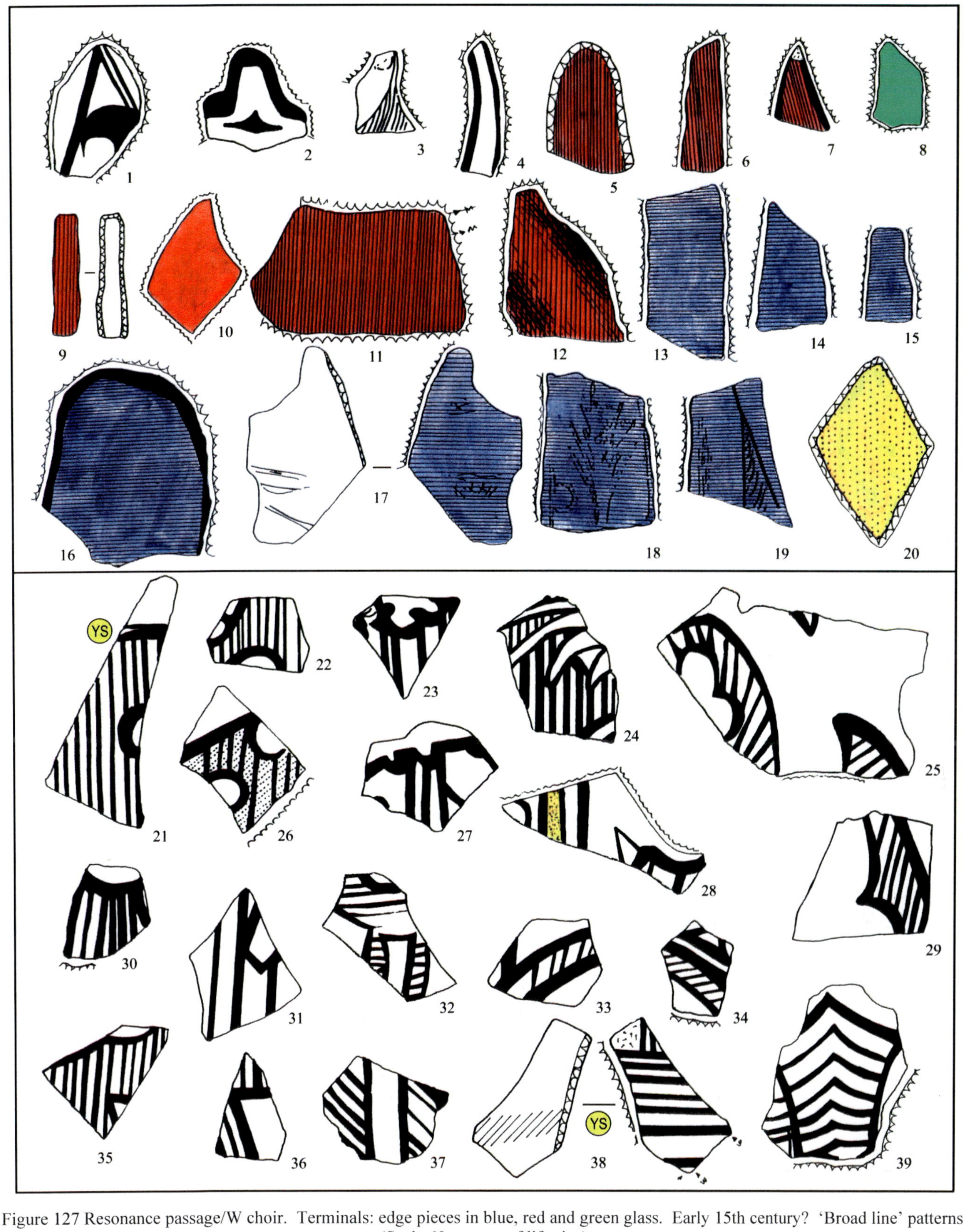

Figure 127 Resonance passage/W choir. Terminals: edge pieces in blue, red and green glass. Early 15th century? 'Broad line' patterns (Scale 60 percent of life size).

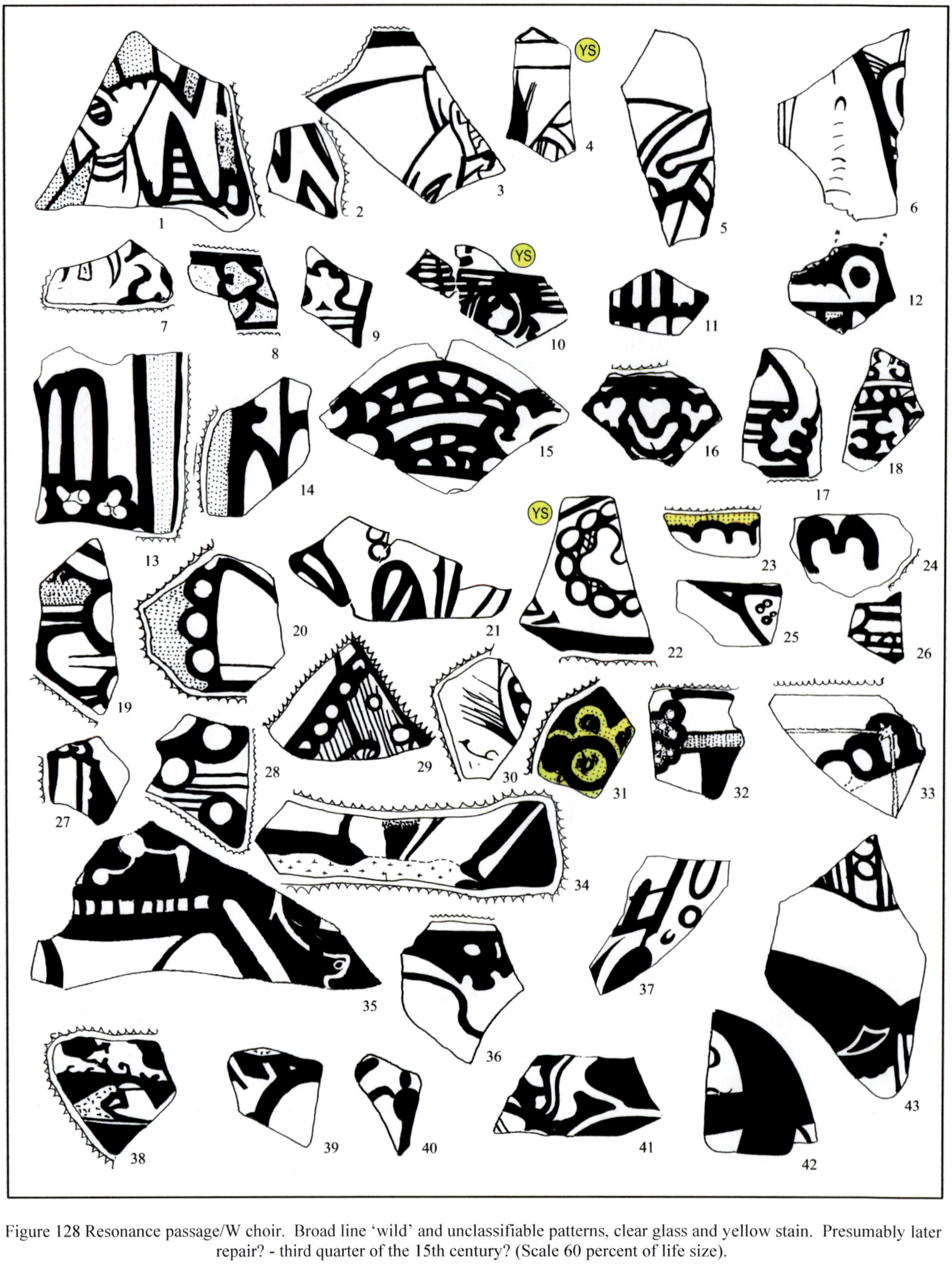

Figure 128 Resonance passage/W choir. Broad line 'wild' and unclassifiable patterns, clear glass and yellow stain. Presumably later repair? - third quarter of the 15th century? (Scale 60 percent of life size).

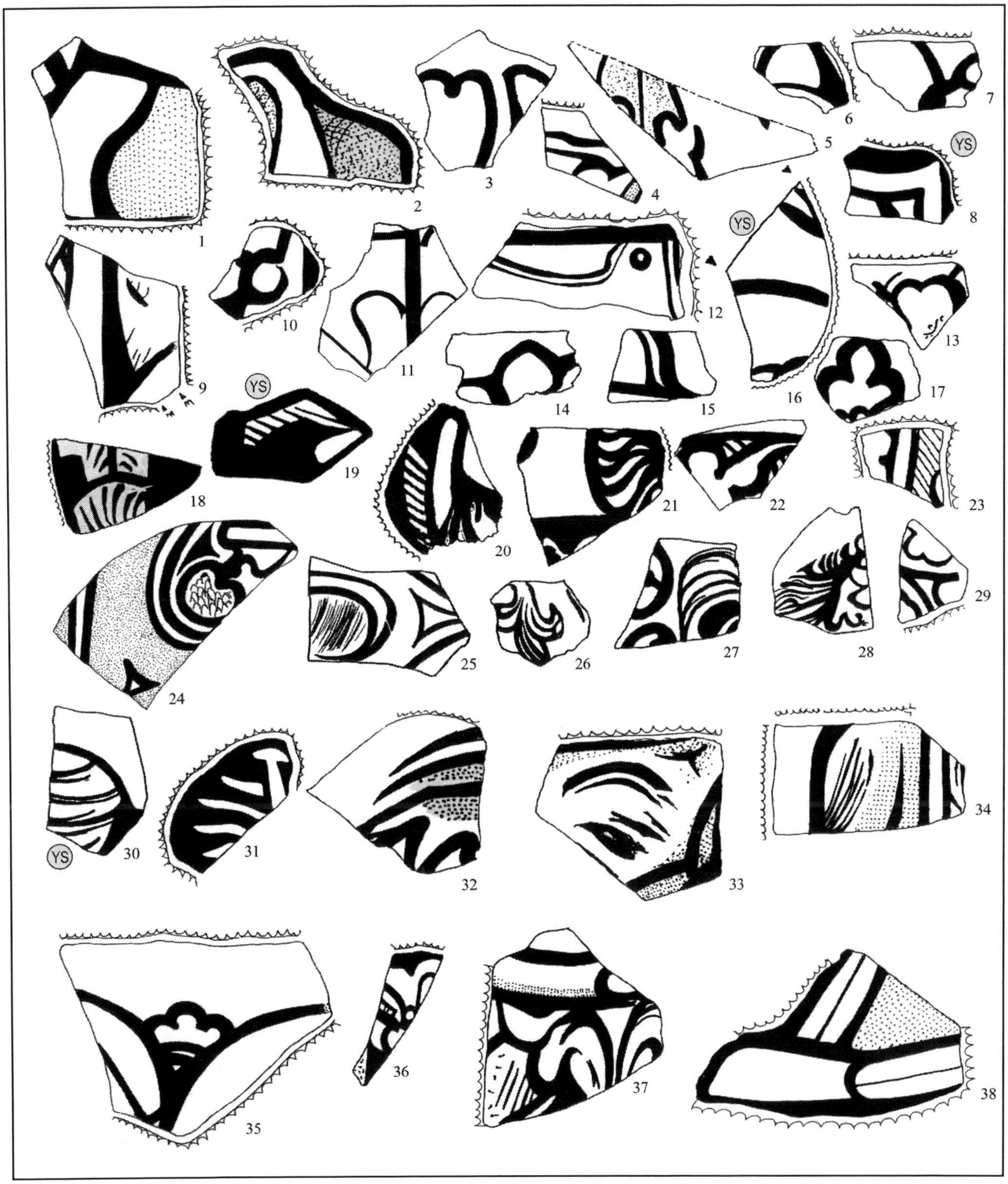

Figure 129 Resonance passage/W choir. Broad line 'wild' and unclassifiable patterns in clear glass and yellow stain. Third quarter of the 15th century? (Scale 60 percent of life size).

Figure 130 1) Window glass from the N transept and N porch/chapel (Nos 1-42). From repaired multi-period windows? Colour is virtually absent. The large leaves are a new style. 15th century, probably post 1423.
2) Window glass from the S transept (Nos 43-56). As above, with larger pieces apparently new types. Colour is virtually absent. (Scale 60 percent of life size).

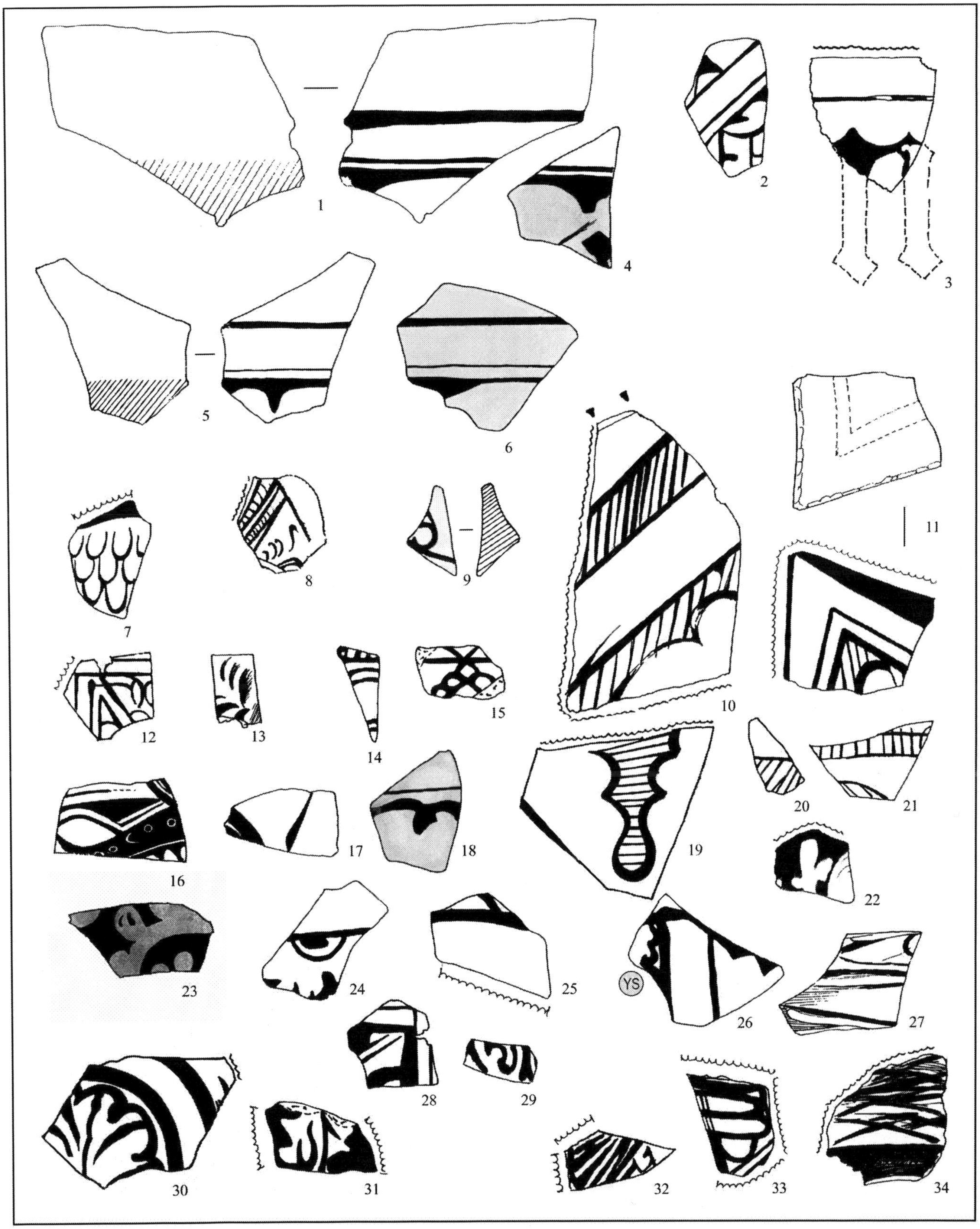

Figure 131 Nave, W end. Glass, mostly of later, 15th century, types (?post 1423), from the western nave. Late yellow stain examples and a ?stray blue fragment (23) (Scale 60 percent of life size).

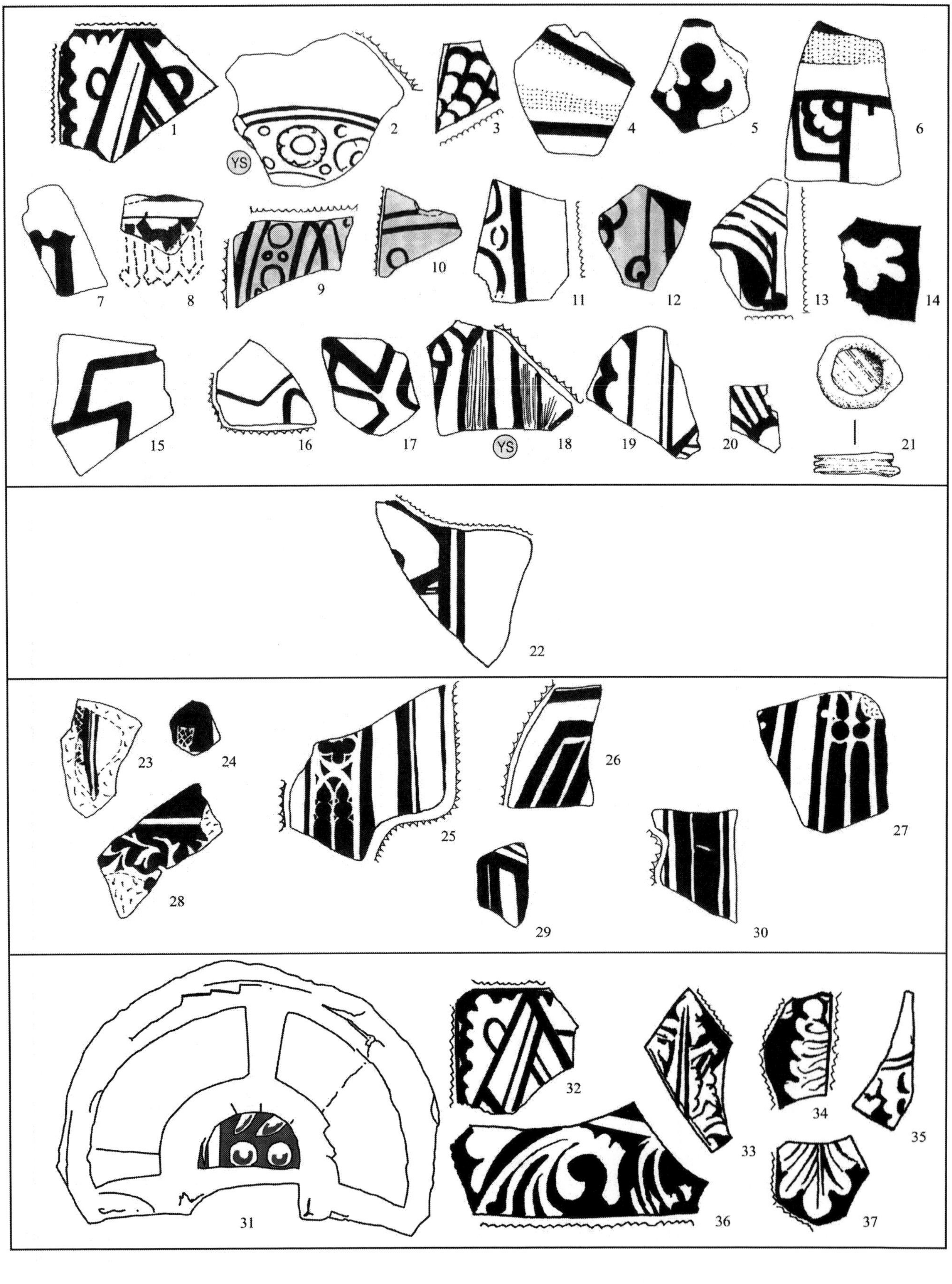

Figure 132 Early and later glass from: 1) E nave, with yellow stain examples (Nos 1-21); 2) NE sacristy (No 22); 3) chapter house (Nos 23-30); 4) pieces on display at Coventry Museum (Nos 31-37). No 32 resembles No 1 and Nos 33-37 are familiar types. No 31 is an unrecognised 18th-century repair. It is probably from the prior's house. The central colour is red. (Scale 60 percent of life size).

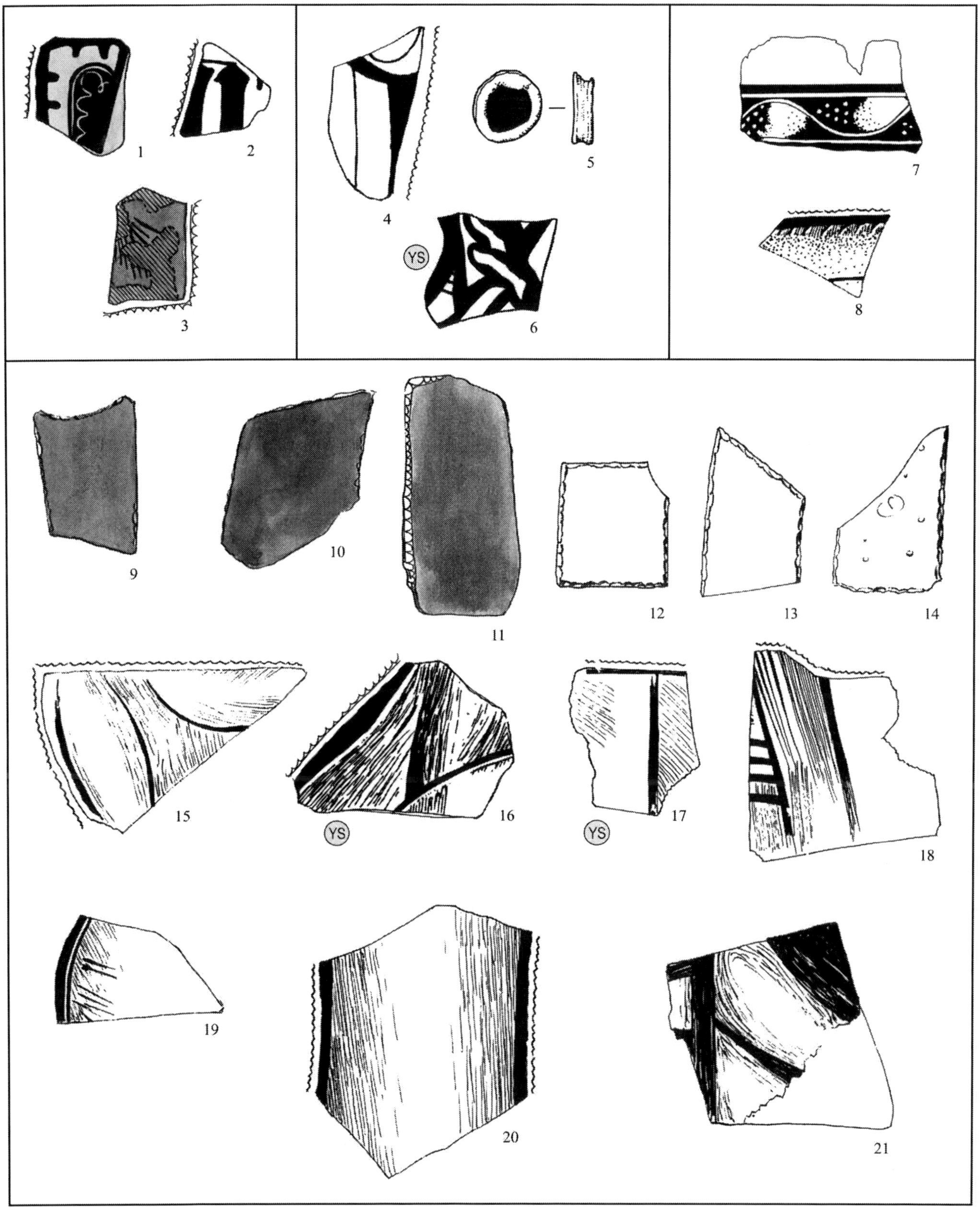

Figure 133 1) Glass (Nos 1-8) from cloister area but the small quantity suggests it is unrelated to the cloister.
2) Late medieval or ?post medieval red (3 and 9), blue and yellow-stained glass (Nos 9-21) of distinctly different style to other glass from the site. As so little has been recovered, virtually all this last group of material has been illustrated, with only 30 additional drawings in archive. (Scale 60 percent of life size).

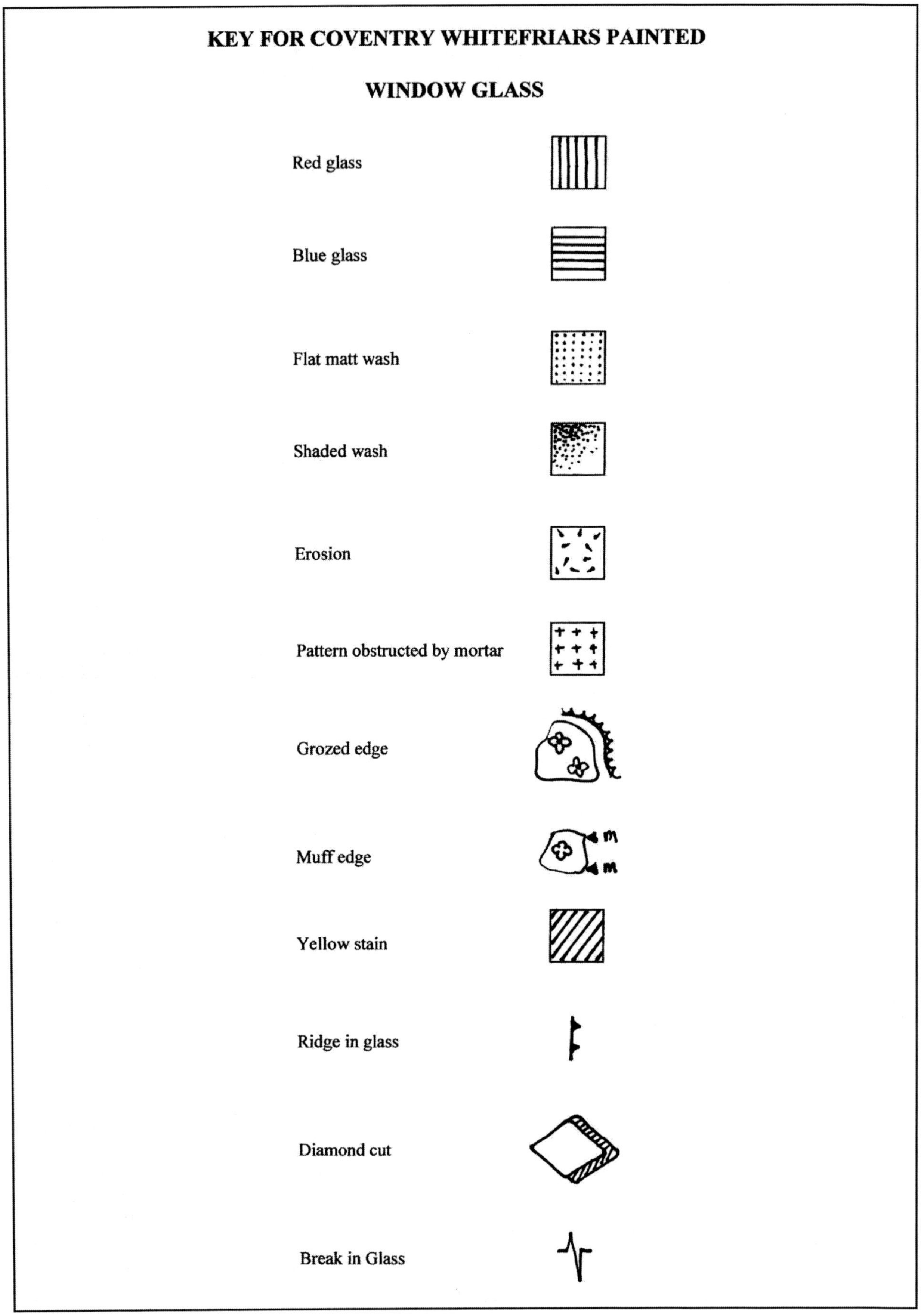

Figure 134 Key to conventions used in window glass illustrations, Figures 95-133.

SECTION K
SCIENTIFIC EXAMINATION OF AN OYSTER-SHELL PALETTE

H. Howard
Conservation of Wall Painting Department, Courtauld Institute of Art.

Figure 135a-e and 135f-g

SUMMARY

Examination of an oyster shell palette from the friary was undertaken in December 1996 at the request of Mrs. Charmian Woodfield.

The palette was found during her 1962 excavations, and came from the northern resonance passage which lay under the choir stalls. Although it was recovered from a Grammar School, 16th-century, deposit, it is almost certainly a medieval artefact.

The palette retains a considerable amount of paint. Most of this is natural azurite, though red lake, lead white, carbon black and gold leaf were also identified. In some areas the pigments have been mixed to provide a range of pale blues and pinks.

Although shells containing pigment survive from some sixteen medieval and Tudor sites in Britain, this is the first case in which red lake and gold leaf have been identified. The materials found in the shell are consistent with a dating between the mid 14th century and mid 16th century. From the context of the painted stonework a date in the later 15th century seems most likely.

METHODOLOGY

Following a detailed examination of the palette in normal, raking and UV light, a small number of minute samples were taken to identify the original materials.

Samples were mounted as dispersions (in *Meltmount*, which has a refractive index of 1.662) and were examined with an optical microscope at 170-2500x magnification; photomicrographs were taken at between 500 and 5000x. A scanning electron microscope (SEM), used with energy-dispersive X-ray (EDX) analysis which provides elemental analysis, was employed to confirm the identifications made with polarised light microscopy (PLM). Analysis of organic materials and additional confirmation of inorganic components were undertaken using Fourier Transform Infrared (FTIR) microspectroscopy.

ORIGINAL MATERIALS

The oyster-shell, Fig. 135a, which measures 55 x 45mm - shows evidence of recent repairs with a modern consolidant, presumably undertaken at some time in the 1970s. The paint contained in the palette is predominantly blue in colour and extends on to the outside of the shell in one place. A tiny trace of gold leaf, scarcely visible to the naked eye, survives on top of the blue pigment in one area. Around the curved perimeter of the shell are remains of pink and white paint, and towards the centre, a zone of black. All the surviving remains of paint exhibit severe wrinkling, of the type usually associated with the contraction of original binding medium during the drying of paint films.

Analysis of paint samples from the palette, Table 1, confirmed the presence of the following pigments: natural azurite ($2CuCO_3 \cdot Cu[OH]_2$); a red lake pigment (possibly on a calcium carbonate substrate); lead white ($2PbCO_3 \cdot Pb[OH]_2$); carbon black (C) and gold leaf (Au). Unfortunately, analysis of any media which may survive has been compromised by the presence of the modern organic consolidants.

TABLE 1 (samples from oyster-shell palette)

Sample No. Accession No.	Description	Original Materials	Comments and Analytical Method
1/1874	Blue pigment	natural azurite combined with lead white	In one area a tiny trace of gold leaf remains on top of the azurite PLM, SEM/EDX & FTIR
2/1875	Pink pigment mixture	red lake combined with calcium carbonate and lead white	The red lake pigment does not fluoresce strongly in UV light. PLM/MCT & FTIR
3/1876	Black pigment	carbon black	PLM & SEM/EDX
4/1887	White pigment	lead white	PLM/MCT & FTIR

TABLE 2 (sample from stone 1159)

Sample No. Accession No.	Description	Original Materials	Comments and Analytical Method
5/1886	Red and blue pigments from stone 1159	•vermilion and natural azurite in a lead white matrix	In some zones the vermilion has been applied over azurite in a lead white matrix PLM/MCT

The blue pigment is natural azurite of larger than average particle size (the majority of particles are 15 x 30µm, with a small number of larger particles of approximately 30 x 50µm, Fig. 135a-c and f. Since azurite was priced according to the intensity of its colour, which depends directly on particle size (Dunkerton *et al.* 1987, 34) the Whitefriars pigment was presumably rather costly. In many areas the blue pigment particles are combined in a white matrix which consists principally of lead white, although a phosphorus peak in the SEM/EDX spectrum suggests that some bone white may also be present.

The pink material around the upper curved surface of the palette consists of a red lake pigment combined with lead white. The particle size ranges from an average of 20 x 30µm to around 40 x 60µm, Fig. 135d and g. Analysis of a single red lake particle by FTIR suggested that the substrate of the pigment may be calcium carbonate.

The white paint consists principally of lead white, although the phosphorus peak in the SEM/EDX spectra suggests that some bone white - composed chiefly of tricalcium phosphate - may also be present.

Examination of the carbon black pigment by polarised light microscopy indicated the presence of charcoal black. The average particle size is 25 x 40µm, though the largest particles are approximately 60 x 110µm, Fig. 135e.

DISCUSSION

Shells containing pigment survive from some sixteen medieval and Tudor sites in Britain, and are discussed in Howard and Park (forthcoming). Examples from more than half of these sites have now been subjected to scientific examination. In most cases they are not precisely dateable, and it is not clear for which type of painting they were employed, though it seems likely that the majority were used for wall painting or polychromed sculpture. Some of the shells only contain a single pigment, and can therefore be regarded as containers, while others have remains of various pigments and were clearly used as palettes. This was certainly true of the Coventry example, where the analysis has shown how the blue and red pigments were combined with white in some areas of the palette to produce a variety of tones.

The main pigment present in the Coventry palette is azurite, which is also the only blue pigment to have been identified in other shells (in the examples from Clarendon Palace, the Greyfriars at Norwich, and St. Augustine's Abbey, Canterbury). The Coventry palette, however, is the only shell in which red lake and gold leaf have been identified. Although the use of red lake pigments in wall painting has been confirmed as early as *c.*800AD (a red lake pigment, thought to be madder, has been identified in the Carolinian scheme of *c.*800 at Müstair (Switzerland), see Mairinger and Schreiner 1986), they are more commonly found in the later medieval period. For instance, recent examination has established the presence of a red lake in the extensive *Doom* painting of *c.*1435-60 over the chancel arch of Holy Trinity Church, Coventry (Howard 1996).

The materials in the palette are therefore consistent with a dating in the period between the middle of the 14th century and the middle of the 16th century. The friary was founded in 1342, and the shell was found in the mid 16th-century Grammar School rubbish fill of the resonance passages constructed beneath the choir stalls (context 62 Tr. I (4)). Associated finds included parts of a South Netherlandish altar vase, pilgrim tokens and other objects clearly from the friary (C. Woodfield, pers. comm). It is not clear for what painting the palette was employed, though a fragment of wall painting in red and black survived on the late 15th-century NE tower pier, and there are various *ex situ* fragments of polychromed stonework, mostly in red, blue and gold, and believed to date from the excavator's Rebuild phase, from *c.*1450 to the early 16th century. These appear to have originated from the choir or tower (C. Woodfield, pers. comm.).

EXAMINATION OF A PAINT SAMPLE FROM EXCAVATED STONE 1159

Analysis of a single paint sample from an excavated stone (No 1159, Fig. 69), a cusping of a cylindrical terminal from the choir, was undertaken. This indicated that the red pigment consists of vermilion (HgS), and that in some places this has been applied over a blue layer of azurite combined with lead white, Table 2.

ACKNOWLEDGEMENTS

I am indebted to English Heritage for its generous funding of access to FTIR facilities at Imperial College, London University, and to David Park of the Courtauld Institute for his assistance in the preparation of this report.

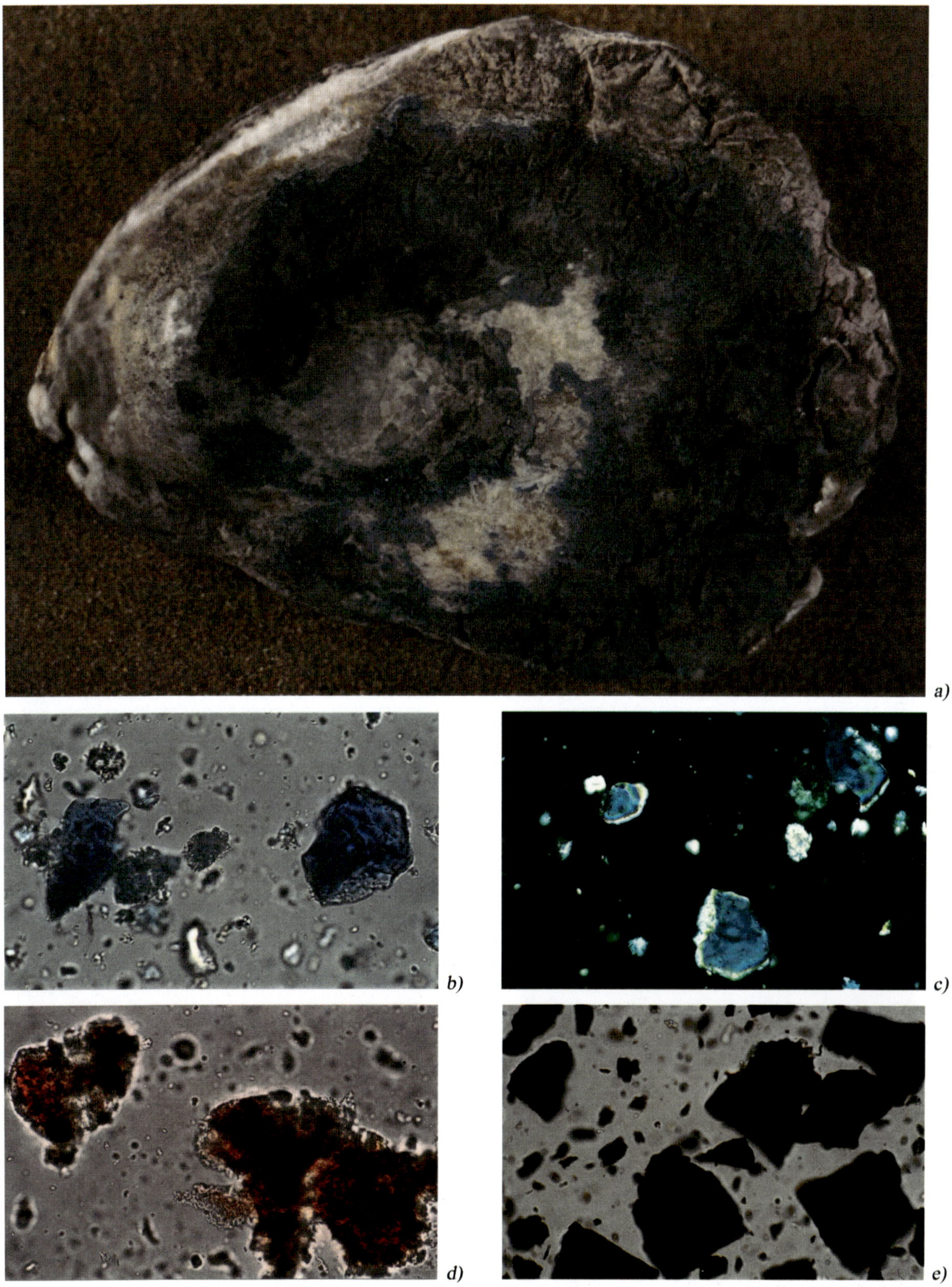

Figure 135 a) Oyster-shell palette (62 I 4; Scale 3:1) and b-e) photomicrographs (Howard 1996): Plates b and c) show dispersion of natural azurite particles from Sample 1. In Plate b) the particles have been photographed in plane polarised transmitted light, and are shown at 5000 x magnification. The striations within the angular structure indicate their mineral origin. With crossed polars (Plate c, shown at 3600 x magnification) the particles exhibit strong birefringence (a rainbow effect, visible around the perimeter). Plate d). Dispersion of Sample 2 shown at 3600 x magnification in plane polarised transmitted light. The particles of red lake pigment vary in colour from a very pale pink to a deep rich translucent red depending on their thickness. Plate e). Dispersion of Sample 3 photographed in plane polarised transmitted light and shown at 3600 x magnification. Large angular opaque particles of a carbon black pigment, probably charcoal black, are clearly visible.

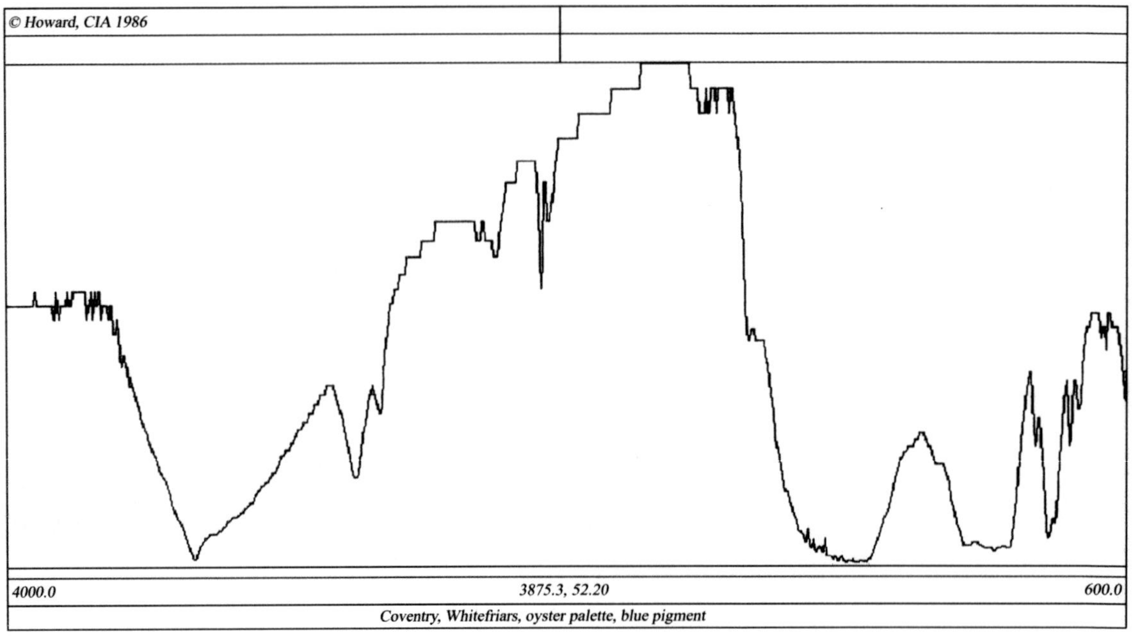

Figure 135f FTIR spectrum of the blue paint from the palette (Sample 1/1874). Bands at 3429cm^{-1}, 1400 cm^{-1} (CO_3), 952cm^{-1}, 837cm^{-1} and 818cm^{-1} are indicative of azurite.

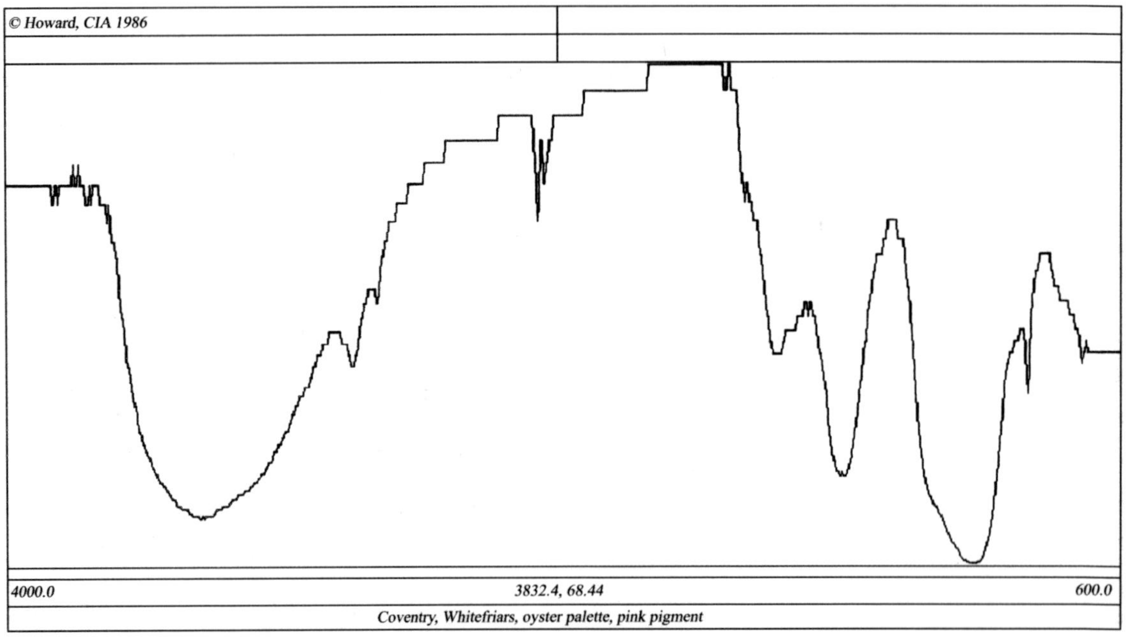

Figure 135g FTIR spectrum of the pink paint from the palette (Sample 2/1875). The broad peak around 1400cm^{-1} and peaks at 875 and 1794cm^{-1} confirm the presence of calcium carbonate which is likely to be the substrate of the red lake colorant.

SECTION L
LATE 14TH AND 15TH CENTURY STAMPED FLOOR TILE

PATTERNS, LAYOUT, CHRONOLOGY, DISTRIBUTION, SOURCE AND DIMENSIONS

C. Woodfield

Figures 136-147 and Tables 3-5

THE SITE AND RECORDING METHODS

The floor tiles from the church with its nine-bay nave with chapels, six bay choir with acoustic passages, crossing and transepts, was excavated, together with parts of the sacristy, and the W and N ranges of the cloister, for MoPBW in the 1960s by the writer (plans in Woodfield 1971, fig. 11; Platt 1978, fig. 49), with full recording of floor tiles from stratified deposits. The, rare, *in situ* tiles and surviving tile matrices were also recorded.

Clearances, in advance of landscaping, by Julian Barnard and John Bateman for Coventry Museum in the 1970s revealed further detail of the three eastern bays of the choir, and also parts of the chapter house and structures to the SE of the standing cloister but with virtually no recording of stratified deposits (see Cattell 1997 and Section C of this report, and the account of the excavations, Section E of this report). However, the brick-patched remains of a medieval tile floor *in situ*, which now appears to have survived to *c.*1800, was recorded in detail in 1978, although its position on the ground was uncertain.

Recent work by the writer on 1977-8 plans and photographs has now made it clear that what the clearances revealed were parts of a second court to the S of the cloister with part of a reredorter adjoining, and has also fixed the position of the tiled floor in what now appears to be the Prior's House, Figs. 136, 37 and 49 (the dotted lines on the W of Fig. 37 indicating the suggested road building threat in the 1960s, and on the E the then suggested area for landscaping). The church and conventual buildings seem likely to have been tiled throughout.

This account of the decorated floor tiles is based on a full set of drawings, records and an interim report made by P. and C. Woodfield from the latter's excavated material of the 1960s, combined with a later interim report prepared by John Bateman in the late 1970s on the floor tiles from the Coventry Museum's clearances and excavations. The City of Lincoln Archaeology Unit in 1995 commissioned N. Griffiths to redraw all the floor tile material that survived at Coventry Museum. This duplication, administratively puzzling, can however be said to have led to a greater certainty than usual concerning the nature and number of die variants, because of the need for consensus, and the writer would like to acknowledge the help and support of Nick Griffiths and Paul Woodfield, without which it would have been difficult to complete this report.

The tile illustrations are therefore now by Nick Griffiths, except for Nos 2, 19, 22, 96, 98 and 116 by Paul Woodfield, and Nos 20b, 51, 104 and 120 by John Bateman. Plans of the structures and of tiles *in situ* have been drawn up by Paul Woodfield from the excavators' records and recent documentary research. The writer is also grateful for Iain Soden's comments (Marked I.S. where they occur in the text).

The choir stalls and misericords are considered elsewhere in this report (Section H) and have also been published by Tracy (1997). There is no correlation between the heraldry there illustrated, and the heraldry of the floor tiles.

THE SOURCE OF THE FLOOR TILES AND THEIR FABRIC

All the tiles appear to be the products of the nearby Coventry Stoke kilns, three miles to the E (Chatwin 1936, 2-3). The eastern part of the friary precinct was known as Old Brickkiln Close in 1748, but there is no evidence either way for its use in the medieval period. Thin sectioning (by Alison Oliver and Caroline Kemp) showed no obvious differences between tiles, confirming the visual impression formed during excavation and previous study. Inclusions consisted of abundant angular and rounded quartz, the last sometimes consisting of actual pebbles, moderate to slight muscovite (mica) flakes, slight black-stained clay pellets, and slight rounded chert. All examples had an oxidised isotropic clay matrix.

An ICPS survey carried out (pers. comm. Dr J. N. Walsh, Royal Holloway College) again showed general uniformity, but did indicate a similarity between the mosaic tiles, Fig. 145.122, the border tiles, Fig. 146.129-131, and the grave 64.31 cover tiles, Fig. 139.36-37 and 38, again confirming the 1960s assumption of a chronologically late grouping of this material, all with reversed designs of 'black' on 'white'. The survey did not suggest any other groupings.

Michael Hughes of the British Museum confirmed *in litt.* to the writer that the fabric analysis of the eight-petalled rosette quarter tile, Fig. 140.56a, and the letter Q, Fig. 146.150. A, matched the analysis of the equivalent rosette and Q tiles from the Stoke kiln undertaken by the

British Museum (WMPRG Newsletter 11, 1988).

The fabric is brick red in colour, the quartz and the black pellets being the most noticeable inclusions, although the mica can also be conspicuous. Despite the presence of Chilvers Coton ridge tiles and louvers, there was no suggestion of the presence of floor tiles from that source. Stoke roof and plain ridge tiles did occur, but not from the primary cloister roof.

MANUFACTURE

Examination of the tiles suggested the following stamp-over-slip manufacturing process:-

1 The work took place on a sanded bench, as the bottoms of the tiles were usually sandy, timber moulds being used. There was no sign of animal footprints to suggest that moulds had been placed on the ground.

2 The moulds were bottomless, as there is sometimes a ridge round the base, where the mould did not exactly meet the bench. Moulds are unlikely to have been individual but could easily be handled in banks of say six, arranged as two rows of three tiles. They were probably of planed timber, the sides highly finished to produce the smooth finish noted on the tiles, and given a slight bevel to aid the easy releasing of the clay from the mould.

3 The clay (whatever preparation took place did not get rid of the pebbles) was thrown into the mould, tamped well down, and struck off (the correct term) using a wooden scraper, its drag lines being often visible across the top of the tiles, though some of these, or perhaps indeed all, may relate to step 7; these were not convincingly brush marks for slip, step 6, although this interpretation cannot be totally discounted.

4 When partially dry, the mould with tiles would be turned over, and the tiles released. Sometimes this had to be assisted with a knife to release the tile, there being quite often a curved line on the side suggesting a knife inserted down the side of the mould; however, the evidence did not suggest deliberate knife trimming, except in the case of the mosaic tiles, Fig. 145.122, where this had clearly taken place. No evidence was noticed for distortion due to the over hasty emptying of the mould, nor for fingers pushing the tiles out; curling at the edges occasionally occurred.

There is no evidence that the tiles were stamped with their pattern whilst still in the mould. The clay almost certainly needed to have dried to a firm outer surface before this could be done, otherwise the clay would stick to the pattern stamp, requiring it to be laboriously cleaned. If left to a surface-dry state only whilst still in the mould, it would be difficult to stamp the pattern without the stamp hitting the edge of the mould, rendering the stamp ineffective on that side. To release the mould at the earliest opportunity, and return it to production, would obviously make the best commercial sense.

5 Assuming the tiles are brought out of the mould in a semi-dry state (when initial shrinkage would aid their release) the next stage, before they dry further, is to stamp them with their patterning. However, it has been pointed out (I.S.) that stamping after removal could create edge damage or surface spreading, and it may be that the whole tile had to have dried to a considerable extent to prevent this. One pattern would probably be used at a time, thus the tile bats would be lined up on the bench close together.

6 It appears that the white clay slip is thinly applied (or just possibly brushed) over the tiles, which are then stamped. There is virtually no sign of slip running down the edges of the tiles, so it must have been of a thick consistency. The impressions vary in depth (up to 3mm) but the arrises of the pattern are often slightly rounded, and lines of the pattern do not meet at a sharp point, so the patterns have not been manually cut out or trimmed. The bottoms of the impressions are smooth and they often bear the grain of the timber stamp.

If the tiles had been stamped first, then flooded with the thinner slip that would have been necessary, the edges of the depressions would not be free of slip, which they are (Drury and Pratt 1975, 139; I am grateful for this reference to Laurence Keen); the same argument also mitigates against 'printing' tiles, when slip would surely have been pressed onto these edges. Additionally runs of slip would surely be seen down the side of the tile, but these are extremely rare and sparse. Also the result would be to bring the level of the slip in the pattern flush with the top of the tile. This is not what is observed, where the slip in the pattern is frequently well below the top face of the tile.

7 The surface of the tile must have been scraped clean, presumably after a further drying period. The clear lead glaze appears to have been applied wet, not dry, for runs down the sides, and even on the backs of the tiles, are frequent. Tiles to be divided are normally cut halfway through before the glazing phase, and show glaze in the cut. There was presumably a further lengthy period of drying, when the whole would be fired in one operation. Stabbing to assist in firing, or scoring to assist keying, are both absent, except for some keying lines on tile 79a.

The white clay print was normally paper thin, and wore badly.

20-26mm was the normal thickness for some 70% of the large tiles, though 15% of the tiles do occur below that range and can be as thin as 15mm, (e.g. tiles 51 and 52); 10% occur above that range and can be as thick as 30mm.

For the smaller tiles the peak, again some 70%, comes between 24 and 27mm, with some 20% still falling below that range down to 16mm, and some 5% above. However a tendency to thicker tiles seems clear.

The maximum difference in thickness of a single large tile was 4mm, and a single small tile was 5mm.

THE BASIS FOR THE CATALOGUE

In multiple tile patterns the descriptions are those of the **complete** pattern (which was what the tile-maker intended and the patron chose) not the single tile. The letters **a** to **h** are used to denote either, other tiles of the same multiple tile pattern, parts of halved or quartered tiles, or die variants of the same stamp, the text making these distinctions clear.

The reconstruction of the appearance of the church at different phases was paramount in the research design for this project, and this has governed the order of this catalogue, which is laid out chronologically starting from known layouts, through the known significance of tile sizes in the main body of the material, and the variety and frequency of occurrence of sixteen, nine, four tile and repeating patterns in those chronologically different sizes, together with a classification of heraldic, mosaic, border and lettered types.

1 THE LARGE TILES

Figures 137-140

Tiles are arranged in this, the 'earlier large tile' section of the Catalogue under the various type categories primarily in order of the frequency of their occurrence in order to help establish the main patterns in primary use. A large tile is here taken to be 120mm or above. It is clear that measurements of hand-made objects will be variable, and that the combination of die stamps and sizes may well be different on other sites. Nevertheless, it is clear that size related to date and fashions of tile laying at the Whitefriars, and the writer has remained mindful of a 1960s on site conversation with the late Philip Chatwin, when she was urged to consider the implication of this size difference.

Mortar samples indicate that the mortar from the tiled floor in the prior's house was of the same group as the mortar from the choir floors. The presence of a somewhat worn coin of 1380 in a foundation trench of the NW choir, and the dating of the choir stalls to the mid 1380s, and possibly post 1388 (Tracy 1997, 89, 93) has led to the suggested date of *c.*1390. It is true that large tiles were still being laid in the easternmost bay of the nave, Fig. 136, and this may take the date of these tiles into the first quarter of the 15th century, but this is not certain. A full discussion of the complexities of the dating of the nave appears in the main body of the report.

It seems certain that the cloister gate, cloister, and buildings to its SE, and the church certainly as far W as the more eastern bays of the nave were primarily tiled with this larger size tile and half tile, laid diagonally on a field of dark green and cream tiles and half tiles, Fig. 136 and discussion below. In some cases the tiles are preserved in place, and in others the original tile matrix survives to show the laying pattern, Figs 136-7. The decorated tile colours are basically pale yellow, the result of the lead glaze over a white stamp, against a brown background, the result of oxidisation of the fabric during firing.

The majority of the 1960s tiles came from stratified Dissolution deposits, though some twenty came from pre-Dissolution contexts; clearly there is a problem in the amount of moving around of material that might have taken place at the Dissolution, but a logical picture still emerges.

The 1997 tiles are virtually all unstratified; nevertheless those then still on site, and in particular those from the chapter house, the reredorter area and from S of the standing cloister, are unlikely to have moved far, and the nave, crossing, W choir, N and W cloister were not then being cleared.

The pre-Dissolution stratified tiles are included throughout where meaningful (some were clearly in residual though medieval deposits).

The Initial Laying Scheme

The conclusion is that a tile floor was laid throughout the convent and church in large tiles (i.e. 120mm square up to 130/135+mm) as a primary undertaking apparently at one go at the very end of the 14th century. Diagonal laying is likely to have continued throughout the nave, but smaller tiles were coming into use before the W end was reached, presumably because they were cheaper and quicker to manufacture. The floor area for the church is some 1500 sq. metres and that of the chapter house and the sacristy some 156 and 54 sq. metres respectively. At approximately 64 tiles per square metre, this gives an estimate of a requirement for some 85,000 tiles. The area of the floors of the cloister and structures to the S is not included because of uncertainty, but is unlikely to add less than some 75% to the combined area given above, suggesting an initial requirement approaching 150,000 tiles. The order would presumably have been given in the Friary 2 building phase and might not have included the western three bays of the nave, although this did have arcade pier bases of that date.

The main evidence for the initial lay-out is the tile floor in the 'Prior's House', surviving in 1978, though it is not clear if it survived later landscaping, Fig. 136. The preservation was best at the S, presumably as it was in the corner of the building where there was little traffic. There has been much later patching and relaying during its 400 year history as a working floor. However, the borders were clearly of alternate dark green and yellow tiles and the corners of the sixteen-tile holly leaf pattern, Fig. 137.3, butt up against this border, using triangular tiles at the junction of the two systems. A single line of green tiles separates the large patterns from a four-tile pattern, Fig. 137.4a. There are traces of two other blocks of the same sixteen-tile pattern in the expected positions, and there are also remnants of a worn repeat of the four-tile 4a pattern to the W of the better surviving sixteen-tile example, but moved one tile to the N. All tiles were worn, and it has not been possible to recover the original glaze colour in all cases; the drawing should not, therefore, be used to interpret medieval wear patterns.

The two St Catherine wheel tiles recorded (9 and 10 - there is some confusion in the recording and the presence of 9 only is a possibility) may have been laid as part of another four-tile pattern (as they are at Wormleighton, pers. ob.). This may also be true of the Boteler tile (8) although there was only one example of this.

There are single tiles representing two nine-tile patterns, acorns (6) and cusping enclosing flowers (7). There are problems in fitting in a nine-tile pattern, but it is possible that we are looking at the remains of the tiling for the high end of the prior's hall, and that a change in the laying design took place further W reflecting this; however we may just be looking at later patching.

It is not suggested that the lay-out pattern indicated by the material from the Whitefriars is standard throughout even Warwickshire, but that it seems to represent not only what occurred at the Whitefriars but perhaps a strong strand in local fashion and tradition.

Tile Floor at South End of Cloister Walk

Figure 136

This floor, situated at the foot of the day stair at the S of the E cloister range, Fig. 136, was planned from a photograph and recognition of the masonry (some half dozen unannotated photographs only survive of the Hobley excavation records). From comparison with the 'Prior's House' floor it would seem likely that the western style of paving is primary, and the eastern style is probably later 15th-century patching. The size of tiles cannot now be determined.

In addition to the above surviving large tile diagonal-laid floors, small areas of diagonal matrix were recorded in 1964, in the SE corner of the N nave chapel and again in the passage between the two chapels, Fig. 142. The size cannot now be certainly determined (as they were recorded at a small scale in the 1964 site notebook and were vandalised before the large scale recording was undertaken) but appears to be large. The tile matrix in the passage between the chapels, which is likely to be primary as there is no immediately adjacent building work, is of particular interest, as it overlies green sand and a wear gully, implying that no floor tiling at all took place before the Friary 2 green sand sub-phase which is unlikely to do more than just predate the turn of the 15th century. The switch of sandstone from the primary red to green in the vault of the Freemen's section of St Mary's Hall - where the ribs of the vault are red sandstone but all the infill is green - dates from about the first decade of the 15th century. All the green sandstone of the Benedictine Priory nave, aisles and cloister appears to be fifteenth century (I.S.).

Summary of Distribution of Patterns in the Large Tiles

Figures 137-140

The details of the distribution of the tiles is presented on Table 3. A plus sign indicates the presence of three or more tiles, and square brackets that only one tile seems to have been present. The following points arise from a consideration of this table.

1 One sixteen-tile pattern (3), the nine-tile pattern (7/15), two four-tile patterns (4 and 11), run throughout all structures. The sixteen-tile pattern 3, is particularly strong throughout, and nine-tile patterns 7/15 and four-tile pattern 11 are also well represented, implying they are basic patterns.

2 Looking next at the entries from both cloister and the chapter house, which continued through the choir as far as the crossing, the sixteen- and nine-tile patterns continue strongly represented and four-tile patterns (19 and 22) are also well represented in this sector; in addition endless-repeating tile (32a) and border tile (56) also occur throughout the sector and indicate that continuity existed through these areas. What is new is that there is a greater variety of four-tile patterns, probably due to the extra floor space available in both chapter house and choir, and an emphasis on endless-repeating patterns, perhaps used on graves; there is again nothing here to suggest a break between the style of tiling of the conventual buildings and the choir of the church, confirmed by the sameness of the floor mortar samples.

3 Running also through the entries beginning with the chapter house and this time taking them as far W as the nave, four-tile pattern 24, new in the chapter house, is still strongly represented in the nave, again indicating continuity from conventual buildings to nave.

4 Considering the entries for the church only, that is from choir to nave, there are three new sixteen-tile patterns in the choir, 12 occurring strongly and continuing into the nave, and 13 and 14 weakly in the choir alone. Presumably the basic lay-out continues, but more space enables a greater variety within that lay-out, without giving up the primary, larger, patterns. There are additionally five new four-tile patterns presumably relating to filling those larger spaces, 21, well represented, and 23, 25, 27 and 28, in the choir. There are also new single-repeating patterns, 39 well represented particularly in the crossing, and 40 and 41.

DISTRIBUTION OF PATTERNS OF LARGE EARLY TILES

	16-tile patterns Total 4				9-tile patterns Total 5						4-tile patterns Total 14													
	3	**12**	**13**	**14**	**6**	**7**	**15**	**16**	**17**	**18**	**4**	**5**	**11**	**19**	**20**	**21**	**22**	**23**	**24**	**25**	**26**	**27**	**28**	**29**
Prior's Lodging	3+				6	7	[15]				4a	5+	11											
Cloister including Gate	3+																22	23						
Reredorter	3+						15+						11				[22]							
Chapter House	3+						15+		17				11	[19]	20+		[22]		[24]		[26]			
Choir	3+	12+	[13]	[14]		7	15		17+		4a		11+	19+	20+	21+	22+	23	24	[25]	[26]	[27]	28	
Crossing	3+	12+					15	[16]	17+	[18]				19+			22	23						
Nave	3+	12+				7	15		17+		4a		11+						24+					[29]

DISTRIBUTION OF PATTERNS OF LARGE EARLY TILES

	Endless repeating patterns Total 9									Simple repeating large tiles Total 3		
	30	**31**	**32**	**33**	**34**	**35**	**36**	**37**	**38**	**39**	**40**	**41**
Prior's Lodging												
Cloister including Gate												
Reredorter			[32a]									
Chapter House	30+		32a		[34]	[35]						
Choir	30	31	[32a]	33+			36			39	[40]	[41]
Crossing			[32a]	[33]						39+		
Nave							36+	37+	38+	[39]		

Tiles 21 (4-tile pattern) and 50 (Heraldic) are recorded for the Sacristy

Numerous examples are indicated by ....+

Scarce examples are indicated by ....[ ]

Tiles lacking provenance are indicated by .....np

DISTRIBUTION OF PATTERNS OF LARGE EARLY TILES

	Single tiles Total 11											Heraldic tiles Total 5					Border tiles Total 4			
	1	**8**	**9**	**10**	**42**	**43**	**44**	**45**	**46**	**47**	**48**	**49**	**50**	**51**	**52**	**53**	**2**	**54**	**55**	**56**
Prior's Lodging		8	9	10																
Cloister including Gate	1+												[50]				2			[56d]
Reredorter	1+		9		42															
Chapter House	1+		9	10	[42]		44+				[48]						2			
Choir	1		9		42+	43+			[46]	[47]	[48]	49	50			np			[55]	[56]
Crossing	1		9					[45]	[46]			49+		[51]	[52]			[54]	[55]	[56]
Nave	[1]											49+	50+						55	56+

Table 2 Distribution of floor-tile patterns of large early types.

These may again come from graves, burials being numerous here. New single tile 43 and a new heraldic tile version 49 are both well represented, the latter continuing strongly through the crossing to the nave.

All this suggests enrichment of the basic framework as the space available increased (but one that did not involve new nine-tile patterns). The evidence does not suggest replacement.

5 In the nave there is a new four tile pattern 29, but nothing to indicate that the established pattern does not continue, Fig. 139.

THE CATALOGUE

Figures 137-140

Parallels are given for Warwickshire (Chatwin 1936), the Coventry Charterhouse (Soden, 1995), the Coventry Benedictine priory (Hobley 1971), the Coventry City Wall (Woodfield, C. 1966), Dudley Castle (Locock 1989), and Leicestershire (Whitcomb 1956). Examples from a limited number of counties' sites are quoted when tiles occur there in meaningful numbers. 'No local parallels' means that tiles are not matched in these publications. 'No Chatwin' means that they do not occur in Warwickshire and 'No Whitcomb' that they do not occur in Leicestershire, as recorded in 1936 and 1956 respectively. Simplified site provenances are listed in Tables 3-5. More specific provenances are retained in the text where they carry extra information. U/P indicates unprovenanced, and U/S unstratified. John Goodall's comments on the heraldry are quoted under his initials. The Woodfield numbers, preceded by W., and the Griffiths numbers, preceded by L, are given below in brackets to tie in to the archive, but normally not the Bateman Coventry Museum numbers. The term 'lost' indicates tiles and records that cannot now be found at Coventry Museum.

It should be noted that all tiles are stamped, not inlaid, and that the Charterhouse parallel tiles are probably in the main of the turn of the 14th and 15th centuries (its foundation date was 1385 (Soden 1995), forty-three years later than that of the Whitefriars, and a painting in the Charterhouse refectory records Prior Soland's completion of the work in 1417 (I.S.)). About a third of the tile types in this section appear to be paralleled at the Charterhouse.

As for spread of distribution of these tile patterns, some fifth of the Whitefriars tile stamps appear to be of types paralleled at Wormleighton, Warks, where the large tile, diagonally-laid phase is clearly to be seen, and, more surprisingly, about some fifth again are paralleled at Chastleton, Oxon, which has almost no tiles that could not be closely matched by those from the Whitefriars - (the tiles are there relaid), and at Bradgate House, Leics.

Some quarter of the tiles illustrated in this section appear to be hitherto unknown tiles or unknown die variants.

A Tiles of earlier 14th-century pattern-type, and size

Figure 137

Two designs occur on exceptionally large tiles for the site, (but they are the norm at e.g. earlier Tanworth in Arden); the designs look earlier 14th century in character, with their suggestion of an architectural origin, particularly tile 2 with the mouchette, and its distribution confirms a primary use.

1a, b (L104 W7). Four roundels containing two designs of eight-petal flowers.- 152 x 156 x 23mm. Poor stamp, slight wear. Nine whole, 1a, tiles, and one half tile cut as a rectangle, 1b, survived. Also four triangular halves, implying diagonal laying near a straight edge, presumably a wall - one of these from the E bay of the nave. Found throughout the site. No local parallels but relates to Chatwin 5.4.

2 (L22, W88). Scroll with circles containing three mouchettes, alternating with circles with foliage in quatrefoils. White edged border tile, 94 x 174 x 23mm. Chatwin fig. 30.2, no Charterhouse, no Whitcomb.

B 1 Primary Tiles Found *In Situ*

The tile floor in the 'Prior's House', Fig. 136. This presumably survived, patched and altered, until the *c.*1800 demolition. All tiles recorded in 1978 fell between 125mm and 135mm.

Sixteen-tile pattern as laid.

3 (L147 156 156a 157, 157a 159. W25A, 25b, 25C vars 1 and 2, 25D). Floral circle with holly berry corners containing a floral quatrefoil enclosing holly leaves. The holly leaves outline a central cross. A popular pattern spread over five counties, (and with many die variants additionally) cf. Chatwin 42.1 to 8, occurring at Kenilworth, Wormleighton, Chastleton (Oxon), and Longborough (Glos). Also in Northants. at Charwelton (pers. ob.), Preston Capes and Catesby (Dryden Collection, 1883, Northampton Library). In Leicestershire they occur at Bradgate House (Whitcomb 1956, 179). Also Charterhouse, fig. 29, and Coventry Benedictine priory, fig. 14, 26.

The variants of this pattern are here included below, as the small scale drawings of the tile floor make it impossible to know which variants were there in use.

3a (L147 W25D.1). Holly leaf spray forming outer corners of design. 128 x 126 x 28mm. An incomplete tile also occurred *in situ* in the N transept, but relaid secondarily relating to the insertion of wall tomb Grave 61.2, Fig. 141.

3b (L159 W25B.1). Formalised leaves, arcs, five-petalled flowers, circles forming top of design. 130 x 130 x 26mm and 125 x 128 x 24mm. A tile of this type was also *in situ* in the S chancel doorway, but relaid.

3c (L.157 W25b var. 1). Reversed version of 3b. 130 x 130 x 26mm and 125 x 128 x 24mm.

3d (L167 W25). Die with smaller-petalled flowers, side of design with different foliage.

3e (L156 W25A.1). Formalised holly berries and leaves forming centre. 130 x 130 x 26mm.

3f (L156 var.). Variant of 3a with small-petalled flowers, small central dot. 125mm.

Some ninety tiles of this large sixteen-tile pattern are known, some 50% *in situ*, and were recovered throughout the site.

Four-tile patterns in situ.

4a. (L109 W9). Three trefoil leaves in corners. Circle enclosing five five-petalled flowers. Centre four hearts with five-spoke wheel motifs, suspended from stems with five-petalled flowers at ends. (two tiles *in situ*). (?) x 122 x 23mm, centre motif in surviving floor. Two others in choir and E nave, 1977 U/P. Variant of Chatwin 20.17, Wormleighton, no Charterhouse, Whitcomb 1956, 200. A tile of this design, but not this die, occurs at the Bristol Whitefriars in the later 14th century (Stopford 1993, 100, fig. 7.16).

4b (L540A and 540). These are basically the same design. 1977, W of passage one, one U/S). Dudley Castle, 15.

4c (L540). 1997 U/P.

No no. The variety with the five-petalled flower, as Chatwin 20.17, was noted in the 1960s but is now lost.

5 (L564 small variant of large L79 W51, catalogue 23). Four-pointed star within an equal armed cross? Central small cross motif, Fig. 136. Flowers and trefoil leaves. Or (J.G. *in litt.*) 'possibly intended for *Ermine a chevron between 3 cinquefoils*, a coat found on a seal of John Fermer 1353-3 in the PRO'. The variant (No 23 below) is 126 x 130 x 21mm but this precise pattern survives otherwise on this site only as a small tile, 80. Four tiles *in situ*. Variant of Chatwin 13.5. No Charterhouse, no Whitcomb. (A recording error is possible here.)

B 2 Tiles Present In Early Floor But Not Now In Original Positions

Figure 137

Nine-tile patterns present but not as originally laid.

In both cases these were represented by one tile only, which could relate to later patching. However, the records in 1978 state that no tiles from the area were smaller than 125mm, and if all the tiles were of the large early type it may be more likely that they are original tiles, disturbed. It is not easy to see how a nine-tile pattern could be fitted in, though the lay-out may change to the W. However, alternating sixteen- and nine-tile patterns did occur at the Coventry Benedictine Priory frater undercroft, apparently of this date (pers. ob.).

6. (L56a W122.B). Circles with oak leaves and acorns. Presumably the W 122 Die Ab version at 124mm. One only in tile floor, Fig. 136. Chatwin 13.2, Chastleton, no Charterhouse, no Whitcomb. See No 61 for general description of this pattern.

7 (L78 W49B). Bands enclosing six-petalled flowers, four floppy triple-leaves outlining unknown central tile. 124mm. Chatwin fig. 31, no Charterhouse, no Whitcomb. This tile occurs at St John's Bablake, Coventry (pers. ob.). One only (but otherwise two known from the choir and W end of the nave), Fig. 141. At the Coventry Benedictine frater there is a similar (but not identical) pattern with Beauchamp as the central tile (pers. ob.).

Single tiles present but not as originally laid.

8 (L92 var. W60 var.). A bend between six covered cups, their bases towards the bend, with a cinquefoil on the bend for difference. J.G. comments 'The plain arms are recorded for Boteler of Warrington and Wem (N962 etc) but the cups should be upright in relation to the vertical axis of the shield and not at right angles to the bend as here. The difference does not seem to be recorded in the rolls'. This tile is presented here as it appears in Chatwin, Soden and Whitcomb, but is, heraldically speaking, as J.G. comments, shown upside down. Chatwin 39.1, Wormleighton. A version only of Charterhouse 11 and Whitcomb 173. This precise form is not recorded elsewhere on this site beyond this single example, see discussion under No 49 below. The Coventry link is presumably Robert the Butler of Randal, Earl of Chester, the cinquefoil equalling the second son.

9 (L118 W18). Catherine wheel, emblem of St Catherine of Alexandria, rather than a water wheel? It contains two confronting flower? motifs, and a rabbit opposite a bird, 125mm. Elsewhere known from the reredorter through to the crossing with two U/S from 1977. Chatwin 20.14, Chastleton, Charterhouse 34, Whitcomb 213 (Bradgate House), Dudley Castle 7.

10 Another wheel, not otherwise known from the site, was recorded by Bateman from the chapter house. The subject matter appears to be the same, but the forms are different. Chatwin 20.13, Wormleighton, no Charterhouse, no Whitcomb. At Wormleighton it is laid

as a four tile pattern (pers. ob.).

It is uncertain if this floor survives the 1980s landscaping.

C Four Tile Pattern Partly *In Situ*

Laid as a primary floor and diagonally as in the 'Prior's House' but here in the E bay of the nave (S nave chapel), Fig. 136.

11 (L.60 W37B). Octofoil containing eight torches? flames at corners? (or seed pods, leaves at corners?). 126 x 124 x 25mm and 129 x 127 x 27mm.

Seven out of the 1960s tiles of this pattern are in the nave. but in 1977 they occurred from reredorter to choir. No exact Chatwin, Charterhouse 81, Whitcomb 199 (Bradgate House). The two 11 tiles *in situ* at the E bay of the nave, Fig. 136, are laid on green sand, putting these at least into the Friary 2 early 15th-century sub phase, and we are here clear of the problem of fitting with the dating of the choir-stalls. There are two small versions L.61a/W 36, and L62/W37a, 79a and 79b, see below, so the pattern continues. One occurs in the NW nave tile feature, Fig. 141.

D Tiles Occurring In Large Sizes, Presumed Of Earlier Type

Whatever the distribution of small tiles from later patching (grave digging and rebuilding would have caused much destruction of the original lay-out) it seems extremely unlikely that workmen would set out to tile an intricate and quality floor with a radical difference in tile sizes of up to 3cm.

D 1 Other Sixteen-tile patterns in large tiles..

Figure 138

These occur thinly, although 12 makes a respectable showing. There is no doubt that pattern 3 above was the dominant early sixteen-tile pattern. No 12 appears to relate to the tiling of the choir, crossing and nave.

12a, 12b, 12c. (L18, 19, 63, W40a, 40b, 40c). Corner device of crown over ostrich feathers. J.G, writes 'probably decorative as the crowned ostrich feather badges were depicted upright supporting the crown. The ostrich feather variously differenced was used by most of Edward III's sons and their descendants and without the colours and other details cannot be assigned to anyone in particular'. Two ostrich feathers in a crown occurred as supporters on a lost misericord in St Michael's (Harris 1927, 264, pl. XXXII). The pattern continues as a band of quatrefoils containing flowers. Interior of design unknown. 125 x 125mm. In the 1960s seven examples, concentrating in the crossing, plus three built into the 62 IX tile feature at the NW corner of the nave; Fig. 141. Chatwin 41.9, Charterhouse 99, 100, Whitcomb 182.

The unused L19/W40b tile was stratified, 61 WF C(e), built into the mortar and tile bedding of the NE tower pier two, confirming its use before the second quarter of the 15th century.

13a (L158 W123). Six-petalled flowers in arcs enclosing large veined leaf. Large veined leaves in external corners. 125 x 123 x 27mm, well made. One only in choir (although one was recorded, reversed, 1977 U/S, now lost). Chatwin 42.16, no Charterhouse, no Whitcomb.

13b (W25c). One.

14 (L112 W13). Spray of trefoil leaves, presumably forming a twelve-leaf centre of a sixteen-tile design. Copper green splashing. 122 x 124mm. One only, choir. Corner fragment 164, (L 42 W.108) is possibly from an outer tile for this design. No local parallels.

D 2 Other nine-tile patterns in large tiles.

Figure 138

15 (L76 W49a lst var.). One tile of this pattern present in *in situ* tiled floor, see 7 above. Six-petalled flowers in band with inward projecting triangles, large corner fleur-de-lys. Throughout from reredorter through to church W end, and one half tile was built into the tile feature at the NW end of the church (Tr.61 IX). Chatwin 31, no Charterhouse, no Whitcomb. Similar, but not identical, tiles also occur in the Coventry Benedictine frater (pers. ob.).

16a (L55 W122Ab). Fruit? and large veined leaf in corners, circle containing scroll with acorns, acorns and oak leaves framing central square (central pattern unknown). Die distinguished by small polygonal acorn and small triangle at base of stem. One from crossing (61 XIII 3), last quarter of the 14th-century packing over N wall of transept. Chatwin 13.1, Chastleton, no Charterhouse, no Whitcomb. For small tiles in this pattern see 61.

16b (L54 var.).

17 A range of related patterns consisting primarily of fleur-de-lys and cables, sometimes with the addition of letters and flower and leaf motifs, and occurring also as a four tile pattern.

17a (L160 W29a, var. b). Corner tile, broken cable, fleur-de-lys, foliage. The large side tiles indicate the pattern would have had an interior motif of nine five-petalled flowers and eighteen formalised ?fleur-de-lys, with the usual vacant central space. A version of this is the only large side tile at the Charterhouse, 110, and is also present at Wormleighton (pers. ob.). The Whitefriars set appears to be different from any illustrated in Chatwin

fig. 9. 124 x 124 x 25mm. Choir through to W nave. Probably as Charterhouse 106. The general type, which occurs also as a small tile, occurs at Burton Dassett and Wormleighton (where the king, 43, is used as the central tile), and Bradgate House (Whitcomb 1956, 189).

17b (L542 W29a var.). Detail of corner of L.160 above.

17c (-- W29.1). Half tile, 124 x 124 x 23. Choir and crossing.

17d (L562 W29b var. b). Top tile as above. 125mm. W29b var. b, has a broken cable, and L562 a continuous one. This recording difference is probably due to wear. 1977, five in presbytery/choir. Charterhouse 110.

17e (L.14, W82). Variant corner of 17d above. One in chapter house.

17f(L.153 W29.4). Half tile, broken cable, ? corner letter 'i'. 124 x 121mm. Chatwin 9.3 indicates this is half of a large lettered fleur-de-lys corner tile. One stratified in 61 VI 4, phase Friary 2, i.e. early 15th century. Version of Charterhouse 107. Choir and crossing.

17g (W 29a). Half tile with fleur-de-lys. Die variant. 1977 U/S.

17h (L592). Version with distorted cable and fleur-de-lys. 124 x ? x 24mm. One only, 1977 U/P.

18a (L 'D'). Circle enclosing trefoil containing fleur-de-lys with trefoils. 1977 U/P. Parallels indicate a large nine-tile pattern, cf. Coventry Cathedral fig. 14.14, but no other local parallels.

18b (W114). Corner fleur-de-lys against band with worn remains of small lozenges. Possibly a corner of the above, 18a. Crossing, one. No precise parallels.

D 3 Other large four-tile patterns.

Figures 138-139

19a, b, c, d (L69, W43, 43a, 106). One 1977 U/P. Order of tiles uncertain. Four grinning green men/wodewose masks in corners, circle containing inscription surrounds four vine leaves and grapes, and four pomegranates? Eight-petalled flower in centre circle. Problems with heavy wear, but the inscription contains the word GAUDIA, and apparently MARIA, possibly some reference to the Seven Joys of Mary. Usual tile size 124mm. Six in tile pit in crossing. 19b is drawn from two overlapping tiles - one is unprovenanced but a 1973 find, so perhaps from the chapter house. 19d, corner, may be part of a 19a tile. No known parallels except tile from Coventry St Michaels used to elucidate drawing of 19a (formerly in possession of the late P. Helmsley).

20a (L532 W77b). A sophisticated pattern. Trefoil, fine crosses and foliage in corners. Circle containing octofoil with four sprays of leaves branching up from the bottom lobes, and four fleur-de-lys with trefoils. Central circle contains eight-petalled flower. Chapter house. Chatwin 42 is of same general type only. No Charterhouse, no Whitcomb.

20b (Variant of L532). Thinner arc, larger triangle at base of leaf spray. 1977 chapter house. Charterhouse 83.

If laid as a repeating pattern, a four-sided figure appears between the circles, with large leaves and trefoils, small quatrefoils, and with a central eight-sided figure with twelve dots. 126 x 125 x 20mm. 1960s one only, crossing pit. 1977 six in chapter house, five in presbytery.

21a (L113, 113a W17a). Ball and pinnacle design in corners, four pairs of confronting stags and birds, divided by arcs, central circle with four-petalled flower. 134 x 134 x 20mm, i.e. particularly large. Five in school acoustic passage in choir, one in sacristy, 1977 six in choir. No exact local parallels.

21b (L113 var.). Choir, one.

Figure 139

22 (L90 W58). Pinnacle like corners with leaves, cusped band enclosing four grotesque human headed monsters in an octofoil, (or can be read, and humour is relevant, as two frontal human faces being attacked by four creatures). Circle encloses four crowns with six-petalled central flower in circle. If the pattern is continued beyond four tiles, an elaborate four-petalled cusped device is formed between the circles. Derivative of mid 14th-century Chertsey type? A large tile, 135 x 133 x 22mm. Cloister to crossing. A complete but worn tile was in place in the packing for a soft area at the bottom of the resonance passage (Fig. 141 and Tracy 1977, fig. 4). Chatwin fig. 26.2, no Charterhouse, no Whitcomb.

23 (L79 W51). Possibly a four-pointed star within an equal armed cross. Central small cross motif; suns/?daisies, four-petalled flowers and trefoil leaves. J.G. comments 'if heraldic, perhaps intended for *Ermine a chevron between 3 cinque foils,* the "sun" being then probably an error by the tile maker' See note on No 5. 126 x 130 x 21mm. Cloister, including one from the Cloister Gate, through to the crossing. Chatwin 13.5, Chastleton, Charterhouse 88, Whitcomb 204, Bradgate House, Dudley Castle 18.

24 (L111 W15a). Foliage corner, wide band with letters read by Chatwin as WGWER reversed, but by J.G. as N E (reversed), W T (on side), ?W repeated four times. Four trees in central roundel. 127 x 125 x 25mm. Chapter house through to W end of nave. Also in the W end tile feature, Fig. 141 (but it is not known if the large

or small version as the 1962 tracing is lost, and the figure. has had to be reconstructed from photographs). 1977, chapter house? one. Dunning believed these letters to be, as others on Midland pottery, the initials of a prophylactic against sorcery (Dunning 1967, 240. I am grateful to Beverley Nenk for this reference) but this is uncertain. Chatwin 17.3, Chastleton, Charterhouse 73, Whitcomb 227, Bradgate House. A copper counter 'WGGER', which may relate in some way, was published in Woodfield, 1981, 124.

D 4 Sparsely represented large four tile patterns.

Figure 139

25 (L64 W39b). Incomplete. Stalked trefoils between two dotted arcs. Central roundel encloses cross of four trefoils. (?) x 122 x 22mm. No local parallels. One unworn tile in resonance passage.

26. (L168 W31a). Formalised leaves in corners, circle containing white triangles, curious bunched ?fleur-de-lys in centre. 127 x 24 x 26mm. Chapter house, choir. Chatwin 43.7, Wormleighton, no Charterhouse, no Whitcomb. A smaller version with a narrower chevron band also existed.

27 (L105 W6). Formalised leaves in corners, black circle with white lozenges encloses four outlined five-petalled flowers surrounded by outlined leaves? Reversed slip. Tile worn. One only, resonance passage. 123mm. Chatwin 19.2, Burton Dassett (a small version with a different die), no Charterhouse, no Whitcomb.

28 (L576). Corner unknown, band of anvil shapes, with quatrefoils in field, enclosing octofoil with small quatrefoils and perhaps part of a fleur-de-lys as 20a? Size uncertain but the design requires a large tile. 1977, two, presbytery and choir. No local parallels.

29 (L106a). Circle with irregular squares/lozenges, enclosing leaves and trefoils. Floppy leaf in corner. 125mm. One, tile pit at W end, and in the NW nave tile feature, Fig. 141. Version only of Chatwin 11.1, no Charterhouse, no Whitcomb.

D 5 Large 'endless repeating' patterns

Figure 139

These seem to have a particular relationship to the chapter house, perhaps for graves?

30 (L580). Guilloche of large and small circles, the large containing four double-vine sprays, and the smaller an eight-petalled flower with sepals. Reversed pattern in the field of four sprays of oak leaves enclosing a circle around an octofoil. 123mm. Chapter house. eleven, 1977 presbytery, two. No local parallels.

31 (L588). Rows of circles, one plain containing eight trefoil leaves, one with fifty-two dots containing a foliage scroll. 120mm. Choir. No local parallels.

32a (L512 W26). Interlacing circles with quatrefoils and trefoils. A half tile 32b found unstratified in 1977 suggests that this also related initially to diagonal laying. The pattern could of course be read as a single tile. 127mm. One relaid straight against the NE transept wall by the wall tomb, Grave 61.2, Fig. 141. Reredorter and four in the chapter house, through to the crossing. Chatwin 22.2, Charterhouse 44, no Whitcomb.

33 (L581 W59/67). Broken cable enclosing eight-petalled flowers and lions'head/?grotesque mask occurring alternately in diagonal lines, four-petalled flowers in the field. 132 x 130 x 21mm. Choir to crossing. No local parallels.

34 (L579). Complex design of interlocking circles, spirals, etc. with rows of circles containing four clips? where lines cross, with quatrefoils and dots. 124 x ? x 20mm. One only, from the chapter house. No local parallels.

35 (L557). Six-petalled flower within circle with four fleur-de-lys, all within a square. Whole within a circle with foliage trails. Smaller circles with nine-petalled flowers in the field. Only known as a large tile. One only, in the chapter house. Chatwin fig. 1.5, no Charterhouse, Whitcomb 104, Bradgate House.

D 6 Large 'endless repeating' patterns covering subsided grave *64.31*

Figure 139

In the E bay of the nave (64 XVIIa 3) against the N wall, Fig. 141.

Dark green and cream tiles and half tiles had clearly originally formed part of the layout. The disturbance seems to indicate reuse of an earlier grave, with an incompetent attempt to replace the tiles. The tiles were used together without any apparent perceived difficulty with their difference in detail. They may well have been designed to do so. The presence of seventeen half tiles (eight patterned, nine plain) suggests that this grave carpet had been fitted into an originally diagonally-laid pattern. The design of these tiles seemed alien, but they were present at Dudley Castle with other Coventry material. The fabric analysis relates them to the mosaic tiles 122, and thus to the Stoke kiln.

36 (L167 W32). Interlocking circles producing additionally stars, squares, vesicas and other shapes. Acorns and oak leaves sprout from these figures. Eight whole and six half tiles, poorly stamped. Some wear. 122 x 120 x 25mm. Additionally and exceptionally for this group, two whole and one half tile were found,

perhaps strays, in the choir resonance passage. Dudley Castle 29.

37 (L172 W33a). Intersecting circles as above, but with berries? and central cross of five dots. Reverse slip. 123 x 123 x 25mm. Slight wear, poor stamp. Four whole tiles and one half. Grave 64.31 only. Dudley Castle 8 has this pattern, reversed, i.e. matching 36.

38 (L171 W33). 123 x 123 x 27mm. Intersecting circles as above, but with ?pears. Reverse slip. Three whole and one half tile.

This grave group also included plain tiles - there being eight whole plain 'black' tiles and six half 'black'; four plain 'white' tiles and one 'white' half tile. No immediately local parallels.

D 7 Simple repeating large tiles

Figure 139

Rare, Could be used singly or as fours, etc.

39 (L149 W27b). Dotted circles enclosing six-petalled flowers, quatrefoils in field. 125 x 118 x 20mm. Two in resonance passage, four in E crossing. One built into 61 IX tile footing at NW nave, Fig. 141. None in 1977. Version of Chatwin 23.9, no Charterhouse, Whitcomb 209, Bradgate House, Northampton Greyfriars (Swann 1952, 4, no 18).

40 (L83 W55). Fleur-de-lys in diagonally set rectangle, quatrefoils at corner of square and in main tile. Two half leaves each corner for foliage background. 123 x 123 x 21mm. One tile only, W choir. Relates to Chatwin 41.13, Charterhouse 38, no Whitcomb.

41 (L224 W53). Lys in diagonal square, quatrefoils and dots in outer square and at tile corners. Half leaves again to provide foliage field in form of eight-sided figure with alternate trefoils and lys. 125 x 123 x 23mm. One tile only in resonance passage. Chatwin 41.13, no Charterhouse, no Whitcomb.

D 8 Single tiles.

Figures 139-140

42 (L103 W1). Traditionally described as the Cross as an anchor? Father Bertram describes it as a cross with an O rune meant to represent a cross with pennants flying, the original rune having been forgotten. The cross is set diagonally, five-petalled flowers in two corners, now with the letters j and n??. These are said (Chatwin fig. 20.16) to stand for Jesus of Nazareth, with the cross symbolising the Resurrection. Bertram believes the initials to be JU or JV. Alternatively, J.G. suggests that it is 'a merchant's mark between the initials d r? It was not in Elmhirst's collection published by the Harleian Society'. Also at Coventry St Michaels and at Chastleton. Reredorter, chapter house to choir. Charterhouse 33, no Whitcomb.

43 (L170 W34). Crowned king's bust, holding a flower in the right hand and a ? jester's rattle in the left, or is it an orb? It is used as the centre piece of the 17 nine-tile design at Wormleighton, but would make a four-tile pattern or could be laid alternating with plain tiles. 125 x 127 x 20mm. Five pieces in the choir. Chatwin 20.16, Chastleton, Wormleighton, Charterhouse 43, no Whitcomb, Dudley Castle 5.

44 (L577). Circle enclosing quatrefoil with four vine leaves, six-petalled flower at centre. Trefoils in corners. 122 x 121 x 21mm. Chapter house only, four. No local parallels.

45 (L11 W80). A heart (possibly the Sacred Heart?) within a circle, stylised fleur-de-lys at corners. 123 x 121 x 21mm. One only from area of SE tower pier. Charterhouse 29? No other local parallels.

46 (L.26 W92). Large fleur-de-lys set diagonally on plain tile. 120 x 120 x 24mm, i.e. on border line of 'large' category. One, very worn, in fill of grave 68.13, choir, below the upper interment, one crossing. Similar to City Wall fig. 12, H, in a 15th century deposit (Woodfield, C. 1966), Chatwin 10.18, no Charterhouse, no Whitcomb.

47 (L 'L'). Single-handled altar vase?, holding lily, the emblem of the Virgin Mary. Scatter of sixteen letters ?meaningless? 120mm. Stoke kiln. 1977 one only, choir. Chatwin fig. 1.6, no Charterhouse, no Whitcomb.

48 (L558). Lion rampant and heart. 122 x 122mm. Also a complete tile from the site in the Shelton collection at Coventry. Chapter house one, one S of choir. Chatwin fig. 1.3, no Charterhouse, no Whitcomb.

D 9 Large heraldic tiles

Figure 140

It is noteworthy that there are no parallels between the heraldry on the tiles, and the heraldry on the commissioned choir stalls. It is just possible that the horseshoe tile 96 may relate to the Ferrers roof boss from the choir, but this is uncertain.

49 (L92 W60). Additional to the tile recorded under No 8 above with the central cinquefoil. *A bend between six covered cups their bases towards* the bend. Boteler of Warrington and Wem. Trefoils and leaves in corners. It is possible that the apparent anomaly of this version (no parallels) with the plain band is due to missing fragments/wear. 126mm. W choir, crossing and nave. A version of this tile with a central star was listed by Bateman as occurring S of the choir. Chatwin gives two versions (fig. 39.1 and 2), one occurring on the tile floor

here (No 8) and at Wormleighton, the other at Chastleton. We have many parallels with both churches and both are likely to have occurred here. No Charterhouse, no Whitcomb.

50 (L84 W56 Die 1). Diagonally set shield, with arms of Beauchamp, Earls of Warwick. J.G. comments '*A fess between six plain crosslets*, apparently a carelessly made version (e.g. the tiler has added an extra crosslet). Found elsewhere in the county, which is surprising as it might have been thought that the correct coat would have been too familiar to be so ill done' I.S. comments 'Even the tile in the antechamber of the Beauchamp Chapel is "inaccurate". There is very little accurate tile heraldry in the sense of that which might pass muster in the College of Heralds'. Quarter of a four-petalled flower in the top corner indicates these tiles are laid with the top of the shields forming a square around a four-petalled flower, the shields then also forming a four-petalled flower shape. Circle and foliage motifs in two corners. 127 x 126 x 25mm. SE cloister through sacristy and choir to nave at W end, where there are four. Chatwin 25.2, Wormleighton, Chastleton, Charterhouse 4, Coventry Cathedral 10; Whitcomb does not have this version.

51 (L8 W72). Diagonally set shield, with eagle, head here turned to the sinister. Leaves in three corners. Arms of Leofric Earl of Mercia for the Benedictine Priory. 125 x 17mm, very thin. One only, crossing, none 1977. Chatwin 25.7, Charterhouse 20; also Ford's Hospital (Chatwin 1941-2).

52 (L88 W57). J.G. comments. 'The fragment is not wholly clear but appears to be: two chevrons and a sinister canton, only recorded with the canton in the dexter corner for Fitton, Moberley and Orby, and also for Criol or Kyriell'. 120 x 15-19mm, very thin. Heavy graining over the pipe clay areas. Intermediate size. One N transept, none 1977. Three different corner motifs, a formalised leaf at the top, a dotted crescent in one corner, and a dotted quarter of an eight-petalled flower in the other (see Charterhouse no 18 for complete version, where Clare (anachronistic) and Fitzwalter of Daventry are suggested). No other precise parallels.

53a (L53 W118). Tile 3 from a four-tile representation. J.G. comments 'Since the heads of all the beasts are missing it is not possible to say whether they were lions passant or leopards. It looks more likely that there were only two beasts'. 123 x 120mm. Drawn from two overlapping tiles. Handed in by a member of the public in 1969. The relationship of the pattern to the tiles is not the same as Chatwin 27, 1-4. No parallels from the Charterhouse and the Whitcomb version is different again.

53b (L53 HAGM). Tile 2, as above. 1977 U/S.

Border tiles

Figure 140

These seem to fall almost entirely in the smaller, later, category of tiles, but there are three tiles with uncut quarters which fall into an intermediate size range. Two have heraldic and floral devices, both at 121mm.. and one is an uncut letter tile at 121mm.

It seems likely that lettering was hardly in use on the primary floors at the Coventry Whitefriars.

54. (L133 W22.1 var.). a T, a Q? an R? and an unidentifed letter. (?) x 121 x 20mm. Crossing, one only, stratified in a Pre-rebuild context (61 WF A (e), presumed residual. None in 1977. No local parallels.

55 (L584). Uncut and unscored. Four quarter tiles of an eagle (cf. 51), a six-petalled flower, a fleur-de-lys and unknown, all presumably heraldic. 121mm. Chapter house one, 1977 choir one. Chatwin 32 includes the eagle quarter. No Charterhouse, no Whitcomb.

56a (L123 W20a/20b). Uncut. J.G. comments 'Shield with a chevron, presumably for Stafford, opposite shield with four chevrons, given for Every (RB 495)'. Elsewhere in Coventry Stafford is represented by their knot (I.S.) Also eight-petalled and seven-petalled flowers, opposing. 121 x 119 x 21mm. Intermediate size . Three in crossing. Cf. Chatwin 32 for eight-petalled flower. No Charterhouse, no Whitcomb.

56b Quarter tile shield with one chevron (Stafford?) as cut from above. The design relates to that on border tile 129. 57 x 58mm. 1977 U/P No parallels.

56c Opposing shield. Every? (tile now lost) recorded from the chapter house and S of the choir in 1977. Chatwin 38.7.

56d (WT 112). Die variant of flower quarter, showing crack damage. Poor stamp, little wear. One, W cloister.

A large tile with a non-symmetrical pattern new to the corpus. and another new tile from a four-tile pattern, with ten dots or perhaps trefoils enclosing a flower or leaf - a version of Chatwin 19.3, occurred *in situ* in the W end tile feature, Fig. 141. Another apparently new white-bordered tile carried the letters L, G (badly worn, drawing in archive).

2 THE SMALL TILES, BORDER TILES, AND TILES OF UNKNOWN SIZE

Figures 140-142 and Tables 4-5

Discussion

It appears therefore that large tiles were used over an area which certainly included the conventual buildings and the church at least as far W as the easternmost bays of the nave, and probably through much of the rest of the nave (the central four bays were largely inaccessible due to tenant hostility): it is also clear that these were laid diagonally to the walls. This scheme seems likely to continue to about 1400. The sequence of tile laying through the later 15th century is indicated below.

Evidence from stratified smaller (below 120mm) tiles

Figures 138-140, 143-145 and 147

Small tiles were found stratified in Friary 2/Pre-rebuild contexts, four from the crossing and one in the SW corner of the chancel. Two were slight variants of the nine-tile pattern 63 (W29a var. a, and W29b) with a large tile predecessor, 17; there was also 103, a heraldic tile, and 60, a new four-tile pattern in a thin linear style. These were all in secondary floor make-up. Tile fragment 171c was built into the secondary step in the NE transept. These presumably relate to retiling after the extensive strengthening works of this phase and suggest a date in the second quarter of the 15th century for their appearance. They seem likely to continue to the end of the century, if we accept the identification of 111a as the arms of Bishop Smith of Coventry in 1491.

Small tiles *in situ*, and the evidence of tile matrices

Small tiles still related to diagonal-laying in the extreme NW corner of the nave, Fig. 141, although here as a footing or setting, perhaps for a holy water stoup?, not as a laid patterned floor. This feature (62 IX 2) as far as can be told from photographs, (the contemporary tracing having been lost), by now contained tiles in both sizes, but with more patterns in the smaller size; however four large tile patterns were still present, represented by a 32a of the 'endless repeating' type, four tiles of the sixteen-tile 12 pattern, one of nine-tile pattern 15, and a new unrecognised pattern. Six patterns in the smaller size occurred; two of the smaller tiles were unused, (both of them from four-tile patterns which had again previously occurred in the large size) that is 71 and 79a. In addition small tiles 66a and 97 were present, and two unrecognised small patterns. It seems, therefore, that this feature was constructed at a transitional period for tile sizes, when there was a movement towards smaller tiles, but before the fashion for laying square to the walls had come in. The date for the construction of the W end is likely to be in the 15th century, probably in the second quarter.

Square-laying replacing diagonal-laying

At the sunken grave 64.31 in the eastern bay of the nave, Fig. 141, large tiles, 36, 37 and 38, were laid straight in order to make a rectangular carpet for the grave (but the presence of intermingled plain square and triangular tiles indicates the previous presence of a diagonally laid floor, presumably involving the surviving tiles). There was no direct dating evidence.

Square-laying combined with diagonal-laying

The square-laid tiles preserved in part as a matrix and in part as worn tiles in the crossing, Fig. 141, are six tiles to a 760mm length, (as opposed to six tiles to a 775mm length in the first bay of the nave described below) and presumably represent bedding for small tiles. The reason for this strip, originally at least three tiles wide and eight tiles long, presumably laid into the original diagonal large tiling which seems not to survive here, is not clear. They may simply be a patch representing a change of fashion in tiling, but it is possible that they might originally have been some form of processional marker. The make-up over which these are laid, 62 VI 11, is of the Friary 2/Pre-rebuild phase, tying in the appearance of these small tiles with a new laying pattern following close on the old. Presumably the mixture of tile sizes and laying patterns was short lived. The presence of triangular half tiles in small tile pattern 63, implying diagonal-laying, is again evidence for an overlap. They are again the only patterned small half tile at Burton Dassett (pers. ob.).

The diagonal-laid mixed tiles which surrounded this strip appear to be very late patching and are described below.

Square-laying

A small tile from a four-tile pattern, 65, occurred *in situ* in Trench XVIIa (1), the easternmost first bay of the nave, at the entrance to the N chapel, with some fifteen others loose in the same general area. The *in situ* tile was laid square to the building, although this was on a step, Fig. 142). The tile matrix to its W appeared, with six tiles in a 775mm strip, to represent an original floor of large tiles laid diagonally. Presumably these pattern 65 tiles represent a later retiling of the Pre-rebuild, post 1423 phase, for the work of buttressing the NW tower pier would have damaged the primary floor.

Contemporary with this, the detailed recording in 61 VI of a surviving eleven-tile matrix pattern, being patching after the parallel strengthening of the NE tower pier, Fig. 141, indisputably showed small size tiles laid straight to the building. There was one tile impression only of 121mm size. This matrix is again of the Pre-rebuild phase, implying a period later than the second quarter of the 15th century.

The relaid floor over the inserted 15th-century wall tomb construction trench, Grave 61.2, in the NE transept, Fig.

141, again reused a large tile, 32a, and a large half tile, 3e, but included the stag and bird tile of intermediate size, 73a, and a small Maltese cross tile, 94. This seems to confirm the contemporaneity of straight-laying with small tiles.

Very late patching

The other, diagonally-laid, tiles in the area E of the second SW tower pier - an area which was much disturbed by alterations in the building plan, and by grave digging - are certainly in part late patching, for they overlie the mouldings of the second SW tower pier, and were a scrappy mixture of large and small sizes and cut pieces, Fig. 141. They must have been relaid late on in the history of the building when money for tiling was hard to come by, for not only are they a bodge of roughly cut fragments but they were all worn completely smooth without trace of glaze or pattern. The continuation of diagonal-laying is probably due to the form of the tower pier, and is presumably 16th-century in date. I.S. further suggests that large numbers of burials and re-use of graves, due to the epidemics of the time, made new floors a waste of money.

Equally rough and worn late patching occurred in the N transept against the E wall, (61 VIII and IX), Fig. 142.

The shape of the small rectangle of six tiles, laid square in the bottom of the S resonance passage, (Fig. 141; Tracy 1997, fig. 4; Woodfield 1981, 118), was perhaps dictated by the form of the soft place in the rock floor that it was designed to fill, for acoustic purposes, but even so it still shows the relationship of straight-laying and small, or mixed, tiles. It contained a 22 large four-tile pattern of early type, and a small, very worn, heraldic two-chevron tile, 99, making this some late medieval activity, probably relating to work on the choir stalls after the mid 15th-century fall of the tower. The presence of small plain tiles here should be noted; there is not enough evidence to establish how they were used in the church, however.

A small area of tiles was recorded on a visit to the site in 1970, laid square in the S of the choir (70 XXIX 19) in the doorway to the sacristy passage, Fig. 43. Their position is possibly post-medieval in view of the survival of this passage into the late 18th century. This appeared to represent very rough patching, including the reuse of a single sixteen-tile pattern 3b with otherwise plain or worn material. However, to the N in the later 1970s (unfortunately the only tile matrix recorded by the Museum) lay a square mortar matrix, representing some eight tiles, tile size unclear, and this is presumably late medieval. It shows that there had been two parallel rows of tiles laid square to the S choir wall, i.e. not the primary pattern as recorded at the Prior's House, nor partially at the S end of the cloister, where again there was only one row of tiles laid square to the walls, Fig. 136. Clearly relaying of floors took place in the choir.

DISTRIBUTION OF PATTERNS OF SMALL, LATER TILES

	New 16-tile patterns = 1 + 1?				New 9-tile patterns = 1			4-tile patterns						
	Total 4				Total 3			Total 18 (5 new versions of old patterns and 13 new patterns)						
	57 (Old 3)	58 (Old 3)	59 ?	60	61 (Old 6)	62 (Old 7/15)	63 (Old 17)	64	65	66	67	68	69	70
Prior's Lodging														
Cloister including Gate							[63]							
Reredorter														
Chapter House						[62]					[67]		[69]	
Passage to Sacristy						[62]		64+			67			
Choir		[58]	[59]	[60]	61+	62+	63+	64+	65+	[66]		68+	[69]	np
Crossing		[58]	[59]	[60]		62+	63+	[64]		[66]				np
Nave			[59]				63+		65+					np
Nave, west end	[57]					[62]	63+			66				

	4-tile patterns (cont.)											
	71 (Old 24)	72	73 (Old 21)	74	75	76	77	78	79 (Old 11)	80 (Old 5)	81	82
Prior's Lodging												
Cloister including Gate												
Reredorter												
Chapter House										[80]		
Passage to Sacristy							77+					
Choir	71+	72+	[73]		[75]	[76]	77	np	78+	80+	[81]	np
Crossing	[71]	72	73					np				
Nave				[74]				np	79+			
Nave, west end				74	[75]				[79]		81	

Table 4 Distribution of floor-tile patterns of small later types (16, 9 and 4 tile patterns).

Numerous examples are indicated by ....+

Scarce examples are indicated by ....[ ]

Tiles lacking provenance are indicated by .....np

This sequence of large tiles laid diagonally to the walls being replaced by small tiles laid square to the walls is borne out by a comparison of the large, early, diagonally laid tiles at Wormleighton with the small tiles at Burton Dassett, where, despite some tidying up after the discovery of the tiles under a timber floor in the 1890s (O'Haughnessy *c.*1987, 12), much of the original floor survives. The large tiles at Chastleton were relaid in the 19th century, but the Victorian replacement in the choir appears to relate to the original diagonal-laying.

Note that in the W range of the cloister a very small 88mm square fleur-de-lys tile, Fig. 146.128, crudely made with a crude stamp, occurred stratified in a Rebuild context, 68 XXVII 16. This may imply a 15th-century date for this exceptional size.

Tables 4 and 5 show that the distribution of these smaller patterns concentrates in the choir, crossing and nave, there being only a scatter of single tiles in the cloister, reredorter and chapter house, where they may well be strays as none of them were in stratified contexts, though in the chapter house the combination of 108 and 109 might just represent intended eagles, and 112 and 113 are new shields probably with the intended arms of Astley, and there are again endless-repeating tiles, now types 120 and 121, Fig. 145.

Pattern of occurrence of small tiles throughout the church

There is little evidence for the use of smaller, later, tiles in the conventual buildings. In the church it is to be assumed that we are dealing with a series of repairs, relayings after building works and burials - these will be widespread over a considerable period of time, be small scale, and possibly not related to any overall concept.

Small tiles in the choir

There are no significant numbers indicating the continuation of the use of sixteen-tile patterns into the small tile phase.

With nine-tile patterns in the choir there is a very strong presence of 63 (cable and fleur-de-lys, a new version of type 7/15); its continued use of triangular tiles suggests that it is of transitional date; also nine-tile patterns 61 and 62 are well represented - a new version of the acorn pattern, indicating a desire for visual continuity, Figs 140 and 143.

With four-tile patterns, three were reasonably represented, 71, 79 and 80, copying old types, and five new patterns, 64, 65, 68, 72, and 76 reflecting a movement of fashion to these, Figs 143-144.

New single-tile patterns, now copious, included 83, the dancer, and fashionable heraldic tiles 92, 103, 106, 108 and 115; there is also an increased fashion for small lettered-tiles, some fifteen small capital letters *in toto* being from the choir, (as probably were most of the unprovenanced small letters), Figs 144-146. They are likely to have surrounded graves.

It appears that considerable re-flooring took place in the choir, presumably as a result of burials, damage from subsidence and falling masonry at the W, and the insertion of the ?reredos wall.

Small tiles in the crossing

Figures 143-145

Much patching would be expected from the many graves and rebuildings. Again there is no convincing appearance of sixteen-tile patterns; but there is again a strong presence of the nine-tile patterns 62 and 63, and a slight presence of four-tile patterns 64, 72 and 73. Monograms 86 and 87, for Maria and Christus, are new types, as are the horseshoe 96, perhaps a prophylactic, or perhaps related to Ferrers, whose arms appear on a vault boss; also the bear and ragged staff, 97, for Beauchamp, and 110, the arms of Edward the Confessor for Westminster Abbey are well represented in the SE transept, the last perhaps related to an altar. Type 111, the arms of William Smith, Bishop of Lichfield and Coventry in 1491, seems to carry the friars' ability to purchase new floor tiles into the late 15th century. Several stylistically late-looking border tiles of large formalised leaves, 124, came from the pulpitum area. Much of this seems likely to relate to later 15th-century reflooring and the setting up of new altars, etc., after the structural problems of the mid 15th century.

Small tiles in the nave

Figures 143-145

Again sixteen-tile patterns in small tiles are virtually absent, but in nine-tile patterns the new, inevitable 63, lys and cable, continues right through to the W end, as does four-tile pattern 79b, a version of old 11, with a cluster in the E bay of the nave; new four-tile pattern 74, for Beauchamp. continues to the W end, and 65 is well represented, known throughout the nave eastwards from its position *in situ*, with sixteen other examples in the vicinity, at the entrance to the N nave chapel.

In single tiles, 86, the Maria monogram, continues well represented, with six within the N nave chapel, presumably identifying the known chapel of Our Lady; No 97, Beauchamp's bear and ragged staff continues to the W end. Other heraldic tiles 111, Bishop William Smith, occurs with five throughout the nave, and 112, Astley, occurs as four in the E nave; 115, Leofric's eagle, for the Benedictine Priory, is also well represented.

The prevalence of Beauchamp, Earl of Warwick, tiles throughout is noteworthy.

	DISTRIBUTION OF PATTERNS OF SMALL, LATER TILES															
	Single Tiles															
	Total 39 (38 new types)															
				Monograms (5 new types)						Semi-heraldic (6 new types)						
	83	84	85	86	87	88	89	90	91	92	93	94	95	96	97	98
Prior's Lodging	n	o	n	e												
Cloister including Gate																
Reredorter																
Chapter House																
Passage to Sacristy																
Choir	83+		[85]			[88]	[89]			92	[93]		[95]			
Crossing	[83]	[84]	[85]	86+	87		[89]			[92]		[94]	[95]	96	97	[98]
Nave			[85]	86+						[92]					97	
Nave, west end														[96]	[97]	

Numerous examples are indicated by ....+

Scarce examples are indicated by ....[ ]

Tiles lacking provenance are indicated by .....np

	DISTRIBUTION OF PATTERNS OF SMALL, LATER TILES																						
	Single Tiles																					Endlessly Repeating	
	Total 39 (38 new types)																						
	Heraldic (Total 21: 20 new types																					Total 2 (new)	
	99	100(Old 52)	101	102	103	104	105	106	107	108	109	110	111	112	113	114	115	116	117	118	119	120	121
Prior's Lodging																							
Cloister including Gate		[100]																					
Reredorter																							
Chapter House						[104]				[108]	[109]			[112]	[113]							[120]	[121]
Passage to Sacristy			[101]												[113]		115						
Choir	[99]			[102]	103+	[104]	[105]	106		108			[111]			np	115+	[116]	np		[119]		
Crossing					[103]	[104]						110+	111+			np			np				
Nave					[103]									112+		np	115		np	[118]			
Nave, west end	[99]								[107]				111										

Table 5 Distribution of floor-tile patterns of small later types (single tiles and endlessly-repeating tiles).

Other sites

Figures 138-140, 143 and 145

Some quarter of the small tiles are of die stamps shared with the Charterhouse. The conspicuous parallels that existed in the large tile category with Wormleighton and Chastleton have now totally vanished.

Burton Dassett, although the floor is in some disarray, gives an indication of what is to be expected in Warwickshire 15th-century tiled floors. Here, significantly, all the known tiles look to be small, Chatwin recording one small sixteen-tile pattern (as at Whitefriars, a small version of the popular earlier holly pattern, our 57). Observation on site shows that it is very sparsely represented, however. Chatwin records only one nine-tile pattern, a version of our 63c, which is actually present in some quantity (C.W.).

Four-tile patterns are the most common at Burton Dassett, (and they include heraldic tiles laid as fours) at least ten patterns in all being represented. There are four obvious four-tile patterns, three being small versions of our large tiles 20b (pers. ob.- not recorded by Chatwin), 22 and 27. Our 69 is also present, previously unrecorded, and there is also an unrecorded four-tile pattern with an inscription. However, the main body of tiles at Burton Dassett are small heraldic tiles, of which at least six are represented - all with the shields diagonal to the tile: a Stafford knot, a chevron, and an heraldic lion as our 107, and inspection suggests the presence of at least three other heraldic tiles, many of the Chatwin fig, 24.17 pattern.

The layout at Burton Dassett therefore seems originally to have consisted largely of four-tile patterns, and heraldic tiles laid as fours, on a plain ground. All tiles here are laid straight to the walls. This is perhaps a version of what we are seeing, through a glass darkly, for the Coventry later tiling phases.

Small tile catalogue

Figures 140-146

It is to be assumed that we are dealing with a series of relayings after building works and burials in the church (there is little evidence for new floor tiling in the conventual buildings) presumably spread over a considerable period of time, of relatively small scale, and not necessarily related to any overall concept. Too much early tile survives to postulate a complete relaying.

There is, as Burton Dassett would suggest, an increase in four-tile patterns, most noticeably heraldic and semi-heraldic tiles, monograms, and an explosion of small letters (some also occurring unrecorded at Burton Dassett), reflecting the fashions of the time. There is an overall sharp decline in the number of sixteen-tile-pattern tiles, but two versions of old forms carry on; the apparently new sixteen-tile patterns are represented by a single tile of that pattern only and may be from a job lot, although they indicate continued manufacture. One certainly, and possibly both may represent old designs. The nine-tile patterns that survive are all of old styles, and presumably come from the intermediate phase. There are some eighty new patterns.

Sixteen-tile patterns

Figure 140

57 (L154/W25c var. 2). Formalised leaf, and attenuated five-petalled flowers in band - small tile version of the common large tile holly leaf design, No 3 in the catalogue. One from the College of Art huts in Whitefriars Street to the W of the site, so not necessarily from the church (though it may be from the tile dump with very large numbers of whole tiles, partially recorded in 60 V, but reported by Rupert Williamson in 1996 to the writer as being destroyed in unwatched late 1960s/70s road works). 117mm. Charterhouse fig. 29 var, no exact Chatwin but Whitcomb 180?

For distribution on site, see Tables 4 and 5. Some extra notes on distribution are given in the text.

58a (L95/W64b var.). Outer band of five-petalled flowers, dotted bands and trefoil leaves - a development of the holly leaf design, using different foliage. No exact Chatwin, perhaps an intermediate form? An example occurred on the City wall at King Street, said to be from the 15th-century wall footings (Woodfield, C. 1966, fig. 7.I). One tile, NE transept, one 1977 choir area. 116mm.

58b (Var. die). Smaller leaves and trefoil. Chatwin 18, Burton Dassett, Charterhouse 116, Whitcomb 184b, Bradgate House.

58c (L95 var.). (A leaf motif has presumably worn away in the corner). Unknown provenance.

59a (L3 W64di). Twelve leaves within a quatrefoil, presumably the centre of a sixteen-tile pattern; no obvious candidates for the twelve enclosing tiles. 112mm. Di, four, between the W choir and the E bay of the nave; Dii, one. No local parallels.

59b (W64dii, die var.). N transept, one.

60 (L9 W71a). Dotted quatrefoil containing foliage, (centre pattern is a large floriated cross), enclosed by a foliage scroll within bands. Attenuated linear style. From the S crossing and choir - may relate to reflooring after strengthening of the SE tower pier. 118 x 115mm. Chatwin 15.8. No Charterhouse, relates to Whitcomb 183 (Bradgate House).

Nine-tile patterns

The distribution is largely choir and crossing.

Smaller versions of earlier types

The centre tile for all these designs is unknown.
The presence of small triangular tiles for various versions of pattern 17, indicate that that small tile pattern may still have been laid diagonally. These triangular tiles were also present at Burton Dassett.

61a (L.54 W122 Aa). Circle containing scroll with small leaves and acorns within bands; spray with unidentified leaves and fruit in corners. 112 x 112mm. Three in choir and one from the Hobley 1973 excavations (possibly chapter house but all records are lost). On this die the red triangle under the fruit extends up to the leaf junction and there is a distinctive notch in the lower arc. Version of Chatwin fig. 13.1-3 series. No Charterhouse, no Whitcomb.

61b (L56 W122 Bi). As above, leaves and acorns below lower band. 110 x 113mm. Ten examples from the choir.

Figure 143

62a (L75 W49a 2nd var.). Small version of No 15 above. Eighteen six-petalled flowers in cusped bands, fleur-de-lys in external corners, floppy trefoil below band. 110mm. Choir three, N transept one, and *in situ* in tile feature in the NW nave, Fig. 141, and one each in the 1970s unstratified, in the chapter house and the reredorter. Chatwin fig. 31.1, no Charterhouse, no Whitcomb. An example from a different die occurs at the Coventry Benedictine Priory at the same period (pers. ob.).

62b (L379 W49b). 113mm. Choir three, crossing two. Chatwin fig. 31,2. An example from a different die occurs at the Coventry Benedictine Priory at the same period, with a Beauchamp tile forming the centre (pers. ob).

62c (L75 var. ?L76).

62d (L76 var. a).

63a (L34 W103). Variant. The cable is angular and flattened, and the corner appears to hold a worn monogram. Cloister, per architect J. Brown. No local parallels.

63b (L162 W29a). Guilloche in bands, fleur-de-lys with letters h and r, Chatwin's suggestion being Henricus Rex? Henry IV and Henry V both had Carmelite confessors, and the Carmelite Thomas Netter accompanied Henry VI to Rouen in 1430 (Sheppard 1943, 29, 44, 46). If the reading is accepted, this could confirm strong Henrican connections in the 1420s and 1430s, and one of these tiles was stratified in 61 XIV 3, in a Friary 2/Pre-rebuild phase context of this date. However, I.S. points out that Coventry's Henrician connections were exceptionally strong particularly from the 1450s and the 1480s, and a later connection is possible. It seems likely that this tile accompanies a Maria tile resembling 63c, as it did at Burton Dassett (cf. Whitcomb 185 a and b). 110 x 108mm. Choir six, eastern bay of nave two. Chatwin 9, 11 no exact Charterhouse parallel.

63c (L163, 550 W 29b var. a). Guilloche within band, M and A for Maria (or perhaps a reversed A M for Ave Maria) with central five-petalled rose between, a device which only occurs on this smaller version, perhaps referring to the *Rosa sine spina.* The corners of the whole design presumably carry fleur-de-lys. 110 x 107mm. Choir eight, crossing seven, nave W end, one. One could expect fairly frequent occurrences in a church dedicated to the Virgin Mary. Chatwin 9,12, no precise parallel at Charterhouse nor in Whitcomb.

63d (L151 W29.3). Half tile, version of No 63b. Fleur-de-lys with letters h and r. 110mm. Choir one, N transept one. Relates to Charterhouse 102. No Whitcomb. This tile also occurs at St John's Bablake, Coventry (pers. ob.).

63e (L186 W 29.2). Half tile, version of 63b. Guilloche within bands, unrecognisable device in corner. 109mm. Choir three, N transept one. Relates to Chatwin 9.11, no Charterhouse, no Whitcomb.

63f(W29 var. W85). Half tile, top of a tile not otherwise represented in the series; fleur-de-lys, band and hint of guilloche 105mm. Three from choir, two from W end of nave. Chatwin 9.8, no exact Charterhouse, no Whitcomb.

63g (L195 W29.5). Half tile. Guilloche. 108mm. Choir two, dump at W end of nave two. Perhaps from the four-tile version?. No Charterhouse, no Whitcomb.

New-nine tile patterns

64 (L121 W11a, 11c). Eighteen eight-petalled flowers, triangles between, enclosed in bands. Fleur-de-lys and trefoils at corners. Style somewhat attenuated. 113mm. Three each from choir and passage to sacristy, one from crossing. One U/S. No Chatwin, Charterhouse 112, Whitcomb 190, Bradgate House.

Four-tile patterns

The four-tile pattern nature of many 'single' heraldic tiles should be noted.

Patterns based on a circle

65 (L169 W35). Large sixteen-petalled flower within dotted circle, simple trefoil in corners. Heavily stamped,

the wood being very coarse grained. Slight wear. 118 x 115mm, intermediate size. *In situ* on step at entrance to the N chapel in the nave. Some fifteen other examples were found in the vicinity, presumably a retiling of the Pre-rebuild phase, after work on the NW tower pier. Also, five in the choir, and one in the tile feature at W end, Fig. 141. Chatwin 23.15, Charterhouse 91, Whitcomb 201, Bradgate House, Dudley Castle 2.

66a (L106 W5a). Band of twenty lozenges (reverse slip) enclosing four six-petalled flowers, four ?oak leaves, and four small trefoils. Large complete leaves in corners. 108 x 110mm. This appears to be a smaller version of an earlier larger type. version of Chatwin 23.14, but different flower. *In situ* in tile feature at W end, one. No Charterhouse, no Whitcomb. This tile also occurs at St John's Bablake, Coventry (pers.ob.).

66b (Nil W5a var. b). Die variant with bungled squares/lozenges. Crossing one.

67 (L560). Band with triangles forming asymmetrical reverse lozenges, enclosing quatrefoil containing eight eight-petalled flowers. Unclear leaf motifs in corners. U/P. 110mm. Charterhouse 95. No other local parallels.

68 (L523 W41). Band of twenty-four line-drawn triangles within double line bands, enclosing collared fleur-de-lys, square motif of squares, rectangles and dots at centre. Formalised leaves at corners. Attenuated style. 118 x 118mm. One stratified in a Pre-rebuild (15th century - not first quarter) context 61 D h W choir. Four others from the choir. No local parallels.

69 (L168a). Version of above. Band of forty two opposing solid triangles, enclosing four fleur-de-lys. Central motif unclear. Formalised ?complete foliage in four corners. Attenuated style. 119 x 19mm, so intermediate in size. 1977 U/P. No local parallels.

70 (L'K'). Circle of thirty-two opposing triangles, enclosing wide circle containing large eight-petalled flower. 1997 U/P. Chatwin 43.9, Charterhouse 75, Whitcomb 202, Bradgate House.

71 (L111 small.). Foliage corner, wide band with letters (Chatwin and Whitcomb read as WGWER reversed, Goodall reads as N E (reversed) W T (on side) W?) repeated four times. Four trees in central roundel;. see notes under 24, the larger version. 110 x 111mm. Choir, crossing, and tile feature in the NW nave, Fig. 141. Smaller copy of Chatwin 17.3?. Charterhouse 73 indicates that most unusually our example has used a large die on a small tile. A variant occurs again at Bradgate House.

Patterns based on a circle, but where the corner motif suggests carpet laying

72 (L67 W42a). Four-sided figure enclosing a patterned sub-square motif, overlaid by a saltire. Trefoils and quatrefoils in field. Enclosed by circle with four groups of four- and three-ringed dots. If laid as a carpet the corner motifs form an elaborate flower, dot and tendril pattern. 113 x 113mm. Choir four, crossing two. Coventry Benedictine Priory, fig. 14 no 27, but no other local parallels.

73a (L115 W 17b). Circle with eight stags chasing each other. Within, circle with eight confronting birds and within that an eight-petalled flower. Complete leaf sprays in corners. Intermediate size, 118-120mm. One in tile pit in crossing, one *in situ* in 15th-century patching over wall tomb foundation in the N transept, Fig. 141. No exact Chatwin, or Charterhouse, Whitcomb 192 (there also dated to the 15th century).

73b (L115a var.). Variant of 73a above, and smaller. 116mm. 1977 presbytery, one. Chatwin 9.20, Charterhouse 85, Dudley Castle 14.

74 (L114 W16). A border circlet enclosing four bears, with ragged staffs and five-petalled roses. J.G. comments that all except the last are Beauchamp badges. There was probably a four-petalled central flower. Probably a nave and crossing pattern. The corner motif suggests carpet laying. 111 x 113mm. Chatwin.9.14 (the Whitefriars original drawing shows matching dots on the cinquefoil petals). No Charterhouse, no Whitcomb.

75a (L117 W17E). Circle with bands enclosing four hounds chasing four stags. Within this a circle of eight confronting birds, within that an eight-petalled flower? Eight half leaves in the corners. 110mm. Poor stamp, wear heavy. Probably Chatwin 9.15, no Charterhouse, no Whitcomb.

75b (L535). Broken bottom corner, apparently of a worn reversed tile of this group, stags etc., showing mortar across break, i.e. scruffy patching. 1997 unprovenanced.

Figure 144

75c (L117A). Version with stag with raised tail. 1977 U/P.

Patterns not involving a circle but where corner motifs also suggest four- tile or carpet laying

76a (L91 W61). Lion rampant with quarter of an eight-petalled flower in corner. Poor impression. 110mm. One only, choir. Probably Chatwin 38.5, Weoley Castle. No Charterhouse, no Whitcomb.

76b (L94 W61a). Variant of above. 113mm. Choir, two. No known parallels.

Patterns based on a quatrefoil

77a (L110 W12). Quatrefoil enclosing four worn

fleur-de-lys, eight-petalled flower in circle at centre. Four grotesque faces in corners. 114mm. Version of Chatwin 11.5 (but with mask instead of leaf), Charterhouse 97, no Whitcomb.

77b (L110 var.). Variant of 71a. 115mm.

77c (L110 var.). Version of grotesque face. A choir and ?sacristy pattern.

78 (L578). Treble band quatrefoil, enclosing four fleur-de-lys. Central motif in circle uncertain. Corner uncertain. Style relates to No 77a above. 1977 U/S, one.

Patterns based on an octofoil

79a (L61a composite drawing, W36). Octofoil with dotted band enclosing eight radiating sprays of leaves in the outer corners. A smaller well-made version of an earlier pattern, one tile unusually with four parallel scratches for keying on the back. 111mm. Choir, three. One *in situ* in tile feature in the NW nave. A 1977 unstratified example had been very roughly cut down and mortared in as a rectangular border tile. Version only of Chatwin 20.20 or Charterhouse 82 or Whitcomb 198 (Bradgate House).

79b (L62 W37a). Version of No 73a, smaller and the quatrefoil without dots. 113 x 110mm. Concentration in first bay of nave, five examples. One in choir. Again no exact parallels.

Other patterns

80 (L564). See Goodall comments for No 23. He notes that the ?rose in the base here cannot be traced in the *Dictionary of British Arms* and that this is not necessarily a heraldic tile. The complete pattern resembles a four-pointed star within an equal armed cross, forming a central elaborated cross motif. Five-petalled flowers, trefoil leaves motif in three corners. Smaller variant of 23. 113mm. Two 1977 complete tiles from the presbytery are now lost; one each in both presbytery and chapter house

(This version looks more like the four correctly set tiles recorded in the Prior's House tiled-floor, Fig. 136, presumably a larger version as all tiles there were recorded as large, A large version exists (Chatwin 13.5, but the pattern is different, e.g. central flower, as is Charterhouse 88); no Whitcomb.

81 (L70 W45). Inscription within bands apparently involving the name JOB or JOHAN (suggested by Father Bertram). Leaves in corners. 113mm. Choir to W end. No local parallels.

4-tilers, Size unknown

82 (L120 W17D). Unidentified animals facing each other presumably within a circle. Central motif unknown. No local parallels.

Single patterns

The 15th-century single tile *per se* is possibly an illusion. It seems more likely that they were used in groups of four, centres of nine-tile patterns, and tiles set as an all-over patterned carpet.

There are five new single-patterns, plus five new monograms, plus six semi-heraldic patterns and twenty-one heraldic patterns - a large increase in the popularity of this class, and a sign of secularisation.

Group of 4?

83 (L66 W44). Man in short tunic and pointed shoes (crackowes (Cracow) or poulaines (Poland)), standing with arms held out, perhaps a dancer?, or if set as a four, a ring of dancers. Scatter of flowers in background. Set diagonal to the tile. The short tunic and the full sleeves indicate a fashion of the late 14th/early 15th centuries; the pointed shoes would be out of fashion early in the 15th century (information Linda Woolley, Victoria and Albert Museum). Doubtless conservatism kept this tile in production for some period after these fashions died. The tile was built into the step in the NE transept in a Pre-rebuild context and the date of this context would probably be second and third quarters of the 15th century. 110 x 113mm. Choir, five, 1977 U/S, two. No Chatwin, Charterhouse 25, Whitcomb 191, Dudley Castle 19.

Centre of nine-tile pattern?

84 (L21 W89). Four ivy leaves emerging from a square with sixteen dots, set square to the tile. 112 x 112mm. This could be the centre of a nine-tile pattern but no obvious candidate presents itself. A distinctive darkened surface gives it a 'foreign' appearance. One only, N porch. No known parallels.

85 (L65 W38). Four ?fruit and four veined leaves radiating from central circles. *c.*115mm - intermediate size. Again a distinctive darkened surface. Choir to E nave. No Chatwin nor Charterhouse, Whitcomb 217, Bradgate House.

Monograms

86 (L74 W47). MARIA monogram set square on tile, in a sunburst (cf. 125). Possibly the centre of 58 above. 110 x 110mm. Their concentration in the NW transept/NE nave area (six) suggests that this northern chapel may be the recorded Chapel of Our Lady. No local parallels.

87 (L125 W21a). CHRISTUS monogram, lower case, set square to tile. 118 x 115mm. Very little wear so may have been used as an edging. Crossing. No local parallels.

88 (L126 W21b). IHS monogram. E choir, one. No local parallels.

89a, b (L127 W 21c). Unidentified monograms, 89a perhaps an M, NE tower pier, one. Fragment 89b from the choir. No local parallels.

90 (L 'J'). No match with existing lettered tiles (and too thin for fleur-de-lys) Perhaps another monogram? Provenance unknown.

Single tile

91 (L 'B'). Intersecting vesicas, six-petalled flower at centre. 112mm. 1977 U/S. A version of this tile occurs at the Northampton Whitefriars now in the Rutland collection at the British Museum. Chatwin 23.13, Charterhouse 42, no Whitcomb; also at the City Wall at King Street. in a 15th-century cess pit (Woodfield C. 1966, fig. 6c).

Semi-heraldic

92 (L549 W86). Fleur-de-lys, with conspicuous veins, set diagonally. 112 x 113mm. Choir to crossing. No local parallels.

93 (L52 W 116). Large fleur-de-lys in square frame, leaves in corners? Probably 112mm ±. A tile of unusual thickness (30mm) and rather foreign in style. Choir, one. No local parallels.

94 (L.536a W19a). Maltese cross in circle, set square to the tile. The triple corner leaves continue right to the edge of the tile suggesting its use in four tile or carpet patterns. 110 x 112mm. One relaid over 15th-century wall tomb foundation (G2), and 1997 unprovenanced. Chatwin 41.19, no Charterhouse, no Whitcomb.

95 (L536 W19). As above, but Maltese cross set diagonal to tile. 112 x 113mm. No Chatwin, Charterhouse 45, no Whitcomb; also Fords Hospital (Chatwin 1941-2).

96 (L73 W46). Horseshoe, set square to tile. Goodall confirms that this is 'a Ferrers badge being taken from the border'. The Ferrers arms appear on a vault boss in the choir, Fig. 71, No 1124, in Section F, *The Architectural Stonework*. 110mm. However, their distribution, three against the door in the N transept and one against the door at the W end, may suggest that it was used to keep witches and other evil forces out of the church. Version of Chatwin 11.10, no Charterhouse, no Whitcomb, though a horseshoe occurs as no 231.

97 (L.150 W28). J.G.comments 'A bear and ragged staff with a double rose at the sinister side, the Beauchamp badge. However without the colours the rose cannot be identified. Might other tiles completing the pattern have provided a clue to this?'; if such 'other tiles' exist they are not obvious. What appear to be short lengths of rope? are perhaps an oblique reference to a chained bear? 111mm. A nave and crossing tile, four. One *in situ* in tile feature at W end, Fig. 141. Always poorly stamped. Chatwin 38.12. no Charterhouse, no Whitcomb.

98 (W74). Unrecognised device, not necessarily heraldic. 112mm. Area of SW tower pier, one. Slight wear. No local parallels.

Heraldic designs

Shields set square to the tile

99 (L33 W121/104). J.G. comments 'Two chevrons, borne by, among other families, Bagot, Chaworth, Grendon and Seymour'. Traces of formalised flower and leaf motifs in corners. Continuous white border suggests its primary use as a border tile. Heavy wear. 113mm. One from group in S resonance passage laid over a soft patch in the sandstone for acoustic purposes, Fig. 141, presumably repair after the collapse of the tower in 1447. One from W end of nave. No local parallels, but cf. Charterhouse 18 (where the two chevrons are equated with Clare. and Fitzwalter of Daventry).

Shields set diagonal to the tile, to be set in fours or as carpet

100 (L87 W57a). As No 99, but set diagonally to the tile, and this example has a reverse-slip background - might this relate to the tinctures? Formal flowers and ?leaves in three corners. Worn. White line edge, presumably a border tile. 108mm. In cloister garth, and one 1977 U/S. No local parallels.

101 (L87). Variant of 100 above. Fragment of ?related tile, passage to sacristy, two.

Figure 145

102 (W56 die 2). Uncertain but presumably as 103, but crosslets have more marked bifurcations. 114mm. W end of choir, one.

103 (L85 W56 die 2a). J.G. writes 'A fess and ten plain crosslets countercoloured, not identified.' Bow tie-like side motifs with two half petals on three corners. 114mm. N transept and E nave, two, choir, four. No exact parallels, but there may be a reference to Beauchamp.

104 (L30 W95). J.G. writes 'A dance between six crosslets fitchy, given for one of the families of Engaine.' Worn parts of ?flower petals in three corners. 112mm. N transept/pilaster buttress, one. Presbytery, one. Chapter house one, and one 1977 U/S. Chatwin 1.4, no Charterhouse. no Whitcomb.

105 (L71 W45a). J.G. writes 'If the fragment is

correctly restored it is not the London mayor Olney who bore a quite different coat in the 15th-century records: Gules bezanty on flaunches two leopards facing inwards Silver (LV2, CRK 932, lost monument in Milk Street church). This is '?On a fess batteled between six crosslets fitchy three crescents, + /jon ol/ne.' This fragment appears to be identical to a tile traced by the Reverend George Rowe in the late 19th century. The tracing is now at the British Museum (I am grateful to Elizabeth Eames for this reference). The Rowe tracing suggests a size of 112mm for the Whitefriars' example. One only in choir. Version of Chatwin 25.16 at Burton Dassett (but the Burton Dassett tile does have the Rowe tracing's three crescents (pers. ob.) not shown by Chatwin). Charterhouse 22, but the attribution to John Only Mayor of Coventry, is a misreading. No Whitcomb.

106 (L585). Shield with a lion, not identifiable without colours. Quarter eight-petalled flowers in three? corners. 110mm. 1977 Choir two. No local parallels.

107 (L8 W8). A lion, as above; sprays of three dotted-petals in upper corners. 118mm. (intermediate size.) One in dump at W end. Chatwin 24.13, Burton Dassett. Charterhouse 19, Northampton Greyfriars (Swann 1952, M.1), no Whitcomb.

108 (L565). Attenuated eagle, presumably for Leofric as No 51, diagonal shield. There is what appears to be a small bird in a surviving corner. 115mm. Chapter house, 1977 choir. No local parallels.

109 (Nil). Attenuated eagle as above, diagonal shield. Grotesque mask in one corner; what appear to be half fleur-de-lys and trefoils in two corners; tile now lost but this is based on a drawing of John Bateman's. 112mm. Chapter house one complete tile. No local parallels.

110 (L80 W52). J.G. writes 'A cross patty between five martlets facing sinister, an eccentric version of the arms attributed to St Edward the Confessor', here representing Westminster Abbey. 119 x 116mm, an intermediate size. Seven pieces from the SE crossing only, possibly relating to an altar. Chatwin 24.1, Charterhouse 14, no Whitcomb. This tile also occurs at St Mary's Hall, Coventry (pers. ob.).

111a (L1 W66a). J.G. writes 'The design is unclear, the chevron, if such it is, being much narrower than usual. I do not find the continental division implied by the drawing in the English medieval records. A chevron between three roses, borne by William Smith bishop of Lichfield and Coventry (1491) and of Lincoln (1496-1514).' 112mm. Five tiles in nave, E and W ends, there possibly relating to the construction of the western three bays. Version of Chatwin 25.10, arms not there identified. No Charterhouse or Whitcomb. This new heraldic identification suggests a date much later in the 15th century than normally considered for some, at least, of these tiles, but it would be in keeping with the previously established date for the W end.

111b (W66b Die var.). Choir, one.

112a, b (L13 W75). J.G. comments 'A pierced cinquefoil, perhaps for Astley, but these fragments look as if there would have been three foils when complete'. Fleur-de-lys in all corners. First and second bay of nave at E, four. Chapter house, one. Chatwin 23.8, Astley church. No Charterhouse, Whitcomb 66.

113 (L402/'A' W 75 var.). J.G. again comments 'A pierced cinquefoil perhaps for Astley.' Part of eight-petalled flowers in corners. 113mm. Chapter house one, sacristy passage one. Charterhouse 17, no other parallels.

114 (L 'H'). Probably corner of above.

Set diagonal to tile, border rather than shield?

115 (L244 W 2). Spread eagle in incomplete shield or border. The motif below the eagle's tail suggests the tiles are laid in fours around a central square motif, forming a short armed cross. Formalised flowers and leaves in corners. 110mm. Whole tiles from the choir, the E nave and the passage linking choir and sacristy. Seven other pieces from the choir. No local parallels.

Heraldic tiles of unknown size

116 (L15 W 81). Apparently Mortimer, (two bars in chief a pale and two gyrons, on a scocheon?) but J.G. comments 'if so there is an additional vertical line in the scocheon.' Shield set straight to the tile, size unknown. Paralleled by Rutland Catalogue 395 (Worcester Cathedral) and 396 (Malmesbury), but these do not have the additional line (identification suggested by Elizabeth Eames). Choir, one. No local parallels.

117 (L89 W57c). Base of shield set straight to tile? Too fragmentary for identification. U/S, one.

118 (L5 W70). The tile is poorly impressed and very worn. A diagonal shield is assumed but is no longer visible. It was postulated that this might refer to the Bassetts of Drayton, but J.G. comments that they bore 'Gold three piles Gules with a quarter Ermine, and the design appears to represent a pily coat.' NE nave, one. No local parallels.

119 (L1 var. a). 1977 S of choir. Version of Chatwin fig. 25.11.

Endless repeating patterns

These now seem to be out of fashion except for:

120 (Bateman 20/29). A simplified version of earlier types, with rows of circles containing eight-petalled

flowers, and masks with protruding tongues in the voids. 112 x 113mm. Chapter house, one, an area where endless repeating tiles seem popular. No local parallels.

121a (L583). Rows of circles containing ?twelve-petalled flowers, four squares (here worn) in centre. 110mm. Chapter house and 1977 U/S. Chatwin 41.17, Charterhouse 36, no Whitcomb.

121b (L583). Smaller version, used for edging(?) mortared in with untrimmed edge. 1977 unprovenanced. A tile of this pattern and size was recovered from a 1990 Evaluation at Hay Lane, Coventry (pers. comm. I.S.).

Mosaic border tiles

Figure 145

122 (L389 and 391-3). W MT 122a-e. Basically a lobed lozenge tile, with four stripes one way and three stripes at right angles; eight stalked trefoils. Combined with a 'butterfly' tile with three stripes at right angles, and four sprays with leaflets and flowers at the spray bases. The reverse slip and general style certainly suggest a later 15th-century date for a floor relaying after the tower fall of 1447.

122a Double lozenge. Four pieces, representing three tiles at least - much variation in the thickness of the parallel lines. These tiles appear, exceptionally, to have been trimmed with a knife after removing from the mould.

122b Half lozenge. 2 pieces.

122c Variant trefoil from above.

122d Whole 'butterfly'. There were two examples of this tile.

In addition one certain and three probable halves and three complete quarters.

All are reverse slip and the white edge lines suggest a border. The evidence for difference in detail of pattern, i.e. different stamps, is reasonably clear (i.e. for the floral motif) on three tiles, and suggested on a fourth but they were very worn. The tiles had been roughly cut through before firing, and broken afterwards.

122e Reconstruction as border. All tiles were from the 16th-century destruction level, 64 XVIa (2), from inside the S chapel against its N wall, except one from the passage between the two chapels. They were not found anywhere else on the site. In view of the narrow limits of their find place, and the high amount of division, it seems more likely that they were a border than a carpet.

The only other known local example of a Butterfly tile is from the Stoke kiln (Chatwin fig. 2). Tiles of this form are known at Sandwell Priory, Warwickshire (Hodder 1991, fig. 26). They are a little larger than No 122, and the butterfly tile is of different form. In appearance they are very different, these being line impressed tiles, the lozenge form depicting what is surely not an angel, but the winged creature of Ezekiel 1, the butterfly tile carrying the spirit wheels of the same vision, as at Basingwerk Abbey (Lewis 1976, fig. 36). The Sandwell figured tiles are glazed green and the floral tiles are glazed yellow, both over a white slip. A post late 14th-century date is suggested. Sandwell is on the eastern boundary of the geographical area where these tiles occur, including Basingwerk Abbey, Flintshire, Buildwas and Lilleshall Abbeys, Wenlock Priory, Tong and Brewood.

Mosaic tiles of the early 14th century at Norton Priory have the lozenge and butterfly forms among others, but are plain themselves though laid in contrasting colours (Greene 1989, fig. 85). They are presumably the link between these decorated mosaic tiles and the earlier well known Cistercian examples.

A mosaic tile pavement almost exactly paralleled at Norton Priory is recorded from the frater of the Chester Whitefriars (Ward 1990, fig. 138).

Catalogue of other border tiles

Figure 146

White edged small border tiles 123-126, and small-tile derived letters 135 to 158, plus other small border tiles 159 to 160, are all new patterns.

The size category cannot be applied to the mosaic tiles nor to tiles 127 to 131, although both the mosaic tiles and the heraldic borders look late with their use of reverse slip.

Standard sizes

Single-tile borders, white edging two sides only

123 (L72 W94/48). Continuous frieze of alternate large and small leaves, between two white edges. 112mm. Choir two, N transept one, N porch one. No local parallels.

Patterns requiring two tiles to make a double white-edged border

124 (L77 W50). Frieze of large formalised cut leaves growing from the border stripe, small formalised leaves in between. Groups of eight dots on background squares. 112mm or 114mm. Crossing/pulpitum six, dump at W end of nave one, choir two. Slight wear confirms edging. Charterhouse border 41 is a reduced version, otherwise no local parallels.

Single tile, white-edged border?

125 (L4 W68). MARIA cypher, roses to left and right of monogram, formalised leaf and flower in corners, cf. 86. 114mm. W end of nave one, cloister one. Chatwin 16, no Charterhouse, no Whitcomb.

126a (L166 W30). *Agnus Dei* within cusped white border. Three tiles SE tower pier and choir, one NE nave. Two stamps are represented. No local parallels.

126b (L548 W30b). Variant of above. No wear. Nave at W.

Non standard sizes

127 (L518 W91). Four trefoils with dotted leaves, each set inside a white border line. Possibly designed originally to be cut and used as corner tiles? 80mm. Two from chapter house, one a half triangular tile; two from presbytery and choir (one another half triangular tile) and one from passage to sacristy. Chatwin 22.1. The tile is also known at Etchingham, Sussex. No Charterhouse, no Whitcomb.

128 (L20 W90). Fleur-de-lys diagonal to tile. No white border. 87mm square. Crude stamp, crudely made. From 68 XXVII 16, a Rebuild context i.e. late 15th century, in the W cloister. Another 1977 U/S. No local parallels.

Another small *c.*100mm fleur-de-lys tile was recorded *in situ* in the tile feature at the NW end of the nave (tracing lost). It resembled Charterhouse no 31 and Whitcomb 153, Bradgate House.

Heraldic, rectangular, multiple tile border

129 (L32 W101). Single strip border; part shield with one chevron, presumably representing Stafford; the tile edge occurs just above the chevron point, so it presumably continued onto another tile in the series? Reverse slip. Two white edges. Width 73mm, rectangular. 1964 unstratified, but probably crossing. Chatwin 38.6, no other local parallels.

130 (L6 W69). As above and presumably part of the same scheme. Shield with a cross, probably for St George but, as J.G. comments, also given for several families. 73mm. Built into NE tower pier two, giving a Pre-rebuild, later 15th-century date. Also 1977 E of passage, and two 1977 U/S. No local parallels.

131 (L571 HAGM). Shield, presumably again part of same scheme as the above. J.G. confirms the three bars are not identifiable without the colours. Width 73mm. E of passage, one. No local parallels.

Heraldic quarter tile borders

These occurred only in the large tile format, catalogue Nos 56a, 56b, for Stafford and Every.

Large letters, presumably used as borders

132 (L81 W54). Capital H, presumably as earlier series with trefoils in background. 118 x 120mm, intermediate size. Crossing one. Series resembles Chatwin 32.5 and, more exactly, Charterhouse 48 to 52 series. No Whitcomb.

133 (L31 W100). Capital A. 112 x 108mm. Choir one, E cloister one. No local parallels.

134 (W119). Capital A, different die. Choir one.

Small letters

An unusually large number and variety. All apparently from small tiles cut into quarters. The white lines here appear often as markings for cutting, not always a border in themselves. Unfortunately many are 1977 unprovenanced, but are most likely to be from the choir or to its S. The Chatwin fig. 32 and the Charterhouse letters appear to be a different series. No Whitcomb parallels.

135a (L138a). Capital E. 50mm. 1977 U/P.

135b (W22.2). Capital E 52mm. Deep stamp, slight wear. E nave, one.

136 (L138b). Capital E. 50 x 54mm. 1977 choir, grave 1, one.

137 (L566). Capital F. 53mm. Choir.

138 (L537 W23.3 var.). Capital G. 55mm. 1960s choir two, 1977 choir, two.

139 (L241a W22). Capital H, 'thin' version. 50mm. Crossing.

140a Capital H. 52mm. 'Fat' version. 1977 U/S.

140b (W22.3). Capital H. 52mm, no wear. 'fat' version, fault on die. 1977 U/S two.

141 (L141 W22.2 var.). Capital H of different form. 59 x 55mm. Dump at W end, one.

142 (L241b). Its resemblance to Chatwin suggests a badly stamped H, but it may be an N, cf. Chatwin fig. 32.15. 53mm. U/P.

143 (L567). Capital I. 50mm. 1977 one in Grave 1, two others in choir.

144 (L128b W22.3). Capital I 54mm. Choir two, E of passage to sacristy, one.

145 (L129). Capital R 53mm. 1977 choir, one.

146 (L129b). Capital L. 53mm. 1977 U/P.

147 (L135 W223). Capital M? or perhaps should be read reversed as a W, cf. No 158. 55mm, 60mm with border. 1977 choir, two, and F.60 tank fill, SE cloister (Fig. 49), one.

148 (L137 W22.2). Capital O 50mm. 1960s dump at W end, one.

149 (L131 W22.4 var.). Capital P. 54mm. Choir and W of passage, three.

150a (L139). Capital Q. 53mm. 1977 unprovenanced.

150b (W22.2). Capital Q. 54 x 55mm. W end of nave dump, one.

151a (L174 W22.2). Capital R. 53mm. W end of nave, one and 1977 U/P.

151b (L129a). Capital R. 1977 U/P.

152 (L180). Capital T. 54mm. 1977 U/P. This appears to be a different die to the T on No 54, or it has become damaged with age.

153 (L136 W22.3). Capital W. Choir, one.

154a (L570). Capital Y 55mm. 1977 choir one, W of passage to sacristy two. Y's of this curious form are attested with a Z on a lettered tile from Northampton (Swann 1952, M.17).

154b Nil. Capital Y 53mm. W of passage, one.

155a (L142 W22.2 var.). Capital Z 55mm. E crossing, one.

155b (L140 W22.2). Capital Z, perhaps here shown reversed? 55 x 54mm. E crossing, one. 1977 U/P.

156 (L546). Incomplete letter, not identical with other examples. 1977 U/P

Small letters - half and whole tiles

157 (L129A W22.3). Capitals R and I. 110 x 54mm. Choir one, dump at W end of nave, one. 1977 U/S, 1. No local parallels.

158 (L128a W22.5 var.). Capitals W (rather than M?) and I survive. 113mm. Per the architect Jimmy Brown, found in works on the cloister. No local parallels.

I am grateful for Beverley Nenk's comments on Nos 54, 142, 144, 145, 147, 154, 155a, 157 and 158.

Other small floral, semi heraldic and symbolic motifs

These were presumably intended to be cut as quarters and used as edging. The quarter tile white borders seem to be complete in these examples.

159a (L99 W3a). Fleur-de-lys, five-petalled flower with foliage. Catherine wheel and lyre? J.G. comments that this resembled depictions of the classical lyre, but the early medieval examples did not have the central support, and the instrument had been replaced by the later Middle Ages with the harp and crowd (crwth) (Roche 1981), illustrating the extreme conservatism of these patterns. 112mm. Choir two, N transept one. 1977 area 1. No local parallels.

159b Die variant. Choir, one.

160 (L100 W3). Formalised flowers and foliage and a lion's tail? (cf. Chatwin fig. 32, bottom line). 117mm. Choir, crossing and E nave, seven, one stratified in a Rebuild context 60,I,15. later 15th century. No local parallels.

Small tile designed to be cut in half for edging

The white edge here seems to be a marker, not a complete border.

161 (L 'F'). Leaves and stags. 112mm. 1977 Unprovenanced. Chatwin 9.17, no Charterhouse or Whitcomb.

Other tile types

The remaining entries in the catalogue consist of single examples of unrecognised tile types, repeat patterns (mainly floral and leaf, but also arc, cable and hunting motifs), and tiles of known designs, but unknown size. Parallels are unknown unless otherwise stated.

Figure 147

162 (L35 W102). Internal point with cusp crowned with trefoil. Sixteen-tile pattern. The piece is covered with mortar on all surfaces. W choir, one. Possibly Charterhouse 101, and so as 12 series above.

163 (L9a). Sixteen tile pattern. Fine arc with fragment of foliage spray. 1977 U/P.

164 (L42 W108). Corner with trefoil leaf, probably from a sixteen-tile pattern. May relate to 14 or 58b (compare with Woodfield, C. 1966, fig. 7, I).

165 (L40 W111.1). Corner with veined leaf. Perhaps corner of 14, a large sixteen tile pattern? Choir, one.

166 (L281 W111.2). Flattened arc with stem and leaf, presumably from a sixteen tile pattern, perhaps as above; also choir, one.

167 (L347). Trefoil leaf, also variant of 14? 1977, Choir, one.

168 (L'R'). Arcs with exterior cusp. Traces of flower and ?foliage. Sixteen- or nine-tile pattern? No known parallels but some resemblance to Chatwin 33, 2, 3 and 6.

169 (L146 W10). Cusped band, enclosing heart-shaped/ovals with six-petalled flowers. Apparently part of a nine-tile pattern resembling 62. Choir, one.

170 (L544). Arc enclosing worn corner motif, perhaps a letter i. Cable within another arc. Another variant of the 63 nine-tile group.

171a (W122 Die Aci). Die variant of either 16a or 61a. N transept one, choir two.

171b (W122 Die Acii). Die variant as above. N transept, one.

171c (W122 Die B2). Tracing from a fragment relaid in the blocked door of the NE transept.

171d (W122 Die Ad). First bay of nave, one.

172 (L38 W107). Dotted band surrounding floral motif. Four-tile pattern. Crossing one.

173 (L'I'). Wide arc from four-tile pattern, trefoil and dot. The pattern is presumably of the 20a family, but closer to Charterhouse 83, which lacks the fleur-de-lys and the corner giant trefoil. The trefoil and dot are however reversed. 1977 U/P.

174 (L'Y'). Corner with wide arc and small trefoils. Also same genre as 20a. No parallels, but analogies are with four-tile patterns. 1977 U/P.

175 (L'X') Corner with quarter of eight-petalled flower, presumably a four-tile pattern. Thin arcs, dots and small trefoils. Same genre as 20a? No parallels. 1977 U/P.

176 (L'S'). Internal corner with convoluted foliage. 1977 U/P.

177 (L'Q'). Thin arc and formalised foliage? Perhaps same family as 20a. 1977, U/P.

178 (L'O'). Complex leaves and dots representing vines. Resembles but does not match 19a. 1977, U/P.

179a (L'Z' W 62). Arc with internal cusp, triple dots, and 'green man' foliage. Again resembles but does not match 19. NE nave and crossing, one.

179b (L'Zb'). As above but perforated cusp. 1977, U/P.

180 (L'T'). Intersecting stems? No parallels. 1977, U/P.

181 (L'V') Intersecting arcs. No parallels. 1977 U/P.

182 (L'C'). Distinctive 'furry' leaf, and arc. Chapter house, one. Probably as top right hand section of Whitcomb 210, an 'endless repeating' pattern.

Uncertain type

183 (L574). Unrecognised corner motif. It is not clear whether this is a reverse slip pattern. 1977 choir, one.

184 (L'P'). No parallel recognised. 1977 U/P.

185 (L'N'). Foliage spray, or even lower part of eagle, or pair of doves as versions of Chatwin fig. 1.1? No exact parallels found. 1977, U/P.

186 (L'AA'). Fragment of inscription and ?foliage. A version of 47? 1977 U/P

Border tiles ?

187 (L92 var.). Cup or vase diagonal to the tile, white border. No parallel known. 1977 U/P

188 (L98 W125b). White bordered corner, formalised leaves and arc. No wear. NE nave. No parallels known.

'Framed' tiles

189 (L29 W93). Large cross and ?crosslets, in a black frame. Reverse slip pattern. N porch. No local parallels.

190 (L573). Unidentifiable pattern in black frame. Perhaps part of above tile. 1977, choir one.

Single tiles ?

191 (L10 W73). Corner with trefoil leaf. Central motif unrecognisable. E bay of nave, one. No local parallels.

192a (W110a). Large leaf with trefoil 'stamens' in a rather wild style, from fill of 15th-century 68 Grave 16 (but some contractor's disturbance) in the W choir. No local parallels.

192b (L44 W110b). Variant die (or different part of same tile?) Crossing, one.

193 (L51 W117). Fleur-de-lys and ?cable. Perhaps missing corner of 97. Very thin. No wear. SW tower pier, one.

194 (L36 W105). Corner piece with cross. U/S.

195 (L39 W105b). Corner piece with suspended leaf (or cross in reversed slip?) Rubble in nave chantry tomb, 64 XXI 3. No local parallels.

Semi-heraldic tiles

196 (L46 W113). Running animal? Possibly a version of the jousting knight, Whitcomb 154, particularly as this is a Bradgate House tile, and also known at the Charterhouse (see also Swann 1952, M.1; might also relate to Whitcomb 117/118?). N transept, one. The number of tile patterns shared with Bradgate House is noteworthy.

197 (L49 W120). Corner with bird's feet? Presumably four-tile pattern. No wear. Nave at W, one.

Additionally a *c.*100mm fleur-de-lys tile was built into the tile feature at the W end. This did not resemble existing fleur-de-lys tiles, but was probably a Charterhouse 31 (tracing lost). Other tiles from that feature indicated (size now uncertain) a ten dot version of Chatwin 19.3, and at least one fragment from an illegible but clearly new tile type.

Cutting of patterned tiles

Patterned tiles were, infrequently, cut diagonally, presumably for edging, e.g. types 15, 17 and 63d-g (all nine-tile patterns) and 36-38, endless repeating patterns from a grave. Types 56 and 127 appeared to be designed with cutting in mind as a possibility, 56 occurring both cut and uncut, as did 127.

Some patterned tiles were cut in quarters to form small squares, e.g. type 1a. Types 134-156, all small letters, were clearly designed to be cut, but uncut letter tiles also survived, i.e. 157-160.

Some tiles were marked out for cutting into squares but remained uncut, e.g. types 54-55 and 56a-c. These included both letters and small decorative patterns.

Plain tiles

These occurred in dark green, yellow and brown. They were quite commonly cut in half, diagonally, for edging, Figs 136 and 141.

Plain tiles were also cut into quarters diagonally, to form small triangles, something which did not happen with patterned tiles. They were found in the robbing of Grave 19, presumably associated with a now lost tile layout around this elaborate stone-built chantry tomb. Another also occurred in the robbing of the S chancel wall E of the passage, presumably related to 1977 Grave 1, or another of the important stone-lined graves in the presbytery. They are not recorded elsewhere, but it must be borne in mind that there has been considerable loss of plain tile.

TILE FEATURE AT W END, N. CORNER (62 IX)

Figure 141

The decorated tiles were numbered 1 to 16, and traced *in situ* by CW and Tony Page. Unfortunately this tracing has disappeared from the Coventry archive.

Where possible tiles have subsequently been identified from slides and black and white photographs.

The tiles were in general in the small sizes, but three were certainly in the larger 5in (127mm) size. There were two tiles of 16-tile pattern WT 15, and if there had been a high correlation of the other tiles with that area, it might have been suggested that these W end tiles were scrap from the construction of the 2nd NE tower pier, which also contained WT 15 in its stonework. However, although several of the other types were present in the crossing, there was a very general distribution of them throughout the church.

Two of the smaller size tiles, were unused, perhaps breakage from recent tile laying? All the tiles were laid chaotically, facing all ways. The sizes are deduced from the inches scale on the photographs.

The laying of these scrapped W end tiles as a footing does not therefore tell us anything about the likely flooring of the late western three bays of the nave, but its diagonal-laid nature does put those western three bays in an early sub-phase of the Pre-Rebuild Phase, i.e. they are going to be before the final finishing off of the NE tower pier work by its associated parallel-laid re-flooring. These tiles include a new large fleur-de-lys, as Charterhouse 31. The tiles represented appeared to be Nos 11, 12 (x3), 15 (x2), 24, 29, 62a, 65, 66a, 71, 79a and 97.

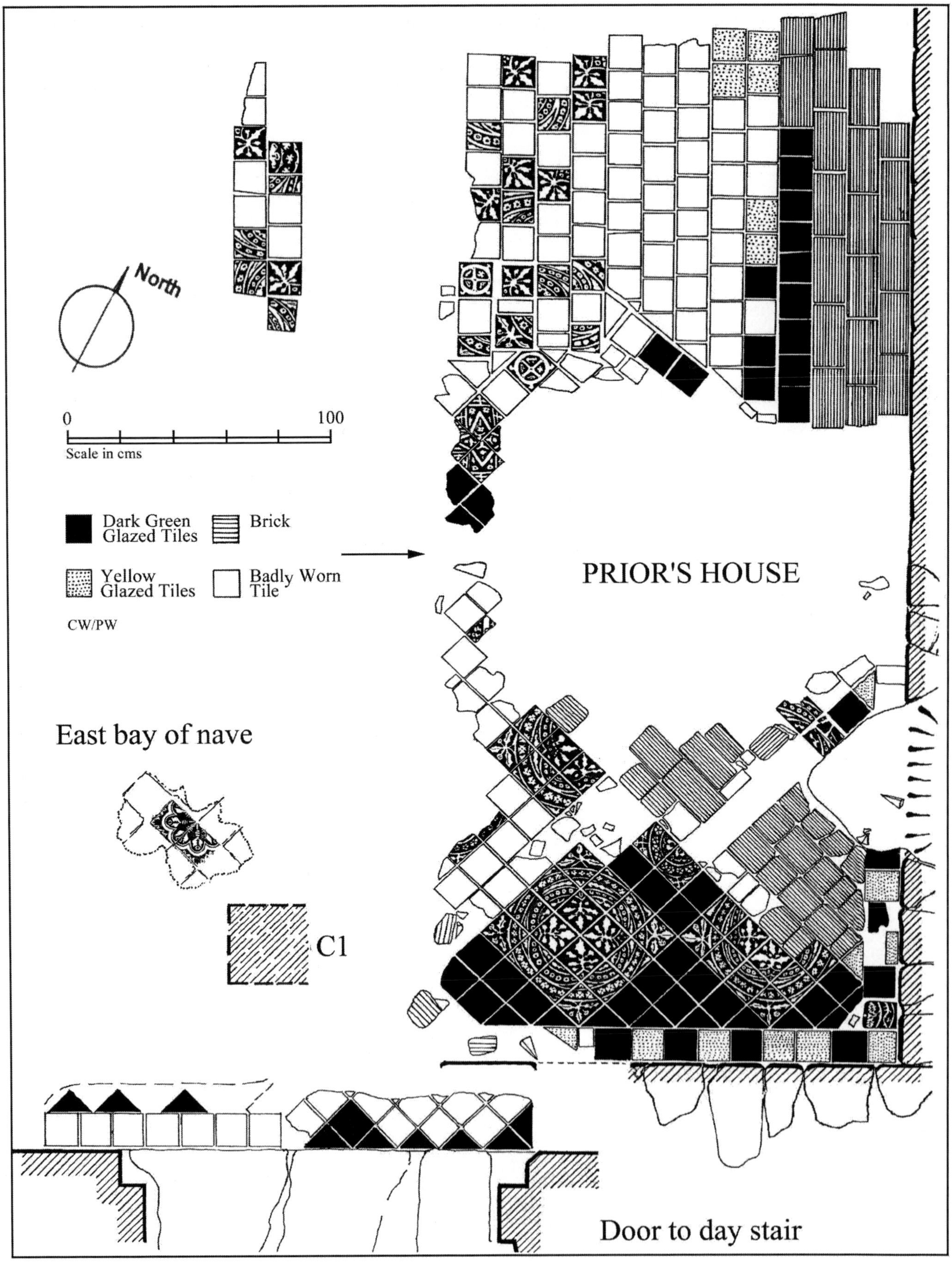

Figure 136 The prior's house plan showing the layout of the floor tiles; also the surviving floor at the foot of the day stair, and the floor fragment east of C.1, the southern wall of the Chapel of the Holy Rood.

Figure 137 Large floor tiles *c*.1395-1400:
1-2 Tiles of earlier 14th-century type.
3-10 Tiles *in situ* in Prior's House: 3 Sixteen-tile pattern,
4-5 Four-tile pattern,
6-7 Nine-tile pattern,
11 Tiles *in situ* in nave Four-tile pattern.

Figure 138 Large floor tiles *c*.1395-1400:
12-14 Sixteen-tile patterns,
15-18 Nine-tile patterns,
19-21b Four-tile patterns.

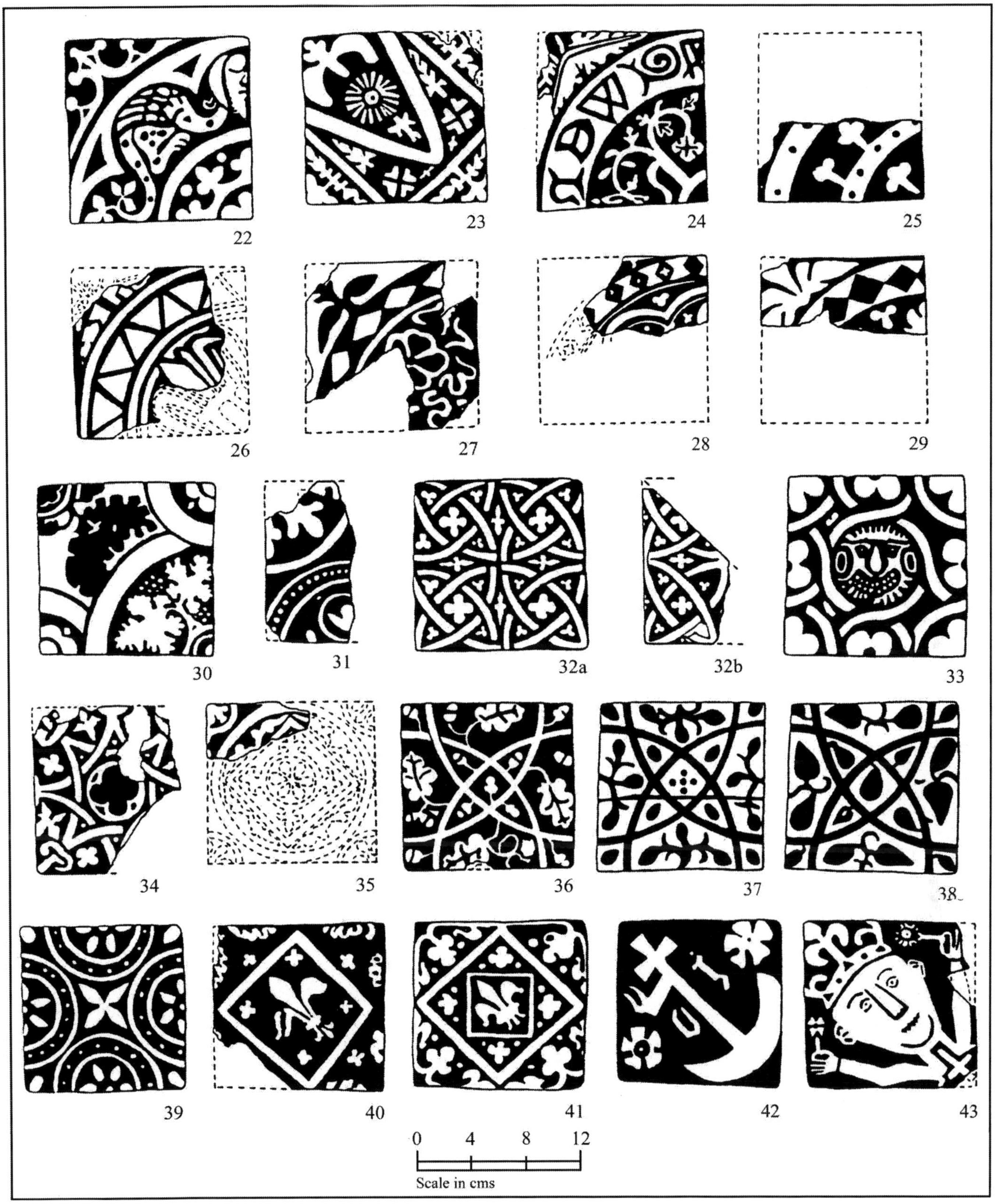

Figure 139 Large floor tiles *c.*1395-1400:
22-29 Four-tile patterns,
30-38 Endlessly-repeating patterns,
39-41 Simple repeating patterns,
42-43 Single tiles.

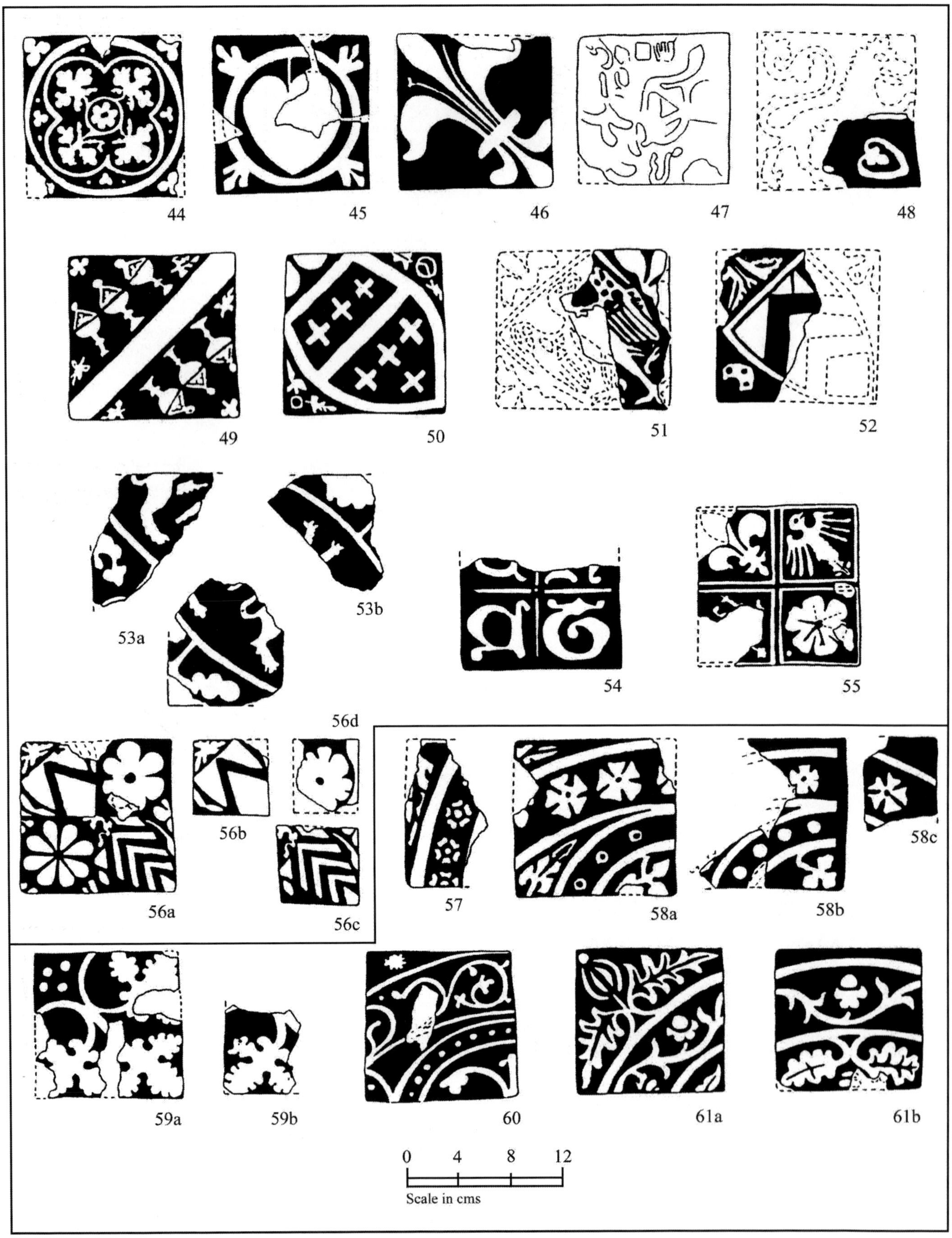

Figure 140 Large floor tiles *c.*1395-1400:
44-48 Single tiles,
49-53 Heraldic tiles,
54-56 Border tiles.
Small floor tiles, from *c.* second quarter of 15th century:
57-60 Sixteen-tile pattern,
61 Nine-tile patterns.

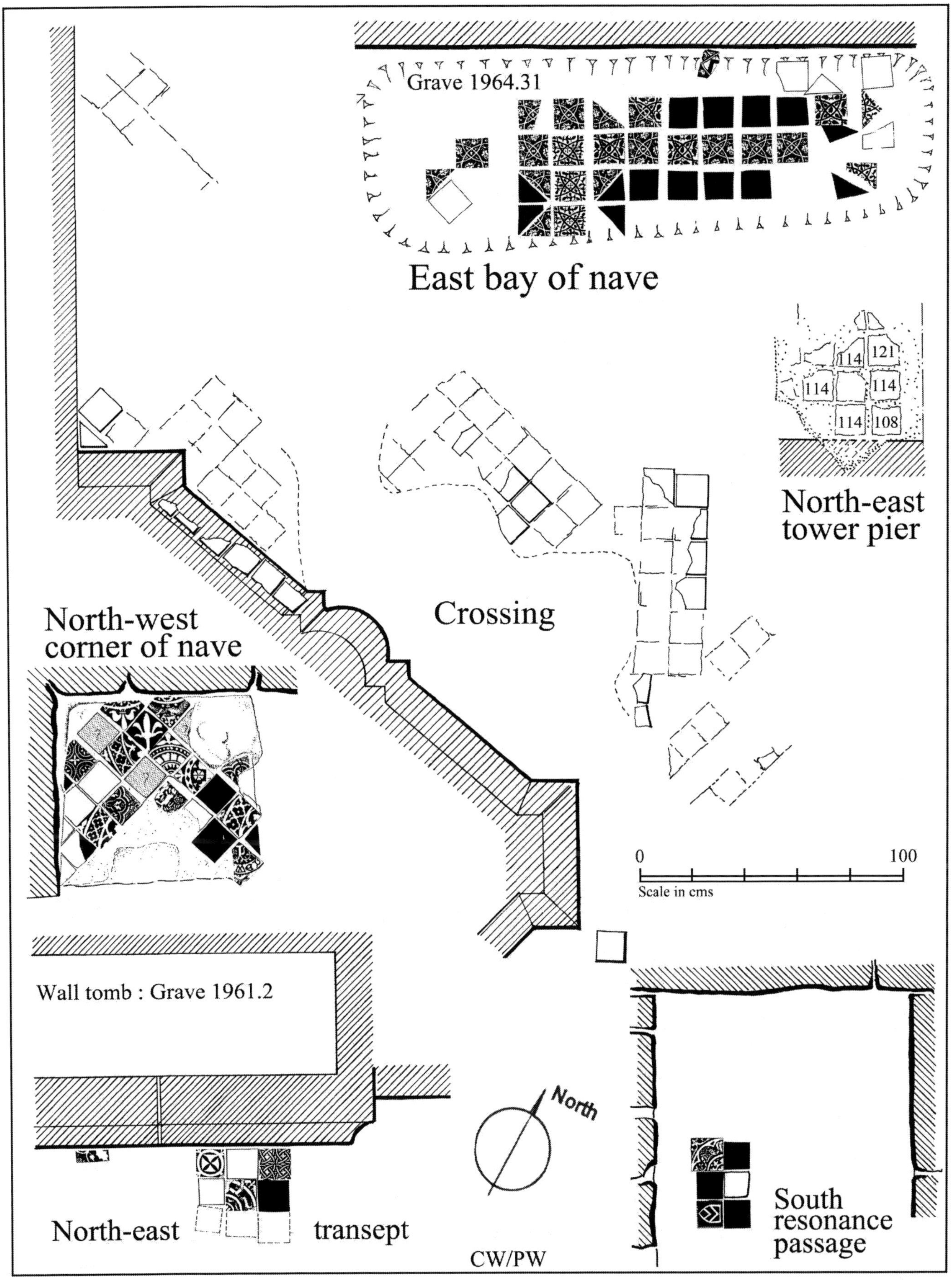

Figure 141 Layout of *in situ* floor tiles surviving within the church.

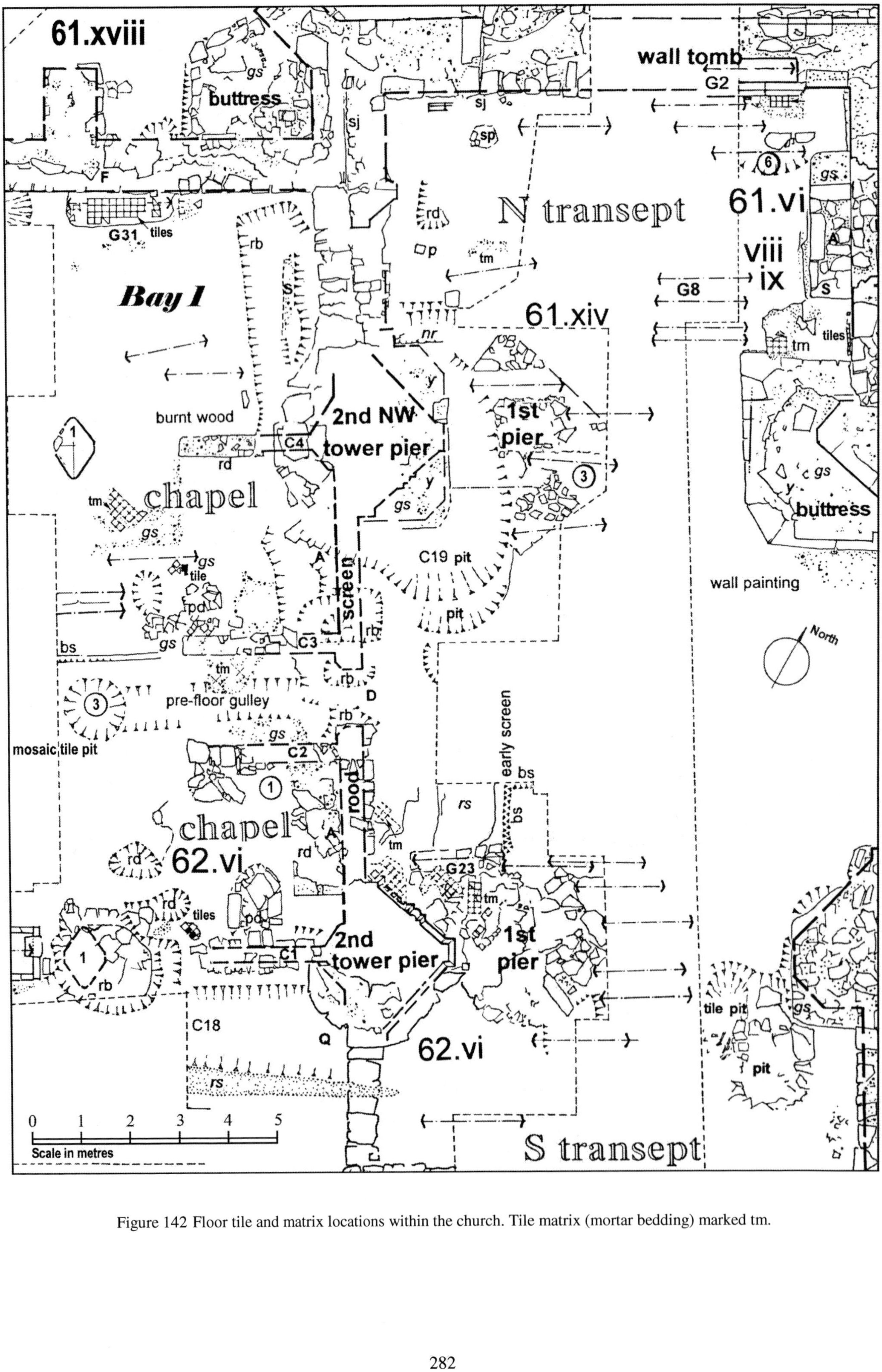

Figure 142 Floor tile and matrix locations within the church. Tile matrix (mortar bedding) marked tm.

Figure 143 Small floor tiles, from *c.* second quarter of 15th century:
62-63 Nine-tile patterns,
64-75 Four-tile patterns.

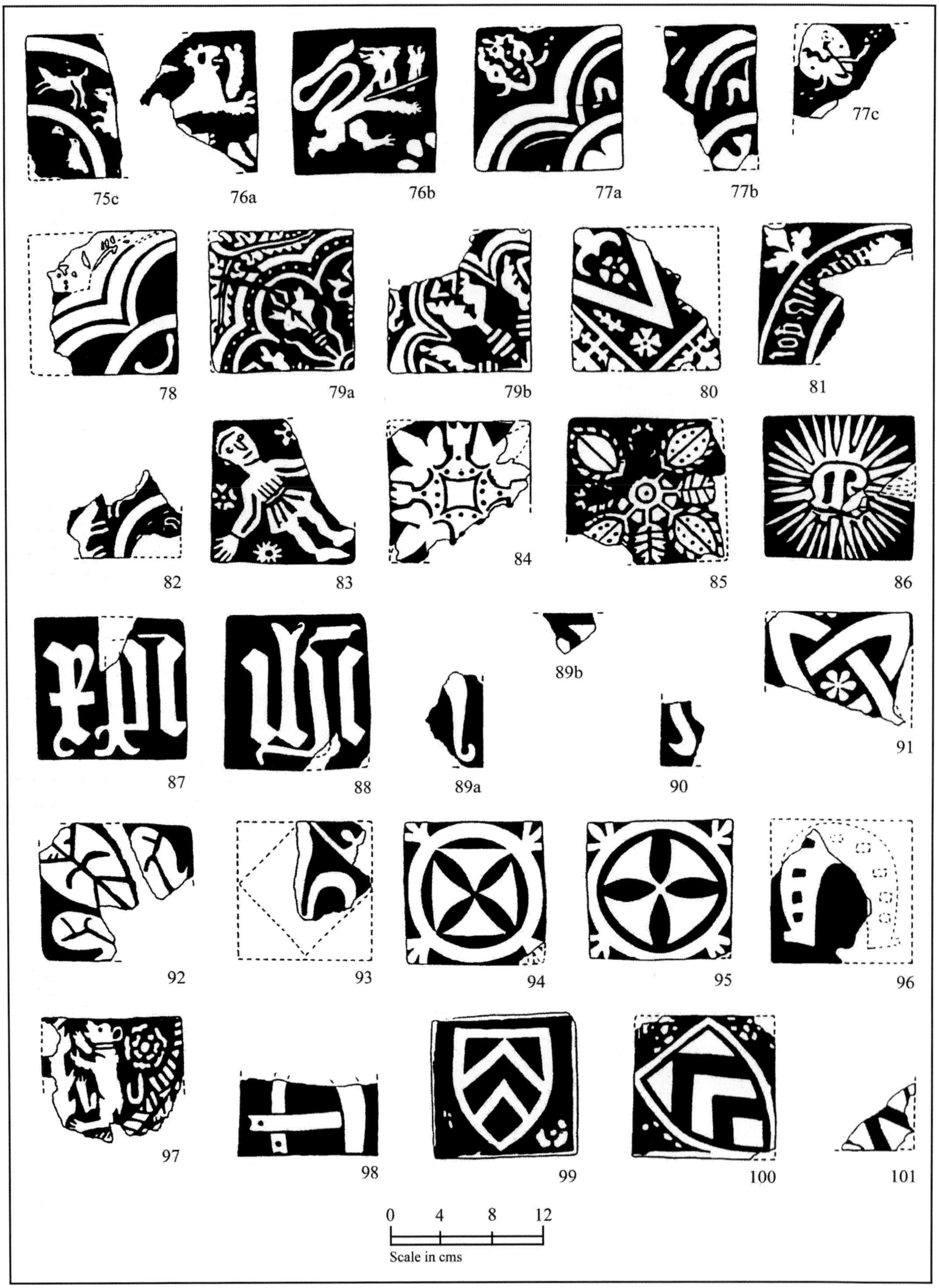

Figure 144 Small floor tiles, from *c.* second quarter of 15th century:
75c-82 Four-tile patterns,
83-91 Single tiles,
92-98 Semi-heraldic tiles,
98-101 Heraldic tiles.

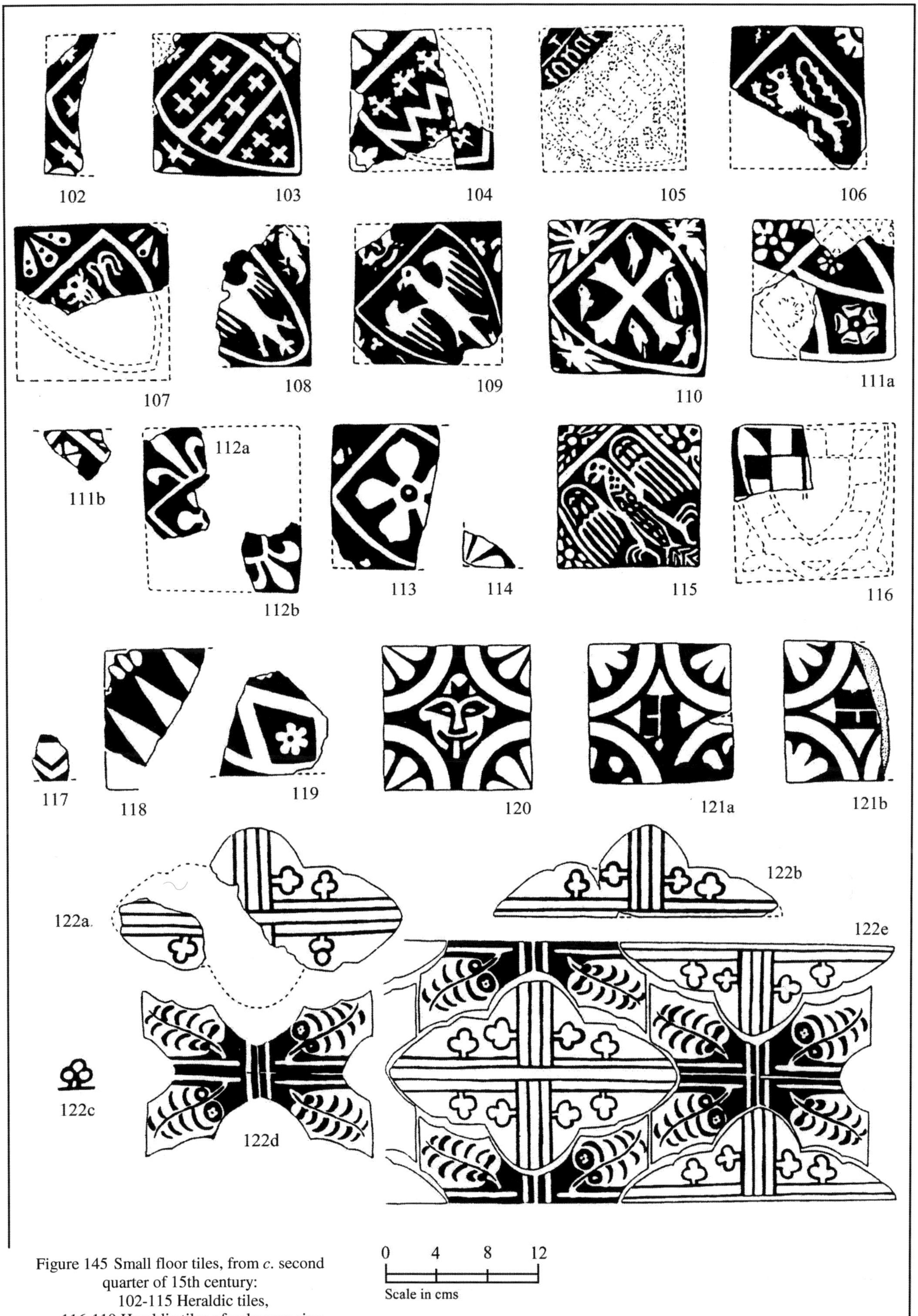

Figure 145 Small floor tiles, from *c.* second quarter of 15th century:
102-115 Heraldic tiles,
116-119 Heraldic tiles of unknown size,
120-121 Endlessly-repeating patterns,
122 Mosaic tiles.

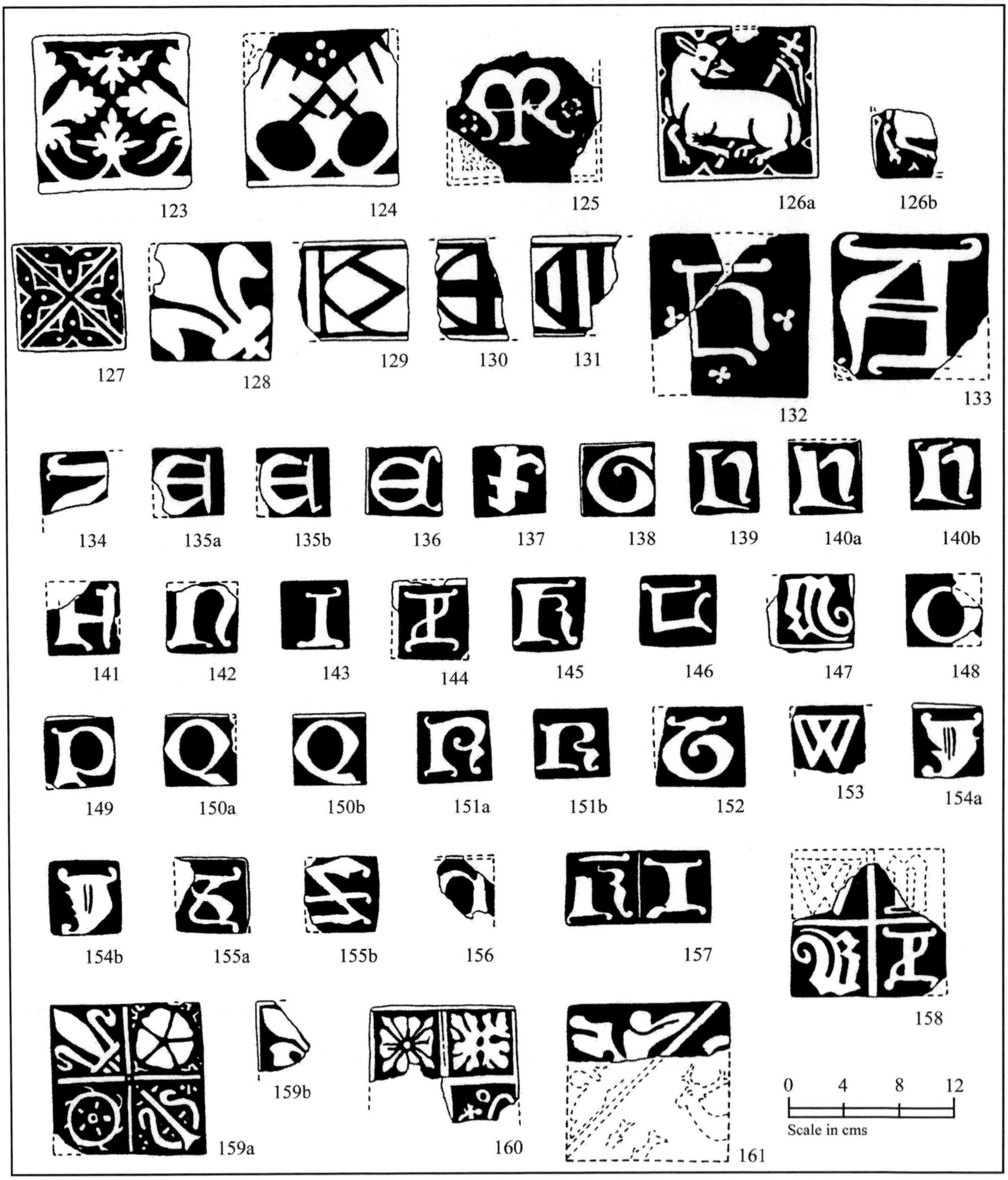

Figure 146 Border floor tiles, from *c.* second quarter of 15th century:
123-126 Border tiles,
127-128 Tiles of non-standard sizes,
129-131 Heraldic border tiles,
132-158 Lettered tiles (probably borders),
159-161 Border tiles.

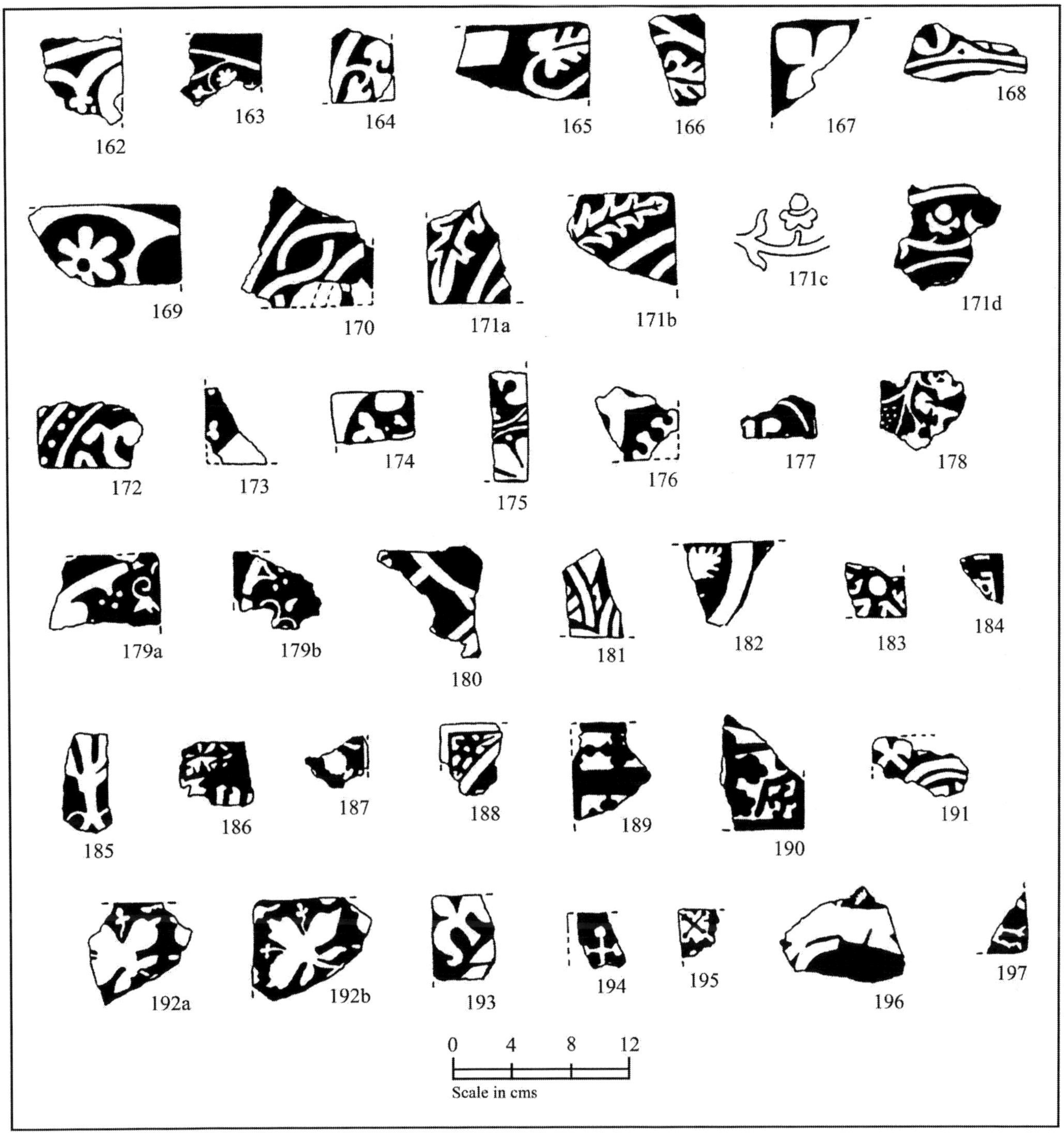

Figure 147 Floor tiles of unrecognised types (162-197).

SECTION M

ROOF TILE

S. Ratkai and C. Woodfield

SUMMARY

Study of the Whitefriars tile has established a chronology for the tile fabrics present, notably extending the date range of Chilvers Coton A to the end of the 14th century; it has established the presence and the form of roof tiles made at the Stoke kilns; it has confirmed the chronology for crested ridge tiles, and suggested a new louver type and other tile types; it draws attention to the presence of 'tiles and a half', their use being a sign of expensive roofing; it has also further indicated the decline of the use of glaze on roof tile in the later middle ages; and has established the use of women and children in the Stoke manufacturing process. The use of roof tile (and roof slate) for levelling courses in masonry walls has also been discussed. What buildings were roofed with tile has been established, together with the appearance of the perforated cloister sky line, with its brilliant glaze colours.

INTRODUCTION AND BACKGROUND

The following report is based on examination of the surviving tile from excavations at Whitefriars, incorporating notes made by C. Woodfield on that roof tile which has now been lost (primarily from the extensive 1964 and the 1968 excavations), and her work on form, use, chronology, stratification and parallels.

In the 1960s excavations roof tile was retained on the basis of form, glaze, and obviously differing fabrics, featureless tile sherds being discarded. There appears to have been no specific collection policy for tile from the Cloister Gate excavation of 1956 nor for the 1966 and 1970s excavations and the little of that material which survives is virtually unstratified.

Much of the surviving tile came from the 16th-century School deposit in the N resonance passage and the 18th-century robbing of this feature. Some of this tile was possibly brought into the choir from elsewhere on site by the school boys for the making of quoits, and does not imply that the choir was tiled, but its presence is further confirmation of the derelict state of the friary buildings at the time. The rest occurred occasionally in late reflooring deposits, grave fills, etc., but most of it came from 16th-century destruction levels. Some had been used to fill the worn post-Reformation pathway through the Great West Door.

A total of 324 fragments of roof tile/roof furniture survives from the excavations. It should be noted that less than a dozen tile fragments survive from the nave, and less than half a dozen from the crossing (excluding the N porch/NE transept area), so that this is a report on surviving material from, primarily, the standing E range of the cloister and areas to its S, immediate N and W, the Grammar School in the choir (Woodfield 1981), and the N porch and the NE transept area.

Each fragment was divided into a simple fabric grouping by eye. Fabric type, tile type and tile thickness and width (where possible) were noted. Details of peg/nail hole type, nib type and glaze type were also recorded. The tile was quantified only by count.

Five fabric types were noted, three of which could be sourced to Chilvers Coton, while a fourth now seems likely to be from Stoke. Seven main tile forms were observed, namely flat tiles with a central nib between two nail holes, flat tiles with a central nib and no nail holes, ridge tiles decorated with looped crests, knife cut crests, or pinnacles. Plain ridge tiles are also likely, and tiles with close set nail holes and probably an eccentric nib. Nibless tiles may have been present but there is no clear evidence. There were also four fragments from at least two louvers/ventilators. A large globular finial was also seen by both authors during the various assessments but could not be subsequently located at Coventry for inclusion in this report.

ROOF TILE FABRICS AND FORMS

Figures 148 and 149

Locally Produced Fabrics

Coarse Red Sandy Fabric

This is a coarse, granular, maroonish/strongly red fabric, with small black non-magnetic flecks, occasionally having calcareous or flint inclusions up to lcm across, often with noticeable golden mica on the surfaces and interior, and usually with rich dark green (less often brown) glazes, these being often brilliant and glossy/iridescent. Two fragments from the NE transept have the upper surface covered in a white slip, making the glaze a bright apple green. There are odd examples of olive glazes and mottled tan and dark green glazes which are reminiscent of Cannon Park ware (Redknap 1985). All the tiles were plain flat tiles with the exception of a dark green-glazed point, Fig. 149.13, possibly from a finial or less likely a 'pinnacle' from a ridge tile, and a flat but tapering tile, also glazed dark green, presumably a hip tile.

The tile thickness in this fabric fell generally between 15-20mm. Tile width varied, with an apparent norm of 170mm, from 165mm up to 220mm; a tile from the N porch was 235mm wide, probably representing the traditional tile-and-a-half for edge laying. Apart from the last, these measurements are approximate, derived from doubling the width from the edge to the estimated centre of the nib. One tile indicated a minimum length of 240mm, accompanying a width of 163mm.

There were thirteen examples of central nibs, Fig. 148.1, and these tended to project more than those on the smooth red sandy tiles (not apparent on the illustrated examples). There were four tiles with a central nib and a nail hole to either side, near to the upper corners. There were three examples of tile fragments with nail holes, All the nail holes were diamond-shaped on the nib side, tapering and ending in a small circular hole. The impression given is that they were formed by pushing a nail into the unfired clay. However, some of the holes were partial, i.e. they only went midway through the tile thickness. These may have been unintended, but evidently did not make the tiles unusable. Not enough material survives to be sure, but it seems possible that the majority of the tiles in this fabric had nail holes.

This appears to be a 13th and 14th-century fabric, see below.

Smooth Red Sandy Fabric (Fabric SMRS)

This was by far the largest surviving fabric group. These tiles are a lightish brick-red colour with a comparatively smooth fracture, and a smooth surface on the tile 'back' as laid, with a sanded 'front' with very variable amounts of glazing. Occasional large quartz grains and black clay pellets are visible in the fracture, and quartz generally is abundant. Some inclusions which appear to be flint/chert are up to 1.4cm across. Sometimes mica is visible on the surface or in the body of the fabric. Although most of the tiles were fully oxidised, a small number had reduced cores.

This fabric appears to the eye, even assisted with a hand lens, to be identical to the floor tile fabric, and is presumably also a product of the nearby Stoke kilns. Indeed one of these roof tiles has been cut diagonally across, as if it had been mixed up with floor tiles that were being halved.

Most of the tiles in this fabric were flat but there were ten examples of ridge tiles, the largest number for any of the fabrics (not illustrated), none of them being certainly crested. There were tiles with a central nib. Fig. 148.4. apparently without nail holes, and tiles with a central nib and two peg/nail holes, one in each upper corner. Fig. 148.3. Of the tiles which were complete across the top section, none could be shown to be without this central nib. These are sometimes rather small, only projecting 1-1.5cm. Many are damaged to the point of disappearance, and there are, as with the earlier fabric, several cases of spalling caused by a large inclusion behind the nib.

A flat tile with strange grooves, Fig. 148.7, occurred in 1968 IIIE 127, a Rebuild/Industrial level in the N porch area. Its use is unknown. Another anomaly occurred in a grey-cored version of this fabric in a destruction deposit in the S chancel, 69 XXIX 15, which also produced Elizabethan rubbed brick. This last tile has an abnormally large nib and the associated brick may indicate it is of 16th-century date, Fig. 148.6.

The shape of the peg/nail holes was not consistent. Some were diamond-shaped on the nib face, tapering to a narrow roughly circular hole, Fig. 148.5, and some were roughly circular and tapering. Two were circular but had a consistent diameter through the tile, but as one was unstratified and one from an 18th-century context, that may well be their date. As with the coarse red sandy fabric tiles (see above) some of the holes went only part way through the tile. There was a single example of two peg/nail holes close together, Fig. 148.5, doubtless an error.

The surviving tiles suggest a proportion of two-holed tiles for every three-unholed, and tiles without nail holes certainly occur. Normally one would expect one in four rows of tiles to be nailed.

A surviving broken off nail still stuck in a tile of this fabric, adjacent to the subsequently successful hole, indicates the method of their making.

Tile dimensions were variable, the width normally falling in the 150-180mm range, Fig. 148.3. There was again an apparent tile-and-a-half of 245mm width from the N porch, interestingly with the print of three small child's fingertips 7mm across, (together with a kitten's footprint 20mm across). There was a second possible tile and a half, 224mm wide. The most common tile thickness was 14-18mm. The tiles were often unglazed. When glazes did occur they were olive or tan/brown, and were on the lower half of the tile.

A dog pawprint measuring some 45 x 50mms across, and another more indistinct example, also occurred in tiles of this fabric. Several small children's or women's finger marks were also noted and suggest the use of female and/or child labour at the tile-works.

A fragment of one of these tiles from WF 60 II 9, a School deposit, had been re-shaped and probably used as a quoit. Fourteen apparent quoits, normally of a diameter of some 45mm, and mainly coming from the same deposit are published in Woodfield 1981 (105, fig. 11.7a).

All nail holes were made pre firing.

Chilvers Coton/Nuneaton Fabrics A, C and D

A description of these fabrics is given in Mayes and Scott (1984, 40). Fabric A with fine sand inclusions is white, cream or occasionally pink. Fabric C is slightly sandy, varying from pink to orange to red. Fabric D is a finely gritted fabric varying from orange to brick red to dark reddish, often having darker edges and surfaces (Midland Purple). In classifying this material the code CCC/D was used to denote a hard fired, pale purplish brown fabric, sometimes known as Proto-Midlands Purple, which is somewhere between fabric C and fabric D. Despite its name there is no firm evidence that it is a forerunner of true fabric D/Midland Purple and must in part, if not wholly, be coeval in the late 14th and 15th centuries.

Just under half the surviving tile fragments in fabric A were either ridge tiles or louver fragments, Fig. 149.10-11 and 14. In addition a sherd resembling a wide jug neck, with the rough internal finish of a ridge tile, but a neat, rilled external jug-like finish, may have come from the open top of a Nuneaton A ventilator of the form suggested for the Leicester Austin Friars (Allin 1981, 63, fig 18.20). All this material was glazed, generally with an apple green colour, often mottled. Tile thickness was generally 10-12mm, thinner than that in the fabrics described above. There was a crested ridge tile with a 'pinnacle' crest, Fig. 149.11, and also a single example of a knife-cut crest, Fig. 149.10, which could just be 15th century; an example in this fabric occurring at Ernesford Grange (Soden 1988, type RC3). Sherds not impossibly from flat tiles were too small for details of their form to be seen, and in the absence of any fragments with nail holes it seems likely that no flat tiles were represented.

How far this 13th-century fabric continued into the 14th century was thought to be uncertain (*ibid.* 43), but its occurrence here must now take it to very near the end of that century.

Half of the surviving tile fragments in fabric C were certainly either ridge tiles or louvers, Fig. 149.8-9, 12 and 15. Most of the tiles were glazed. Glazes varied between primarily olive greens and browns, often mottled. Tile thickness was generally in the same range as those in fabric A. There were three crested ridge tiles. One, from context 1969 XXIX 13 from E of the sacristy, was badly abraded and it was not possible to work out the shape of the crest. Two had double looped crests, Fig. 149.8-9 (cf. Mayes and Scott 1984 figs 114 and 118). This fabric was thought to extend from the 13th to the 15th centuries (*ibid.* 41), but its use in the 15th century at the Whitefriars is uncertain.

The typology of crests is reasonably well attested, and is supported by what survives of the Whitefriars crested material. The swan neck form, where loops curl round to touch the main body of the crest is 13th century at Chilvers Coton (Mayes and Scott 1984, fig. 117), Ernesford Grange (Soden 1988, figs 15 and 18-19) and the Leicester Austin Friars (Allin 1981, fig.15.1) but is not present at Coventry Whitefriars. The upright horned form (Woodfield, C. 1966, fig. 10 no. F, 117) there in a reduced Chilvers Coton C fabric, was dated to the (?earlier) 14th century, and was again not present at the Whitefriars.

The form where loops are made on either side of the crest stem, the points being smoothed outwards along the tile, is represented by Fig. 149.8. The loop flattening of Fig. 149.9 here is probably a late 14th-century feature.

The form with 'pinnacles' in Chilvers Coton A ware, Fig. 149.11, was thought to be also late 14th century by Mayes and Scott (1984) but interestingly first appears in a post 1400 context at the Leicester Austin Friars (Allin 1981, 60).

There were two louver/?chimney pot fragments both with a grey reduced Chilvers Coton fabric, Fig. 149.15. Their findspots were quite close and it is highly likely that the two fragments are from the same louver. A fragment of another louver, Fig. 149.14, in Chilvers Coton A fabric also came from the NE cloister.

The roof furniture in proto Midlands Purple fabric was negligible and was made up of ridge tiles and ?flat tile sherds in the same proportions as above, but there were only some half dozen occurrences of this fabric. Glazes were purplish, brown, or dark olive. Tile thickness ranged from 10-18mm. Presumably this fabric is 14th and 15th-century in date.

No tiles in Chilvers Coton fabrics survived here with nail holes; nail holes do occur in Chilvers Coton roof tiles (Mayes and Scott 1984, fig. 118, from F.74, mid 14th century), and their absence, together with the absence of nibs, makes the presence of flat tiles here uncertain.

A Chilvers Coton 'Midland Purple' tile fragment from WF 1960 III 4, the N porch, carried a possible batch mark in the form of an incised Roman V.

The attested loss of the more complete and elaborate examples of tiles, apparently not replaced after being put on display, makes the discussion of forms difficult throughout this report. It is known that there were sherds from one other finial, at least, in the School deposit.

Other Tile Fabrics

Not all the tiles fitted neatly into the above categories. At the W end of the nave in a 16th-century clearance pit, a 3cm thick ridge tile occurred in a fabric that appeared different to the eye, though still local, with conspicuous mica, white inclusions up to 7mm across and grey and black inclusions up to 3mm across. Its surviving length of 24cms showed that it had not been crested, and it was unglazed.

DISCUSSION, DATING, AND SITE DISTRIBUTION

Roof tile is not discussed in Hobley 1971(Benedictine Priory), Bateman and Redknap 1986 (Town Wall), Soden 1995 (Charterhouse), nor in Rylatt and Stokes 1996 (Broadgate), and this must put a restriction on discussion. It is however briefly discussed in Woodfield, C. 1966 for the Town Wall (fig. 10 F, 117 and 127), and more extensively in Soden 1988 (figs 14 and 15, 50 and 53).

It should also be noted that only ten tile fragments, all in the smooth red sandy fabric, survive from the nave, and that likewise only four tiles in coarse red sandy and smooth red sandy fabrics survive from the crossing (apart from the N porch/NE transept area), so it is not possible to discuss these areas. However a lead roof is to be expected for the main body of the Church.

The Coarse Red Sandy Ware Tiles

The loss of virtually all of the 1960 prefriary material from the quarry is particularly unfortunate. One fragment alone survives in this fabric, from 1960 II 16, a context well down in a pre-friary quarry fill, Fig. 148.2. This is slender evidence for the early date of this fabric, but tiles in a coarse red sandy fabric also with a central nib and nail holes in the corners occurred at Ernesford Grange, Coventry where they were thought to be of mid to late 13th-century date (Soden 1988, fig. 14.1-3).

Additionally this coarse fabric occurs again in a grave fill, WF 61 VI 8, grave 61/5; the grave is of the Friary 2 period, i.e. after *c.*1390; but the tile and medieval pottery from the grave fill are more likely to be residual from the Pre-friary quarry backfill into which the grave was cut. In the Pre-rebuild period (*c.*1430 to the later 15th century) this fabric was also found in WF 61 VI 3b (collapse of the N transept and the N porch/chapel) and in WF 61 IX 1 (over the cut-down step in the N porch before rebuilding), presumably residual from the first roof of that porch.

The amount of this material recovered makes it clear that this fabric was used in the earlier periods of the Friary, rather than all predating it. It is likely that flat tiles in this fabric with their iridescent green and brown glazes were used on the eastern cloister and chapter house with Chilvers Coton ridge tiles, whose distribution suggests that this roofing phase should extend as far S as the Prior's house. Three pieces of this tile presumably extend this roofing phase westwards to include the Cloister Gate. Five boxes of roof tile, now lost, were noted from here in the 1992 assessment, and it must be assumed that the Cloister Gate was also tiled.

This combination of coarse red sandy flat tile with Chilvers Coton crested ridge tiles also occurred at Ernesford Grange (Soden 1988, 50-53) although there only the Chilvers Coton A fabric was represented, and plain ridge tiles in the local coarse sandy fabric also occurred, there thought to be of mid to late 13th-century date.

These coarse sandy tiles appear also to have been used for the first roofing of the N porch, which would probably have occurred not long after the roofing of the cloister. Though only a single Midlands Purple tile survives from the porch itself, Chilvers Coton ridge tiles occur nearby in the N transept. Ridge tiles in this coarse red fabric are however also not directly associated with the porch, except for a possible pinnacle, Fig. 149.13. The loss of material makes discussion difficult.

The Smooth Red Sandy Ware Tiles

This fabric occurs stratified for the first time in level WF 62 VI 11 (a reflooring level E of the SW tower pier). This reflooring probably dates from the first half of the 15th century. The use of tiles in this fabric continues through into the late 15th/early 16th century with the rebuild of the N porch as a structure of uncertain use at this time, and here these tiles survive, even with the loss of material, in three rebuild levels, 60 III 7, 68 IIIE 115, and 68 IIIE 127, of the late 15th/early 16th centuries. A smooth ridge tile with no external glaze from the W cloister (68 XXVII 2) looks like a later development of this fabric for a later building phase.

It appears therefore that the Coarse Red Sandy fabric is replaced by the Smooth Red Sandy fabric sometime in the early 15th century.

These tiles may also have been used in the (?)second quarter of the 16th-century Rebuild period, as part of a workshop then attached to the porch, and tiles in this fabric are copiously represented in the mid 16th-century destruction levels of this rebuilding in that area, i.e. in levels 60 III 4, 68 IIIE 105, 107, 109, and 110. A contemporary comment on excavating level 68 IIIE 109 records that 70% of the glazed tiles had a bright ginger glaze with a late medieval air.

Some of these tiles appear also to have been used as levelling courses in masonry walls. A tile covered with mortar and with a smoothed face on one edge survives from 62 VI 11, a phase Friary 2 (less likely Rebuild) makeup level probably of the second decade of the 15th century, this being for the floor E of the SW tower pier. Another came from 68 XID WCG, the lower fill of grave 14, where 22 pieces of roof tile were recorded at the time 'the majority with mortar on both sides, apparently from use as levelling'; the phase here is Rebuild of the mid to later 15th century.

Much of the mortar on all tiles is on backs and edges and relates to torching in the majority of cases. However, in all surviving examples where the use was clearly for levelling all the examples were in this Smooth Red Sandy fabric, although this may be fortuitous. These smooth sandy levelling tiles occurred in the N and S resonance passages (where the mortar deposits were over lcm thick), in the SE transept and the SW chancel, presumably relating to adjacent 15th-century building works.

Both roof tile and Stockingford shale 'slate' wasters were used for levelling courses, and can still be observed in the surviving masonry.

Additionally there was much built-in roof tile recorded on plans and photographs in the late 15th/early 16th-century pentagonal reinforcement buttress at the W of the N transept (WF61 XI Be), but unfortunately the samples taken do not seem to survive. It appears that clay tile wasters may have become cheaper or more easily available than shale tile wasters sometime before the later 15th century, for the shale does not seem to have been used in later phases of construction.

Tiles in this fabric appear from their distribution to have been used for re-roofing the N porch, and presumably for repairs to all roofs including the Cloister Gate. The western cloister was probably roofed in these *de novo*.

Their manufacture, apparently at Stoke, where the floor tile kilns of 15th-century date at Harefield Road (Chatwin, 1936, 2) are known to have been constructed from both roof and floor tile wasters suggests both are being manufactured together, and also, with other evidence, that they may be reaching Whitefriars from the early 15th century. This might not coincide with the arrival of the first group of the larger floor tiles from Stoke, which were presumably going into recently roofed buildings, but would coincide with the second group of smaller floor tiles which are thought to have arrived on site at that date, continuing probably into the early 16th century.

Chilvers Coton Tiles

The eastern cloister and areas to its immediate N, less so to its S but probably extending to the Prior's house, and related sacristy/passage/SE transept areas, seemed to have a higher concentration of Chilvers Coton tile than elsewhere. In addition these areas also produced ridge tiles in fabric C, and crested ridge tiles and at least two louvers in fabrics A and C (although ridge tiles in these fabrics did occur in the N transept, suggesting that the first tiling of the N porch might also have involved this fabric). This roofing is likely to have occurred in the last decade and a half of the 14th century.

These tiles and roof furniture occur largely in levels related to a post-Reformation (1540s) possible total re-tiling of that eastern cloister range by Hales, implying that they had remained in use, doubtless with some replacement during rebuilding work for many timbers were replaced in the 1470s-90s, for some century and a half before being finally discarded when the late medieval roof was destroyed. This roofing would have been undertaken before the tiling of floors and so was not accompanied by an influx of Chilvers Coton floor tiles, which in any case had perhaps ceased to be produced by this time (Eames 1984, 185).

Chilvers Coton Fabric A was thought to stop *c.*1300 at Ernesford Grange (Soden 1988, 37 and 50) but this cannot now be maintained. The Whitefriars seems to take this fabric almost into the 15th century. It is likely that roof furniture in this fabric was standard on high status buildings, and looped crests are known at the royal manor of Cheylesmore (Coventry Museums Archaeology Unit, 1992, fig. 10).

THE ROOFING OF THE MAIN BODY OF THE CHURCH

Evidence for lead roofs usually completely disappears at the Reformation and only some three offcuts of roofing lead were found in the 1960s excavations, together with a sliver used by a schoolboy as a tally (Fig 162.66). The assumption must however remain that the main choir, crossing and nave were not tiled.

EVIDENCE FOR POTTERY AND TILE PRODUCTION IN THE COVENTRY AREA

This has been summarised both by Redknap (1985) and Soden (1988, 53). This evidence suggests production at Canley, Coundon, Little Park, Potters Green, Potters Harnall and Stoke, all within five miles of the city. The general picture concerning its production remains clouded, and we do not know the source of the coarse red sandy fabric, but have established that the fine red sandy fabric is likely to come from Stoke.

CATALOGUE OF ILLUSTRATED ROOF TILE AND LOUVERS

C. Woodfield

Figure 148

A Tiles in the earlier coarse red sandy fabric

Prefriary and early friary. 13th to late 14th century.

(Descriptions carrying the mark ** are of tiles that are now lost).

1 Tile with large nib and remains of nail hole, of the apparently standard diamond shape for this fabric, c.f. Soden 1988, fig. 14.3. Unglazed, but a rich iridescent green glaze is common in this fabric, and a brown glaze can occur. 1960 II 8. Residual in 16th-century destruction in S resonance passage.

2 As above, showing nail hole. This frost damage to nibs was common. 1960 II 16, fill of pre-friary stone quarry.

Apparent hip tiles were noted in this fabric, but no obvious ridge tiles occurred, although No 13 is a possible ridge tile or finial fragment. The accompanying ridge tiles and louvers at this period are from Chilvers Coton, and it appears that the cloister buildings and the first N porch used this combination. The Stone House at nearby Much Park Street (Wright 1982, 19, fig. 56 No. 3 and 101) was also thought to have had a roof of local red tiles, with Chilvers Coton green-glazed looped finial ridge tiles in the later 14th century.

B Tiles in the later smooth red sandy fabric

(Stoke) Early 15th into early 16th century.

3 Tile with two nail holes (shape more variable in this fabric) with the now more common smallish nib. Unglazed, but these tiles are normally only glazed on the lower half, often not reaching the tile edge. A note in 1968 on now lost material commented that the piercings in this fabric only occurred 'occasionally, and were usually sub-rectangular or square but set diagonally, the holes being mostly incomplete. The tiles had been set on the roofs with mortar over the lower 30mm or so'. 1960 II 9, residual in 16th-century School deposit in N resonance passage.

4 Tile without nail holes and smallish nib. Unglazed, torched at back. The fabric is a little coarser than usual. 1960 III 4, Rebuild phase, mid to later 15th century, at the N porch/chapel, which it is assumed was re-roofed in this material.

5 Tile with two adjoining holes - one of only two examples. Shiny tan glaze, the commonest glaze colour in this fabric, although a dull blue green glaze does occur. 1968 Ga 2.1. 16th-century robbing of grave 17.

C Anomalies.

6 Tile in a late-looking reduced, grey-cored, smooth sandy fabric, spots of blackish glaze. Very large nib. 1969 XXIX 15, found stratified with rubbed Elizabethan brick in the S chancel, so probably 16th century. One only.

7 Tile with grooved edges, unglazed, and roughly made. Mortar on back. 1968 IIIE 127, an industrial context of the mid to later 15th century. N porch.

The presence of 'tiles-and-a-half' for edge laying, with widths of e.g. 245mm was noted in 1968 in this fabric at the N porch/chapel, paralleling their occurrence here in the earlier coarse sandy fabric. Their use implies expensive roofing for both the first phase as a porch and the second phase as a late 15th-century chapel.

D Ridge tiles in the smooth red sandy fabric

A thin scatter of ten apparently plain ridge tile fragments occurred in this fabric, and were presumably made at Stoke (not illustrated). The fragments were generally unglazed, but with two examples of tan/dull green glazes. The absence on the site of Chilvers Coton decorated floor tiles suggests an inability to cope with the competition from Stoke in the field of both roof and floor tiles from *c.*1395, the assumption being that the Chilvers Coton ridge tiles were replaced by these Stoke products. Certainly the last occur in relation to the W cloister built about the second quarter of the 15th century (68 XXVII 2).

Figure 149

E Chilvers Coton Ridge Tiles

Apparently contemporary with the earlier coarse red sandy fabric.

8 Ridge tile with swan's neck loops in the Chilvers Coton C fabric, with brownish glaze.** The typological development is that the loops open out and flatten, see No 9. A mid to late 14th-century date is suggested at the Austin Friars (Allin 1981, 59), a later than mid 14th-century date being more likely here. This form is confirmed as the next stage on from the earlier, pre-friary, Ernesford Grange ridge tiles (Soden 1988, fig. 15, no 19), and is paralleled at the royal manor of Cheylesmore (Soden 1992, 41, fig. 10). Context WF 61 A d, residual in N resonance passage.

9 As above, but with the loops flattened, again in the

Chilvers Coton C fabric with a dull olive glaze (not shown), a later type than No 8.** 1973 Tr II, uncertain but possibly chapter house.

10 Crested ridge tile fragment with knife cuts.** It does not however resemble true knife cut ridges (c.f. Steane 1967, fig. 9). Might it be from another cloister finial or louver? Chilvers Coton fabric A, dull apple green glaze. Crest form not attested at Chilvers Coton. Residual in 1962/63 Cloister Bay 7 (1), 16th-century destruction related to re-roofing.

11 Ridge tile with pinnacles, a later type than loops, and unlikely before late on in the 14th century.** Chilvers Coton A fabric, glaze colour unknown. It cannot now be established if the pinnacles were or were not dowelled. The standard length for Midland ridge tiles is stated to be between 380-480mm (Dunning 1971-2, 38). 1960 I 13/13a probably from the sealing over of the quarry in the SE transept in the late 14th early 15th century.

12 Ridge tile in Chilvers Coton C fabric, partial (not shown) olive glaze.** 1973?/1977, i.e. uncertain, but NE cloister or chapterhouse.

F Louvers and Finials.

13 The small size and the fabric date suggests the top of a finial rather than a pinnacle from a ridge tile. The coarseness of the local red sandy fabric, and the dark green glaze, together with the find place, suggests a later date in the 14th century. 1968 IIIE 109, 16th-century roof tile tip at the N porch.

14 Chilvers Coton A fabric, glazed, colour not recorded.** Its form suggests it is from the base of a louver/ventilator as No 15, and it is incorporated in the reconstruction of that form. 1962 Cloister Bay 8 (1), N end of standing cloister, removed in 16th-century re-roofing.

15 Two fragments apparently of the same louver, in reduced Chilvers Coton fabric C, with greyish brown surfaces, and dark shiny olive-green overall glaze with brown iron specks, external but with some internal splashing. Traces of coiling, a break along a coil line, and the run pattern of the iron inclusions in the glaze were indicators for the placing of the two upper sherds (I am grateful to John Cotter for this suggestion). Two knife-cut edges indicate adjacent large holes, outlined by single thumbed strips, one hole a long oval and one a rounded oval. The long oval hole is recorded at Chilvers Coton (Mayes and Scott 1984, fig. 120). The base is assumed in this reconstruction to have resembled the sherd 14 base. The louver diameter appears to have been some 35cm, and the height some 50cm. The suggested terminal is based on a trefoil form in Fabric C (Mayes and Scott 1984, fig. 118). It may however have terminated as No 16. 1961 XI D s, residual in 18th-century level N. of the standing cloister, and WF 77 Area 4 U/S, N of standing cloister.

Both louvers from their find places are likely to be from the dorter roof and to date from the later 14th century. This fits well within the date range of up to 1425 for their manufacture (Dunning 1971-2, 34). There is no immediately obvious parallel in Dunning 1961, nor in Mayes and Scott 1984. The unusual feature of the larger sherd is that it cannot be reconstructed with the holes occurring in the usual horizontal zones. The firing of the louver on its side would seem unlikely.

16 Upper part of a comparative, probably friary, finial or louver, drawn from a photograph in the Dunning archive at the British Museum. Described as 'light brick-red ware' (presumably Chilvers Coton C) 'spike not glazed - thick uneven dark green glaze covers surface and the flanges, which are finger printed. Solid spike, deeply slashed - parallel knife cuts. Between the flanges a single opening'. Presumably later 14th century. From Greyfriars Lane Post Office, Coventry.** Coventry Museum A/254/1. I am grateful to Barbara Hurman for the information on this terminal.

Tiles 1-5 and 7-14 were drawn by David Watts, and tiles 6, 15 and 16 by Paul Woodfield.

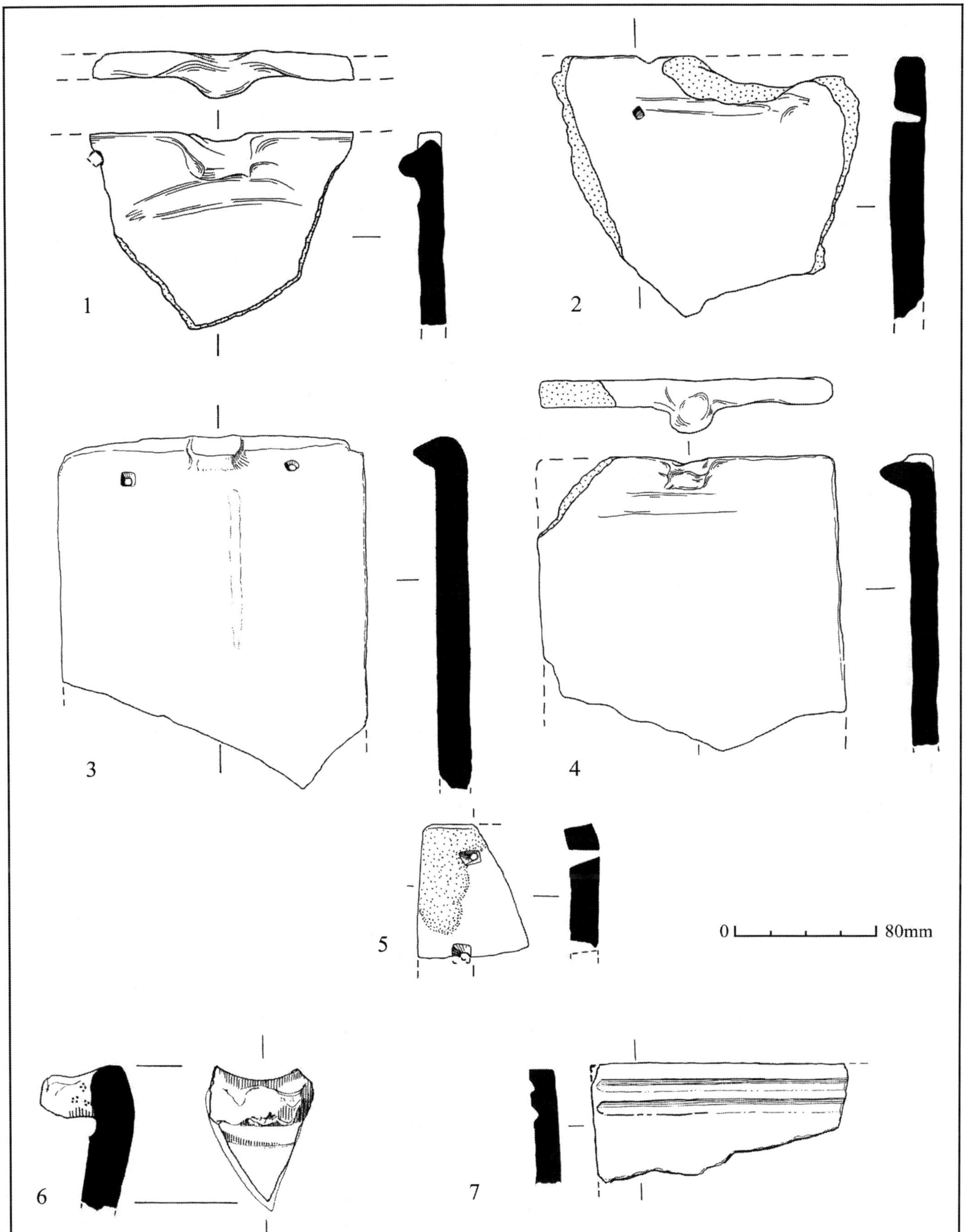

Figure 148 Roof tile:
1-2 13th to late 14th-century coarse red sandy tiles; rich green and brown glazes; cloister and N. porch,
3-5 Early 15th to early 16th-century smooth red sandy tiles (Stoke); unglazed; N porch,
6-7 Anomalies,
6 Elizabethan, large nib, black glaze on grey fabric,
7 Later 15th-century, grooved edge tile, unglazed.

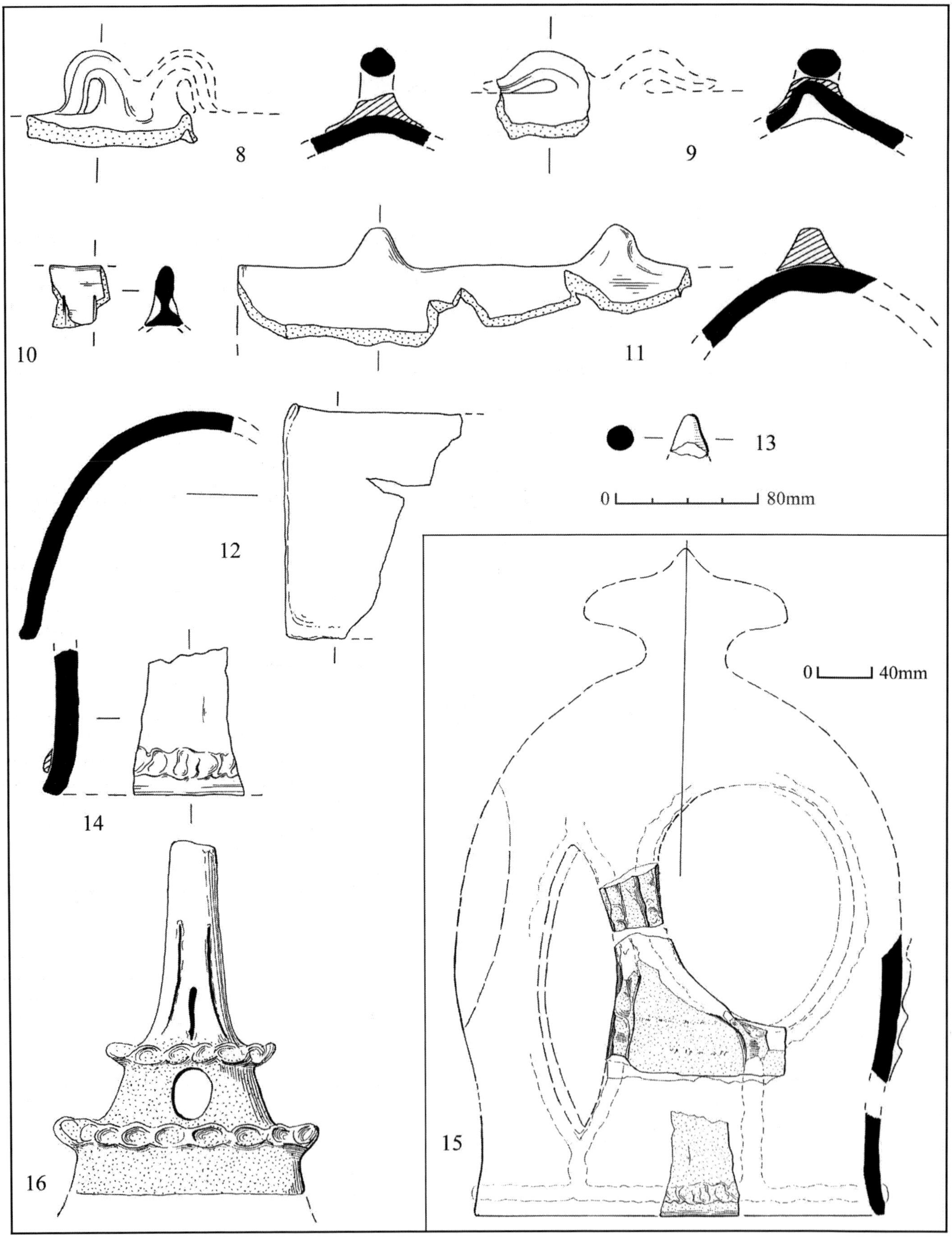

Figure 149 Ridge tiles and roof furniture:
8-12 Chilvers Coton ridge tiles, 9-10 and 12 green-glazed, from standing cloister,
13 Finial ?, green-glazed, from tile tip,
14-15 Chilvers Coton louvers, green-glazed, from standing cloister,
16 From Coventry Greyfriars.

SECTION N
BRICK

P. Woodfield

Ten late medieval or Tudor bricks or portions of bricks were recovered from the resonance passage, and were published in Woodfield 1981, with descriptions of the fabric and manufacture, as coming from pre-Reformation alterations to the friary buildings, or from the alterations to Hales' Place. They were of virtually standard width at 125mm (5in) width, and between 44 and 57mm (1¾ and 2¼in) thickness. The only two complete bricks were both 260 – 267mm (10¼ to 10½in) long.

Deductions as to date cannot safely be made on the basis of the dimensions of early bricks, and there is the added complication of the inevitable distortion that takes place during firing. Various attempts were made from time to time to regulate the size, from the 15th to the late 20th century, which were often ignored or relapsed, and the size 'comfortable' for a bricklayer to handle has remained the approximate size, surviving even attempts at metrication (see Lloyd 1983 for an account of the regulations up to 1800). In 1426 a given size was laid down in Chelmsford for 'tile' (i.e. walling brick). The Tudor brick was standardised in 1571 at 9 x 4in (*c.* 230 x 100mm) (Cave 1981, 114). Slightly earlier, the bricks used in Henry VIII's work at Hampton Court from about 1530 are 10 x 4 x 2½in (Wight 1972, 214); those used at Little Wenham Hall, Suffolk, are significantly smaller, at 8-9¾ x 3¾ x 1¾-2 ½in; whilst those used at Lambeth Palace in the 1480s were 10 x 5 x 2¼in (Wight 1972, 311).

Brick structures of the 16th century in the wider Coventry region include part of John Spencer's manor house of *c.*1512 at Wormleighton, Warwickshire, and the manor house at Compton Wynyates some eight years later (Wight 1972, 390). Sheldon Hall, near Birmingham is of a similar period (Wight 1972, 391). The presence of 'hand-made brick burnt blue' is recorded from the 1970s excavations at Coventry Whitefriars, from over the pitched paving apron immediately N of the reredorter's N arcade where it occurred in levelling to form a workshop of just pre-Reformation date. Unfortunately this brick is lost, but it suggests the possible employment of diaper or even decorative work, as in the Bishops of Lincoln's works on the palace at Buckden, Cambs. of 1472-80 (Wight 1972, 279).

No monastic buildings purely of brick are known from Warwickshire, although the surviving building of Coventry Charterhouse has ribbed brick flues rising from the stone chimney stacks. This may perpetuate the earlier construction, as elaborate chimneys of brick are shown on antiquarian drawings (Birmingham Reference Library, Aylesford Collection). The excavations there identified a brick-lined drain outside cell III leading to a central well but without dating evidence (Soden 1995, 61, fig. 21).

These findings suggest that construction in brickwork during the last phases of the friary, and possibly even diapered brickwork, is a distinct possibility at the Coventry Whitefriars. Certainly, brick (5in wide and 2¼in thick) set in lime mortar appears to have been used in the chantry tomb, in the SE nave, Fig. 42 (Grave 64.19).

The hand-made bricks from the rectangular ash pit, F.112, perhaps used in conjunction with the Workshop itself fall, within a similar size range, 9½ x 4¾ x 2¼ (240 x 120 x *c.*55mm); and similarly those from an ash pit on the S side of the workshop, F.122 (not shown on plan due to the uncertainty of its recording). Unfortunately the fill of both pits, including the ash and leather offcuts, was bagged up with adjacent material of 16th to 18th-century dates. The position of F112, Fig. 49, suggests the earlier date.

The patching of the partly medieval tiled-floor of the Prior's house, Fig. 49, using bricks 230-250mm in length, is presumably of the 18th century, the building surviving until *c.*1800 when it was demolished. Also shown on Fig. 49, is the drain F.24, which had a brick base of three parallel runs of brick probably dating from the Workshop period as it seems to represent a drain to a new latrine made necessary by the disappearance of the reredorter in *c.*1535.

SECTION 0
SLATE

P. and C. Woodfield

Figure 150

Stockingford Shale is a sandy shale of upper Cambrian age which forms the core of the Nuneaton inlier, overlying the Hartshill quartzite, and is found thinly in a bed N of Bedworth, running SE of Nuneaton and terminating in the region of Atherstone, under the Coal measures (Sylvester Bradley and Ford 1968, 29-37); the Coventry slate was identified in 1964 by the late Prof. F W Shotton, (Geology Dept., University of Birmingham).

At Coventry Whitefriars, this varied laminating shale generally of a green colour, is used to provide a roofing slate, whilst offcuts and laminates are used extensively for packing and levelling, a role usually played by oyster shells in the medieval period (Salzman 1967, 89).

The amount of roofing slate is not easy to determine as the proof of this particular use lies in the chance appearance of a distinctive shape and a fixing hole for wood, bone or iron nails. The quantity is not large, for if any large building on the site had been slated, it is more than likely that very much more material would have been recovered. It is of course possible that the few distinctive slates had been brought on to the site from an earlier building for the specific purpose of breaking them up for the use of the masons in packings for levelling purposes.

Two distinctive pieces of roof slate, Fig. 150, complete with fixing holes were found in 69 XXIX 4, the rubble N of the sacristy N door and a position which suggests it may have been used on the night stair, while another, retaining the head of a nail, occurred in a slot in the area of the N chapel (IIIE 109), a roof tile tip from the destruction of the church. The thickness of the slate in this last case, is confirmed by the corrosion of the nail, and is remarkable as being 3mm only, raising some doubts as to whether this is really adequate for roofing, although 'farewells' need not be particularly thick. The others are more in the region of 6mm thick, one being shaped to an acute angle with the 6.5mm diameter hole at the apex, Fig. 150.2.

Pieces of slate without distinctive features occurred widely elsewhere, some still adhering to stonework and having clearly been used for levelling and packing, where a choice of thicknesses would have been necessary. One piece (62 VI 10) is, 11mm thick, stratified in the Friary 2 phase in the eastern nave; another from the rubble in the choir (1977 Area 3) is up to 15mm, but otherwise the normal thickness is around 5mm - 6mm. Other pieces had been used to pack around ironwork before running in with lead (see Section Q, *Structural Metalwork*).

One piece of roofing slate exhibits mortar adhering to one side, and one side only. This may just be evidence of strip mortar bedding in roofing, a normal practice with roof tiling, but unfortunately it cannot be said that this is not the result of secondary use as packing, and further, it is unlikely that the mortar would be placed closely around the fixing hole.

Slate was used for some roofing at the Aberdeen and Perth Whitefriars, but was of a different type and up to 20mm in thickness (Stones 1989, 149, 151, fig. 92; the slating at Perth was carried out in 1513). Mortar bedding was noted there, as well as the slates being 'shouldered' i.e. the top corners of the rectangular slate broken off.

The distribution at Coventry is largely confined to the W chancel and night stair areas, with a thin scatter in the crossing and E nave, largely the areas of the first phase of building, where of course much remained in place, Table 6. Other loose surviving material came from stratified 15th-century contexts, or from the main 16th-century destruction contexts.

Stockingford slate used for levelling purposes was noted in the excavations at Much Park Street, occurring there from the early fourteenth century (Wright 1982, 99), also at Coventry City Wall (Woodfield 1966, 129-30) and at Kenilworth Castle (Rahtz 1963-4, 66).

This material, which has also been observed by the writers in the late 12th-century Chapter House of Combe Abbey, seems likely to represent a substantial but unlocated and undocumented medieval industry, based probably in the Nuneaton area, the nearest source being Griff (Warwicks.). The material was further identified but not dated at the Coventry Benedictine Priory excavations in destruction levels (Hobley 1971, 101). This industry thus appears to have already been established by the late 12th century.

Table 6 Distribution of Surviving 15th-century Stockingford Shale

The subsequent loss of all the 1964 material at the museum is unfortunate.

Trench	**Layer**	**Quantity**	**Context/Phase**
62 VI	10	1	E nave. Phase Friary 2, 15th century.
68 IIIE	109	1	N porch. Destruction tile dump.
77	2 (U/S)	3 small pcs mortar (pink)	Area E of passage to sacristy.
77	3 (U/S)	-	Rubble in choir.
69 XXIX	4 (U/S)	1	Passage to sacristy.
69 XXIX	4 (U/S)	1	Passage to sacristy, rubble from the night stair area.
From Stephanie Ratkai's list (not seen):-			
60 II	8	25 pcs	Destruction over S resonance passage.
60 III	4	2 pcs	Destruction N of N porch (tile dump).
61	Ad	2 pcs	N resonance passage: School level.
61	Ag	1	Destruction levels in N resonance passage.
61 VI	(U/S)	1 large fixing hole, M	Area N transept.
61 VI	10	1	E nave, phase Friary 2. 15th century.
61 VI	3B	1, M	NE transept: Pre-rebuild phase. 15th century.
61 XII	8	-, M	NW chancel destruction level.
62 1	4	1	N resonance passage: School.
62 III	-	1, 9mm thick	E end, destruction level.
62 VI	11	1, M	Crossing. Phase Friary 2.

M = mortar adhering

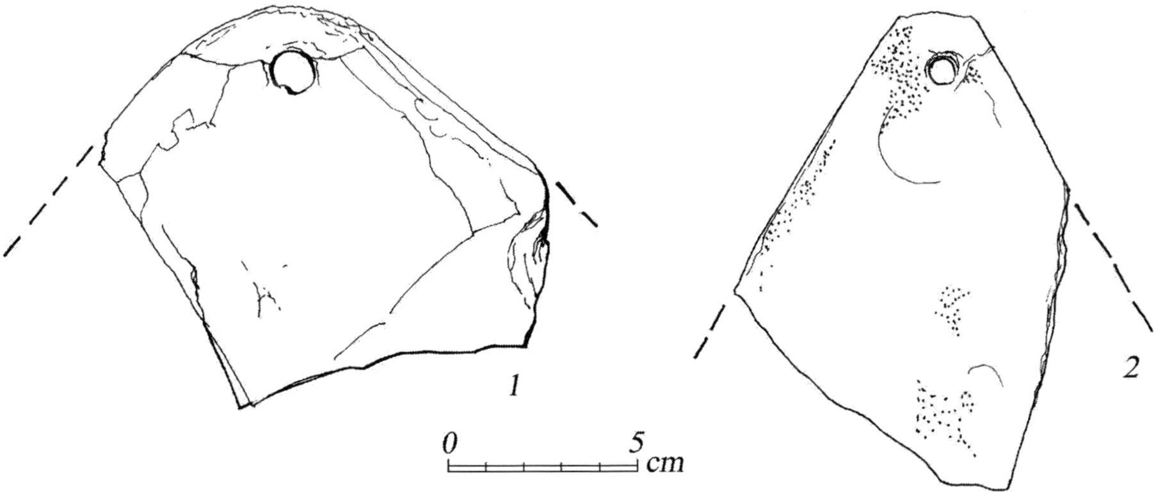

Figure 150 Two piece of Stockingford Roof Slate with fixing holes, from 69 XXIX 4. Scale 1:2.

SECTION P
PLASTERWORK

C. Woodfield

Two small pieces of plaster were found amongst the recovered window glass. The first, 77 F95(h), in glass box IZ, and the second, 77 95(h), in glass box 12.

One provides a finished surface on the front, unpainted, and is the final coat applied over what appears to be slit timber lathing, either a ceiling or an internal partition wall. No variation of coat-work is to be seen in the total thickness before the rear extrusion break of 13mm. The second is less clear, but of similar thickness, one side looks as though it has been cut down after setting, alternatively is pressed close to a finely cut surface. It is possible that one or both pieces may relate to the setting in of the window glass into the reveals.

SECTION Q
STRUCTURAL METALWORK AND ITS IMPLICATIONS

C. and P. Woodfield

This category of finds includes those items of iron and lead used in the construction of the building, and its fixtures and fittings. Lead calmes for glazing are discussed with the window glass in Section J: *Medieval Window Glass from the Church and Cloister.*

No structural metalwork was included in the report on the finds from the Grammar School (Woodfield 1981), as it was assumed that the structure was already in place before its use by the School, and no modifications were made during their 12-13 years tenancy, except for the probable construction of a light timber screen (Figs 43 and 93c).

IRONWORK

Figure 151.1-7, 9-14 and 17-24

The use of iron for nails, hinges and all matter of fittings was of course routine, but in the medieval period, the usefulness and strength of structural iron was well appreciated, and when deemed necessary builders had little hesitation in resorting to its use in the primary construction of major buildings, particularly where movement was both anticipated and was deemed unacceptable or threatening to the stability of the work.

In stone construction, cramps, crampettes, ties, bars and anchors were often necessary in a distinct variety of situations, such as where stresses were concentrated, as at the gathering of vaulting ribs, on sloping constructions like spires, for cantilevering as on corbel tables, and where external stresses such as wind pressure or leverage created tensile stresses within the fabric, situations where stonework was quite inadequate. Iron was also resorted to in complex timber construction, where, for instance, a number of elements come together at one point, and the size of the recipient timber was insufficient to allow the normal methods of jointing to be made within its compass.

Salzman (1967, 286) quotes prices for imported French and Spanish iron varying from 2/4d (1280) to 15/6d (1285) per cwt.

Cramps and Ties

A total of nine 'ties' of iron were recorded in the field notebooks; some have been subsequently lost. All nine, interestingly, were recovered from the mass of rubble from the fall of the tower over the W end of the choir and the SE transept (61 D 1, 61 Di, 60 II.4, 61 XI DB5, 68 XID; another from 68 XID, embedded in lead; and four further ties, also from 68 XID).

Two that do survive are true stonework cramps of traditional form, being of bar iron with down-turned ends. One (61 XI, area of the SE tower tile pit; Fig. 42) is illustrated at Fig. 151.1 and another from the second bay of the choir (61 XI DB5) at Fig. 151.2. They are of heavy wrought iron bar (11.5 x 11.5mm, and 12 x 16mm respectively), both with 45mm long down-turned ends for letting into pockets cut into the upper surface of adjacent stones, and secured by running in with lead. Both bars are 160+ mm (approximately 6½in) long. The cut chase on the upper face of the stones would have needed to be 26mm wide, allowing for 5mm of lead each side; at the ends the lead had been driven in after cooling with a 15mm-ended cold chisel or bolster, and once the joint was finished it had apparently been flushed over with mortar, probably merely the result of the joint made with the next stone above. These stout cramps may have served any one of the mentioned uses, and the place of recovery suggests they may have been employed on the tower or spire structure.

A further three cramps are recorded in the notebooks for the Coventry Museum excavations of the 1970s, also from the area E of the crossing (SF Nos 21-22, and 24, Area 3, the last in place, set into red sandstone). These do not survive for study.

Two further shaped iron bars were found, one with the mouldings in the western area of the chancel (60 II 4; Fig. 151.3); this iron bar is 11 x 3.5mm in section, with legs at right angles 48mm long, one at least neatly ended, the other rusted. The rusted leg is splayed, clearly the result of trying to remove it. The other example, Fig. 151.4, (61 XI D1, SE tower pier, W chancel) is remarkably similar, even to the splaying of the damaged leg, but is of 7mm square section iron.

A similar but larger example, Fig. 151.5, was found, unstratified from Grave 13 in the western end of the choir (68 XI.D). The strap iron is 16 x 6mm in section, and has one finished square end on a leg some 65mm long, looping round 200mm, to the other end, also probably misshapen during its removal.

The purpose of these last three objects is not clear. They

are too slight to be cramps in the usual sense, and it seems they are ties for some unknown purpose. There are no perforations or indications of timber in the rust, and at least the two smaller are, by their size, unlikely to be shelf suspension straps or indeed handles, as the legs are not sharpened for driving into timber. The unfinished state suggests that they may well have been built into masonry, and could be to anchor back elements of the superstructure of an elaborate tomb or monument, but could also have been for holding back a timber or suchlike against the wall. They could relate to the pulpitum or choir stalls.

Another true cramp, Fig. 151.6, not x-rayed, is only 90mm long overall, with 56mm deep downturns set at 65mm centres. This must represent the joining together of small elements, although it is difficult to believe that large drillings would have been placed so close to the arrises of constructional stonework. It resembles the fixings of some door fittings, where two drillings into the same stone were often necessary to avoid a pivoting movement. The absence of any ironwork projecting from the top face rather precludes this idea and it is more probable that the joint was made between two finely cut stone elements or mouldings. The presumed iron bar, totally concealed in lead, cannot be much more than 10 x 15mm wide, and the legs filled 25-26mm diameter drilled holes. The lead had similarly been driven in to the cavities after pouring with a small (15mm wide blade) bolster, in the customary way. The find spot is uncertain, but probably was in the W choir area, and may be additional to the nine recorded.

The end of a much stouter iron bar, Fig. 151.7, 35 x 22mm in section was found in 1977, from Area 3 in the choir on the E side of the vestry passage. This has been set in a 50 x 45mm socket in masonry and run in with lead, which had leaked in two runnels from the bottom of the socket, indicating that the socket was on a vertical face. The lead had been driven in manually when cool, with some air bubbles forming. It has all the appearance of being the supporting arm of a door pintle, and the location suggests it may just be from the door from the choir into the S vestry passage.

From the resonance passages came other items of structural iron.

An example of a decorative door stud was recovered from the destruction level in the area of the nave to crossing screen.(64 XVIIa 2), Fig. 151.9. It is identified as such by its large head, approximately 25mm square, and relatively slender short square shank. The decoration of doors with studs is a well-established medieval practice (*vide* St Albans Cathedral (S transept) where they are 22mm square).

Fig. 151.10 (62 Ad, School deposit in the N resonance passage) shows what appears to be a broken part of an iron tapering strap, 58mm wide at its maximum, and tapering sharply through its surviving length of 130mm. X-ray examination shows that it had been beaten out, thinning at the centre, but with no surviving fixing holes. It is judged to be too thin and insubstantial to stand the stresses of a working hinge, and may well be strap decoration applied to the face of a door or chest, as was popular in the 13th century and represents the long tradition from the earlier doors of Staplehurst and Stillingfleet (pers. ob.). A much narrower section, clearly a strap hinge complete with the pivot ring at one end, came from the robbing for the E nave pier masonry, Fig. 151.11 (62 VI 9). The width of the strap barely reaches 1in (23mm), and the pintle is only 5mm in diameter. This is unlikely to be sufficiently robust to support a full-sized door, and it more probably comes from an aumbrey cupboard or other such item of furniture, perhaps from the adjacent S nave chapel. This is not the only indication of furniture; a small piece of iron from the School deposit in the N resonance passage, Fig. 151.12 (61 XI Ad), here drawn from the x-ray plate, appears to be part of a harr-hung door where the 6mm diameter pintle has been lost leaving a hole in the 11mm wide strap, which itself has two small nail holes for securing on the top (or bottom) of a cupboard door leaf. Another hinge (now lost) is recorded from the area of the doorway leading directly into the N transept or porch (61 VI 6).

The split tail of the door pintle in the rebate of the eastern door from the N transept remained *in situ*.

Another object of iron, Fig. 151.13 (60.I.2), perhaps related to door furniture, appears to be a latch key, with a circular handle 23mm outer diameter, and some 85mm long in the shank, the end being deeply grooved on four faces.

Fig. 151.14 is a 10mm square section iron bar, 170mm long which had been reduced to a circular section at one end. This was recovered during the 1977 investigations of the S resonance passage, and is probably a saddle bar to support glazing, although the working down of one end to the round suggests that it has been inserted into a drilling in another related bar, perhaps during assembly of *ferrumenta*.

Nails

The remaining structural metalwork, Fig. 151.17-24, mostly consists of nails in a large variety of sizes. The larger are clearly used in constructional work; such as the huge spike 250mm long from the rubble in the choir (77.3A) with a head, Fig. 151.17, and a similar large-headed nail from an E nave destruction level (64 XVIIa 2). These must have been used to join substantial timbers. Also there is a 50mm long nail from the N choir found in 1977, Fig. 151.18. These are exceptional and the 1977 stratification cannot be taken as certain.

There is some indication that nails came in defined lengths, increasing by increments of 10mm from the shortest at 30mm with oval to round heads, 40mm with square or sub-rectangular heads, 50mm with sub-square heads of 15-25mm, 60mm and a smaller number of around 70mm long, also square-headed. The most plentiful group is within the range 40-60mm. The smallest sizes such as sprigs cannot be identified, probably not due to their absence, but because small items of iron are more likely to rust away. The shanks of all nails are usually square. Some nails preserve in the iron corrosion, evidence of the thickness of timber they originally penetrated. One from the choir, Fig. 151.21 (1977 Area 3), 50mm long, passed through a board 25mm thick across the grain, but others from the same general context had been driven a depth of 18mm behind the head, where no evidence of timber had been preserved, into the end grain of timber. Other nails had been distinctly clenched (61 XII.7; school deposit in the N resonance passage) having penetrated a thickness of 40mm, probably from a counter-boarded door.

Lost-headed nails also appear, but whether they were actually nails remains uncertain. They were probably used, as today, to secure floor boarding.

A 1989 assessment (in archive) identified some 70 nails from the church, with an additional 300 nails recovered from the resonance passage deposits, and the question arises whether the Grammar School was at times reduced to burning items of joinery for warmth. Pupils were expected to provide their own charcoals, for which there was much evidence (Woodfield 1981, 118 and 156 n 46) and *A Fifteenth-century School Book* (Nelson ed. 1956) alludes to chilblains. The Coventry statutes insisted on the burning of charcoal only (Nelson ed. 1956, 6) but the fact that coal was prevalent in School deposits (Woodfield 1981, 156, n 46) means these statutes were not strictly adhered to.

Nails were very sparse in the medieval building levels, but occurred thinly, often singly, in the following contexts: N transept (61 VI 6, 61 XIII 3), the N porch/chapel (60 III 3) including a 125mm nail, all of the Rebuild phase. Outside the church nails were recovered from the W cloister (68 XXVIII 1). They also occurred thinly (only eleven) in 16th-century levels (62 Cl Bay 3 (1) and 64 XXIII 11 - a 16th-century ground level to the NW of the cloister). These last two levels certainly represent Hales' activity. This all suggests that nails were not considered to be lightly disposable.

Within the church itself, excluding the 16th-century school deposits, the nails mostly come from 16th-century destruction levels. They survived in an unscattered cluster in the area of the timber screen or pulpitum, which must have continued to have provided the western wall to the school room, and indicates that this medieval feature was retained until after the school's departure for St John's in 1557-8 (60 II 8, and more strongly in 61 Ca and Cb), Fig. 151.19-20. There was also a similar concentration at the E end of the nave in the area of the Rood and chapels (62 VI 2), including several clenched nails. This latter clustering was particularly marked in the area of the southern chapel (64 XVIa 1, 64 XVIa 2 and 64 XVIIa 2). In this position they suggest that the chapels were divided by timber screens, and may have had boarded doors and even floors before their final destruction by fire, evidenced by carbonised wood in this area. As these groups of nails survived it is suggested that the main cross screen in the Rood position probably survived the initial destructive zeal and continued through the life of the school, although what purpose the space between it and the so-called pulpitum screen, under the tower, served is not known. This supports the view that the screen illustrated on Fig. 93c came from the Whitefriars. The screens, no doubt embellished with panel painting, were presumably whitewashed over as was the fragment of wall painting on the S face of the adjacent NE tower pier.

A clustering of nails in the N transept and in the area of the N porch presumably relates to the demonstrated dumping of building materials in these areas (60 III 4). Much roof tile occurred at the latter position, and some nails in the 40-50mm category could well be associated with the nailing of every fourth tile course in the traditional way for a plain tiled roof, but there were also two exceptionally large nails or spikes, one of 90mm, another of 125mm.

Some nails, also in the 40-60mm range, are doubtless from timber coffins, rather than from structural work but these two uses cannot be distinguished, Fig. 151.22. Those from the grave in the N transept (61 VI 8) suggest, by the shank being curved along its full length, that the nail was drawn out of the timber, perhaps as a concomitant of grave-robbing. There was also a suggestion of this again from the Renaissance chantry tomb in the second bay of the nave, Fig. 151.23 (64 XXI 3). This was thought at the time of excavation to be the result of despoilers opening a wooden coffin (Grave 64.19, Fig. 42, chantry tomb in the SE nave).

Nails from levels associated with the final collapse.

These deposits were mostly of rubble, filling the top of the N resonance passage before the final collapse of the central tower in 1572 (61 XI Af; Ag, 62 I 1). Elsewhere such deposits occur only very thinly, as in the N transept (64 XVIII 1), the great W door (61 IX.1) and in the first bay of the nave (64 XVIIa (1)). Most timber of any use had presumably been carted off the site by then.

Apart from SF 45 recorded as 'possibly 3 iron nails' found in the S resonance passage, there is no further information extant on the Coventry Museum excavations.

LEAD

Figure 151.8, 15-16

The use of lead on its own to prevent masonry joints from moving is demonstrated by an unstratified find from the area of the choir in 1962, Fig. 151.8. It had a 20mm square dowel, from which two v-shaped runnels radiate on the top and bottom faces of the fine 5mm joint. The lead must have been poured from the top dowel, and the dowel hole filled with the pink mortar characteristic of the first building phase. The trouble taken to prevent all movement suggests that this was critical, and may be from a pinnacle or spire.

A further and incomplete piece of lead (not drawn) was recovered in 1962 from Trench I, 1, the collapsed tower material fallen into the N resonance passage. This piece was shapeless, but measured approximately 20mm wide x 12mm, and had apparently been used for the running in of a vertical iron stay, perhaps *ferrumenta*. In this case, the ironwork appears to have been packed around with slivers of slate before the molten lead was poured, as the ends of the slate were left exposed.

The main large roofs of the church were probably of lead, as tiles, had they been used, would have been found in much greater quantities then was the case. The lead was reserved to the City of Coventry in 1538/9 (PRO (E318/19/967, Sheet 7). In 1560 Coventry Corporation petitioned Queen Mary for the covering of lead of the Church of the Whitefriars (See Section B, *The Whitefriars in Coventry - Historical Background*); this must have been very efficiently removed for only one recognisable piece of roofing lead survives.

Leadwork requires some nailing of soakers, flashings and lead clips for rolls and welts but these were not identified as such, although a strip of lead, 30mm wide by about 170mm long, was recovered from outside the N side of the chancel (61 X), in an unstratified context, Fig. 151.15. It had been nailed four times at one end, using small 5mm headed nails. This is interpreted as either a lead welt clip, multiple nailing still being a recommendation in the trade, or a tingle for securing a displaced tile on a long established roof.

Melted lead was found in a 16th-century gully in the presbytery (62 II 1a) which was in industrial use contemporary with the school. There were also lead shavings in the N resonance passage where it suggests it may have been whittled or reworked by the boys; one pointed offcut of what appears to be light weight (approx. Code 4) roof lead from this position had six equally-spaced nicks, a long nick and two holes. Perhaps it was used as a tally (62 I 4; school deposit in the resonance passage), Fig. 151.16.

Four small pieces of sheet lead were also recovered (not illustrated):

1 Triangular fragment, one face, and edges, set in mortar, total length 5cm, maximum width 3cm, thickness 5mm. A groove on one edge indicates some connection with glazing, apparently where calmes met (60 II 8, Destruction level in N resonance passage).

2 Small fragment, pointed both ends, use uncertain, 3.5cm long, 5cm wide, 2mm thick (61 XII 4, Main School fill of resonance passage).

3 Thin roofing lead, one roughly cut edge, 1.5mm thick, widest dimension 8mm, rough surfaces (61 VI 4, Destruction level in N crossing).

4 Thin (1.5mm) lead strip, neatly cut, 8.8mm long and 2.7mm wide; resembles a tingle, but there is no hole (Unstratified 1961).

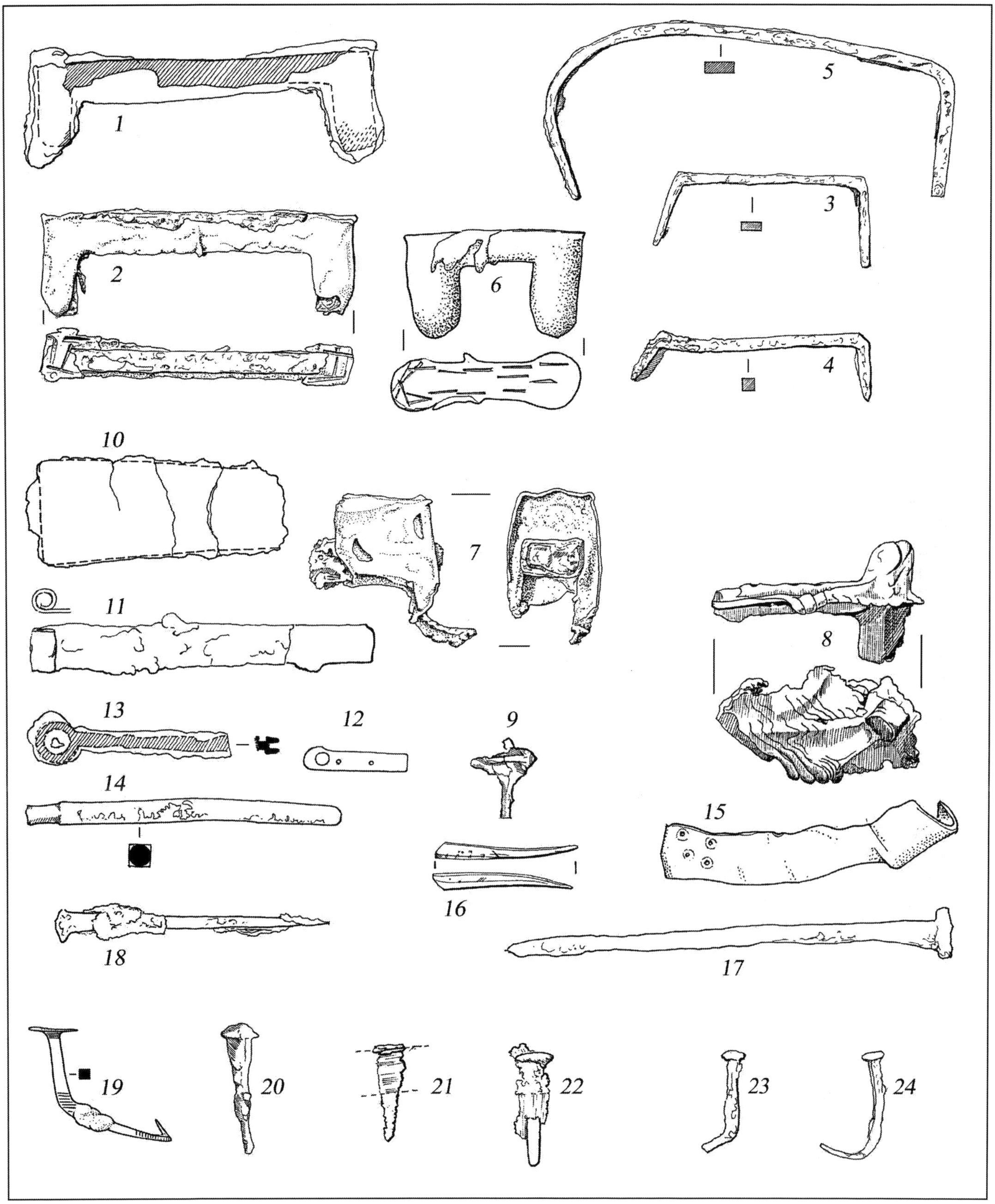

Figure 151 Structural metalwork of iron and lead: 1-7, iron bars and cramps (6 and 7 were run in with lead); 8, lead dowel; 9-14, iron studs, straps, bars and hinges; 15-16, lead straps and offcuts; 17-24, iron nails. Scale x⅓.

SECTION R
THE POTTERY

INTRODUCTION

This assemblage of late medieval and early post-medieval pottery is of particular importance because of its association with clear and often closely dated building phases. As such it has a value well beyond Coventry itself, as a guide to the ceramic chronology of the West Midlands.

The Fabric Analysis and Discussion section is written by Stephanie Ratkai, and the Catalogue of Illustrated Vessels section by Charmian Woodfield incorporating Ratkai's preliminary notes, there being no funding available for completing the Catalogue and its accompanying figures.

PART 1

CATALOGUE OF ILLUSTRATED VESSELS

C. Woodfield and S. Ratkai, with a contribution by the late J. Hurst.

The pottery has here been grouped into three sections:

1) the Woodfield 1960s excavations of church, sacristy and cloister (some 350 stratified contexts);
2) the Telford Cloister Gate excavation of 1956; and
3) a sample from the Coventry Museum 1977-78 pre-landscaping clearances/excavations in the presbytery, sacristy, and an area SE of the cloister (2 and 3 producing only some 10 stratified contexts).

The 1960s material is arranged under the site phasing, the other two sections under pottery fabric type, arranged under fabric chronology. The information about the illustrated vessels is arranged as follows: illustration number; form description; fabric code; details of glazing; excavation year; trench and layer number (areas in 1977-78); phase and area within the building complex. The Woodfield area codes are normally arranged to run from E to W on the site.

Table 7 (CW) indicates how the 1960s pottery fabrics relate to the structural phases. The table includes unillustrated sherds not listed in the Catalogue, and some dozen sherds of fabrics A02 and A03 from the 1977-78 excavations of the reredorter.

The identifications of Nos 78-86 are by David Barker, Keeper of Archaeology, Stoke on Trent City Museum; further information on no 86 is provided by R. J. C. Hildyard of the Victoria and Albert Museum. C.W. has also benefited from discussion with Dr Richard Ivens.

THE 1960s EXCAVATIONS (WOODFIELD)

The drawings are largely by David Williams; additionally sixteen (Nos 3a, 11-12, 15-16, 18, 20, 28a, 38, 40, 63a, 73a, 74, 93, 101-102) are by June Burbidge; eight (Nos 21, 21a, 22, 68-71, and 86) are by Paul Woodfield, and one, 103, is by David Watts.

The areas indicated by the trench numbering are as follows. 'Passage' is the passage between the presbytery and the vestry, 'Lane' is the strip between S nave and cloister, and 'Yard' the area between choir, cloister, S transept and passage. NRP and SRP are the N and S resonance passages respectively. The pottery from the N resonance passage lower fill is already published (Woodfield 1981).

PRE-FRIARY PHASE: Pre second half of the 14th century

These are illustratable vessels whose dating can be safely assumed but which do not themselves occur in Pre-friary contexts - see Table 7 for the occurrence of Pre-friary sherds in Pre-friary contexts.

Chilvers Coton Wares

Figure 152.1-16a

The illustrated examples occur mostly residually, but these wares occurred stratified in Pre-friary contexts, i.e. 13th and earlier 14th-century quarries in the SE transept, 60 II (16) and 60 I (13) and in a cess pit in the NW nave (64 XII (3). Vessel 13 occurred in a primary Friary construction context of the later 14th century; the lime plaster contents, suggesting contemporaneousness. Otherwise these fabrics occurred chiefly residually in disturbances throughout church, vestry and cloister. However, D02 continues in such numbers, e.g. in the Cloister, as to raise questions as to the likelihood of so much being residual.

1 Jug, fabric D02, 68 XI Ga 2.2, rob of grave 17, 16th-century destruction, W chancel.
2 Jug, fabric D02, 69 XXIX +, Unstrat., passage.
3 Jug, fabric D02, 69 XXIX +, Unstrat., passage.
3a Slashed jug, fabric D02, 63 C1 B8 1, Residual, cloister.
4 Jug, fabric D02, 69 XXIX +, Unstrat., passage.
5 Decorated jug, fabric D03, 62 VIII 3, Rebuild, lane. External rich copper glaze, elaborate raised decoration.
6 Decorated jug, fabric D03, 62 VIII +, Unstrat., lane. Copper green glaze and wavy underglaze combing.

STRUCTURAL PHASES AND THEIR ACCOMPANYING POTTERY FABRICS

	Chilvers Coton D.2-4. to 15th century	**Sandy Glazed Wares** D.11-14 12th to late 13th century	**Coventry Tripod Pitcher Ware** D.31	**Brill** D.41 14th-15th century	**Non Local (? Brill)** D.43	**Developed Stamford Ware** D.44	**Late Red Wares** A.21-25 Early 15th to 16th century	**Tin-Glazed enamels including S. Netherlands, Andalusian** 15th century and later	**Tudor Green** C.2-4 15th-16th century	**Midland Purple** A.2-5 Late 15th-16th century	**Midland Purple** A.12 Late 15th-16th century	**Cistercian/Blackwares** A.13-14 Late 15th-16th century	**Proto Coarse Wares** B.12 Late 15th century and later	**Late/Post Medieval Wares** B.2 Late 15th century and later	**Late/Post Medieval Wares** B.11a-11c Late 15th century and later	**Late/Post Medieval Wares** B.13-16 Late 15th century and later	**Blackware/Cistercian** A.11 16th century and later	**Proto Coarse Wares** B.11 16th century and later	**Yellow Wares** Y.2-5 *T. a. q.* 1570s-17th century	**Rhenish Stonewares** X.1-3 16th century and later
PRE-FRIARY Quarries and clay pit. 13th-14th century or earlier.	D.2 (17) D.3 (13) D.4 (1)	D.12 (1) D.14 (2)		D.41 (1)	D.43 (1)	D.44 (1)														
FRIARY Cloister/SE transept. 1342 - *c.* 1380/85, but quarries present.	D.2 (3)																			
FRIARY 1 and 2 N transept, grave and N porch/chapel. E nave. 1385 - 1423, but quarries present.	D.2 (11) D.2b (2) D.3 (5)						A.21 (2) A.23 (1) A.25 (3)													
PRE-REBUILD *c.* 1423 - late 15th century.																				
REBUILD 1 Tower, sacristy, W cloister wall Late 15th early 16th century.	Grave 17 D.2(17) D.2a (3) D.2b (1) D.3 (2)						A.21 (1) A.23 (4) A.24 (2) A.25 (3)	TGE (1)	C.2 (8) C.3 (1)	A.2 (3) A.3 (1) A.5 (1)	A.12 (2)	A.14 (4)	B.12 (2)	B.2 (2)	B.11a (2)	B.13 (1) B.13a (1)				X.3 (1) But 1977
REBUILD 2 Workshop E of N transept 16th cent. Pre-reformation.	D.2 (5)						A.25 (2)					A.14 (1)								
REREDORTER SHORTENING THEN REPLACEMENT BY WORKSHOP *c.* 1540.	D.2 (1) D.3 (1)						A.23 (2) A.25 (5)			A.2 (1) A.5 (2)										
SCHOOL in Choir *c.* 1545- *c.* 1558 Presbytery (AO3) goes on another decade ? Sacristy. Industrial.	D.2 (2) D.3 (1) D.4 (1)		D.31 (1)	D.41 (12)			A.21 (5) A.22 (2) A.23 (1) A.24 (3) A.25 (16)	TGE (4)	C.2 (3)	A.2 (1) A.3 (1) A.4 (1)		A.13 (139) A.14 (1)	B.12 (10)		B.11a (40) B.11c (1)	B.13 (1) B.15 (4)	A.11 (47)	B.11 (3)		X.1 (1) X.2 (6) X.3 (2)
HALES Mainly Cloister. 1540s to 1571.	D.2 (11) D.3 (2)			D.41 (1)			A.21 (4) A.22 (1) A.23 (6) A.24 (4) A.25 (8)		C.2 (7)	A.2 (3)		A.13 (18) A.14 (34)	B.12 (4)	B.2 (2)	B.11a (2)	B.13a (1) B.13b (1) B.14 (1) B.15 (1)	A.11 (5)		Y.5 (3)	X.2 (3)
DESTRUCTION Mainly Church. Contemporary with Hales.	D. 2 (17) D. 2a (1) D. 2b (1) D.3 (2) D.4 (1)	D.12 (3)		D.41 (1)			A.21 (5) A.23 (7) A.24 (3) A.25 (7)	TGE (1)	C.2 (1) C.3 (1) C.4 (1)	A.2 (7) A.3 (2) A.4 (4)		A.13 (47) A.14 (5)	B.12a (2)	B.2 (3)		B.13 (2) B.13a (3) B.14 (1)	A.11 (32) A.13a (3)	B.11 (1) B.11a (3) B.11c (5)	Y.2 (1) Y.4 (1)	X.2 (2) X.3 (2)
COLLAPSE Church, mainly tower. Earlier 1570s							A.25 (1)			A.2 (3) A.2a (1)		A.13 (4)		B.2 (1)		B.13 (1) B.16 (1)	A.11 (4)		YW (1)	SR CW

It should be remembered that pottery is not normally deposited in great churches while they are in religious use.

Table 7 Table showing the distribution of pottery fabrics across archaeological phases.

7 Rouletted jug, fabric D02, 60 II 3, residual in 18th century context, area SRP. Partial external glaze.
8 Jar/cistern, fabric D02, 62 +, Unstrat, crossing?
9 Jar/cistern, fabric D02, 68 XI Ga.2.2, rob of grave 17, 16th-century destruction, W chancel.
10 Cooking pot/jar, fabric D02, 60 III 8, Rebuild, NE transept. Sooted, and with hammer scale, soot and lime accretions internally.
11 Cooking pot/jar, fabric D02b, 68 IIIE 127, Rebuild, N porch/chapel. Glaze on top of rim only.
12 Pipkin? with traces of handle, but angle indeterminable. Fabric D02, 60 III 8, Rebuild, NE transept.
13 Wide mouth bowl, fabric D02, 60 II 15, Friary, SRP construction. A dollop of white lime plaster in the interior, partly wiped off, suggests it was a vessel contemporary with the construction of the SW chancel wall which formed the S wall of the S resonance passage. Sherds show a bright orange interior glaze.
14 Bung-hole, fabric D02, 61 VI +, Unstrat. NE transept. Traces of stamped elongated diamonds?
15 Wide mouth bowl, fabric D02, 60 I 14, Friary 2, SE transept.
16 Bird whistle, fabric D03?, 60 I 6, residual in 18th century, SE transept. The fabric is unusually fine and white. The surviving part is from the unseen interior of a hollow vessel, normally in the shape of a bird. What survives of the (fluted) vessel wall has a bright mid-green copper glaze. The form is not recorded in Mayes and Scott (1984).
16a ?Bird whistle, fabric D03, 62 III 5, ?Residual in School/ Industrial deposit at E. end. Presumably Pre-friary. Possibly the external part of a whistle as 16, or perhaps from a spouted vessel.

INITIAL FRIARY PHASE: Second half of the 14th century

No 13 above (60 II 15, construction of SW chancel wall) is the only illustrated vessel of this phase. One could assume it was residual, but if so the lime plaster on the internal surface is puzzling.

FRIARY 1 and 2 and PRE-REBUILD PHASES: Later 14th to later 15th century

Nothing illustratable, except 13 and 15 above. Layers of this phase, 60 I 14 (construction of SE transept), 60 II 15 (construction of SW chancel), 61 VI 7 (construction of NE transept) and 64 XVA 1 (make up for W crossing floor), produced only residual (D02) and possibly residual (D03) sherds. An A21 sherd was, however, recovered from 62 XIV 3 (make up for floor over the 1st NW tower pier).

THE REBUILD PHASE: Late 15th - Early 16th century.

Late Red and Proto-coarse Wares

Figure 152.17-20

17 Jug, fabric A23, 61 VI 6, Rebuild, NE transept.
18 ?Jar, fabric A14, 61 VI 6, Rebuild, NE transept. For possible jar form see Woodfield 1966, vessels 23 and 78.
19 Wide-mouthed bowl, fabric A24, 61 VI 6, Rebuild, NE transept. External sooting.
20 Pancheon, fabric B12, 61 VI 6, Rebuild, NE transept.

Imported maiolicas and lustre wares

Figure 152.21-2

All are presumably here ecclesiastical vessels.

21 Lustreware dish, Late Andalusian, 68 XI Ga2.3, Rebuild, W chancel. From the undisturbed fill of grave 17. with a B11 late 15th-century sherd. Blue green arc decoration on rim, external rim red-brown (decayed lustre). Areas of red-brown pigment under rim. A rare vessel.

John Hurst writes - ‘Small rim sherd from a flanged dish with a bevelled rim. Hard buff sandy fabric with schist inclusions (confirmed by Alan Vince). This was previously identified as Valencian (Woodfield 1981, 109-10) but the schist inclusions now show that it was definitely made at Malaga (Vince 1995, 282). Bevelled rims and interlace border patterns are common on both Andalusian and Valencian vessels but an Andalusian source for the Whitefriars dish is certain from the buff fabric with schist inclusions, and the typical rough tin glaze. Early Valencian Lustreware usually has a pink fabric with buff surfaces and a much finer glossy tin glaze.

This Late Andalusian Lustreware type can be dated to the mid 15th century, (although likely to be later 15th century in this context) as is shown by a dish with the same form and decoration found at Sluis, the outport of Bruges, Belgium (Hurst and Neal 1982, 86, no. 51). At least two other similar dishes have been identified in England, from Polsloe Priory, Exeter, Devon, and Glastonbury Abbey, Somerset (Allan 1995, 305, nos 11 and 12), interestingly both monastic sites. These dishes were for decorative use, often to show off imported Mediterranean fruits as is shown by the collection of the Dukes of Burgundy illustrated in the Book of Hours for Engelbert of Nassau of similar date (Alexander 1970, 80) which also depicts an early Valencian Lustreware dish again with the interlace border.

All three Late Andalusian Lustreware dishes have been found in the western part of England (cf. the differing distribution of albarelli given below).

This might suggest that these decorative dishes had a different marketing pattern.'

21a Albarello, Late Andalusian, 61 XIA d(e), Rebuild, NRP, W chancel.

John Hurst comments that 'the sherd has the typical Andalusian small black schist inclusions, pink fabric and blue underglaze decoration as the Coventry Shelton Collection albarello, (itself not impossibly from Whitefriars and on which the reconstruction is based), and the matt appearance. There are also parallels with another similar albarello from Coventry and one from Weoley Castle (Hurst 1977, fig. 27, nos 14-16), and from Old Bolingbroke Castle, Lincs. (Coppack, 1976, 7-8, fig. 4, no 1) A band, and part of the typical interlace decoration (as in the Shelton Collection albarello) survive quite distinctly. This form of decoration appears to be of the later 15th century, albarelli of later date having simple bands.

This vessel clearly falls into the group of Late Andalusian Lustreware albarelli, which are known from about eleven sites in England, being at the NW extremity, as listed and mapped in Allan (1995, 283 and fig, 20.2B). It is of considerable interest that four have been found in Warwickshire, two from other sites in Coventry and one from Weoley Castle (Hurst 1977, 83, nos 14-17). The date range extends into the early 16th century. As they would have come in as containers the albarelli might have been expected to have a shorter period of use than the dishes, e.g. as No 21 above. They were doubtless also used for flowers, see discussion in Hurst (1977, 95), e.g. the Portinari altar piece in the Uffizi.

These are not normally monastic finds, though one is known from a Dissolution deposit at Denny Abbey, Cambs. (Coppack 1980, 236 and 241, fig. 42 no 190). In this case the albarello was perhaps also used as a vase, although it would originally have been a container for spices or medicines. It is of particular interest to have vessels 21 and 21a together on the same site, a situation not known elsewhere in Britain.'

Imported Spanish maiolicas are rare, but not unknown, in friaries, for example the two Valencian vessels listed (Hurst 1997, 84, 92) in later medieval levels from the Dominican friary in Boston. Additionally a pre-Dissolution Spanish lustreware is known from Chester Blackfriars (Axworthy Rutter 1990, fig. 94, no 24).

22 Altar vase, S Netherlands maiolica, 61 XII 7, Rebuild, residual in NRP fill, W chancel. Piece of round-section ring-handle, bluish white, glossy, crackled tin glaze on a soft buff fabric, with, unusually, blue and blue green underglaze blurred trails on outer margin of handle. First half of 16th century. Different forms of decoration - e.g. instruments of the Passion and floral motifs - to that suggested are, of course, possible.

John Hurst comments that Neutron Activation Analysis has shown that some examples are Italian (Hurst 1999, 93-5) but the fabric of this is rather more friable than Italian examples. See also Woodfield (1981, fig. 13, 1).

Local and other imported wares

Figure 153.23-8.

+ implies may continue into the 16th century later than the Rebuild phase's normal termination in the early years of that century.

23 Jug base, fabric A23, 64 XV 1, Rebuild?+, Yard. Vessel imitating imported stoneware; virtually unglazed. A similar jug in a red sandy fabric was found at Dudley Castle in a 15th-century level (Ratkai 1985; 1987).

24 Jug handle, fabric A25, 64 XV 1, Rebuild?+, Yard.

25 Jug handle, fabric A25, 64 XV 1, Rebuild?+, Yard.

26 Cup, fabric C02?, 64 XV 1, Rebuild?+, Yard. White with a poorish quality mid-green internal and external glaze with brown flecks, perhaps a local copy? (a lobed cup is a possibility). Cups increase in number (as do small jugs) in this phase.

27 Cup/?small bowl, fabric A25, 64 XV 1, Rebuild?+, Yard, Unglazed.

28 Industrial base, fabric A03, 64 XV 1, Rebuild?+, Yard. Unglazed and unusually well potted ?industrial base/cucurbit, evidence for distilling? A possible alembic distilling-base was published in 1981 from the mid 16th-century deposit in the N resonance passage (Woodfield 1981, fig. 13, no 17), in 'red ware with an orange glaze'.

Other sherds in fabrics A02 and C03 were present in this level. A German stoneware sherd of 'early' type, fabric X02 Raeren/Siegburg, takes this deposit into the 16th century.

Other ceramically dated Rebuild levels are:

69 XXIX 6 (construction of secondary narrow N. wall) and 69 XXIX 20 (secondary floor make-up - sacristy/Hales' chapel). 60 III 3 (secondary floor make-up). 60 III 4, 60 III 7, 68 IIIE 112, 68 IIIE 113 and 68 IIIE 116 (fill and overlying construction trench to

triangular buttress). 68 IIIE 115, 68 IIIE 120 and 68 IIIE 122 (demolition of first porch). 68 IIIE 127 (metalworking activity of this period). 68 IIIE 128 (N porch/chapel). 60 I 10 and 60 I 15 (SE transept construction levels). 68 XXVII 4 (construction trench to unfinished W. wall of the NW cloister, presumably built with the Thomas Bond money of 1506). 62/63 Cloister Bay 8, 2. Construction of triple width window? (Note the cloister material does not represent cooking activity). 62 VII 3b (NW nave).

SIXTEENTH CENTURY REBUILD

Figure 153.28a

28a Jar, fabric B14, 69 XXIX 6, 16th-century Rebuild, Hales' chapel. This sherd may be later in the sixteenth century than this pre-dissolution phase, and so could be post Dissolution. It was built into the footings of the new N. wall, which could be of Hales' construction. However antiquarian drawings show window tracery which appears to be late medieval.

SCHOOL: *c.*1545 to *c.*1558

Figure 153.29

The Grammar School pottery from the N resonance passage was published in the early 1980s (Woodfield 1981, 108-116), and is **not** accurately reflected in Table 7 due to much loss of this material after its return to Coventry Museum. Pottery from deposits that were probably, but less certainly, School are now published here, the difficulty in precision of dating being caused by the fact that the industrial use of the presbytery possibly continued for some dozen years after the School had left the choir. Pot 29, from a certain School deposit (not previously made available) adds tripod pipkins to the 1981 body of material. During the School period two-handled cups were the most common form (40%), together with jugs/drinking mugs (22%), storage jars with simple everted flat topped rims and rims with lid seating (18%), narrow-necked bottles (12%) and, pancheons (8%).

29 Pipkin foot, fabric B11a, 60 II 9, School, NRP. Base of foot burnt, internal black glaze.

SCHOOL/?INDUSTRIAL: *c.*1545 to *c.*1573?

Figure 153.30-36

This shallow gully was recorded in the easternmost presbytery bay (with 62 III 5 and 62 III 7). It seems to relate to light industry as well as to casual school losses, and the date is likely to run into the early 1570s. The adherence of kiln detritus to 'Cistercian/ developed Midland purple wares' noted in 1981 (Woodfield 1981, nos 13 and 18b) is again apparent.

30 Mug, fabric A11, 62 II 1a, School?/industrial, E chancel. External and internal glossy dark brown glaze. Originally 2 handles?

31 Jug base, fabric A11, 62 II 1a, School?/industrial. Kiln detritus adhering, including 3 sherds inside the base. Internal and external dark brown glaze.

32 Cistern base, fabric ?A02, 62 II 1a, School?/?industrial. Hole made before firing. Unglazed.

33 Pancheon, fabric B14, 62 II 1a, School?/industrial. Unglazed.

34 Pancheon, fabric B15, 62 II 1a, School?/industrial. Unglazed. Very large vessels with base diameters of up to 41cm were published in Woodfield 1981 (nos 18d, 18e, 21).

35 Rim, angle unknown, fabric B15, 62 II 1a, School?/industrial. Sherds of fabrics A03, A13, B11a and B12 were also present in this gully.

36 Jug handle, fabric A25, 68 XXVII 2a, Industrial?, W cloister. An A23 sherd was also present here.

HALES: *c.*1545 to *c.*1558

Figures 153.37-43 and 154.44-51

These levels appear to relate to John Hales' activities which appear to be distinct from the School. It should be noted that no tankards or flared rim cups occur in the School

37 Jar, fabric ?B15, 69 XXIX 16, Hales', cobbles in passage. Int. glaze.

38 Wide-mouthed bowl, fabric B12, 69 XXIX 16, Hales', cobbles in passage. Unglazed. A13 sherds were also present. The blocking of the sacristy door produced an A11 cup sherd.

39 Cup, fabric A13, 69 XXIX 13, Hales', rubbish E of chapel. Int. and ext. glaze. Several A21, A24 A25 and C02 sherds were also present, the forms being mainly cups. This deposit may relate to nearby Well 2, Fig. 43

40 Jar/cooking pot, fabric A24, 69 XXIX 9, Hales', Passage/yard.

41 Bowl?, fabric B13a, 69 XXIX 9, Hales', Passage/yard. Unglazed.

42 Pancheon, fabric B12a, 69 XXIX 9, Hales', Passage/yard. Tan/brown int. glaze. Much distorted, as Woodfield 1981 no 21.

43 Cistern base, fabric B02, 69 XXIX 9, Hales', Passage/yard. Unglazed. Also present were sherds of A02, A11, A13, A14, A21, A23, A25, B11, B14 and yellow ware. Iron-working debris adhered to some sherds. Unfortunately layers 9, 15 and 18, were muddled before marking, during storage at Coventry Museum. They do however appear to be all of this date, and are grouped together under XXIX 9. The material included sherds of crucibles used in copper working.

44 2-handled cup, fabric A11, 1962 VIII 2, Hales', Lane. Bifurcated terminal to handle. Metallic but

dull pitted int. and ext. glaze. As Woodfield 1981 no. 15?

45 Base of cup?, fabric A11, 62 VIII 2, Hales', Lane. Int. and ext. dull metallic glaze - kiln detritus adheres to base.

46 Flaring-mouth cup, fabric A11, Cloister Bay 8.1/2, Hales', NE cloister. Int. and ext. black pitted glaze.

47 Cup base, fabric C02?, Cloister Bay 8.1, Hales, NE cloister. Buff fabric, grey core. Dark green int. copper glaze and limescale. Light green ext. dots. Resemblances to Potterspury and Brill.

48 Albarello?, fabric D41?, Cloister Bay 8.1., Hales', NE cloister. The fabric remains a puzzle. Brill, C02 and an over-fired yellow ware, perhaps an import, have been suggested. The fabric is white, with a yellow green overall glaze, and bright green copper patches, unlikely in a yellow ware. This is form 13 in the 'Tudor Green Type Series' from Farnborough Hill, Hants (Holling 1977).

49 Wide-mouthed bowl, fabric ?B14, Cloister Bay 8.1, Hales' NE cloister. Unglazed. Sherds of fabrics A25, A13, A14, A21, A23, B02, B13b, B14, C02, and D41 were present.

50 Jar, fabric A24, 64 XXIII 4, Hales', NW cloister. Patch of int. glaze only. Construction trench of Hales' enclosing wall 68 IV. A13 and B02 sherds were present.

51 Wide-mouthed bowl, fabric A24, 68 XXVII 15, Hales', NW cloister. Unglazed. A13 and B02 sherds and an A14 unglazed lid were also present.

DESTRUCTION: *c.*1545-1572/74

Figure 154.52-61

The presence of re-used architectural pieces cut down to make inkwells, and the copious presence of smashed window glass and decorated floor tiles mixed together in the School deposit in the N resonance passage indicates that destruction of structure continued through the life of the School as well as afterwards, i.e. from *c.*1545 intermittently until the great collapse of 1572/74. This period produced a wide range of domestic forms from the church, many cups and other drinking vessels, but also cisterns and sooted jars suggesting cooking.

52 ?Chamber pot, fabric A11, 62 II 1, Destruction?, E presbytery. Metallic dark brown all over glaze. Found with wire so possibly an industrial context. Not a sealed deposit and a later date is possible.

53 Jug, fabric A13, 69 XXIX 12, Destruction, S presbytery. All over metallic glaze. Sherds of German stoneware (X03) were also present.

54 Jug rim, fabric A23, 68 IIIE 107, Destruction?, N porch/chapel. Possibly industrial. Unglazed.

55 Pedestal salt (?), fabric A13, 68 IIIE 107, Destruction?, N porch/chapel. Dark brown int. and ext. glaze. Sherds were also present in fabrics A11 and A14.

56 Jar, fabric A14, 61 XI D(i), Destruction, SE transept. Ext. tan glaze.

57 Cup, fabric A13, 64 XVIa (1), Destruction, S chapel in E nave. Traces of ?decoration formed by underglaze raised dots. Int. and ext. brown glaze.

58 Cistern, fabric A02b, 62 VI, Destruction/contam., SW tower pier. Purple int. glaze. The adhering sherd and kiln detritus confirms this as a mid 16th-century vessel.

59 Cup? Base, fabric A11, 62 VI 2, Destruction, SW tower pier.

60 Jug?cup handle, fabric A25, 64 XVIIa 2, Destruction, NE nave. Sherds of fabric A14 were also present. Some sherds from this deposit were covered with white lime, perhaps from lime burning.

61 Drinking jug, fabric X02, 62 IX 1, Destruction, W end of nave. Ext. salt glaze, grey with brown patches.

COLLAPSE: 1572/74

These are the levels associated with the fallen stonework from the collapse across the chancel and to the NE of the tower in 1572/74.

Figure 154.62-67

62 Jar? Base, fabric A02a, 62 II 2, Collapse, outside NE chancel. Black pitted int. glaze. Adhering kiln detritus, and large glaze bubbles.

63 Jar rim, fabric A02a, 62 II 2, Collapse, outside NE chancel.

63a Tankard base, fabric A11/A13, 62 II 2, Collapse, outside NE chancel. Bright brown int. and ext. glaze.

64 Jug or figurine, fabric YW, 62 II 2/3, Collapse, outside NE chancel. It was originally assumed that this represented a belted female figure, with a pleated skirt (the 'skirt' is glazed inside, roughly finished but not moulded). The non-joining handle suggests a small jug, although European figurines are handled. The form is Woodfield Dc, this sherd having been previously published in Woodfield, P. 1966.

65 Pipkin foot, fabric A04, 62 XII 8b, Collapse, outside NW chancel.

66 Cup?, fabric C03, 68 XI Ga 2, Collapse, E of grave 17, W chancel. White fabric, yellow-green int. and dark green ext. glaze. The vessel turns outward at the base of the sherd.

67 ?Tankard ?beaker, fabric A11, 61 X 1, Collapse, NW chancel. Int. and ext. black glaze, 'white' slip decoration under glaze appearing yellow/brown. Other sherds of this type are known from the W. cloister, but they are rare on the site.

LATE 16TH - EARLIER DECADES 17TH CENTURY

The material from F.130 was rescued from inside a well by the road contractors. It lay some 10m NE of the N. porch.

Figure 155.68-75

68 Tankard, Cistercian, 68 F.130, Well NE cemetery. Dark brown ext. and int. glaze. Also one other residual in an 18th-century context in the W. chancel.

69 Mug, Cistercian , 68 F.130, Well NE cemetery. Black metallic int. and ext. glaze.

70 Jar/?stool pot, Cistercian, 68 F.130, Well NE cemetery. Dark brown to black metallic and pitted int. and ext. glaze.

71 Cup?jug rim, fabric A11, 68 F.130, Well NE cemetery. Black metallic int. and ext. glaze.

72 Tankard, fabric A11, 69 XXIX 11, Pit, W of passage. Metallic dark brown int. and ext. glaze.

73 Cup, handle missing. Fabric YW, 69 XXIX 11, Pit, W of passage. Good int. and ext. yellow glaze, browning at edges.

73a Large cup?, fabric YW, 69 XXIX 11, Pit, W of passage.

74 Porringer?, fabric YW, 69 XXIX 11, Pit, W of passage. Good yellow int. glaze; fire damaged around ex. rim.
Also 7 X03 Frechen/Cologne drinking jug sherds, and 74a.

74a Clay pipe, 69 XXIX 11, Pit, W of passage. The form is Oswald's Type 3 of *c.*1630 to 1660 but the wheel mark on the pipe is as on a Dutch example of *c.*1625 (Atkinson 1972, fig. 81, no 14). Unfortunately the rather fine collection of pipes from the 1960s Coventry Whitefriars excavations are now dispersed.

75 Bartmann jug, fabric X04, 69 XXIX 1, W of passage. Mottled brown ext., grey body.

There were no other certain levels of this date, when presumably much was gardens/orchards, but the period was represented at the Cloister Gate, see vessels Cloister Gate nos CG1 to 4.

18th-CENTURY PHASE

The garden wall construction trenches. The single sample (no 76) now illustrated of this material, recorded in the 1960s as 'copious' but much now lost, is important, as it dates to the 18th century the right-angled wall running N and then W of the standing cloister, i.e. establishing that it is neither medieval as confusingly appears on site, nor 16th century.

Figure 155.76

76 Joggled slipware platter, construction trench of garden wall, sectioned as 60 I 9, 60 I 11, 69 XXIX 1 and 77 F.10. Three other slipware dishes are illustrated in archive.

The material listed below is evidence for:
a) the continued use of the passage to the area of the former chancel, and its recobbling, into the late 18th century, and
b) the unexpected 'gentry' nature of the occupation of Hales' Place at that period.
From 69 XXIX 8a, lying directly on late cobbling in N. half of the passage.

Figures 155.77-86 and 156.87-88a

77 Dish, dark interior slip, white slip decoration over, mainly under glaze. Three other slip ware dishes are illustrated in archive.

78 Cream ware plate, slightly concave profile to edge, *c.*1780-1800?

79 Small bowl, pearlware. Turned band to rim with green glaze touches. Underglaze swirls of cobalt blue with ?sponged iron oxide, *c.*1780-1800.

80 Tea bowl, Worcester soft paste porcelain, underglaze blue painted decoration. An expensive piece, 1770s but a long life can be expected.

81 Bowl, pearlware, underglaze blue painted decoration, *c.*1780-1800.

82 Teabowl, underglaze blue printed decoration, oriental style. *c.*1790-1800.

83 Teabowl, creamware or pearlware. Burnt, *c.*1780-1800.

84 Bowl or saucer, creamware or pearlware, probably *c.*1780-1800.

85 Saucer, pearlware, underglaze blue-painted decoration, *c.*1780-1800.

Some 150 other 18th-century sherds were present, over a third cream wares, and a sixth tea bowls including porcelain. Salt glaze and delft wares were also present.

86 Transfer printed pearlware teapot. From related 1977 Area 4, N passage. The decoration and shape of the teapot (cf Miller and Berthould 1985, pl. 426) appear to be typical of transfer printed pearlwares of *c.*1800 made by potteries in Staffordshire, Yorkshire and elsewhere (pers. comm. R. Hildyard). However, it is not a Staffordshire Potteries product and may be from N Derbyshire (pers. comm. D. Barker). The transfer decoration has been crudely applied to the teapot and cut to fit. This indicates that it was made in one of the smaller factories, not for example, Spode, although they did produce pottery 'in the Greek taste' (pers. comm. R. Hildyard). The transfer decoration appears to represent a fighting Amazon and a victorious Amazon. There is a blue-painted 'shell edge',a device much used on pearlware plates, etc. The shoulder is decorated

with a Greek key pattern, containing at least five oval cartouches.

87 Pancheon, fabric B11b, 64 XV 3, 18th-century pit cut in S transept wall. Black metallic int. glaze.

88 Pancheon, fine orange fabric with white inclusions, 60 I 8, 18th-century gully in the SE transept. Note the more complex rim forms of this date (although simpler forms can also occur). Both have black metallic int. glaze.

88a Jar, fabric buff, cream streaks, 60 I 8, 18th-century gully, SE transept. Int. black metallic glaze. Note rectangular rim form. Another from the 69 XXIX 8a, 18th-century deposit. 60 I 8 also included fine wares, i.e. part of a Whieldon teapot, early cobalt wares, Chinese export porcelain, delft, salt glaze and cream wares, and fragments of delft tiles hinting at refurbishment in the second half of the 18th century.

Residual and unstratified pottery

Figure 156.89-103

Medieval - Pre-friary.

Cannon Park?

89 Dripping tray, fabric D12, 60 II 2, residual in W. chancel. Cannon Park?, 13th to 14th century. Roughly made, ext. knife trimming, int. orange glaze, heavy sooting.

90 Dripping tray or skillet handle, fabric D12, 64 XXI 3, residual in nave chantry tomb (Grave 19). Cannon Park. Unglazed. 12th to late 13th century.

91 Decorated jug, fabric D12, 69 XXIX 9a, residual in passage. Cannon Park, 13th to 14th century. Incised lines under thin green glaze.

Coventry Sandy ware

92 Cooking pot/jar, fabric D22, 62 III +, E presbytery. probably ex Pre-friary clay pit fill. Unglazed. First half 13th century.

93 Cooking pot/jar, fabric D22, 64 XVIIa 2, residual in NE nave. Roughly made, unglazed.

94 Cooking pot/jar, fabric D23, 62 VI +, SW tower pier. Unglazed.

Medieval, ? Rebuild phase

Late Red Ware

95 Rouletted jug, fabric A25, 62 VIII, SE nave. The rouletting resembles poorly observed lettering. Purplish ext. glaze.

Midland purple

96 Flat rimmed bowl, fabric A02, 61 XI Dn/Ds, SW choir.

16th-century pottery from 18th-century robbing of North and South Resonance Passages

97 Jug, fabric A02, 60, II 5a, rob of S resonance passage. Also the base of a small Cistercian ware cup.

98 Cup, fabric A13, 61 XI D f, rob of S resonance passage and wall. Brown int. and ext. glaze.

99 ?Bowl, fabric A14, 60 II 5, rob of S resonance passage. Knife trimming on base. Unglazed.

100 Storage jar, fabric B15, 60 II 5, rob of S resonance passage. The adhering kiln detritus, including sherds, confirms the date. Int. and ext. dark brown glaze.

100a Small jar, fabric A11, 61 Ad(d), N resonance passage (disturbed). Int. dark brown glaze.

Unstratified late 16th-17th-century pottery

101 Possett pot lid, fabric A11, 62 unstratified, probably crossing. Underglaze white slip dots, yellow on brown mottled ext. glaze.

102 Cup?, fabric A11, 69 XXIX +, Passage. Black/purple pitted metallic glaze, underglaze slip dots read as pale green. The pre *c.*1558 Grammar School knob had traces of white slip ((Woodfield 1981. 116).

103 Base of handle, fabric YW, 69 XXIX +, Passage. Little-finger impression on base of handle, cut-off with a knife below. All over yellow glaze.

MUSEUM 1977-78 EXCAVATIONS

Figure 157 M1-4

This pottery is covered by the discussion section of the report. As virtually all this ceramic material is unstratified or from contaminated or uncertain contexts, it has not been thought worth while to illustrate more than the four vessels below, which a) illustrate an unusual ?Pre-friary vessel from SE of the cloister, and b) relate to the continued use of the passage from the sacristy to the N.

Drawings M.2-M.3 and Cg. 1-3 are by David Williams, M.1 by June Burbidge, and M.4 by David Watts.

Medieval Pottery

M.1 ?Industrial vessel, fabric D02, 78 F.59a. Residual, apparently at junction of F.59/F60 tank and drain, SE of cloister.

M.2 Jar, Midlands purple, 77 Area 2, unstratified, E of Passage.

Coarsewares

M.3 Jar, fabric B11a, 77 Area 2, unstratified but joins 69 XXIX 16, and so is Hales', Passage.

Tin glazed earthenwares

M.4 Dish, tin glazed, 1977 Area 17 unstratified, Passage.
John Hurst comments, *in litt* to CW, 'a blue-dash charger, probably Anglo Netherlandish, and first

half of the 17th century. It is odd in not having a lead-glazed back and in having a pale palette.'

Virtually no material survives from the Museum excavations in the Chapter House, Cloister E range, Lay Cemetery area, ?Prior's House, S resonance passage, reredorter, the shortened reredorter and its overlying workshop. However, some dozen sherds of fabrics A02 and A03 do survive to hint at an early and a mid 16th-century date for the two latter features, and they are included on Table 7. From the F.60 tank, perhaps related to that workshop, come sherds of a Martincamp flask and a drinking jug in fabric X03, for which a mid 16th-century date again seems likely. A cup base in fabric D41 and a cup rim in fabric C02 survive from F.18. This is from red clay, E of the sacristy in the Well 2 area, (but the clay extends outside the well yard wall, so they do not necessarily relate.).

1956 TELFORD EXCAVATION THE CLOISTER GATE: Seventeenth Century Occupation

Layer numbers are known, but the main site records were lost by 1958

Figure 157 CG1-4

CG1 Drinking vessel, yellow ware, probably handled, and Woodfield, P., 1966 type H. h. 1956 layer 9. 2nd quarter of 17th century. As no 4?

CG1a Base, perhaps also a yellow ware cup, but not the same vessel as 1.

CG2. Chafing dish fragment, preserving neck and shoulders, and an underglaze tress of hair, cf. the Rainbow portrait of Elizabeth I at Hatfield House of 1586. Yellow ware, Woodfield, P., 1966 type C(L). 1956 layer 16.

CG2a Is a suggested reconstruction of CG2 (P. Woodfield).

CG3 Drinking jug, fabric X02. Frechen, seventeenth century. 1956 layer 3.

CG4 Bartmann drinking jug, with arms of Amsterdam. Dr. Gaimster suggests (pers. comm. to C. Woodfield) a date of *c.*1650 or a little before. Frechen. 1956 layer 9. The reconstruction is based on Hurst, Neal and Van Beuningen 1986, 220, pl. 44, a Frechen find, and Gaimster, 1997, 200, no 67.

The 17th century is more apparent at the Cloister Gate than elsewhere, confirming its continued use as a major entry point.

SECTION R
PART 2
THE MEDIEVAL AND LATER POTTERY
and its implications for building sequences

S. Ratkai

All the pottery which was available from Woodfield's excavations, some unfortunately having been lost during museum storage, was examined in detail and recorded, including material already published (Woodfield, 1981). A type series was formed and sherds allocated to fabric groups by macroscopic examination. Non local, i.e. fabrics from outside Warwickshire, were examined under x20 magnification. At a later stage of revision the medieval fabrics were compared with the Warwickshire medieval pottery type series (Ratkai and Soden 2000). In the text comparative material where cited is given both the county fabric number and the fabric number under which it was first recorded. The fabrics were divided into three main groups: Medieval Wares, Late Medieval/Early Post-medieval transitional wares and Post-medieval wares. There was some overlap between each group. The well-documented building phases, particularly in the Late Medieval/Early Post-medieval transitional period, provide a framework for the understanding of the development and chronology of Coventry's ceramics, see Table 7 where well-stratified pottery and those phases are correlated.

The pottery which survived from the Herbert Art Gallery and Museum's excavations (1956, 1966 and 1973-1978) was also examined, but in less detail as most of the pottery was effectively unstratified. Semi-stratified groups which could be located more or less accurately within Whitefriars, some ten contexts, were recorded in as much detail as material from Woodfield's excavations.

The pottery, and a copy of the written archive, has been deposited at Coventry Museum.

The fabric-founded quantification of the pottery that follows is based on combined sherd numbers recovered, and surviving, from all the excavations. This amounted to a total of 1080 sherds. The material has been divided into three main fabric groups overlapping in date:

1) Medieval to *c.*1500,
2) Late Medieval/early post medieval transitional, 15th to 16th centuries,
3) Post-medieval wares *c.*1550 to *c.*1700,
There are two sub-groups,
4) Late 17th and 18th-century wares, and
5) Imports.

1 THE MEDIEVAL FABRICS (POST CONQUEST - *c.*1500)

Fabrics D02-D04: Chilvers Coton Wares (130 sherds)

Fabric D02 corresponds to Chilvers Coton fabric 'C' (dating from the end of the 13th century but predominant in the 14th and 15th centuries) and fabric D03 to Chilvers Coton fabric 'A' (dating mainly to the 13th century but with some production in the 14th century) (Mayes and Scott 1984). Fabric D04 is distinguished from D03 by a slightly sandier fabric and a distinctive copper green and yellow-green mottled glaze. There were no examples of Chilvers Coton 'B' fabric. This was thought to have had a limited distribution confined to the immediate vicinity of the kiln sites. However, excavations at Burton Dassett in SE Warwickshire disprove this (Ratkai forthcoming), and it is possible that this fabric was no longer being produced by the time of the establishment of the friary, especially since it has been found at Broadgate East, Coventry (Redknap and Perry 1996).

Forms, Fig. 152.1-16a and Fig. 157.M1, in fabric D03 were confined mainly to jugs, often highly decorated but there were also examples of bowls and cooking pots/jars. Sherds in both fabric D03 and D04 were usually small, making a fuller form analysis almost impossible, although a decorated jug and a bird whistle were identified in fabric D03. Forms in fabric D02 were more varied, consisting of cooking pots/jars, jugs, wide-mouthed bowls with flanged-rims, cisterns, a dripping pan and a possible pipkin. These fabrics are also found among the roof tiles and roof furniture. Both fabrics D02 and D03 occur and there seems to be no reason why the two cannot be coeval. If this is the case then this perhaps further strengthens the argument that whitewares (fabric D03) continue to be produced well into the fourteenth century. Tiles in this fabric were found associated with the E range of the cloister and structures to its S and came also from the passage and sacristy, all of which date to Phase I, Friary, *c.*1342 to *c.*1385.

Fabrics D11-D14: Sandy Glazed Wares (10 sherds)

Figure 156.89-91

Fabric D11 is a sandy red ware, sometimes partly reduced. It contains rounded pink ?clay pellets. The external surface is coated with a thick white slip over which is a rich green glaze sometimes slightly mottled. One similar example to this fabric has been found in the Coventry area (pers. comm I. Soden and inspection by author). Sandy fabrics with clay pellets are also known in Worcester (pers comm V Buteux and inspection by author) and in Stratford-upon-Avon (Ratkai 1992b) but the fabrics tend to be lighter firing and sandier. Dating evidence from Stratford-upon-Avon would suggest that this is a 12th to late 13th-century type. The source or sources for these fabrics are as yet unknown. Fabric D12 is probably a Cannon Park product (Redknap 1985) and can be matched to kiln wasters in the Warwickshire county type series. It is likely that fabric D13, a fine clean oxidised fabric, with sparse, ill-sorted sub-angular quartz grains, less than 0.25mm, is also of local manufacture, although it could not be paralleled in the county type series. Sherds were generally undiagnostic but bowls, jugs and a dripping pan are represented. Fabric D14 could be paralleled in the county type series (fabric Sg13, Warwick. fabric 143 (Ratkai 1990)). It is a sandy fabric containing moderate to abundant ill-sorted quartz grains, sparse burnt-out organic material and sparse ?clay pellets. It has light brown oxidised surfaces and a mid grey core. The glaze is a dull olive colour. Most of the sherds were undiagnostic. One unstratified sherd (marked WF 1977) came from a bowl with an internal glaze. Three sherds of fabrics D12 and D14 occurred in Pre-friary contexts, the rest residually. This suggests that the quarry pits date from at least the 13th century and possibly the 12th century.

Fabrics D21-25: Sandy Cooking Pots (16 sherds)

Figure 156.92-94

Fabric D21, although sandy, appears to contain igneous/metamorphic rock fragments. It does not resemble Malvernian Wares. A similar fabric was found at nearby Much Park Street, Coventry, (Wright 1987) where petrological examination suggested the Caldecote volcanic series as the source. Recent work at Wolvey (Ratkai 1998) which lies very close to the volcanic outcrop also produced pottery with similar inclusions. The fabric is represented in the county type series (fabric StR11) and has also been found in the SE of the county at Burton Dassett (Ratkai forthcoming).

Fabric D22 (county type series fabric Sq203) is often known as 'Coventry Sandy Ware' (Redknap 1985; Redknap and Perry 1996, for full fabric and form descriptions, where fabric D22 is the same as fabric A.1 (Much Park Street fabric type 3)). However, there are no known kiln sites. Previous work in Coventry has tended to group together all sandy cooking pots under this heading, although Redknap and Perry (1996) have four sub-divisions.

However there are clear variations. Fabric D23 (county type series fabric Sq202; Redknap and Perry 1996 fabric A4) contains moderate- frequent red ?ferrous inclusions which are particularly visible on the sherd surfaces. This fabric is common in the Coventry area but has also been found at Burton Dassett in the SE of the county (Ratkai forthcoming, fabric 5). Another variation, fabric D24 (possibly the same as Redknap and Perry 1996 fabric A3), is a much finer ware, with dark grey/black smoothed surfaces and a brown core. This type has a wide distribution in Warwickshire (county type series fabric RS01) in the same range of forms. It is common in Warwick (Ratkai 1990; Ratkai 1992a, fabric 121) but is also found in Stratford (fabric 13, Ratkai 1992b), Alcester (fabric 26, Ratkai 1994b) and Burton Dassett (fabric 14, Ratkai forthcoming). This fabric is also known from Birmingham (Ratkai 2000, fabric gw4). It is possible that the source for this fabric is the Forest of Arden. Forms are mainly cooking pots although there was one example of a jug in fabric D23 (not illustrated).

Fabric D25 is a grey ware sometimes with brown oxidised surfaces. The fabric contains abundant quartz grains and sparse-moderate brown clay pellets. It is similar to but sandier than Coventry tripod pitcher ware (see fabric D31 below) and as such should be classed as a Coventry sandy ware variant. It is most probably a 12th-13th-century fabric.

With the exception of fabric 21, the other fabrics in this group occurred chiefly in Pre-friary deposits (six sherds in total). Three sherds of fabric D21 and three of D22 were found in Friary contexts. It is most likely that they are residual and represent disturbed material associated with the quarries, i.e. Pre-friary activity.

Fabric D31: Coventry Tripod Pitcher Ware (1 sherd)

There was only one small sherd present, residual in a Grammar School context. For a full description of this ware see Redknap (1985) and Redknap and Perry (1996).

Fabrics D41, D42, D44: Non Local Glazed Wares (12 sherds)

Figure 154.48?

Fabric D41 is a product of the Brill-Boarstall industries in Buckinghamshire (see Mellor 1994) and for general description and gazetteer of published sources see McCarthy and Brooks (1988) - primarily Ivens, R. J. and Jope, E. M., (1953-4; 1981; 1982). In Woodfield (1981) this fabric is described as a 'Tudor Green type' because of the rich copper green glaze. However, it has a pink fabric unlike true 'Tudor Green'. Forms are mainly restricted to jugs and cups, the jugs usually having a yellowish green glaze (also Woodfield 1981, 113, nos 2 and 4).

Fabric D42 is a very fine, very sandy buff ware and appears to be a product of the Potterspury kilns (cf. McCarthy 1979 and Mellor 1994 for full fabric and form descriptions; also Jope, E. M. and Ivens, R. J. (1995)).

These are likely to be superseded when the massive Ivens' and Woodfields' work undertaken at Potterspury since 1995 can find funding for publication. Both bowl and jug forms were represented. This fabric dates to the later 14th and 15th centuries, although there are no stratified sherds from the site. Until now Brill-Boarstall and Potterspury products have not been identified in Coventry. However, as Brill-Boarstall products have been found throughout the county, as far as Warwick, it is perhaps surprising that these appear to be the only recorded occurrences in Coventry.

Fabric D43 is similar to fabric D42 above but is coarser with larger less well sorted quartz grains, sparse red ferruginous inclusions and moderate irregular voids. Surfaces and margins are buff and the core pale to mid-grey. It has an olive glaze with dark green speckles. This fabric cannot be paralleled in the county type series and it is likely that it was a non-local product. One sherd was stratified in Pre-friary levels, giving a *terminus ante quem* of 1342.

Fabric D44 (Developed Stamford ware) bears a rich external copper green glaze. A single sherd occurred stratified in a Pre-friary context (for full description see Kilmurry 1980).

D51: Calcareous Ware (1 sherd)

This was represented by a single unstratified sherd containing shelly-limestone. This type of pottery is commonly found in Northampton (McCarthy 1979) but also the SE Midlands (e.g. Baker and Hassall 1979). It is virtually impossible to tell the various shelly wares apart on fabric alone, and the presence of a single sherd only at the Whitefriars is not conducive to a detailed study of its source. However, the propensity of Coventry's trade to focus to the E (Wright 1987) probably means that this sherd originates in Northampton where the shelly ware T2 tradition lasted until *c.*1400 (McCarthy 1979). Other post-Conquest shelly ware finds in Warwick suggest a 12th-13th century date (Ratkai 1990).

2 LATE MEDIEVAL/EARLY POST-MEDIEVAL TRANSITIONAL WARES (15TH-16TH CENTURY)

Fabrics C02-C03: White wares (22 sherds)

Figures 153.26? and 154.47? and 66

Fabric C02 is a southern white ware or 'Tudor Green' type ware. The fabric is very fine with abundant fine quartz and is very similar to 14th-15th century Potterspury ware which may be a nearer source than the Surrey/Hampshire borders (Pearce 1992). Fabric C03 is iron-poor, firing to pale orange or cream. It is quite fine with sparse rounded quartz grains. It is similar to Brill-Boarstall ware and may be a late product of that industry. One vessel, possibly a bowl, in this fabric has an external copper green glaze and internal yellow glaze. A similarly glazed iron-poor vessel from Burton Dassett was identified as a product of Nettlebed, Oxon. (pers. comm. Maureen Mellor) and this is another possible source for fabric C03. Forms in these fabrics are mainly cups but there is also a possible chafing dish. Eight sherds of C02 and one of C03 came from Rebuild levels of the late 15th-early 16th centuries. There are over thirty sherds in stratified 16th-century levels of *c.*1540-1570.

Fabrics A02-A05, A.12: Midland purple and related wares (53 sherds)

Figures 153.28, ?32; 154.58, 62-63, 65; 156.96-97 and 157.M2

Fabric A02 has a dark purplish brown, sandy, hard-fired fabric. There are two variants, one with very little sand (A02a) and the other with noticeable yellowish rounded inclusions (A02b). Fabric A03 is not strictly a Midland Purple ware but a very hard-fired red ware with grey bands in the section, usually between margin and core, giving a sandwich effect. It is probable that under slightly different firing conditions it would become a true Midlands Purple. Fabric A04 has a rough pimply surface and dull purplish brown glaze. Fabric A05 has purplish surfaces and glaze but a hard-fired 'dirty buff' fabric, often with lighter streaks within it, but few visible inclusions. Fabric A12 was another reddish ware, but sandy with rough surfaces. Forms in these wares may best be described as 'functional domestic' or kitchen and storage wares. They consist largely of jars and cisterns (it is difficult to differentiate between the two when body sherds alone are present), but pipkins, bowls and jugs are present. There was a handle in fabric A03 from a pipkin or skillet and a possible alembic. Fig. 153.28.

These fabrics first appear in Rebuild layers of the late 15th-early 16th centuries. They are possibly present in the pre-Reformation workshop which succeeds the reredorter but are most common in the 1540s to 1570s levels.

Fabrics A11, A13, A14: Cistercian and related wares (237 sherds)

Figures 152.18; 153.30-31, 39; 154.44-46, 52-53, 55-57, 59, 63a, 67; 155.68-72 and 156.98-99, 100a, 101-102

These fabrics are all characterised by very fine red or maroon fabrics. Fabrics A11 and A13 are Cistercian/Blackware types, the latter being distinguished from the former by a denser fabric and the occasional presence of rounded yellowish inclusions. However, there did not seem to be any chronological significance in the apparent difference nor a clear distinction between forms in one and forms in the other. Fabric A14 is a fine red ware with a rich tan/warm brown mottled glaze. It has also been found at Burton Dassett in the form of a flat-backed costrel, but here the forms are jars, jugs and bowls (Ratkai forthcoming). Forms in A11 and A13 are predominantly cups, together with 'corrugated' mugs, two-handled and flaring-mouthed cups, chamber pots, jugs, tankards, possett pots and a salter. Some of the cups have a distinctive handle formation, the terminal of which resembles a fish tail, Fig. 154.44. This seems to be a peculiar local trait. The only other example is from Stafford Castle (Ratkai, in preparation) where it is unique. Some glazes had a silvery metallic sheen. Such a glaze is always less frequently found, but seems to occur in most W Midlands Cistercian/Blackware assemblages. It is difficult to know whether the metallic quality of the glaze was thought desirable or occurred accidentally. Some cup forms imitate Rhenish stone wares and have globular bodies and a pronounced ridge at the neck-shoulder junction. A mug, Fig. 154.67, and a cup, Fig. 156.102, had external white slip decoration, as did a possett cup lid, Fig. 156.101, all in the A11 fabric. The mug came from a pre 1572/4 level. Other forms present are a short length of tubular spout possibly from a puzzle jug (though it might be from a large flask). There were also a number of sherds with an external glaze only, which may have come from jugs or flasks (see Woodfield 1981, fig. 13.9-10). There was a possible chamber pot from a later 16th-century level, but this was not sealed, Fig. 154.52, another in fabric A11, and a stool pot from a well, Fig. 155.70. This last was recovered by contractors (with vessels Fig. 155, 68-69, and 71) from the bottom deposits in that well, but could be intrusive. Chamber pots are more usually a 17th-century form. Fabric A13 occurs first, and in large quantities, in the Grammar School deposits and is frequent in other 16th-century levels. Its forms included a possible pedestal salt, Fig. 154.55.

Fabric A14 forms were generally made up of bulkier items, e.g. jugs, jar/cisterns, and a bowl, Figs 152.18; 154.56 and 156.99. Fabric A14 occurs first in a Rebuild level of the late 15th-early 16th centuries. As Woodfield (1981) has rightly said, the distinction between some of the Midland Purple Wares, Cistercian wares and Blackware is often tenuous and much more work on ceramics of this period needs to be undertaken.

Fabric A21-25: Late Red Wares (95 sherds)

Figures 152.17, 19; 153.23-25, 27, 36, 40; 154.50-51, 54, 60 and 156.95

These fabrics have a wide distribution in the W Midlands. Fabric A21 is perhaps a Cistercian Ware variant or forerunner, less hard-fired, thicker-bodied, with a tan glaze. Fabric 22 is a very fine light orange fabric, with smoothed surfaces, represented by only four sherds. It resembles 'bottle' fabrics found in the NW Midlands at Shrewsbury Abbey (pers. comm. V. Buteux) and Haughmond Abbey, Shropshire (Ratkai forthcoming). The three remaining fabrics A23 A24 and A25 have a wide currency from Stafford Castle (Ratkai, in preparation) and Dudley Castle (Ratkai, 1985; 1987) in the NW, to Burton Dassett in the SE (Ratkai, forthcoming). Fabric A23 (county type series fabric SLM11) has pale orange surfaces and margins and an orange core with sparse quartz and ferruginous inclusions less than 0.5mm. Fabric A24 (county type series fabric SLM20) is reddish orange throughout with moderate well sorted round quartz *c.*0.5mm. Fabric A25 (county type series fabric SLM13) has an orange core with slightly paler surfaces and margins. Its fabric is very clean and paste-like with very sparse rounded quartz generally less than 0.25mm. It is not possible to say whether each fabric originates from a specific kiln site or whether there are several production centres for each fabric. Certainly a fabric similar to A23 and A25 was produced at Wednesbury during the 15th century (pers. comm. Mike Hodder and inspection by author). The forms, method of manufacture and glazing in each fabric are consistent throughout the W Midlands.

Forms in fabric A21 are jugs and a cup. However, there were many sherds which could not be assigned to form and the full range of forms produced probably included cisterns, bowls and jars. An unusual form in this fabric was published by Woodfield (1981 fig. 13:17 (bowl or perhaps an alembic distilling base/cucurbit?)). Fabrics A23, and A25 share a similar range of forms, namely jugs, including an A25 jug with square rouletted decoration, jars/cisterns, and wide-mouthed bowls/pancheons. In addition there was a possible pipkin in fabric A23. Fabric A24 had a smaller range of forms, consisting of jugs, cooking pots/jars and bowls with elongated S-shaped rims, Fig. 154.50-51. This form too has a wide distribution in the W Midlands, and examples are known from Much Park Street (Wright 1987), where they have been published as lids. These fabrics occur first in early 15th-century Friary 2 levels and continue throughout the 15th and 16th-century levels, but are most common in the School, Destruction and Collapse levels of the 1540s to 1570s.

Fabrics B11, B12: Proto Coarsewares (23 sherds)

For B11a to B11c see below.

Figures 152.20; 153.38 and 42

These fabrics represent the appearance of early attempts at what was later to develop into the Post-medieval coarseware tradition. They have sandy pinkish red fabrics but the surfaces are unslipped and the glazes in consequence are a patchy tan and olive. The fabrics were divided by degrees of sandiness. Fabric B12 contains finer, more frequent and better sorted quartz than fabric B11. The only remotely diagnostic form in fabric B11 was a glazed base which may have been from a jug or a chafing dish. Fabric B12 provided a wider variety of forms, consisting of jugs, jars/cisterns, and bowls/pancheons, Fig. 152.20 and Fig. 153.38 and 42. These fabrics are found first in Rebuild levels of the late

15th-early 16th centuries and are commonest in the Grammar School and Destruction levels, although they are never plentiful.

3 POST-MEDIEVAL WARES (*c.*1550-*c.*1700)

Fabrics B02, B11a-B11c, B 13-B16: Coarsewares (147 sherds)

Figures 153.28a, 29, 33-35, ?37, 41, 43; 154.?49; 156.87-88, 88a, 100 and 157.M3

Fabric B02 is a pale orange sandy fabric with slipped surfaces which fire purplish brown. This fabric is found first in Rebuild levels of the late 15th-early 16th centuries but is commonest in the 16th-century levels, although examples are never plentiful. Forms include cisterns, Fig. 153.43, and pancheons.

Fabric B11a to B11c. These fabrics seem to be variations of the same fabric. Fabric B11 (see above) may be the forerunner. Fabrics B11a and B11c both have slipped surfaces which fire to a purplish brown, often quite lustrous. Fabric B11c is less sandy than B11a and contains ferruginous inclusions. Both fabrics contain yellowish rounded inclusions but B11c has a higher quantity and they are larger. Fabric B11b looks like a poorly mixed version of fabric B11a with noticeably pale and occasional red streaking through the clay matrix. Fabric B11a has been found at both Dudley Castle (Ratkai 1987) and Stafford Castle (Ratkai in preparation) associated with 16th-century pottery and has also been published by Woodfield (1981, fig. 13:18, jar). Forms are divided between pancheons, Fig. 156.87, and lid seated jars, although there are also examples of chafing dishes and tripod pipkins, Fig. 153.29. Fabric 11a occurs first in Rebuild levels but is commonest in Grammar School levels.

Fabric B13 is a hard fired buff fabric with a grey core similar to fabric A12. Fabric B13a has a smooth pale orange fabric with rounded whitish and ferruginous inclusions. The unglazed surfaces have a purplish brown bloom. Forms are restricted to pancheons, jars and a possible bowl, Fig. 153.41. These fabrics occur first in a Rebuild context, but are associated primarily with School, Hales' and Destruction levels predating the 1570s.

Fabric B14 is an orange coarseware with partial reduction towards the core and ferruginous inclusions. Forms appear to be limited to pancheons, Figs 153.33 and 154.49?, and a jar, Fig. 153.28a. It is not present in the School deposits but is found in Hales' and Destruction deposits, which run some fifteen years later.

Fabric B15 is similar to fabric B11a but has noticeable dark rounded inclusions and occasional light fire streaks in the clay and purplish brown unglazed surfaces. As with the other coarsewares, forms are pancheons, Fig. 153.34, dripping trays and jars, Figs 153.37 and 156.100. Fabric B16 is a fine buff fabric with few noticeable inclusions, in a similar range of forms to the other coarsewares (not illustrated). Fabric B15 occurs first in School deposits, and is very scarce thereafter. Fabric B16 is found somewhat later in a Collapse deposit of the early 1570s.

The coarsewares are all similar and differences within the clay matrix may be of dubious importance. However, it was thought that there might be some chronological significance, and it did seem to be the case that earlier coarsewares have purplish brown surfaces which become redder through time. The coarseware fabrics continue much the same into the 18th-century stratified deposits. However, rim forms on both jars and pancheons are different and stratified examples have been published here for comparison, Fig. 156.87-88 and 88a. It is also noticeable that the application of slip to the 18th-century vessels is much more carefully done, often with a clear horizontal line externally where the slip ends.

The pancheon form develops from the late medieval wide-mouthed bowl with a flanged almost horizontal rim. These became larger, and deeper, with a marked ridge at rim and body junction. The glazes also change from tan/olive to a treacly brown to dark brown mainly as a result of slipping the surface below the glaze. The latest (i.e. 18th-century) forms have much more elaborate rims, Fig. 156.87-88, in general.

Fabric YW:Yellow Wares (37 sherds)

Figures 154.64; 155.73, 73a, 74; 156.103 and 157.CG 1, 1a, 2 and 2a

The Yellow Wares were initially subdivided into fabric groups but there seemed little significance in them, either chronologically or related to form. Yellow wares were not well represented at Whitefriars, probably due to a lack of excavation in areas of 17th-century activity, except at the Cloister Gate. However, there was a wide range of forms, e.g. chafing dishes (Fig. 157.CG 2), jars, cups (Figs 155.73 and 156.103), a ?skillet or pipkin handle and porringers, Fig. 155.74. Yellow Wares are not present in the Grammar School deposits but are found in Hales', Destruction and Collapse deposits, giving a *terminus ante quem* of the early 1570s.

An unusual vessel was also found in a Collapse context of the early 1570s, Fig. 154.64. It was originally classed, probably correctly, as a Yellow Ware by both P. Woodfield and the author (Woodfield, P. 1986, type Dc, where it was published without the (non-joining) handle). The fabric of the vessel is rather yellowish and the glaze has a somewhat brownish tone. Neither of these traits is normally associated with Yellow Wares. The form has always remained uncertain, and the lack of parallels may just imply a Continental source in Northern France, particularly in view of the presence of sherds from Martincamp. This form, a 'fluted' drinking jug or cup?, is also unusual if not unique for Yellow Wares but resembles continental forms, particularly the prominent (in this case decorated) ridge at the junction of the neck and shoulder. However, the resemblance to a pleated dress and studded belt has also led to it being thought of as a figurine, or even possibly, when complete, a salt.

4 POST-MEDIEVAL WARES (EIGHTEENTH CENTURY)

Figures 155.76-86; 156.87-88a; and 157.M4

The usual range of late 17th-18th-century types were found associated with robbing and rubbish disposal at the Whitefriars, namely feathered slipwares, dark on light slipwares, Fig. 155.76-77, multi-coloured slipwares, manganese mottled wares, and tin-glazed earthen wares, Fig. 157.M 4. Also white salt glaze and blue scratch-glazed wares, cream ware plates, Fig. 155.78, and pearl and cream wares often as Chinoiserie tea bowls, Fig. 156.82-83, and, less commonly, porcelain, including Worcester, Fig. 155.80. A transfer printed, pearlware teapot, Fig. 155.86, was also a relic of the last, final, gentry occupation of the site at the very end of the 18th century.

5 IMPORTED POTTERY

Late medieval maiolicas (5 sherds)

Figure 152.21, 21a, 22

An Andalusian lustreware dish, Fig. 152.21, was recovered from the undisturbed fill of stone-lined grave 17 in the W chancel (68 Ga.2.3) of the Rebuild phase. It was referred to as Valencian in Woodfield 1981, 110, but opinion has changed in the last twenty years or so, and it is now identified as Late Andalusian. The S Netherlands altar vase, published as residual by Woodfield in 1981, fig. 13:1, is included here, Fig. 152.22, as a rare find likely to have been of friary ritual use. The Late Andalusian Spanish albarello sherd also referred to by Woodfield in 1981, and now fully published, may also have had a similar function, Fig. 152.21a. All these will be of the Rebuild phase.

Imports of just pre- or post- Dissolution date: Fabrics X02 X03 X04 X12, X21

Rhenish Stonewares (35 sherds)

Figures 154.61; 155.75 and 157.CG 3-4

Fabric X02 appears to be the earliest type, from either Raeren or Siegburg. Fabric X03 vessels consist of 16th-century Frechen/Cologne drinking jugs. Fabric X04 sherds are from seventeenth century Bartmann type jugs.

The earliest example of Rhenish stoneware comes from an apparently 16th-century tank, 77 F.60, but it is not known from what part of its fill. It may be of an earlier monastic 16th-Century Rebuild phase. The remaining Rhenish stonewares appear in Grammar School, Hales' and Destruction levels.

Fabric X12 (Martincamp flask) from Neufchâtel-en-Bray. This fine grey fabric, with a thin yellowish glaze, is represented by only a few sherds from the largely unstratified material from the 1977 excavations, although it was apparently again present in the tank fill, F.60, with Rhenish stoneware, presumably there of 16th-century date.

Also from the 1977 excavations was part of a Malling jug (fabric X21) with blue and brown mottles on a white tin-glaze background. A very similar vessel to this was found in a ?17th-century context at Stafford Castle (Ratkai, in preparation).

See also Table 7: 'Structural phases and their accompanying pottery fabrics' for the chronology of fabrics. This table does not include unstratified material so the sherd numbers will not match those given above.

B CHRONOLOGIES: INTERRELATION OF CERAMIC AND STRUCTURAL EVIDENCE

It was decided to study four groups of pottery in greater detail in view of their relationship to clear and often closely dated building phases. These were from the church up to the 16th-century destruction, the porch/chapel attached to the E of the N transept, the claustral area, and the Sacristy /Hales' Chapel.

The Church

Pottery from the church was divided into three groups. Group 1 up to the tower collapse of 1447 (phases Pre-friary, Friary and Friary 2 - ignoring the Pre-rebuild phase from which no pottery was recovered). Group 2 was the post-tower collapse up to 16th-century Destruction levels (Phases Rebuild, 16th-Century Rebuild and post Reformation School). Group 3 consisted of 16th-century destruction levels (Phases Hales', Destruction and Collapse). The material from the resonance passages published by Woodfield (1981) is not included although some material from the later robbing of the resonance passages is illustrated, Fig. 156.97-100a.

In the first group the pottery was divided between medieval 'D' wares and the later Medieval Red Wares. Some of the 'D' wares, e.g. D21 and D03, may be residual, i.e. pre-date the construction of Whitefriars. Although D03 is problematic, in that it is dated by the excavation of Chilvers Coton (Mayes and Scott 1984) to the 13th and 14th centuries, but appears in a small but consistent quantity throughout Whitefriars, though this is in part due to the disturbance of earlier features, e.g. when grave or foundation digging. It has been suggested (Ratkai forthcoming and above) that this dating may need to be revised.

However, there are other examples of sherds which considerably pre-date the construction of Whitefriars, e.g. Developed Stamford Ware (Fabric D44) and Coventry Tripod Pitcher Ware (Fabric D31). These are only represented by single sherds which have presumably come from Pre-friary quarry and clay pits beneath the Whitefriars' structures. Only one context, originally thought possibly to belong to the pre-tower collapse phase, seemed misplaced. This was 60 III (8), a ground surface by the NE transept. It contained sherds of fabric D02 but also a sherd of coarse ware fabric B11c, suggesting that this level should now be seen as post-dating the tower collapse and to be of the Rebuild phase.

The presence of B11a and B12 in 62 VIII 3, a green sand builders' trample of the Rebuild phase, confirms the suggested later 15th-century date for the added buttress in the lane, normally without buttresses, and most probably belongs to the late 15th century-early 16th century, being strengthening work in the S nave caused by the collapse of the tower. Additionally 61 (VI) 6 is confirmed as unlikely to be pre-N transept and more likely to belong to the transept and tower rebuild of the later 15th century. The presence of B11a and B13 confirms the impression that these must be the earliest types of coarseware. The information from this early period is useful for giving a *terminus ante quem* for the introduction of Late Medieval Red Ware and suggests a date in the Rebuild phase for the introduction of the Midlands purple tradition. It would also seem to confirm that Cistercian ware was not introduced until the second half of the 15th century at the earliest. Apropos, Glyn Coppack writes (*in litt.* to C, Woodfield) 'the earliest Cistercian ware that I have ever seen from a dated deposit comes from the Bishops' Palace in Lincoln (Drewett, Chapman and Coppack, 1976). That was in a construction context in the privy kitchen of 1452. It was only a single sherd but it was securely stratified below a primary brick floor'.

The Rebuild phase sees the introduction of imported Spanish and Netherlands tin-glazed enamel earthenware, and of 'Tudor Green' type ware. The following periods (School, Hales', Destruction) are characterised by the preponderance of Cistercian wares, Late Medieval Red wares, Midland Purple wares and coarsewares. There are, however, some forty sherds of residual medieval 'D' sherds from the church and more than double that number from the whole site. Most of the coarseware fabrics are represented and this period witnesses the introduction of German stoneware.

Information from the excavation of the church is also of regional importance in the dating of Midland Yellow Wares. Six Yellow Ware sherds are present in a phase which ends in the early 1570s.

Four robbed graves within the church, Grave 8 (61 VI 8), Grave 19 (64 XXI 3), Grave 17 (68 Ga.2.3) and Grave 12 (68 XId 4) contain 15th and 16th-century material. Although we cannot be certain how much of this robbing-disturbed material derives from the original grave fill, the presence of fabrics A13, A23, B11a and B12 would tend to indicate a date of the late 15th or early 16th century. Also of interest is a possible Nettlebed sherd (Fabric C03) and a sherd of Andalusian lustreware of late 15th-century date, this last at least from the undisturbed grave fill of Grave 17, Fig. 152.21. The pottery from these graves is in marked contrast to that from graves to the E, excavated in the 1970s, which cut Pre-friary industrial dumps, some of which was incorporated into their fills; all these graves were apparently cut into an old clay pit.

The Porch/Chapel at the North East Transept

The information here from pre-tower collapse, tower collapse and late medieval robbing levels concurs with that from the church, with a further indication that the Late Medieval Redware tradition began before 1447. In the 16th-century levels there is once more the dominating presence of Cistercian wares, coupled with the presence of coarsewares. Context 68 IIIE 127 contains fabric A14 and would seem to confirm the suggested date of the 16th-Century Rebuild of the third N porch/chapel wall as a workshop wall built after the tower collapse. i.e. in the earlier 16th century.

The Cloister, including the adjoining 'raft' for the south east transept

Excavations in the claustral area took place over several years. The earliest, by Priscilla Telford for MPBW in 1956 has little stratigraphic information in view of the loss of the site records. This pottery consists mainly of 15th to 18th-century material, all from the area of the then standing cloister gatehouse, now demolished, and its site under the ring road.

The earliest context from this area is 60 I 16, a Pre-friary quarry fill, the quarry partly underlying the E range and projecting to the N. Also early is 60 I 13. The lowest levels here are 60 I 10 and 60 I 14, levels of the 'raft' to support the SE transept built against the pre-existing cloister. However, the presence of fabrics A25, B13 and B13a in these layers confirms the view that the 'raft' is not of primary 14th-century date, and indeed there is structurally a straight joint between it and the cloister wall. Nor is it of Friary 2 phase, the original date of the transept, but of the late 15th century Rebuild phase and a strengthening after the tower collapse. Again 60 I 15, a higher level of the 'raft', also contained a 15th-century sherd, in fabric A14.

Pottery from the 1962/1963 trial holes, undertaken to establish the original external ground and internal floor levels to the standing cloister W face, during reconstruction, consists mainly of Late Medieval-early

Post-medieval wares, mainly coarsewares, Midland Purples and Late Medieval Redwares. It would perhaps be surprising to find a build-up of pottery in the cloister whilst Whitefriars was still a religious house and it would therefore seem most likely that the pottery accumulated during Hales' ownership. In relation to other areas of the site there was comparatively little Cistercian ware; however, these deposits were in many cases the make-up for floors and could have come from anywhere and do not reflect normal use and discard patterns.

The NW cloister garth ground level, 64 XXIII(1), contained a sherd of Cologne/Frechen stoneware and would therefore appear to be contemporary with Hales rather than medieval.

In 1964 and 1968 excavation revealed the walls of the NW cloister range. Context 68 XXVII(4), which appeared to be a small construction trench for wall I, contained a single 15th-century sherd in fabric A21. This confirms the stratigraphical impression that cloister wall I was begun late but that work was abandoned; money was found to 'finish' the cloister in 1506, and this perhaps relates to this unfinished westernmost wall, but if so the intention was not realised. Context 68 XXVII (3), red clay over the garth wall, contained a single Midland Purple sherd from its demolition deposits. Context 68 XXVII (2) is a tipped workshop level and contains a single 15th-century sherd, possibly residual. The latest level, context 68 XXVII(6), probably the construction trench for Hales' enclosing garden wall IV, contained a single Cistercian ware sherd and the certain construction trench for Hales' wall also contained a single Cistercian ware sherd, a coarseware sherd and a Late Medieval Redware sherd.

The sequence of the walls seems to begin with wall III (internal cloister garth of the late 14th or early 15th century), then continue with wall II (external cloister garth built before 1450), in turn followed by wall I. This was a wall for the double range but only the foundations for this were built. It belongs to the 16th-Century Rebuild phase. The last wall in the sequence was Hales' garden wall, wall IV of the mid 16th century.

The Sacristy (also known as Hales' Chapel) together with the Passage joining the Sacristy to the Presbytery

The earliest surviving context associated with 'Hales' Chapel', context 69 XXIX (20), was an external late 14th-century level related to the first medieval S wall, and contained a single Chilvers Coton 'C' fabric sherd (fabric D02). However, this sherd is harder-fired than usual and resembles a proto-Midland Purple ware. This is normally thought to belong to the 15th century. However the sherd in question may have been accidentally overfired or it may be that steps towards Midland Purple ware began to be taken in the late 14th century.

The rebuilding of the foundation to the N doorway in the N wall of the predecessor (but second phase) of Hales' Chapel (context 69 XXIX (6)) contained a sherd of coarseware fabric B02. This presents a similar picture of rebuilding to the material from the 'cloister raft'. Fabric B02 (a slipped coarseware jar) is unlikely to be earlier than the late 15th century and more probably belongs to the early years of the 16th century, i.e. the Rebuild phase.

Sixteenth-century levels from the passage contain the usual mixture of Cistercian wares, coarsewares, Tudor Green type wares and Late Medieval Red wares, with very few residual medieval 'D' wares. The largest group of sherds, from context 69 XXIX (9), a ground level, was unfortunately mixed, after excavation, with other bags of Trench XXIX 16th-century material, when handed out to school children at Coventry Museum. This is a pity as it is not now possible to relate the Yellow Ware sherds to their original precise group. However, it is apparent both from the association of Yellow Wares with this mixed 16th-century group and with its occurrence in a layer (69 XXIX (5)) over 16th-century Hales' paving, that Yellow Wares have a *terminus ante quem* of the later 16th century.

In the late 16th century-early 17th-century levels, mainly in the passage, there is a much more limited range of fabrics. The evidence from Hales' Chapel suggests that fabric A11 continued in use, whereas fabric A13 did not. Yellow Wares also now become more plentiful. The paucity of coarseware material is surprising but presumably reflects the source from which the sherds came, i.e. the pottery present is made up of tablewares rather than 'kitchen' wares, (a phenomenon reproduced again in the passage in the late 18th century).

The evidence for the date of the top layer beneath the 18th-century flint cobbling and over the 16th-century sandstone cobbling, context 69 XXIX (8), is insufficient for dating, although it should be of later 16th-17th-century date. However, the layer above these cobbles, 69 XXIX 8a, is unequivocally late 18th century and contains sherds from cream ware plates, fine tea bowls and porcelain. This shows that the passage survives until this date, as does gentry occupation of Hales' Place at this time, although the passage itself was presumably not in polite use, since rubbish had started to accumulate there, doubtless on its way out to vegetable gardens.

C POTTERY FROM THE 1970s EXCAVATIONS

Two possible Pre-friary contexts were identified in the presbytery, 77F.77, probably a Pre-friary level exposed by the removal of the overlying floor make-up rather than the suggested 'unused grave' of friary date; this lay N of grave 1977/5; also 77F.79 adjoining, apparently again a patch of clay pit fill. There were three sherds, representing two vessels, from 77F.79, two in fabric D02/Chilvers Coton 'C' fabric and one in D03/Chilvers

Coton 'A' fabric. Both vessels were jugs. The other context 77F.77, contained more pottery. There were fourteen sherds, which were made up of Chilvers Coton 'A' and 'C' wares, sandy cooking pots and a single developed Stamford ware sherd, all of which would fit quite happily with a Pre-friary date. However, there was a single proto-Midlands Purple ware sherd, which was of much later, 15th-century date. This may date the cutting of this feature into the early clay pit fill as a piece of post Reformation robbing, (floor tile was also present) or, given the circumstances of the excavations, have been intrusive.

Vessel forms were a mixture of jugs, bowls and cooking pot/jars. Two of the bowls were sooted on the exterior as were two of the cooking pots, an indication of nearby habitations of this date.

Unfortunately there is a great deal of contamination in the 1977 'contexts' and this is not made easier by the habit of grouping pottery under a number which is that of a wall, which happened in the case of some twenty-five exposures of medieval structures, e.g. Fs 9, 23, 100, 103, etc. The material 'from' F.100, a 14th-century wall, contained thirty-seven 18th and 19th-century sherds, and context 'from wall F.23' was also contaminated with late post-medieval material. However F.66, Grave 1977/4 in the presbytery, could be dated broadly to the Friary phase by the presence of D02/Chilvers Coton 'C' ware. Some earlier 12th-13th-century residual material was apparent, from the underlying clay pit, e.g. sandy cooking pots/jars in fabrics D22 and D23.

At the SE corner of the cloister, pottery from F.59a, the 'bottom stones of tank F.60' consisted of D02/Chilvers Coton 'C' and Late Red ware, the latter suggesting a 16th-century date. F.60 is the fill of the same tank. This produced again D02/Chilvers Coton 'C' sherds together with sherds from a Cologne stoneware drinking jug and from a Martincamp flask. There was also a Cistercian type sherd from a hollow ware vessel probably dating to the late 15th-16th century. The tank seems likely to date initially from close on the Dissolution and may relate to the Workshop.

The Workshop material deriving from the taking down of the N-S baulk running across this feature and the reredorter below, seems to contain mainly late 15th-16th-century pottery, but as elsewhere contamination with later pottery is apparent, noticeably in F.91c, which should be the demolition of the reredorter. Additionally the fill of F.110, a rubbish pit most likely related to the Workshop, was contaminated. The late 15th-16th-century pottery consisted of a Late Red Ware jug and Midland Purple ware. There was a single Chilvers Coton 'C' sherd. In view of the structural interpretation of this area as a workshop replacing a Reredorter, the range of fabrics, forms, etc., repays further study. The fabrics are all hard-wearing utilitarian wares, largely unglazed. The forms consist of cisterns, jars and jugs. The vessels from F.91c, demolition of the reredorter, all had a thick white internal lime deposit, presumably representing the heating of water for ablutions. A jug from this context as well as having an internal deposit was also sooted on the exterior. The range of forms and fabrics are not paralleled anywhere else on the site, suggesting a particular and discrete use of this area in the sixteenth century.

In this same area, F.93a, an area of red sandy soil outside the workshop to the E, of unknown relationship to the buildings, shows some evidence for 16th-17th-century activity, although the ceramic finds are difficult to interpret. They consist of a residual shelly ware sherd and a small 38mm diameter ?albarello base which has had its bottom knocked out. It survives to a height of 30mm and is in a hard, high-fired, pale grey fabric with a patch of thin yellowish clear glaze, possibly an import.

Other 'stratified' deposits may relate to Destruction levels or friary Collapse. However they are all highly contaminated. Some 18th-century phases could be identified but many of these were also contaminated.

D CONCLUSION

The pottery from the Woodfield excavations at the Coventry Whitefriars provides a useful chronology for the late Medieval-early Post-medieval period. It can be seen that the Late Red Ware tradition had already begun before the tower collapse of 1447, and probably before the 1420s, but seems to have died out during the 16th century. It seems likely that the coarseware tradition had begun in the closing years of the 15th century and was flourishing by the mid 16th century. Although differences in coarseware fabrics were noted there seems to be little chronological significance in this.

The pottery from Whitefriars provides further evidence for answering the question of the introduction of Cistercian wares in the Midlands. An early introduction of *c.*1450 postulated at the Austin Friars, Leicester (Woodland 1981) does not seem likely in Coventry. However, at Fountains Abbey (Coppack 1986), in the Wool House, the likely date of deposition was the 1480s on coin/jetton evidence, and in the church the early to mid 1490s. Cistercian ware appears at Whitefriars at a similar date, i.e. in the late 15th century, in very small quantities, although there are few contexts which can be dated to between the tower collapse of 1447 and the Dissolution. The preponderance of Cistercian wares in the period of Hales' and the School suggests that the presence of Cistercian Ware is largely a 16th century phenomenon and would support Brear's (1983) dating of post 1485 for its introduction. What is particularly interesting is the concurrence of the Cistercian forms with Blackware forms, i.e. the Blackware tradition was developing quite soon after the introducion of Cistercian wares. This must be by the 1540s as they occur together in School deposits. Many of these Blackware forms are directly paralleled at both Dudley Castle (Ratkai 1985) and Stafford Castle (Ratkai, in preparation). One source of production is Wednesbury (Hodder 1992), in the W Midlands, which is almost certain to be the source of supply for Dudley Castle. Whether Wednesbury products travelled to Coventry as well is at present impossible to say.

Evidence for the introduction of Yellow Wares is scanty but would seem to occur in the later 16th-century in levels associated with Hales (see above) but significantly not with the earlier School deposits. There is not a large quantity of Yellow Ware from the site, either stratified or residual, and this probably reflects a real lack of 17th-century material in the areas excavated, a time when Yellow Wares are common. It is possible that different methods of waste disposal were in use in that century or it may point to a shift in the focus of activity on the site, for example to the Cloister Gate main entrance and the Passage from the Sacristy to what was by then gardens.

Most of the earlier medieval 'D' wares are presumably residual and represent material from disturbed Pre-friary deposits and date to the 12th and 13th centuries. D02/Chilvers Coton 'C' ware is found throughout the life of the friary. It also occurs in 16th-century levels and it is difficult to be certain with such small groups whether this represents contemporary usage or residuality. The former should certainly not be ruled out.

Despite more local pottery production, e.g. Cannon Park (Redknap 1985), the dominant medieval fabric is Chilvers Coton 'C' ware (fabric D02). This is unusual in that it was believed that only the more elaborate Chilvers Coton 'A' ware jugs found a market in Coventry. It is possible that there is an ecclesiastical link between the Whitefriars and the Nuneaton area especially as in some cases the production of pottery can be linked to the influence of religious houses.

However, the overall picture of medieval ceramic supply at Whitefriars is fairly parochial with most of the pottery coming from more or less local sources (if Chilvers Coton about eight miles distant, is counted as local) with less than 10% of pottery being non-local. A local supply pattern is evidenced at Much Park Street (Wright 1987) although the pottery is not quantified making it difficult to assess relative proportions of Coventry sandy ware to Chilvers Coton wares. However Wright herself (1987, 40) remarks on '*t*he extreme paucity of regional imports and 'exotic' material' At Broadgate East (Redknap and Perry 1996) the pottery was said to be predominantly of local manufacture with a smaller component derived from Chilvers Coton (this pottery is also not quantified). However, Perry (1996, 43) indicates that 'at some point Nuneaton (i.e. Chilvers Coton) wares appear to take over from local wares, which then only appear in small quantities if at all'. On the neighbouring (unpublished) Derby Lane site 'no contexts have produced Nuneaton wares in the same quantities as local sandy wares'. The picture regarding the relative frequency, popularity and dating of local Coventry and Chilvers Coton wares is clearly still unresolved.

In comparison the town of Warwick, which was of less commercial importance than Coventry in the medieval period, had a much wider range of non-local ceramics (Ratkai 1990) although local products form the greater part of the pottery. Late 13th-14th century Brill-Boarstall jugs form *c*.5% of the assemblage but there are also sherds from Wiltshire, S Staffordshire, the Cotswolds, Oxfordshire and Deritend, Birmingham, in addition to pottery from Chilvers Coton and the Coventry area. Ratkai (1990, 58) suggests that one possible stimulus to the movement of non-local pottery to Warwick may have been caused by the fact that several religious houses in Leicestershire, Northamptonshire, Staffordshire, Worcestershire and Wiltshire held property in Warwick. It is of no little interest that Wright (1987, 40) suggests that Coventry enjoyed a period of economic buoyancy in the later 14th and 15th centuries 'partly at the expense of Warwick' and shows the difficulties in interpreting ceramic data, particularly when the dataset is small, as indicators of trade, exchange and economics.

The range of vessel forms was fairly typical. The early residual Pre-friary pottery was made up chiefly of cooking pots with a smaller percentage of jugs, some decorated. A bird whistle was an unusual form. In the 15th century exotica (Netherlands and Spanish maiolicas) appear in the form of an altar vase, a bowl and an albarello. Towards the end of the 15th century there is a bias in favour of jugs and bowls; there is a possible industrial vessel base, and cups make an appearance. In the 16th century the range of forms favours particularly cups, mugs, drinking jugs, coarseware pancheons, some very large, and jars or cisterns. Cucurbits/industrial bases are present, and a possible small albarello. Pipkins are rare.

Less common forms such as salts, chafing dishes and stool pots are found, but only rarely, and all in post-Dissolution contexts. It is perhaps surprising that no urinals have been found associated with the monastic occupation of the site as they are often found in assemblages from religious houses, but there are of course virtually no domestic friary contexts here.

The phases of industrial activity both pre- and post-friary have not resulted in groups which could be said to reflect that activity very clearly, although there was an early 16th-century industrial base/cucurbit stratified in 64 XV 1 in the 'yard' between cloister and choir, and 16th-century crucible fragments, with copper alloy detritus adhering, came from 69 XXIX 9, stratified in the same 'yard'. Unfortunately no funding was available for a specialist report on these vessels.

Posset pots appear by the middle of the 16th century. By the 17th century a greater number of dishes were present together with drinking vessels, chafing dishes and porringers. The 18th-century groups contained a preponderance of table wares e.g. plates, dishes, tea bowls and teapots, although utilitarian kitchen wares in coarse ware fabrics were also present.

There was little in the pottery which would have marked out this site as either religious, (except perhaps for the altar vase, although these do occur elsewhere as flower vases) scholastic (except here perhaps the Cistercian ware flasks from the Grammar School (Woodfield 1981) but absent from other contexts) or seriously industrial. It consisted of a mix of kitchen wares, e.g. pancheons, jars and cisterns and of table wares, e.g. cups, jugs, chafing dishes and salts. It is the presence of tablewares and of more 'sophisticated' cooking vessels, e.g. tripod pipkins, which suggests a moderately affluent occupancy of Whitefriars in the 16th and probably 17th centuries. Firstly because the use of table wares, particularly salts and chafing dishes, indicates a certain formality in dining arrangements and social aspirations and secondly the use of pipkins suggests more elaborate or careful cooking methods. As Gaimster (1999, 214) summarises 'In terms of its status we see the migration of ceramics from the kitchen...to a central position on the table... By this stage (1450-1650) ceramics were being used as an active cultural medium. Ceramics were employed in the gentry residence and urban merchant house as part of the social emulation progress'. However the destruction without record, in the final thirty years of the 20th century, of the domestic areas of both friary and great house has precluded any chance of expanding the picture we have of the Coventry Whitefriars or the succeeding great house.

The spatial distribution of vessel forms was undistinguished throughout the medieval and early post-medieval periods. However, this is not to say that the study of the vessel forms is in itself flawed but rather may, in this case, represent the rather truncated nature of the evidence from the 1960s caused by working largely in the church, where pottery rubbish is unlikely to be dropped, and in a situation where the main thrust was towards uncovering the plan of the church and NW cloister, both threatened with imminent destruction.

No conclusions can be drawn from the material from the 1956 and the 1970s excavations/clearances, since there is insufficient stratigraphic data.

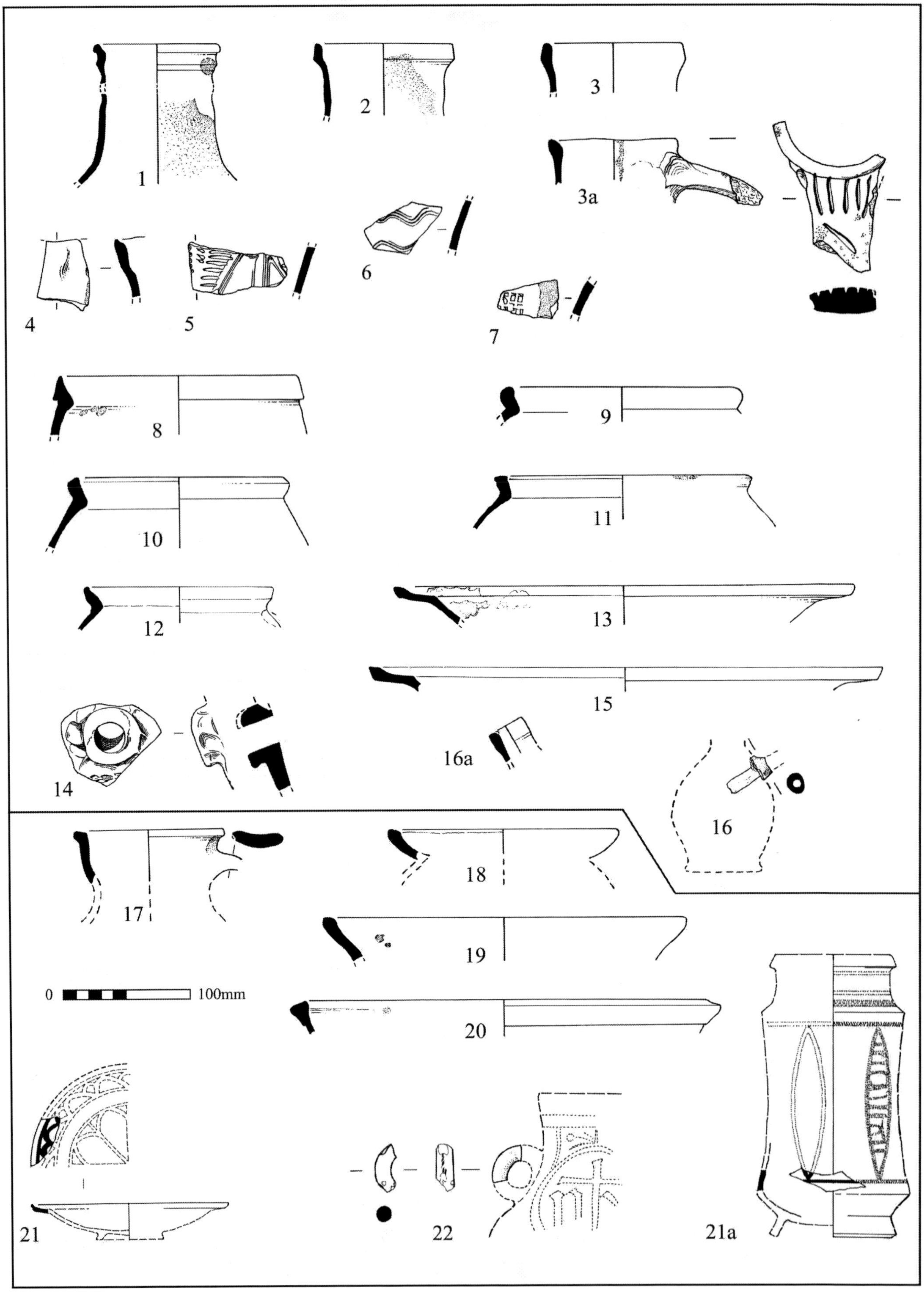

Figure 152

1-16a Chilvers Coton wares from Prefriary phase, pre second half of 14th century; (some possibly Friary phase, second half of 14th century ?); jugs with green glazes, jars and bird whistles; bowl 13 contained lime plaster.

17-20 Late Red Wares, and proto coarsewares from Rebuild phase, late 15th and early 16th century; jug, jar bowl and pancheon.

21, 21a Rare Hispano-Moresque (Late Andalusian) lustrewares; decorated dish and albarello.

22 South Netherlands Maiolica altar vase Rebuild phase. Scale 1:4

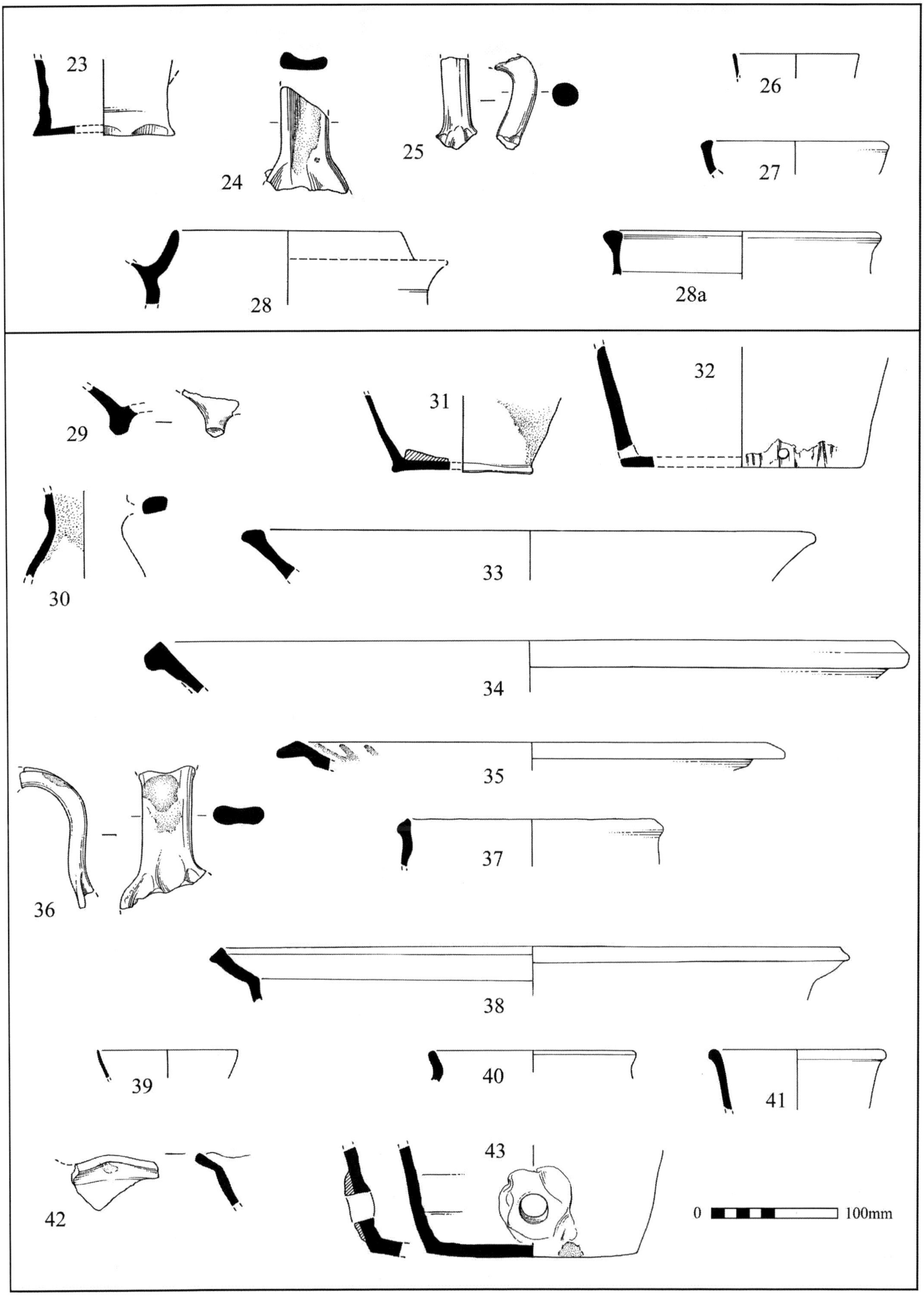

Figure 153

23-28 Late Red Wares and 'Tudor Green'. Rebuild phase, late 15th and early 16th century; jugs, cups, curcubit.

28a Post-medieval coarse ware. 16th-century Rebuild phase; jar.

29 Post-medieval coarse ware. School phase, *c.*1545-*c.*1558; tripod pipkin.

30-36 Cistercian, Midland Purple, late Red Wares and post-medieval coarsewares. School/?industrial phase, *c.*1545-*c.*1570; jugs, pancheons, cisterns, mug.

7-43 Proto coarsewares, coarsewares, Cistercian wares. Hales' phase, *c.*1545-*c.*1558, but distinct from Grammar School; jars, bowls, pancheon, cistern, cup. Scale 1:4

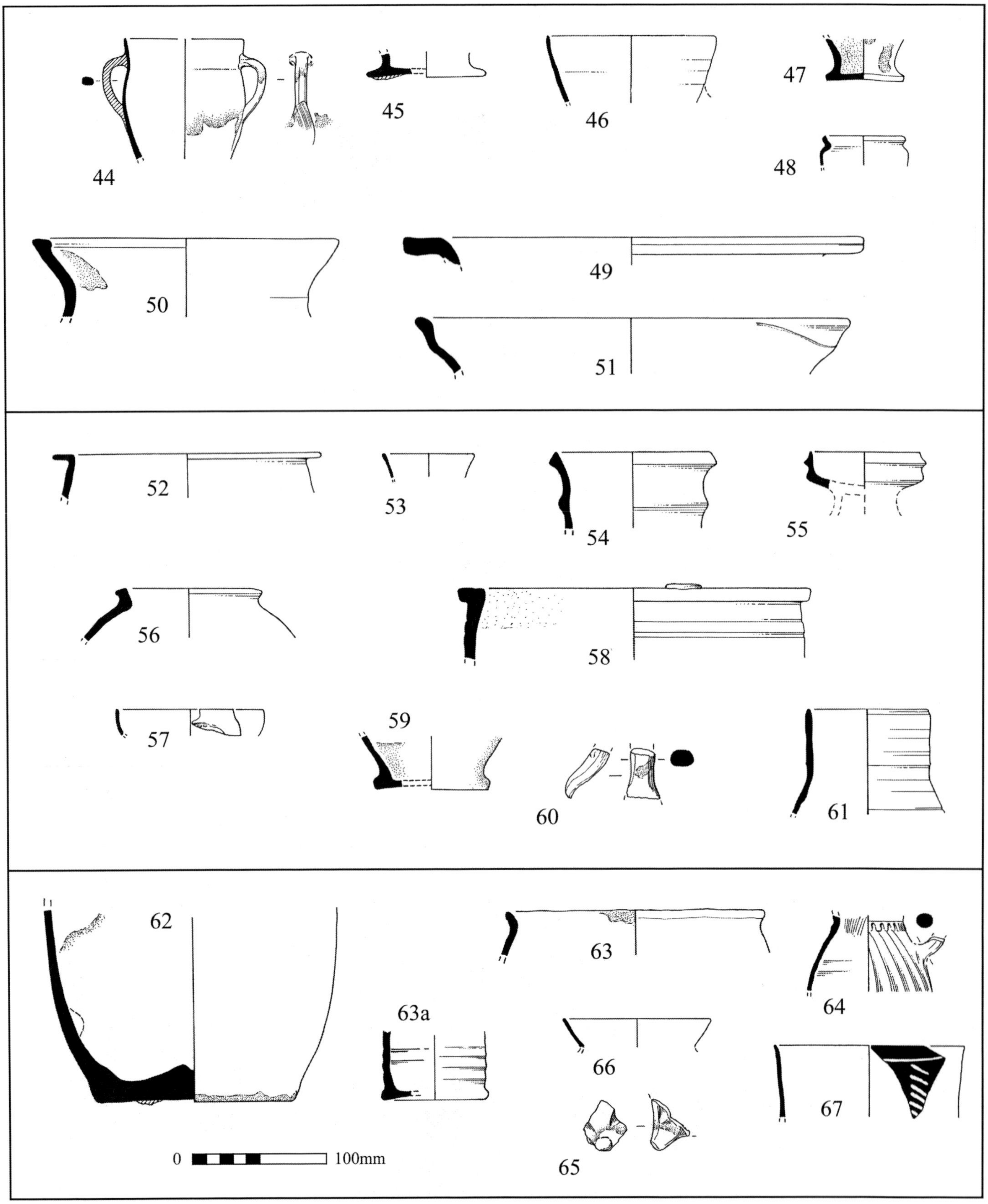

Figure 154

44-51 Cistercian, 'Tudor Green', coarsewares, late Red Wares. Hales phase, *c.*1545- *c.*1558; cups, bowls, albarello?; black and green glazes.

52-61 Cistercian, Late Red wares, Midland Purple, and Rhenish stoneware. Destruction phase, *c.*1545-*c.*1572/74; jugs, cups, jar, cistern, chamber pot, salt; brown and purple glazes.

62-67 Midland Purple, Cistercian, 'Tudor Green', and Yellow wares. Collapse phase, *c.*1572-74; jars, tankards, pipkin, rare figurine/jug.

Scale 1:4

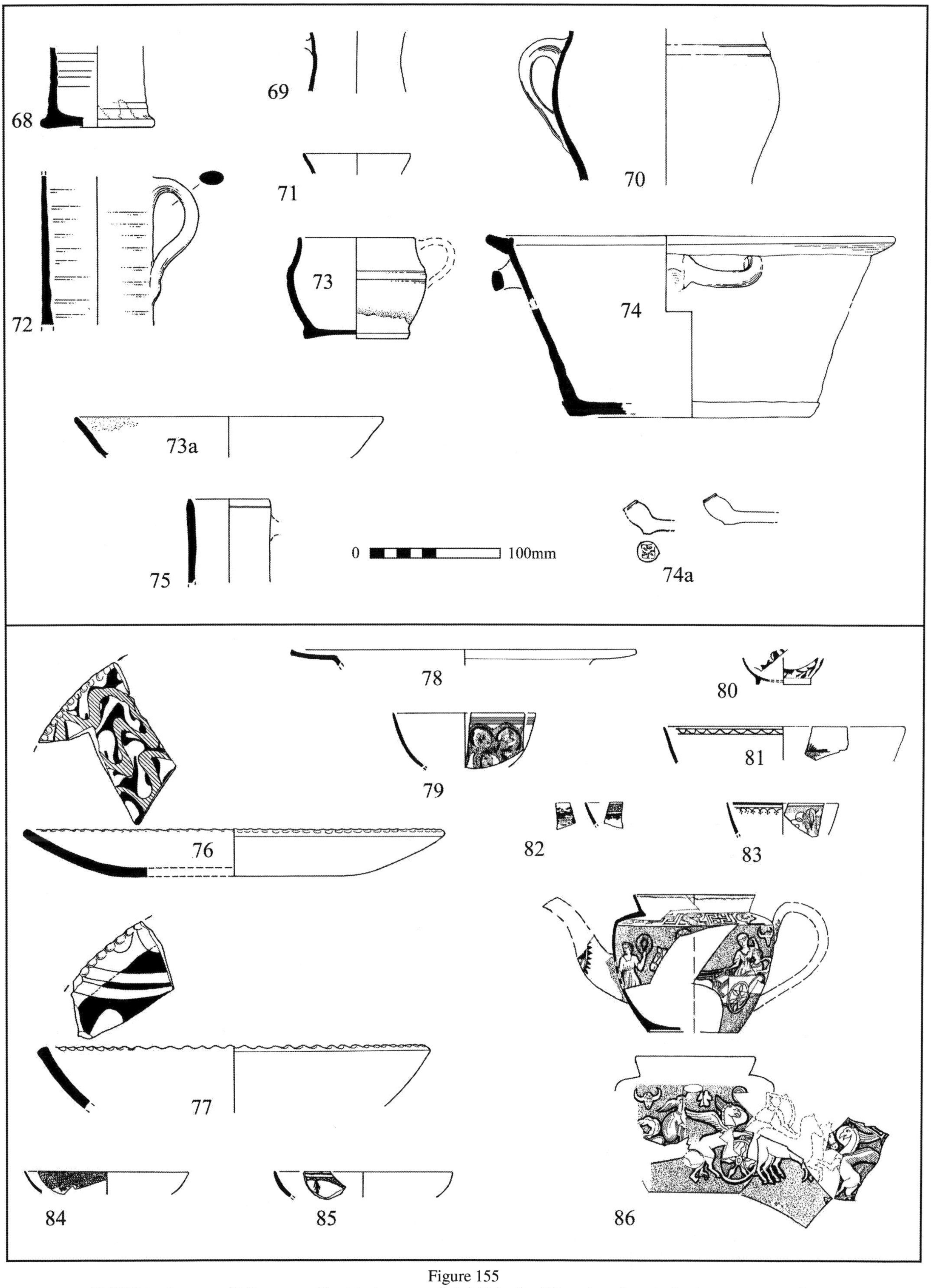

Figure 155
68-75 Cistercian wares, Yellow wares, Rhenish stonewares. Late 16th/earlier 17th century phase; tankards, cups, mug, porringer, Bartman jug, clay pipe, *c.*1625, found with 72 to 74.
76-86 Wares of 1780-1800 gentry occupation of Hales Place; tea pot, tea bowls, plates, saucers, dish.
Scale 1:4

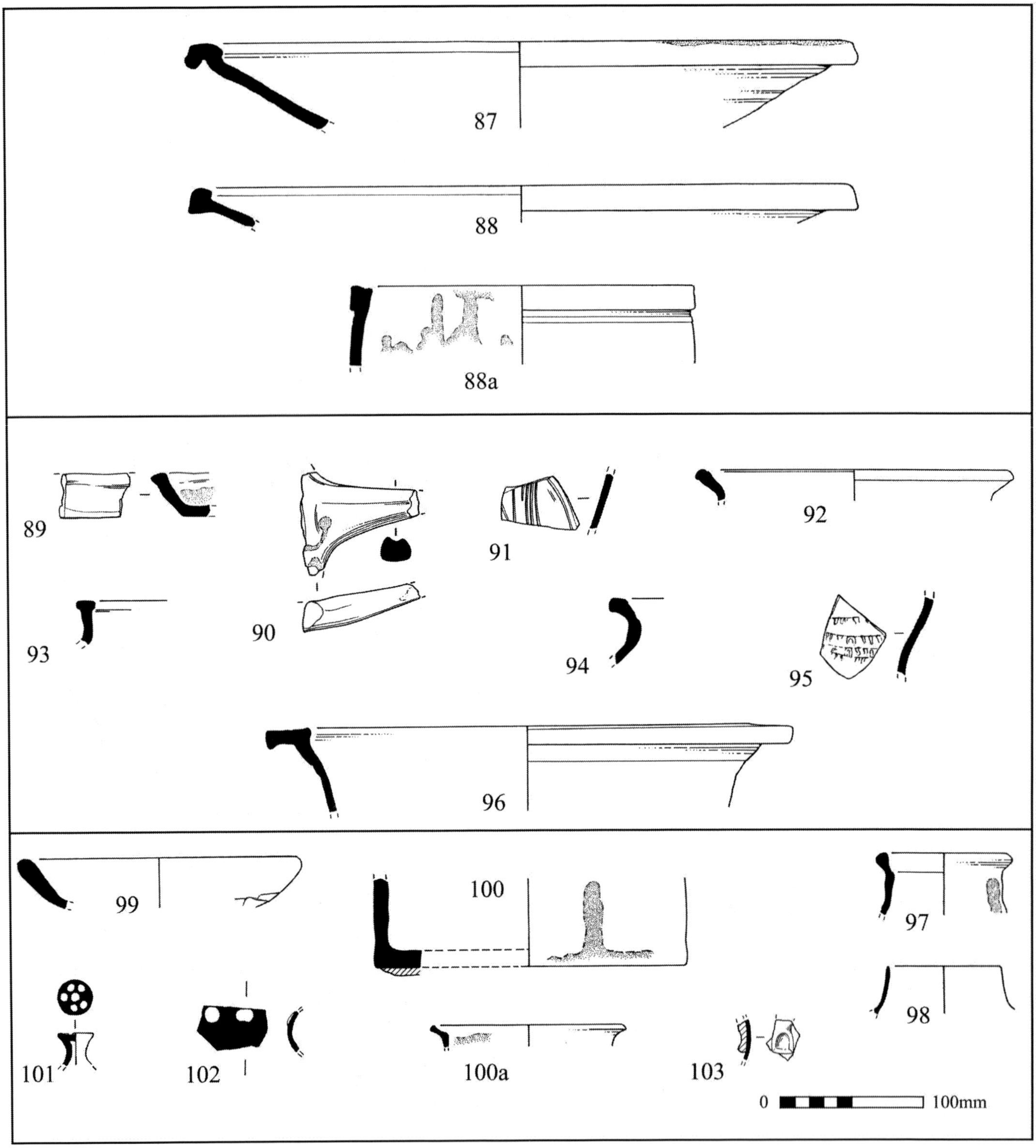

Figure 156

87-88a Coarse wares of the 18th-century phase; pancheons and jar.

Residual and Unstratified Pottery

89-94 Cannon Park? and Coventry sandy ware. Pre-friary? Phase, pre 1340s.

95-96 Late Red Ware and Midland Purple. Rebuild? Phase, late 15th century.

97-100a Midland Purple, Cistercian/Blackware, coarsewares. School? Phase, mid 16th-century pottery from 18th-century robbing of Resonance Passages.

101-103 Cistercian and Yellow Wares. Late 16th-17th-century pottery. Unstratified.

Scale 1:4

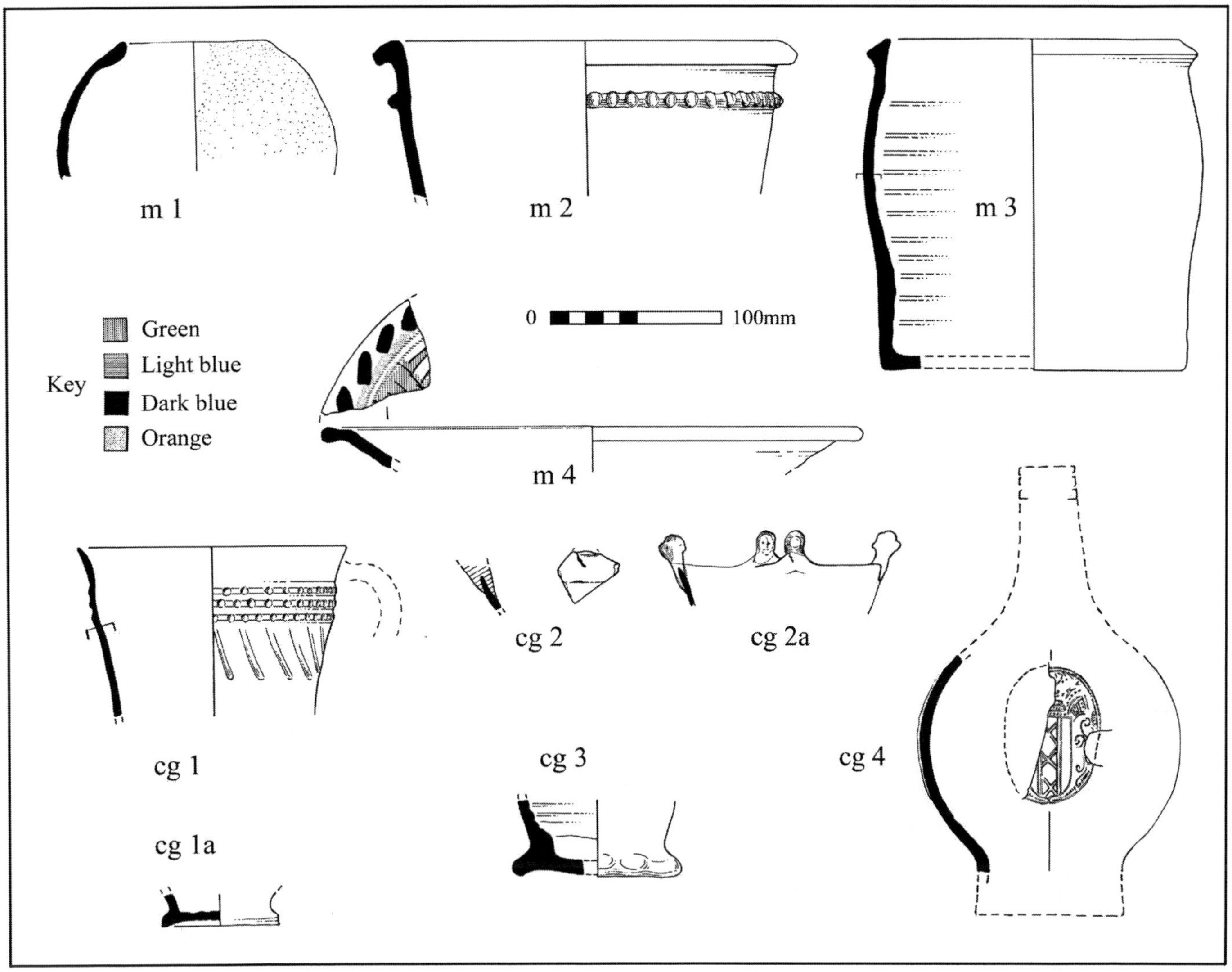

Figure 157
MUSEUM EXCAVATIONS, 1970s.
M1-M4 Chilvers Coton, Midland Purple, 16th-century coarseware, 17th-century tin-glazed enamel. M3 is Hales phase, *c.*1545-58, others unstratified. Forms include an industrial vessel (m1); m4 may be an import,

TELFORD EXCAVATIONS 1956. 17th-century occupation of Inner Cloister Gate.
CG1-CG4 Yellow wares and Rhenish stonewares. Forms include a chafing dish (cg2) and a Bartman jug (cg4) with the arms of Amsterdam
Scale all 1:4 except cg2a at 1:8

SECTION S

THE VESSEL GLASS

Dr H. Willmott

Figure 158

A total of eighty fragments of vessel glass was recovered from the excavations at Whitefriars, and these constitute a minimum number of between twenty and twenty-eight vessels, Table 8. Although several fragments are demonstrably later in date, as a whole the majority of the glass can be dated to the first half of the 16th century and relates to early post-monastic activities on the site. The glass can be divided into two distinct types. The first is a high quality soda glass that was almost certainly imported from Venice, whilst the second is potash glass which was likely to have been domestically produced. All the glass has suffered severe weathering and, in the case of some of the potash fragments, complete devitrification. It is probable that these vessels represent a small proportion of those originally used at the site, the remainder not having survived burial in adverse archaeological conditions. Although ten of the vessels from Whitefriars have been previously published (Woodfield 1981, 107-8), this report considers all the surviving glass found at the site, but note that Woodfield (1981) 14 (Venetian), 21 (tumbler) and 22 (urinal) are lost. The seventy surviving pieces are detailed in the catalogue (Nos 1-43).

Table 8 Relative Number of Vessels

Glass Type	Vessel Type	No
Soda Glass	Goblets	3-4
	Jugs	1
	Bowls	1
Potash Glass	Beakers	3-4
	Dishes	1
	Jugs	1
	Lamps	4-8
	Plain Flasks	2-4
	Wrythen Flasks	2
	Jars	1
	Phials	1
	Total	**20-28**

VENETIAN IMPORTS

Six fragments of high quality early 16th-century soda glass were found in the resonance passages and date to the School phase of occupation. Three are decorated with coloured *filigrana* canes, Fig. 158.1-3. This was a technique initially developed during the latter 15th century in Venice, and subsequently adopted by many European glasshouses throughout the 16th century. However, the early date and forms of these vessels makes them most likely to be Venetian rather than *façon de Venise* products. A clear paraison of glass was overlaid with rods, or canes, which were either in plain or twisted colours and then marvered flat into the surface. The paraison was then further inflated and formed into the final shape of the vessel.

Two fragments from Whitefriars, which may well have come from the same vessel, were decorated in an identical way. The first, Fig. 158.1, is the folded-under base-ring from a pedestal footed goblet that is overlaid with vertical running bands of alternating opaque white *vetro a fili* and twisted *vetro a retorti*. The second, Fig. 158.2, is from the everted or trumpet-shaped bowl of a similar goblet. A further fragment, Fig. 158.3, is also decorated in this way, although it is from a different vessel, with the bands of *fili* and *retorti* being much more closely grouped and the fragment sharply curved. Goblets with *filigrana* decoration are occasionally found on high status sites in England. Interestingly, close parallels to the Whitefriars examples can be seen in the post-dissolution layers of the Augustinian priory at Canons Ashby, Northamptonshire (Taylor 1974) as well as other sites such as the moated manor at Acton Court (Courtney 2003).

Two further fragments of imported Venetian glass were also found at the site. The first, Fig. 158.4, is a small section of body made from *millefiori* glass, possibly from a goblet. Originally a Roman technique, *millefiori* glass was revived at the end of the 15th century in Venice and continued to be made into the early 16th century. Glass canes incorporating a variety of colours were prepared much in the same way as modern seaside 'rock' and sliced into small thin sections. A paraison of glass was rolled over these and then marvered so that they were flattened into the surface giving the vessel the flower-like appearance of the technique's name. The small fragment from Whitefriars is decorated with sections of cane containing blue, olive green, brown and opaque white glass. *Millefiori* glass is exceptionally rare archaeologically, and only one other parallel for this example has been found, at Southampton (Charleston 1975, 218 no 1523).

A further import, Fig. 158.5, is a single curved fragment made in opaque white, or *lattimo*, glass, another Venetian innovation dating to the end of the 15th century. *Lattimo* glass continued to be produced into the 17th century, particularly in the Low Countries. However, the contextual date and the form suggests that this vessel is an earlier and rarer Venetian product. It appears to be part of a narrow and vertical neck, probably from a jug or flask. Although fragments of a *lattimo* goblet were found at the Carmelite friary at Maldon (Andrews 1999, 124; I am grateful to Charmian Woodfield for this reference), the nearest parallel for the Coventry vessel can be seen in a ring-handled vase with a tall cylindrical neck, now in the British Museum (Tait 1991, 159-60). This vessel is decorated with the arms and portrait of Henry VII and might have been a diplomatic gift. However, given the small size of the fragment, it is impossible to be certain whether the Whitefriars example is of similar form.

The final soda glass vessel, Fig. 158.6, is represented by a small fragment of solid tooled base-ring. The glass is a deep sapphire-blue colour, although obscured by a heavy iridescence, and the diameter of the base-ring suggests that it comes from a pedestal bowl. Unfortunately the fragment is too small to provide a more detailed reconstruction of its form and provenance. Nevertheless, given its occurrence in the school phase resonance passage, it is likely to be Venetian and of early 16th-century date.

ENGLISH POTASH GLASS

The majority of the vessel glass is made from a potash metal. Potash, or forest, glass was made in England from the 13th century onwards and was the only type of domestically produced glass in the country until the establishment of a fineware industry in the late 16th century. Although some potash glass was imported from the Continent, it is likely that most found at Whitefriars was of local origin. By the early 16th century potash glass was used to make a wide variety of forms including drinking, storage and other domestic vessels. Despite being a relatively small and fragmented assemblage, the potash glass from Whitefriars includes many of these diverse types.

Fragments of between three and four beakers were recovered. The first, Fig. 158.7, is a thin fragment of a tubular base-ring from a pedestal beaker. The vessel was formed from a single paraison of glass with a pushed-in base that was folded to create a stable footing. The rest of the vessel would have had a vertical side. Pedestal beakers were popular throughout the 16th and early 17th centuries, although earlier examples, such as Fig. 158.7, tended to have taller bases and more cylindrical sides. A second fragment, No 8 (not illustrated), is also from an earlier pedestal beaker and is the upper portion of the basal push-in. Both were found in contexts dating to the school phase. A further fragment of pedestal beaker body, Fig. 158.9, is slightly later in date. The side is more tapered and decorated with optic-blown vertical ribbing. This is a later variation of the pedestal beaker dating from the mid to late 16th century and was correspondingly found in the destruction phase of the resonance passage. Earlier pedestal beakers are relatively uncommon finds in England, although several similar examples with enamelled decoration on their bodies were found at Poole (Charleston 1992, 139 nos 30 & 34). Later pedestal beakers with optic-blown vertical ribbing are known from the dissolution phases of Norton Priory as well as more ordinary domestic contexts, such as at St Peter's Street, Northampton (Oakley and Hunter 1979, 299 no 57).

The final fragment of beaker, Fig. 158.10, is more problematic in its identification. It is a slightly everted rim with a rounded in-folded edge and made from a completely devitrified potash glass. It does not resemble any known beaker form of the 16th century, as suggested by its School phase context. However, the rim corresponds to a type found in large numbers at the monastery near Schaffhausen in Germany and thought to be produced in that region during the 14th and 15th centuries (Tyson 2000, 88). The bodies of these beakers were barrel-shaped and decorated with small applied prunts, but the absence of the rest of this vessel from Whitefriars makes more certain identification difficult. If indeed an imported Germanic beaker, it must be a residual find in the 16th-century context, which is not unlikely.

Two further potash glass tablewares were also found. The first, Fig. 158.11, is a small dish or saucer. The vessel has a shallow well, broad brim and a rim that is folded-under to produce a tubular edge. Dishes are relatively uncommon and when found archaeologically are usually 17th century in date. However, earlier examples are referred to in some 16th century sources. For example 'platers dishes and sawcers of glasse' were listed amongst the 1542 inventory of Henry VIII (Hartshorne 1968, 465), whilst in 1594 Sir Hugh Platt advised his readers to place vinegar in 'sawcers of glasse' at the table as they were more resistant to the acidity (Platt 1979, bk. III 35). The rim of a very similar dish was found at the Carmelite Friary at Maldon (Andrews 1999, 124 no 12), although this was from an unstratified context. The final tableware, No 12 (not illustrated) , is a very small fragment of oval-section handle originally from a small jug. Although other vessels, such as mugs and tankards, also had handles, the width of this piece is too small for these and it is likely that it came from a small cruet or similar vessel.

Perhaps the most distinctive vessel type to be found at Whitefriars was the hanging lamp. Four fragments from different rims, Fig. 158.13-16, were found which are all either vertical or slightly everted. These would have led to a hemispherical or shouldered body. Fragments from four bases were also recovered, Fig. 158.17-20, and these are thick and tapered with distinctive external pontil marks. Iconographic evidence suggests that lamps were often suspended by the use of chains, although the pointed base would have allowed insertion into any suitable holder. First occurring in the 13th century, lamps were in common usage until at least the early 16th century. Their association with ecclesiastical sites has tended to overshadow their domestic function, as has the assumption that they ceased to have been used with the Reformation (Tyson 2000, 144). Although lamps have been found in large numbers in certain 16th-century Dissolution contexts, such as at Battle Abbey (Charleston 1985, 139-40 nos 1-8) and Denny Abbey (Charleston 1980, 208-9 nos 1-5), they also occur elsewhere. Interestingly a 16th-century example was found on the site of the former City of London Boy's School at Carmelite Street, London (Tyson 2000, 147 g434), whilst a nearly complete example came from a tannery in Northampton and dates to the late 16th or early 17th century (Oakley & Hunter 1979, 298). Given the finding of all but one of the Whitefriars' lamps in the School phase resonance passage, there is little reason to suppose that they date to prior to the Dissolution.

Between four and six flasks were also excavated. Three, Fig. 158.21, 25 and No 22 (not illustrated), are plain everted rim and narrow neck fragments, whilst two, Fig. 158.23-24, are decorated with heavy optic-blown wrythen ribbing. The now missing bodies of these flasks would have been globular in shape and the bases, Fig. 158.26 and Nos 27-29 (not illustrated), were formed by a simple push-in to create stability. Potash flasks were first produced in England during the late 12th century and remained largely unchanged in form until the 17th century. However, all the examples from Whitefriars were found in the School phase of the resonance passage and consequently can be dated from the early to mid 16th century. Flasks were common vessels and found on many types of site. They appear to have been used for the storage of all types of liquid including foodstuffs and beverages.

The final two vessels recovered from Whitefriars were also both for storage. The first, Fig. 158.30, is the everted rim and short shoulder from a cylindrical jar. This form closely imitated the ceramic *albarello* and would have been used for many similar purposes, such as storing drugs. Although from an unstratified context and phase, this vessel dates to the 16th century and similar examples have been found at Sandal Castle (Moorhouse 1983, 229 no 69) and Norwich (Haslam 1993, 102 no 645). The last vessel, Fig. 158.31, is later and dates to the 17th or early 18th century. It is a narrow base with a pointed pushed-in kick from a tall cylindrical phial. Phials were first produced during the late 17th century and soon became a popular form. By the 18th century they are found in large numbers, particularly on urban sites, where they would have been used for a variety of domestic functions, including the storage of tinctures and medicines.

A further thirty-seven fragments of potash vessel glass were also excavated at Whitefriars, Nos 32-47. However, these are all undiagnostic body pieces that are too small for positive identification. They may relate to the already discussed vessels or represent other unidentifiable forms.

CATALOGUE

Figure 158

Diagnostic Fragments

Note that Nos 8, 12, 22 and 27-29 are not illustrated.

1 One fragment of pedestal base with a folded-under base-ring from a goblet. The surface is decorated with alternating opaque white vertical *vetro a fili* and *retorti* marvered trails. Clear soda glass. Base diameter around 80mm.
Resonance Passage. *Phase* School. *Date* Early to mid 16th century.

2 One fragment of curving bowl from a goblet. The surface is decorated with alternating opaque white vertical *vetro a fili* and *retorti* marvered trails. Possibly from the same vessel as No 1. Clear soda glass.
Resonance Passage. *Phase* School. *Date* Early to mid 16th century.

3 Two fragments of thick curved body from a vessel of uncertain form. The surface is decorated with alternating opaque white vertical *vetro a fili* and *retorti* marvered trails. Clear soda glass.
Resonance Passage. *Phase* School. *Date* Early to mid 16th century.

4 One fragment of curved body fragment from a vessel of uncertain form. The surface is decorated with marvered sections of *millefiori* canes of blue, olive green, brown and opaque white glass. Soda glass.
Resonance Passage. *Phase* School. *Date* Early to mid 16th century.

5 One fragment of vertical neck? Possibly from a jug. Opaque white soda, or *lattimo*, glass with minimal weathering.
61 A (d) Resonance Passage. *Phase* School. *Date* Late 15th to early 16th century.

6 One fragment of applied pedestal base-ring, probably from a bowl or standing dish. Sapphire blue soda glass with quite heavy surface iridescence. Base diameter 76mm.
61 A (d) e Resonance Passage? *Phase* School. *Date* Early 16th century.

7 One fragment of folded tubular base-ring from a cylindrical pedestal beaker. Green potash glass with very heavy weathering. Base diameter 75mm.
62 II Unstratified. *Phase* School ? *Date* Early to mid 16th century.

8 One fragment of upper basal push-in and the body lead-off, from a pedestal beaker. Green potash glass with very heavy weathering.
62 I (4) Resonance Passage. *Phase* School. *Date* Early to mid 16th century. Not illustrated.

9 One fragment of body from a pedestal beaker. Decorated with optic-blown vertical ribbing. Green clear potash glass with medium weathering.
62 III (4) Resonance Passage. *Phase* Destruction. *Date* Mid to late 16th century.

10 Two joining fragments of rim with an in-folded edge, possibly from a beaker. Completely devitrified potash glass. Rim diameter 70mm.
61 A (d) e Resonance Passage? *Phase* School. *Date* Residual 15th century?

11 Three fragments of a folded-under rim, flat brim and curved well from a small dish. Clear green potash glass with heavy weathering. Rim diameter 170mm, well diameter 90mm.
63 CL? (2) Uncertain provenance. *Phase* Hales ?. *Date* Mid to late 16th century.

12 One small fragment of oval-section handle, probably from a flask. Green potash glass with very heavy weathering.
62 I (4) Resonance Passage. *Phase* School. *Date* Early 16th century. Not illustrated.

13 One fragment of plain vertical rim from a lamp. Green potash glass with very heavy weathering. Rim diameter 160mm.
62 I (4) Resonance Passage. *Phase* School. *Date* Early 16th century.

14 One fragment of plain vertical rim from a lamp. Green potash glass with very heavy weathering. Rim diameter 110mm.
61 A (d) Resonance Passage. *Phase* School. *Date* Early 16th century.

15 One fragment of plain vertical rim from a lamp. Green potash glass with very heavy weathering. Rim diameter 150mm.
61 A (d) Resonance Passage. *Phase* School. *Date* Early 16th century.

16 One fragment of slightly everted plain rim, probably from a lamp. Green potash glass with extreme weathering. Rim diameter *c.*120mm.
62 I (4) Resonance Passage. *Phase* School. *Date* Early 16th century.

17 One fragment of slightly tapering and thickened side from the stub end from a lamp base. Green potash glass with very heavy weathering.
62 I (4) Resonance Passage. *Phase* School. *Date* Early 16th century.

18 One fragment of thick stub end from a lamp base, with heavy external pontil mark. Completely devitrified potash glass.
? Resonance Passage. *Phase* School. *Date* Early 16th century.

19 One fragment of lower tapering and thickened side from the stub end from a lamp base. Green potash glass with extreme weathering.
? Resonance Passage. *Phase* School. *Date* Early 16th century.

20 Five fragments of thick broad stub end from a lamp base, with a heavy external pontil mark. Devitrified potash glass.
62 Bay 8 (1) Cloister. *Phase* Hales. *Date* Late 15th to early 16th century.

21 Two joining fragments of everted rim from a flask. Completely devitrified potash glass. Rim diameter 38mm.
61 A (d) e Resonance Passage? *Phase* School. *Date* Late 15th to early 16th century.

22 One fragment of everted rim from a flask. Green potash glass with very heavy weathering. Rim diameter uncertain.
61 A (d) e Resonance Passage? *Phase* School. *Date* Early 16th century. Not illustrated.

23 One fragment of everted rim and start of shoulder from a large flask. Decorated with heavy optic-blown wrythen ribbing. Green potash glass with heavy weathering. Rim diameter 75mm.
? Resonance Passage. *Phase* School. *Date* Late 15th to early 16th century.

24 One fragment of everted rim and start of shoulder from a flask. Decorated with heavy optic-blown wrythen ribbing. Green potash glass with heavy weathering. Rim diameter 65mm.
? Resonance Passage. *Phase* School. *Date* Late 15th to early 16th century.

25 One fragment of upper tapering neck from a small plain flask. Green potash glass with very heavy weathering.
62 I (4) Resonance Passage. *Phase* School. *Date* Early 16th century.

26 Four fragments of basal push-in from a plain flask. Green potash glass with very heavy weathering. Base 70mm.
? Resonance Passage. *Phase* School. *Date* Early 16th century.

27 One fragment of small basal push-in, probably from a small flask. Green potash glass with extreme weathering.
62 I (4) Resonance Passage. *Phase* School. *Date* Early 16th century. Not illustrated.

28 One fragment of small basal push-in, possibly from a small flask. Green potash glass with extreme weathering. Not illustrated.
62 I (4) Resonance Passage. *Phase* School. *Date* Early 16th century. Not illustrated.

29 One fragment of small basal push-in, possibly from a small flask. Green potash glass with very heavy weathering. Not illustrated.
62 A (d) Resonance Passage. *Phase* School. *Date* Early 16th century. Not illustrated.

30 One fragment of everted rim and concave short neck from a cylindrical jar. Green potash glass with very heavy weathering. Rim diameter 90mm.
62 VI + Unstratified. *Phase* Uncertain. *Date* 16th century.

31 One complete base with a pointed kick from a tall cylindrical phial. Blue green potash glass with medium weathering. Base diameter 24mm.
60 II (1). Phase 18th century. *Date* Mid 17th to mid 18th century.

Undiagnostic Fragments

Not illustrated

32 One small curved fragment, possibly from a flask neck. Green potash glass with very heavy weathering.
62 I (4) Resonance Passage. *Phase* School. *Date* Early 16th century.

33 One fragment of thick curved body, possibly from a shoulder of a plain flask. Green clear potash glass with heavy weathering.
62 I (4) Resonance Passage. *Phase* School. *Date* Early 16th century.

34 One thick body fragment, possibly from a flask. Green potash glass with very heavy weathering.
62 I (4) Resonance Passage. *Phase* School. *Date* Early to mid 16th century.

35 Five fragments of curved plain body from an uncertain vessel form. Green potash glass with heavy weathering.
61 A (g) Resonance Passage. *Phase* School/Destruction. *Date* Early 16th century.

36 One fragment of curved plain body from an uncertain vessel form. Green potash glass with heavy weathering.
62 II (2) Resonance Passage. *Phase* School/Destruction. *Date* Early 16th century.

37 One fragment of curved plain body from an uncertain vessel form. Green potash glass with heavy weathering.
62 II (9) Resonance Passage. *Phase* School. *Date* Early 16th century.

38 One fragment of curved plain body from an uncertain vessel form. Green potash glass with heavy weathering.
61 D (j) S Resonance Passage. *Phase* School. *Date* Early 16th century.

39 One fragment of folded edge from an uncertain vessel form. Green/clear potash glass with some weathering.
62 I (4) Resonance Passage. *Phase* School. *Date* 16th century.

40 One fragment of plain body from an uncertain vessel form. Green potash glass with heavy weathering.
62 I (4) Resonance Passage. *Phase* School. *Date* 16th century.

41 One fragment of curved body from an uncertain vessel form, with subsequent heat distortion. Green potash glass with very heavy weathering.
60 II (9) Resonance Passage. *Phase* School. *Date* 16th century.

42 Twelve fragments of undiagnostic plain curved body, from several vessels. Green potash glass with heavy weathering.
? Resonance Passage. *Phase* School. *Date* Early 16th century.

43 One fragment of curved plain body from an uncertain vessel form. Green potash glass with heavy weathering.
62/63 III (4a) Resonance Passage. *Phase* Destruction. *Date* Early 16th century.

[It is known that the schoolboys picked up intriguing objects which dated from the Friary and which subsequently found their way into the Resonance Passage. This should be borne in mind when considering the Glass Report. CW]

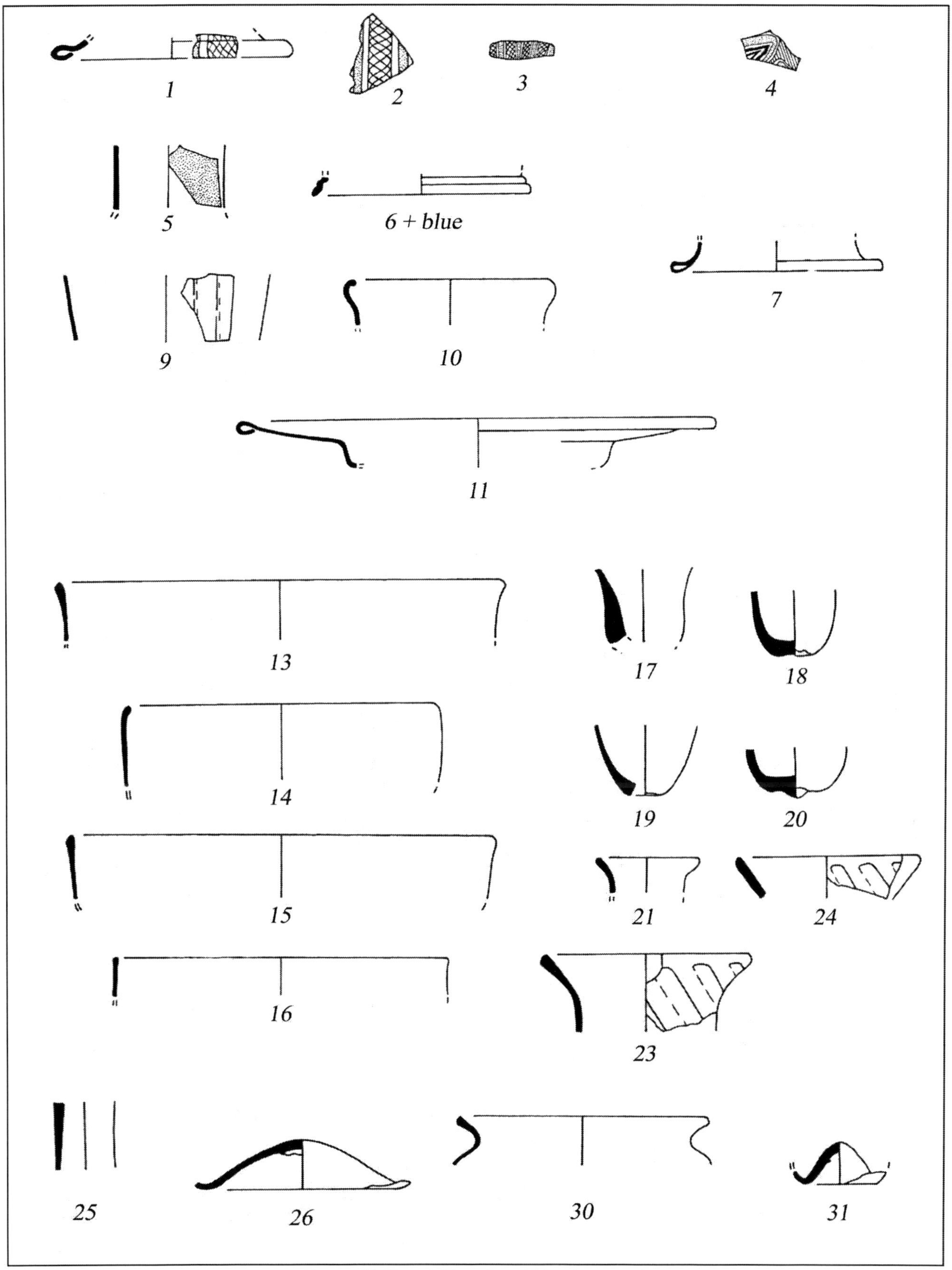

Figure 158 Vessel Glass: Late 15th-16th centuries.
Venetian Glass: 1-3. high status goblets with *filligrana* decoration; 4, ?goblet with *millefiori* decoration; 5, ?jug or flask, *lattimo* glass.
English Potash Glass: 6, ?standing dish; 7 and 9 pedestal beakers; 10, ?beaker; 11, dish; 13-20, lamps; 21 and 23-26, flasks; 30, cylindrical jar.
17th-18th Century Glass: 31, cylindrical phial. Scale 1:2. Nos refer to Willmott catalogue (Section S, *The Vessel Glass*).

SECTION T
OBSERVATIONS ON SOME OF THE SMALL FINDS

by
G. Egan (Museum of London Archaeology Service) with C. Woodfield

with contributions by
J. Ables, M. Curteis, I. Goodall, E. Holmes, D. Moore, and M. O'Hara

The principal writer (GE) was invited by the City of Lincoln Archaeological Unit to examine finds from the excavations undertaken by Charmian Woodfield and others in the 1960s and 1970s. Much of the material was published by Mrs Woodfield in her 1981 paper in *Post Medieval Archaeology*, which covered material from mid 16th-century Grammar School and related 16th-century deposits, but it was suggested that residual and additional items relating to the medieval religious house might be further defined and perhaps some other perspectives might be added. Structural and coffin nails (Woodfield 1981, 89) are discussed and illustrated elsewhere in this report (*Structural Metalwork* and *Human Skeletal Analysis*, Sections Q and W). A coffin handle (WF 1960, III 4A, 18th century robbing in the NE transept; Fig. 165.135), if correctly identified, goes awkwardly with the history of the site, although a map of *c.*1800 in the Birmingham Central Library Aylesford Collection (LBB97/6254) refers to 'Lady Hales' Church Yard' to the N of the vanished church (pers. comm. C. Woodfield); (these fittings are generally attributed to the 17th century and later). Did burials continue?

Re-examination of published material can be an invidious task, particularly when it is the subject of a first-rate paper less than 25 years old (and one to which current researchers regularly turn, both for basic identifications and for the remarkable series of well chosen extracts from contemporary sources - many of which provide insights not matched by subsequent investigations for details of usage of a range of artefacts. It is a pity that it was felt necessary to restrict these extracts at the time of publication. It is inevitable that advances have been made during the 25 or more years since that report was prepared and much of what follows is concerned with suggesting new emphases for published items. Thanks are offered to Charmian Woodfield for her co-operation during this part of the work, which relied heavily on her original paper.

A few finds can be attributed to the period of the Carmelite Friary from their primary contexts (Section 1 of this report, Fig. 159.1-18). Other items can be identified as probably residual in 16th-century contexts by comparison with evidence elsewhere (Section 2 of this report, Figs 159.19-24 and 161.25-38; several of the latter items were noted in Woodfield 1981).

These two categories include a range of finds which are emerging from a number of excavations across Britain as characteristic of medieval ecclesiastical sites. This leaves a number of items of forms which may have remained unchanged through the early 16th century or longer, or forms for which the precise chronology of definable changes around this time remains un-established (Section 3 of this report, Figs 162.39-67 and 163.68-69, 73, 80, 82, 87-98 and 101-104). Several of the characteristic religious-house categories of finds are also probably going to recur among assemblages from early-modern educational establishments. This includes objects relating to reading and writing, like the spectacle frames (Fig. 162.61 and Woodfield 1981, 93, fig. 5, no 37) which could be of late 15th-century date. There is scope therefore for confusion on this point for finds from the present site in particular and its immediately post-Reformation deposits, because it comprised both sorts of institution. However, the black humus-like School deposit in the N resonance passage carried down to the natural rock, and no earlier level was discernible, the earlier material being perhaps picked up by the boys.

A series of items from the Whitefriars/Grammar School excavations taken together provide evidence for metalworking locally, in the years preceding and contemporary with the friary as well as in the years following the Dissolution (Section 4 of this report, Figs 163.68-69, 73, 80, 82, 87-98, 101-104 and 164.106-109; this does not, of course, imply that all other metal objects described in Sections 2 and 3 are not of local manufacture). Copper-alloy working is represented by a number of pieces of wire, sheet fragments, etc., along with a single hint of casting, and there are also parts of two moulds for casting spoons and tokens in lead/tin (pewter), Fig. 163.102-103. Pinmaking, which required wire, but few tools, and little if any fixed plant is attested here (Figs 159.10 and 163.73, 80, 82; 164.108-109; and cf. Woodfield 1981, 91) as it is on at least two London sites of former religious houses (St. Mary Clerkenwell and Bermondsey Abbey, and perhaps also at St. John's Clerkenwell). It now begins to look as if this light industry catering for the growing urban markets was one of the regular commercial users of space newly available following the Dissolution, and at Coventry Whitefriars apparently from just before. Caple's detailed analysis and discussion of the wound wire-headed pins found on the site is presented in Section U, *The Wound Wire-headed Pins*.

A small group of copper-alloy accessories with a distinctive black coating which has also been recognised elsewhere is discussed separately (Section 5 of this report, Fig. 164.110-113). Finally a few further observations are offered on what may appear a random selection of finds, which otherwise lack coherence as a group (Section 6 of this report, Figs 164.116-120, 123-126 and 165.127-129, 131-132), although they are all from 16th-century deposits, or related thereto.

Note: Sequential Catalogue numbers are given to each item or category of items discussed below (objects mentioned only summarily are not included in this sequence); the second, underlined number for each item is from a single, running series given to such excavated objects as could be found in 1995/96; GE's catalogue has subsequently been expanded by Charmian Woodfield, and these items do not carry underlined numbers.

** indicates unillustrated objects, some known from records, but where the finds themselves could not be produced by Coventry Museum for examination, and this includes the great majority of the finds from the Museum excavations of 1973 and 1977/78. No finds appear to survive from the Museum excavations of 1956, 1965, 1966, 1967 and 1975. Where this class of object is included, the descriptions are by Charmian Woodfield.

The phasing codes used throughout the main Report are indicated here. They are as follows:

Pre-friary indicates pre 1342,
Friary, when not used in a general sense, indicates *c.*1342-*c.*1385,
Friary 2 indicates *c.*1385 to c.1425,
Pre-rebuild indicates *c.*1425 to later 15th century,
Rebuilding indicates late 15th-early 16th century,
Pre-Reformation *c.*1520 to *c.*1542,
School passages (i.e. School deposits in the resonance passages under the choir stalls) indicates a deposit of *c.*1545-*c.*1558,
Destruction indicates 3rd quarter of the 16th century,
Hales indicates from *c.*1540-*c.*1571,

The drawings are by Paul Woodfield, with the exception of Nos 37-38, 65, 69, 73, 83, 87, 88, 123a and 129, which are by David Watts.

SECTION 1: MEDIEVAL

This section lists items found in medieval contexts from the period of the Whitefriars (therefore not described in Woodfield 1981).

As most of the 1960s excavations were in the church and not in the conventual buildings, there are few stratified domestic friary finds from this period, 50% of those being from the Woodfield NW Cloister watching brief. However, the finds do include items of categories found at sites of other medieval religious institutions, these relating to water supply management (spigot tap, Fig. 159.4) and religious observance (bell, Fig. 159.5); also the candle holder, Fig. 159.3, might be claimed as an elaborate furnishing appropriate for an institutional milieu.

Figure 159

Seal

1 Seal of the Coventry Carmelite House, 35 x 50mm, red wax. Attached to E322/65 Court of Augmentations - October 1st 1538 (Ellis 1986, 27, M.257). 'Broken and very much flatted' as described in PRO 1837, 18, but shows the Virgin and Child under a canopy, with a shield to the left. On the Oxford Carmelites' prior's seal, held at the Ashmolean, and which this resembles, the shield's place is taken by a kneeling figure, and the arched space below contains a winged beast. This may have been the case here, as there does not seem to be enough room in the equivalent space for a figure, even if kneeling. Surviving Carmelite seals are known from Perth (Stones (ed.) 1989, frontispiece and 154), Aberdeen and Linlithgow (ibid. 6, table 64 mf, 12E). They also survive from Appleby (Ffinch 1984), Northampton (V.C.H 1906, 148-9, seal now in the British Museum LXIX, 91) and Marlborough (Ashmolean).

Copper-alloy

Buckle

2 342. WF 1964 XXIII 6, built into NW Cloister internal garth wall. Phase Friary 2. Oval frame 14 x 14mm, with lip and notch for wire pin, integral with forked spacer for missing sheet plates, *c.*23 x *c.*8mm, cf. No 21. The pin is probably a replacement (see Nos 69-70). This small buckle is similar to a series attributed to the late 14th/early 15th century in London (Egan and Pritchard 1991, 78-82 nos 322-30) and is a useful confirmation of the anticipated date of this Cloister wall.

Candle Holder

3 326. WF 1968 XXVII 2, very late medieval rubbish (? industrial) tip, external to Cloister W range, Fig. 52b. Phase Pre-Reformation ?, though a Dissolution date is not impossible. Turned cup with decorative bands and grooves, ht 44mm, internal d. 17mm; riveted at tapered base to fragment of horizontal arm. Probably from a stick for a pair of candles (cf. Bangs 1995, 55-6 and 202 no 10 - an English stick of the 15th-century).

Spigot Tap

4 324. Context as No 3. Incomplete: Ht 54mm, d. of plug at base 11mm and at top 14mm, d. of hole for liquid 4mm. The cock-shaped handle, from which the tail is broken off, has ring-and-dot motifs for eyes. The breakage of the handle, which would have made turning difficult or impossible without a tool, would have taken considerable force, possibly the violence of Dissolution destruction. A tap with a cock-shaped handle is depicted

in Dürer's woodcut of *c.*1497 *The Men's Bath* (Kurth 1963, no 101).

Clapper Bell

5 339. WF 1962 VI 6, piscina drain in Chapel of the Holy Rood. Phase Pre-rebuild. Ht 40mm, d. at mouth 42mm; cast and turned, with pair of grooves near top, and ridge defining flare of mouth; a rusted iron clapper is not illustrated. Presumably for use during religious observance (see Biddle and Hinton 1990, 725-7, fig. 207, nos 2207 A-B and D). It is of interest that the Whitefriars Great Bell 'survives' (after sundry recastings during the period 1573 to 1966 at Holy Trinity, Coventry) in the peal of Christchurch Cathedral, New Zealand. (Pickford 1987, 465, 468).

Shroud Fasteners?

6 1977 SF 92, soil near feet of skeleton, stone-lined Grave 1977.6 in presbytery. Phase Pre-friary or Friary. Double-ended loop of strip bronze 2.25 x 2.75mm. Length of loop 30mm. Resembles Woodfield 1981 fig. 5, no 59.

7** 1977 SF 86, stone-lined grave 1977.5 in presbytery. Phase Pre-rebuild. Hooked bronze pin of 1.5mm wire, length 41mm, hooks both to one side.

Such hooks were not recorded from earth graves.

It is possible that these items are not shroud fasteners, but debris from Pre-friary metal working from clay pit material redeposited in the grave fills. These graves probably overlay such a clay pit, Fig. 51, Section J.

Stylus?

8** 1977 SF 80, F.38, chapter house, in feature possibly related to seating? Stratification uncertain. 50 x 2mm, one end rounded the other pointed, with an apparent band of 3 mouldings about 10mm behind the point.

Ring

9** WF 1961 VI 6, Phase Rebuild context in NE transept. Diameter 20mm, thickness 1.5mm, thin strip ring, as No 42, but here in a pre-Reformation context.

Pins

10 298. WF 1962 VI 4, construction trench to nave screen wall I. Phase Friary2. Unfinished pin, 50mm.

11** WF 1964 XXIII 3. Phase Rebuild level in the cloister garth. Pin, 'Long'.

12** WF 1968 XXVII 16. Phase Rebuild level in the W cloister. Pin, 'Long'.

13** WF 1968 XXVII 16b. Phase Rebuild in W cloister. Pin, 'Short'.

These are rare at this period, but do occur, mainly in friary late 15th-century Rebuild levels, being generally longer than their 16th-century successors.

Bone

Styli

14 WF 1964 XXI 2, construction trench for first SW tower pier. Phase Friary, late 14th century. Stylus, surviving length 76mm, but broken at top end, tapering with sharpened point.

15 WF 1968 Ga 2 (2). From fill of Grave 17 (disturbed in 16th century) of high status 15th/16th-century stone-lined double grave in SW choir in front of Prior's seat. Phase Pre-Rebuild. Stylus, length 61mm, d. 5-6mm, very little taper. An ?ornamental top has been broken off. Very sharp, knife trimmed at top, and turned neck. Might a scribe have been buried with this?

Stone

Hones

16 WF 1964 XXIII 5, from a rare ?late friary domestic level in the NW cloister garth. Phase Friary 2?. Hone, 16 x 37mm, length unknown, but presumably perforated at one end. David Moore (British Museum (Natural History)) writes, post thin-sectioning. 'A muscovite-sericite/illite-chlorite 'coal' bearing sandstone. It is probably from a Coal Measures Sandstone, from a nearby Midland coalfield' and this may relate to an unknown local medieval industry. This small size of hone was apparently carried on the person. A comparable hone is known from the Perth Carmelite house, length 90mm, (Stones (ed,) 1989, fig. 104).

17 WF 1968 XXVIII 2, (as 68 XXVII 1, Fig. 52b, probably quarry tip NW cloister area - initial machining). Phase Hales ? Hone, 30 x 45mm, length unknown. David Moore writes 'A lithic greywacke sandstone, which could be from Wales or some area of similar rocks (Lake District, Southern Uplands of Scotland). It could however have been a glacial erratic'.

Hones did not occur in any of the certain post Dissolution deposits, and presumably they were no longer carried on the person by the mid 16th century. What then was the means of sharpening the School's known 27-30 knives?.

Sandstone handle

18 WF 68 IIIE 113, a late medieval ?industrial/rebuilding level at the N Porch. Phase Rebuilding. Handle, length including curve 30mm, ovoid section, thickness 15mm. A puzzling find. A handle to a sculptured stone lantern has been suggested (Helen List) or possibly part of a pestle. However, it is in the normal Period 1 red sandstone used for building and sculpture.

SECTION 2: MEDIEVAL OBJECTS FROM 16th-CENTURY CONTEXTS

These artefacts were mainly recovered from the fill of the School Passages (acoustic chambers) or from 16th-century destruction levels. Descriptions are normally kept brief in cases where these items were published in Woodfield 1981.

The potential for residuality in the School deposits in the resonance passages built for acoustic purposes below the choir stalls is demonstrated by the numismatic items published in 1981 (Rigold 1981, 118-25), which included a mention of nine medieval coins from the resonance passages, dating from the 13th century onwards with only five dating from the School period (see also *Numismatica*, Section V, for a fuller account).

However jetons in the passages included only five attributed to the medieval period (six if lead item Woodfield 1981, fig. 9, O is included) compared with 87 16th-century examples. (The jetons noted by Rigold (1981) included, 'for the sake of completeness' 13 listed as from the 16th-century non-School destruction levels, and 16 from the presbytery 16th-century ?industrial gullies, all before the 1570s; 2 were from the cloister and 13 were unstratified. These do not affect the residuality proportions of the School passages material.)

Figures 159-160

Enamelled gilt bronze, with silver outlined cloisons

19 School passages fill (Woodfield 1981, 99, fig. 7, no 119). Original phase probably Rebuild. High quality roundel, or mount, d. 26mm, from the base of a medieval chalice? Dark blue enamel four-pointed star, floriate centre, pale blue dots within motif and inside gilded margin, the cloisons being outlined with twisted silver wire. This is a specifically Hungarian technique, the best known parallel being the reliquary bust made *c.*1405 for the tomb of Saint Ladislas, King of Hungary, now in the cathedral at Gyor (pers. ob. C. Woodfield; S. Mihalik, 1961, 20-21, figs 22 and 23; CW is indebted to Marian Campbell, Victoria and Albert Museum, for this reference). Stud at back for attachment. Post 1981 cleaning has revealed two opposing holes suggesting re-use as brooch? Fig. 160 features an X-ray of this roundel.

This item had been identified as 14th-century Hungarian work of unusual occurrence in Britain by Charles Oman, formerly head of the Department of Metalwork at the Victoria and Albert Museum. However Dr Mihaly-Nagy of the Magyar Nemzeti Museum, Budapest, (*in litt.* to C. Woodfield) expressed the opinion that this was too early.

Copper alloy

Possible Tomb Brass Fragment
20 111. School passages fill (Woodfield 1981, fig. 6, no 91), Fig. 51, Sections F and E. Filed on three sides, broken off on the other; the back has a series of triangular pits made by a sharp instrument. If correctly identified this is one of the items which directly relates to the religious institution. The reason for the filing and pitting on this tiny fragment is unclear.

Buckle
21 91. School passages fill (Woodfield 1981, fig. 5, no 30, when identified as residual). Copper alloy: oval frame, forked spacer category, as No 2 above (sheet plates missing). Probably late 14th/15th century; this type seems to represent the best quality among mass-produced, late-medieval buckles. The sheet pin is probably a replacement. The shape of the aperture between the broken fork springs corresponds with those in buckles attributed to the late 14th century in London (Egan and Pritchard 1991, 78-80, nos 323-4). These top-of-the-range accessories may have been kept in use for somewhat longer than cheaper versions.

Mount
22 112. WF 1960 II 8. 16th-century Destruction level associated with S resonance passage (Woodfield 1981, fig. 6, no 72). Square copper alloy sheet with round relief decoration; possibly from a book cover. A near parallel from London is from a deposit attributed from ceramics to *c.*1400 (Museum of London, G+S88 site, acc. no 257).

Lead/tin

Pilgrim Badges
23 102. School passages fill (Woodfield 1981, fig. 8, no C). Lead/tin glove, one of an originally joined pair. Several further parallels for this souvenir, from different moulds, have been found in London since its original publication, and its identification as a Canterbury badge in the form of a pair of gloves belonging to Archbishop Thomas Becket is confirmed (see Spencer 1998, no 120, which is from a deposit attributed to the late 14th century, and Spencer 1990, 23 and 72, no 31, fig. 38, for an example from Salisbury). The present glove is notable in having not only the monial - the jewelled mount (wrongly depicted on the front of the glove) - but part of a second decorative motif on the side as well (my thanks to Brian Spencer for help with this item).

24 A sheet copper-alloy badge from School passages fill. This depicts a Madonna and Child, and is also of pre-Reformation date, probably late 15th/early 16th century, as previously published (Woodfield 1981, fig. 6, no 94).

Figure 161

Thimbles
25 1973 Tr. M? Chapter House? Base of 16th-century Destruction Phase level. Ht 16mm, d. at base 20mm. 13 horizontal rows of pits. English, 1350 to 1400

(Edwin Holmes, pers.comm.). The only surviving 1973 small find.

26 55. School passages fill. Cast; ht 18mm, d. at base 19mm; central hole in damaged top; unevenly drilled pits in vertical rows; faint band around base; transverse groove in bottom (Woodfield 1981, fig. 6, no 107). Holmes (pers.comm.) believes this to be a 15th-century Nuremberg import.

27 School passages fill. Sewing ring, ht 6mm, d. at top 16mm, d. at base 22mm. 3 rows of large pits (Woodfield 1981 fig. 6, no 108, now lost). Holmes (pers.comm.) believed this, from the drawing, more likely to be 15th than 16th century, and probably a Nuremburg import. See also Nos 49 and 50.

The last two are paralleled by finds of thimbles near the choir stalls at Thornholme Priory, Yorks. (McAleavy 1996, 20) where it is suggested that mending took place during services. Holmes (nd) thinks it is more likely that thimbles in churches relate to the sewing of shrouds. Sewing was performed as much by men as by women at these dates (Holmes pers. comm to C. Woodfield).

Jetons
It is possible that some of the earlier Jetons (Woodfield 1981, 119-120) were used for the casting of friary accounts. See *Numismatica*, Section V.

Lead

Lead Calmes
28-29 The majority of the excavated window leading (some 400 pieces survive) is of the medieval tradition, i.e. cast, ready for use. No 28 shows the light section of the first period calmes (Friary phase, late 14th/early 15th century, e.g. Great East Window). The heavier and unique section, No 29 (WF 1969 XXIX 3), is from Hales' work at the NW angle of the sacristy wall, apparently third quarter of the 16th century.

The calmes occur in 16th century Destruction levels throughout, including the cloister and the reredorter/prior's house area, all of which were presumably glazed. Some 270 of these were in School deposits emphasising the dilapidated state of the building at the time of the school.

Lead pins.
30 Thirty-one lead pins (Woodfield 1981, 99-100, fig. 8a-j) were recorded with necked or pierced heads for attaching line, and one sharpened end, frequently some 50mm in length. It seems likely that these are mason's pins or plumb bobs, probably dating from the general friary period. They were almost all found in the School phase fills of the resonance passages, although there were two outliers together in the E nave, and this remains puzzling. Were they left in place in walls, to be released by later demolition? Similar objects were excavated in 1996 at Southwick, Northants (pers. comm. Gill Johnson) apparently from a 14th-century context.

Iron work

Jew's harp.
31 School passages fill (Woodfield 1981, 89, fig. 3, no 22). A late 15th-century painting in the church at Harkeberga, Uppland, shows a man playing a jew's harp, and a residual friary date cannot be entirely ruled out. The friars were paid for singing at Guild feasts (Fretton 1872, 66).

The *Structural Metalwork* (Section Q) is the subject of a separate report by Paul Woodfield.

Beads
32a-o Several of the beads, in various shapes, of bone (a, g, 1, n, and o), jet (d-e, h and j), amber (d, f, and k,), glass (b, d, h, i and m,), quartz (i), faience (c) and red paste (d) (Woodfield 1981, fig. 10, nos 1a-o) from the School passage fill may well be residual, and from rosaries as suggested previously, (Woodfield 1981, 102-103), the main period of popularity for which was pre-Reformation. Additionally necklaces of e.g. amber beads are known to have been presented to images of the Virgin in Carmelite friaries.

Bone and shell.

Stylus
33 School passages fill (Woodfield 1981, fig. 10, no 4). Bone, iron point missing; for use with wax tablets; identified as possible stylus and residual in Woodfield 1981 (103). It is not impossible that it is a damaged 'pricker' relating to the production of manuscripts. In either case the form probably did not last after the Dissolution.

Oyster shell palette
34 WF 1962 I 4, found in the School passages fill under the N choir stalls, to the decoration of whose canopies it may refer. Pre-Reformation, possibly 14th century. This object is the subject of a separate report by Helen Howard, Section K, Fig. 135.

Glass

Vessel glass
35a-d The fragments of expensive imported Venetian or *façon de Venise* glass from goblets and other vessels found in the School passages fill (Woodfield 1981, fig. 12, nos 12-16) seem likely to be liturgical vessels and to date from the last decades of the friary (Woodfield 1981, 107), though a source from Hales' Great House is not impossible. *Latticino* glass evolved in the 15th century and in the 16th century spread over Europe, but would have represented very high status gifts at that time, and would have been rare even in the 1540s.

36** White *latimo* glass was also recovered from the resonance passages (Woodfield 1981, 107).

Glass Lamps
37 School passages fill (Woodfield 1981, fig.12, no 22). Base fragment (with fragments of three others, and another base from 1962 cloister bay 8 (1), a 16th-century Destruction deposit in the cloister E range).

The form is characteristic of late-medieval hanging oil lamps (cf. Keys in Egan 1998, nos 344-355).

A rim fragment, School passage fill (Woodfield 1981 fig. 12, no 17) may be from this or another lamp.

A later full updated report by Hugh Willmott on the glass is presented in Section S, written after glass previously missing had surfaced.

38 337. WF 1962 I 4, School passages fill. Wire-chain link; this may well be from a pendant holder made entirely of links for lamps like the preceding item (cf. Egan 1998, nos 358-64, especially the first of these, which is dated to the late 14th century).

SECTION 3: OBJECTS FROM GRAMMAR-SCHOOL PERIOD DEPOSITS

Figure 162

Gold or gilt bronze

Brooch pin
39 WF 1964 XVIII 3, 16th century Destruction pit in the N transept. 25 x *c.*1.5mm, slightly tapered; three incised lines behind hook and one just short of point. This, with a small '?gold' fragment (1977 SF 5**, ? residual in a 16th-century level, F.1, choir, now lost, and possibly the base of a heraldic badge) were, with the Hungarian roundel, the only hint at the former presence of precious metals.

Copper alloy and iron

As well as the items listed individually, the objects in this category include lace chapes (including Woodfield 1981, no 36c, a lace chape with horizontal ribbing), parallels for which have now been found in London in mid/late 14th-century and later medieval deposits (Egan and Pritchard 1991, 281-90, nos 14077 ff) meaning that this accessory does not necessarily post-date *c.*1520 (cf. Woodfield 1981, 93) as most lace chapes appear to do from their find spots at the Coventry Whitefriars.

However, as with the wound wire-headed pins (Section U, *The Wound Wire-headed Pins* and Woodfield 1981 no 35) (all the pins found were not however of this form) the large number of finds at the Whitefriars site of both these items, i.e. chapes and pins, appear here to form in the main a coherent group from the mid 16th-century School period (see Section 4 of this report: *Metalworking and other Industrial Activity,* below). They include fine ruff pins, (Woodfield 1981, fig. 5 (c) an unusual survival (pers. comm. Avril Hart, Victoria and Albert Museum).

Strap end
40 182. School passages fill. Probable roulette-engraved strap end fragment (Woodfield 1981, fig. 6, no 88, then thought to be medieval).

Drape rings
41-44 51, 100, etc. School passages fill. Drape rings perhaps from church hangings (Woodfield 1981, nos 34 and 114-16 - the first is here re-identified from a brooch - cf. Egan 1998, nos 91-129, dated to the late 14th/early 15th century).

Iron Buckle
45 School passages fill (Woodfield 1981, fig.3, no 13). Iron: Small circular frame. This type was standard for shoe fastenings from the late medieval period to the (?) early 16th century (cf. Egan and Pritchard 1991, 60-2, fig. 38, nos 60-113).

Locking buckle
46 School passages fill (Woodfield 1981, 98 n. 73, fig. 6, 106). A pin bar and part of the swivelling arm from a 'locking buckle' is also probably late medieval, as suggested in Woodfield 1981.

Key
47 325. WF 1968 XXVII 5, Fig 52b, a mid 16th-century buried ground level related to Hales's alterations to the friary. Cloister W range. Incomplete: surviving length 33mm, oval bow 27mm wide and with thickened top, square shaft having on opposed faces a saltire cross in a panel defined by grooves; working end broken off at constriction; worn. The form may be less appropriate for a rotary-mechanism lock than a slide one (cf. Shortt 1973, 27, fig. 58, especially lower two). Probably residual.

Calibrated scale
48 School passages fill (Woodfield 1981, 97, fig. 6, 104). 31.5mm long, 7mm wide. The bottom end is rounded and pierced at the centre point as if it was intended to pivot. On the one finished face is a scored vertical line and cross calibration lines, apparently numbered, as surviving, 36, 30, 24, 20, 16, making a progression first in fours and then in sixes. There is a short mark between the marks for 16 and 20, which might represent 17. The figures are in 16th-century style Arabic, one digit each side of the median line, as seen on scientific instruments of the period. The spaces between the calibration lines are 8mm (from the rounded bottom), 6.7mm, 3.5mm, 3.7mm and 3.4mm.

This object was published in 'The Last Word' section of *The New Scientist*, No 2077 12.4.97, the replies being printed in the same section of issue No 2139, 20.6.98, and on Planet Science, New Scientist's Web site at http://www.last-word.com/. The answers were summarised by Mick O'Hare - 'Many correspondents noted that the instrument looks somewhat like a modern dipstick and that there is a non-linear relationship between the units marked on the scale, and their distance along the scale. That suggests the instrument might have been used for measuring the volume of a fluid or powder in a vessel with sloping sides.'

Jon Ables had concluded that this was a 'dipstick for measuring fluids in a small conical glass cup. Such cups, looking like a short-stemmed, narrow-cone Martini glass, were common in apothecary shops and alchemy laboratories of the mid 16th century'. He describes the manufacture of these glasses with a 45 degree vertex angle, a short hollow stem and a disc-shaped foot. 'The implied fluid unit' (for a 45 degree vertex-angled cup) 'is precisely one fluid ounce. One has to marvel at the quality of the work. The average error is less than 200 micrometres.'

It is possible that this might have related to distilling, of which activity there are hints from the early 16th-century pottery vessel, Fig. 153.28, and from one of the mid 16th century (Woodfield 1981, fig. 13, no 17).

Thimbles and Sewing Rings

Cast thimbles were produced from the late medieval period to *c.*1550. More than half of those known from the site seem likely to date from the Friary period. See in addition Nos 25-27 above, which appear to be residual medieval.

49 54. 1977 unprovenanced. Accession number 86/11/226. Cast; ht 24mm, d. at base 23mm; drilled pits in a spiral; worn. The largest of the thimbles. Medieval or early Tudor and probably an import (Holmes, pers. comm.).

50 56. 1977 unprovenanced. Accession number 86/11/227. Sewing ring. Ht 16mm., d. at top 14mm, d. at base 18mm. Six lines of triangular perforations, worn/eroded through. Ridge at base. Nuremberg, 16th century (Holmes, pers.comm.).

Book Cover Accessories

51-59 From School passages fills, and 60 (Woodfield 1981, no 46) from the overlying pre 1570s Destruction rubble.

51-54 Four book mounts with double or single rivets - three with incised circles (Woodfield 1981, fig. 5, nos 48-51).

55-56 Two parts of book clasps (Woodfield 1981, fig. 6, nos 102-3, there identified as book hinges).

57-58 79 and 81. Two rods, respectively of copper alloy and iron, set through mounting plates (Woodfield 1981, fig. 6, 84-5).

59-60 94 and 101. Two (?)clasps in the form of strap plates with central holes (Woodfield 1981, fig. 5, nos 43 and 46).

The above may all be from book covers (see Egan 1998, nos 919-25 and fig. 214 for the function of pins of this form together with a different category of clasps - though perhaps the present clasps could equally have been used with them).

A 1507 Carmelite binding of Duns Scotus' *Super Sententiarum* with a similar but undecorated mount to No 52 (Woodfield 1981, no 49) is preserved at Aberdeen (Stones 1989 157, fig. 97).

Like the spectacle frame, these finds are all appropriate for bookish institutions, either lay or religious.

61 Spectacle frame (Woodfield 1981, fig. 5, no 37). School passage fill. This could be as early as the late 15th century, cf. the late medieval spectacles held by St. Peter in the Master of the Saint Bartholomew Altarpiece at the National Gallery. Or, they could be as late as the 2nd quarter of the 16th century, cf. Holbein's painting of St. Thomas More, pre-1535, again at the National Gallery.

Lead

Cloth Seals by G. Egan

Lead seals were attached to individual traded cloths as quality-control marks (cf. hallmarks) in a system of industrial regulation that was in operation in textile-producing countries across Europe (Egan 1994; Endrei & Egan 1982). Four incomplete seals or fragments recovered from the Whitefriars excavations were re-examined. All four were catalogued from the School passage fills in Woodfield 1981, though none of them were then identified with the textile trade (Woodfield 1981, 101-2, fig. 9, nos I, and L-N) except that an impression of woven fabric was noted for a similar seal to I. This, together with numbers H, J and K, further cloth seals in the same illustration, have not been located. H has no device indicated, while J has an incomplete privy mark with no identified letters, and K has blackletter initials b(?t) to the sides of an unidentified device; the last two are probably clothiers'/weavers' seals (Egan 1994, 9 and 78ff). O in the figure is a late medieval token as published, while P is a round piece of lead of some other category, impressed with a partial heraldic device.

Three of the available seals have stamps that are at least partly legible, enabling one to be identified as a French import, while the other two are probably corporate seals, possible English/alnage issues (Egan 1994, 2; Endrei & Egan 1982, 55). None of the seals including those mentioned above is certainly of local origin, though Coventry's important textile trade is represented by finds in London and perhaps elsewhere locally (Hulton 1995, 69-70, Museum of London acc. no 93.142/429 is a

Coventry seal unearthed in the capital).

62 School passages fill (Woodfield 1981, 101-2, fig. 9, I). Corroded second disc from a two part seal, d. *c.*19mm; ?no stamp.

63 School passages fill (Woodfield 1981, 102, fig. 9, N). Second disc from a two-part seal, d. 21mm; (crude) arched crown. It is not possible to tell from the remaining portion whether this is an offstruck main device or (as its position implies) it was intended to be over another one. The most likely interpretation is that it is an English alnage seal, from a series which in the 16th century included issues with a variety of crowned devices (roses, fleurs-de-lis, etc.) some of them surprisingly crude for official usage.

64 School passage fill (Woodfield 1981, 102, fig. 9, L). Fragment probably of the second disc of a two-part seal, d. *c.*18mm; edge legend (Lombardic lettering) ...A... The A with its horizontal line at the top appears on some English alnage seals and also on a number of Continental ones. Too little of the stamp survives to narrow the field of possibilities.

65 School passages fill (Woodfield 1981, 102, fig. 9, M). Second disc of a two-part seal, d. 18mm, imprint on the back of a very fine fabric with *c.*14 threads per 5mm in the system that has registered. The stamp, which is offstruck, has about half of a device which identifies the seal as being from Valenciennes in NE France. This device, a lentoid outline with two vertical lines through it, was known locally as the mark of the staple (*étaple*). It was used by the civic authorities on stamps to show that commercial weights were accurate and on the town's medieval coins as well as its cloth seals (Egan 1994, 105 no 307). Part of what may be a fleur-de-lis appears on the seal in the central area of the staple mark (not shown on drawing).

A number of Valenciennes seals have been found in Britain, notably in the London area (*ibid.*) and most have a version of the staple mark and on the other side the town's symbol, a swan. Dating appears to focus on the 16th and 17th centuries, and imprints from the textiles to which they were originally attached indicate a variety of lightweight fabrics; the impression on the present seal being the finest of those noted. Valenciennes' worsteds rivalled those of Norfolk on the English market from the mid 16th century and the finds of seals in this country provides clear evidence that they achieved a significant penetration here, presumably with varieties of fabric that were unavailable from English looms or that could be purchased cheaper than native products. The fact that there was a sister Carmelite house at Valenciennes might have some relevance.

Musket and pistol balls

These lead shot (Woodfield 1981, 100, fig. 8 B, a-c) did not occur outside the choir. Their use, presumably for shooting at pigeons in the partly windowless church, is unlikely to be pre-Reformation. School passages fill.

Small shavings of lead were found in the School deposits so lead was perhaps being reworked by the schoolboys in class (rather than the friars in choir).

Tally?

66 School passages fill. Sliver, 78mm long, shaped, with bevelled edges, as a pointer? with 4 tally marks and a longer nick on a longitudinal line on one side, and 3 thin lines on the other; compass marks each side.

Stone

Tessera

67 School passages fill. Green stone irregular cube with cone boring one end, *c.*10 x 20mm. Use and residuality uncertain.

SECTION 4: METALWORKING AND OTHER INDUSTRIAL ACTIVITY

The following items are mainly from deposits attributed to the mid 16th century, the period of the Grammar School and of John Hales' occupation of the site, which extended into the 1570s (Woodfield 1981, 81-84). Although it may seem improbable that the light industries they appear to represent were at any time carried out within an educational establishment, the contemporary (jeton evidence) and apparently industrial wire- and scrap-producing gullies in the presbytery recorded in the 1960s, together with the screen wall cutting the School off from that presbytery, indicate that these activities might be close neighbours. Wire additionally was present in some quantity in the school resonance passages. There were further indications in the 1960s of 16th-century light industrial activity outside the choir, to the N (e.g. 62 III 4, 20 pins) and to the S (69 XXIX 13, 12 fragments of wire with pins and twists); there is also evidence for metalworking outside the N transept, and outside and to the W of the NW cloister. Some of these, and certainly the last, were possibly fairly short-lived activities in operation between the Dissolution and the establishment of the School. There is little information on the use of the Nave, but a flurry of some 40 pins from its N and W extremities may indicate yet more light industrial activity.

Figure 163

The Pre-Friary industrial activity, now seen to be represented by material in the fill of an apparent clay pit (labelled as F.23) beneath the presbytery (unrecognised in the 1977 excavations, but appearing as refill of graves), is discussed in the main report. Despite losses some material survives.

Copper alloy

68 1977 SF 78, from Pre-Friary clay pit beneath presbytery cut by reredos wall. Piece of 1.5mm square section wire 120mm long. A 27mm length of 'wire knotted at one end' (SF 81**) came from presbytery grave 1977.4, which was cut into the same clay pit fill. Additionally scrap items of strip copper alloy came from 60, I 13, the top fill of the pre friary stone quarry N of the cloister E range, Fig 51, Section E.

Interpretation of the industrial history of the site is further hampered by the failure to plan in any detail the workshop that replaced the reredorter, on documentary evidence in the immediately pre-Reformation period, together with the machining away of evidence for its working floor.

Some of the now unprovenanced material listed below may be from these areas.

The very large number of small copper alloy objects and fragments recovered, in the main, from the School passages fills, particularly simple dress accessories - pins of which over 1,500 were published (Woodfield 1981, no 35) and lace chapes with over 400 published (Woodfield 1981, no 36) - include several arguably unfinished examples of both the main categories. Post-excavation losses have made it difficult to calculate the full number but it must have stood at over 1,700 for pins, and 450 for chapes.

The overall impression is of a heterogeneous collection of finished items, used and recycled items (some perhaps collected from around the church or even in the streets), and a few unfinished pieces, some of which give an indication of the process of manufacture having gone wrong in individual instances - detritus from the tradestock of someone, possibly near the poverty line, who was just about making do with recycled scraps and newly made items which could be produced without expensive tools and equipment.

A single casting runnel 132a from School passages fill (Woodfield 1981, fig. 11, no 12), here No 102, Fig. 163, would have required specialised plant to reach melting temperature and its source may well be unrelated to the other finds.

Items which suggest active working are:

Sheet Buckle Pins
69 176. School passages fill. Cut to shape but profile unfinished.

70** 179a. School passages fill. Cut to shape but profile unfinished.

71** 169. School passages fill. The smallest of four strips in the group, may perhaps be the first stage of manufacture of the two preceding items.

It may be no coincidence that the (?replacement) pin on buckle No 21, Fig. 159 (also from a School period deposit and recognised as residual in Woodfield 1981) is of sheeting.

It is of course not impossible that some of this material is derived from the pre-friary industrial level in the presbytery, floorless and disturbed in the school period. It is unfortunate that much 1977 material is unprovenanced.

Pins
i) shafts not sharpened
In London in the late 15th/16th century sharpening appears to have been the last process in pinmaking (cf. evidence from the BOY86 site, Museum of London archaeological archive); it is possible that points have been broken off these items, but the shafts are of appropriate length for usable pins.

72** 139. School passages fill.

73 118. Provenance uncertain.

74** 357b. 1977 Provenance lost. (two examples in group)

ii) heads apparently uncrimped
The wire is wound round but not as smoothly rounded (as by a specialised crimping tool or drop hammer) as in the majority of the excavated pins. These arguably unfinished pins might have functioned perfectly well, or the heads might have slipped the shaft or come completely off, as in the following category.

75** 118. WF 1961 D f. 18th-century robbing of 16th-century S resonance passage.

76** 139. School passages fill (seven examples in group).

77** 357b. 1977, provenance lost.

78** 357c. 1977, provenance lost.

iii) heads misplaced
The wire heads have slipped some way down the shaft, as a result of inadequate fixture by solder or crimping with pliers, (?) drop hammer, etc., possibly after finishing but maybe prior to fixture (cf. Woodfield 1981, 91).

79** 244. School passages fill.

80 247. School passages fill.

81** 257. Provenance lost.

82 282. WF 1968 IIIE 125, a 16th-century

industrial level, N porch/N transept.

83** 309. School passages fill. Length 30mm. The top end of the shaft is hammered flat, making it impossible to set the head there.

Some 30 pieces of wire from the School passages fills are known, in both fine and medium gauge (Woodfield 1981, 98-99), and two pin-holding bones are known, Nos 108 and 109 below, from the choir and the night stair areas.

For further discussion on the manufacture of these articles, see Caple in Section U, *The Wound Wire-headed Pins*.

An additional 1075 pins were discovered packed (without context comments) in the 51 boxes of window glass. They are presumably of 16th-century date.

Lace chapes
The following are sheet rectangles bent lengthways into a U shape, presumably in preparation for fixture on laces. No parallel elsewhere has been traced for this stage of manufacture.

84** 121. School passages fill.

85** 132b-d. School passages fill (three examples).

86** 143. School passages fill (two examples).

87 249. School passages fill, (three examples).

Some lace chapes contained twisted cord as well as leather so both these materials were in use for laces for doublets, etc.

The sizes of pins, lace chapes, twists, and gauges of wire are discussed in Woodfield 1981, 91-93 and 98-99.

The following items may perhaps, but need not necessarily, be related to local metalworking -

Mounts
88 177. School passages fill (Woodfield 1981, fig. 6, no 69). Oval sheeting with domed area which is off-centred relative to the outline. Possibly a second, discarded because of the misplaced relief shaping.

89 165. School passages fill. Sheet waste from stamping of discs; presumably used as mount, (Woodfield 1981, fig. 6, no 64).

A possible additional mount is known, 1977 SF 82**, top fill of grave 1977.4 in presbytery. Oval strip 17 x 9mm, hole for fixing either end, central wider domed area, carrying a 'lattice or grid design'. From pre friary or 16th-century metal working?

90 School passages fill (Woodfield 1981, fig. 6, no 83). This appears to be unused, as the rivet is not bent or hammered.

Cut or broken scrap sheets with bosses and perforations
Unavailable for Woodfield 1981 report.

91 School passages fill. 30 x 25mm. The decoration of little bosses is made from the rear with a small punch.

92 School passages fill. 16 x 13, x 1mm. Pentagonal simple strap end, perforated with slot and hole, ?broken one end.

93 WF 62 I 1a, ?industrial gully in presbytery. School or Hales phase. 23 x 16mm. This item was made from re-used metal (simple linear decoration now on the reverse side) and has then again become broken/scrap.

94 WF 1962 II 2, rubble N of choir, pre 1572-74. Phase Destruction. *c.*25mm square overall. Originally a highly decorated fitting, moulded, with large linear and ?circular perforations, and linear decoration perforated with fine holes.

95 WF 1964 XVIa 1, 16th-century Destruction in chapel of the Holy Rood. 24 x *c.*20mm, perhaps part of strap end. This had been roughly shaped, folded and twice riveted.

96 WF 1962 XIV 4, robbing of NW tower pier, but 16th century. Phase Destruction. 15 x 11mm. Simple strap end with two perforations.

97 WF 62 U/S, but 16th century(?). 3 x 8mm. Sheet attachment, decorative band, perforation at centre.

Unused Rivet
98 School passages fill (Woodfield 1981, fig. 6, no 109). Rolled sheeting form (this type is characteristic of the late 15th/early 16th century onwards, and was normally used on sheet vessels and other kitchen equipment).

Book mount (?)
99 101. 62 I/II 2, 16th-century Destruction rubble in presbytery. A possible book mount already illustrated as No 60 above (Woodfield 1981, fig. 5, no 46), has four rivets, a most unusual repair for such an accessory (and it is probably not of particularly high quality).

Scrap and sheet offcuts
Numerous pieces were recovered, e.g.

100** 171 and 178**. School fill of passages (both with two pieces).

101 1977, SF 27, S resonance passage fill ?. Scrap sheet, 0.5mm thick, 33 x *c.*33mm, broken one end.

Tin or lead casting

Two fragments of stone moulds for casting lead/tin products have been identified from the resonance passages. These were probably fairly expensive pieces of equipment, and they presuppose at least a temporary hearth to melt the metal (perhaps the workshop overlying the reredorter which is known from photographs to have had tile hearths). They supplement an impressive series of finds of stone moulds from Coventry, both published (Telford 1956) and unpublished (Coventry Herbert Art Gallery and Museum collection, Iain Soden pers. comm.). The excavated evidence in Coventry for casting a variety of decorative accessories and other items in lead/tin is particularly abundant and a reassessment of the historical evidence to put this in perspective would now be useful.

102 School passages fill. Fragment with part of trough for (?hexagonal-section) spoon-handle (Woodfield 1981, fig. 11, no 12). See Muldoon and Brownsword 24-5 no 49/190/132 for another spoon mould found in Coventry, there provisionally dated to the late 16th century.

103 School passages fill. Fragment with part of engraved cobweb-like design (Woodfield 1981, fig. 11, no 10). For producing rough tokens. The 'cobweb' device is a common and widespread one on these, though it is usually attributed to the 17th or 18th centuries. See Dean 1977 for discussion of similar tokens.

Smithing

Iron slag from the quarry fill in the N transept (61 VI 10) and below the presbytery (77. F.23) attests to pre-friary iron-working on the site. A concentration of iron slag was also found in the N porch (60 III 3 and III 4) and N transept (61 VI 6) in the later medieval period, where it seems to relate to the reconstruction of the N transept. Were iron ties and bands for cramping together the superstructure (see *Structural Metalwork*, Section Q) perhaps being made on the spot, or was it merely residual?

Sixteenth-century levels produced slag also in the N resonance passage, the N porch (68 IIIE 105), and in the Cloister W range (68 XXVII 13), though this last might be late medieval (this level also producing iron rings and buckles).

Iron hardy with owner's stamp

104 WF 68 130. From a well located by contractors to NE of church, but within precinct. Length 138mm, width of 'blade' 45mm. The stamp is raised by just over 1mm. Found with late 16th-century pottery and pins, probably dating from a late Hales' phase. Ian Goodall writes: 'Blacksmith's hardy, iron, a tool with a tapering shank and a rectangular-shaped blade tapering in side view to a flat edge. One face of the blade has an inverted shield-shaped stamp with the letter 'A' on one face. The hardy, one of a number of anvil tools available to the blacksmith, is a form of chisel. The shank was dropped into a hole in the surface of an anvil, and the hardy was used with a hammer to cut cold or hot iron (Bradley Smith 1966, 121, 127-8; CSIRA 1955, 11)'.

Figure 164

Bone-working

105** A bone waste panel (1962 unstratified, now lost) from the turning of beads or discs of *c.*9mm diameter, attested local working (cf. Egan and Pritchard 1991, 311-5). The products of the 1962 fragment would have been smaller than those described by Woodfield (1981, fig. 10 nos j, l and n).

106 Fragmentary bone waste panel. WF 1962 VII 3, phase Pre-rebuild, a late medieval context external to the NW nave. Diameter of discs would have been *c.*12mm, and could have produced simple disc beads as Woodfield 1981, fig.10.

107 Bone disc bead. WF 62 III 4, E end, a 16th-century Destruction level. Diameter 13mm, *c.*4mm thick, unusually with two perforations at right angles, possibly a workman's error. A similar bead with more than one perforation occurred in the School passage fill (Woodfield 1981, fig. 10, n).

108 Pinner's bone. 1977 night stair area, unstratified. Ox metatarsal, trimmed to reduce shaft to a rough 13mm square. Length 148mm.

109 Pinner's bone. WF 1961 XI Ag, red clay seal post-School deposit in resonance passage. Destruction Phase. Ox metatarsal. Cut on each of four faces to reduce shaft to a rough 18 x 20mm square, each cut at the same angle. Length 140mm. The find spot implies industry moving into the choir when vacated by the School. There was 'much wire' from this level.

SECTION 5: BLACK-COATED SHEET COPPER ALLOY FINDS

by G. Egan

Half a dozen of the sheet copper-alloy finds, mainly fragments of dress accessories, have the remains of a distinctive black coating on one face. This coating, which appears to be a late 15th/early 16th-century fashion (possibly continuing slightly later) may be linseed oil. It is possible that originally this gave a translucent (?reddish) brown colour, rather than the opaque black which now meets the eye (cf. the '*vernis brun*' coating of Romanesque metalworkers). The present coating is probably distinct from that on some of the pins (Woodfield 1981, 91) which may well be tin.

A London manufacturing assemblage of buckles and plates (Clark 1991, 11, fig. 1.6; Margeson 1993, 25, pl. 9), recently dated to *c.*1500 from associated pottery, has close parallels with the first two items here.

Figure 164

110 109. School passages fill (Woodfield 1981, fig. 6, no 87) Crumpled (?) buckle plate, with relief design (?including roundel) and zigzag engraving.

111 62. School passages fill (Woodfield 1981, fig. 6 no 71). Rectangle, with relief design and zigzag engraving; an iron rivet suggests reuse; (?)cut from buckle plate.

112 32. School passages fill (Woodfield 1981, fig. 5 no 53). Folded (?)strap end, with three wire hooks, possibly originally to hold bells (cf. Woodfield 1981, fig. 7, bell no 121, and Margeson 1993, 37-8 no 245, fig. 21).

113 45. School passages fill (Woodfield 1981, fig. 5, no 44). Strap end.

114** 170. School passages fill. Crumpled fragment.

115** 40. 1977, SF 72, fill of S resonance passage. Book clasp, (identical to Woodfield 1981, fig. 5, no 50, illustrated as No 53 above) may relate to this group, but without analysis it is not possible to confirm whether or not the coating, possibly tin, is the same as that on the other items here, which does not seem to have been noted on book clasps elsewhere.

Single buckle plate parallels for the London assemblage have also been found in Northampton (Oakley 1979, 251 and 253, fig. 108, no 34 and 257-8, fig. 111 no 88) in Norwich (Margeson 1993, 24-5 and 27-8, no 147, fig. 14) and on the Isle of Man (Egan 1996, 31 no 2 and 30, fig. 15). These and the Coventry parallels are so close to the London finds that it is possible they were all shaped from the same templates. It is uncertain whether completed objects or partly finished components would have been sent out to provincial centres, but the former seems more likely. Alternatively, a number of templates may have been produced at one workshop for distribution to manufacturers across the country. The engraving on two of the above items and the Norwich parallel is an embellishment not found in the London assemblage.

The Whitefriars pieces, most perhaps a generation or more old at the time of deposition, may be a by-product of recycling buckle frames (none of the appropriate size for the plates and strap ends having been recovered during the excavations).

SECTION 6: OBSERVATIONS ON OTHER FINDS AND FURTHER IDENTIFICATIONS

Numbers 116-129 all appear to be from the School period, except No 121 (not published in Woodfield 1981) which is an intrusive later item, while Nos 131-132 from the same deposit are much earlier in origin and may well have been kept as curiosities. The dating for Nos 123-125 is open to question for they may be earlier. No 133 is probably 17th century.

Figure 164

Button
116 110. School passages fill (Woodfield 1981, fig. 5, no 41). The moulded head is actually of very dark ('black') glass, imitating a metal form. Copper alloy and glass. This is a very unusual survival, perhaps from before the earliest period of manufacture of glass buttons in England (cf. Godfrey 1975, 32; Margeson 1993, 20-2, nos 105-6, fig. 11; and Henkes 1994, 319, for Dutch finds of slightly later date).

Pin
117 WF 1964 XVIa/XVIIa 2, 16th century Destruction levels (normally no later than *c.*1572/74) in nave (Woodfield 1981 fig. 5, 35f). Copper alloy, with rough, cast head; the thistle-like head is not uncommon in pins from contexts attributable to the late 16th/early 17th century, and, if the proposed dating for the present one is a little early, it is tempting to see the series as favours for the new Scottish dynasty in the early years of James I.

Clasp
118 98. School passages fill (Woodfield 1981, fig. 6, no 86). Copper alloy: elaborate outline; knop for attachment; foliate decoration. Two iron rivets may indicate that this accessory had been remounted. Possibly from a sword belt. The form of the other, corresponding part of this form of clasp is uncertain.

Twisted Wire Loops
119 Fifteen of these from the School phase fills of the resonance passages were published by Woodfield (1981, fig. 7, no 117), and five more are now known. There was only one outlier, 69 XXIX 13, an industrial level of the Hales Phase, S of the choir, but their relationship on this site to the school seems clear despite this. They can tentatively be identified as a form of protection against cut-purses, from the ones sewn on to the covering of a purse found at Southampton (Egan forthcoming in Moir, D. (ed.), no 317).

Chain for Seal (?)
120 37. School passages (Woodfield 1981, fig. 5, no 39, where so identified). Despite its resemblance to a watch chain, at the date in question the use of portable time pieces had not developed. A parallel in a contemporary deposit in Southampton is cited in Woodfield 1981.

Watch
121** 165. No 2 of eight items now packed as WF 1962 I 4 (the most common School passage numbering); not included in Woodfield 1981. Fragment of an enamelled watch face retaining part of one numeral. The relatively thin sheet copper alloy is characteristic of timepieces from the 19th century (Chris Ellmers pers comm) and is therefore intrusive, presumably wrongly bagged.

Spoon
122** 63. School passages fill. Copper alloy, fragment of bowl; tin coated.

Box Lids
123a 60. School passages fill (Woodfield 1981, fig. 6, no 61). Oval sheeting; hole for attachment of hinge strip (broken off); rabbet for (or broken off from) catch; this has rough but lightly engraved decoration of two, six-armed spiral motifs (object cleaned subsequent to 1981 paper). Perhaps from a container for a folding balance (cf. Egan 1998, nos 484-6, which are earlier).

123b-c School passages fill (Woodfield 1981, 124-5, fig. 15, nos 1 and 2). 123b: wt 3.65g, appears to be a latten half-ryal weight converted into a crown weight, date probably 1527-42, and 123c: a latten weight of 3.45g for the gold florin of Florence, late medieval.

Tenterhook(?)
124 School passages fill (Woodfield 1981, fig. 3, no 25). The form of this iron object has been identified as a tenterhook (Woodfield 1981) but Goodall (1990, 234-5) suggests it is a variant of a nail for roof-tiles; however, only one was recovered among the 300± nails in the passage fill.

Weight
125 88. School passages fill (Woodfield 1981, fig. 5, no 42). Disc, (?) central knop broken off; filed on base to achieve accuracy; present weight 3.60g; traces of two stamped 'E's' (not illustrated). Presumably from the reign of Edward VI from the regulatory stamps and the site dating.

Bone Die
126 School passages fill (Woodfield 1981, fig. 10, 2). The numbers on the die are as on modern dice, viz. opposite numbers add up to 7, 6 being opposite 1, etc.

Figure 165

Marbles
127a-b Stone and ceramic: The mid 16th-century dating for these ten published marbles (diameters 11 to 30mm) from the School passages fill (Woodfield 1981, fig. 11, 8a, 8b) is among the earliest in Britain; they become common from the middle of the next century onwards. The earliest marbles so far claimed in this country seem to be a couple of ceramic ones found at Merstham in Surrey, which are attributed to the period 1270-1350 (Opie 1976, 65, nos 161-2; four naturally spherical flint nodules, diameters *c.*40mm, found together at the same site and discussed under the same period heading, are tentatively suggested to be toy balls). Another ceramic marble, excavated at Beeston Castle, was thought perhaps to be intrusive in a deposit of similar date (Courtney 1993, 156, fig. 197, no 25).

Apart from these isolated finds, there is nothing until the present items and a provisional 16th-century attribution in London (Museum of London ER no 1318).

The marble game board surviving cut into the reading desks of the choir stalls may be of this date. (Woodfield 1981, p.105 - 106). This is fully described in Section I, *'Marbles' Gaming Board*, accompanying the consideration of the Choir Stalls, Section H.

Slate counter
The cutting of tile quoits and slate counters is also firmly attested as being related to the Grammar School (Woodfield 1981, 105-106), the slate counter distribution tying in the presbytery/?industrial gully 62 II 1a as contemporary. There is the occasional outlier.

128 62 VI 10, on floor make-up eastern bay of nave. Polygonal and incomplete, d. 75mm, thickness 11mm, i.e. the largest of all the slate counters. The make-up is of Phase Friary 2, however. Is this intrusive or an object of a different category?

Toy Sword
129 59a. School passages fill. Sheet copper alloy: the second strip of the hilt is probably intended to represent a form current in England from *c.*1500 (Anthony North pers. comm.). A remarkable survival of a flimsy, one-off toy, of a category very little known from this date. (cf. Egan 1996B).

Keyhole Cover
130** 44. WF 1961 XII+, disturbed fill of resonance passage (Woodfield 1981, fig. 6, no 63). This is indeed an intrusive object, as previously suggested; it is probably of late 18th/19th century date.

Curiosities from Earlier Periods
131 School passages fill. Coarse micaceous stone weight of Roman form (Woodfield 1981, fig. 11, no 9).

132 36. School passage fill. Copper-alloy pin (Woodfield 1981, fig. 5, no 40). This may be of prehistoric or Saxon date (cf. Norwich 1977, no 105 and Dunning 1965, 62, fig. 10) - thanks to Jon Cotton for help with this object.

These antiquities were presumably kept as curiosities from the past, though it is doubtful whether their true significance would have been known in the mid 16th century.

Prehistoric Flints

by Mark Curteis

133** Possible borer made from utilised flake. A translucent grey-brown flint flake with abrupt retouch (45 degrees) on bulbar side. Flat cortical platform produced by soft hammer blow. Bulb of percussion. Length 22mm, width 21mm, maximum thickness 4mm. WF 77 95e.

134** Side/end scraper. Heavy utilised flake from a hard hammer blow. The piece is of grey brown flint and plano-convex in profile with a pronounced bulb of percussion. Retouch is on three edges nearly at right angles to each other in effect giving three working edges. The abrupt retouch has been produced by soft pressure flaking with an angle of retouch of 60-90 degrees. Most retouch is on the bulbar side but there is also retouch on the dorsal side. Curved cortical striking platform. Length 32mm, width 27mm, maximum thickness 9mm. WF 64 XVII (1).

Neither flints have strong dating diagnostic features and could date to any prehistoric period from the Neolithic to the Iron Age. Both residual in 16th-century destruction levels in the choir and nave.

No material was recovered from the site between the date of these flints and pottery of the 12th/13th centuries, except for 131 and 132 above.

From a Later Period

135 WF 1960 III 4a Post medieval robbing of NE transept. This iron coffin handle of ?17th-century date suggests the continued use of the N cemetery.

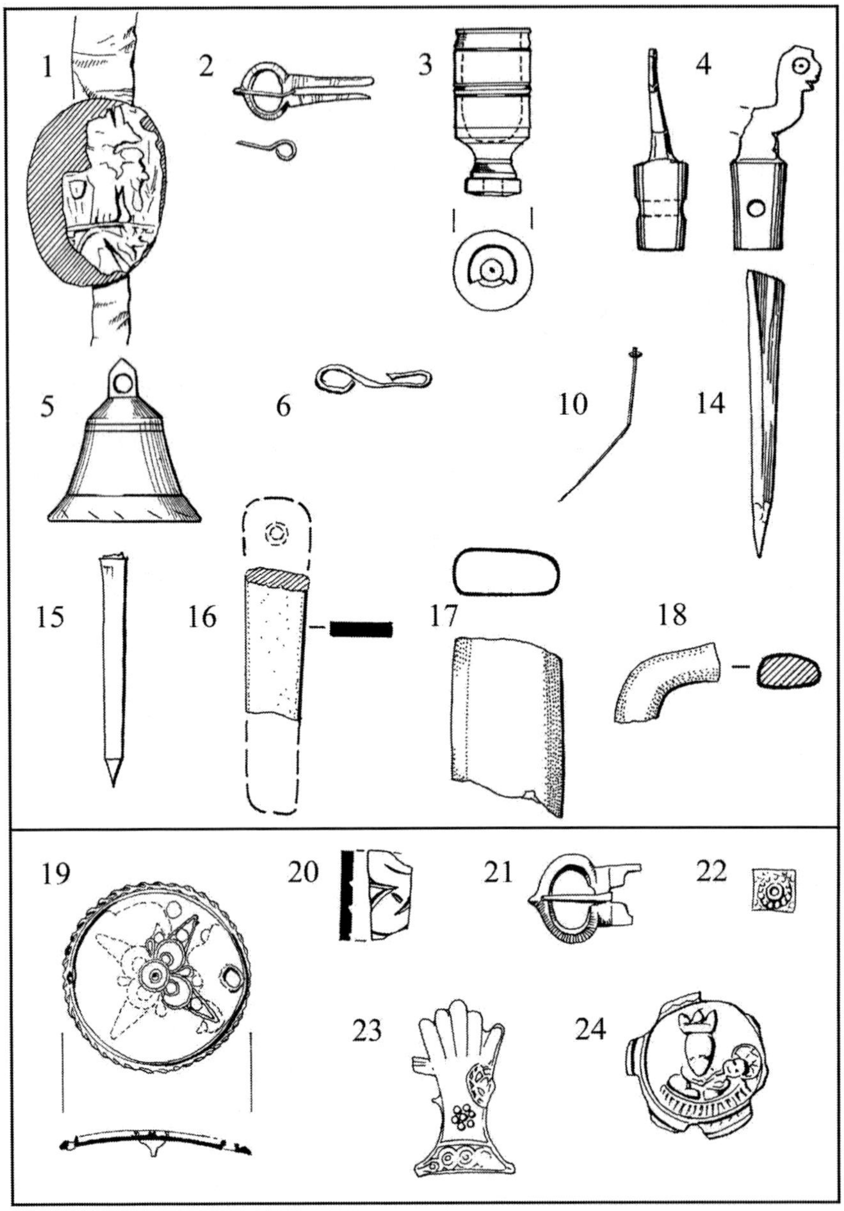

Figure 159 Medieval Small Finds.
1, wax seal. 2-6, 10 and 21-22, copper alloy: 2, buckle; 3, candle holder; 4, spigot tap with cockerel; 5, clapper bell; 6, shroud fastener; 10, pin; 21, buckle; 22, mount. 14 and 15, bone styli. 16 and 17, stone hones. 18, stone handle. 19, a high quality very rare Hungarian roundel with cloisons outlined in silver wire, enamelling and gilding. 20, fragment of tomb brass?. Pilgrim badges - 23 Canterbury (lead), 24 Virgin and Child, cu alloy..
Scale 1:2, except 19 and 23 at 1:1.

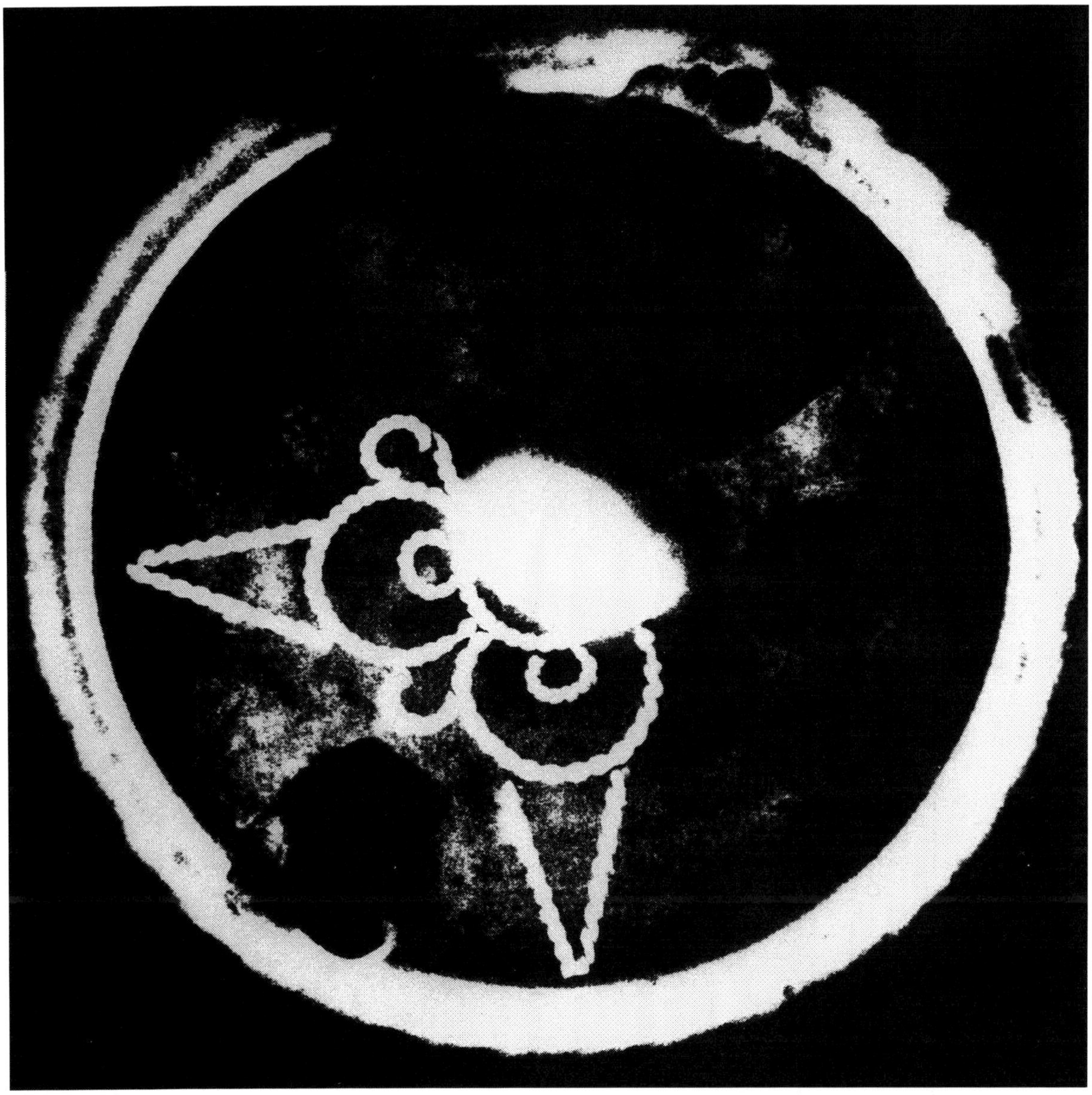

Figure 160 Medieval Small Finds. X-Ray of silver wire outlining cloisons on Hungarian roundal (Fig. 159.19). Scale c. x6.

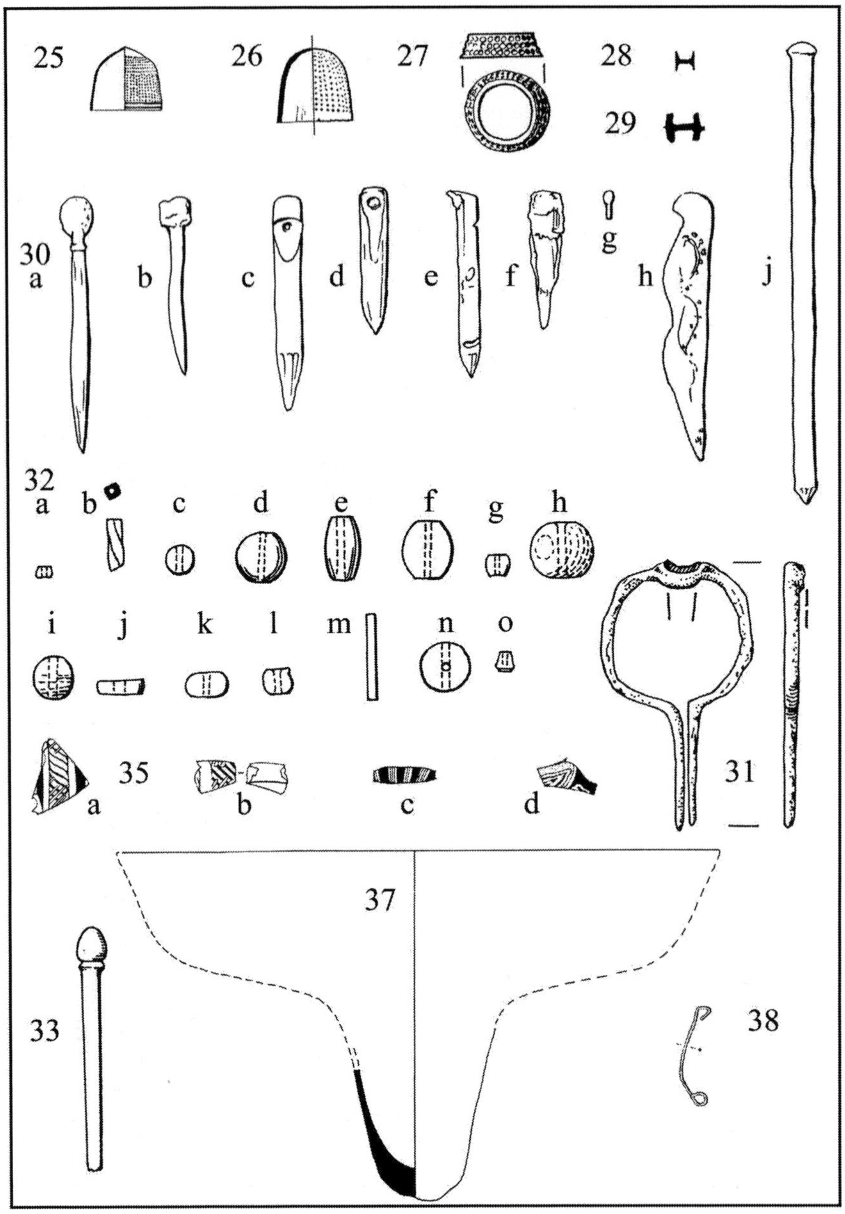

Figure 161 Medieval Small Finds.
25-27, two thimbles and one sewing ring in copper alloy, Nuremburg and English; 28-29, lead window calmes; 30a-j, lead pins; 31, jew's harp (iron); 32a-o, beads of bone, jet, amber, glass, quartz, faience and red paste; 33, bone stylus; 37, glass lamp; 38, copper alloy lamp link.
Scale 1:2.

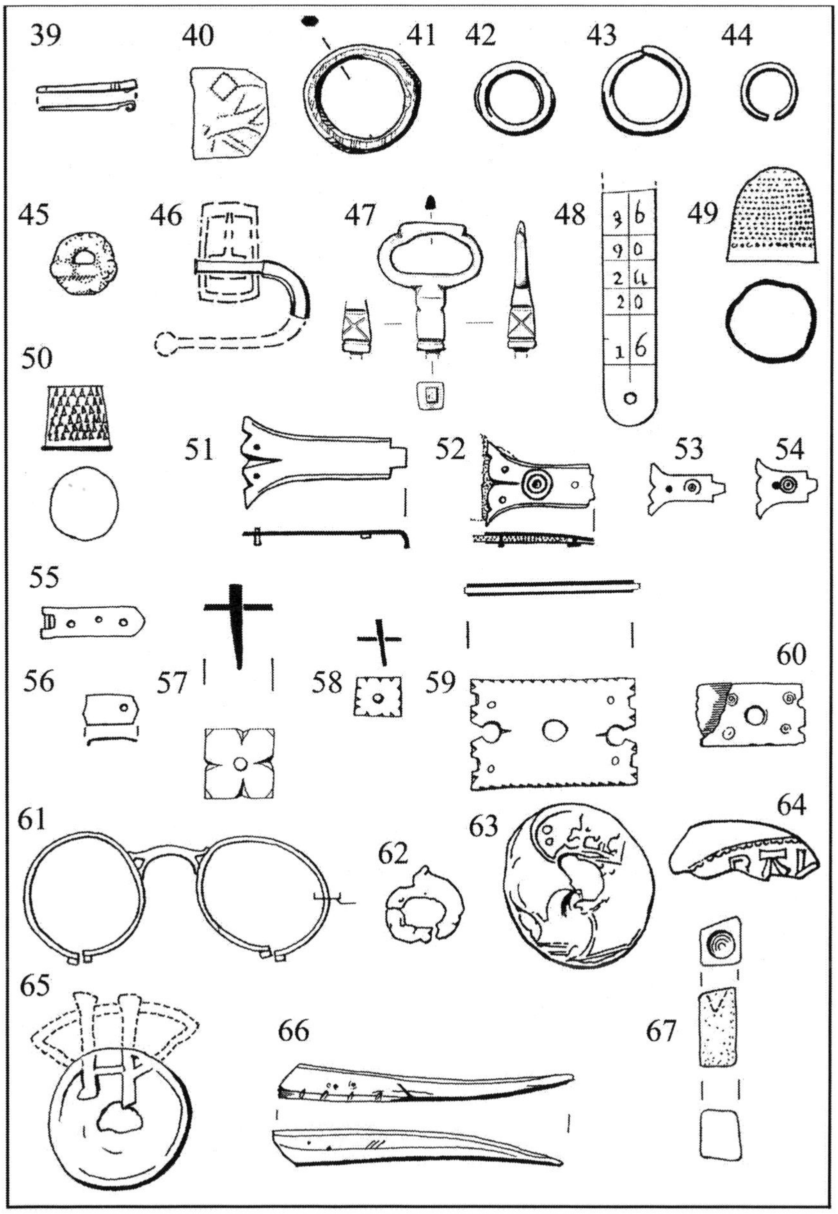

Figure 162 Small Finds from Grammar School Period deposits.
39, gold brooch pin. Copper alloy objects: 41-44, drape rings; 45-46, buckles (45 iron); 47, key; 48, calibrated scale with 16th-century Arabic numerals; 49-50, thimble and sewing ring; 51-60, book cover accessories; 62, spectacle frame. 62-65, lead cloth seals, one from Valenciennes; 66, lead? tally; 67, stone tessera.
Scale 1:2, except 48 and 62-64 at 1:1.

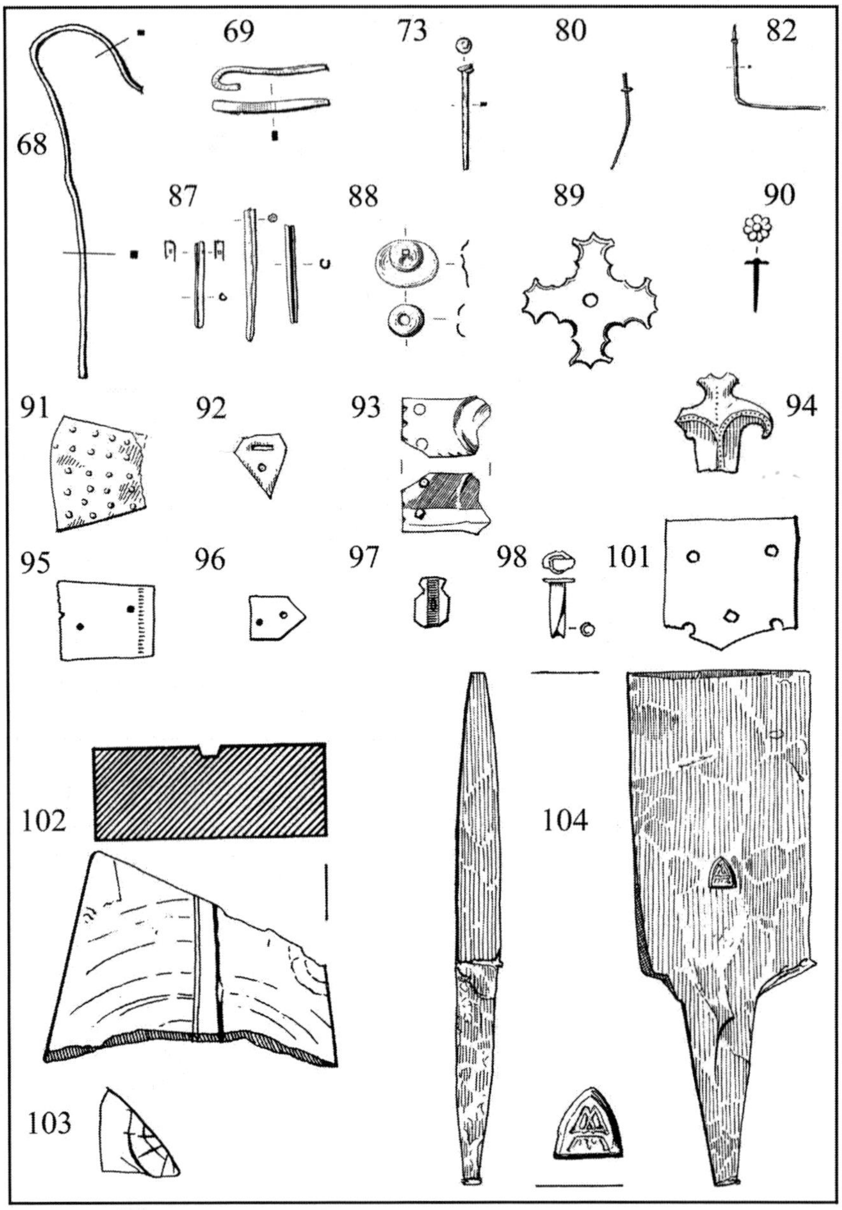

Figure 163 Small Finds from Grammar School Period deposits.
Copper alloy objects: 68-82, pins and pinners' wire; 87, lace chapes; 88-90, mounts; 91-97 and 101, scrap sheets; 98, rivet. 102-103, stone casting moulds. 104 iron hardy with stamp 'A', late Hales' phase.
Scale 1:2.

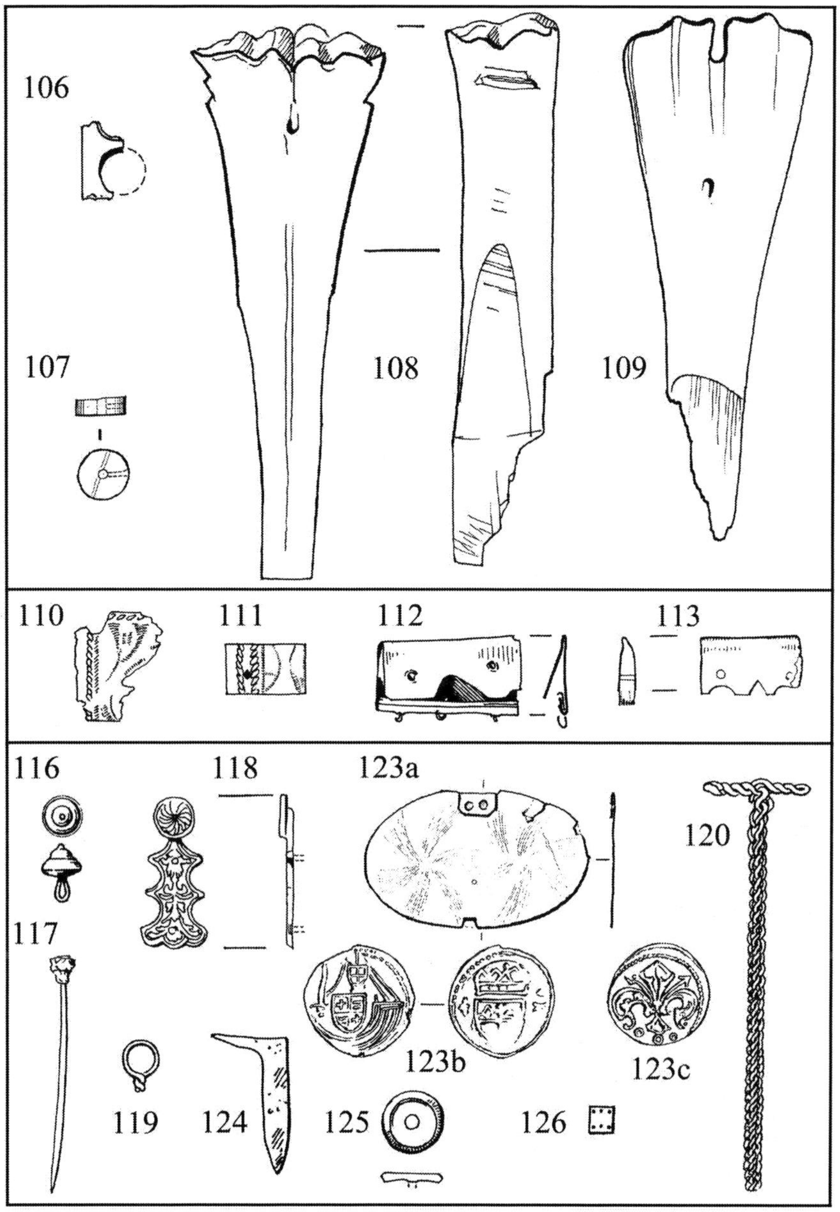

Figure 164 Small Finds from Grammar School Period deposits.
106-109, bone waste and pinners' bones; 110-113, black-coated copper alloy dress accessories; 116, copper alloy and glass button. Copper alloy objects: 117, thistle head pin; 118, decorated clasp; 119, twisted wire loops; 120, chain for seal; 123a, box lid. 123b-c and 125, copper alloy/latten weights; 124, iron tenterhook or roof nail; 126, bone die.
Scale 1:2.

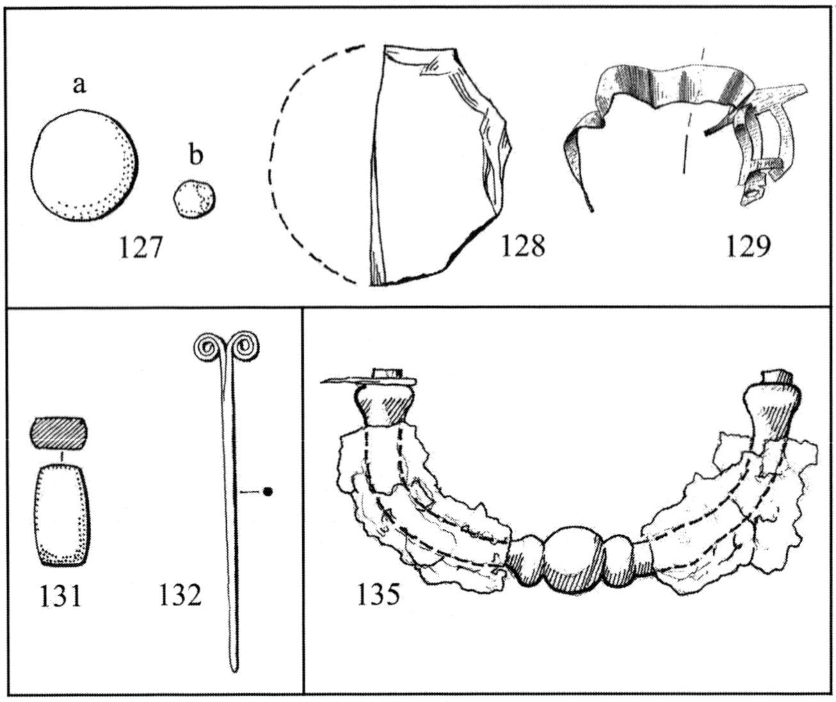

Figure 165 Small Finds from Grammar School Period deposits.
127a-b, stone and ceramic marbles; 128, slate counter; 129, rare copper alloy toy sword; 131-132, Roman/Prehistoric; 135, 17th century iron coffin handle.
Scale 1:2.

SECTION U
THE WOUND WIRE-HEADED PINS

Dr C. Caple
Department of Archaeology, University of Durham

Typology, metrology, alloy composition changes - with parallels in brasses and jettons; manufacturing sources - and imports from North-west Europe; Coventry pinners; dating.

The conclusions here are based on 880 pins recovered from the 'Grammar School' deposits found in the 1960s excavations of the resonance passages at Coventry Whitefriars, dating from *c.*1545 to *c.*1558. Such close dating is rare, making it worth while for these to have been studied in some detail (Caple 1986; 1991).

These pins are of the type known as wound wire-headed pins (Tylecote 1972; Caple & Warren 1983); they are made of copper alloy (brass) wire and are usually between 15 and 50mm long. They have a head composed of a tightly wound spiral of wire (usually two turns), stuck or crimped on to the top of the shaft. The earliest wound wire-headed pins come from 13th and 14th-century contexts at Southampton (Platt and Coleman Smith 1975). Such pins become common in post 15th-century contexts (Tylecote 1972; Goodall 1984; Williams 1979; Caple 1983; 1985).

An assemblage of 198 pins was analysed, with the head type and twenty-two visual and metrical parameters being recorded. Thirty-eight pins were cut up to form metallographic sections.

TYPOLOGY

Earlier work (Caple and Warren 1983) established that there are three major head-form variants for wound wire-headed pins:

A. 2 twists of wire stuck on to the top of the shaft with a flux or adhesive, 32% of the Coventry examples;
B 2 twists of wire loosely crimped on to the top of the shaft, 57% of the Coventry examples;
C 2 twists of wire tightly crimped on to the top of the shaft forming a spherical head, 10% of the Coventry examples.

This confirms earlier suggestions (Caple 1986; 1991) that 'A' type heads are mainly 15th century, that 'B' type heads are prevalent in the 16th century, and 'C' type heads do not become dominant until after 1700.

METROLOGY

Pins of between 20 and 32mm length were the most commonly utilised, and pins 25mm long were commonest at the Whitefriars. A comparison of mean pin lengths from dated sites - St Peter's Street, Northampton (Williams 1979, 256-62), Sandal Castle (Caple 1983, 269-78), Moulsham Street, Chelmsford (Caple 1985) and Ludgershall Castle (Caple 1986) indicates that pre 1500 pins have mean pin lengths over 40mm., but in our period, within the phase 1500 to 1630, pins are generally slighter shorter (29-35mm). This gradual shortening may have resulted from the increasing fineness of cloth, or a change in fashion to have less visible pins and smaller folds and pleats in garments.

There is also a general diminution of the shaft wire diameter. This is again gradual; the shorter the pin the thinner the wire and vice versa.

MANUFACTURE

It appears that there is a high level of variability in the manufacture of 'A' type wound wire heads which is consistent with being a handmade craft product. Historical evidence (Caple 1986, 1991) indicates that early pin production of the high medieval period was undertaken in small urban workshops, which were present in most urban centres in England. Records of the trade of 'pinner' and of the activities of the 'Guild of Pinners' occur from the 14th century onwards in many English towns. Conversely the regularity of 'B' type and 'C' type headed pins is consistent with a regularised, even mechanised, manufactured product. There is also a correlation between the marks of manufacture associated with the use of punches to crimp the head wire into position and 'B' and 'C' type wound wire-headed pins. Given that the 'C' type pins become predominant in deposits dated later than the mid 17th century, the date after which mechanised production of pins is believed to have started in England, it may be possible to correlate the 'C' type headed pin with automated pin machine manufacture, and this would suggest pins of this type in the Whitefriars assemblage are imports. Records of pins being imported from Continental Europe from the 15th century have already been noted (Caple 1986, 1991). The 'B' type headed pins, so prevalent in this mid 16th century Whitefriars assemblage, probably represent pins made, like the preceding 'A' type, by hand, and with the head wires crimped into place using hand-held hollow punches. Such pins were probably made locally by the 'pinners' of Coventry, medieval craftsmen still producing a hand-made product as efficiently as possible in competition with cheap imports. The presence of the Pinners Guild in Coventry throughout the 15th century (and presumably on into the 16th) is attested in the Coventry Leet Book (Harris 1907-1913) where 10 pinners are recorded as present in the city in 1450 (Caple 1986).

ALLOY COMPOSITION

Analysis of the alloy composition of the metal used in the manufacture of the pins was undertaken using pins prepared as metallographic specimens and analysed using an energy dispersive X Ray fluorescence analysis (EDXRF) system (see Caple and Warren 1983 and Caple 1986 for an account of this technique). The vast majority of the Whitefriars pins were made of brass containing low levels of lead.

The compositions from Whitefriars - copper 68-83%, zinc 15-29%, lead 0.8-5.5% - are typical of those seen for pins and wires of this period. From the large number of analyses of copper alloy pins and wires from this period it has been shown (Caple 1986; 1991; 1995) that:

i) There was a large level of compositional variation within any group of pins analysed.

ii) Copper alloy pins of this period show exactly the same range of compositions as those used for wire. Neither pins nor wires yet show any significant regional variation within any group of pins analysed and thus pins were being made from the standard brass wire which was available throughout NW Europe.

iii) These alloys are also similar to those used for many of the few sheet and wrought metal analyses obtained for this period. In the High and Later medieval period most brass production was concentrated in the Aachen and Liege regions. Port records indicate that brass was imported in bar, sheet, ribbon, wire or as ready manufactured objects into England (Caple 1986).

iv) Since many of the alloy compositions used for cast objects have similar levels of zinc to those of pins it can even be suggested that a consistent supply of brass for all forms of copper alloy manufacture existed. For creating cast items greater quantities of lead were added to this alloy. The higher levels of tin also seen in some castings indicate that it was also usual to add scrap metal (Caple 1995).

v) If the mean values of the alloy constituents for pins and wires are examined a clear consistent overall change in composition is discernible for the two major alloying elements, zinc and tin (Caple 1986).

During the high to post-mediaeval period there is a change in the metal used for wire and pin production from a medium zinc brass with a low level of lead and a small percentage of tin to a high zinc brass with a low level of lead and virtually no tin. Similar developments in the composition of copper alloys have been noted for memorial brasses (Cameron 1974) and jettons (Pollard 1983). Whitefriars, with its mean zinc content of 22.3% (from 37 samples) clearly demonstrates the rising zinc contents of brass wire of this period.

One pin shows a markedly different alloy composition with no lead, a significant percentage of nickel, the presence of arsenic and a low zinc content. A small number of pins and wires with similar compositions were found at Sandal Castle (Caple 1983), as well as examples from Moulsham Street, Chelmsford and Salisbury (Caple 1986). This alloy is probably derived from an unusual copper ore which was rich in nickel and arsenic, and these particular lower zinc brasses appear in 15th and 16th-century contexts. The source of the arsenic- and nickel- rich copper has not yet been determined.

CONCLUSION

The pins from Whitefriars show the range of head forms, length and alloy composition typical of the mid 16th-century period. They are the product of an urban based industry which was present in many British medieval towns whose hand-made product was facing competition from continental imports. The pins of the period were becoming shorter and finer due probably to the increasing complexity of fashions and the increasing fineness of cloth. The metal of which the pins were made was a widely exported material present through much of NW Europe and whose composition reflected underlying developments in the brass alloys of the European brass industry.

The original, fuller, version of this report is lodged with the Archive.

SECTION V
NUMISMATICA

P. Woodfield

The excavations produced a total of 20 medieval and sub-medieval coins (up to 1550) from stratified contexts which provide a valuable date for certain features, discussed below. There were, however, in addition, a large number of jettons, most from the lower fill of the acoustic chambers, which apparently accumulated there during the period of the School's occupation, and also spread throughout the 16th-century levels and gullies in the eastern part of the church. These post-medieval finds were reported on at length by S. R. Rigold in Woodfield (1981, 118-25) and are only dealt with in summary here. The pervading blackness of the rotted floor coverings of the deposits in the acoustic chambers, largely accumulated during the period of occupation by the School, left no identifiable earlier deposits pertaining exclusively to any earlier friary occupation, although it is likely that some deposits accumulated before the Reformation, but were absorbed by the black deposits of rotting rubbish of the School's occupation. There was no trace of a separate lower layer - some coins may have been picked up and later discarded by the schoolboys.

CATALOGUE I: MEDIEVAL

A Coins recovered from the acoustic chambers, with 13, 14, and 17 from the presbytery in the Hales' period

1 JOHN. Cut quarter penny. Short cross. 1199-1216. ?Class V.
Residual, from the school occupation (62 I 4).

2 HENRY III. Half penny. Long-cross issue of 1247-1272, Class IIIC.
Reverse illegible.
Residual, from the school occupation (62 I 4).

3 Edward III-Henry V, but probably of RICHARD II. *c.*1350-1420.
Penny of York mint. Extremely worn and pierced off-centre for suspension.
Possibly a keepsake from the friary period (62 I 4) and so residual.

4 RICHARD II. Penny of York mint, 1377-1399.
Very worn, pierced for suspension but probably from a local die of Group A. X before CIVI. (North 1991 II 1330).
Possibly lost during the Friary period or the school occupation (61 XI Ad).

5 Richard II(?) – Henry VI. Quarter penny, ?1377-1461.
Pellet each side of the crown.
Possibly lost during the Friary period (62 I 4) and so residual in School occupation.

6 Fragmentary penny in very poor condition and unidentifiable.

7 HENRY VI. Penny of York. Leaf-pellet issue of 1445-1454.
Class A, possibly with a residual reverse die. Fairly fresh, so lost in the third quarter of the 15th century, probably by dropping through the floor boarding of the choir stalls.
(North 1991 II 1510)
Friary period (61 XI Ad) and so residual in School occupation.

8 EDWARD IV. Penny of ?Durham mint. 1461-1470.
Appears to be struck from local dies, but worn and clipped.
Probably lost during the Friary period (62 I 4) and so residual in School occupation.

9 EDWARD IV. Penny of York, of Archbishop George Neville. 1465-1470.
B (G) and key by bust. Clipped. The record gives this as of Booth of York and initial B, but this type does not exist.
Possibly lost during the Friary period (62 I 4) and so residual in School occupation.

10 EDWARD IV. Penny of Dublin. *c.*1473-1478.
'Cross and Pellets' issue. ....LIN. Pellets by neck.
Very clipped (Dowle and Finn 1969, 136).
Possibly lost during the Friary period (62 I 4) and so residual.

11 EDWARD IV. Penny of Dublin. *c.*1478-1483.
Rose l and sun r of the neck, and a rose at the centre of the reverse.
Clipped and in poor condition. (Dowle and Finn 1969, 166).
Possibly lost during the Friary period (62 I 4) and so residual.

12 JAMES III of Scotland. Bronze penny of Bishop Kennedy of St Andrews, *c.*1450 -1488.

(The Crosraguel penny). Type I.
Obverse: IACOBVS:DEI:GRA:REX, around a tilted orb, reverse: /CRVX:PELLIT:(OMNE:C)RIM, around a Latin cross in a quatrefoil. The spandrels of the orb are void. The stops are in the form of colons each side (Stewart 1967).
From the destruction phase associated with the N acoustic chamber (60 II 8).
Friary period, and so residual.

13 EDWARD VI. Groat. 1547-1549.
Bust of Henry VIII, Type 5. Initial mark arrow.
Industrial gully of the period of John Hales' occupation (62 II 1a).

14 EDWARD VI. Groat of London (Tower) mint. 1549.
Bust 6 of Henry VIII. Initial mark – grapple.
From an industrial gully in the presbytery (62 II 1a).
Period of John Hales' occupation.

15 EDWARD VI. Penny of London, Tower mint or Southwark [SR], 1547-1549.
Old portrait of Henry VIII. Initial mark – arrow.
Period of John Hales' occupation, before the school moved out (62 I 4).

16 EDWARD VI. Base penny of London. 1550-1552.
i.m. scallop. Cracked and broken. (North 1991 II 1943/1).
Period of the School occupation (60 II 9).

17 CHARLES V. Double-korte of the Spanish Netherlands. 1547.
Radiate bust. Reverse, a lion.
Very worn and bent.
Unstratified, from chancel, period of John Hales' occupation (77 Area 3).

B Coins from other areas:

18 RICHARD II. Penny of York. G. 1380s.
Not struck up but probably fresh when lost.
From the builder's trample for the construction of the S wall of the NE transept chapel/porch, and/or the N wall of the chancel at the western end (68 IIIE 116a).
Early Friary period.

19 RICHARD II. Halfpenny, probably of the 1380s.
Early style, and little worn when lost. (North 1991 II 1331).
Unstratified but from the area of the S wall of the choir, fourth bay from the W (77 Area 3a).

20 HENRY VI. Penny of York, ?1430-1434.
Quatrefoil centre. Probably of the pinecone-mascle issue but the symbols are not distinguishable through wear.
From the make-up following the fall of the tower (68 IIIE 118).
Rebuild phase.

Comment

The two groats on display in Coventry in 1966 were not accessible for checking but are almost certainly Nos 13 and 14 in the above catalogue, from the Tudor industrial gully which was open while part of the chancel was used as a workshop.

The Richard II coin of the 1380s, Catalogue No 18, lost in builder's trample, provides a very useful confirmatory date for the building of the first phase of the E chapel to the N transept, and for the NW choir wall. The other two coins of this reign, although not closely stratified, suggest activity in the choir at this period, probably connected with the primary construction.

The occurrence of the Irish coins is of particular interest. Coventry is on one of the routes from Ireland to London, and travelling Irishmen, as today, might well seek hospitality from the friars. Rigold writes (*in litt.* to P. Woodfield) 'I expect that Irishmen, as ever, would have patronized the Carmelites, but there weren't many Irish in England in the Middle Ages. There was a coin found by Rahtz at Beckory – a site with Irish connections, that was so feeble – a bad imitation sterling cut down – that it could never have passed for a penny in England'. Irish coins, after their weight had sunk below the English standard, were of little use and are hardly ever found in England.

The incidence of the Scottish copper penny of St Andrews, the type formerly called the Crosraguel penny, is however of particular interest as they are very rarely found in England, where there was no familiarity with the use of base metal for coins. It was found in association with a destruction level over the N acoustic chamber (60 II 8). Again, it may have come with a wayfarer from the N. Rigold believed, in 1977, that it may be the only one actually found in England.

CATALOGUE II: THE JETTONS

All 112 jettons recovered from the early excavations were listed and reported on by S. R. Rigold in Woodfield (1981, 118-125) covering all excavations up to 1977. Additions since that date have not been kept apart in Coventry Museum.

The earliest is a jetton of sterling type, Class Fox 14, (SF69) of the time of Edward I and was recovered in 1977 from a 'brown' level in the presbytery. This level was under the clay make-up for the chancel floor, and was between, and at the E of graves 1 and 2. The date assigned to the piece is 1318-1320s. This is of particular interest in that it here is presumably from the dark fill of the pre-friary clay pit. These English jettons did however continue to circulate in use until replaced by continental types in the later 14th century. Not being currency or precious metal, there was no incentive to call them in.

One jetton of Group A.2 (*Residual Late Medieval)* of the French Derivative type (later 15th century) was found in the construction trench of the seventh N nave arcade pier from the E (64 XXV 3). This provides evidence for the earliest date of the pier's construction. Structural details show it is probable that the nave was extended by two or three bays at the W end section at this date, faithfully repeating the detail of the earlier, eastern piers.

Jetton No 109 in Rigold's 1981 report, from the destruction levels at the W end of the nave, could be as late as 1610 and is unlikely to occur before 1570. This suggests that the building stood longer than we currently believe.

Sixteen jettons were found in the industrial Tudor gullies (62 II 1a; 62 III 5; and 62 III 7). They were of the Nuremberg Group C, 'Venetian' type, group D 'French' type, Group E 'Normal' type and Group F, the subtype cut down and ground smooth on one side. All these date from the 1550s, but the two Edward VI groats, Nos 15 and 16 above, indicate that this activity continued after the school had moved out.

One Group D 'French' jetton in an early style, with a legible inscription reading 'Volge la Gallée' and dated to *c.*1520-30, came from the disturbed fill of the S acoustic chamber. It probably relates to School activity where jettons would have been in constant use for reckoning and the casting of accounts, and doubtless, games.

A later Group D jetton came from the 16th-century levels in the crossing, as did a 'Normal' Nuremberg jetton from the destruction levels, both dating from the mid 16th century. The destruction levels at the W end of the nave contained a Krauwinkel 'Normal' jetton of the 1570s. Of the ten jettons from the 1977 excavations in the chancel area, five are of pre-reformation date in England, and could possibly relate to the last days of the friary.

Five jettons from the acoustic chambers were issued in the late 15th century before the demise of the Friary and may well have been acquired and used by the friars before they were finally expelled. Others, of pre-Reformation date were found in the crossing, in the cloister garth, - a group B Nuremberg of *c.*1525, - and one at the foot of the night stair.

Jettons, are regular, if sparse finds on other friary excavations, although unusually plentiful at Coventry. At the Carmarthen Greyfriars, one was found in an 'acoustic gully' in the choir, (Manning 1998, 23); three Nuremberg jettons in demolition rubble at the Ludlow Carmelite house (Klein and Roe 1987, 63), and a 16th century jetton at the Whitefriars of Linlithgow (Lindsay 1989, 89). Medieval jettons were recovered from the 3B phase at the Leicester Austin Friars (Mellor and Pearce 1981, 130), whilst a range of nine jettons dating from the early official English series to one late Nuremberg appeared at the Guildford Blackfriars (Poulton and Woods 1984, 81). The Oxford Dominican house produced eight jettons, four of which were from the Nuremberg series, of which one was found in dust beneath the choir stalls (Lambrick and Woods 1976, 220-1). It is not always clear whether they are from very late medieval or post dissolution contexts, but the assumption, based on Coventry, is that they may well have been used for reckoning in the decades prior to the closure of the houses.

CATALOGUE III: COIN WEIGHTS

Figure 164

The excavations produced two coin weights from the N acoustic chamber which were fully reported upon in the earlier article by S. R. Rigold (Woodfield 1981 124-5). One, 15mm in diameter, and weighing 56.34 grams, has a crude semblance of the ship type of the noble or ryal, although the king's head on the reverse has become a crowned shield as on the Crown of the Double Rose of 1527-42. The weight appears to have been pared down on one side, and is probably intended to correspond originally to the half-ryal (of 120g), then converted into a crown, which weighed 57.3g. It cannot therefore date to earlier than 1527, and is probably of the latest phase of the Friary, Fig. 164.123b.

The second weight, Fig. 164.123c, is of latten, uniface, 13mm in diameter, weighing 3.45 grams. It bears a fleur-de-lys above three annulets on the obverse. It appears almost certainly to be the weight for the consistent and much copied gold florin of Florence, of 3.45g, and bears the same insignia. The gold florin and its imitations were in wide circulation throughout Europe from the mid 13th century. It is probably also of the late Friary period as it is unlikely that the school would be weighing such coins, particularly in the mid 16th century.

SECTION W
HUMAN SKELETAL ANALYSIS

P. Kiberd, MSc.

All skeletal material available was assessed and detailed in skeletal inventories (for the methodology see, Bass 1987; Manchester 1983; McMinn and Hutchings 1991; Roger *et al* 1967.). Metric and non-metric traits and morphologies were examined and are listed in the archive. The following report details the main findings.

Many of the skeletons in store at the Herbert Art Gallery and Museum from post 1969 excavations were unwashed and remain so, as facilities to clean skeletons were not available to the author. Equally most of the skeletons were in a poor state of preservation, as a result of post-deposition damage or damage during exhumation and storage. Due to the small number of skeletons and the unequal preservation from individual to individual very little comparative analysis is applicable.

Since 1960 there have been a number of excavations, which have revealed human remains at Coventry Whitefriars. Between 1960 and 1964 excavations took place in the area of the church and cloister. Due to excessive vandalism and very slender resources the policy was to plan the position of graves, Figs 42 and 43, and leave them for a later period when the problems would have lessened, and arrangements were made, at Charmian Woodfield's departure for Sarawak in 1965, for their excavation by Don Brothwell. Unfortunately this arrangement was discontinued. Brothwell was interested because of the likelihood of these being priors, benefactors, the wealthy, and their families, so giving an interestingly narrow social range, and because of the comparatively late date of foundation and short life of the friary (pers. comm. C. Woodfield).

In 1966 Brian Hobley located, and presumably excavated, graves in the E cloister range. No material of this date was found for study.

In 1968 rescue excavation was undertaken by the Woodfields immediately on their return from the Far East, with the assistance of Bob Thompson. This recovered the human remains from stone-lined graves 68/12? (a probable but badly damaged grave), 68/13-15 in the SW area of the choir, and graves 68/16-17, a previously located double stone grave a short distance to the E, Figs 42, 61a-b and 166. Additionally, from an area severely damaged by the road contractors' machinery came skeletal material from a grave or graves in the angle formed by the SW choir and the S transept, graves 68/42-43, Fig. 42. All this material was recorded on record cards in 1968, and this forms the basis for their data in this report. The original material, when it consisted of reasonably complete skeletons, was re-interred by the Friars at Aylesford.

In 1969 a second Woodfield short rescue exercise was undertaken in the area of the sacristy/vestry, which was being damaged by building work. This recorded a disturbed body W of the night stair in an enclosed yard (Grave 69/46), an unusual location, Fig. 43. This body could not be located at Coventry Museum for analysis.

Forty-six graves were noted by Woodfield throughout the church, cloister and lay cemetery (but no material survives for examination from cloister and lay cemetery).

1973 saw the excavation of the W chapter house by Brian Hobley. Some plans and photographs survive, but there are no written records. Nine skeletons from seven? graves (apparently an error) were noted. No material was located for study.

In 1975 there was further clearance in the chapter house. Limited material, apparently from this work, was available for study (Grave 75/3), Fig. 48.

In 1977 clearance work was carried out in advance of landscaping in the presbytery. The majority of material that survived to be studied in the late 1990s came from this work, Fig. 43.

No records of the 1978 investigations seem to have been made, but some material from this survived for study.

DATING

Of the material examined Graves 68/13-17 are 15th century in date. Graves 77/2 and 77/6 are of 14th-century date.(C Woodfield, pers. comm.).

NAVE AND CROSSING

Figure 42

Vandalism and lack of resources did not allow for the excavation of graves in this area, although the site of some half dozen were planned in the eastern bay of the nave, and some score in the crossing. There will have been many more, now destroyed by road works. The material described here is from disturbance, both before and after the Reformation.

62 VI (6)
Disturbed material from piscina drain, S chapel in nave. Phase Friary 2. Premolar from mandible probably PM2. Presumably from a burial disturbed during the life of the friary.

62 XIV 4
Robbing of NW tower pier. Phase Destruction. A proximal 1st phalanx from the left side (?).

64 XVIa (3)
16th-century robbing fill (mosaic tile pit). Phase Destruction. Redeposit of Reformation disturbance of two children's graves. From the passage between the two E nave chapels. An infant humerus, sub-adult first rib, sub-adult metacarpal, sub-adult phalanx, two sub-adult incisors; a second infant first rib, sub-adult vertebra, sub-adult unfused fibula epiphysis, malleolus, infant rib fragments. Infant age approximately 3.5-4.5 years and sub-adult approximately 7-17 years were represented. Might these have been dumped from a reliquary?

WEST CHOIR

The skeletons recovered during the 1968 watching brief (listed above) were reburied at Aylesford Friary in 1968 and were therefore not available for re-examination. A total of six skeletons were briefly described in archive form by P. Woodfield in 1968, and these skeletons are detailed in this report largely on the basis of that data, but with some added comments based on photographic evidence.

Elaborate stone double tomb

The northern side of the W choir (Fig. 42) contained two certain burials, graves 68/13 and 68/14, and one probable burial, 68/12, over these, this latter having been robbed at the Reformation. Curiously there had been no burials at all in the southern and larger tomb, 68/15, Fig. 61b and 166.

Lower grave 68/14
15th or possibly 16th century, Fig. 166. The burial, which was in a ?pine coffin (see Morgan, Section Y), was damaged, presumably by the later insertion of grave 68/14. The cranium was particularly fragmented and it was not possible to assess morphometrics. The post-cranial skeleton was more complete.

Dentition x7x54321/12345678
87654321/12345678

Slight periodontal disease was noted on teeth, as was slight calculus. Evidence for underbite was noted, also a supernumerary tooth germ was observed in the right palate. There was an unusually large attachment for the deltoid muscle on the left humerus indicating a left handed individual. The skeleton was of an adult male, 30+ years old. Stature based on femur length (femur:stature ratio, my determination) is given as 5ft 9in or 1.78m.

Severe osteoarthritis was noted in the cervical and thoracic vertebrae resulting in ankylosing and lipping of vertebral bodies. The skeleton was briefly examined in 1968 by Mr Sargent, an Orthopaedic Surgeon at the Coventry and Warwickshire Hospital, who reported that the individual suffered from *Spondylitis deformans*. Slight periostitis of the metarsals was noted. No other pathologies were seen.

Following examination of site photographs a reassessment of the evidence was possible. It is now probable that rather than *spondylitis deformans* the individual suffered from a condition called DISH (Diffuse Idiopathic Skeletal Hyperostosis). The main spinal change observed in this condition is the presence of massive vertical osteophytes on the right antero-lateral surface of the vertebral bodies of the thoracic spine (where both sides of the vertebrae are affected it is known as Forestiers spine).

A definite classification of DISH cannot however be given as the skeleton was not personally observed and the record card makes no mention of extraspinal manifestations of new bone which must be present for DISH to be recognised. Such manifestation would take the form of new bone growth in ligaments, in tendinous insertions or in cartilage. Osteoarthritis can of course develop in someone with DISH, and when this happens the OA changes are generally extreme. DISH at a fully developed stage is unlikely to be seen under the age of 45. The individual concerned is described as 30+.

It is likely that the condition is DISH rather than Ankylosing Spondylitis as in AS the condition is more prominent in lower thoracic to sacral vertebrae, whereas DISH is found in the thoracic vertebrae, as in this skeleton. AS causes the vertebrae to square-off creating a 'bamboo' spine with calcification at the corners. DISH creates lesious growths over bone flowing down the spine like candle wax, much as seen in the photographs and described to me. The other option would be Reiters syndrome which produces similar lesions visually to DISH; however, Reiters syndrome affects more central to lower thoracic vertebrae whereas DISH occurs predominantly in upper thoracic and lower cervical vertebrae, again as apparent in the photographs of the skeleton.

If the individual suffered from DISH it would have resulted in severe movement restrictions especially in the spine, both in terms of moving forwards and backwards (bending) or from side to side (twisting or turning). In addition the extraspinal manifestations which affect ligaments and tendinous insertions would also severely restrict movement. The condition would have been, and is, painful, frightening to the person concerned (especially so, pre-modern diagnosis) and would have required individual care being given to the patient, who would have needed help with many basic tasks.

Middle grave 68/13
15th or possibly 16th century, Fig. 166. There had been some damage from Reformation robbing. This was recorded as an extended burial partially lying on the right side with hands in the pubic region. The coffin was again thought to be pine (see Morgan, Section Y: *Wood and Charcoal Analysis*). The cranium was incomplete, lacking the face, and the post-cranial skeleton was very fragmentary. The dentition showed considerable occlusal wear and one small caries cavity on a molar (?). The number of teeth present was not recorded. The individual was recorded as a probable female, 40+ years of age, stature not discernible. Slight periostitis of the metatarsals was noted.

Upper grave 68/12
The robbing disturbance was very visible above grave 68/13 and implied the removal of a body some 5ft long, Fig. 166. A fragment of an immature vertebra was retrieved from here, and a juvenile parietal from the contractor's machining which had caught the NW end of the grave. It appears that this is a family burial, presumably benefactors.

The second stone double tomb

Another double tomb (68/16 and 68/17, Fig. 166) occurred some 1.75m to the NE of the above and this was smashed through by the road contractors' machinery.

68/16, the northern burial
Here the machines entirely removed the grave walling at the N, and the skeletal material here described was recovered from the spoil heap. Skeletal finds included a largely complete cranium with slight cribra orbitalis on orbits. Recovered post-cranial bones were thought to belong to this skull, but there was no certainty under the circumstances. These were described as those of a male 50+ years, uncertain stature, no post-cranial disease.

68/17, the southern burial
15th century, Fig. 166. The evening break in the contractor's machining allowed for the excavation of the lower burial. A complete skull was recorded, but only a partial post-cranial skeleton survived due to decaying of the 'underside' within the grave. Stature 1.56m or 5ft 2in (based on femur:stature ratio, my determination): previous estimate 5ft 4in.

Dentition 8x6x4321/123456xx
87654321/1234567-

Described as female, aged 30+ years. No pathology noted except dental.

This was again a double burial of male and female individuals, probably man and wife, and therefore not from the religious friary community.

Graves 42 and 43

Apparently earth graves with one body lying above the other situated some 5m south of Grave 68/17, Fig. 42. The lower part of the bodies was removed by the road contractors.

Grave 42, upper burial
Note that if coffins had existed they would not have been observed in these conditions. Apparently a complete skull and largely complete post-cranial skeleton. Described as male, age 40-50 years, stature estimated at 5ft 10in. Report states that no pathology was evident, but also indicates the presence of cribra orbitalis and osteoporosis.

Dentition -7654321/12345678
87xxx321/12345678

Grave 43, lower burial
Complete skull and incomplete post cranial bones recovered from below Grave 42. Described as sub-adult due to bones not being fully fused. Possibly male.

Dentition --654321/--------

?Grave? 44

This material was recovered from the spoil heap emanating from the area of graves 42 and 43. The bones included 4 fused (ankylosed) thoracic vertebrae.

Area of graves 68/12-15

Unstratified, from road works contractors' machining in the W choir, was a right (juvenile?) parietal bone. This may relate to the destroyed grave 68/12, a robbed juvenile burial which overlay grave 68/13. There has been loss of bone from this context.

EAST CHOIR/PRESBYTERY

The 1977 Presbytery graves show post-excavation damage and loss of skeletal material. Nevertheless it has been possible for the writer to describe four burials in some detail in 1998, Figs 43 and 167.

Grave 77(2): stone grave with rare moulded stone pillow

Figures 43 and 71 No 1123

This comprised a very damaged late 14th or early 15th-century skeleton of an apparently elderly person, with most body parts present but in a fragmentary state. The skull is largely intact with the temporal and occipital absent and all internal facial bones missing. Both scapulae are absent, as is the sternum and manubrium.

No ribs were present. All other bones are present but incomplete.

Dentition xx66x3xx/x23x56xx
xx654321/12345xx8

The teeth are in a very poor state. There is complete loss and resorption of two molars on each side of the mandible and maxilla. This has led to an increased use of the frontal teeth, incisors, canines and pre-molars, which have been worn down to the pulp cavity. More mandibulary teeth are present than maxillary. These show extremely flat and excessively worn occlusal surfaces, and the pulp cavity is clearly exposed on eight teeth. Those molars which have survived show a state of wear, apparently preserved at the time of the loss of the molars, and reliance on the frontal teeth.

Caries was evident on the left mandibular M3 at the medio CEJ and on the right maxillary M3 at labial-distal CEJ. Also on the left maxillary I2 and C occlusal surfaces. Full resorption had occurred at the mandibulary right M2/M3 and left M2?M3 and maxillary right PM2/M1/M3 and left PM1/M2/M3.

Based on dental wear of molars and subsequent wear on incisors, an age of 35-50+ is given. Cranial sutures give an age of 18-50.

Many characteristics were not present to aid in determining the sex of the skeleton. Those present were indeterminate, but favour a female? designation. However, the presence of the stone pillow and its inscription, Fig. 71 No 1123, makes this unlikely (pers. comm. C. Woodfield).

A stature, based on femur:stature ratio and tibia, a height of 1.68-1.72m or 5ft 6-7in(±5cm) is given.

Pathology
Extremely severe pathology of the lower spine was noted. Five lumbar vertbrae (L1-5?) were seen to have been affected. L1/L2 were severely affected, L.2 being flattened. All show union of the articulatory processes and loss of spinous processes and transverse processes, indicating probable spondylosis due to vertebral trauma. They have collapsed anteriorly and would have resulted in a kyphosis. Of the thoracic vertebrae, T.3-12 are present, ten of which exhibit evidence of collapse and bone strengthening. This is all suggestive of vertebral trauma, possibly as a result of osteoporosis of the spine or severe trauma from an outside force, such as a severe fall.

The lateral condyle of the left tibia shows extensive pitting and degeneration of the articulatory surface, which has largely been destroyed. The medial condyle does not exhibit degeneration. Pitting and destruction of bone is evident at the fovea capitis of the left femur head. This is also quite extensive, evidence possibly of the tracking of disease down the ligamentum teres via the psoas muscle, rather than O/A as no eburnation is evident. The right femur head was not visible.

A fracture, (healed) is evident on the left proximal fibula. This was a linear, probably closed (no evidence of infection) fracture, resulting in some displacement and shortening of bone; natural splinting of the fibula and tibia no doubt helped in the healing of this trauma. The fibula has rotated medially and adducted distally. The fracture is well healed, but resulted in a near 180° displacement, despite which a stage 6 healing and full functional reconstruction was achieved.

Avulsion fractures to the left talus at the tibial articulation and navicular articulatory surface were noted. Both occurred at the margin. Slight deformation of the navicular inferior surface was also seen. The left calcaneus is narrow and exhibits bone spurring on the inferior surface, 23mm breadth and 73 mm length.

All the injuries may well be connected and it is certainly not unlikely that the spinal collapse resulted in the fibula fracture and tarsal pathologies. The vertebral trauma may have been caused by an external source of a specific infection. Tuberculosis can lead in severe cases to weakening of the body cavities of vertebrae and collapse. The combination of the spinal collapse and the destruction of bone around the knee point heavily towards TB as a likely source for the pathologies.

Grave 77(4): earth grave in presbytery

Figures 43 and 167

This was a well preserved complete skeleton, within an oak coffin, in front of the High Altar.

Cranial bones. A well preserved nearly complete skull. All bones present. Nasal bones incomplete, as are zygomatic and inferior nasal concha.

Post-cranial bones. Sternum and manubrium not present, right patella also absent. Phalanges, ribs and scapulae incomplete but present. 11 other bones complete.

Dentition x7654321/-2345678
87654321/12345678

All mandibulary teeth are present. The maxilla has all except right M3 and left I1. All teeth exhibited mild-severe calculus. Slight hypoplasia was noted on the maxillary M2 right and M1 left.

Across all the maxilla periodontal disease was evident, with slight pitting of the alveolar on the buccal and labial side. The mandibular right M3 is small and peg-like. The mandible also exhibited overcrowding; this was most evident at the incisors, resulting in rotation of right I1 and I2. The right maxillary M3 was probably lost ante-mortem.

Age. Based on dental wear 17-25, cranial sutures 18+, medial clavicular epiphysis 18-25. An age of 18-25 is given.

Sex determination. Cranial morphology and metric traits of post-cranial bones unambiguously indicate a female skeleton.

Stature. Based on femur:stature ratio a height of 1.64m or 5ft 4in (±5cm) is given.

Pathology. No definite pathology was determined. Bowing of the right distal fibula and left distal humerus may indicate well-healed (greenstick?) fractures.

Metric and non-metric traits. Facial indices indicate an individual with a narrow slender face and orbits, but with otherwise average cranial indices.

Discussion. The skeleton represents a young adult female, who suffered from poor dental hygiene.

Grave 77(5): earth grave in presbytery

Figures 43 and 167

The remains comprised a now incomplete and largely fragmented skeleton, which had also been buried in front of the High Altar. Those bone parts that were present were largely damaged.

Cranial bones. The skull was damaged but with most components present. There was no mandible.

Post cranial bones. The post cranial skeleton was in a mixed state. The only complete bones were as follows: right scapula, left ulna, left radius, right and left femorae and tibiae, left fibula. The vertebrae were largely lacking with only cervical 1-5 and first thoracic present. No ribs were present.

Dentition 87654321/1234567-
--------/--------

All maxillary teeth were present, except left M3. Advanced caries were noted on the right and left PM1 and 2 distal and medial. Other than the caries on the premolars which are severe, little wear on other teeth was noted, especially molars. Occlusal wear was most evident on the incisors, especially I1 on the left side. All molar cusps were clear. M3 left appears to have only recently erupted and M3 right has been lost post-mortem.

Age. Based on dental wear, 18-25 years; on cranial sutures, 18-50 years. An age of 18+ is given.

Sex determination. Cranial morphology and post-cranial metrics all indicate a female skeleton.

Stature. Based on Lundy-Femur:Stature Ratio, a height of 1.61m or 5ft 3in is given (±5cm).

Pathologies and non-metric traits. No pathologies (other than dental, previously mentioned) were observed.

Discussion. The skeleton is that of an adult female, young to early middle age, who suffered from poor oral hygiene.

Grave 77(6): stone grave in presbytery

Figure 43

This comprised an incomplete 14th-century skeleton now in a largely fragmentary state.

Cranial bones. The cranium is largely present but fragmentary. The maxilla and most of the facial bones are missing.

Post-cranial bones. The upper body consisted of largely incomplete bones, the left scapula and all ribs being absent, along with the manubrium and sternum. The lower body was in a better state of preservation. Both femurs, the left tibia and both sets of tarsals and metatarsals were complete. All the other lower body bones, except the left patella, were present but incomplete.

Dentition ----4321/12345---
87654321/12345--8

The maxillary right premolar 2 and all three molars, and left molars were absent, lost post-mortem. Also lost post-mortem were the mandibulary left second and third molars. Caries were present on 5 of the 23 teeth. On mandibulary right M1 and M2 were large caries on the left I2 mesial, large and PM1 and PM2 CEJ mesial, large. Calculus was present on the right mandibulary teeth, I1/2 and C and left I1/2, C and PM1 and 2. On all teeth it was slight on buccal and lingual surfaces. The third molars on the mandible had only recently erupted and show no signs of wear. The caries present are very severe and have on the mandible eroded the main body of the teeth involved. The teeth also exhibit evidence of severe overbite and uneven tooth wear.

Age. Based on molar wear: 35-45+, uneven wear. Cranial suture closure 50+. An age of 40-50+ is given.

Sex determination.. Many characteristics were unavailable for study. Those characteristics present gave mixed results and a sex of probable Male/Male? is given.

Metric and Non- Metric traits. All bones were too fragmentary and eroded to assess for metrics or non-metrics.

Pathologies. A single body fragment of a lumbar vertebrae (unplaced) exhibits evidence of severe spinal collapse on the right side of the body, posteriorly. This indicates spinal trauma, whose cause is uncertain, but is either external or possibly from specific infection such as TB. It would have resulted in a scoliosis and possible kypho-scoliosis.

Discussion. This skeleton was that of a probable middle aged male, who suffered from poor dental hygiene and spinal problems, possibly caused by specific infection.

Note. There is no surviving material from graves 77/1, 77/3, 77/7 and 77/8.

CHAPTER HOUSE

Figure 48

Partial Grave 75(3): earth grave in chapter house

Most of the skeletons in the western chapter house had been excavated, and lost, (or possibly not excavated?) in 1973. This was what remained under the eastern baulk.

Fragmentary skeletal, representing the majority of the cranium and very eroded tibiae and a right femur. The skull consisted of a complete mandible, maxilla, nasal bones, palate and frontal bone. All other cranial bones present were fragmentary. A right femur and right and left tibiae were present but incomplete. No other bones survived. Due to the lack of bone parts only an age of 18+ was determinable. The majority of characteristics and morphometrics necessary to determine sex were absent. A determination of male is given on the basis of chin shape alone. No pathology and no non-metric traits were observed. Given the location of this burial it is likely to be that of a friar.

WF 78?

A box marked 'CHAPTER HOUSE' contained the remains from three graves of unknown nature, apparently from underneath the blocking of the gap in the cloister range E wall, built after the 18th-century demolition of the Chapter House. No other information is recorded, nor do they occur on any plans. It is not impossible that one may have been of the well-known Carmelite William of Lubbenham, Head of the English Order, known to have been buried at the entrance to the Chapter house (C Woodfield, pers. comm.).

The bones of an unsexed and incomplete skeleton represented the lower limbs. Right and left damaged tibiae were present, possibly from a single individual. In addition there were shaft fragments of fibulae and femorae. It is not impossible that all bones were from a single individual. Only the tibiae were measured. These were 399mm long and give an estimated stature of 1.79m (5 ft 10.5in) if male. They are adult bones 18+ years. Sex of the bones was not discernible and no pathologies were evident.

Box 001

This box contained the fragmentary remains of two individuals, an adult and a juvenile. No records survive but they are presumably also from the Chapter House or other 1978 clearances SE of the cloister and E of the chapter house. However the burials of women and small children are not very likely in a Chapter House, and their provenance should be regarded as uncertain.

The juvenile skeleton consisted of a fragmentary cranium with all parts present but incomplete, complete right and left ribs, incomplete right scapula and humerus, and a complete right clavicle and manubrium and all vertebral bodies; all other bones were absent.

Dentition -DCBA/---DE, erupting 6 right and left
EDCBA/ABC--, erupting 6 and 5 right, 6 left, 1 right due to erupt.

The maxillary deciduous dentition consist of only the first left molar and right first and second incisors, canine and first molar, with both first permanent molars erupted. The mandible holds deciduous right incisors, canine and molars, and left incisors and canine with both left permanent first molars erupted and the second premolar erupting and permanent incisors formed and close to eruption. One carie was visible on the left deciduous mandibular molar which was large and mesial. No other pathology was visible but wear on the deciduous teeth was heavy.

Based on dental eruption and size of humerus and clavicle an age of 6 years ±24 months is estimated. Sex was not determinable, nor were any non-metric traits observed.

The adult skeleton consisted of an incomplete cranium with a damaged right parietal and right side of frontal and temporal. The face was missing and the occipital damaged. Post-cranial bones included the left humerus, atlas and axis, left side of the mandible, left distal half of femur, damaged left scapula and left coronoid half of clavicle. Metrics deduced were for head of humerus at 41mm and glenoid cavity at 33mm, suggesting a female skeleton. Morphologically there was a small nuchal crest, a low long vault to the skull and small mastoid processes, again suggesting a female individual.

DISCUSSION

The skeletal population analysed and detailed below, is both too small and too fragmentary to discuss in any detail. The percentages given above need to be considered with caution, as they are very reflective of the poor state of preservation, and lack of complete recovery from the site.

Broad themes can be noted for the population. There are more males than females, but equally as many skeletons were unsexed as designated to be male. A total of 40% had pathologies which is quite a high figure and may indicate both an environment of high disease threshold, poor diet (though presumably not in the sense of poverty) and hard physical activity/work.

Equally those with pathologies had carried them for some time, as all were either in an advanced state, or, in the case of fractures, had healed. Thus a degree of care may have been available and medicine which may have contained, if not cured, disease. It also suggests that these skeletons had good immune systems, possibly as a result of early exposure to disease in infant and youth life. Of the pathologies over 70% were dental, which implies poor dental hygiene, and no doubt bad breath. Caries were noted in all ages and equally between sexes. This may well be a reflection of diet. However, the number of caries per person was only on average, two, suggesting dental health was not that bad. Yet where it had occurred it was severe and was present in all age groups. There was also a very small percentage with calculus.

The individuals detailed are from the presbytery and choir, with a small survival from the chapter house; they are not from the Lay and Friars cemeteries. They are therefore of presumably higher status. This may in part account for the low level of severe (occupational) pathologies, and may also account for the high level of tooth decay, which may reflect greater access to sugar-rich products.

Stature between the sexes was in the order of 3-8in difference. This may be a reflection of genetics or differential access to food in youth, or may be largely skewed by the sample available.

Figs 42 and 43 record the position of planned graves, both excavated as described above and unexcavated. Fig. 48 shows the known position of most of the excavated W Chapter House graves, now lost. It is possible that the eastern Chapter House graves survive *in situ* and an altar tomb was recorded at its E end in 1800. A full list of graves in contained in the archive. The painted and carved fragments of stone thought to come from the more elaborate graves are considered by P. Woodfield under *Architectural Stonework* (Section F).

SUMMARY

Total number of individuals: 21.
Number and percentage of females: 5 (23%).
Number and percentage of males: 8 (38%).
Number and percentage unsexed: 8 (38%).
Stature ranges: Males 5ft 7in to 5ft 10in and Females 5ft 2in to 5ft 4in.
Number and percentage with pathologies: 9 (42%). A total of 15 pathologies were evident.
Number and percentages with non-metric traits: 4 skeletons (19%).
Percentage of pathology types: 7 pathologies were dental, 77% of pathologies. 2 pathologies were trauma related, 22%. 2 were degeneration, 22%. 3 possible specific infections were noted, 33% of individuals with pathologies. 1 evidence of non-specific infection was seen, 11%.

Tabulated details of skeletons

Year	**Grave**	**Sex**	**Age**	**Stature**	**Pathology**
78?	Box 1	F?	18+	n/a	n/a
78?	Box 1	?	6 ±24 mnths?	?	dental
77	PRES 77/6	M?	45-50	5ft 8in	dental
77	PRES 77/5	F	18+	5ft 3in	dental
77	PRES 77/4	F	18-25	5ft 4in	trauma dental
77	PRES 77/2	M?	40-50	5ft 7in	trauma spec.inf. dental
75	CH.HO. 75/3	M?	18+	n/a	none
78	CH.HO. ?	M?	18+	5ft 9in	?
62VI	NAVE Rob ?.	?	adult	?	?
64	NAVE tile pit ?	?	3.5-4.5	?	?
64	NAVE tile pit ?	?	7-12	?	?
62 XIV	NAVE ?	?	adult	?	?
63	E.CLOISTER ?	?	adult	?	?
68	CHOIR u/s ?	?	juvenile	?	?
68	CHOIR u/s ?	?	adult	?	?
68	CHOIR 68/13	F	40+	n/a	Non-spec.
68	CHOIR 68/14	M	30+	5ft 9in	dental degen.
68	CHOIR 68/16	M	50+	n/a	n/a
68	CHOIR 68/17	F	30+	5ft 2in	spc.inf. dental.
68	CHOIR 68/42	M	40-50	5ft 10in	spec.inf. degen.
68	CHOIR 68/43	M?	sub-adult	n/a	n/a

Number of teeth: 204 from ten individuals.
Number and percentage of caries: 20 (9.8% of teeth) plus 1 from skeleton 68/13, with unspecified number of teeth located.
Percentage of skeletons with calculus: 4 skeletons (19% of all skeletons, 57% of skeletons with dental pathology).
Percentage of skeletons with hypoplasia: 1 (4.7% of all skeletons, 14% of skeletons with dental pathology).

Non metric traits.

Trait	**Number of Skeletons**	**Skeleton Numbers**
Wormian bone	1	68 Upper grave 68/13
Supernumerary teeth	1	68 Lower grave 68/14
Os Lambdoid suture	2	77 Graves 2 and 4
Supra-orbital foramina	1	77 Grave 2
Metopic suture open	1	77 Grave 2
Parietal notch bone	1	77 Grave 4
Supra-orbital notch	1	77 Grave 4
Acc.infra-orbital foramina	1	77 Grave 4
F. spinosum open to f.Lacerum	1	77 Grave 4
Multiple zygomatico-facial Foramina	1	77 Grave 4
Lateral tibial squatting facet	1	77 Grave 4
Medial talar facet	1	77 Grave 4
Atlas double facet	1	77 Grave 4
Ant calcaneal facet double	1	77 Grave 4
Inf. talar artic. surface	1	77 Grave 4

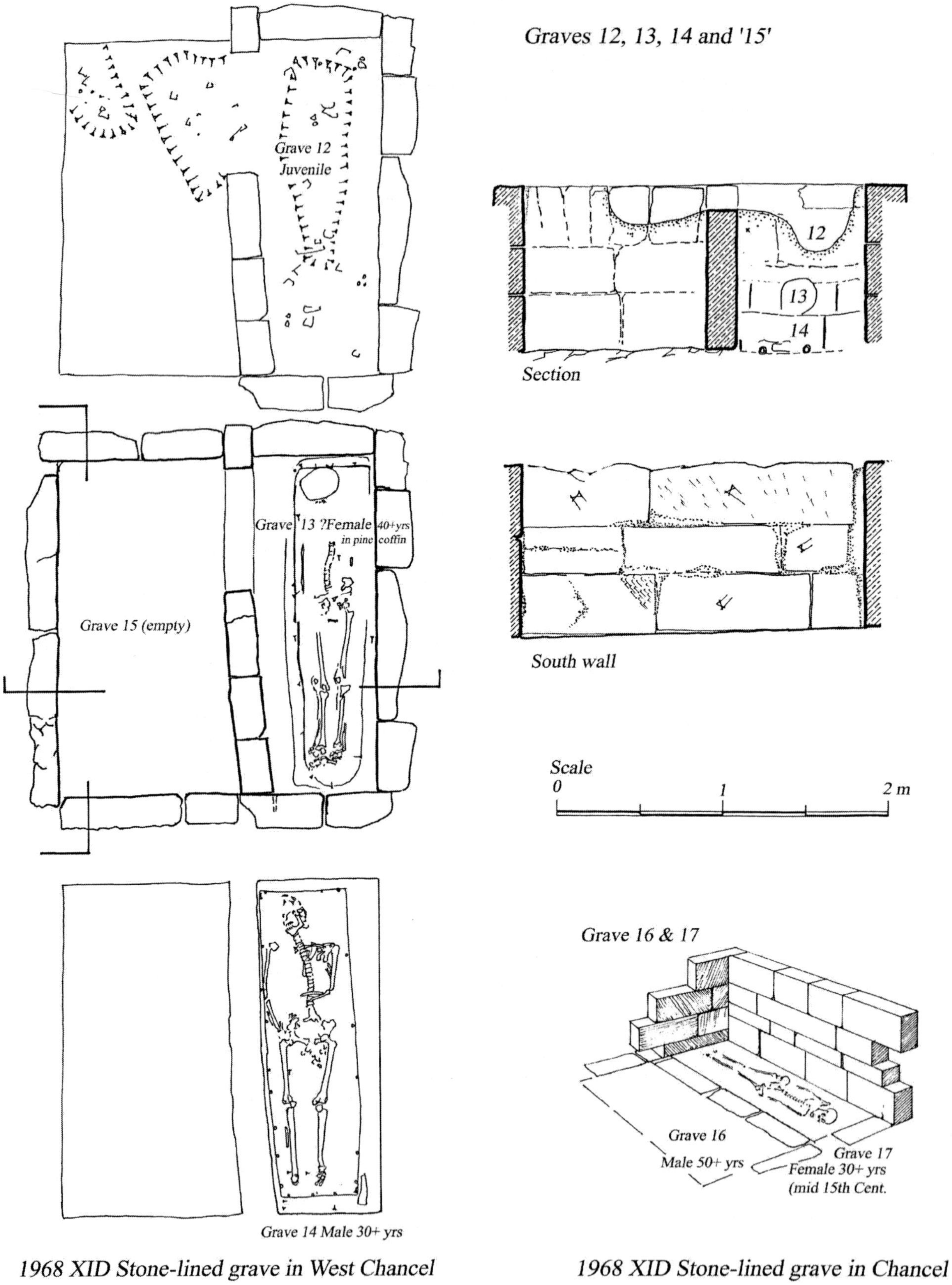

Figure 166 The stone-lined graves in the Chancel: 12-15 and 16-17 (68 X1 D).

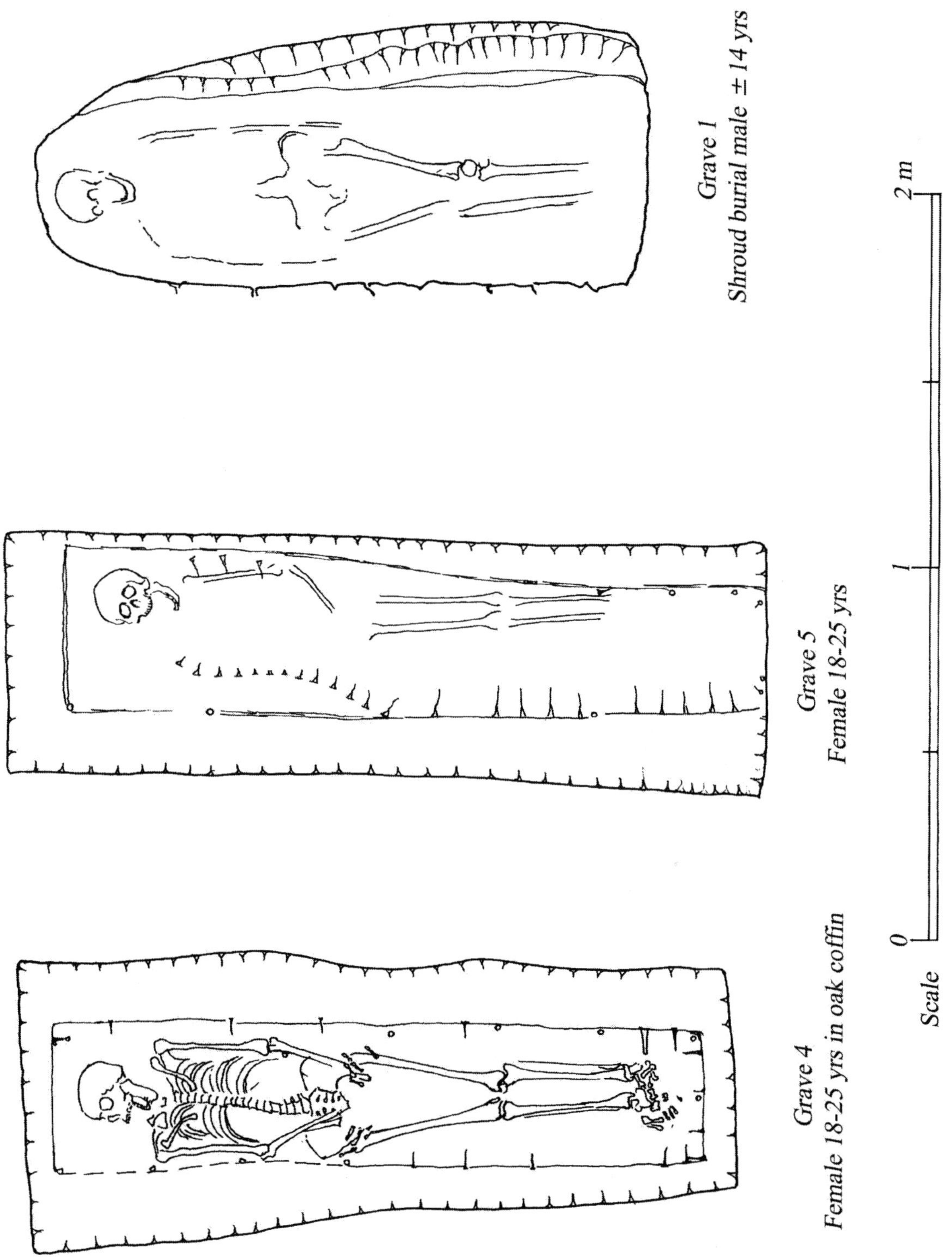

Figure 167 Plans of Graves 1 (1960 II, in doorway to chancel) and 4-5 (1977, in front of High Altar).

SECTION X
THE ANIMAL BONE

J. Rackham

INTRODUCTION

The main requirements for this report were:

a) to identify specimens of mammal bone and shell from the surviving unpublished material from the Whitefriars excavations, for the Pre-friary to Friary Destruction phases. Unfortunately less than 10% of the excavated material from the period of the Friary has survived, Table 9.

b) to identify wild bird and fish species for the Friary and subsequent 16th-century phases, chiefly from the Grammar School, Table 10.

c) to re-examine and identify wild bird and fish species not covered in Holmes' 1981 publication of bone from the School phase, Table 11.

Further:

d) The preparation of a brief report on significant assemblages, e.g. the sheep bones from the School deposit.

e) The study of the butchery of the bones in the School deposit, previously identified by Stephanie Pinter-Bellows (pers. comm. to C. Woodfield) as warranting further study.

d) and e) are available in archive.

The bulk of the surviving material from the site was reported on by Jonathan Holmes (1981), then of the Cambridge University Veterinary School, a report comprehensive for its period. This material was derived from excavations in 1960-1962, although the bird bones, other than domestic species, and virtually all the fish bones, were not then identified; this report, on a unique deposit of the Age of Transition, for no other Grammar Schools are thought to have been excavated, was concerned only with material related to those Grammar School deposits of *c.*1545 to *c.*1557/58 found in the resonance passages under the choir stalls, deposit (a), some 2,150 items, together with material from the clay seal over that deposit, (b), 70 items, with a *terminus post quem* of 1572, and from the small scale robbing disturbances overlying that clay layer which contained 95% 16th-century material (c), some 150 items. Subsequent rescue work at the Whitefriars site by Woodfield in 1968 and 1969, and excavation by Coventry Museum in 1977, was known to have produced further animal bone which had not been studied. The material originally studied by Holmes had been sorted at Cambridge into species groups for teaching purposes, irrespective of original archaeological context. Fortunately all the material excavated in the early 1960s by Charmian Woodfield had been individually marked by her, and except for a few fractured fragments could be assigned to their original contexts. It seems that the complete assemblage originally studied by Holmes cannot be totally accounted for, but it is evident that the vast majority of this material, returned to Woodfield in 1993 and so surviving, has been located. However, Holmes records 351 bird bones from the Grammar School deposits of the resonance passage, while only 295 have been recorded in this exercise, so it is clear that some bird material has been lost, and a small number of rabbit bones also appear to be missing.

RECORDING OF UNPUBLISHED MATERIAL

This material was identified and recorded (in archive), but it presents considerable problems. None of the material from the large-scale 1964 excavations (nave, crossing, NW cloister) survives in the Museum stores, except for the bone from 16th-century robbing of the vaulted tomb, grave 19, 64 XXI 3, Fig. 42. Twenty-five of the 1968 contexts had been mixed at Coventry Museum and put under one context number, combining some six hundred years of activity. From the Woodfield 1969 excavations virtually only the material collected by the road contractors from the late Hales' period well to the N of the church, 1969.130 (with the inevitable cat bones) survived, together with a humerus of a very large robust ram from a Hales' context, 69 XXIX 5, Fig. 43; sadly the only survivor of what would have been an interesting wealthy Renaissance household sample.

The bulk of the Museum 1977/78 excavations' material is from unstratified clearance 'areas', and none of it can now be related to periods in the life of the friary, or later centuries. There are, however, five apparently stratified contexts from the 1997/78 excavations. Material from the fill of the 1977/8 presbytery grave, Fig. 43, is likely to be from the underlying Pre-friary clay pit. F.23 is the 15th-century reredos wall, and the worked red deer and cattle longbone indicate an industrial relationship to that clay pit, into which the reredos footings would have been dug.

Species Name	PHASE: Pre-friary	Friary	Friary 2	Rebuild	Fabrica	Hales	Hales/Industrial, Late Friary	New School (material)	School/ Industrial	Destruction	Collapse	Late Hales	18th Century
Human	-	-	-	-	-	-	-	-	-	-	-	-	-
Horse	-	-	-	-	-	-	-	-	-	-	-	-	-
Cattle	5	-	-	-	9	-	3	-	1	2	2	2	1
Sheep/Goat	7	-	2	-	12	4	1	2	-	3	5	2	3
Sheep	-	-	1	-	3	1	1	-	-	-	-	-	4
Pig	-	-	1	-	11	-	-	3	-	3	-	1	-
Cattle Size	13	-	1	-	54	5	-	2	-	5	1	1	1
Sheep Size	5	-	1	-	18	1	-	5	-	4	-	-	-
Red deer	1	-	-	-	-	-	-	-	-	-	-	-	-
Fallow deer	-	-	-	-	-	-	-	-	-	1	-	-	1
Dog	-	-	-	-	-	-	-	-	-	1	-	-	-
Cat	1	-	-	-	1	-	-	-	-	-	-	1	-
Brown hare	-	-	-	-	-	-	-	-	-	-	-	-	-
Rabbit	2	-	-	-	1	-	-	-	-	-	-	-	-
Small animal rabbit/cat size	-	-	-	-	2	-	-	-	-	-	-	-	-
Elephant ivory	-	-	-	-	-	-	-	-	-	-	-	-	1
Unidentified	1	3	-	-	-	18	-	1	-	4	-	-	-
Snail, *Cepeae sp.*	-	-	-	-	-	-	-	-	-	1	1	-	-
Snail, *Helix sp.*	-	-	-	-	-	1	-	-	-	5	2	-	-
Cockle	-	-	-	-	-	-	-	7	-	-	-	-	1
Mussel	-	-	-	-	-	-	1	4	-	1	-	-	-
Oyster	-	-	-	-	-	2	1	3	-	8	2	-	7
Contexts	62 II 5 F. 23 (77)	61 VI 8 62 VI 10 62 VI 11		Nil	F. 110 F. 92c F. 24 All 1977	62 II 3 62 VIII 2 69 XXIX 5	62 Cl. Bay 8.1 68 XXVII 2	?? Ex window glass boxes	62 III 7	64 XXI 3 62 III 4 62 VI 2 62 VI 3 Grave 3 (77)	62 II 2 62 III 1	69 XXIX 13	69 XXIX 1 69 XXIX 8 F. 10 (77) F. 15 (77)

Table 9 Identified specimens of mammal bone and shell from the surviving material from Coventry Whitefriars

	PHASE											
Species Name	Pre-friary	Friary	Friary and Friary 2	Rebuild	Fabrica	Hales	New School (material)	School/ Industrial	Destruction	Collapse	F. 130	18th Century
Chicken	6	-	1	1	10	-	120	15	6	4	-	-
cf juv. chicken	-	-	-	-	3	-	5	1	-	-	-	-
Chicken size	18	-	1	-	49	4	1	2	1	1	1	-
Turkey	-	-	-	-	-	-	4	-	-	-	-	-
Duck sp. domestic ?	-	-	-	-	3	-	4	1	-	-	-	-
cf Mallard	-	-	-	-	(2)	-	1	-	1	-	-	-
Juv. - duck size	-	-	-	-	1	-	-	-	-	-	-	-
Goose	1	-	-	-	2 (1 Juv.)	-	101 (1 Juv.)	9	3	1	1	2
Goose size	-	-	-	-	2	-	5 (1 Juv.)	4	-	-	-	-
Grey Heron	-	-	-	-	1	-	1	-	-	-	-	-
Swan	-	-	-	-	-	-	1	-	-	-	-	-
cf Teal	-	-	-	-	-	-	5	-	-	-	-	-
Kite	-	-	-	-	-	-	1	-	-	-	-	-
Sparrowhawk	-	-	-	-	-	-	1	-	-	-	-	-
Galliformes	-	-	-	-	-	-	2	-	-	-	-	-
Grey partridge	-	-	-	-	-	-	1	-	-	-	-	-
Woodcock	-	-	-	-	1	-	3	2	1	-	-	-
cf Woodcock	-	-	-	-	-	-	2	-	-	-	-	-
cf Snipe	-	-	-	-	-	-	1	-	-	-	-	-
Pigeon sp.	-	-	-	-	2 (Juv.)	-	2 (1 Juv.)	-	-	-	-	-
cf Pigeon	-	-	-	-	2	-	-	-	-	-	-	-
Thrush family	-	-	-	-	-	-	2	-	-	-	-	-
cf Crow	-	-	-	-	-	-	1	-	-	-	-	-
Jackdaw	-	-	-	-	2	-	4	-	-	-	-	-
cf Jackdaw	-	-	-	-	1	-	3	-	-	-	-	-
Crow or Rook	-	-	-	-	-	-	1	1	-	-	-	-
Unidentified bird	-	-	-	-	2	-	22	4	-	-	-	-
Gadidae (cod size)	-	-	-	-	-	-	2	-	1	-	-	-
Large gadid size	-	-	-	-	-	-	12	-	1	-	-	-
Cod	-	-	-	-	5	-	3	-	-	-	-	-
Roker (Ray)	-	-	-	-	-	-	1	-	-	-	-	-
Pike	-	-	-	-	1	-	-	-	-	-	-	-
Conger eel	-	-	-	-	1	-	-	-	-	-	-	-
Unidentified fish	-	-	-	-	5	-	1	3	-	-	-	-
Contexts	60 I 16 Quarry 62 II 5 77 F. 23	Nil	60 II 10 Grave 62 VI 11	60 III 4	F. 110 F. 92c F. 24 All 1977	62 II 3	60 II 9 61 XI Ad 61 XI Add 61 XI Ade 61 XII 4 61 XII 7 62 I 4	62 II 1a 62 III 7	60 II 8 61 XI Ag 62 I 3 62 VI 3 64 XXI 3 77 Grave 3 (disturbed)	61 XI Af 62 II 2		60 II 7 60 II 8 Disturbed SRP

Table 10 Bird and fish species identified from Coventry Whitefriars

No 1977/78 material survives from the period of the friary, but material does survive from the Dissolution period, related to the conversion of the reredorter to a workshop, Fig. 49. F.24 is the fill of the ?latrine drain F.35, which appears to relate to the Fabrica (workshop) phase of the late 1530s/early 1540s, as does F.92c (levelling over the reredorter to form the workshop floor, Fig. 52). Pit 110 (position known, but no plan) seems likely again to be associated with the Fabrica phase. The above five contexts are included in Tables 9 and 10.

Unfortunately the material from two or perhaps three wells excavated in 1977/78 does not survive, and no material survives either from the Museum excavations of 1956, 1966, and 1975.

Table 9 summarises the surviving previously unpublished assemblage (wild birds and fish are excluded since these are dealt with below), i.e. mammals and shells.

Table 10 lists bird bones and fish species from the 16th-century School, Fabrica (workshop),and Destruction deposits.

Table 11 lists bird bone elements from the School and School/Industrial phases.

Since the bird bones from the resonance passage had been sorted at some period into 'species groups' the question was raised as to the accuracy of some of the original identifications, and so it was decided to re-record all the bird bones in the entire stratified assemblage. This material is summarised in Table 10. Table 11 lists the elements of the bird bones from the school and school industrial phases. Wild bird and problematic specimens were compared with the reference material in the Natural History Museum collection at Tring.

It is noted above that there has clearly been some loss of bird bones from the School collection. The bulk of this material appears to be a loss from the chicken component identified by Holmes, since Holmes' analysis produced a ratio of goose to chicken in the School sample of 88:187, while in the present study it is 98:125. The increase in goose bones and a few more duck bones present is insufficient to account for the drop in chicken of some 60 bone fragments. A quantity of fragmented bird bone was not catalogued in this present exercise and it is possible that some of this material was identified by Holmes as chicken which may account for at least some of the missing material. The data recorded during this study from the School phase is presented in a similar format to that of Holmes so that the results can be directly compared.

A single carpo-metacarpus of a peacock was identified by Holmes. A bone that was thought might be this has now been re-examined and, along with three other bones, has been identified as turkey. Three of the turkey bones are derived from the School resonance passage deposits, and the fourth from the red sand overlying this deposit, 61 XI Ag. However, I am informed by Charmian Woodfield of a sentence in her March 1993, acknowledgement list of returned material, sent to Holmes 'Six boxes from the Free Grammar School resonance passages published in 1981 divided up into species. This is not quite complete, e.g. peacock and fish are certainly missing'. The peacock therefore has to remain an enigma, but Charmian Woodfield also reminds me that Peter Brears, on the Radio 4 Seasonal Food programme of December 29th, 1998, commented that turkeys were of the same food status as peacocks and swans at this period, making the presence of such a bird not unlikely.

Thirsk (1967) records that turkeys were introduced into Britain in the 1520s and Maltby (1979) found one specimen in a deposit dated to the middle 16th century in Exeter. The School deposits, dating from *c.*1545-*c.*1558, are broadly contemporary with this find. Whether all the turkey bones derive from a single specimen could not be established. Concerning the status and cost of turkeys at this period, Brears refers (*in. litt* to Charmian Woodfield) to 'Archbishop Cranmer's constitution of 1541, as quoted in R. Warner, *Antiquitates Culinariae*, (London 1791), XVIII. This instructed both archbishops and all the bishops, deans and archdeacons to modify the fare served at their tables, and also provided that "of the greater fyshes or fowles, there should be but one in a dishe, as crane, swan, turkey cocke, hadocke, pyke, tench;.....*Memorandum*, that this order was kept for two or three monethes, tyll by the disusyng of certaine wylful persons it came to the olde excesse". M. C. Anne Wilson (1976, 118) notes that turkeys appear in the lists of market prices in London in 1555, when turkey cocks were 6/- each and chickens 2/6d'. Turkeys appear quite frequently in background landscapes of this period, e.g. in a German 16th-century painting of Orpheus in the Castelvecchio Museum, Verona.

Only a single swan bone was identified, and this a carpo-metacarpus (not the tarso-metatarsus identified by Holmes) which could not be taken to species. Holmes records 12 bones of pigeon, but only seven have been identified during the present study.

A number of small game birds present in the assemblages must derive from food consumption, including teal, woodcock, snipe, grey partridge and pigeon. Larger food species include heron and mute or whooper swan. Of these bones only a heron tarso-metatarsus shows physical evidence of butchery. Most of the other non-game birds appear likely to have been living in or around the church and conventual buildings, probably nesting in these structures. This would have been even more likely if parts were becoming ruinous. The jackdaws and crows would happily have frequented this habitat, as would the pigeons. A number of juvenile bones among the jackdaw suggest fledgling casualties, or perhaps juveniles that may have been caught and eaten. Kite and sparrowhawk would not have been out of place and could have nested

Name	CHIK	CHSZ	CKSZ	GALL	PART	TURK	CYGN	GOOS	GSZE	cMALL	DUCK	cTEAL	UNIB	HERO	COLUM	cCROW	CORV	JACK	cJACK	WOOD	cWOOD	cSNIP	KITE	SPHK	TURD
skull	-	-	-	-	-	-	-	-	-	-	-	-	-	-	-	-	-	-	-	-	-	-	-	-	-
mandible	1	-	-		-	-	-	1	-	-	-	-	-	-	-	-	-	-	-	-	-	-	-	-	-
tracheal rng	-	-	-	-	-	-	-	-	-	-	-	-	1	-	-	-	-	-	-	-	-	-	-	-	-
atlas	-	-	-	-	-	-	-	-	-	-	-	-	-	-	-	-	-	-	-	-	-	-	-	-	-
axis	-	-	-	-	-	-	-	1	-	-	-	-	-	-	-	-	-	-	-	-	-	-	-	-	-
cervical vert.	-	-	-	-	-	-	-	-	-	-	-	-	-	-	-	-	-	-	-	-	-	-	-	-	-
thoracic vert.	-	-	-	-	-	-	-	-	-	-	-	-	-	-	-	-	-	-	-	-	-	-	-	-	-
lumbar vert.	4	-	-	-	-	-	-	-	-	-	-	-	-	-	-	-	-	-	-	-	-	-	-	-	-
caudal vert.	-	-	-	-	-	-	-	-	-	-	-	-	-	-	-	-	-	-	-	-	-	-	-	-	-
vertebra	3	-	-	-	-	-	-	2	-	-	-	-	-	-	-	-	-	-	-	-	-	-	-	-	-
rib	9	-	-	-	-	-	-	-	8	-	-	-	1	-	-	-	-	-	-	-	-	-	-	-	-
sternum	7	1	-	-	-	-	-	3	-	-	-	2	-	-	-	-	-	-	-	-	-	-	-	-	-
coracoid	7	-	-	-	1	-	-	1	-	-	-	1	2	-	1	-	-	1	-	-	-	-	-	-	1
clavicle	5	-	-	-	-	-	-	1	-	-	-	1	-	-	-	-	-	-	-	-	-	-	-	-	-
scapula	6	-	-	-	-	-	-	2	-	-	-	-	-	-	-	-	-	-	-	-	1	-	-	-	-
humerus	11	-	-	2	-	1	-	20	-	-	4	1	1	-	-	-	-	-	-	-	-	1	-	-	-
radius	5	-	-	-	-	-	-	3	-	-	-	-	2	-	-	-	-	-	-	3	1	-	-	-	-
ulna	7	-	-	-	-	-	-	5	-	1	-	-	1	-	1	-	-	-	1	-	-	-	1	-	1
metacarpus	-	-	-	-	-	1	1	23	-	-	1	-	-	-	-	-	-	-	-	-	-	-	-	-	-
wing phalanx 1	-	-	-	-	-	-	-	7	-	-	-	-	-	-	-	-	-	-	-	-	-	-	-	-	-
phalanx 1, digit 1	-	-	-	-	-	-	-	3	-	-	-	-	-	-	-	-	-	-	-	-	-	-	-	-	-
phalanx 1, digit 2	-	-	-	-	-	-	-	4	-	-	-	-	-	-	-	-	-	-	-	-	-	-	-	-	-
lumbosacrale	16	2	-	-	-	-	-	16	1	-	-	-	-	-	-	-	-	-	-	1	-	-	-	-	-
femur	11	-	-	-	-	1	-	1	-	-	-	-	1	-	-	-	1	-	-	-	-	-	-	1	-
tibia	29	-	1	-	-	-	-	7	-	-	-	-	1	-	-	1	-	2	-	-	-	-	-	-	-
fibula	5	-	-	-	-	-	-	4	-	-	-	-	-	-	-	-	-	-	-	-	-	-	-	-	-
metatarsus	12	-	-	-	-	-	-	3	-	-	-	-	-	1	-	-	1	1	2	1	-	-	-	-	-
phalanx 1	-	-	-	-	-	-	-	-	-	-	-	-	-	-	-	-	-	-	-	-	-	-	-	-	-
phalanx 2	1	-	-	-	-	-	-	-	1	-	-	-	-	-	-	-	-	-	-	-	-	-	-	-	-
long bone fragment	-	-	-	-	-	-	-	-	2	-	-	-	4	-	-	-	-	-	-	-	-	-	-	-	-
unidentified	-	-	-	-	-	-	-	-	2	-	-	-	14	-	-	-	-	-	-	-	-	-	-	-	-

Table 11 Bird bone elements from the 'school' and 'school/industrial' phases at Coventry Whitefriars

Table 12

Key to Table 11.

CHIK	Chicken
CHSZ	Chicken size
CKSZ	Chicken size
GALL	Galliformes (pheasant, etc.)
PART	Grey partridge
TURK	Turkey
CYGN	Swan sp.
GOOS	Goose, dom.
GSZE	Goose size
cMALL	cf Mallard
DUCK	Duck
TEAL	cf Teal
UNIB	Bird indet.
HERO	Heron
COLUM	Pigeon sp.
cCROW	cf Crow
CORV	Crow or rook
JACK	Jackdaw
cJACK	cf Jackdaw
WOOD	Woodcock
cWOOD	cf Woodcock
cSNIP	cf Snipe
KITE	Kite
SPHK	Sparrowhawk
TURD	Turdidae, thrush

in the church tower, or the superstructures of other buildings. The thrush bones, on the basis of their size probably song thrush *(Turdus philomeles),* could have been either a natural casualty or a food item).

Referring to domestic birds, the question of whether the schoolboys indulged in cock fighting is raised, for three cockerel spurred tarso-metatarsi, are recorded. The two, unusually matching, tarso-metatarsi found together in the 61 XI Ad School resonance passage deposit being perhaps more likely to be a fight casualty from the site rather than food discards.

As regards geese, in two of the School phase wing phalanges there are axial cut marks which may be related to the removal of the feathers, particularly the primary feathers which may have been important as quills. Pen knives for cutting quills were recovered from the resonance passage (Woodfield 1981, fig. 4).

FISH BONES FROM THE 16TH-CENTURY SCHOOL, FABRICA (WORKSHOP) AND DESTRUCTION DEPOSITS

All the fish bones clearly derive from food waste. Apart from the pike these are marine species and include cod, conger eel, skate (now lost) and thornback ray. They indicate a supply of dried or salted fish to the city.

As to shell fish, cockles only survive from the School, but this apparent absence from other periods is probably due to material being discarded post-excavation.

The range and frequency of the species eaten at the School appears unlikely to reflect the general diet in Coventry at this time. The presence of the wild game birds, the frequency, recorded by Holmes, of rabbit bones, goose bones, and occasional bones of hare, red and fallow deer suggest a higher standard of fare than the general urban population. Interestingly there appears to be a wide diversity of sheep populations being exploited. Holmes (1981, Table 7a) notes a wide range for the withers height estimates, and although some of this can be expected to be taken up by dimorphism between the sexes and some changes during growth this wide range is likely to be due to animals coming from a number of different sheep populations, a not unexpected situation for the food supply to a large city; see archive report for a further discussion of this point.

CONCLUSIONS

It will be clear that there is not enough material to make any serious basis for the discussion of the friars' diet, nor for convincingly contrasting the School deposits with other 16th-century groups, e.g. working parties concerned with the destruction of the buildings in the 1540s to 1560s, and the light industry of the 1540s. All that can be said is that the Pre-friary bones suggest, for industrial workers in the first half of the 14th century, a diet of sheep, chicken, beef, rabbit, and the occasional red deer and goose, and for industrial workers of the Fabrica, in the late 1530s and early 1540s a diet mainly of chicken, pork, mutton and beef, with goose, duck, squabs and cod in small quantities, and an interesting range of single occurrences, e.g. heron, woodcock, conger eel, pike and rabbit, with the usual shell fish, oyster and mussels (although this latter group may also include rubbish from the nearby friars' kitchen). The pike and heron probably relate to the nearby friary fish ponds.

For what it is worth when dealing with such small quantities, the light industrial activity contemporary with the School in the presbytery hints at chicken, geese, duck, beef, woodcock (and possibly rook), but there is much loss of material, while for the workmen concerned with the Destruction phase of the church from 1538 to the early 1570s, pig, chicken, sheep, beef and deer are present, with oysters and mussels known to have been very numerous. The material from 64 XXI 3 was of particular interest, being apparently the pork, mutton and beef picnic of those smashing up and burrowing into a fine chantry tomb in the SE nave (Grave 19, Fig. 42), and this evidence for loutish eating in a former holy place is significant.

THE GRAMMAR SCHOOL

The presence of crows, jackdaws, sparrowhawk, kite and possibly pigeon among the bird bones from the School assemblage, along with evidence of both rodent (rat bone was present just N of the chancel, 62 II 3) and probable cat-gnawing on the bones indicate that these animals, both of which were listed by Holmes along with dogs, had access to the deposits at the time they were accumulating. This suggests that the birds could then fly in and out of the church, possibly nesting in the roof structure, and scavenging off the floor of the choir. The sparrowhawk might additionally have been used for hawking at the School, as a hawking bell (Woodfield 1981, fig. 7 no.121) was recovered from the resonance passage. The very large amount of window glass found by Woodfield in the resonance passages, and the presence of pistol balls, used at the time as hail shot in sporting guns (Woodfield 1981 fig. 8, 100-101) confirms the likelihood of shot-out windows giving these birds easy access to the church; the ten hunting arrow heads, (Woodfield 1981, 87 and fig. 3, nos 1-10) may also imply the shooting of birds within the former choir.

The diet of the pupils was fairly diverse, although the incidence of fish may be under-represented. Wild game birds and mammals were eaten in addition to the domestic species, with sheep, chicken, rabbit and goose comprising the most frequent species, although beef and pork may have been brought to the site off-the-bone, and therefore be under-represented in the assemblage. Some of the diversity may be attributable to the range of pupils in the school. Most of the pupils are likely to have been from upper class families, although some poor scholars may also have won places (Woodfield, pers.comm.).

The primary butchery of the sheep carcasses into sides, with the removal of the feet and head, can be recognised in the assemblage, but identification of whether the further butchery of the meat of this and other species was carried out by butcher, school kitchen or pupils' households has not been possible. It may be that a combination of home and school prepared food was being consumed. The beef, pork and some of the mutton, chicken, goose and rabbit may have been prepared as a hot stew or gruel in a school kitchen but there was no sign of such, nor of food preparation, in the vicinity, and for example, no cooking pots were found, although there were storage vessels, and a possible chafing dish (Woodfield 1981, fig. 13). There was also much charcoal and coal, but these could be for heating. Food might have been prepared at Hales' adjacent great house, which would have acquired its supplies from the butchers and perhaps occasional lambs, calves, rabbits and chickens as donations; meanwhile pupils may have brought in cold meats of cooked snipe, woodcock, duck, turkey, swan, perhaps peacock, rabbit, chicken drumsticks, goose wings, venison, shoulder of mutton, etc., as snacks or supplements to the 'school meals'. Some of this variety may reflect the different social status of the pupils, with food provided at the school for the poor scholars while the richer schoolboys brought their own midday meal.

The identification of an elephant ivory knife handle (WF 77 15, 18th-century pit) is of interest as its find place relates to the anomalous fine 18th-century porcelain discovered in that area.

ACKNOWLEDGEMENTS

I should like to thank Charmian Woodfield for her help and discussion of the site, the Natural History Museum Bird Department (Tring) for assistance and use of their reference collection, and Alison Locker for the identification of the fish bones.

SECTION Y

WOOD AND CHARCOAL ANALYSIS

Dr G. Morgan *(University of Leicester)*

Timber from coffins, presumably of benefactors

Figure 42

Grave 13 (1968 XID). High status multiple interment in green sandstone-lined grave in the W chancel. Upper, (possibly middle) probably female grave. The two coffin-wood samples are softwood, probably pine, *Pinus* spec., as there are suggestions of resin ducts in places. If so the wood is either imported or of sixteenth-century date.

Grave 14 (1968 XID). As above, but the lower, male, interment. The sample is again softwood, probably pine.

Figures 43 and 167

Grave 4 (1977). Earth grave of young female, sited in front of high altar in eastern choir. The coffin sample is oak, *Quercus* spec.

Grave 5 (1977). Earth grave, again of young female, to the N of Grave 4, but still in front of high altar. The coffin sample is again oak.

These last two samples are probably from earlier, or more expensive, coffins than those from graves 13 and 14.

Fuel from School deposits.

Dark sand deposit in resonance passage; charcoal derived from School heating or cooking (WF 62 I 4).

Hazel	*Corylus avellana*	10mm dia.	4 rings	4 years
Hazel	*Corylus avellan*	20mm dia.	10 rings	10 years
Poplar	*Populus* spec.	25mm dia.	12 rings	12 years
Oak	*Quercus* spec.	40mm dia.	9 rings	9 years

BIBLIOGRAPHY

Alcock, N. W. 1994. 'Assessment of visual and documentary evidence', 33-7 in *An assessment of the potential of excavations at Coventry Whitefriars 1955-78* (City of Lincoln Archaeology Unit Archaeological Report No 125).

Alcock, N. W. and Woodfield, P. 1996. 'Social Pretensions in Architecture and Ancestry: Hall House, Sawbridge, Warwickshire and the Andrewe Family', Antiquaries J **76**, 51-72.

Alexander, J. J. G. 1970. *The Master of Mary of Burgundy: A Book of Hours for Engelbert of Nassau* (New York).

Allan, J., 1995. 'Iberian Pottery Imported into South-West England', 299-314 in Gerrard, Gutierrez and Hurst 1995.

Allin, C. E. 1981. 'The Ridge Crest Typology', 56-62 in Mellor and Pearce 1981.

Anderson, M. D. 1938. *Animal Carvings in British Churches* (Cambridge).

Andrews, D. 1999(a). 'The window glass', 92-3 in Isserlin 1999.

Andrews, D. 1999(b). 'The vessel glass', 123-4 in Isserlin 1999.

Anon. 1998. See *Coventry Whitefriars Medieval Window Glass.*

Arundel, Philip, Earl of,? (16th century). *The Wracke of Walsingham* (Bodleian Library, MS Rawl. Poet. 291, fol. 16).

Aston, M. 1988. *England's Iconoclasts,* Vol. **1**., *Laws against Images* (Oxford).

Atkin, M. W. 1978. 'The Carmelite Friary, Whitefriars. Excavations in Norwich', *Norfolk Archaeol.* **37**, Part I, 20-24.

Atkinson, D. R. 1972. 'A Brief Guide for the Identification of Dutch Clay Tobacco Pipes Found in England', *Post Medieval. Archaeol.* **6**, 175-182.

Axworthy Rutter, Janet A. 1990 'Other finds from the Dominican Friary; Pottery', 138-163 in Ward 1990.

Baker, E. and Hassall, J. 1979. 'The pottery', in Baker, D., Baker, E, Hassall, J. and Simco, A. 1979. 'Excavations in Bedford, 1967-1977', *Bedfordshire Archaeol. J.* **13**, 147-241.

Bangs, C. 1995. *The Lehr Collection, a Study of Copper Alloy Socket Candlesticks AD 200-1700* (Easton; Pennysylvania (USA).

Bartra, R. 1994. *Wild Men in the Looking Glass, the Mythic Origins of European Otherness* (Michigan).

Bateman, J. and Redknap, M. 1986. *Coventry: Excavations on the Town Wall 1976-78* (Coventry Museums Monograph Series **2**).

Bass, W. M. 1987. *Human Osteology: A Laboratory and Field Manual* (Special publication No. 2 of the Missouri Archaological Society, Columbia, USA).

Bennett, J. H. E. 1935. 'The White Friars of Chester', *J Chester and North Wales Archaeol. Soc.* **31**, 5-54.

Bernheimer, R. 1952. *Wild Men in the Middle Ages: a Study in Art, Sentiment and Demonology* (Harvard).

Biddle, M. (ed.) 1990 *Object and Economy in Medieval Winchester* (Winchester Studies **7.2**; Oxford).

Biddle, M. and Hinton, D. 1990. 'Copper Alloy Bells', 725-8 in Biddle (ed.) 1990.

Bliss Burbidge, F. 1950. *Old Coventry and Lady Godiva.* (Cornish, for the University of Birmingham).

Bond, F. 1910. *Wood Carvings in English Churches* **I***: Stalls and Tabernacle Work* (London).

Bony, J. 1979. *The English Decorated Style; Gothic architecture transformed 1250-1350.*

Bottomley, F. 1981. *Abbey Explorer's Guide.* (London).

Bradley Smith, H. R.. 1966. *Blacksmiths' and Farriers' Tools at Shelburne Museum. A History of their Development from Forge to Factory* (Shelburne; Vermont).

Brears, P. C. D. 1983. 'Post-medieval pottery', 215-224 in Mayes and Butler 1983.

Britton, J. and Brayley, E. W. 1810. *Beauties of England and Wales,* Vol. **XV**, Part 1 (Vernor, Hood, Sharpe; London).

Brown, R. A. and Colvin, H. M. 1963. 'The King's Works 1272-1485', 161-292 in Brown, R. A., Colvin, H. M. and Taylor, A. J.1963. *The History of the King's Works* **I** (HMSO; London).

Butler, Lawrence. 1984. 'The houses of the Mendicant Orders in Britain: recent archaeological work', 123-36 in Addyman, P. V. and Black, V. (eds) 1984. *Archaeological papers from York presented to M. W. Barley.*

Butler, Lawrence. 1987. 'Medieval urban religious houses', 167-76 in J Schofield, J. and Leech, R. (eds) 1987. *Urban archaeology in Britain.*

Butler, Lionel and Given-Wilson, C. 1979. *Medieval monasteries of Great Britain.*

Cameron, H. K., 1974. 'Technical Aspects of Medieval Monumental Brasses', *Archaeol. J.* **131**, 215-38.

Caple, C. 1983. 'Pins and Wires from Sandal Castle', 269-78 in Mayes, and Butler, 1983.

Caple, C. 1986. *An Analytical Appraisal of Copper Alloy Pin Production: 400 to 1600 AD.*

Caple. C. 1991. 'The Detection and Definition of an Industry: The English Medieval and Post Medieval Pin Industry', *Archaeol. J.* **148**, 241-255.

Caple, C. 1995. 'The Principal Components of Brass Pin Production', *Trade and Discovery* (British Museum Occasional Paper **109**, 221-234).

Caple, C. and Warren, S. E. 1983. 'Technical Observations on the Method of Production of Wound Wire Headed Pins', 273-83 in Aspinall, A. and Warren, S. E. (eds) 1983. *Proceedings of the 22nd Symposium on Archaometry.*

Carter, J. 1844. *The ancient architecture of England.* (Part II).

Cattell, J. 1997. *An Architectural Analysis of the Former Cloister of the Coventry Whitefriars* (RCHME Survey

Report. NBR Index 94782).

Cautley, H. M. 1937. *Suffolk Churches and their Treasures* (Ipswich).

Cave, L. F. 1981. *The Smaller English House* (Robert Hale Ltd.).

Chambers, E. K. 1923. *The Elizabethan Stage* Vol. **4**(Oxford).

Charleston, R. 1975. 'The Glass', 204-26 in Platt and Coleman-Smith 1975.

Charleston, R. 1980. 'Vessel Glass', 208-11 in Christie and Coad 1980.

Charleston, R. 1985. 'Vessel Glass', 139-46 in Hare, J. 1985. *Battle Abbey*. HMBC.

Charleston, R. 1992. 'The Glass', 134-45 in Horsey, I. *Excavations in Poole, 1973-83* (Dorset Natural History and Archaeology Society Monograph **10**).

Chatwin P. R. 1928. 'Recent Discoveries in the Beauchamp Chapel, Warwick', *Trans Birmingham Archaeol,. Soc.* **53**, 145--147.

Chatwin, P. 1936. 'The Medieval Patterned Tiles of Warwickshire', *Trans. Birmingham Archaeol. Soc.* **60**, 1-41.

Chatwin. P. 1941-2 'Medieval Tiles discovered as a result of Air Raids in Coventry', *Trans. Birmingham and Warwicks Archaeol. Soc.* **64**, 116-117.

Chaucer, G. 1380s *Canterbury Tales, Prologue* (Oxford University Press, 1942).

Cherry B and Pevsner N. 1989. *Devon: Buildings of England* (Penguin; Harmondsworth).

Christie, P. M. and Coad, J. G. 1980. 'Excavations at Denny Abbey', *Archaeol. J.*, 137, 138-279.

City of Coventry Leisure Services n.d. *The story of Whitefriars.*

City of Lincoln Archaeology Unit. 1995. *St. Mark's, High Street, Lincoln. Archaeological Investigations*, (City of Lincoln Archaeological Report No **338**).

Clapham, A. W. 1910. 'The topography of the Carmelite Priory of London', *J. British Archaeol. Assoc.* **16**, new series, 15-32.

Clapham, A. W. 1912. 'On the topography of the Dominican Priory of London', *Archaeologia* **63**, 57-80.

Clapham, A. W. 1913. 'The Friars as builders. The London houses of Blackfriars and Whitefriars', 241-67 in Clapham, A. W and Godfrey, W. H. (eds) 1913. *Some famous buildings and their story....*

Clapham, A. and Godfrey, W. n.d. *Some Famous Buildings and their study* (Technical Journals Ltd.; London).

Clark, J. 1991. 'Saxon and Medieval', 8-11 in Murdoch, T., *et al.* 1991. *Treasures and Trinkets* (Museum of London exhibition catalogue).

Clark, J. W. 1897. *The Observances in use at the Augustinian priory of St Giles and St Audrey at Barnwell, Cambridgeshire* (Cambridge).

Clarke, R. A. 1992. *Illustrating a city: Edward Rudge and art in Coventry c.1760-1830.*

Coldstream, N. 1994. *The Decorated Style; architecture and ornament, 1240-1360.*

Coppack, G. 1976 'The Pottery', 6-24 in Drewett 1976.

Coppack, G. 1980, 'Medieval and Post-Medieval pottery', 223-247 in Christie and Coad, 1980.

Coppack, G. 1986, 'The Excavation of an Outer Court Building, Perhaps the Wool House, at Fountains Abbey, North Yorkshire', *Medieval Archaeol* **30**, 46-87.

Copsey, R. 1992. 'The visit of the Prior General, Peter Terrasse, to England in 1504-5', 176-204 in Fitzgerald-Lombard (ed.) 1992.

Courtney, P. 1993. 'The Medieval and Post-Medieval Objects', 134-61 in Ellis, P. (ed). 1993. *Beeston Castle, Cheshire, Excavations by Lawrence Keen and Peter Hough 1968-85* (English Heritage Report **23**).

Courtney, P. 2003. 'Vessel Glass', in Bell, R. and Rodwell, K. 2003. *Acton Court. The Evolution of an Early Tudor Courtier House.* English Heritage.

Coventry Leet Book (see Harris, M. D. 1907-1913).

Coventry Whitefriars Medieval Window Glass. Conservation Report and Site Archive (Lincs. C.C. Education and Cultural Services Directorate, Conservation Department).

Cracknell, S. 1990 (1987-8) 'Bridge End, Warwick: Archaeological excavation of a medieval street frontage', *Trans Birmingham and Warks Archaeol. Soc.* **95**, 17-78.

Cracknell, S., 1991-2 ''Bards Walk', Wood Street, Stratford-upon-Avon. Medieval structures excavated in 1989', *Trans Birmingham and Warks Archaeol. Soc*, **97**, 57-75.

Cracknell, S. (ed), 1996 *Roman Alcester: Defences and Defended Area* (CBA Res. Rep. **106**. Roman Alcester Series **2**).

Cracknell, S. and Bishop, M. W. 1991-2 'Excavations at 25-33 Brook Street, Warwick, 1973', *Trans. Birmingham and Warks. Archaeol. Soc.* **97**, 1-40.

Cracknell, S. and Mahany C. (eds). 1994. *Roman Alcester: Southern Extramural Area. 1964-66 excavations* (CBA Res. Rep. 97 Roman Alcester Series 1).

Cropper, C. 2001. 'The window glass', 46-54 in Poore and Wilkinson 2001.

CSRIA. 1955 (revised edition). *The Blacksmith's Craft* (Council for Small Industries in Rural Areas; London).

Dean, M. 1977. 'Lead Tokens from the River Thames at Windsor and Wallingford', *Numismatic Chronicle* 7th series **17**, 137-47.

Deloney, T. 1593. 'A pleasant dialogue between Plaine Truth and Blind Ignorance', in *The Garden of Goodwill* (Mann, F. O. 1912. *The Works of Thomas Deloney* (Clarendon Press; Oxford)).

Demidowicz, G. 1996. *Management Plan for London Road Cemetery, Coventry* (Coventry City Council).

Dickinson, J. C. 1968. 'The buildings of the English Austin Canons after the Dissolution of the Monasteries', *J. Brit. Archaeol. Assoc.* **31**, third series, 60-75.

DNB 1975. *Dictionary of National Biography*. (Oxford compacted., 1975, 2 vols).

Dowle, A. and Finn, P. 1969. *A Guide Book to the*

Coinage of Ireland, from 995 AD to the Present Day
Dornier, A. 1971-2. 'Donington le Heath', *Trans. Leics. Archaeol. Hist Soc.* **47**, 22-42.
Drewett, P. L. 1976. 'The Excavations of the Great Hall at Bolingbroke Castle, Lincolnshire, 1973', *Post-Medieval Archaeol.* **10**, 1-33.
Drewett, P. L., Chapman, H. and Coppack, G. 1976. 'Excavations at the Bishops' Palace Lincoln', *Occ Papers in Lincs Hist and Archaeol* **1**.
Druce, G. C. 1915. 'Some Abnormal and Composite Forms in English Church Architecture', *Archaeol. J.* **72**, 135-186.
Drury, P. J. and Pratt, G. D. 1975. 'A late 13th and early 14th-century tile factory at Danbury, Essex', *Medieval Archaeol.* **19**, 92-164.
Dugdale, W. 1580-1 (ed. Caley, Ellis and Bandinel, 1846). *Monasticon Anglicanum*, **VI ii** (London).
Dugdale, W. 1656, and 1730 eds. *The Antiquities of Warwickshire*.
Dugdale, W. 1765. *The Antiquities of Coventry: Illustrated from Records, Ledgers, Manuscripts, Charters, Evidences, Tombes and Armes, beautified with many Curious Copper-plate Cuts* (Jones; Coventry).
Dunkerton, J., Roy, A. and Smith, A. 1987. 'The unmasking of Tura's "Allegorical Figure": a painting and its concealed image', *National Gallery Technical Bulletin* **11**, 5-35.
Dunning, G. C. 1961. 'Medieval Chimney Pots', 78-93 in Jope (ed.) 1961.
Dunning, G. C. 1965. 'Heraldic and Decorated Metalwork & Other Finds from Rievaulx Abbey, Yorkshire', *Antiquaries J.* **45**, 53-63.
Dunning, G. C. 1967. 'Late medieval jugs with lettering', *Medieval Archaeol.* **11**, 233-241.
Dunning, G. C. 1971-2. 'A pottery ridge tile with vents in the sides', 37-41 in Dornier 1971-2.
Eames, E. 1984. 'The Decorated Floor Tiles', 173-185 in Mayes and Scott 1984.
Eames, E. 1992. *English Tilers* (British Museum Press: London).
Egan, G. 1994. *Lead Cloth Seals and Related Items in the British Museum* (British Museum Occasional Paper **93**; London).
Egan, G. 1996a. 'Non Ferrous Metal', 29-35 in Davey, P. J. *et al.*, 1996. *Excavations in Castletown, Isle of Man, 1989-1992* (University of Liverpool).
Egan, G. 1996b. *Playthings from the Past* (London).
Egan, G. 1997a. 'Non-ceramic finds', 201-210 in Thomas, C. *et al. Excavations at the Priory and Hospital of St .Mary Spital, London* (MoLAS Monograph **1**).
Egan, G. 1997b. 'Children's Pastimes in past times – medieval toys found in the British Isles', 413-21 in de Boe, G. and Verhaeghe, F. (eds) 1997. *Material Culture in Medieval Europe* (Medieval Europe, Brugge, 1997, **7**; Zellik (Belgium).
Egan, G. 1998. *The Medieval Household* (Medieval Finds from London Excavations **6**).
Egan, G. (ed.). forthcoming. 'Post Medieval Finds *c.*1450-*c.*1700, a Selection from City of London Sites 1972-82', *Post Medieval Archaeol.*
Egan, G. and Michael, R. L. (eds). 1999. *Old and New Worlds* Historical/Post-Medieval Archaeology Papers from the Societies' joint conferences at Williamsburg and London 1997 (Oxbow; Exeter).
Egan, G. and Pritchard, F. 1991. 'Dress Accessories', *Medieval Finds from London Excavations* **3** (London; HMSO).
Egan, K. J. 1992. 'Medieval Carmelite Houses in England and Wales', 1-148 in Fitzgerald-Lombard (ed.) 1992.
Ellis, R. A. 1986. *Catalogue of Monastic Seals* **I** (HMSO).
Elmhirst, E. M. 1959. *Merchant's marks* (Harl. Soc. 108).
Emery, P. forthcoming. *The Excavations at the Greyfriars, Norwich* (East Anglian Archaeology Monograph Series).
Endrei, W. and Egan, G. 1982. 'The Sealing of Cloth in Europe, with special reference to the English Evidence', *Textile History* **13.2**, 47-75.
Evans, D. H. 1995 *Valle Crucis Abbey* (CAOW Official Guide).
Everyman's Encyclopaedia (Aldine Press, 1961).
Fawcett, R. 1999. *Elgin Cathedral* (Historic Scotland Guide).
Fitzgerald-Lombard, P. (ed.) 1992. *Carmel in Britain. Essays on the medieval English Carmelite Province.*
Ffinch, M, 1984. *Appleby in Westmorland and Warcup* (Titus Wilson; Kendal).
Flitcroft, M. 1998. *An Archaeological Evaluation at Gulson Hospital, Coventry* (Coventry Museum Archaeology Unit Report 98/29).
Forrester, H. 1972. *Medieval Gothic Mouldings: A Guide* (Phillimore; Chichester).
French, T. 1995. *York Minster The Great East Window* (*Corpus Vitrearum Medii Aevi.* Great Britain. Summary Catalogue 2, published for the British Academy by Oxford University Press).
Fretton, W. G. 1871. *Illustrative papers on the History and Antiquities of the City of Coventry: Collected by Thomas Sharp Esq* (Birmingham).
Fretton, W. G. 1872. 'Memorials of the Whitefriars, Coventry', *Trans Birmingham and Midland Inst. Archaeol. Section* **3**, 63-78.
Fretton, W. G. 1890. 'The monastic institutions of Coventry', *Archaeol. J.* **47**, 17-27.
Fretton, W. G. 1891. 'Memorials of St. Mary's Hall Coventry', *Trans. Birmingham and Midland Inst. Archaeol. Section.* **17**, 14-30.
Friedman, J. B. 1981. *The Monstrous Races in Mediaeval Art and Thought* (Harvard).
Gaimster, D. R. M. 1997. *German Stoneware 1200-1900* (British Museum Press).
Gaimster, D. R. M. 1999. 'The post-medieval ceramic revolution in Southern Britain c.1450-1650', 214-225 in Egan and Michael 1999.
Gerrard, C. M., Gutierrez, A. and Hurst J. G. 1995. 'Andalusian Lustrewares', 283-289 in *Spanish Medieval Ceramics in Spain and the British Isles*

(British Archaeol. Rep. International Series **610**).

Gibson, P. 1979. *The Stained and Painted glass of York Minster* (Norwich).

Gilchrist, R and Mytum, H. 1993. *Advances in Monastic Archaeology* (British Archaeol. Rep. British Ser. **227**)

Gilyard-Beer, R., and Coppack, G. 1986. 'Excavations at Fountains Abbey, North Yorkshire; the Development of the Early Monastery', *Archaeologia* **108**, 147-88.

Godfrey, E. S. 1975. *The Development of English Glassmaking, 1560-1640* (Oxford).

Goodall, I. H. 1990. 'Tenterhooks', 234-9 in Biddle (ed.) 1990.

Graves, C. P. 2000 *The Window Glass of the Order of St. Gilbert of Sempringham. A York-based Study* (York Archaeological Trust and the Council for British Archaeology).

Greene, P. 1989. *Norton Priory, The archaeology of a medieval religious house* (Cambridge University Press).

Halliwell, J. O. 1841. *Coventry Mysteries.*

Harbottle, B. 1968. 'Excavations at the Carmelite Friary, Newcastle 1965 and 1967', *Archaeol. Aeliana* **46**, series 4, 163-223.

Harris, M. D. 1907-1913. *The Coventry Leet Book*, Pts 1-2 (Early English Text Society **135-6**).

Harris, M. D. 1927. 'The Misericords of Coventry', *Trans Birmingham and Midlands Inst. Archaeol.* **52 pt 2**, 246-66

Harris, M. D n.d. 'Coventry's ancient buildings and their story. VI. The friary of the Carmelites' (*The Coventry Herald.*).

Hartshorne, A. 1968 (2nd ed.). *Antique Drinking Glasses, A Pictorial History of Glass Drinking Vessels* (Brussel and Brussel, New York).

Harvey, J. 1978. *The Perpendicular Style 1330-1485.*

Harvey, J. 1984 (2nd revised ed.). *English Medieval Architects: a biographical dictionary down to 1550.*

Harvey, J. and King, D. 1971. 'Winchester College Stained Glass', *Archaeologia* **102**, 148-177.

Haslam, J. 1993. 'Glass Vessels', 97-117 in Margeson 1993.

Henkes, H. E. 1994. 'Glaz zonder flans', *Rotterdam Papers* **9** (Rotterdam; Netherlands).

Hills, G. M. 1871. 'Report on British Archaeol. Assoc visit to Fountains Abbey', *Collectanea Archaeologica*, **2**, 294-5.

Hills, G. M. 1881-2. 'Earthenware Pots (Built into Churches) which have been called acoustic vases', *RIBA Trans, Session.*

Hobley, B. 1971. 'Excavations at the Cathedral and Benedictine Priory of St. Mary, Coventry', *Trans. Birmingham Archaeol. Soc.* **84**, 45-139.

Hodder M. A., 1991. 'Excavations at Sandwell Priory and Hall, 1982-88', *South Staffs Archaeol. and Hist. Soc.* **31**, for 1989-90.

Hodder, M. A. 1992. 'Excavations in Wednesbury, 1988 and 1989: The Medieval and Post-Medieval Settlement, and the 17th Century Pottery Industry', *Transactions of the South Staffordshire Archaeol. and Hist. Soc.* **32**, 1990-91 (1992), 96-115.

Holling, F. 1977. 'Reflections on Tudor Green', *Post Medieval. Archaeol.* **11**, 61-66.

Holmes, E. F, nd. *Sewing Thimbles* (Finds Research Group 700-1700 Datasheet **9**; Oxford).

Holmes, J. M. 1981. 'Report on the animal bones from the resonance chambers of the Whitefriars Church, Coventry', 125-154 in Woodfield 1981.

Hope, W. H. St J. 1890. 'On the Whitefriars or Carmelites of Hulne, Northumberland', *Archaeol. J.* **47**, 105-29.

Howard, H. 1996. 'Scientific examination of the "Doom" wall painting in Holy Trinity Church, Coventry' (Conservation of Wall Painting Department, Courtauld Institute of Art, unpublished report).

Howard, H. and Park, D. forthcoming. 'The medieval shell palette', in Emery, P. forthcoming.

Hughes, M., Cherry, J., Freestone, I. and Leese, M.1982. 'Neutron activation analysis and petrology of medieval English decorated floor tiles from the Midlands', in Freestone, I., Johns, C. and Potter, T. (eds) *Current Research in Ceramics: thin section studies* (British Museum Occasional Paper, **32**).

Hulton, M., 1995. *True as Coventry Blue* (Coventry and County Heritage **21**; Historical Association, Coventry Branch).

Hunter, K. 1987. 'The Friars Park Window: conservation and reconstruction of a 13th century window', *ICOM Committee for Conservation.*

Hurst, J. G. 1977. 'Spanish Pottery Imported into Medieval Britain', *Medieval Archaeol.* **21**, 68-105.

Hurst, J. G. and Neal, D. S. 1982. 'Late Medieval Iberian Pottery imported into the Low Countries', *Rotterdam Papers* IV, 83-110.

Hurst J. G., Neal, D. S. and Van Beuningen, H. J. E. 1986. *Pottery Produced and Traded in North-West Europe 1350-1650. Rotterdam Papers VI* (Rotterdam).

Hurst, J. G. 1999. 'Sixteenth-Century South Netherlands Maiolica Imported into Britain and Ireland', in Gaimster, D. (ed.), 1999. *Maiolica in the North: The Archaeology of Tin-glazed Earthenware in Northern Europe c.1500-1600*, British Museum Occasional Paper **122**, 91-106.

Husband, T. 1980. *The Wild Man: Medieval Myth and Symbolism* (Museum of Modem Art).

Ingram, R. W. (ed.) 1981. *Records of Early English Drama. Coventry* (University of Toronto, Toronto).

Isserlin, R. 'The Carmelite Friary at Maldon: excavations 1990-1', *Essex Archaeology and History* **30**, 44-143.

Ivens, R. J. 1981. 'Medieval Pottery Kilns at Brill, Buckinghamshire', *Records of Buckinghamshire* **23**, 102-106.

Ivens, R. J. 1982. 'Medieval Pottery from the 1978 excavations at Temple Farm, Brill', *Records of Buckinghamshire* **24**, 145-170.

Jarrett, B. 1921. *The English Dominicans.*

Jenkins, H. M. 1951. 'Dr. Thomas's edition of Sir William Dugdale's 'Antiquities of Warwickshire', *Dugdale Soc. Occ. Papers*, **3**.

Jope, E. M., 1953-4, 'Medieval Pottery kilns at Brill,

Buckinghamshire', *Records of Buckinghamshire* **16**, 39-42.

Jope, E .M. (ed.) 1961. *Studies in Building History* (Odhams Press; London).

Jope, E. M. and Ivens, R. J. 1995. 'A later Medieval Pottery kiln at Potterspury, Northamptonshire', *Northamptonshire Archaeology* **26**, 141-148.

Kettle, A. J. 1980. 'The Carmelite Friars of Chester', in *The Victoria History of the Counties of England: a History of Cheshire.* Vol. **III**, 176-8.

Kilmurry, K. 1980. *The Pottery Industry of Stamford, Lincs.* (BAR British Series **84**).

Klein, P. and Roe, A. 1987. *The Carmelite Friary, Corve Street, Ludlow; its History and Excavation,* Research Paper **6.**

Knowles, D. 1948. *The Religious Orders in England.*

Knowles, D. and Hadcock, R. N. 1971. *Medieval Religious Houses; England and Wales.*

Kurth, W. (ed.) 1963. *The Complete Woodcuts of Albrecht Dürer* (Dover Edition, originally published in German in 1927; New York, USA).

Lambrick, G and Woods, H. 1976. 'Excavations on the Second Site of the Dominican Priory, Oxford', *Oxoniensia* **41**, 168-231.

Lancaster, O. 1949. *Drayneflete Revealed* (John Murray; London).

Langland, W. see Schmidt 1978.

Le Couteur, J. D. 1922. 'Notes on the E. Window of Winchester College Chapel', Supplement to *The Wykehamist*, No **21**, No **626**, 273-276.

Lee, L., Seddon, G. and Stevens, F. 1989, *Stained Glass York* (London).

Lewis, J. M. 1976. *Welsh Medieval Paving Tiles* (National Museum of Wales: Cardiff).

Lindsay, W, J, 1989 'Linlithgow: The Excavations', 53-94 in Stones 1989.

Lloyd, N. 1925 (reprinted 1983). *A History of English Brickwork.*

Locock, M. 1989. 'Medieval Floor Tiles from Dudley Castle. A preliminary Report', *West Midlands Pottery Research Group Newsletter* **12.**

Lowe, A. 1859. *History and antiquities of the City of Coventry.*

McAleavey, T. 1996. *Life in a Medieval Abbey* (English Heritage).

McCaffrey, P. R. and Carm, O.1926. *The White Friars: an outline Carmelite history with special reference to the English-speaking provinces* (M. H. Gill and Son; Dublin).

McCarthy, M. R. 1979. 'The Pottery', 149-240 in Williams 1979.

McCarthy, M. R., and Brooks, C. M. 1988. *Medieval Pottery in Britain AD 900-1600.*

McMinn, R. M. H. and Hutchings, R. T. 1991. *A Colour Atlas of Human Anatomy* (Wolfe, London).

Mairinger, F. and Schreiner, M. 1986. 'Deterioration and preservation of Carolingian and medieval wall paintings in the Müstair Convent. Part II: materials and rendering of the Carolingian wall paintings', 195-196 in Brommelle, N. S. and Smith, P. (eds) 1986. *Case Studies in the Conservation of Stone and Wall paintings* (Preprints of the Contributions to the IIC Bologna Congress, 1986).

Maltby, M. 1979. 'Faunal studies on urban sites; the animal bones from Exeter. 1971-75', *Exeter Archaeological Reports* **2**, (Dept. of Prehistory and Archaeology, University of Sheffield).

Manchester, K.. 1983. *The Archaeology of Disease* (University of Bradford, England).

Manning, A. 1998. *Excavations at Carmarthen Greyfriars 1983-1990* (Dyfed Archaeological Trust Occasional Paper).

Margeson, S. (ed.). 1993. *Medieval Norwich Households: The Medieval and Post Medieval Finds from Norwich Survey Excavations 1971-78* (East Anglian Archaeology **58**).

Marks, R. 1993. *Stained Glass in England during the Middle Ages* (University of Toronto).

Marks, R. 1998. *The Mediaeval Stained Glass of Northamptonshire* (Oxford).

Martin, A. R. 1937. *Franciscan Architecture in England.*

Mayes, P., and Butler, L. A. S. 1983. *Sandal Castle Excavations 1964-73:a detailed archaeological report* (Wakefield Historical Publications).

Mayes, P. and Scott, K. 1984. *Pottery Kilns at Chilvers Coton* (Medieval Archaeol. Monograph **10**).

Medieval. Archaeol. 1964. 'Warwickshire: Coventry, Whitefriars', **8**, 245.

Medieval. Archaeol. 1967. 'Warwickshire: Coventry, Whitefriars', **11**, 278 and fig. 79.

Meliton, (Claude Pithoys). 1662. *L'apocalypse de Méliton où Révelation des mystère cénobitiques* (Sainct Leger).

Mellor, J, E, and Pearce, T. 1981. *The Austin Friars, Leicester* (CBA Research Report **35**).

Mellor, M. 1994. 'A Synthesis of Middle and Late Saxon, Medieval and Early Post-medieval Pottery in the Oxford Region', *Oxoniensia* **59**, 17-217.

Mihalik, S. 1961. *Old Hungarian Enamels* (Budapest).

Miles, D. W. H. 2002. *The Tree-Ring Dating of Whitefriars, Coventry* (English Heritage Centre for Archaeology, Report 40/2002).

Miles, D. W. H. and Worthington, W. 2002. 'List 26: Oxford Dendrochronological Laboratory, General List', *Vernacular Architecture* **33**, 88-9.

Miller, P. and Berthoud, M. 1985. *An Anthology of British Teapots* (Micawber Publications; Wingham).

Minns, G. 1872. 'Acoustic Pottery', *Norfolk Archaeology* **7**, 93-101.

Möller, Lise Lotte. 1964. 'Die wilden Leute in der deutschen Graphik des ausgehenden Mittelalters', *Philobiblon* **7.4**, 260-264.

Moore, B. 1992 'Wild Men in the Misericords of St. Mary's Church Beverley', *Yorkshire Archaeol. J.* **64**, 135-144.

Moorhouse, S. 1983. 'Vessel Glass', 225-30 in Mayes and Butler (eds) 1983.

Morris, R. K. 1978-9. 'Development of Later Gothic Mouldings', *Architectural History* **21-22**, 1-48.

Morris, R. K. 1988. 'St Mary's Hall and the medieval

architecture of Coventry', *Trans Ancient Monuments Soc.* **32**, new series, 8-27.

Morris, R. K. 1994. 'Art Historical value of the standing building', 29-33 in *An assessment of the potential of excavations at Coventry Whitefriars 1955-78.* City of Lincoln Archaeology Unit Archaeological Report **125**.

Muldoon, S. and Brownsword, R. nd. *Pewter Spoons and Other Related Material of the 14th-17th centuries, in the Collection of the Herbert Art Gallery and Museum, Coventry* (City of Coventry Leisure Services).

Nelson, W. (ed.) 1956. *A Fifteenth-century School Book c. 1500*

Newton, P. 1971. 'The Glass', 107-111 in Hobley 1971.

Newton, P. 1979. *The County of Oxford. A Catalogue of Medieval Stained Glass* (*Corpus Vitrearum Medii Aevi*, Great Britain, No. 1).

Newton, S. M. 1980. *Fashion in the Age of the Black Prince : a Study of the Years 1340-1365* (Woodbridge; Gloucester).

New Scientist. 1997. 'The Last Word', *New Scientist,* **No 2077** (12th April 1997).

New Scientist. 1998. 'The Last Word', *New Scientist,* **No 2139** (20th June 1998).

Nicholls, J. 1823. *The Progresses and Public Processions of Queen Elizabeth* (Soc. Antiquaries of London)

Norfolk Museum Service. 1977 (2nd ed.). *Bronze Age Metalwork in Norwich Castle Museum* (Norwich).

North, J. J. 1963. *English Hammered Coinage* **1**.

Oakley, G. E. 1979. 'The Copper Alloy Objects', 248-64 in Williams 1979.

Oakley, G. and Hunter, J. 1979. 'The Glass', 296-302 in Williams 1979.

Opie, I. 1976. 'Children's Marbles', 248-64 in Ketteringham, L. L. 1976. *Alsted: Excavation of a 13th/14th century Sub Manor House* (Surrey Archaeol. Soc. Research Vol. **2**).

O'Shaughnessy, F. *c.*1987. *The story of Burton Dassett Church* (Coventry Printers).

Page, W. (ed.) 1908. 'The Carmelite Friary of Coventry', *Victoria County History of Warwickshire* **II** (Archibald and Constable; London).

Paley F. A. 1902 (6th ed.). *Paley's Gothic Mouldings.*

Patten, J 1978. *English towns 1500-1700.*

Pearce, J. 1992. *Post-medieval pottery in London, 1500-1700: Border Wares* (Museum of London).

Peck, Rev. F. 1727. *Academia tertia Anglicana or the Antiquarian Annals of Stamford in Lincoln, Rutland and Northampton Shires* (Jas Bettenden; London).

Pevsner, N. 1962. *North-West and South Norfolk: Buildings of England* (Penguin; Harmondsworth).

Pevsner, N. 1968. *Bedfordshire and the County of Huntingdon and Peterborough: Buildings of England* (Penguin; Harmondsworth).

Pevsner, N. 1989. *Yorkshire West Riding: Buildings of England* (Penguin; Harmondsworth).

Pevsner, N. and Harris, J. 1973. *Lincolnshire: Buildings of England* (Penguin; Harmondsworth).

Pevsner, N. and Verey, D. 1970. *Gloucestershire: Buildings of England* (Penguin; Harmondsworth).

Phipson, R. M. 1866 *The Builder.*

Phythian-Adams, C. 1979. *Desolation of a city. Coventry and the urban crisis of the late Middle Ages.*

Pickford, C. 1987. 'The Lost Bells of Holy Trinity, Coventry', *The Ringing World,* No. 3969 (22nd May 1987).

Platt, C. 1978. *Medieval England. A Social History and Archaeology from the Conquest to 1600 A.D* (Routledge and Kegan Paul: London).

Platt, C. 1996. *King Death and its aftermath in late-medieval England.*

Platt, C. and Coleman-Smith, P. 1975. *Excavations in Medieval Southampton, 1953-1969.*

Platt, H. 1979. *The Jewell House of Art and Nature, 1594* (Theatrum Orbis Terrarum; Amsterdam).

Pollard, M. 1983. 'Investigation of the Brass used in Medieval and Later European Scientific Instruments' (Paper presented to the UKIC meeting on 'Conservation of Scientific Materials').

Poole, B. 1870. *Coventry: its history and antiquities.*

Poore, D., and Wilkinson, D. R. P. 2001. *Beaumont Palace and the Whitefriars: Excavations at the Sackler Library, Beaumont Street., Oxford* (Oxford Archaeological Unit Occasional Paper **9**).

Poskitt, M. E. 1992a. 'The English Carmelite Province: 15th century', 149-54 in Fitzgerald-Lombard (ed.) 1992.

Poskitt, M. E. 1992b 'The English Carmelites, houses of study and educational methods', 155-65 in Fitzgerald-Lombard (ed.) 1992.

Poulton, R. and Woods, H. 1984. 'Excavations on the site of The Dominican Friary at Guildford in 1974 and 1978' (*Surrey Archaeol. Soc. Research* Vol. **9**).

Prideaux, E. K., Shafto, G. R. and Holt R. 1909. *Bosses and Corbels of Exeter Cathedral* (Exeter).

Public Record Office. 1847. *Eighth Report of the Deputy Keeper of the Public Records,* Appendix II (Clowes and Son; London).

Rackham, B. 1930-1, 'The Glass Painting of Coventry and its neighbourhood', *Walpole Society*, **19**, 89-110.

Rahtz, P. 1963-4 (1966). 'Kenilworth Castle, 1950', *Trans. Birmingham and Warwickshire Archaeol. Soc.*, **81**, 55-73.

Ratkai, S. 1985. 'Medieval and Post-Medieval pottery from Dudley Castle', *West Midlands Pottery Research Group Newsletter* **5**, (unpaginated).

Ratkai, S. 1987. 'The Post Medieval Coarsewares from the Motte and Keep of Dudley Castle', *Staffs. Archaeol. Studies Mus. Arch. Soc. Rep.* New Series **4**, 1-11.

Ratkai, S. 1990. 'The Medieval Pottery', 33-72 in Cracknell 1990.

Ratkai, S. 1992a. 'Medieval Pottery', 8-26 in Cracknell and Bishop 1992.

Ratkai, S. 1992b. 'The Medieval Pottery', 62-73 in Cracknell 1991-2.

Ratkai, S. 1994 'Medieval Pottery', 154-156 in Cracknell and Mahany (eds) 1994.

Ratkai, S. 1996 'Medieval Pottery', 2 in Cracknell. (ed)

1996.

Ratkai, S. 1998. 'The Pottery', in Coutts, C., and Jones, C. 1998. *Evaluation at the church of St. John the Baptist, Wolvey, Warwickshire* (Warwickshire Museum).

Ratkai, S. 2000. 'The Pottery', in Burrows, R. and Mould, C. *An archaeological evaluation at Hartwells Smithfield Garage, Digbeth, Birmingham,* 1999 (Birmingham University Field Archaeology Unit internal report 336.03).

Ratkai, S. forthcoming. 'The Pottery', in Palmer N., *Burton Dassett: a deserted Medieval settlement in SE Warwickshire* (Soc. Medieval Archaeol. Monograph).

Ratkai, S. forthcoming. 'The Pottery', *Haughmond Abbey, Shropshire.*

Ratkai, S. in preparation, 'The Pottery', in Darlington, J., and Hill, C., *Excavations at Stafford Castle*, Vol. **2**.

Ratkai, S. and Soden, I., 2000. *Warwickshire pottery fabric type series* (Unpublished typescript and type series held by Warwickshire Museum Field Service).

Réau, L. 1956. *Iconographie de l'art chrétien,* **II pt. I** (Paris).

Read, H. 1926. *English Stained Glass.*

Reader, W. 1823. *New Coventry Guide.*

Redknap, M. 1985. 'Twelfth- and thirteenth-century Coventry wares, with special reference to a waster group from the Cannon Park Estate (Lychgate Road) Coventry', *Medieval Ceramics* **9**, 65-78.

Redknap, M. and Perry, J. G. 1996. 'Medieval and later pottery', in Rylatt, Stokes and Alcock. 1996.

Remnant, G. L. 1969. *A Catalogue of Miserecords in Great Britain* (Oxford).

Rickert, M. 1952. *The Reconstructed Carmelite Missal* (University of Chicago Press; Chicago, Illinois).

Rigold, S. E. 1965. 'Two Kentish Carmelite Houses; Aylesford and Sandwich', *Archaeol. Cantiana* **80**, 1-28.

Rigold, S. E. 1981. 'The Coins', 118-25 in Woodfield 1981

Roche, A. and E. 1981. *A dictionary of early music* (London).

Roger, J., *et al.*, 1967. 'Arthropathies in Palaeopathology: The Basis of Classification According to Most Probable Cause', *Jnl. of Archaeol. Science* **14**, 170-193.

RCHM. 1926. *Huntingdonshire.*

Russell J. C. 1944. 'The Clerical Population of Medieval England', *Traditio.*

Rylatt, M., Stokes, M. and Alcock, N W. 1996. *The Excavations at Broadgate East, Coventry* (Coventry Museums Monograph Series **5**).

Salway, P. 1996. 'Sidney before the College', 3-34 in Beales, D. E. D. and Nisbet, H. B. 1996. *Sidney Sussex College, Cambridge: Historical Essays in Commemoration of the Quatercentenary* (The Boydell Press; Woodbridge).

Salzman, L. F. 1967. *Building in England down to 1540* (Clarendon Press; Oxford).

Schmidt, A. V. C. 1992. *William Langland: Piers Plowman* (Oxford World Classics).

Sekules, V. 1990. *The Sculpture and Liturgical Furnishings of Heckington Church and Related Monuments: Masons and Benefactors in 14th-Century Lincolnshire* (PhD. thesis London).

Sharp, T. 1793. *Gentleman's Magazine*, **63**, 397.

Sharp, T. 1816/1825.,*A Dissertation on the Coventry Mysteries*

Sharp, T. 1871. *Illustrative papers on the history and antiquities of the City of Coventry.*

Shepherd, E. B. S. 1902. 'The Church of the Friars Minors in London', *Archaeol. J.* **59**, 238-287.

Shepherd, J. 1995. 'The Window Glass', 119-120 in Soden 1995.

Sheppard, L. C. 1943. *The English Carmelites* (Burns Oates; London).

Shortt, H. 1973. *Salisbury Heritage, Illustrations from the Museum Collection* (Salisbury Museum)

Simpson, A. 1986. 'The Carmelite Friary at Maldon, Essex', *Maldon Archaeol. Group*, 1986.

Sir Thomas Smythe of Hill Hall, Essex, Notebooks.

Skeat, W. W. (ed.) 1867. *Pierce the Ploughman's Crede* (Early English Text Soc., Original Ser **30** (Trubner; London).

Society of Antiquaries. 1992-in progress. *Dictionary of British Arms: Medieval ordinary,* Vol. **1**.

Soden, I. 1988. *Excavations at Ernesford Grange, 1971-1973* (Coventry Museums Monograph Series **4**).

Soden, I. 1992. *Cheylesmore Manor Excavations, 1992* (Unpublished Coventry Museum Archaeol. Unit Report No. 10).

Soden, I. 1995. *Excavations at St. Anne's Charterhouse, Coventry, 1968-1987* (Coventry Museum and Galleries).

Spencer, B. 1990. *Pilgrim Souvenirs & Secular Badges* (Salisbury and South Wiltshire Museum Medieval Catalogue **2**; Salisbury and South Wiltshire Museum).

Spencer, B. 1998. *Pilgrim Souvenirs and Secular Badges* (Medieval finds from Excavations in London **7:** HMSO; London).

Steane, J. M. 1967. 'Excavations at Lyveden, 1965-67', *J. Northants. Museum and Art Gallery* **2**, 2-37.

Stewart, B. H. I. H. 1967. *The Scottish Coinage* (2nd edition with supplement).

Stones J. A. (ed.) 1989. *Three Scottish Carmelite Friaries. Excavations at Aberdeen, Linlithgow and Perth 1980-86* (Soc. Ant. Scot. Monograph **6**).

Stopford, J. 1993. 'The potential for studies of medieval tiles', 87- 106 in Gilchrist and Mytum 1993.

Swann, J. 1952. 'Medieval Paving-Tiles in Northampton Museum', *J. Northants. Nat. Hist. Soc. and Field Club* **32**, (no 235), 124-134.

Sylvester Bradley, P. C. and Ford, T. D. 1968. *The Geology of the East Midlands.*

Tait, H. (ed) 1991. *Five Thousand Years of Glass* (British Museum Press; London).

Taylor, S. 1974. 'An Excavation on the Site of the Augustinian Priory, Canons Ashby, Northants', *Northamptonshire Archaeology* **9**, 57-65.

Telford P. J. 1956. 'Medieval Stone Moulds from the Herbert Art Gallery and Museum Site, Coventry',

Proc. Coventry and District Natural History and Scientific Soc .**2.10** (reprint).

The Master of Game by Edmund, Second Duke of York (mid 14th century, printed London 1904) ed. William, A. and Baillie-Grohman, F.

Thirsk, J. 1967. 'The farming regions of England', in Thirsk, J. (ed) *The Agrarian History of England and Wales*, Vol. **IV** 1500 - 1640 (Cambridge University Press, Cambridge, 1967).

Tickner. N. nd. *M. S. Annals.*

Tracy, C. 1987. *English Gothic Choir-Stalls, 1200-1400* (Woodbridge).

Tracy, C. 1997. 'Choir-stalls from the 14th-century Whitefriars Church in Coventry'. *J. British Archaeol. Assoc.* **150**, 76-95.

Tracy, C. and Goodall, J. A. 1997. 'Appendix I: The misericords of the Whitefriars Church, Coventry', 89-94 in Tracy 1997.

Tylecote, R. F. 1972. 'A Contribution to the Metallurgy of 18th and 19th Century Brass Pins', *Post Medieval Archaeol.* **6**, 183-90.

Tyson, R. 2000. *Medieval Glass Vessels Found in England c. 1200-1500.* CBA Research Report **121**.

Turpin, P. 1917. 'Ancient Glass in England', *Burlington Magazine* **30**, 214-218.

Valentine and Orson (1937). Dickson, ed. A. *Early English Text Society no 204.*

Victoria History of the Counties of England: a History of the County of Northamptonshire 1906. Vol. **II**.

Victoria History of the Counties of England: a History of the County of Warwickshire 1969. Vol. **VIII**.

Vince, A. G. 1995. 'Andalusian Fabrics', 282-4 in Gerrard, Gutierrez and Hurst 1995.

Ward, S. W. 1990. *Excavations at Chester. The Lesser Medieval Religious Houses* (Chester City Council).

Warner, R. 1791. *Antiquitates Culinariae.* XVIII (London, 1791).

Wayment, H. 1994. 'Ten Carmelite Roundels at Queen's College, Cambridge', *Proceedings of the Cambridge Antiquarian Soc.* **82**, 139-156.

Webster, L. and Cherry. J. 1974. 'Medieval Britain in 1973: Bristol Greyfriars', *Medieval Archaeol.* **18**, 189-190.

Wellander, D. 1991. *The History, Art and Architecture of Gloucester Cathedral.*

W. Midlands Pottery Research Group Newsletter, No. **11** of October 1988, 'The British Museum and Midland tiles'.

Whitcomb, N. 1956. *The Medieval Floor Tiles of Leicestershire* (Leics. Archaeol. Hist. Soc.).

White, H. 1972. 'The forms of Wildness: Archaeology of an Idea', 3-38 in Dudley, E and Novak, M. E. 1972. *The Wild Man Within. An Image in Western Thought from the Renaissance to Romanticism* (Pittsburg).

Whitley, T. W. 1870. *Plan of stalls in St John's, Coventry.*

Wight, J. 1972. *Brick Building in England, Middle Ages to 1550* (John Baker (Publisher) Ltd.).

Williams, J. H. 1978. 'Excavations at the Greyfriars, Northampton 1972', *Northamptonshire Archaeology* **13**, 96-160.

Williams, J. H. 1979. *St. Peter's Street, Northampton. Excavations 1973-1976* (Northampton Development Corporation 1979, Monograph **2**).

Wilson, C. 1989. Unpublished PhD thesis. University of London.

Wilson, M. C. Anne. 1976. *Food and Drink in Britain* (Penguin; Harmondsworth).

Woodfield, C. 1966. 'Coventry City Wall Excavation Report', in Gooder, E., Woodfield, C., and Chaplin, R. E. 1966. 'The Walls of Coventry', *Trans. Birmingham. Archaeol. Soc.* **81**, 88-138.

Woodfield, C. 1971. 'Report of the Summer Meeting of the Roy. Archaeol. Inst., Warwick, 1971. The Whitefriars, Coventry', *Archaeological J.* **128**, 251 and fig. 11.

Woodfield, C. 1981. 'Finds from the Free Grammar School at the Whitefriars, Coventry, c.1545-c.1557/8'. *Post-Medieval Archaeol.* **15**, 81-160.

Woodfield, P. 1966. 'Yellow Glazed Wares of the Seventeenth Century', *Trans. Birm. Archaeol. Soc.* **81**, 78-87.

Woodfield, P. 1984. 'Recent Researches on Midland Yellow wares', *West Midlands Pottery Research Group Newsletter* **2**, 2-6.

Woodland, R. R. 1981, 'The Pottery', 81-129 in Mellor. and Pearce 1981.

Wright, S. M. 1982 (1988). 'Much Park Street, Coventry: the development of a medieval street. Excavations 1970-74'. *Trans Birmingham and Warwickshire Archaeol. Soc.* **92**, 1-132.

Youngs, S., Clark, J. and Barry, T. 1986. 'Medieval Britain and Ireland in 1985', *Medieval Archaeol.* **30**, 194-196.

Zimmermann B. 1904. 'L'ancien couvent des Carmes de Coventry (Angleterre)', *Chroniques du Carmel* **16**, 149-151.